NEW CLASSIC CARS

The Icons of the '70s, '80s, '90s and the Youngtimers

The author expresses his gratitude to many people, including Giorgio Ferrero, Valeria Manferto De Fabianis, and Paola Piacco of White Star; his co-workers at *AutoWeek* magazine, iZoom.com, and the ClassicCars.com Journal; his editors at *The New York Times*, *Detroit News*, and at Motorbooks; and to the automotive industry executives and public relations staffers who shared their knowledge and insight throughout his reporting career.

Editorial Project
VALERIA MANFERTO/CONSULTING D&D

Editorial assistant
GIORGIO FERRERO

Graphic Design
PAOLA PIACCO

Piazzale Luigi Cadorna, 6
20123 Milan, Italy
www.whitestar.it

ISBN 978-88-544-2187-5
1 2 3 4 5 6 30 29 8 27 26

Printed in China

LARRY EDSALL

NEW CLASSIC CARS

The Icons of the '70s, '80s, '90s and the Youngtimers

whitestar

CONTENTS

'80s 92

'90s 150

Author, Photo Credits, Bibliography 238

INTRODUCTION

You cannot be faulted if you find the title of this book to be confusing. *New Classic Cars*? Isn't that oxymoronic? Yes, it could appear so.

After all, doesn't "classic," by its very definition, infer something that is old, and if not classic in the sense of being historic as in ancient Greek or Latin literature or art, or perhaps being music of the era of Mozart or Beethoven, then at least, as the dictionary puts it, "having enduring worth, timeless"?

And yet we've heard and accepted classic rock. We enjoy watching classic movies. We've even tasted and accepted (well, at least some of us) Coca-Cola Classic. So, indeed, why not New Classic Cars?

Although Leonardo da Vinci sketched out the design of a self-propelled cart in the fifteenth century, the first practical example of what has come to be recognized as an automobile didn't appear until 1885 when Karl Benz rolled out his Patent-Motorwagen. (Actually, the practicality of Benz's engineering marvel didn't come for another three years, when his wife, Bertha, took her husband's invention, and their two teenage sons, and drove a little more than 100 kilometers to visit her mother, then drove back home in a display of its usefulness.)

It took a few decades, but the automobile replaced the horse and buggy as the primary mode for family transportation on a global basis. Even more recently, the automobile has become cherished as something to collect, to display in car museums, to provide thrills at rallies and vintage races, and to show off at events ranging from local car gatherings to prestigious concours d'elegance, or to buy or sell at collector car auctions.

So what makes a car "classic"?

"The Classic Car Club of America defines a Full Classic as a 'Fine' or 'Distinctive' automobile. American or foreign built, produced only between 1915 and 1948. Many factors come into play, but generally, a Classic was a high-priced, top-end vehicle when new and was built in limited quantities. No 'mass produced' assembly-line vehicles are

considered Classics. Other factors, including higher engine displacement, custom bespoke coachwork, and luxury accessories. Mechanical developments such as power brakes, power clutch, and 'one-shot' or automatic lubrication systems, help determine whether a car is considered to be a Classic."

The club lists around 125 such vehicles that it accepts, all of them of European or American heritage.

Less restrictive is the Fédération Internationale des Véhicules Anciens (FIVA), the global organization "dedicated to the protection, preservation, and promotion of historic vehicles and related culture, as well as their safe use."

According to the FIVA website, "For many decades, the transition of a vehicle to a 'historic vehicle' has been determined by the passage of time. While most vehicles would end up being scrapped after their period of use, some would survive to be enjoyed as a part of history and to pass them on to future generations as a rolling museum.

"But from the use period and until the vehicle reaches the status of a historic vehicle, there is a range of years where protection and preservation is equally important if the vehicle is to survive to become a historic vehicle. This is the 'youngtimer' period."

FIVA defines a youngtimer vehicle as a mechanically propelled road vehicle:

- between twenty and twenty-nine years of age;
- which is in good condition and preservation;
- which is usually used during leisure time;
- and may become eligible for a FIVA Identity Card upon reaching thirty years of age.

"The classification of 'youngtimers' is essential to ensure the continuity of the historic vehicle park and of our motoring heritage."

FIVA does not restrict country of origin as the Classic Car Club of America does and thus recognizes cars produced in Asia as legitimate youngtimers.

The global organization adds in its website this note:

"National scrappage schemes, designed to promote the introduction of more efficient vehicles, which causes less emission of environmental harmful substances, may threaten the survival of youngtimers. It is the view of FIVA that it is the sole right of the vehicle owner to determine the end-of-life of any vehicle."

Among the car collectors around the globe is a younger and growing generation of men and women, people who grew up in the latter half of the twentieth century and who have advanced to the point that they can afford to buy the cars they coveted while in secondary or high school, cars that were just as classic to them as a 1920s Pierce Arrow was to their grandfathers or as a '50s Ferrari was to their fathers.

As indicated above, in Europe, collectible cars from the later years of the twentieth century are called "youngtimers," a term apparently first used in Germany to signify newer vehicles and to differentiate them from old-timers.

In the United States in 2016, a quartet of friends who had attended high schools in the 1980s and 1990s decided to hold a car show for the vehicles of their youth. Inspired in part by a song title from their school days and by the vintage vehicle events at England's Goodwood racing circuit, they hosted a car show they called "RADwood." The event was so popular it generated similar events across the country; some they organized, some they did not.

Regardless, those events helped to identify and unify a new group of car collectors and enthusiasts who loved the cars of the last decades of the twentieth century.

Perhaps classic, like beauty, is best defined as residing in the eye of the beholder. And with that introduction, we present our new book, this one focused on more modern classics, and we hope you find its contents pleasing to your eyes.

Our focus is on the final three decades of the previous century, a period that many might describe as a time of automotive malaise.

After the 1960s and such exciting extremes as the Detroit muscle cars and the European exotics, including James Bond's Aston Martin, Jaguar's XKE, or Ferrari's Daytona, the '70s brought increasing safety regulations, oil embargoes and fuel crises, and worries about automotive exhaust emissions and their impact on the air we breathe.

It seemed the carefree and classic days of the motorcars were over. But as you'll see on the pages that follow, automotive designers and engineers and production techniques and technologies were able to adapt and evolve to work within the restrictions to find ways to make cars fun to drive again while also being safe and clean.

In 1988, in his book, *The Automobile Age*, professor and cultural historian James J. Flink pondered the future of the automobile. He noted "the renaissance in automotive technology is making cars safer, less polluting, and more energy efficient with every model year. Predictions of the imminent death of the automobile have given way to a new optimism."

However, he added that the automobile and the industry producing it were changing: "The current renaissance in automotive technology is a renaissance almost entirely engendered by electronic and aerospace technology...the computer, the robot, the laser beam, and telecommunications."

As you'll see, such things have worked to make the automobile even better, not obsolete. Professor Flink expected the Automobile Age to be nearly over. Instead, technology has produced more of a rebirth and a new fleet of automotive classics.

In 2019 classic car insurer and value tracker Hagerty published a series of essays under the title *Never Stop Driving: A Better Life Behind the Wheel*. The first page of the first chapter includes this: "These vehicle are beautiful and unique, imperfect and infuriating in equal measure, a mirror for our days."

Perhaps that's the true definition of "classic," something—be it a work of art, of music, of literature, or even an automobile—that is a mirror of our days, our lives. The classics are our heritage from those who have gone before us and will be part of our heritage to those who will come after us.

Following pages ■ In the 1950s, Jaguar named one of its cars the XK120 because it could be driven at 120 mph (193 km/h). In the 1990s, the XJ220 nearly lived up to its numbers.

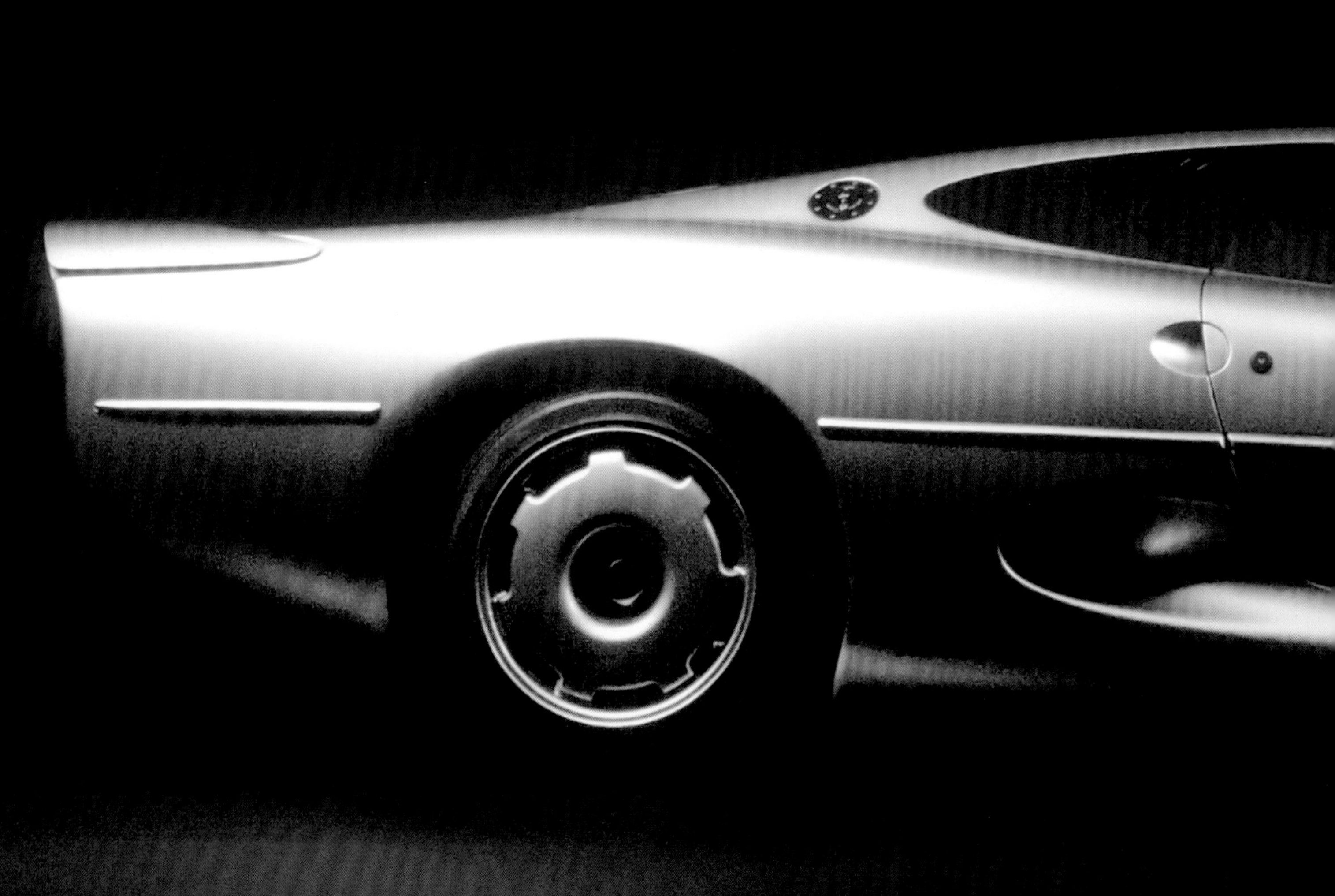

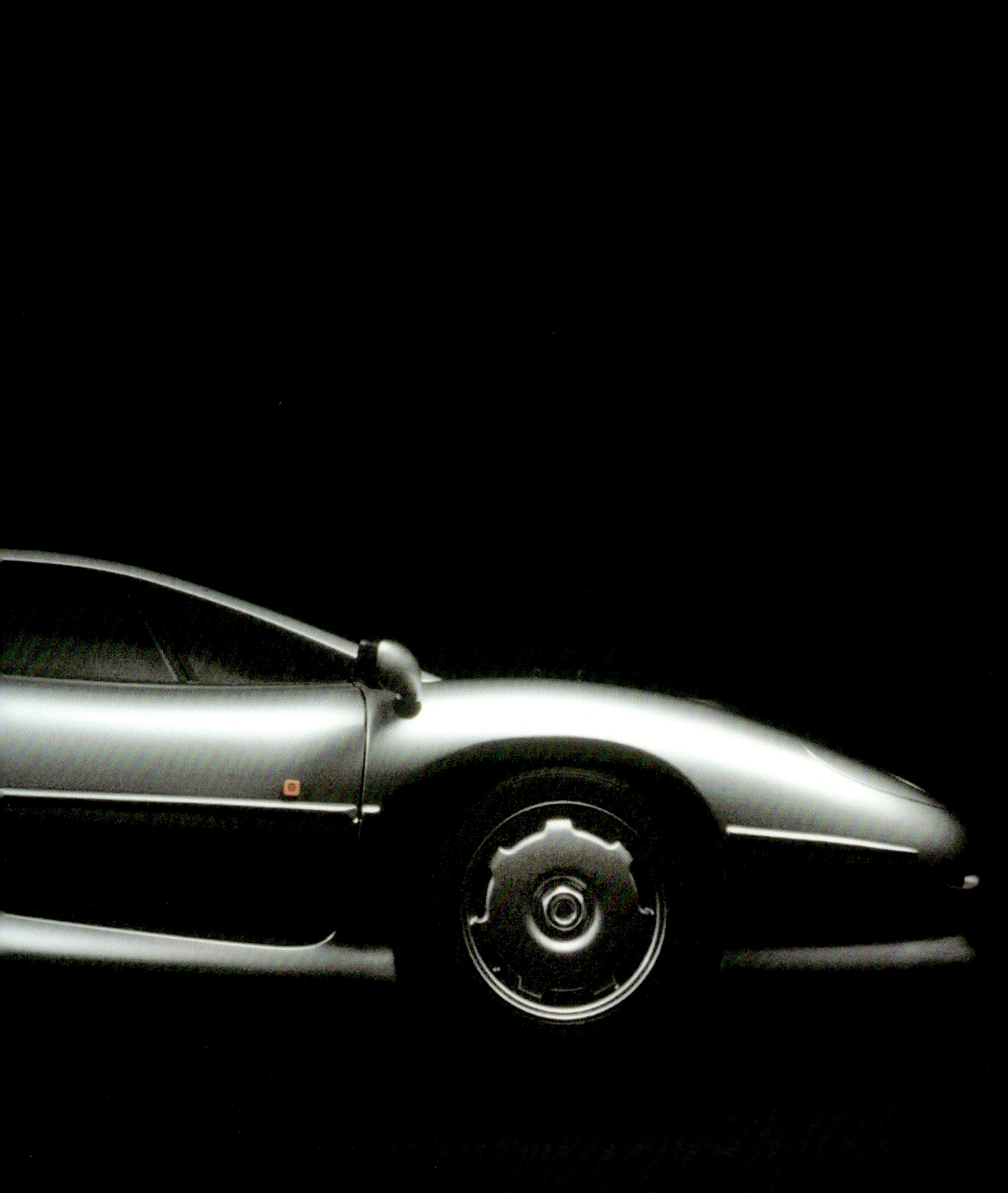

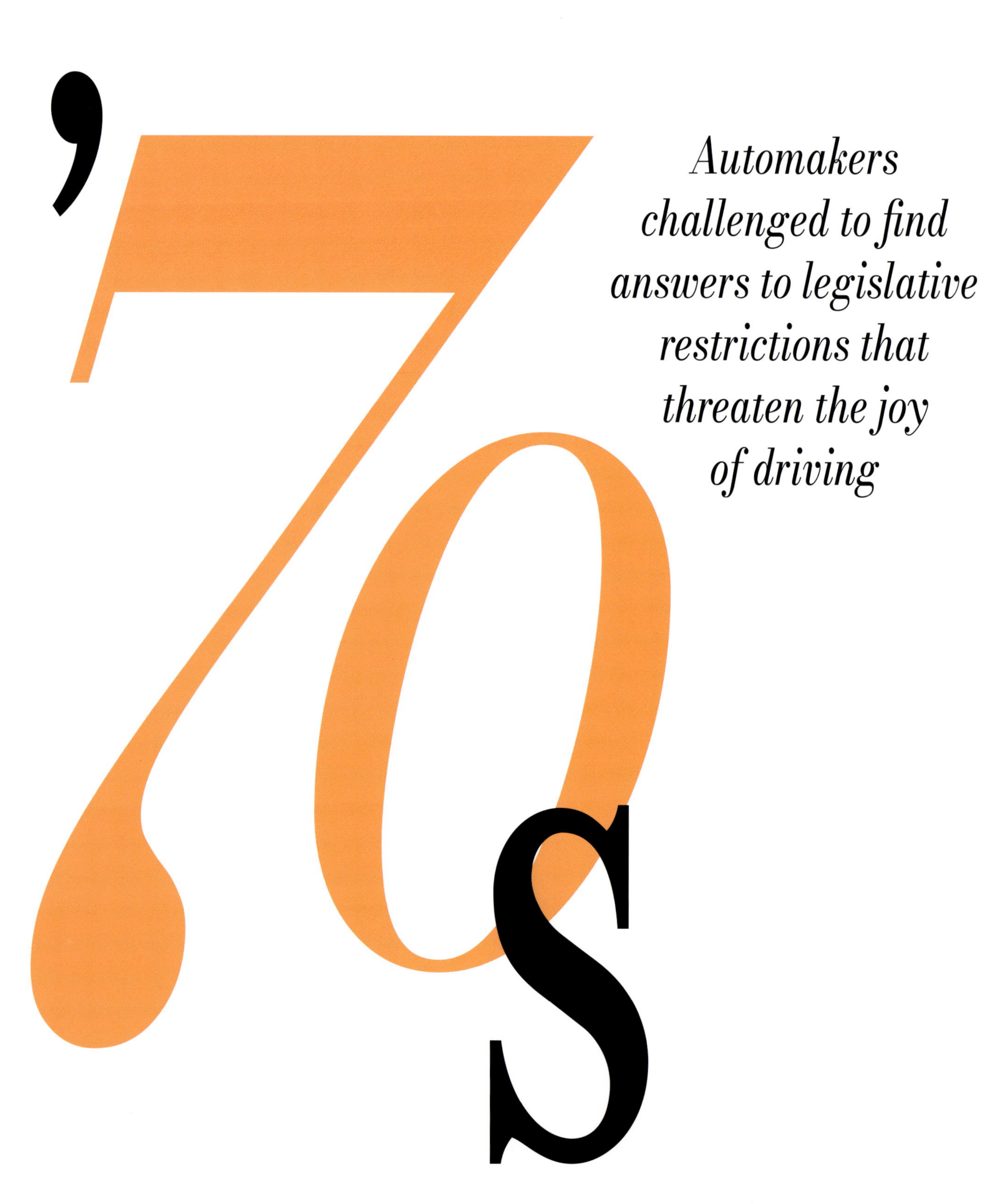

Automakers challenged to find answers to legislative restrictions that threaten the joy of driving

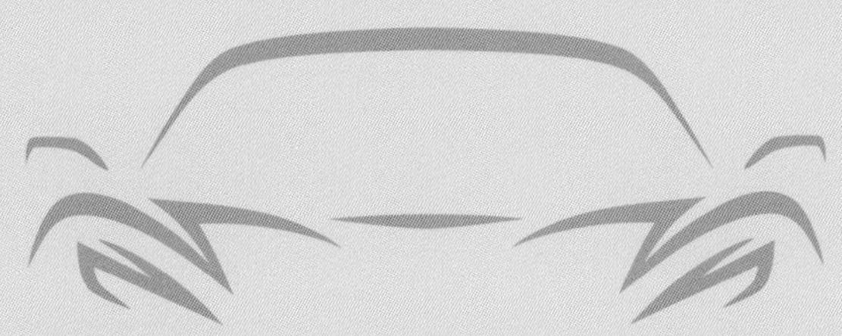

Economists tell us that by the 1970s, the postwar economic boom had ended. Historians point to a world in turmoil: Watergate, the Fall of Saigon, the Munich Olympic Games murders, the Yom Kippur War, the oil crisis, genocide in Bangladesh, a cyclone claiming half a million lives in East Pakistan, the Shah of Iran overthrown and the establishment of an Islamic state, the Soviet invasion of Afghanistan, and well, even the rise of disco music.

People couldn't be blamed for looking back nostalgically at the '60s, the Swinging Sixties with The Beatles, the summer of love, surfing songs, *Mary Poppins*, Brigitte Bardot, "spaghetti" westerns, the debut of *Doctor Who*, hippies in flowered Volkswagen vans, "muscle cars," and not just the Man on the Moon, but mankind actually landing and walking on the Moon.

In the later half of the 1960s, consumer advocate Ralph Nader published his book, *Unsafe at Any Speed: The Designed-In Dangers of the American Automobile*. In 1972, a record 54,589 people died in automobile crashes in the United States, and there were similar statistics reported from other countries as well. New vehicle safety regulations were passed not only in the United States but in auto-producing European countries and Japan.

To punish Western countries for supporting Israel in the Yom Kippur War, Arab oil producers imposed an embargo in 1973 that restricted the flow of fuel and, at least in the United States, led to a national 55-miles-per-hour speed limit designed to reduce fuel consumption. American automakers also reduced the size of their vehicles to make them lighter and more fuel efficient. Another energy crisis resulted from the Iranian Revolution in 1979.

A trifecta of sorts was completed as major cities were chocked by smog. Concern over automotive emissions, be it from lead or carbon monoxide or diesel particulates, led to demands that they be reduced.

As design historian and professor Penny Sparke noted in her book, *A Century of Car Design*: "As far as automotive design was concerned, the last three decades of the twentieth century experienced a period of despondency followed by a time of enormous and unexpected exhilaration. Fears about car safety and urban pollution in the 1960s had been followed by the sudden oil crisis of the early 1970s which had served to augment the anxieties of the anti-car lobby. No longer was the car the potent symbol of modernity and progress but rather the enemy, there to be feared and mistrusted rather than adored.

"While this turnaround was undoubtedly part of a more widespread loss of belief in the future and a crisis of conscience that was felt across many aspects of contemporary culture, its effects were particularly intense in the arena of car design."

The result, she continues, was blandness "that with only a few notable exceptions, made one car virtually indistinguishable from another."

On the following pages, we present some of the most notable exceptions, cars from the 1970s that distinguished themselves in design aesthetics, in engineering innovation and excellence, and in their dynamic performance.

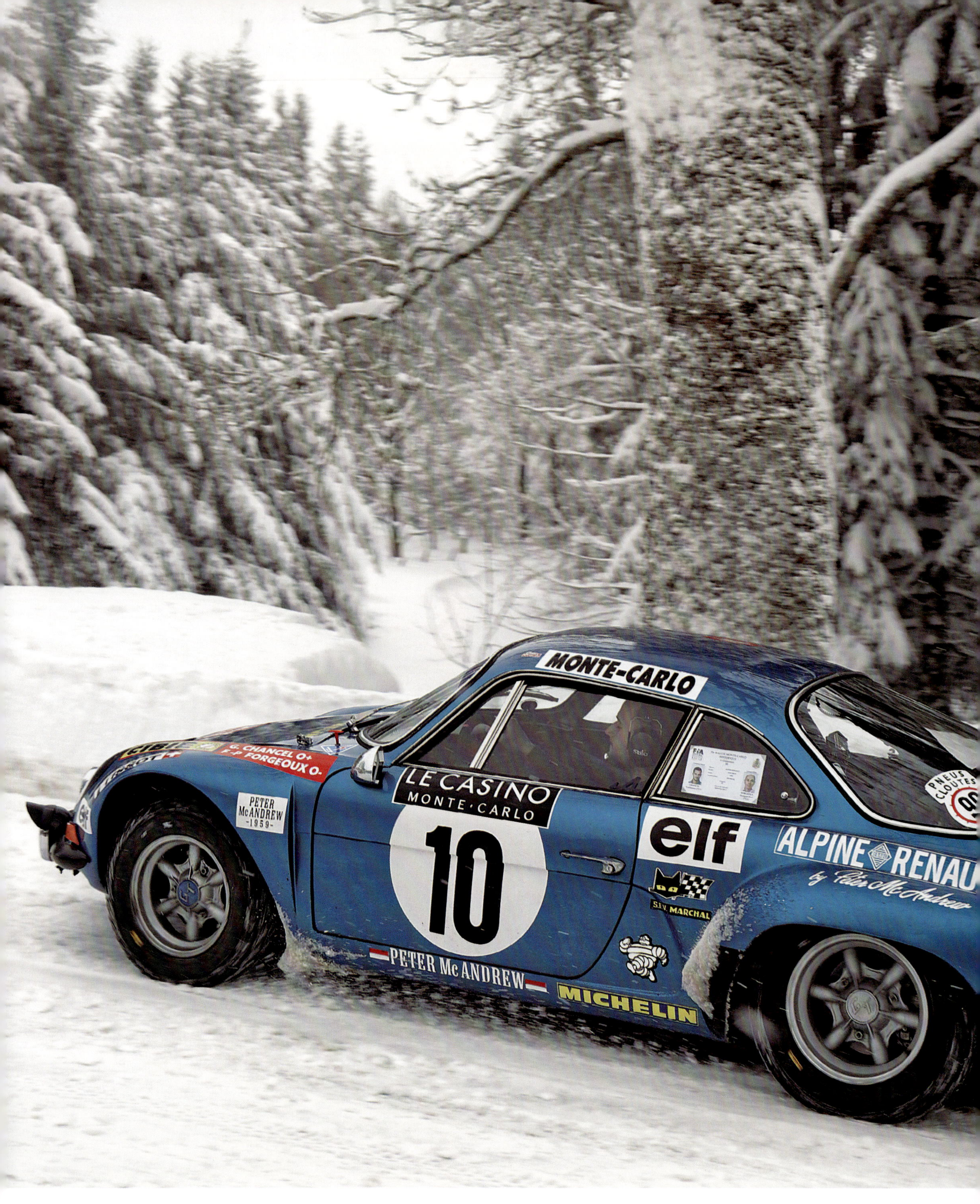
MONTE-CARLO
LE CASINO
MONTE-CARLO
10
elf
ALPINE
PETER
McANDREW
-1959-
PETER McANDREW
MICHELIN
S.E.V. MARCHAL
PNEUS CLOUTES

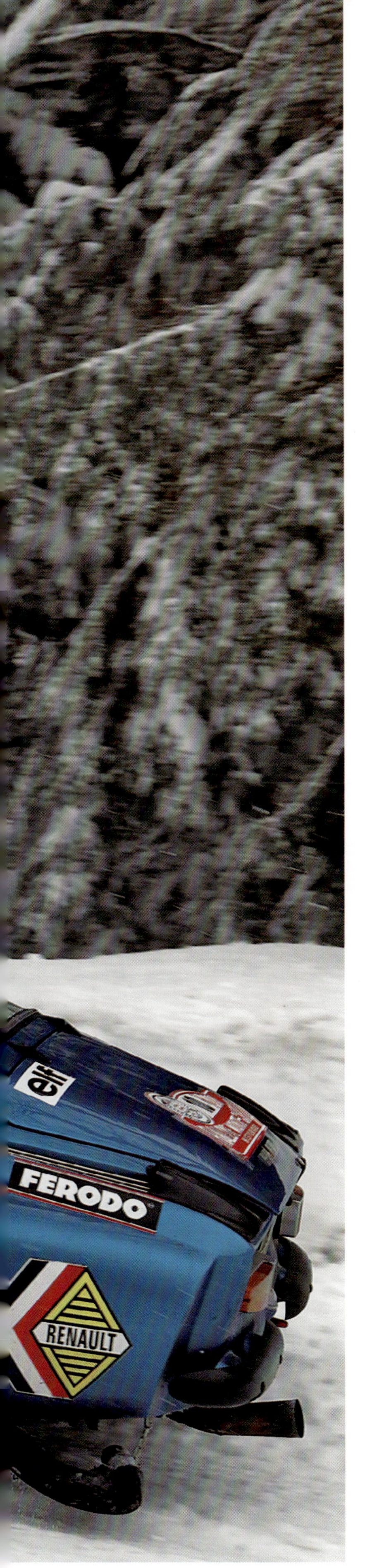

1970 ➤ 1979

RENAULT ALPINE A110

Jean Rédélé took Renault components and made a championship racer from them

Jean Rédélé was a French engineer who operated from a garage in Dieppe, from where he sold Renault cars (he was the youngest Renault dealer in France) and also competed in automotive competitions including the Alpine Rally (which he won in 1954), the Mille Miglia, and the 24 Hours of Le Mans as well as in the Sebring event in Florida.

In 1955 he founded the Société des Automobiles Alpine, contracting none other than Italian designer Giovanni Michelotti to create new coachwork for a Renault 4CV he was modifying with hopes of going into series production. Production of Alpine's A106 didn't begin for two years, and then started very slowly at a rate of two cars a week.

But by 1963 Rédélé had another new car ready, the A110, again based on Renault mechanicals, though he replaced the standard 3-speed transmission with a 5-speed unit. And now Michelotti's sleek, taut, and aerodynamic design was lightened with aluminum rather than steel body panels (and then lightened even further with fiberglass coachwork).

The cars weighed only 620 kilograms (1,367 pounds). With engine tuner "Le Sorcier," Amédée Gordini, tweaking Renault's rear-mounted R8 engines for all the power they might muster, the A110 did very well in motorsports competition.

In 1971, Renault contracted Alpine as its official racing team, and Alpines finished first, second, and fourth in the Monte Carlo Rally that year and in 1973 took four of the top five positions and won the inaugural World Rally Championship ahead of Porsche, Lancia, and Ford.

However, like so many other small specialist automotive producers, Alpine was hit hard by the global gas crises of the early 1970s, and also by the fact that it was using aging designs while other larger com-

■ In the early 1970s, French automaker Renault contracted Alpine as its official racing team and in 1973 was rewarded with the inaugural World Rally Championship.

panies were developing competing vehicles such as the Lancia Stratos, which also had the advantage of using Ferrari engines. As a result, Renault ended up purchasing Alpine in 1974 and merged it with another holding, Gordini's engine tuning operation, which Renault had acquired in 1968, to create Renault Sport.

In 1978, a year before Amédée Gordini's death (Jean Rédélé lived until 2007), Didier Pironi and Jean-Pierre Jaussaud drove a Renault Alpine A442 B to victory in the 24 Hours of Le Mans race, and by more than a 76-kilometer margin for the runner-up Porsche 936.

Production of the A110 had ended in 1977. A new and updated Alpine model, the A310, had been introduced in 1971 and remained in production until the mid-1980s. In the early '80s, Renault used Alpine's Dieppe facility to produce its heralded Renault R5 Turbo while also serving as the headquarters for Renault Sport and its vehicle production.

■ Alpine's A110 took advantage of the use of lightweight materials and the rear positioning of its Renault-sourced engine to excel in rally competition.

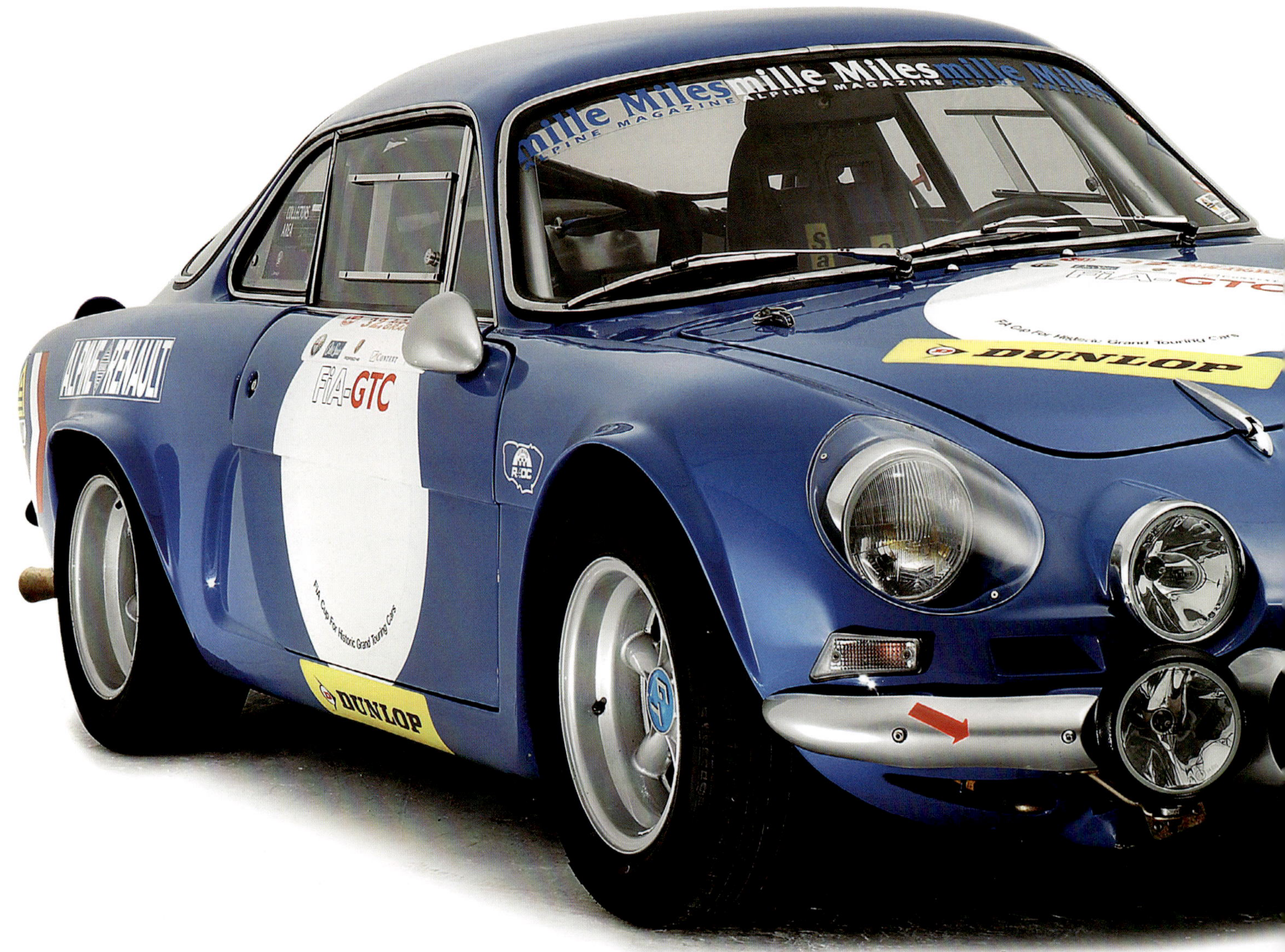

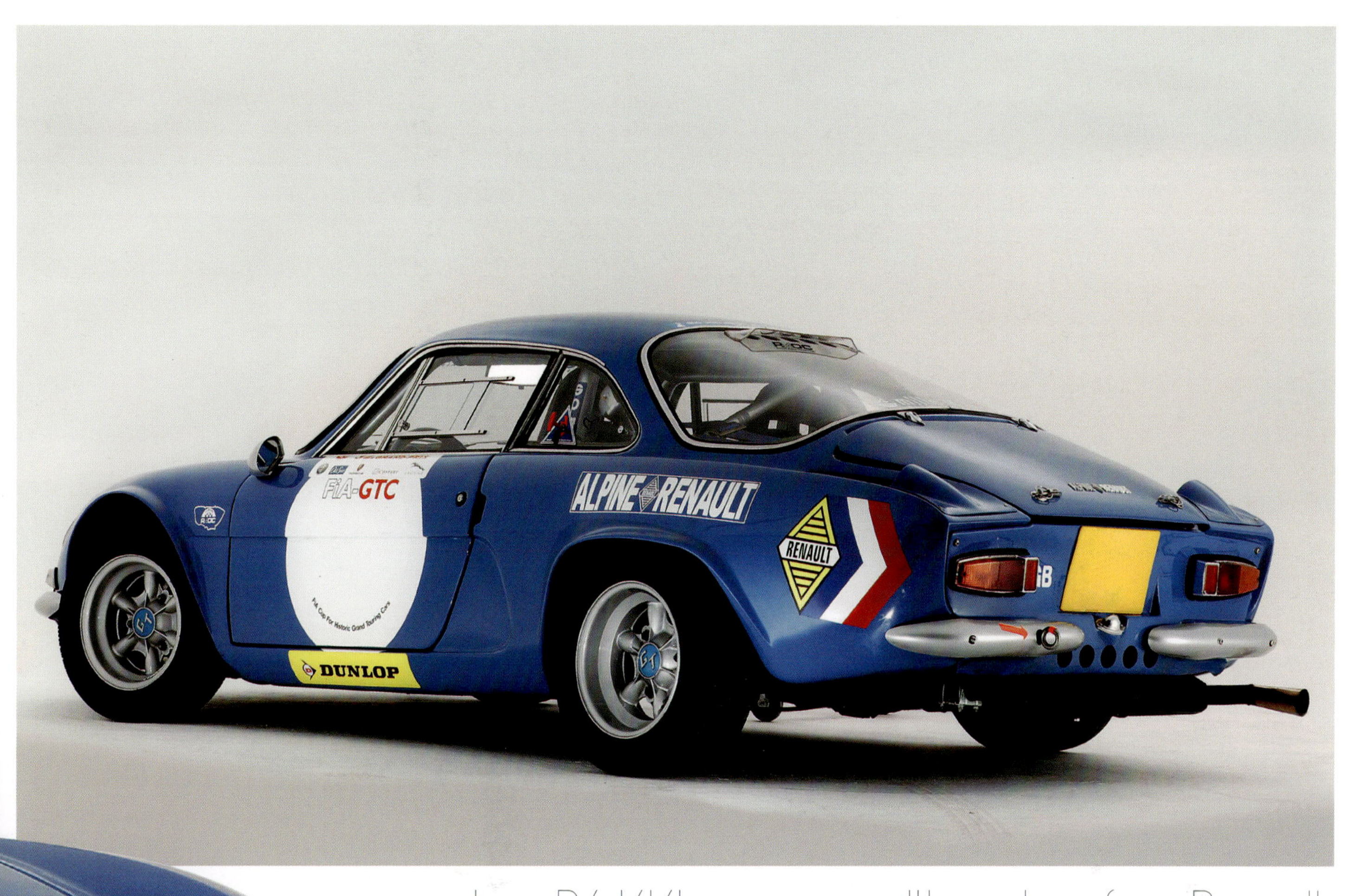

Jean Rédélé's cars won with engines from Renault, which celebrated Alpine's fiftieth anniversary with a new and contemporary A110.

Decades later, in 2012, Renault would celebrate the fiftieth anniversary of Alpine's A110 by unveiling at the Monte Carlo F1 circuit a concept car, the A110-50. Five years later it would celebrate an Alpine revival by showing a new version of the A110 at the Geneva Auto Show and before putting the car into series production later that same year as a thoroughly modern sports car powered by a mid-mounted, 1.8-liter turbocharged 4-cylinder engine rated at 249 horsepower.

In the spring of 2022, the French National Gendarmerie took delivery of a fleet of more than two dozen specially equipped Alpine A110 vehicles and added another dozen or so to the fleet the following year.

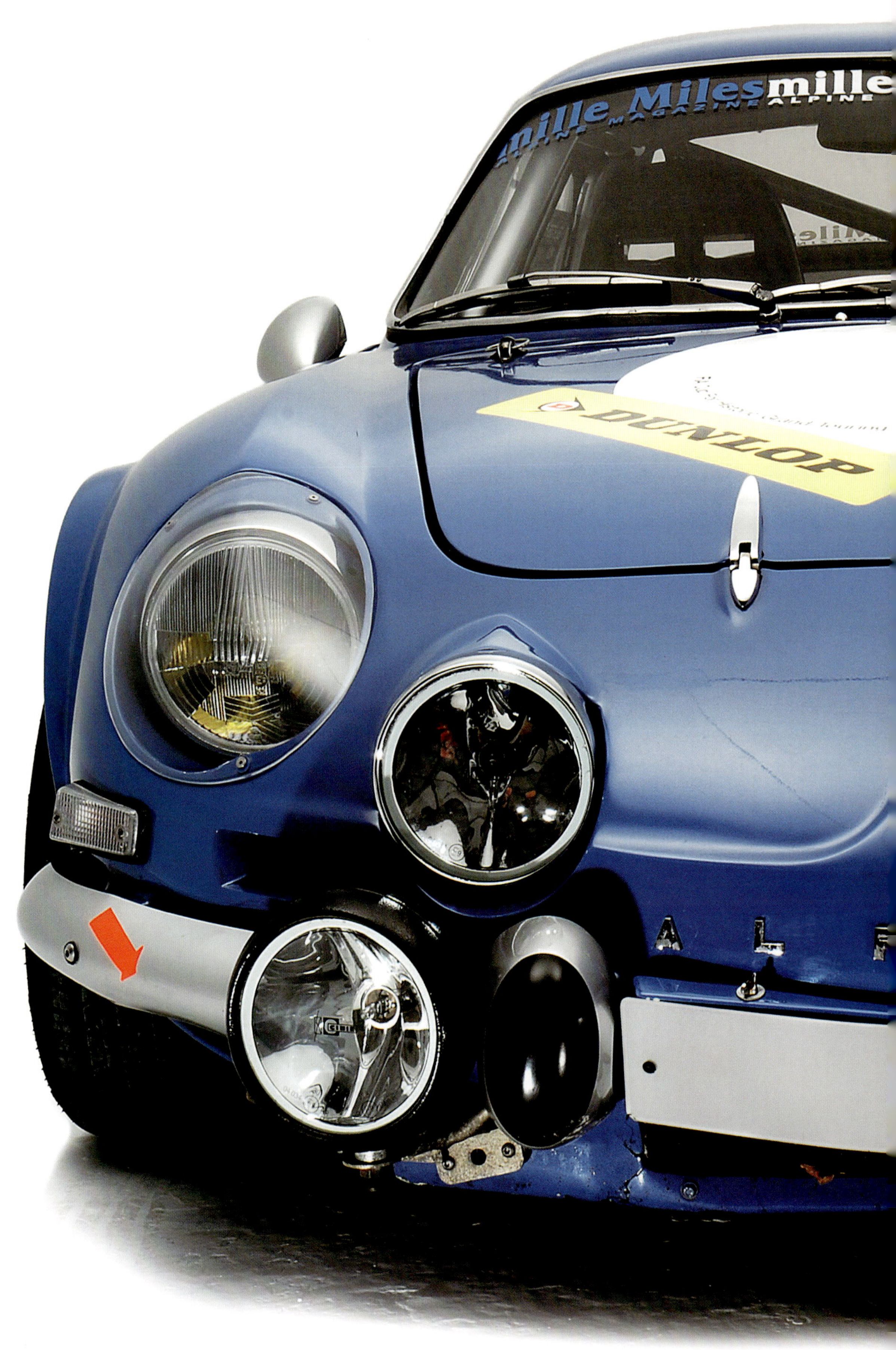
Miles mille
MAGAZINE ALPINE
DUNLOP

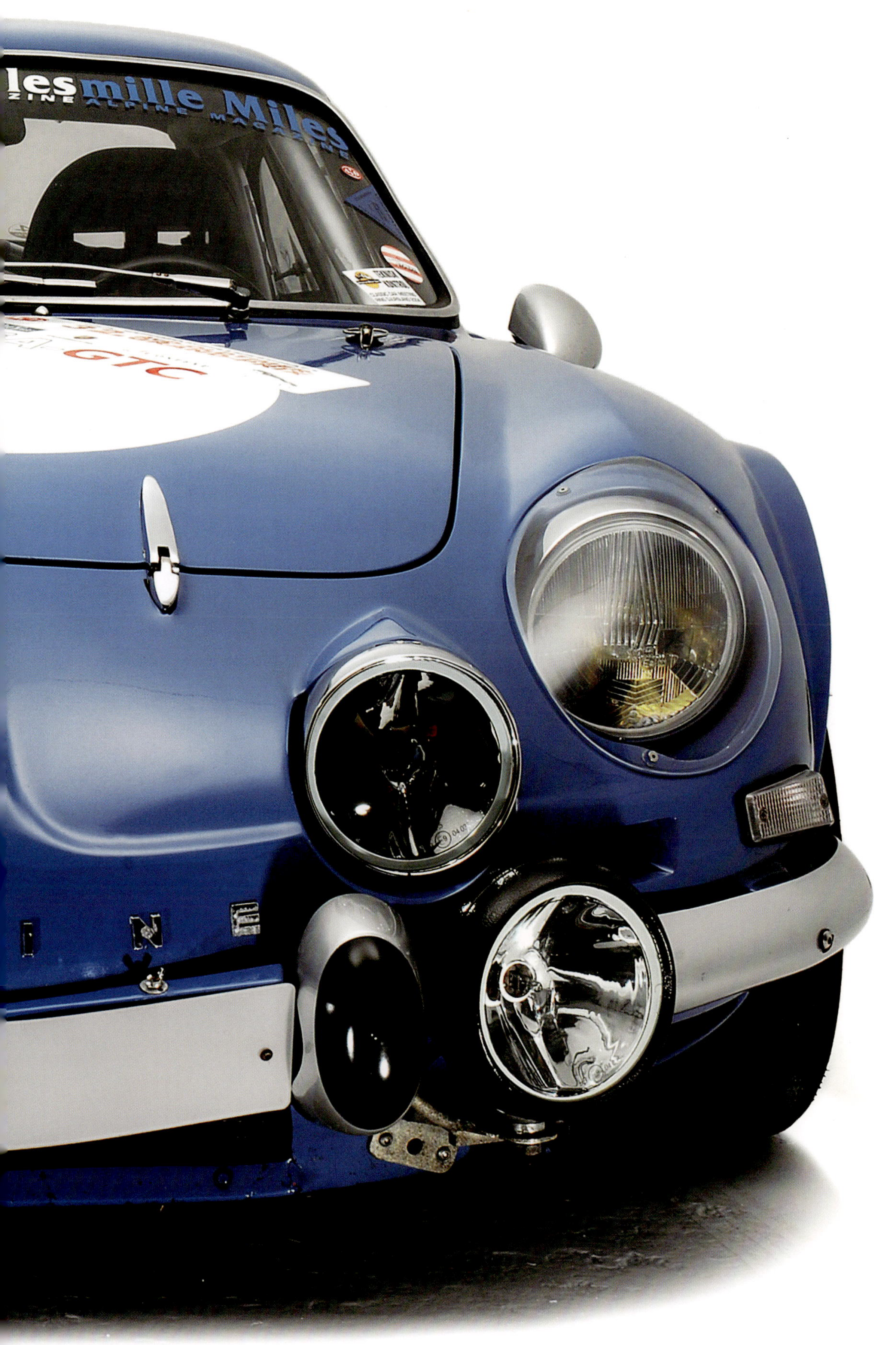
lesmille Miles
GTC

CITROËN-MASERATI SM

Proof that front-wheel drive could provide high performance

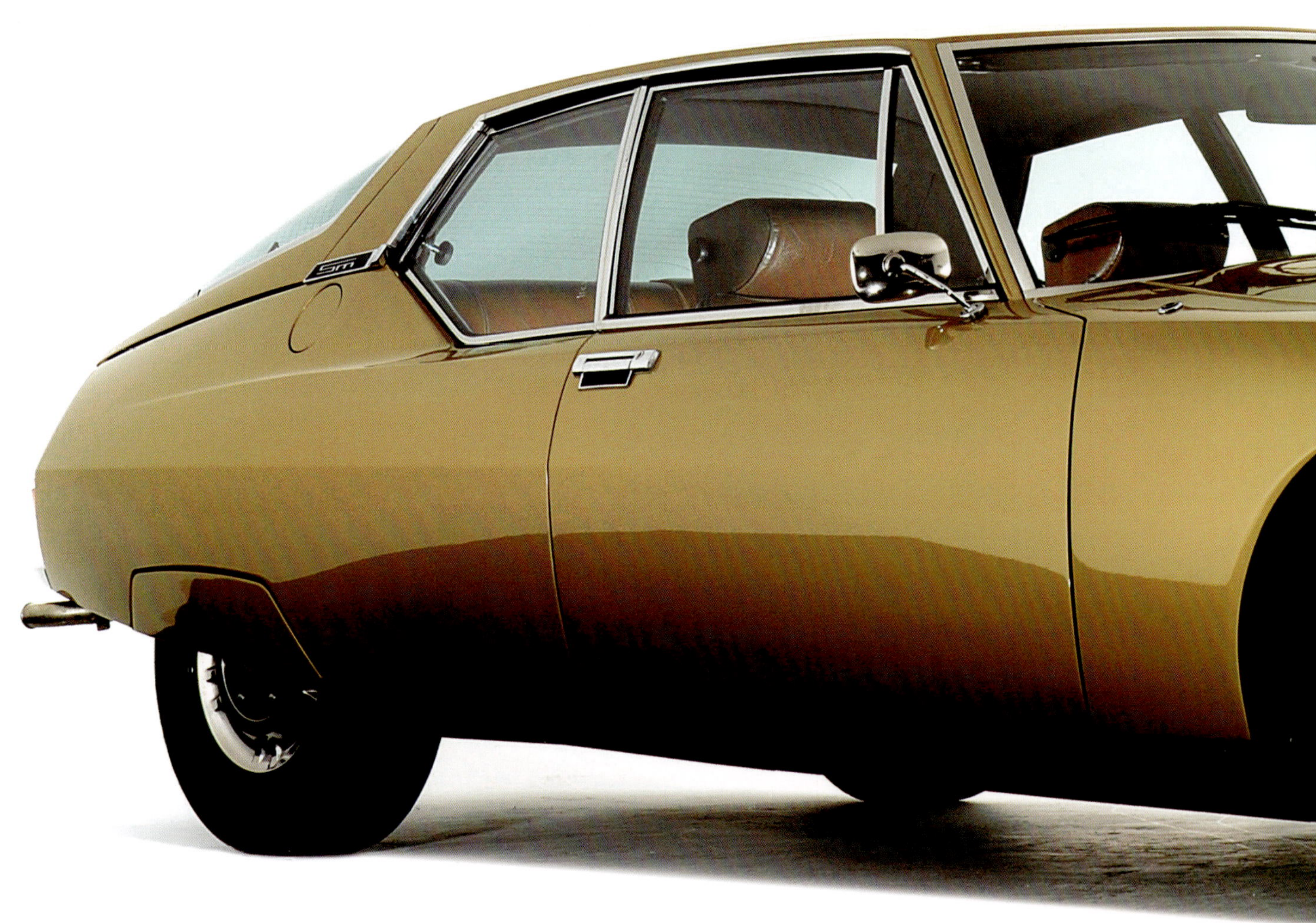

1970 ➤ 1979

André Citroën was born in Paris to a Dutch father and a Polish mother, his mother dying soon after giving birth, and Citroën's father committing suicide when André was six years old. The orphaned child would be raised by relatives. He would study at the École Polytechnique in France. Afterward, while visiting his mother's family in Poland, one of his uncles shared with Citroën his patented gear system, which André would put into production upon returning to Paris.

Called up for military service in 1914, Citroën soon saw that ammunition was in short supply. He convinced the French Army to let him set up a factory and he promised to supply 20,000 shells a day. Instead, he delivered more than double that number.

Even before the end of the hostilities, Citroën's company had begun producing motorcars. In the ensuing years, his company would create some of the most important and revolutionary vehicles of the twentieth century, among them the Traction Avant (which demonstrated the practicality of front-wheel drive), the 2CV (which, just as Henry Ford's Model T, put the everyman resident of France on wheels), and the DS (short for Derivation Special and featuring revolutionary height-adjustable suspension, new radial tires, disc brakes, crumple zones, and more, and which was credited with saving the life of French President Charles de Gaulle during an assassination attempt).

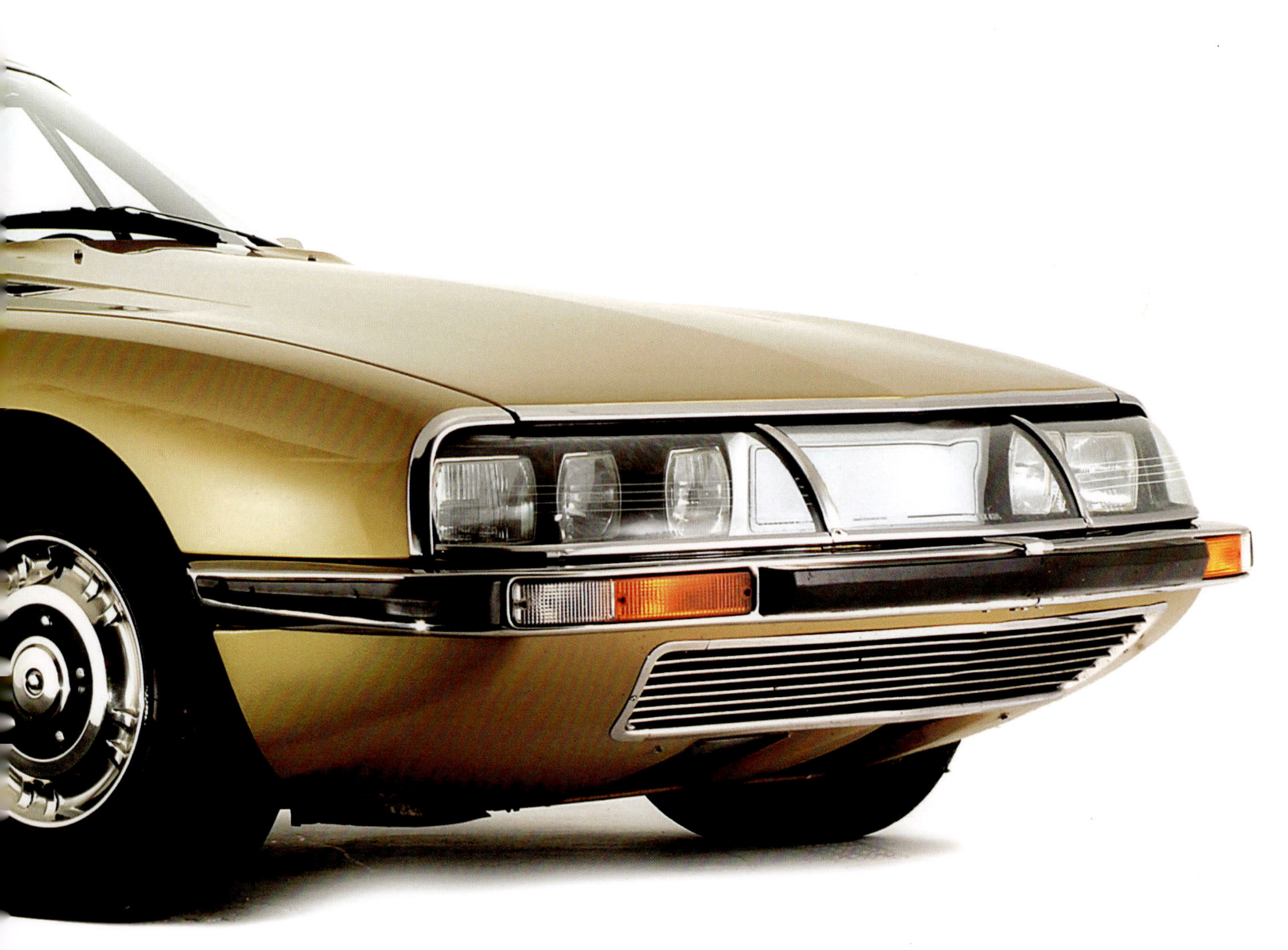

Citroën's SM could reach 140 mph (225 km/h), making it the fastest of front-driven automobiles.

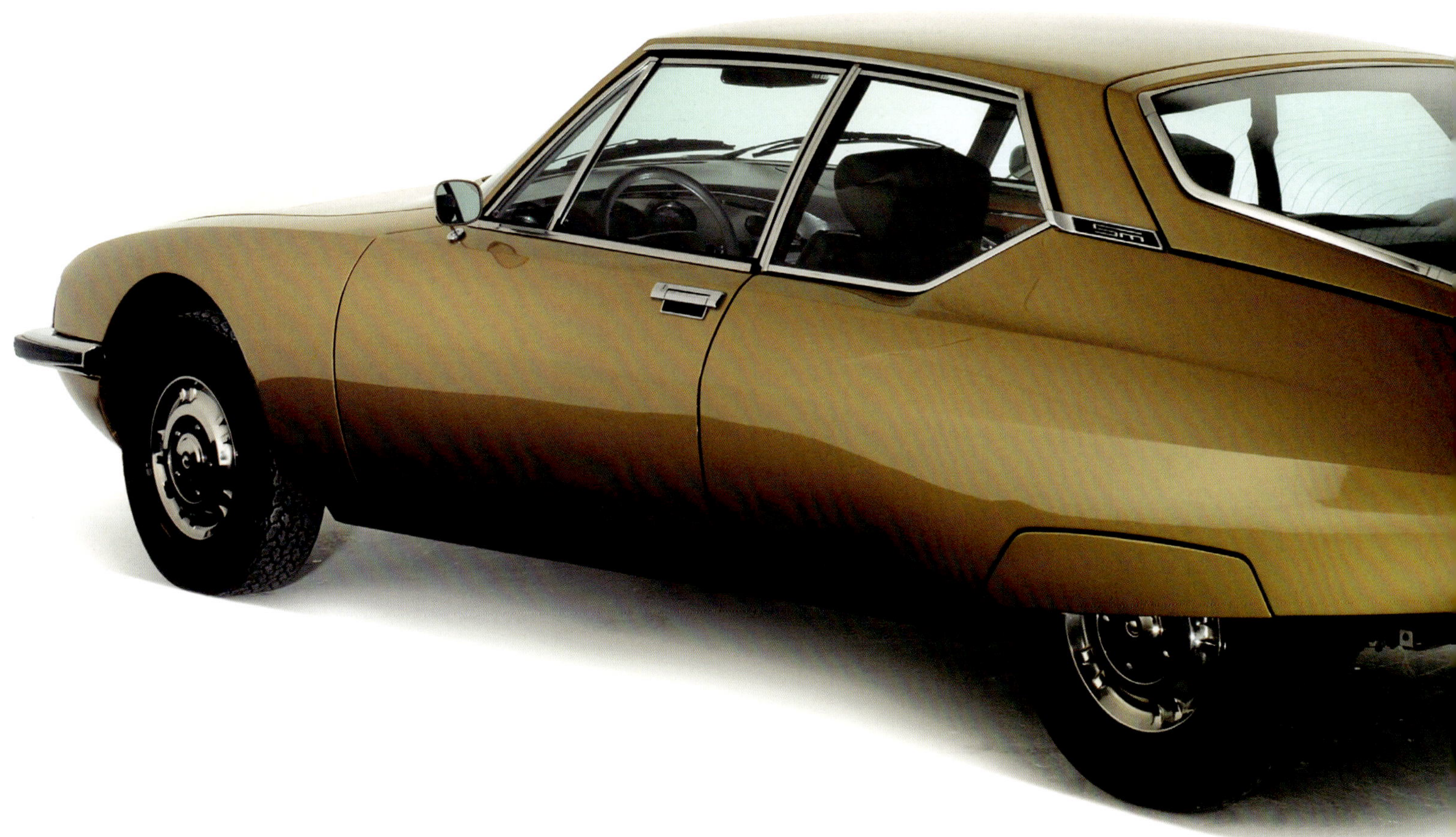

While leading automakers in the development and deployment of front-wheel drive, there were those at Citroën who fretted that there might be a limit to how much power could be safely delivered in a vehicle that pulled rather than pushed its way down the road. The basic question was, could a front-driven vehicle also be a high-performance automobile?

The answer was the Citroën SM, the model name most likely created by taking the S from Citroën's Project S title for the effort and the M from Maserati, the Italian auto company that Citroën purchased in 1968, or it was simply short for *Sa Majesté*, French for Her Majesty, which some prefer since it relates more closely to the naming of the DS from *La Deesse* (French for The Goddess).

Regardless, the SM was a breakthrough luxury grand touring machine that featured Citroën's revolutionary suspension, variable assist power steering (with headlights that turned as the car turned), and also demonstrated that front-wheel drive could handle the nearly 180 horsepower provided by the Italian engine in French-legal road guise (during the car's development, a test car had successfully used a Maserati V8 rated at more than 250 horsepower).

In 1972, *Motor Trend* magazine awarded the Citroën SM its Car of the Year

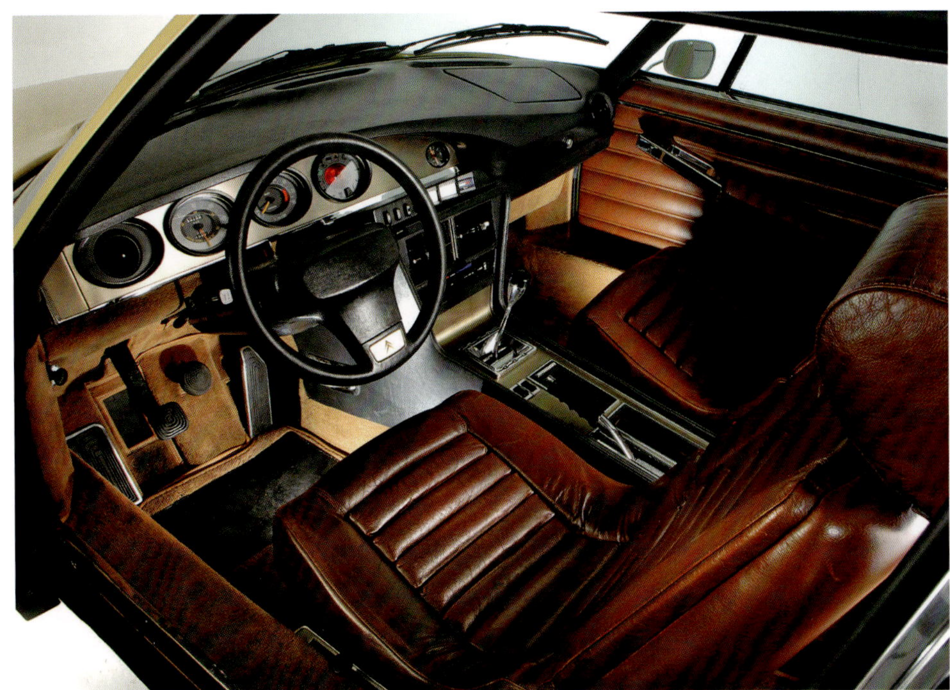

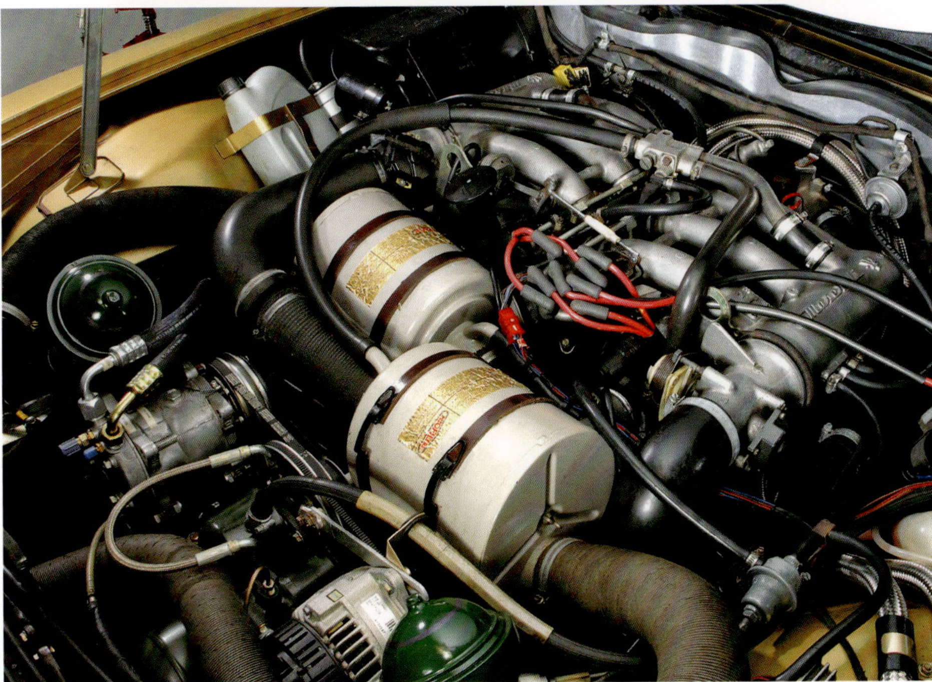

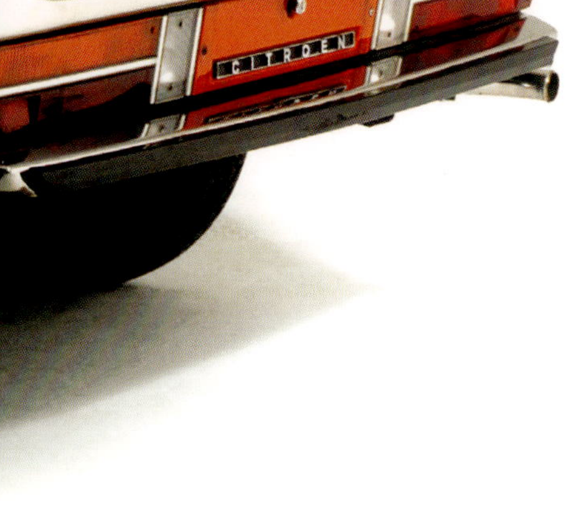

Previous and these pages ■ Citroën's SM was remarkable for its era, offering such features as automatic height-adjustable suspension and headlamps that pivoted to better illuminate corners.

■ The SM offered a luxurious interior for its occupants (top) and a Maserati V6 to enhance the driver's enjoyment (bottom).

trophy. Hagerty's website labeled the Citroën SM as "the great," adding that owners of the car usually say it's the best one they've ever owned.

Or as *Top Gear* put it, "Imagine then, that you wanted a grand tourer. A car to motor from Paris to Nice. Because that's what the SM was designed for. And boy does it do it well. In every action of every control you sense this approach. Complex and innovative it might have been, but boy does the whole thing gel together. There was nothing like it at the time and nothing since either. But you've got to be happy that the SM existed and that it played its role so well."

However, the SM was in production only during the first half of the 1970s. Citroën was enfolded into Peugeot in 1975, and Maserati was sold to Alejandro de Tomaso.

1970 ➤ 1979

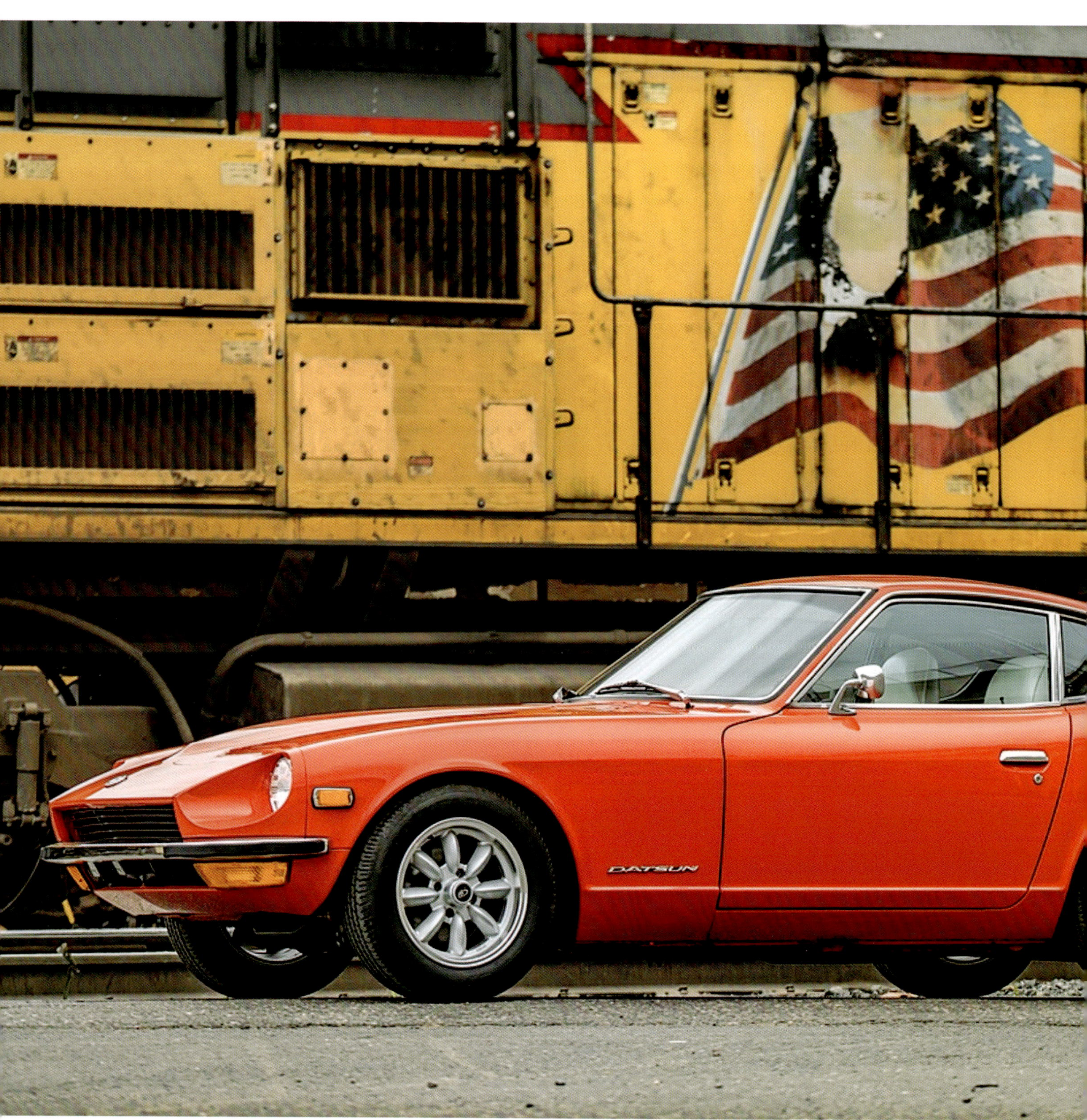

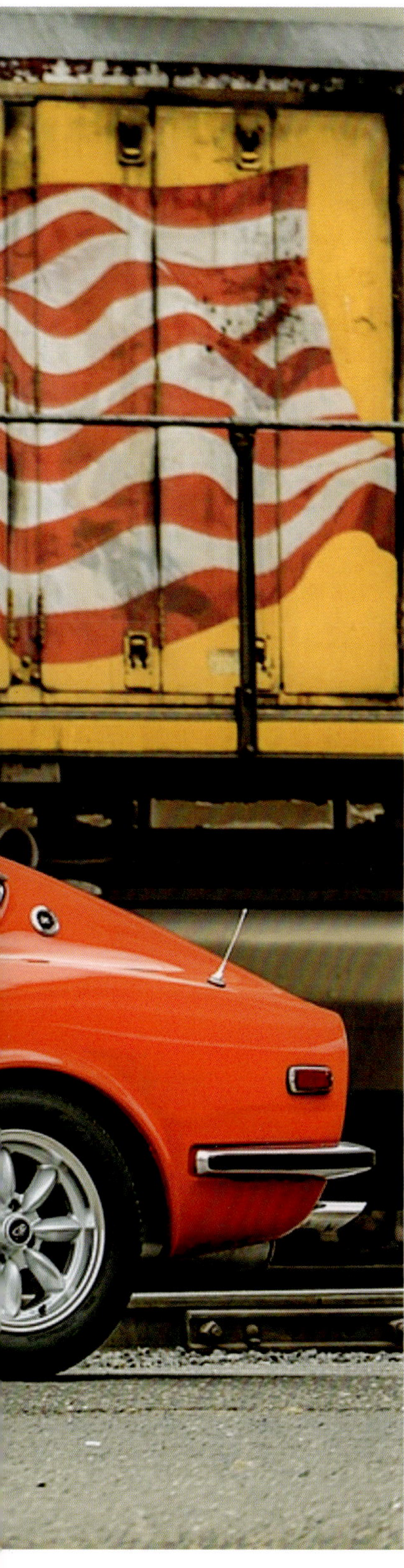

DATSUN 240Z

Japan develops a world-class sports car for the mass marketplace

Founded in 1914 and enfolded into Nissan industries two decades later, Japanese automaker Datsun displayed outside Japan for the first time at the Los Angeles Auto Show in 1958 and began to sell vehicles overseas in 1960, when Nissan Motor Corporation USA was founded with marketing executive Yutaka Katayama as its president.

Until that time, Datsun had labeled its sporty two-seat roadsters as the Fairlady, in tribute to the popular musical *My Fair Lady*. But in the late 1960s, as it got ready to launch its new sports coupe, "Mr. K" objected, arguing that Fairlady was not a fitting name for a true sports car that was to compete with the likes of the Ford Mustang and Chevrolet Camaro. He won, and the Datsun 240Z was launched.

Katayama had grown up riding horses and sought to install the same feeling into Datsun's sports car.

"After all, horses have to be controlled by humans," he explained in an interview. "The rider needs to bring out the horse's best and compensate for its weaknesses. Cars are the same. They become good cars if drivers handle them well. As a result, a driver can experience a sense of jubilation beyond all reason, sort of like adding one and one to get not two but say, five or ten, which is the joy of driving a car that a driver can only feel if he and the car become like one."

Although they were grasping a car's steering wheel instead of a horse's reins, buyers of Datsun's 240Z could appreciate and enjoy Katayama's words. The 240Z was sleek and nimble, with drivers making the most of the 150 horsepower provided by the 2.4-liter inline 6-cylinder engine, especially when it was linked to a 4-speed manual transmission.

■ A Fairlady no longer, the 240Z offered aggressive styling and provided the power and agility to match its design.

DE TOMASO PANTERA

The exotic Italian sports car, available at a much more affordable price tag

Alejandro de Tomaso's grandfather had emigrated from Italy to Argentina, where the family became politically prominent, with Alejandro's father serving as Minister of Agriculture in the 1930s. But in the middle of the 1950s, Alejandro was implicated in an attempt to overthrow Argentine dictator Juan Perón and fled to Italy, his ancestral homeland, where he pursued his passion for automobile racing.

De Tomaso raced in Formula One, first for a privateer team and then for OSCA, the Officine Specializzate Costruzione Automobili team founded by the Maserati brothers.

It was also in Italy that he met and married Elizabeth "Isabelle" Haskell, herself an accomplished racing car driver and also the daughter of William C. Durant, the founder of the General Motors company.

Soon thereafter he founded De Tomaso Automobili SpA, building prototype and racing cars and, beginning in 1963, a series of high-performance sports cars, including the Vallelunga, Mangusta, and in 1971, the Pantera. He also produced a limited run of the Pampero, an open-topped sports car named for the wind that blows across the Pampas in his native Argentina.

De Tomaso's holdings would expand to include the Ghia and Vignale design and coachbuilding companies, Benelli and Moto Guzzi motorcycle manufacturers, Innocenti (the company that built British Minis in Italy), and eventually even Maserati.

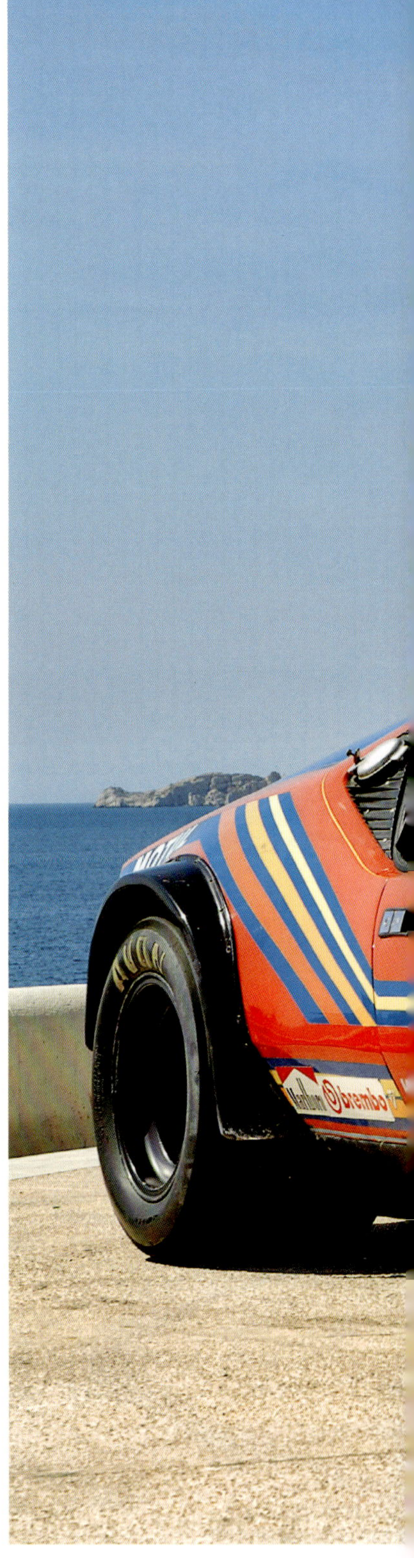

■ The Pantera GTS was a special version the company developed for motorsports competition.

1970 ➤ 1979

MICHELIN
MICHELIN
MAGNETI MARELLI
WEBER
Garage Cavallino

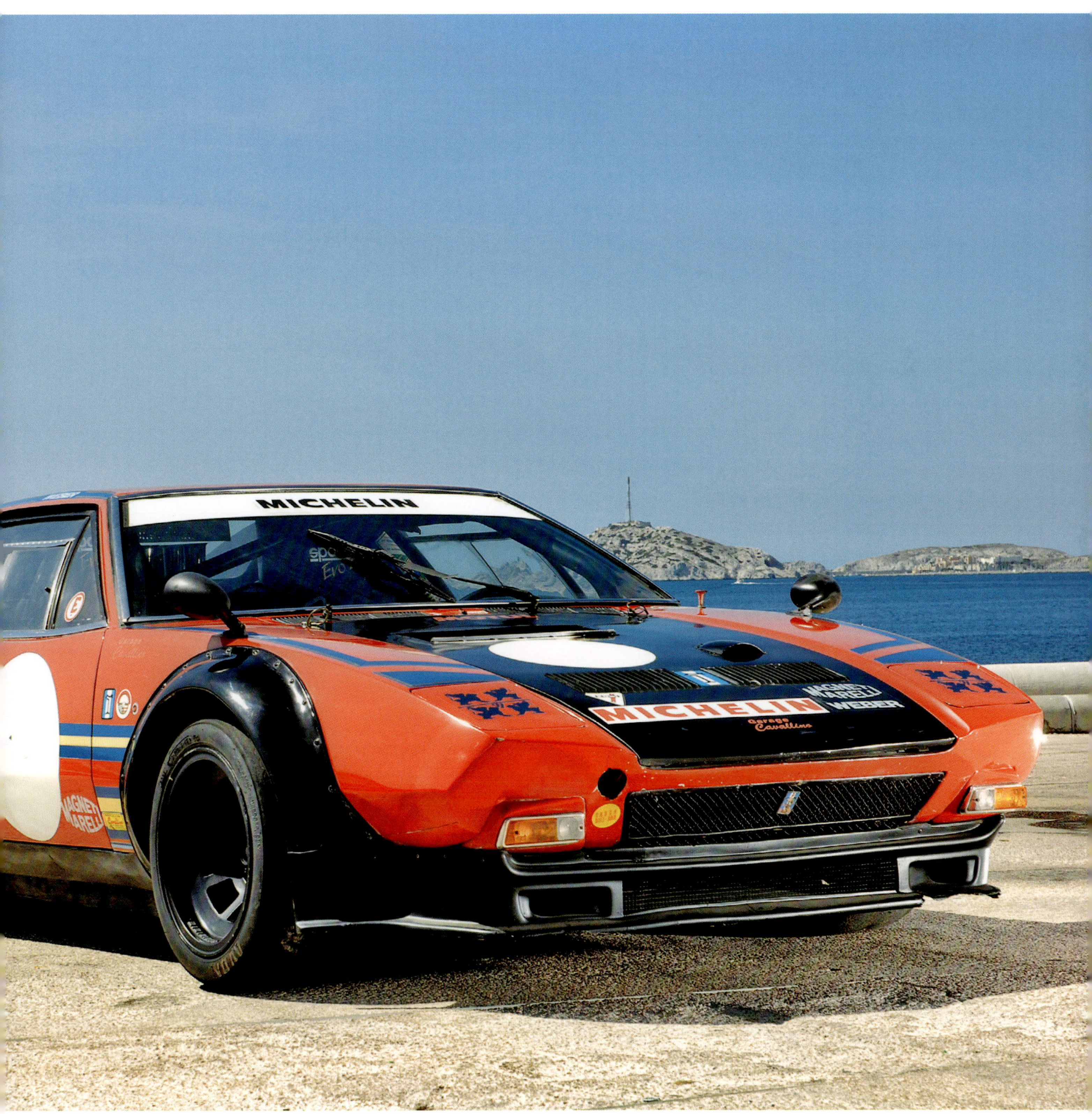

To power his various sports cars, de Tomaso acquired engines from the Ford Motor Company, a relationship that eventually led to Ford's acquisition of Ghia and, after Ford's frustration with its attempt to buy Enzo Ferrari's automaking company, the American automaker's support and an equity stake in De Tomaso, which was located in the same town as Ferrari.

In 1970, de Tomaso announced plans for a new exotic sports car, one with a sleek body design by Ghia and powered by a Ford V8, but one that would be affordable for a wider customer base. The car, the De Tomaso Pantera, would be sold and serviced in the United States by specially selected outlets of Ford's network of Lincoln-Mercury dealers.

■ In standard guise for the road, the Pantera offered luggage compartments on either side of the Ford 5.8-liter V8 engine. Room for luggage wasn't needed on the racetrack.

At one time, De Tomaso was Italy's fifth-largest automaker and also produced motorcycles.

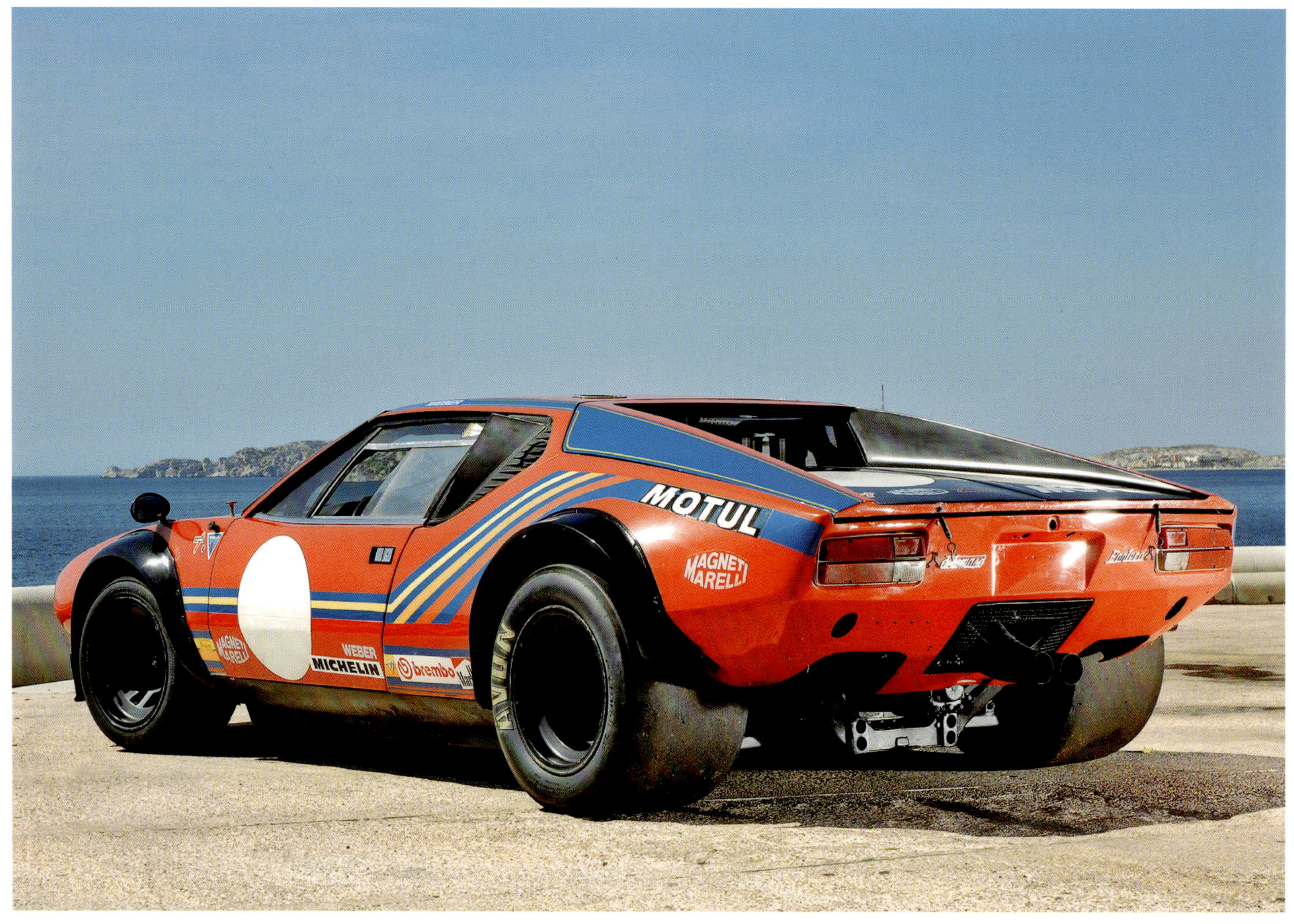

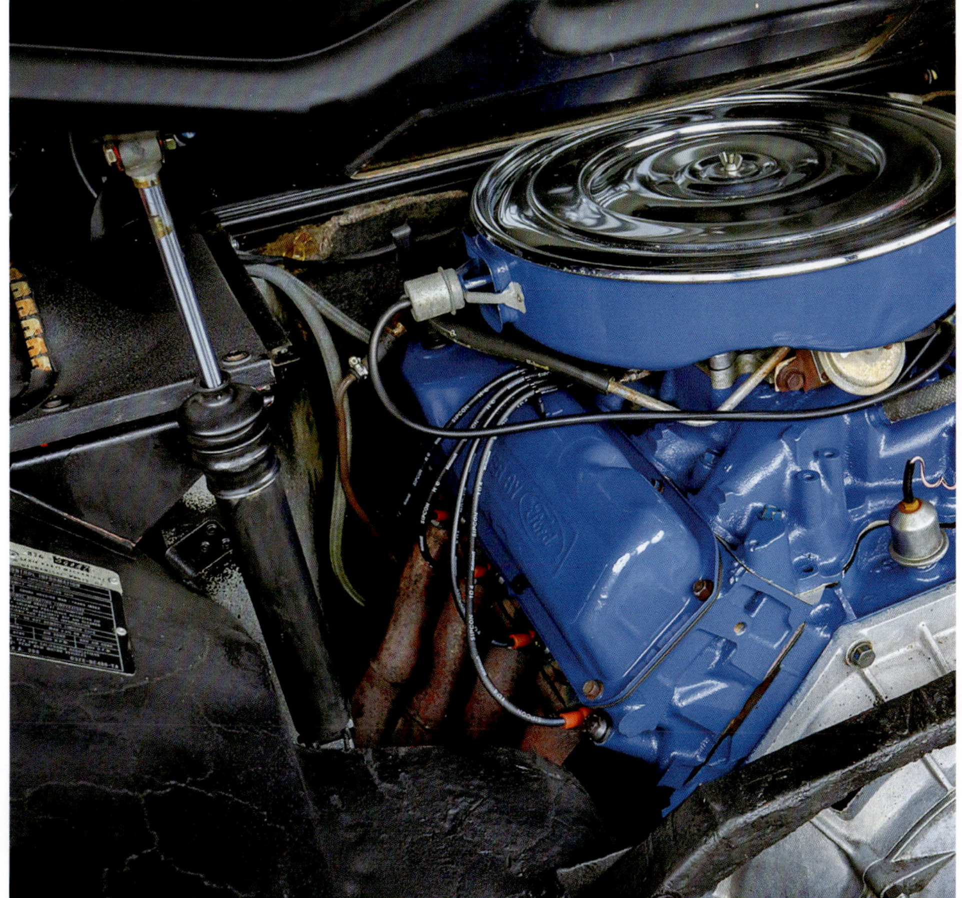

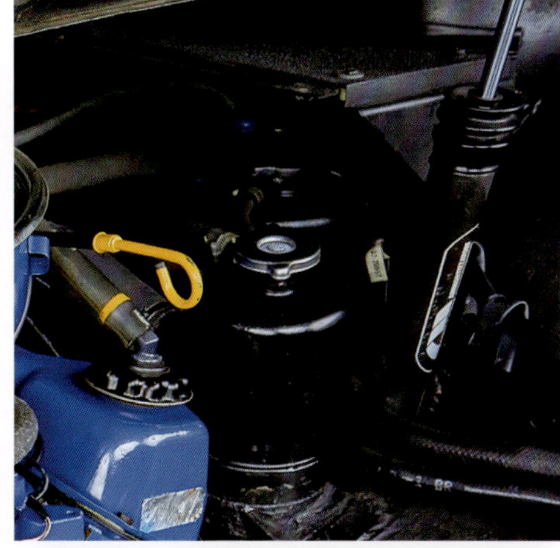

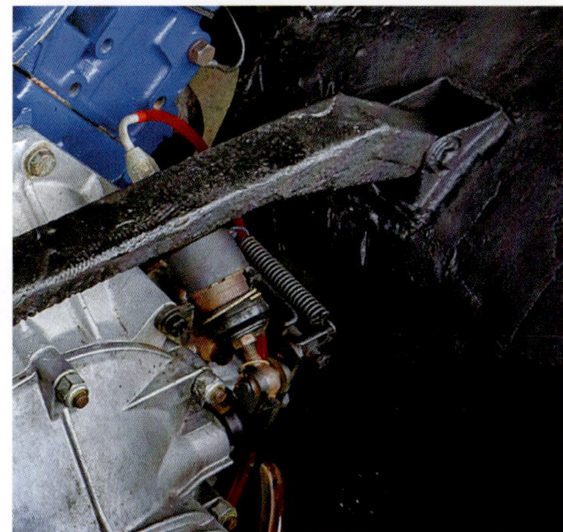

The Pantera's rear-mounted 351-cubic-inch (5.8-liter) "Cleveland" V8 engine pumped out nearly 350 horsepower, propelling the car to 60 mph (96 km/h) in 5.5 seconds on its way to a top speed of nearly 150 mph (235 km/h), and all for an American price of $9,995, less than half the cost of a Maserati Ghibli and only a third of what someone had to pay for an exotic Ferrari such as the Daytona.

Through the years, the car evolved, including a more luxurious L version, higher-performance GTS, GT5, and GT5-S models, and as production was ending, the Pantera 09 Si propelled by Ford's 302 cubic-inch/5.0-liter V8 and with other revisions.

In 1981, America's *Popular Mechanics* magazine staged a ten-car comparison test of exotics. The competitors included a BMW M1, a Porsche 928, and Lamborghini Countach, as well as three Ferraris, a Maserati, a Lotus, a Jaguar, an Aston Martin, and a Mercedes-Benz. The winner was a De Tomaso Pantera GTS.

By the 1980s, De Tomaso had become Italy's fifth-largest automaker. De Tomaso suffered a stroke in 1993 and retired from his company. In 2014, the De Tomaso brand was acquired by a Hong Kong–based company that in 2019 unveiled a limited-production sports car called the De Tomaso P72.

BMW
2002 tii

Finally, a sporty and fun car for a couple with children

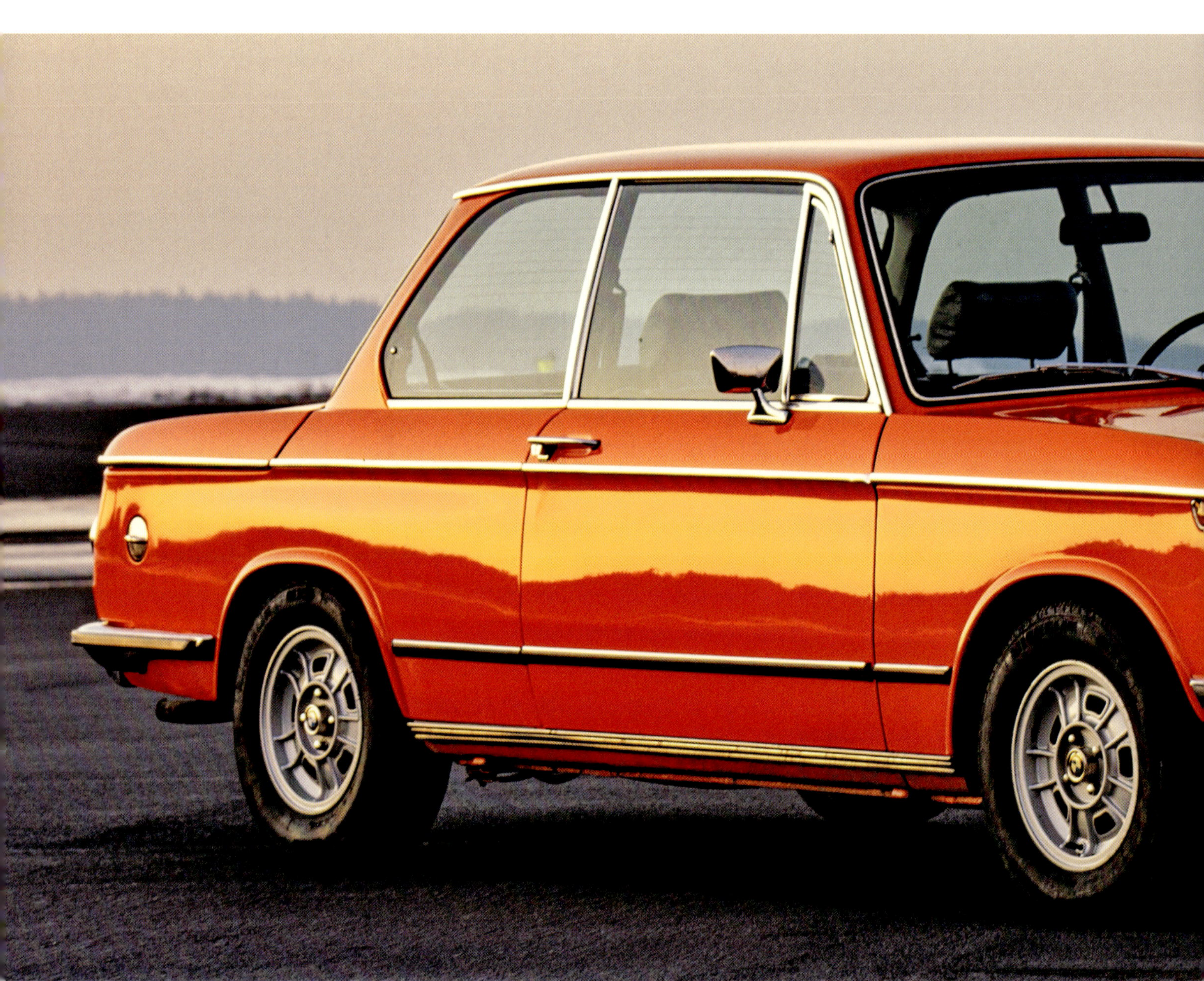

1970 ➤ 1979

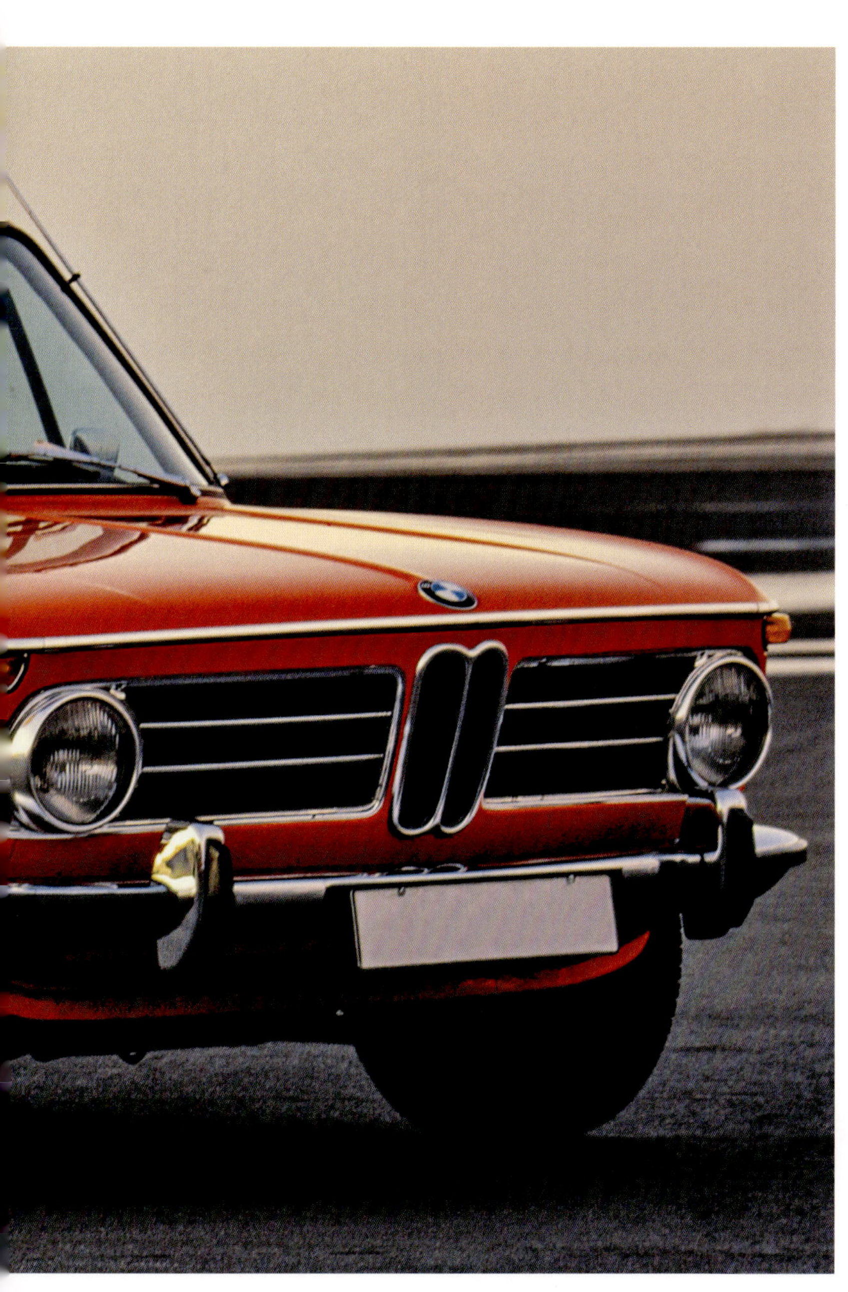

People who enjoy driving owe a debt of gratitude and appreciation to Max Hoffman, a Vienna-born American automobile dealer who in the 1950s was among the first to import European cars to the United States. But he didn't just sell cars, he eagerly made suggestions about potential improvements and new, higher-performance models.

For example, in the early postwar years, there were sports cars and there were other cars. Sports cars had two seats and were fun to drive. Other cars had back seats and were, well, dull but dutiful at best.

As *AutoWeek* magazine put it, "If you had a sports car, you could have a spouse, but if you found yourself with a spouse and a child, you had to drive something that wasn't as much fun."

German auto and motorcycle maker BMW was struggling after World War II, especially with the Soviet Union taking control of BMW's manufacturing plant in what was now East Germany. If that wasn't enough of a blow, the Allies took BMW's plans for a new sedan to England, where it indeed was produced—complete with a double-kidney grille—by British automaker Bristol.

BMW struggled. Sales were slow for its luxury model. While it survived with a license to build Italian-designed Isetta bubble cars, it very nearly found itself enfolded into Mercedes-Benz.

But BMW carried on, although it would take until nearly 1960 for it to develop a popular new model, launched as the 1500 and so named because of its 1.5-liter (1,500 cubic centimeter)

■ Traditionally, sports cars only had room for a driver and a passenger, but the 2002 from BMW added a back seat without subtracting from the driver's enjoyment.

New York importer Max Hoffman suggested BMW fit the engine from its luxury model into its small coupe.

4-cylinder engine. That car begot the 1600, and then along came Max Hoffman, who suggested that BMW could compete very well with the likes of the Mini Cooper, the Lotus Cortina, and the Alfa Romeo GTA—all cars that combined sedan styling but sporty performance—if only it would transplant the 2.0-liter powerplant from its holdover 5 Series luxury model into the compact body shell of its 1600-2 (the 2 signifying a two-door coupe).

BMW's director of product planning and its head of engineering each had an example built for his personal use, and each was so pleased with the performance that they went to the company's board of directors for series production approval. And thus was the launch of the BMW 2002, which not only provided a back seat and a trunk but sports car–level performance, an accomplishment verified when the 2002 became the first sedan to lap the historic Nürburgring racing circuit in less than ten minutes.

Car and Driver magazine proclaimed the 2002 to be "one of modern civilization's all-time best ways of getting somewhere sitting down."

The 2002 debuted as a 1968 model...but wait, there's more—much more.

In 1971 BMW enhanced the car's performance even further with the 2002 tii, the letters behind the numbers representing turismo internazionale (and fuel) injection. Now, instead of 114 horsepower, the driving experience was enhanced by the availability of 130 horsepower.

But there was even more to come: In 1974 and 1975, BMW offered the 2002 turbo, which boasted 170 horsepower and was outfitted with fender flares, rally lights, and wider tires.

After doing its road test in 1972, *Car and Driver* offered very high praise indeed for the 2002 tii, proclaimed this car could be driven "as if you had diplomatic immunity."

■ The BMW 2002 proved quite competitive in motorsports competitions, winning the inaugural 1970 twenty-four-hour race at the Nürburgring and the 1971 European Rally Championship.

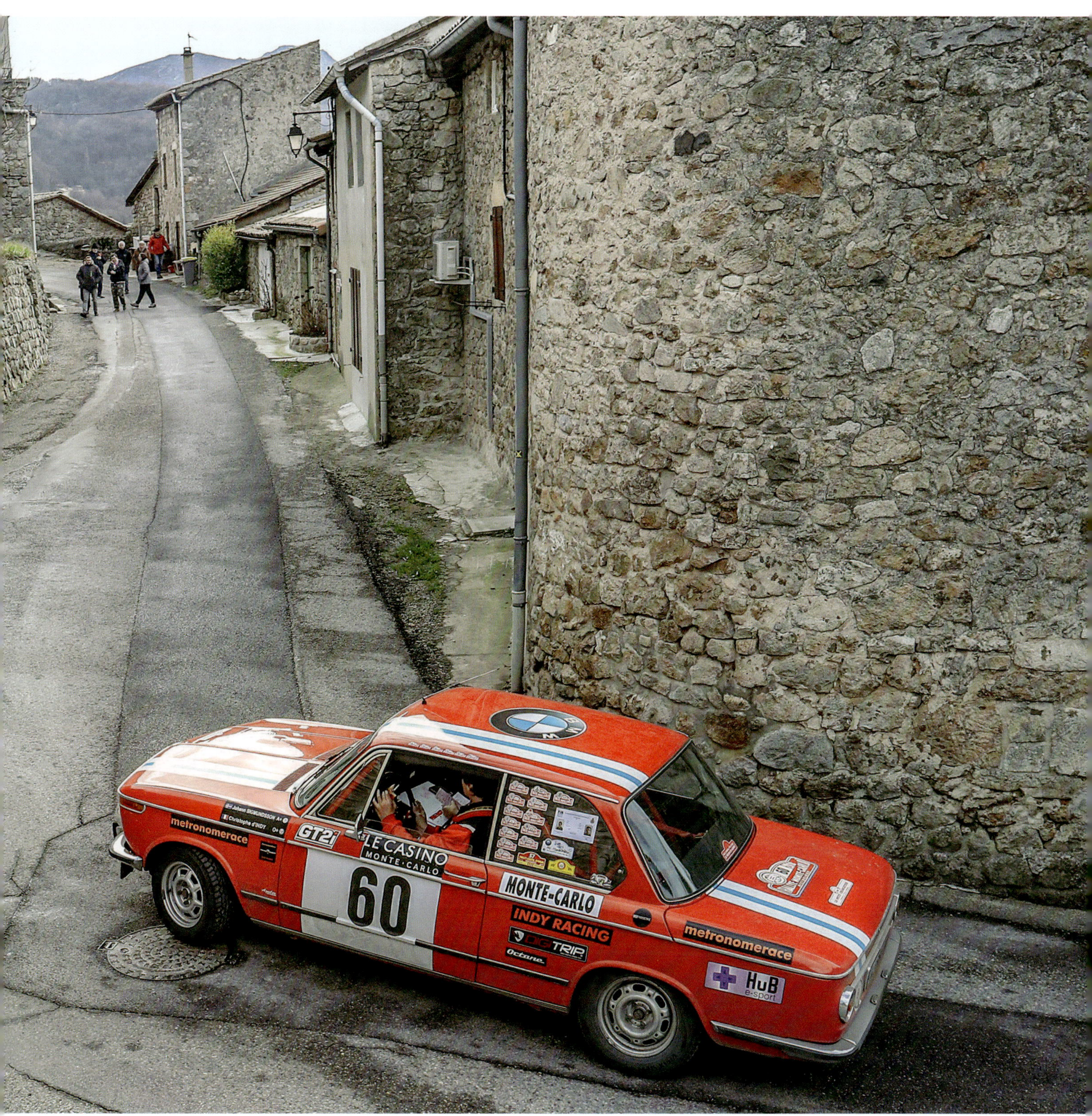
metronomerace
GT2i
LE CASINO
MONTE-CARLO
60
MONTE-CARLO
INDY RACING
metronomerace
HuB
e-sport

PORSCHE
911 CARRERA RS 2.7

Adding a "ducktail" not only tamed this Porsche but made it iconic

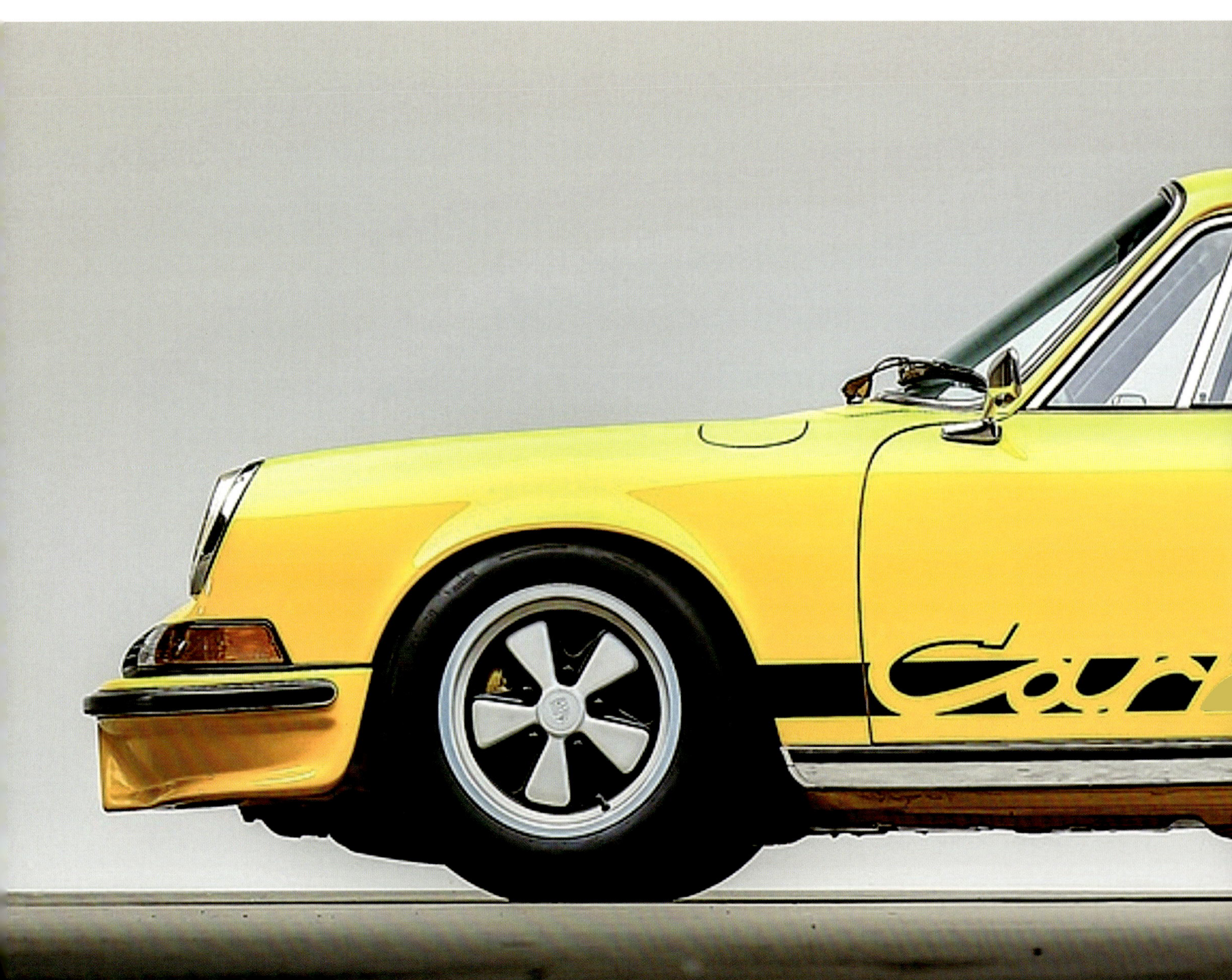

"Everybody was laughing at this 911 on the test track," Tilman Brodbeck said in an interview with *Octane* magazine. "They said there's no way it can be faster with that strange thing on the rear...But it turned out well."

Well indeed, and it was Porsche that would have the last laugh as it showed its new "ducktail" rear spoiler to the rest of the field in global sports car racing.

Brodbeck was a young engineer back in the early 1970s when he was part of the team, small in size and in budget and with tight deadlines, nonetheless instructed to fix the 911's misbehavior on the racetrack. Their solution helped to create a car model that *Octane* magazine termed "the most iconic 911 of all," the Carrera RS 2.7.

The work on a solution began in May 1972, and the result was displayed that October at the Paris Auto Show. Not just a race car, but a new road model as well, and wearing a distinctive rear spoiler and badging that harkened to the famed La Carrera Panamericana road race in Mexico and to the German word for "racing sport"—Rennsport. The 2.7 numbers represented the engine displacement in liters. This was the first time any Porsche model carried both the Carrera and RS badges.

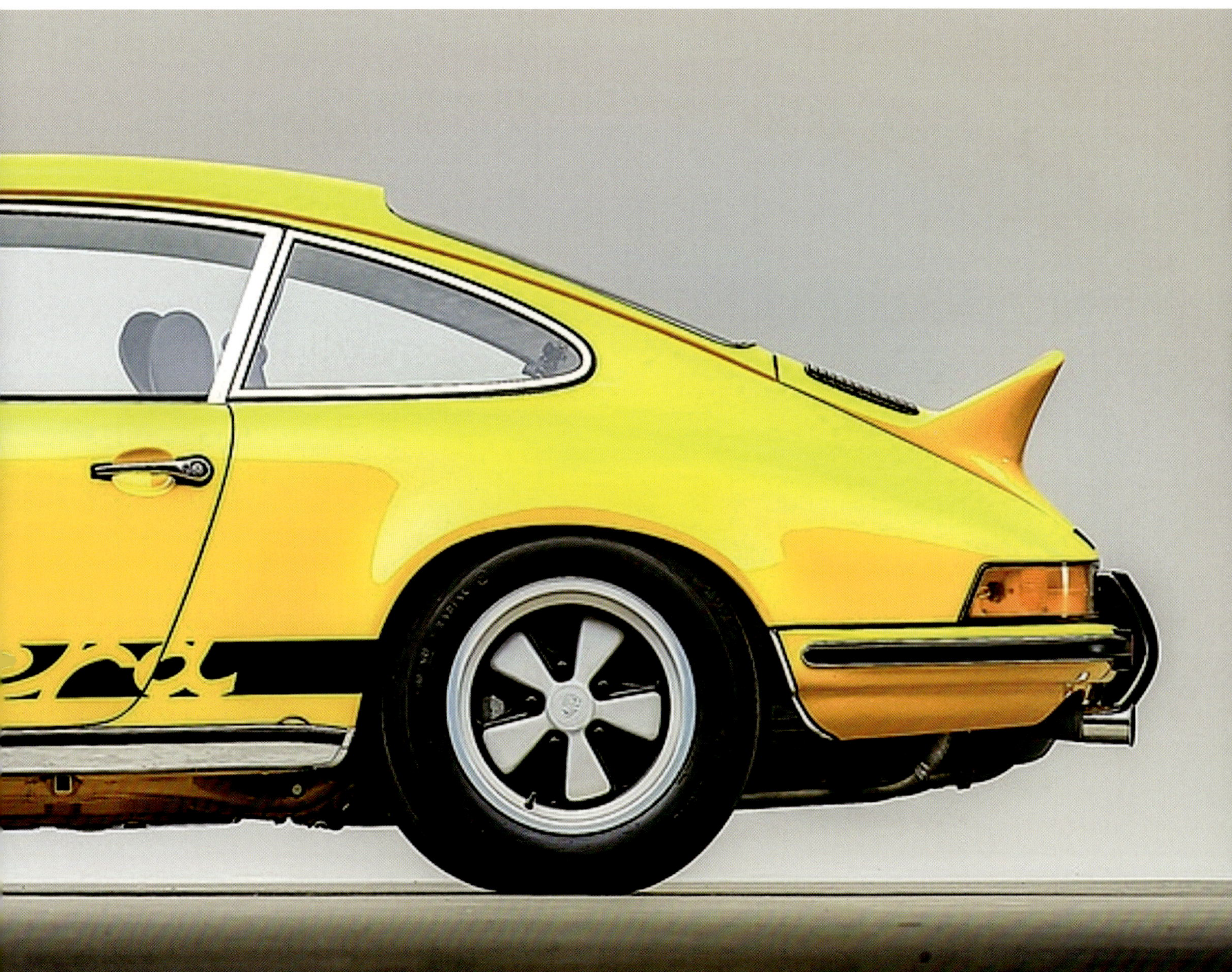

As it turned out, the new if rather large rear-mounted aerodynamic device not only improved high-speed handling, but the way it directed airflow around it helped to cool the car's air-cooled engine.

To make the car eligible for international sports car racing, Porsche would have to produce 500 cars, the Touring version, for road use. In an effort to try to meet customer demand, it would produce more than three times that many.

"At the time," recalled Porsche engineer Hermann Burst, "I thought the spoiler was just a solution to a technical problem. It took me a long time to realize that we had created an icon."

In addition to the rear ducktail, the Carrera RS 2.7 was equipped with wider rear tires (and flared rear-wheel arches to cover them), enhanced suspension components, and thinner glass, and in the Sport version such weight-saving actions as the elimination of carpeting and rear seats, not even a dashboard clock or glove box lid.

The standard 2.4-liter 911 engine was replaced with a 2.7-liter version good for nearly 210 horsepower. *Car and Driver* magazine proclaimed it to be "one of the quickest sports cars on the planet."

How effective were the changes? In 1972, only a single Porsche 911 S was among the top forty in the

Previous pages ■ Flared rear-wheel arches to cover wider tires were one of the visible signs that this Porsche 911 was something special.

Bottom ■ The ducktail rear spoiler not only calmed the car's rear end at high speeds but directed cooling air to the engine bay.

Opposite page ■ To make the car lighter, thinner glass was used, and carpeting, rear seats, and even the dashboard clock were eliminated.

Following pages ■ Porsche's 911 Carrera RS 2.7 also proved its capabilities on the racetrack.

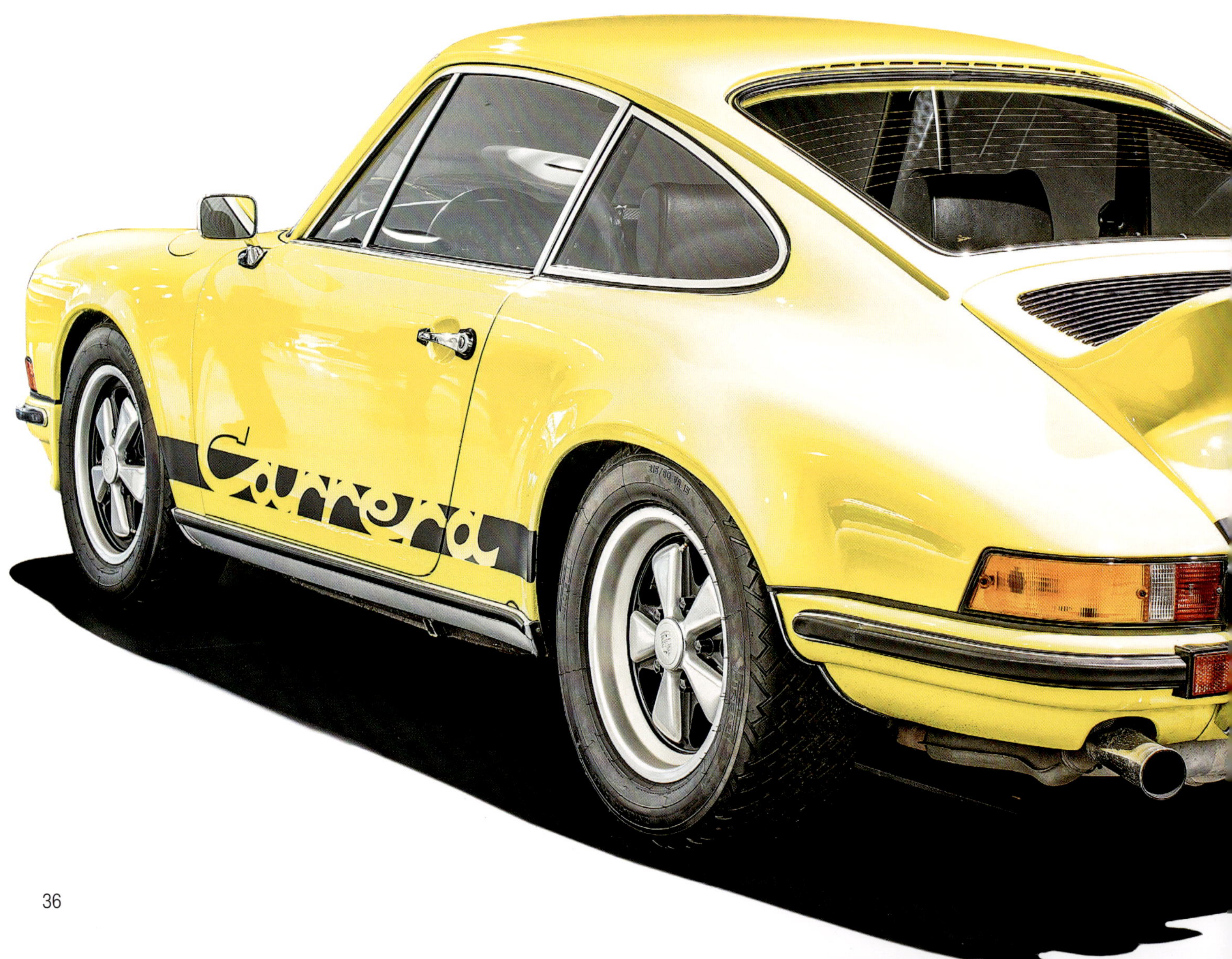

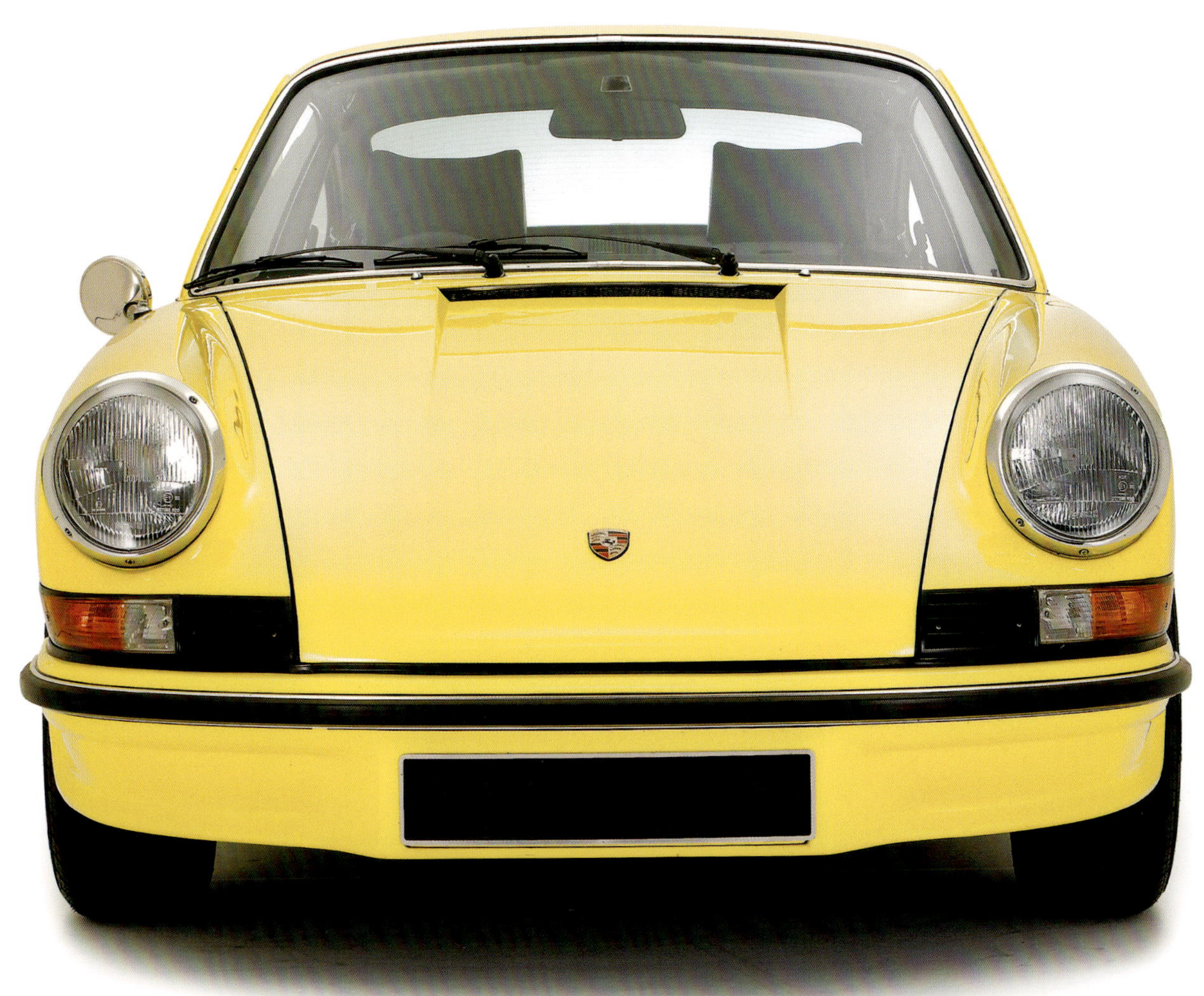

Porsche needed 500 road-going copies to make the car eligible for racing but needed many more to satisfy customer demand.

24 Hours of Le Mans race. The following year, equipped with the ducktail spoilers, three Carrera racers were among the top ten, one of them beaten to the finish line only by three of the sport prototype racers with their 12-cylinder engines.

For the RS's fiftieth anniversary, Porsche invited automotive journalists to drive examples from its museum. "Older cars often feel like a museum piece when viewed through the prism of modern experience—slow and soft and imprecise, even if replete with the cultural associations we love them for," *Car and Driver* observed. "But the 911 Carrera RS 2.7 is a museum piece that has both huge cultural resonance and a compelling driving experience. The various lightweight 911 derivatives that have followed, through GT and RS incarnations, have been faster and grippier. But none have possessed the significance of this early pioneer."

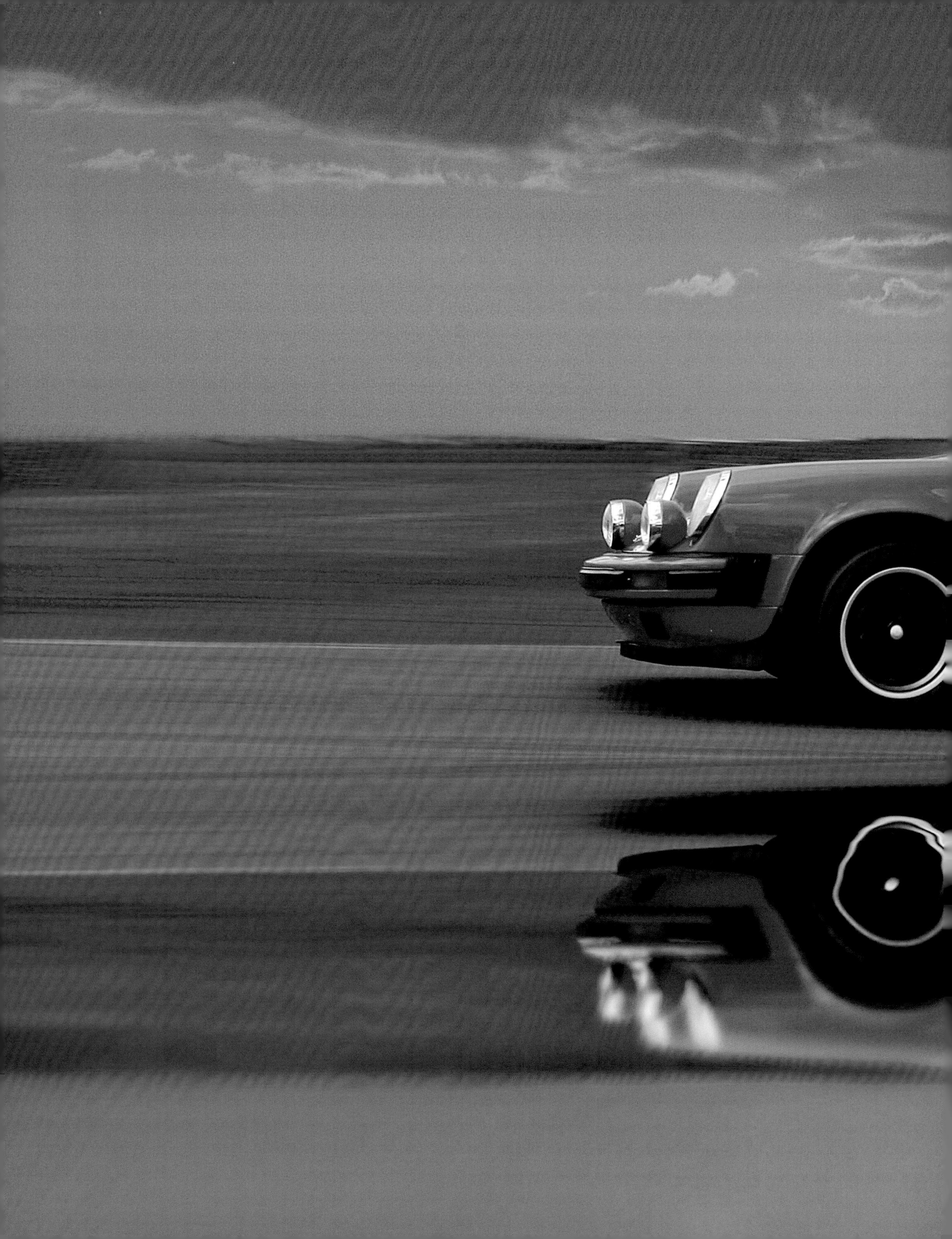

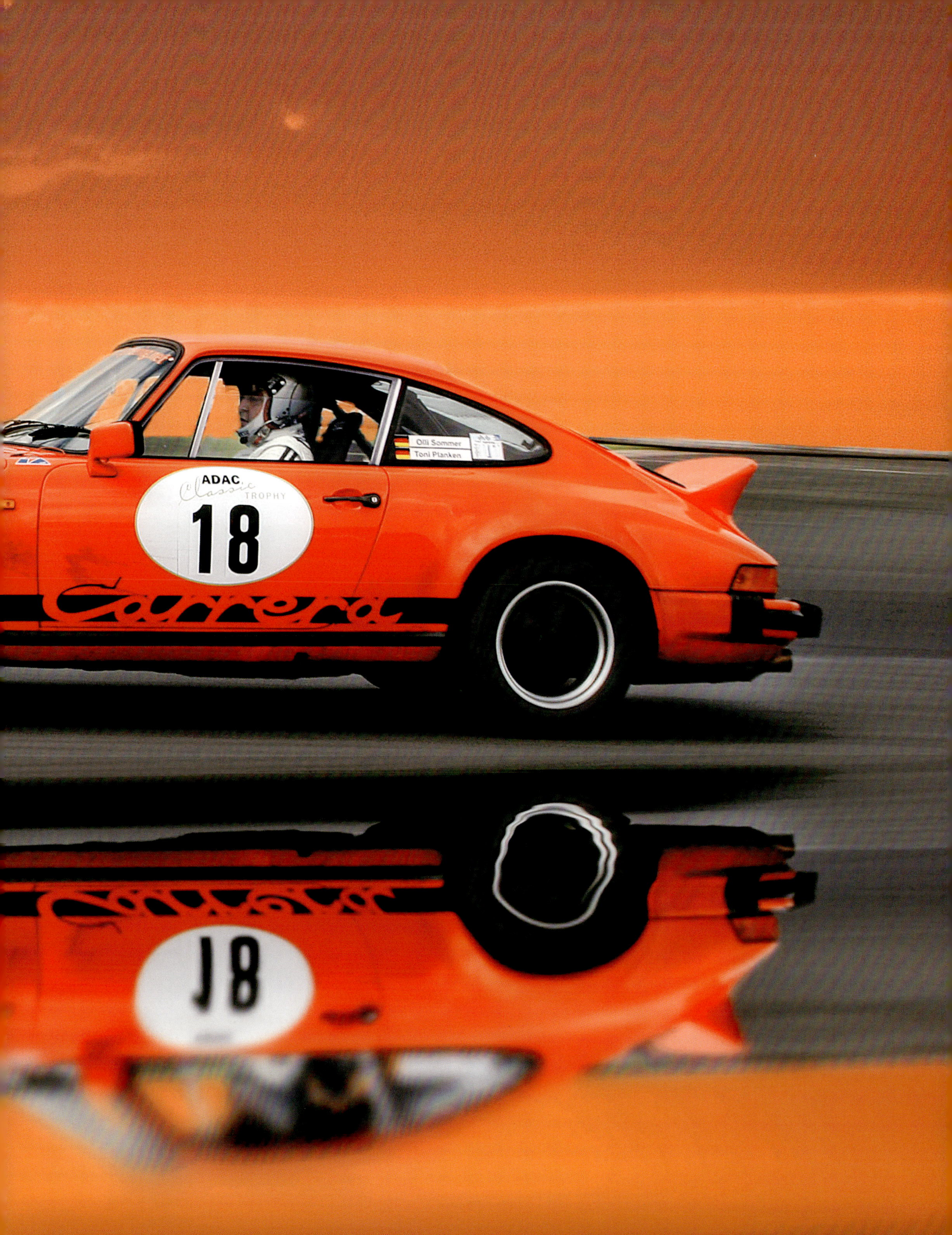
ADAC
Classic
TROPHY
18
Carrera
Olli Sommer
Toni Planken

LANCIA STRATOS

A car so low slung it drove under the guard-gate bar when it visited the factory

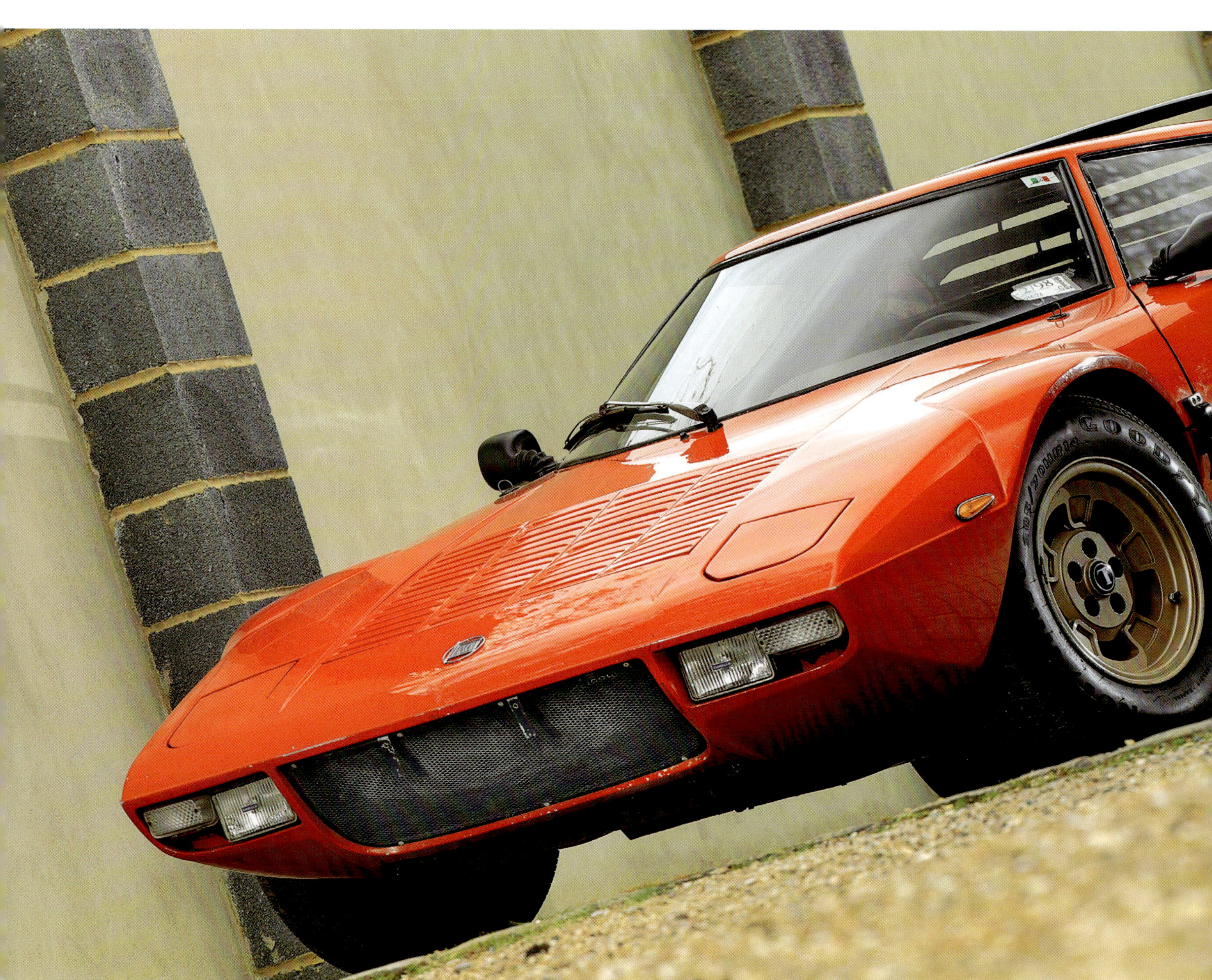

1970 ➤ 1979

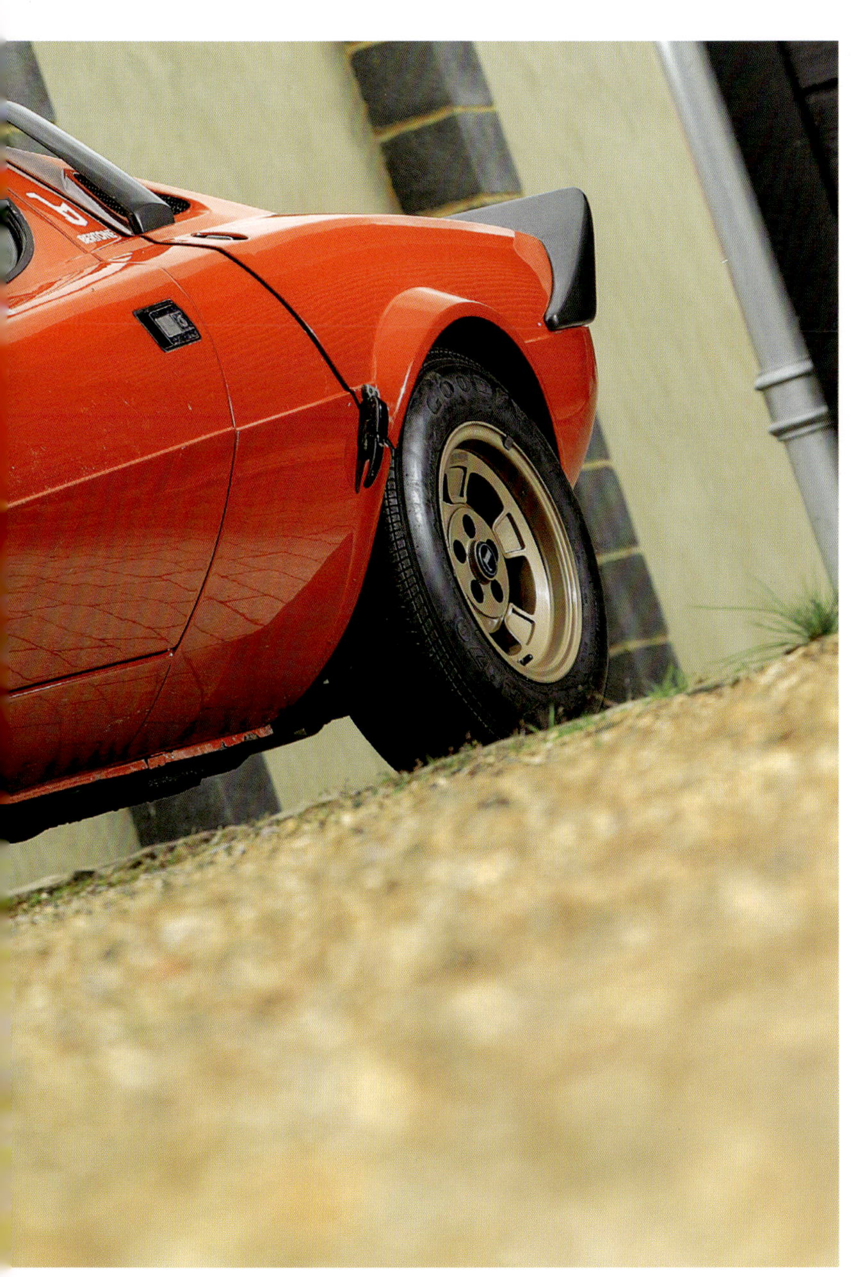

Vincenzo Lancia was the youngest child born into a wealthy soup-making family in Turin, Italy, but for whatever reason, at age seventeen, he went to work as a bookkeeper for Turin's new automobile company, Ceirano. But instead of keeping track of numbers, young Vincenzo spent much of his time as an unofficial apprentice to the company's designer, Aristide Faccioli.

Within a year, Giovanni Ceirano and his brothers sold their fledgling company to Giovanni Agnelli and his Fabbrica Italiana Automobili di Torino (FIAT), where Lancia won the job as chief vehicle inspector and test driver. It is likely through that later duty that he started racing cars, winning the Coppa Florio in 1904.

Friends told Lancia he should start his own car-making company. However, he thought he needed more experience. Finally, in 1906, he bought a car-making facility, hired a staff of twenty, and built a car—only to have his workshop and his car destroyed in a fire.

He started again from scratch and seven months later had produced another car, and then another, and then many more. In 1930 he provided financial support to Battista Farina and his new Carrozzeria Pininfarina. But seven years later, Vincenzo Lancia died of a heart attack, and in 1955 his heirs sold the automaking company, which five years later would be enfolded into Fiat.

■ Marcello Gandini designed the Stratos around parts pilfered from a friend's Lancia Fulvia coupe.

The Italian industrial giant supported Lancia's motorsports heritage, which led to the development of a new model, the Stratos. It was a mid-engine sports car designed with success in rallying as the target.

Instead of Pininfarina, this car's design was done at Bertone by Marcello Gandini, who at the same time was working on the Lamborghini Countach. Gandini, designer of the Lamborghini Miura, the world's first "supercar," borrowed a friend's Lancia Fulvia coupe and used it to create a design concept, the Stratos O, which was a low-slung wedge, so low that when he drove it to the Lancia factory one day, it passed beneath the closed guard-gate arm.

Soon the Lancia Zero would create a sensation when it was officially unveiled at the Turin Auto Show.

A prototype for the Stratos HF rally car was dis-

■ Designed for rallying, the Stratos dominated the World Rally Championship and the historic Monte Carlo Rally in the mid-1970s.
In civilian guise on regular paved roads, the Stratos driver may have felt as if the Ferrari Dino engine was "strapped on your back."

Vincenzo Lancia started as a bookkeeper but soon became chief vehicle inspector and test driver at Fiat.

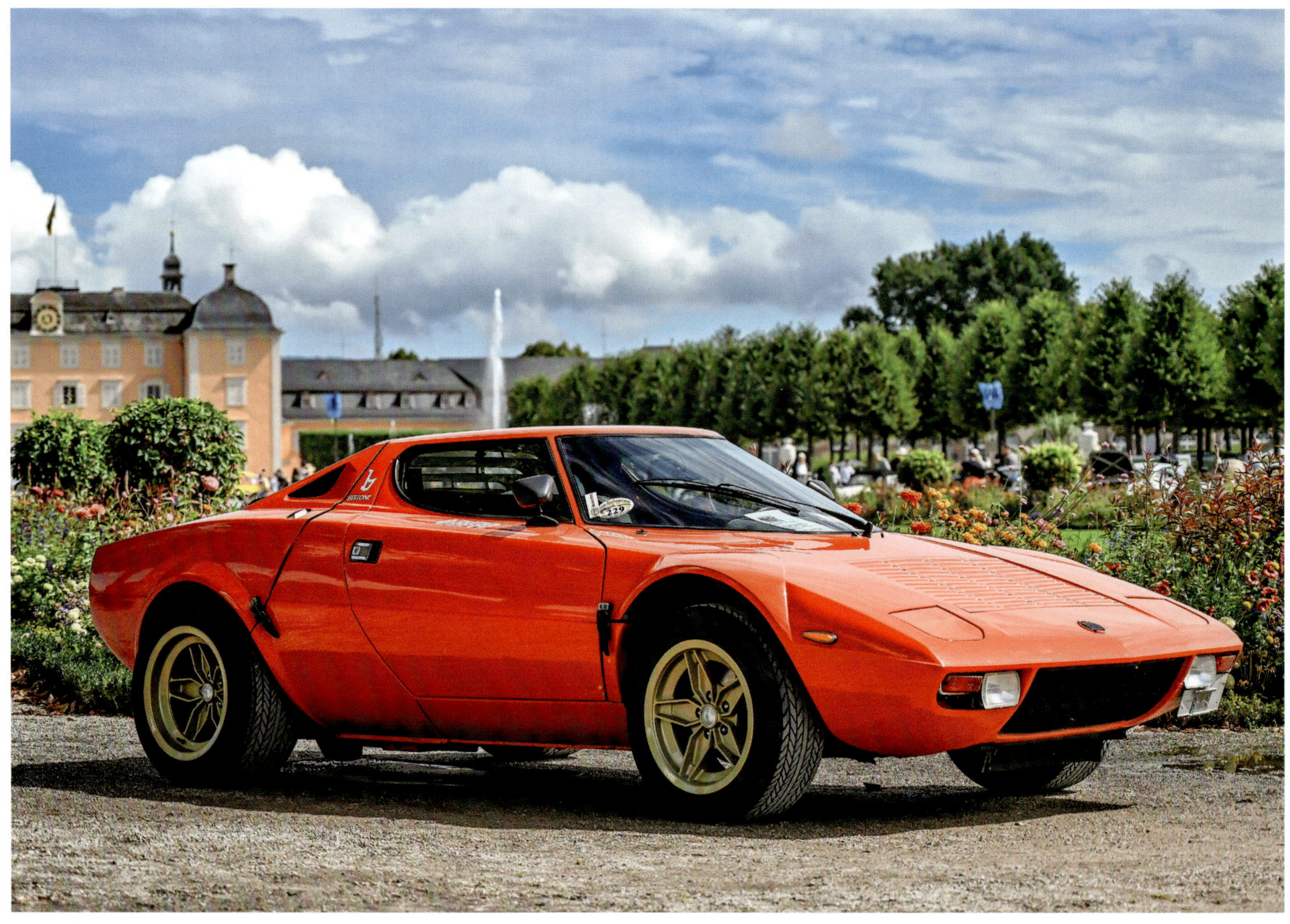

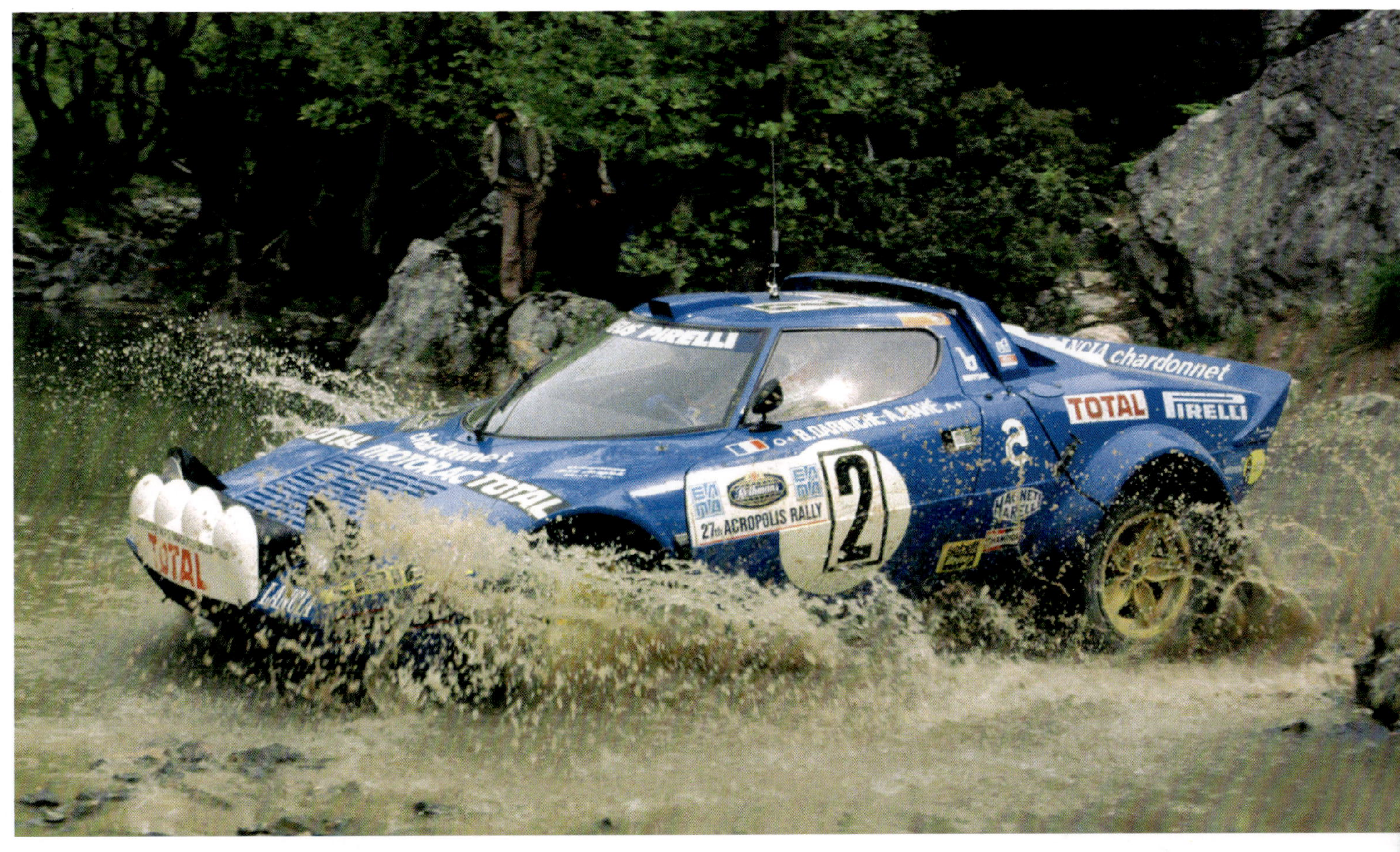

played at Turin a year later. Three different engines were tested, and Enzo Ferrari finally approved use of his company's Dino V6.

The Stratos is considered the first car specifically designed for rallying, with Lancia team manager Cesare Fiorio, British racer/engineer Mike Parkes, Lancia engineer Nicola Materazzi, and factory rally driver Sandro Munari as the key developers.

The car weighed less than 950 kilograms and dominated competition, even with its engine detuned from street-use levels in compliance with rally rules.

The World Rally Championship launched in 1973. Alpine won the inaugural title, and Lancia swept the next three, with Munari taking the inaugural driver's championship in 1977. He also dominated the prestigious Monte Carlo Rally, winning the event for Lancia in 1974, 1975, and 1976.

The string might have been extended but for the internal rivalry within Fiat, resulting in Fiat-branded cars winning the manufacturers' crown in 1977 and 1978. But Lancia would come back later with its Delta Integrale, sweeping the maker's title from 1987 through 1992.

Car and Driver magazine reported on the Stratos in a 1975 issue: "Just riding in a Stratos, its Ferrari Dino engine strapped virtually on your back, is a searing, inebriating experience that assaults every sensory perception you possess. You sit in the confines of a gun turret. The steeply inclined windshield wraps around you like the faceshield of a Bellstar helmet. Looking forward, the nose of the car is invisible; all you can see are the two bulges in the body that cover the front tires...

"Step on the pedal and the asphalt conveyor belt in front of the car starts passing under the lower edge of the windshield with ever-increasing velocity."

LOTUS ESPRIT

Sports car–turned–submarine became famous for its role as James Bond's ride in The Spy Who Loved Me

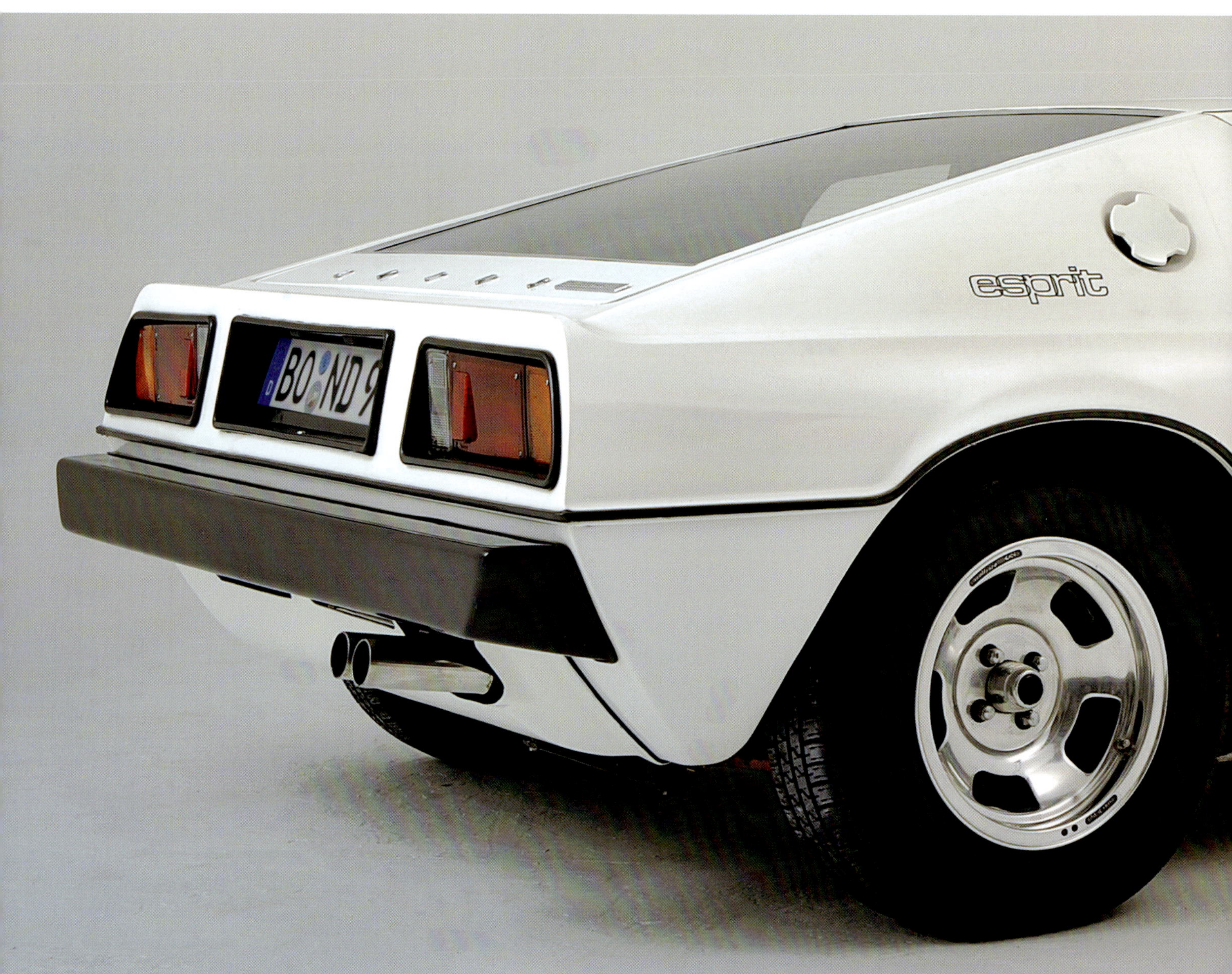

1970 ➤ 1979

Automotive enthusiasts know Lotus as the maker of racing cars that won in Formula One and in the Indianapolis 500 and of some of the world's most exotic sports cars. But perhaps there are just as many if not more people who know Lotus for the role a Lotus Esprit S1 played in the 1977 James Bond movie *The Spy Who Loved Me*.

The 007's Esprit was nicknamed "Wet Nellie," a homage to "Little Nellie," an autogyro flying device deployed in the earlier Bond film *You Only Live Twice*. The word "wet" was justified because this particular wedge-shaped Lotus sports car could be driven on land or from land into the water, where it functioned as a submarine. In typical Q Division engineering creativity, the car's weapons were designed to be used on land or underwater.

While at university, where he studied engineering, Chapman started modifying and racing cars. In 1951, about a year before Ian Fleming's publisher shared James Bond with the world, Chapman launched Lotus Engineering, which built cars for its own motorsports projects and to sell to other racers. Like Ferrari, it also built some cars for the road, the income helping support the racing effort.

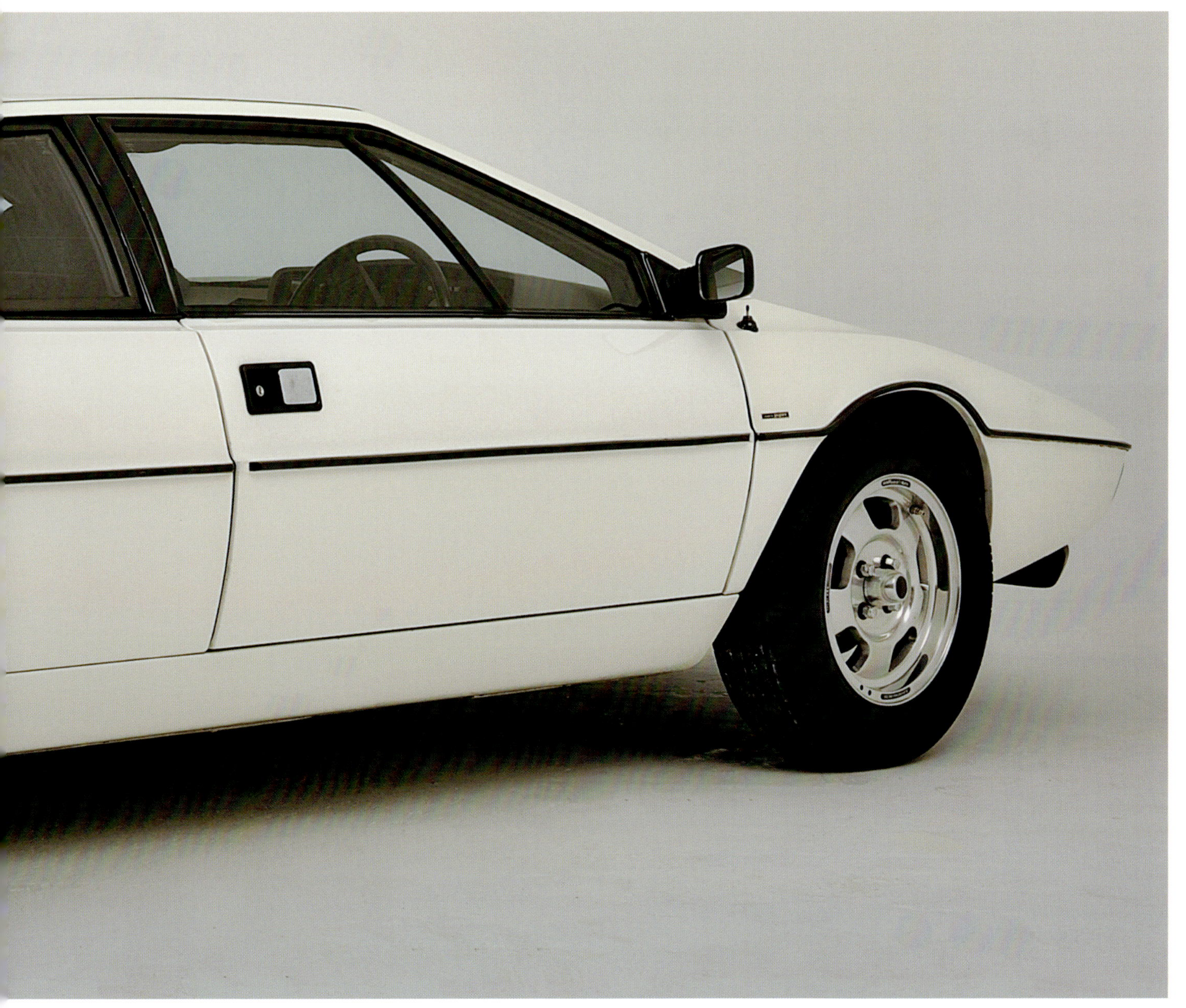

Chapman entered a car at Le Mans in 1955 and again in 1956, when a second Lotus finished seventh overall, and in 1957 the two-car team again had success, one car in the top ten and the one Chapman co-drove winning its class. Chapman then retired from driving race cars but started producing them in real earnest with the Lotus 7, which was designed for road and track. His race cars would win in Formula One (seven Constructors' Championships between 1963 and 1978) and at Indianapolis (where in 1965 Lotus was the first rear-engined winner of the world's most prestigious motor race).

Launched in 1957, the Lotus Elite was Chapman's first car designed primarily for street use. It would be followed by the Elan, Europa, Elite, Éclat, and in 1976, the Esprit.

The Esprit was a mid-engine car with a 4-cylinder engine and sharply creased fiberglass coachwork designed by Giorgetto Giugiaro and his Italdesign studio (Giugiaro later would do a restyling for the Esprit, and the Esprit's chassis would be adapted for use as the basis of the stainless-steel bodied DeLorean DMC). The Esprit would get more power, including turbocharging and eventually a V8 engine and three other redesigns, with smoother coachwork first by Peter Stevens of McLaren F1 fame, and continue in production into the twenty-first century.

In 2013, Britain's *Evo* magazine published an article about its recent drive in a first-generation Esprit, noting that as the car was launched, "Team Lotus had won six F1 Constructors' Championships; Ronnie Peterson was driving the wheels off a JPS Lotus 76 every other weekend...these were the halcyon days, and Lotus was bristling with potential and bathed in glamour."

It noted the engine was the Lotus-tweaked version of the one used in the Citroën SM, and while perhaps underpowered, the car is "light, alive with agility and poise...you feel millimeters above the ground. And like the coolest person in Norfolk; possibly the world."

In other words, just like 007 himself—well, except for the underwater bit.

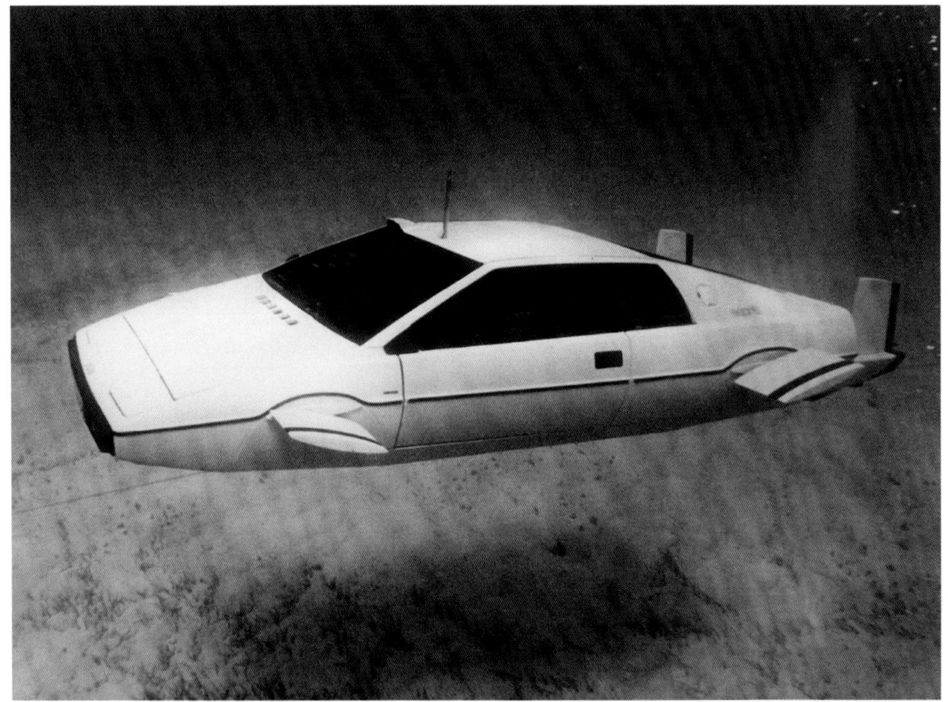

Previous pages ■ Giorgetto Giugiaro was voted Car Designer of the Century, and the Lotus Esprit was just one example of his work.

This page ■ Sports car morphed into a submarine for its role on the road and in the water in *The Spy Who Loved Me*.

Opposite page ■ Throughout its twenty-eight years in production and several styling revisions, the Esprit would retain its pop-up headlamps. License plates bearing the name BOND or even WETNLY were popular with Esprit-driving fans of 007.

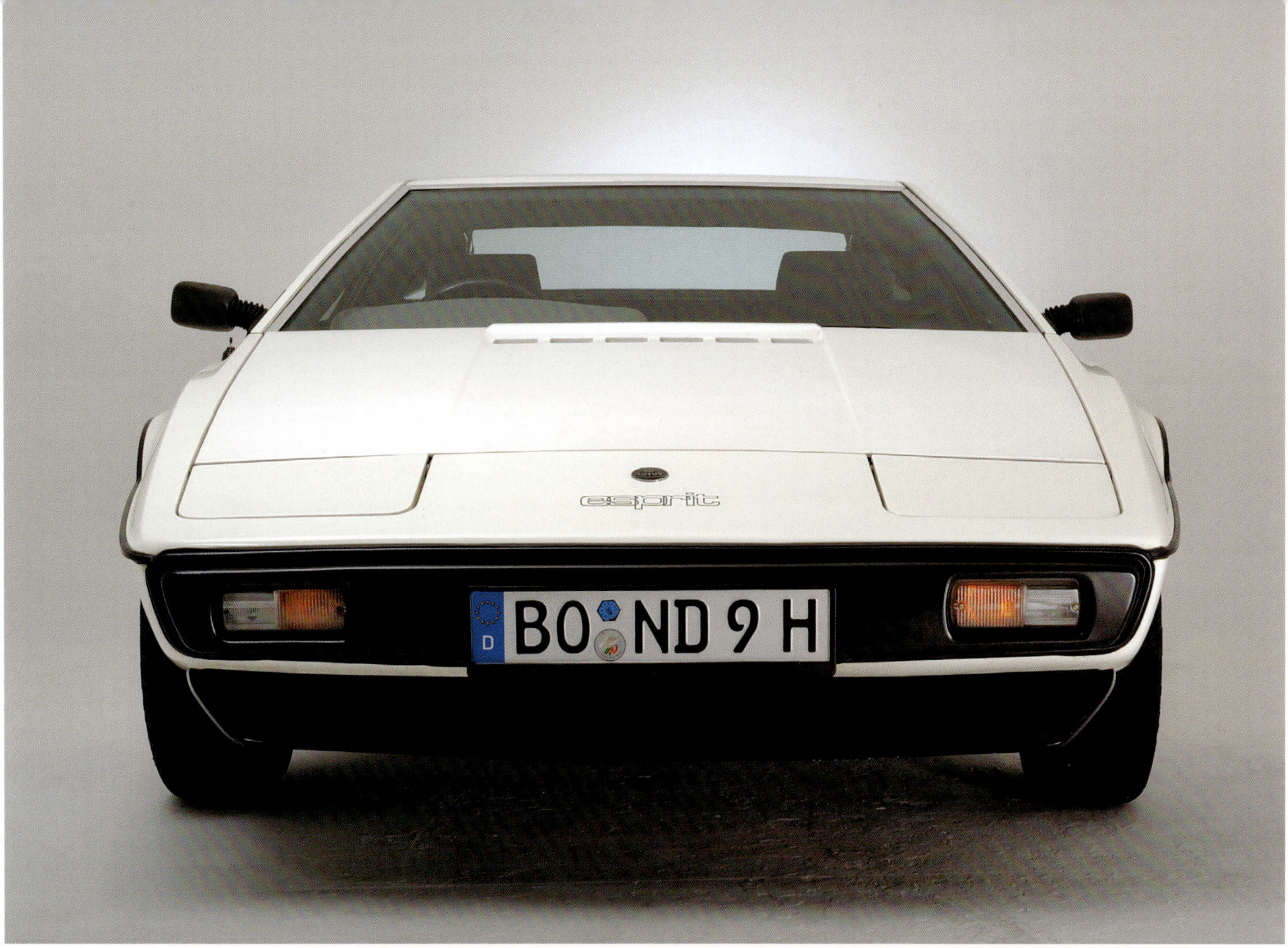

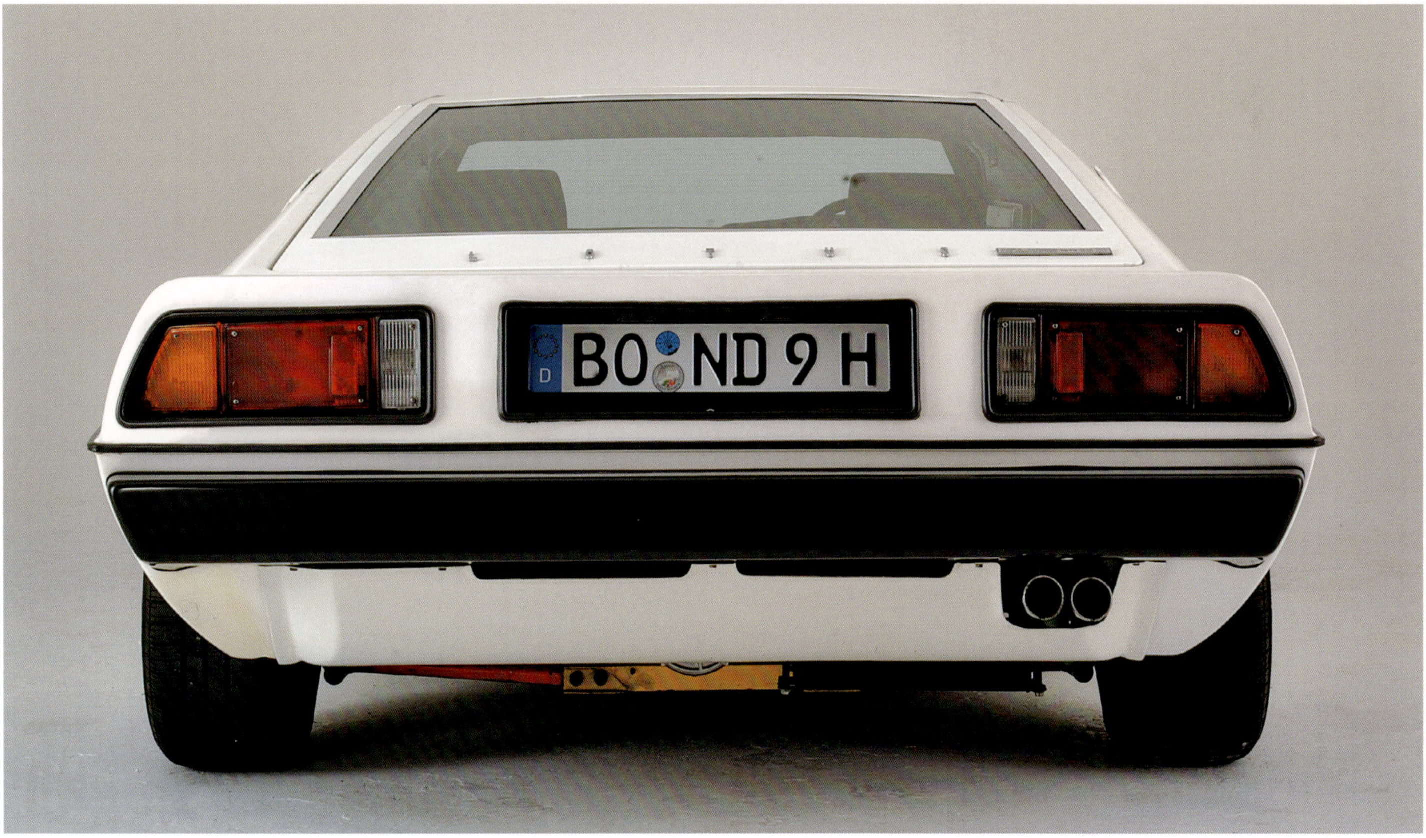

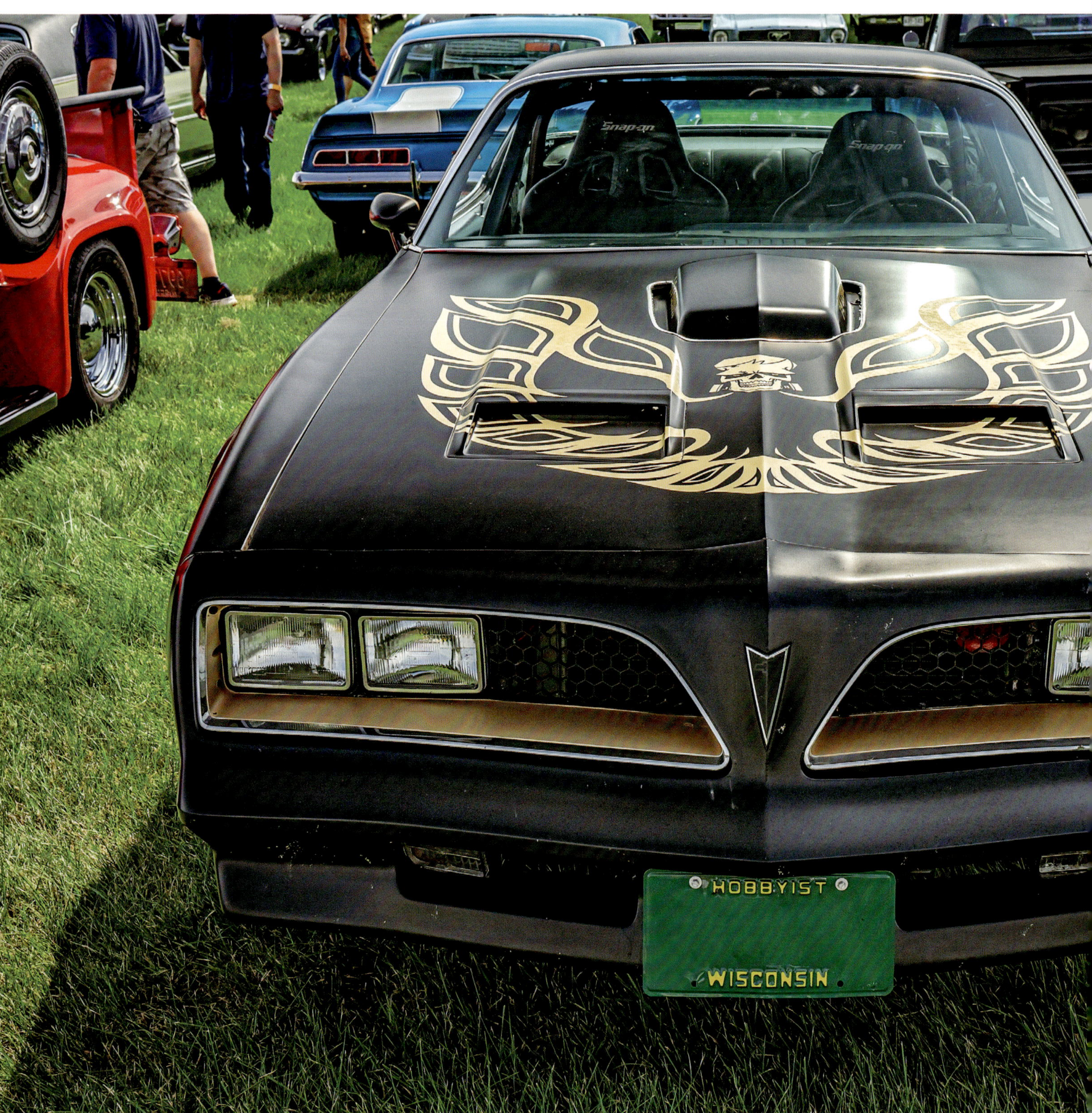
Snap-on
Snap-on
HOBBYIST
WISCONSIN

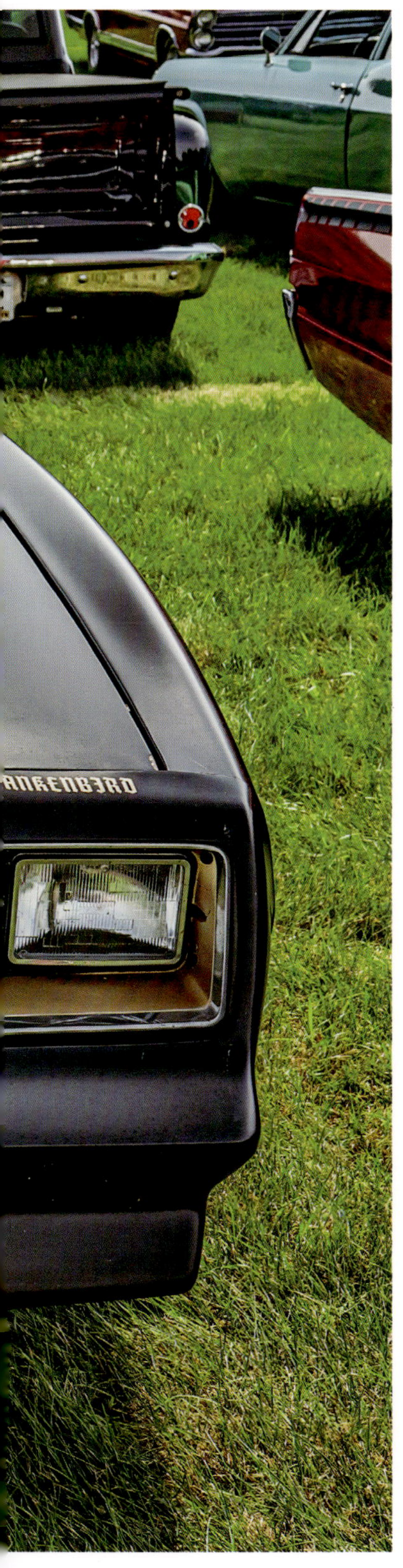

PONTIAC FIREBIRD

Like 007's Aston Martin, this car was made famous by its role in the Smokey and the Bandit *movies*

In the 1980s, the tagline for advertising by the Pontiac Motor Division of General Motors was "We Build Excitement." That phrase certainly was justified after the design, development, production, and popularity of vehicles such as the Pontiac GTO, Firebird, and Trans Am of the 1960s and '70s.

Midway through the 1964 automotive model year, Ford had stunned the car world with the unveiling of its Mustang, a sporty coupe and convertible that for 1965 became even more striking with a new fastback roofline. The car was so popular that it spurred an entirely new car category, the pony car.

It would take until 1967 for rivals such as General Motors to catch up and offer their own entries in the category—first the Chevrolet Camaro and then a few months later, the Pontiac Firebird. Initially, the Firebird was offered during the 1967 model year as a coupe or convertible and with an inline 6-cylinder engine or with V8s rated at 250, 285, or 329 horsepower.

Late in the 1969 model year, Pontiac added a high-performance Trans Am version of its Firebird. The performance upgrade included a heavy-duty, floor-mounted 3-speed shifter, high-performance rear axle, heavy-duty suspension and fiberglass-belted tires, variable-ratio power steering, engine air exhaust louvers, rear deck air foil, and special exterior trim, as well as the availability of a 400-cubic-inch, 345-horsepower engine.

While Firebird was a name General Motors had used on a trio of futuristic concept cars in the 1950s, the Trans Am borrowed its name from the Sports Car Club of America's Trans-Am (Trans-American Sedan Championship), a sports car racing series that featured the new pony car class. Pontiac paid the SCCA a licensing fee for badging each of the Trans Am cars it produced.

■ General Motors responded to the popularity of Ford's Mustang with cars such as the Pontiac Firebird (left) and the Chevrolet Camaro.

The Firebird's original "Coke-bottle" styling changed for 1970 with what was termed a "swoopy" design that would last for more than a decade. It was during this decade that Hollywood forever enhanced the Firebird's image.

Hot Rod magazine termed that second-generation version "the most popular...Its combination of beautiful styling, superb handling, and strong Pontiac V-89 performance makes Firebirds and Trans Ams of this era highly coveted by collectors and performance traditionalist alike."

As if that wasn't enough, in 1977 director Hal Needham signed actors Burt Reynolds, Jackie Gleason, Jerry Reed, and Sally Field to star in a movie titled *Smokey and the Bandit*. However, many considered the real star of the film to be the Pontiac Trans Am that Reynolds drove in what became a race against time (and pursuing police) across the American South and back.

Pontiac credited the movie for increasing sales by 25,000 units in 1978. It's likely that just like the Trans Am from the movie, many were equipped with a huge Firebird hood decal, optional since 1973 and nicknamed the "Screaming Chicken" for its flamboyant graphics. Auto insurer and evalua-

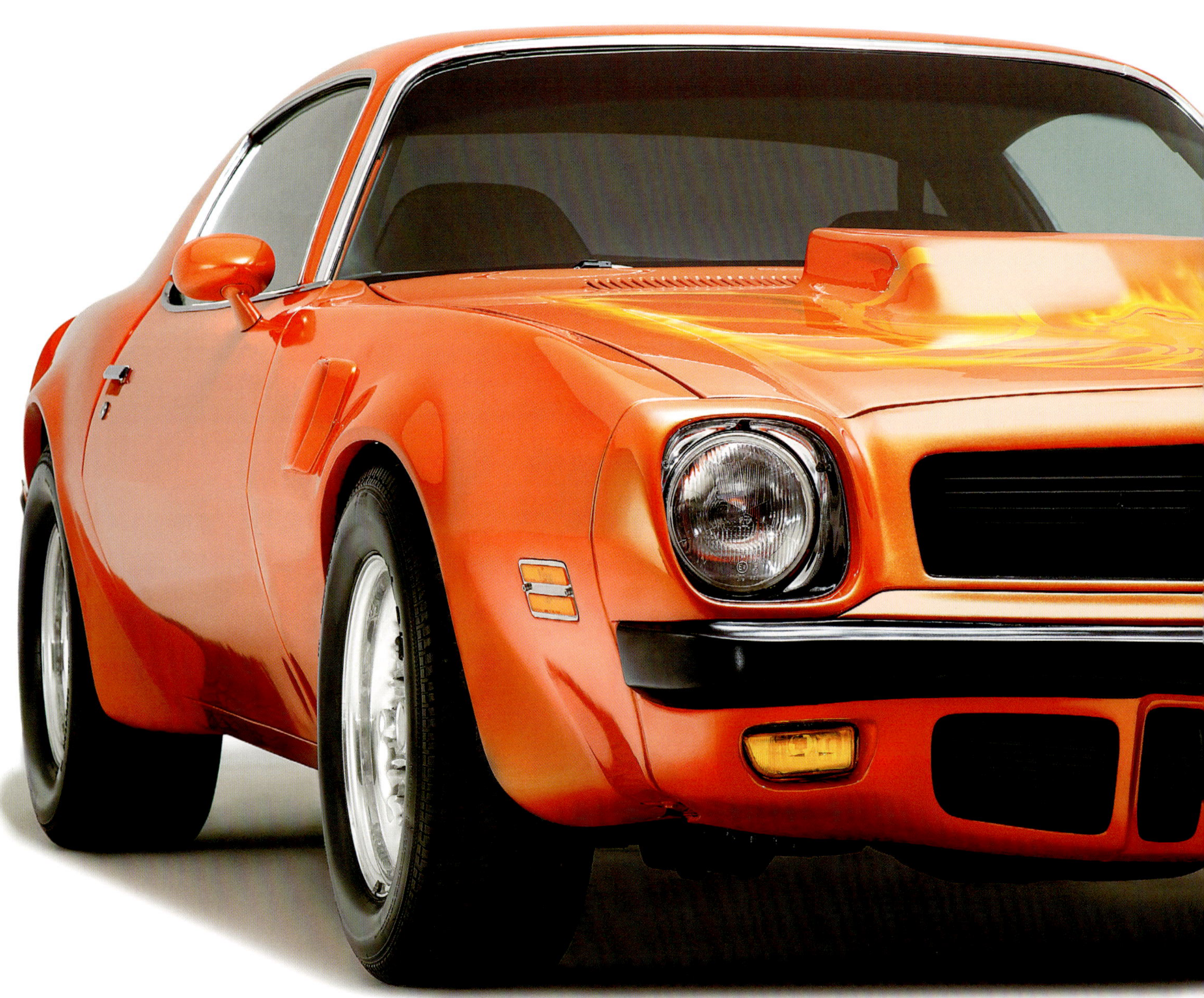

tor Hagerty called the huge hood ornament "the largest and most recognizable decal in automotive history," adding, "It's gaudy. Garish. Tacky...And we love it."

The movie was so popular that it inspired two more, both again featuring the Pontiac version of the pony car.

The Firebird was redesigned again from 1982 to 1992, and again from 1993 to 2002, when its production ended. General Motors would pull the plug on the entire Pontiac Division in 2010.

This page ■ The Pontiac Firebird entered its second generation in 1970 with a new Coke-bottle body styling and an Endura rubber grille surround.
Bottom ■ Fans of the rock band KISS pose with their Pontiac Firebird during a 1975 event in Cadillac, Michigan, staged to promote the band's new *Kiss Alive!* album.

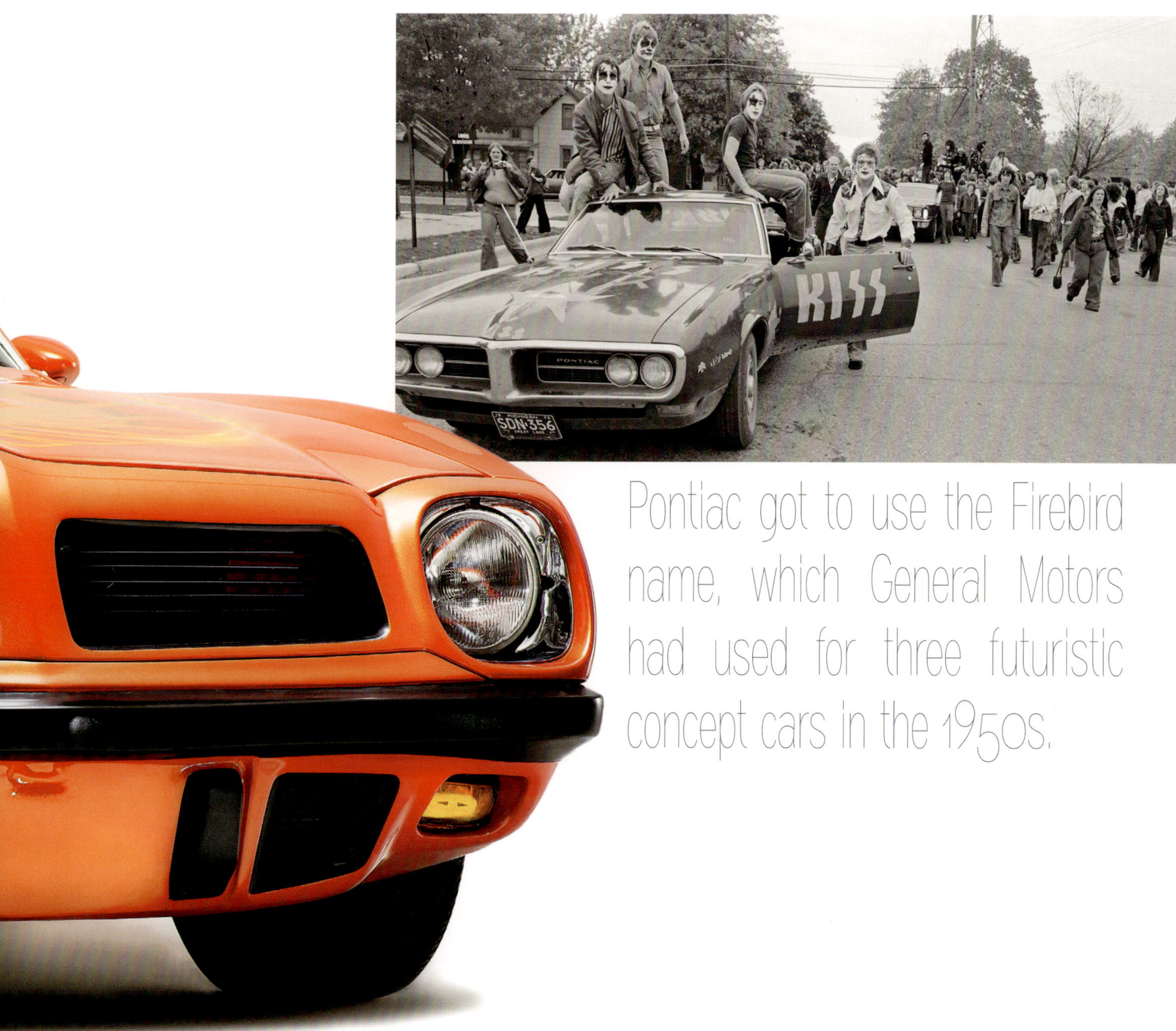

Pontiac got to use the Firebird name, which General Motors had used for three futuristic concept cars in the 1950s.

FORD MUSTANG

Pony car was so popular it was the fastest to gallop to 1 million sales

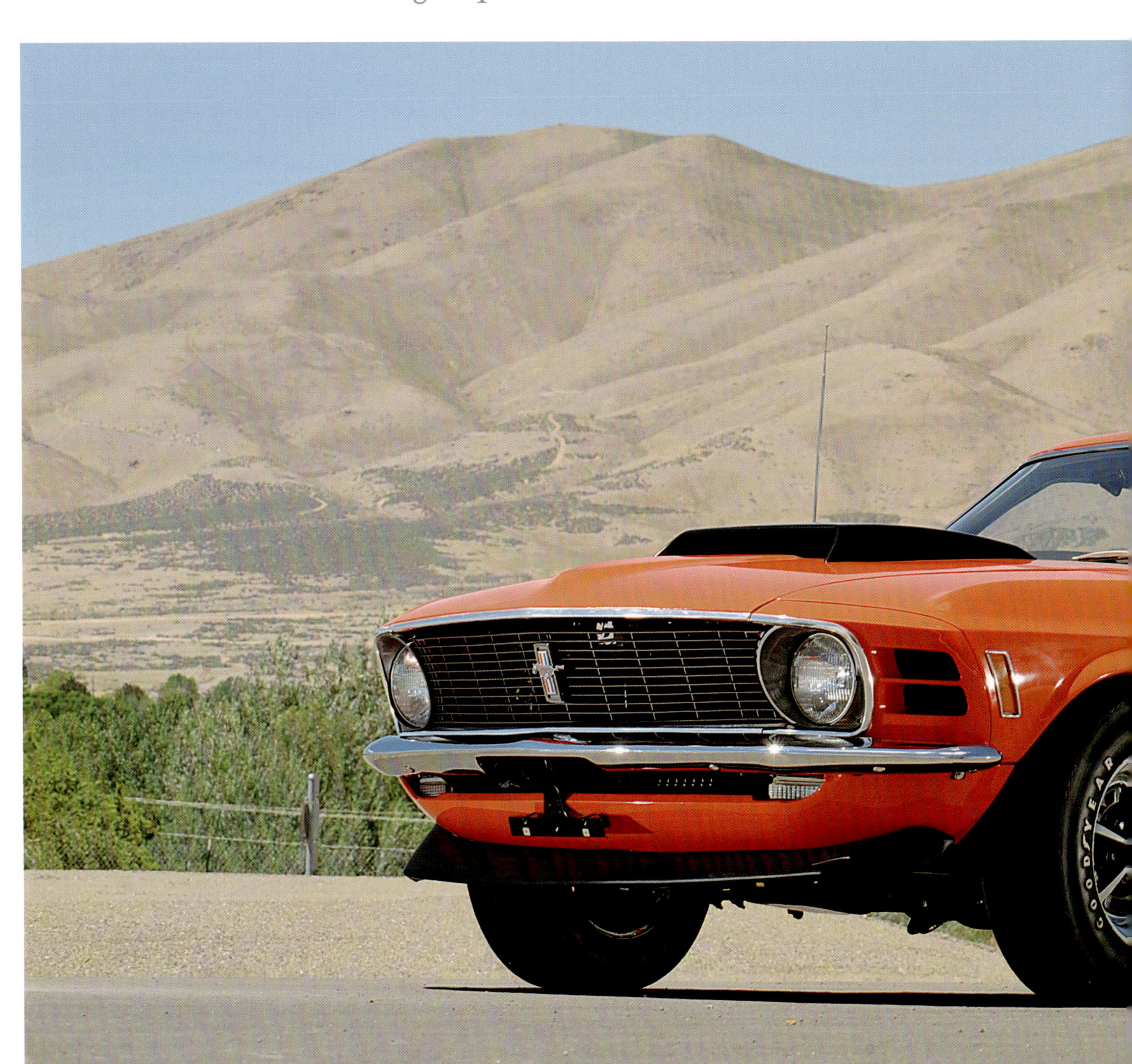

1970 ➤ 1979

The Ford Motor Company needed a winner, and needed it desperately. It had invested manpower and money to develop the Edsel, a luxurious alternative for those shopping at General Motors' Oldsmobile or Buick dealerships or at Chrysler. Seeking to be more competitive with its Detroit competitors, Ford figured it needed a car more comparable to those offered by GM's Oldsmobile or Buick or at Chrysler's DeSoto dealerships. Ford's response was the Edsel, an expensive car hobbled with a horsecollar-styled grille. The car, introduced for the 1958 model year, was a debacle, and it was discontinued after only three years.

As the Edsel was tanking, Lee Iacocca was rising through Ford's executive ranks. Though trained as an engineer, Iacocca found his calling in sales and marketing. By the fall of 1960, he was promoted to general manager of the Ford Division. He needed a marketing success and realized it would come from cars that appealed to a younger (or at least young-at-heart) customer. He also pushed Ford back into auto racing, winning on Sunday and then selling on Monday.

As Iacocca took over at Ford Division, its archrival, Chevrolet, was launching a new car, and one unusual for American roads. It was the Corvair, a compact car but

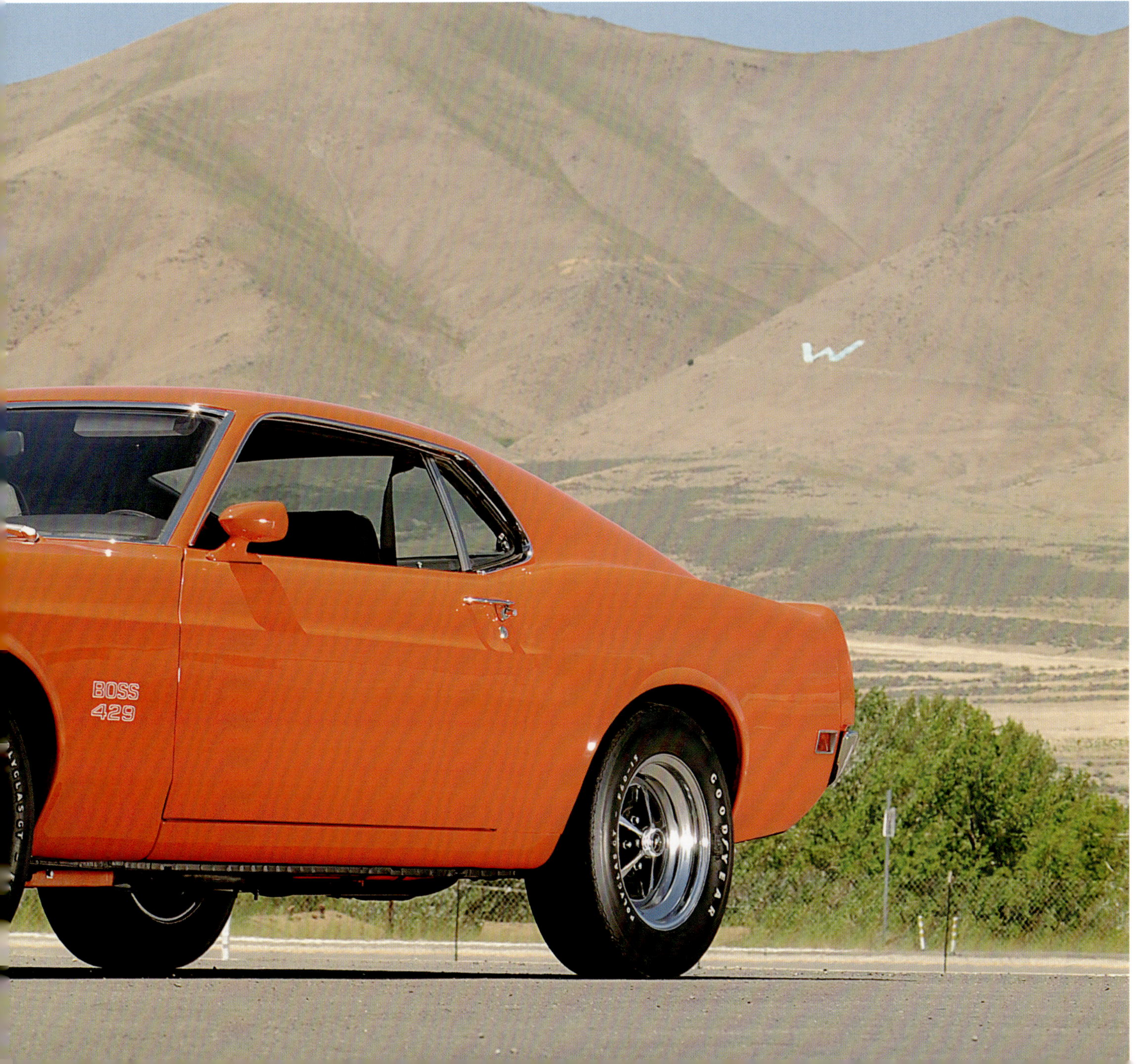

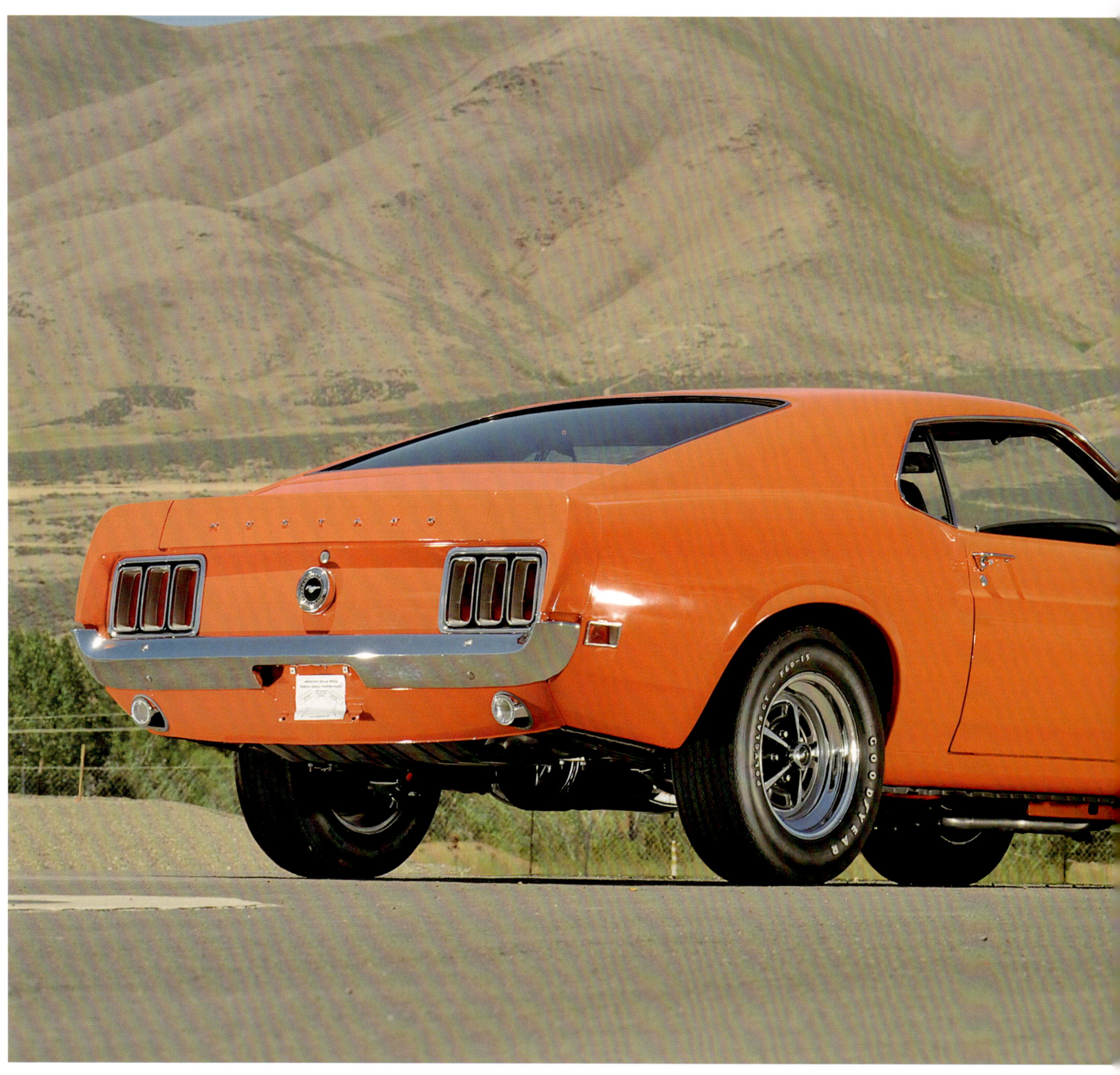

with its air-cooled engine located in the rear rather than in front of the passenger compartment. *Time* magazine displayed the Corvair on its cover and *Motor Trend* awarded it Car of the Year. But there were issues, including critic Ralph Nader's *Unsafe at Any Speed* book about the car's dynamic capabilities.

Ford took a more conventional approach and in the process created an entirely new niche in the automotive marketplace. Using its compact Falcon as a platform, Iacocca's team designed what appeared to be a new low-slung sports car—long hood, short rear deck—but in between were two rows of seats. The car, named the Mustang, was unveiled in coupe and convertible forms and was soon available as well with a sleek, sexy fastback roof. The Mustang wasn't simply rolled out to dealerships—it was unveiled at the New York World's Fair, with live coverage by all major television networks and cover stories on the weekly news magazines. A few weeks later, it served as pace car for the Indianapolis 500.

Soon the car was starring in movies such as *A Man and a Woman*, *Bullitt*, and *Gone in Sixty Seconds*, and even if you didn't go to the cinema, you likely heard "Mustang Sally" being sung on the radio.

Some saw the Mustang as a "secretary's car," but Ford reached out to auto racer Carroll Shelby, who turned it into a competitor for Chevrolet's Corvette on the

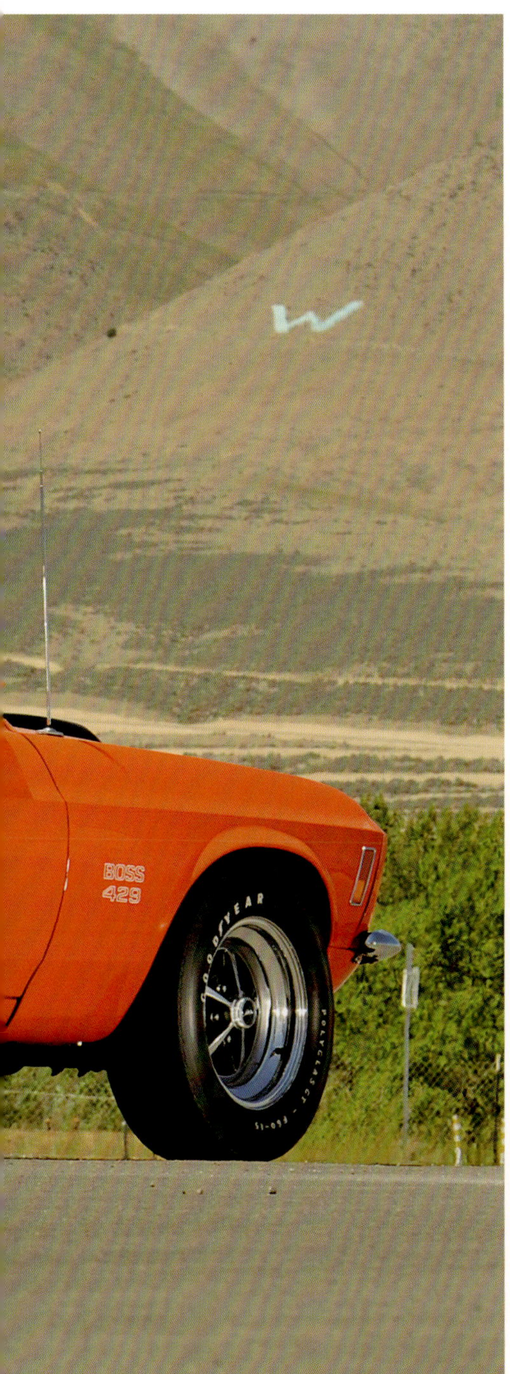

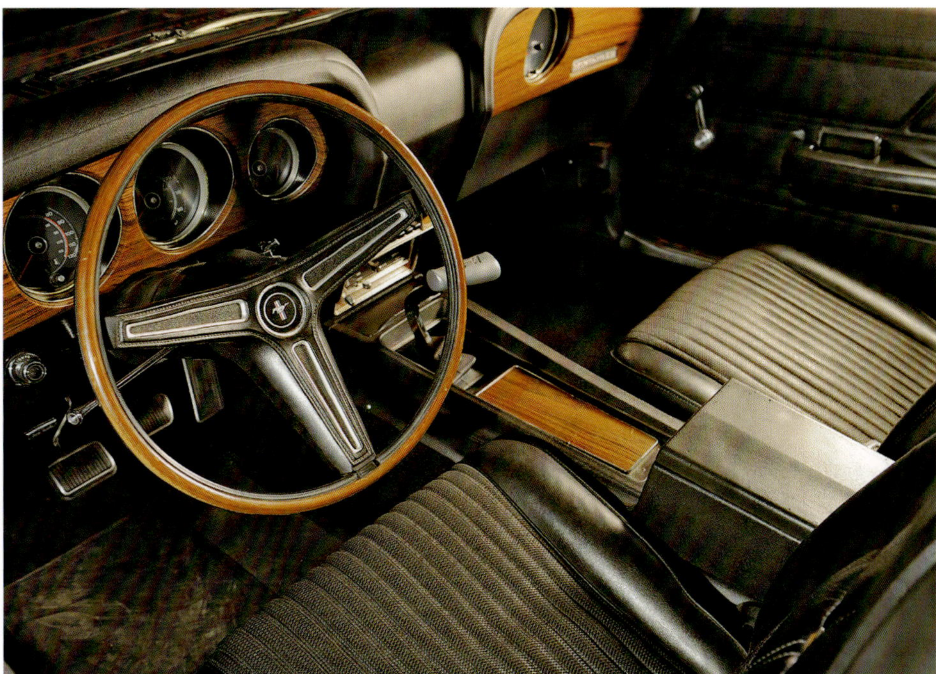

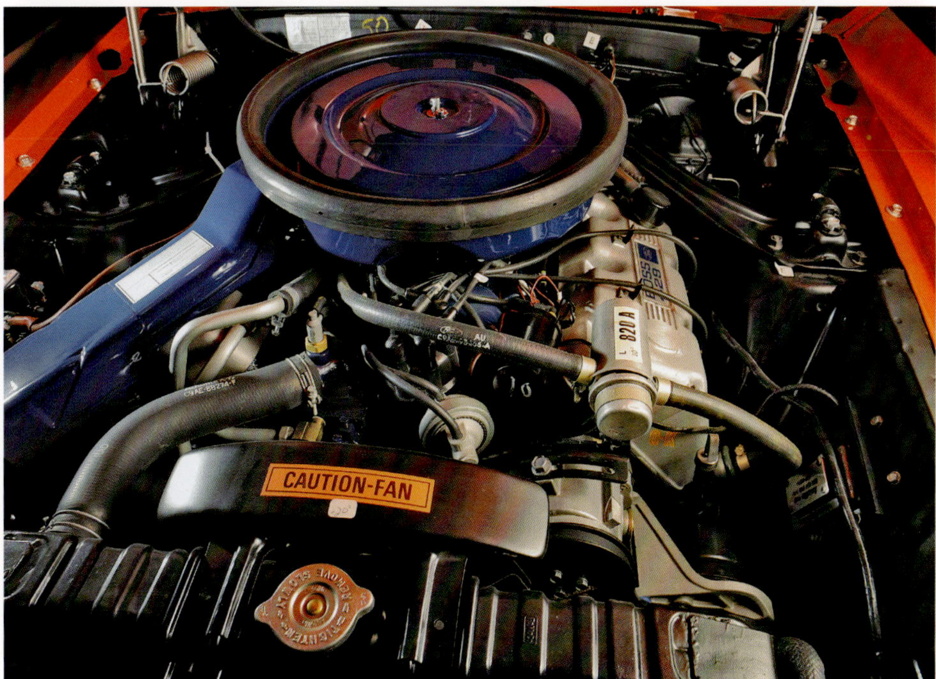

Previous and these pages ■ For the 1969 and 1970 model years, Ford offered the Boss 429 version of its Mustang. The car was equipped with a 429-cubic-inch (7.0-liter) "big-block" V8 engine originally developed for auto racing. This version was twice as expensive as the base-model Mustang.

racetrack. Not only did this "pony car" win there, but it created an entirely new automotive segment that soon included the Chevrolet Camaro, Pontiac Firebird, Plymouth Barracuda, Dodge Challenger, American Motors Javelin, and others.

In the process, the Mustang became the fastest car to reach the 1 million mark in sales, a figure accomplished in just two and a half years.

Like so many other American cars, the Mustang would be downsized in the form of the Mustang II, supposedly "the right car for the right time," from 1974 until 1979, at which point it returned to its size and appeal on Ford's larger Fox platform. The "Fox-bodied" Mustangs have become sought after by youngtimer car collectors.

LAMBORGHINI COUNTACH

A car so beautiful it bumped one of Charlie's Angels *off teenage boys' bedroom walls*

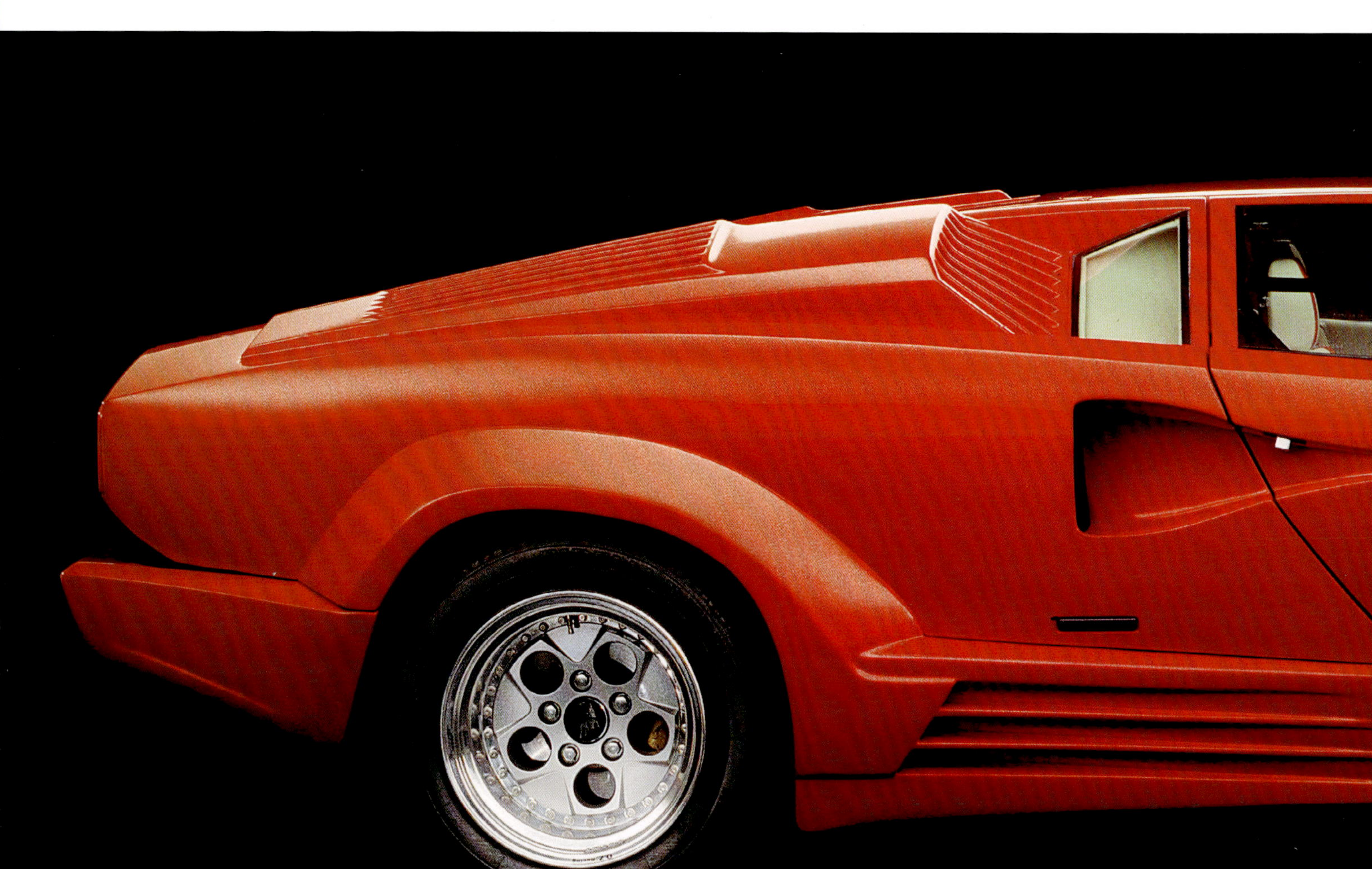

1970 ➤ 1979

Pinup girls were popular in the 1940s and '50s; images of attractive women in bathing suits (or less) were painted on the sides of military aircraft or plastered on the walls of automotive repair garages, and teenage boys around the world had posters of movie and television stars on their bedroom walls.

At least that was the case until Lamborghini unveiled the Countach, and those very popular images of *Charlie's Angels* star Farrah Fawcett were replaced by those of this sexy Italian sports supercar.

During the car's development, it was code-named Project 112. But one day a Lamborghini staffer got his first glimpse of the prototype and all he could say was "Countach," a Piedmontese expression that roughly translates to "That's it," which was typically used by men as an expression of appreciation upon the entrance to a room by an exceptionally beautiful woman.

Ferruccio Lamborghini grew up on a northern Italian farm that grew grapes, but he was more interested in the machines used in farming than in the growing of crops. In 1948 he founded a company to produce tractors and other agricultural equipment, and later added other manufactured products, including air conditioners, to the portfolio.

He also tinkered with cars, modifying one to enter the 1948 Mille Miglia race across Italy. In 1958, he bought a Ferrari but was dissatisfied with what he saw as the constant need for repairs. As the story goes, he complained to Enzo Ferrari about it and was told that if he thought he could do better, then he should go ahead and try.

In 1963, he founded Automobili Lamborghini and hired leading automotive engineers and designers. They produced several sleek grand touring cars, and in 1966

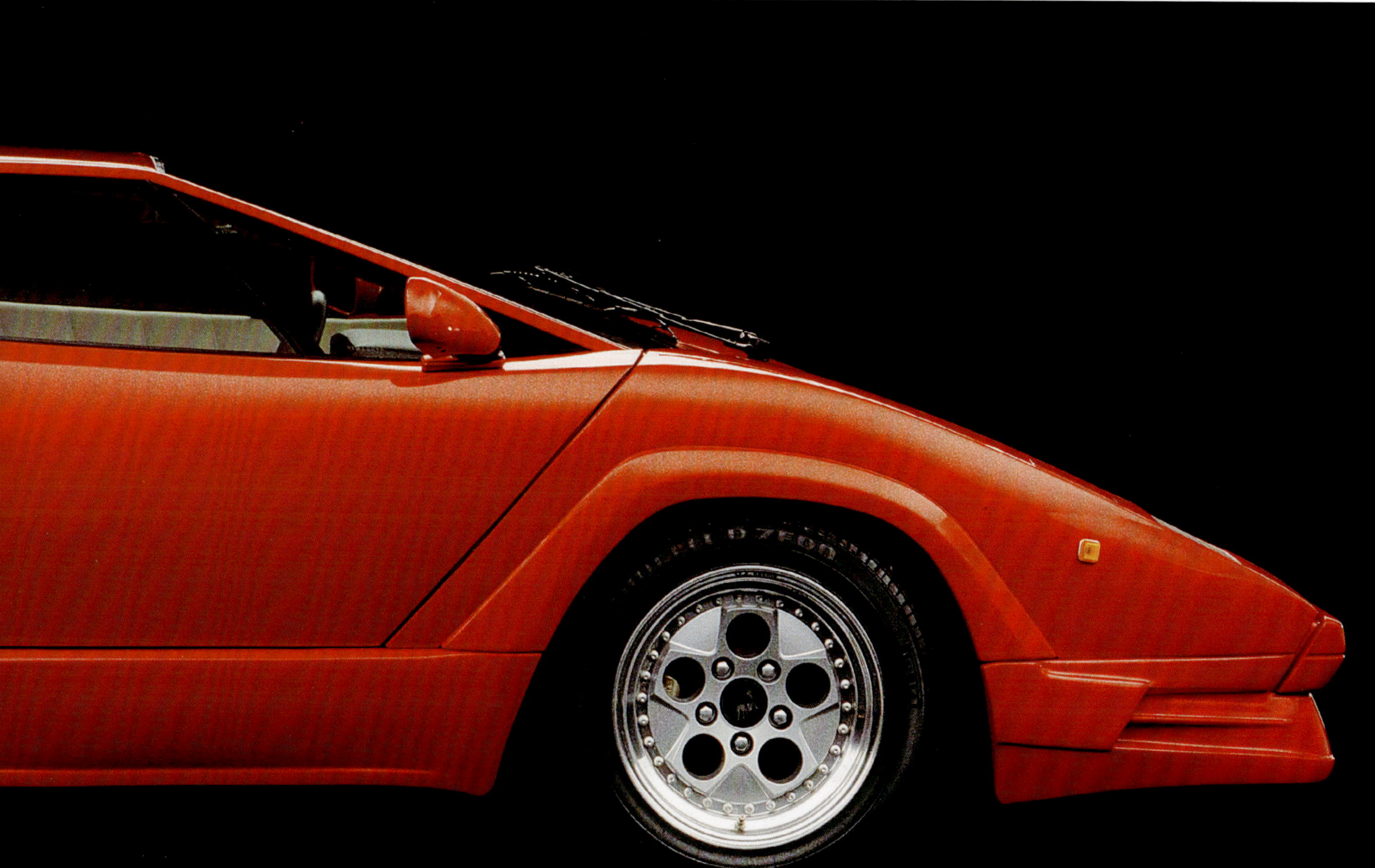

the world's first "supercar," a mid-engined, 175-mph, Marcello Gandini–designed rocket named Miura, the first in a series of Lamborghini sports cars named in honor of famous Spanish fighting bulls (the naming series would be broken by the Countach but resumed thereafter).

By the 1970s, Lamborghini was ready for a worthy successor to the Miura. Gandini again fashioned the design, an exotic wedge shape, again with the engine mid-ship behind seats for the driver and passenger.

The Countach was unveiled in concept car form at the Geneva Motor Show in 1971. It would be two years before the car would go into production with an exotic wedge shape, doors that lifted and opened like butterfly wings, and creative ducting to cool the engine.

Motor Trend magazine reporter Jonny Lieberman recalled his first view of the car: "As a little boy, I once saw an orange Countach parked on some gray cobblestones in Old Montreal. My father was kind enough to let me stand there, jaw on those same cobblestones, as gobsmacked as a nine-year-old human can be.

"How could such a shape, let alone on a car, exist?" he wondered as he wrote about his road test of the car as an adult. "Moreover, how could I be standing next to it? Most crucially, how would I get myself behind that steering wheel? Because suddenly, right there and then, I had a pretty good and clear notion of what I wanted to do with my life."

The engine was Lamborghini's V12, mounted mid-ship longitudinally behind the seats for the driver and passenger, a first for a car designed for the road and not the racetrack. The car was capable of speeds approaching 180 mph (290 km/h).

The original version was the LP400, followed by a higher-performance S version, then the LP500 with even more power, and then the LP500S QV (quattro valvole), again with a performance boost.

The Countach remained in production through Lamborghini's twenty-fifth anniversary, when it was succeeded by the Diablo, a car developed for Lamborghini by Horacio Pagani, a man we will encounter again later in this book.

Most Lamborghinis were named for Spanish fighting bulls, but this car's name was inspired by its beauty.

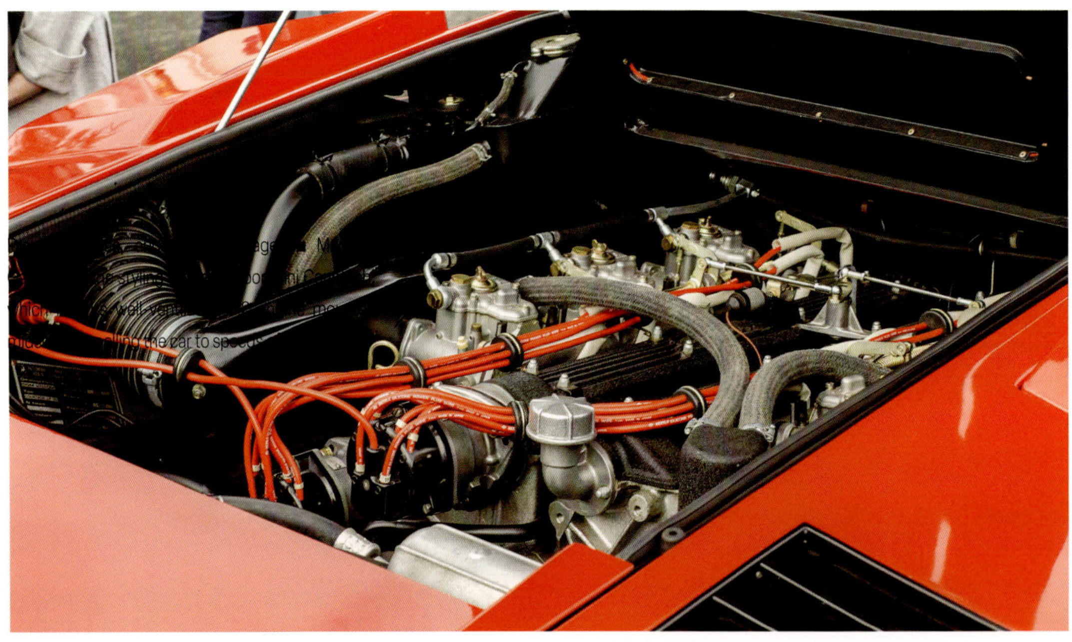

Previous, these, and following pages ■ Marcello Gandini did the styling of the Lamborghini Countach, which had its well-ventilated V12 engine mounted midship, propelling the car to speeds of 180 mph.

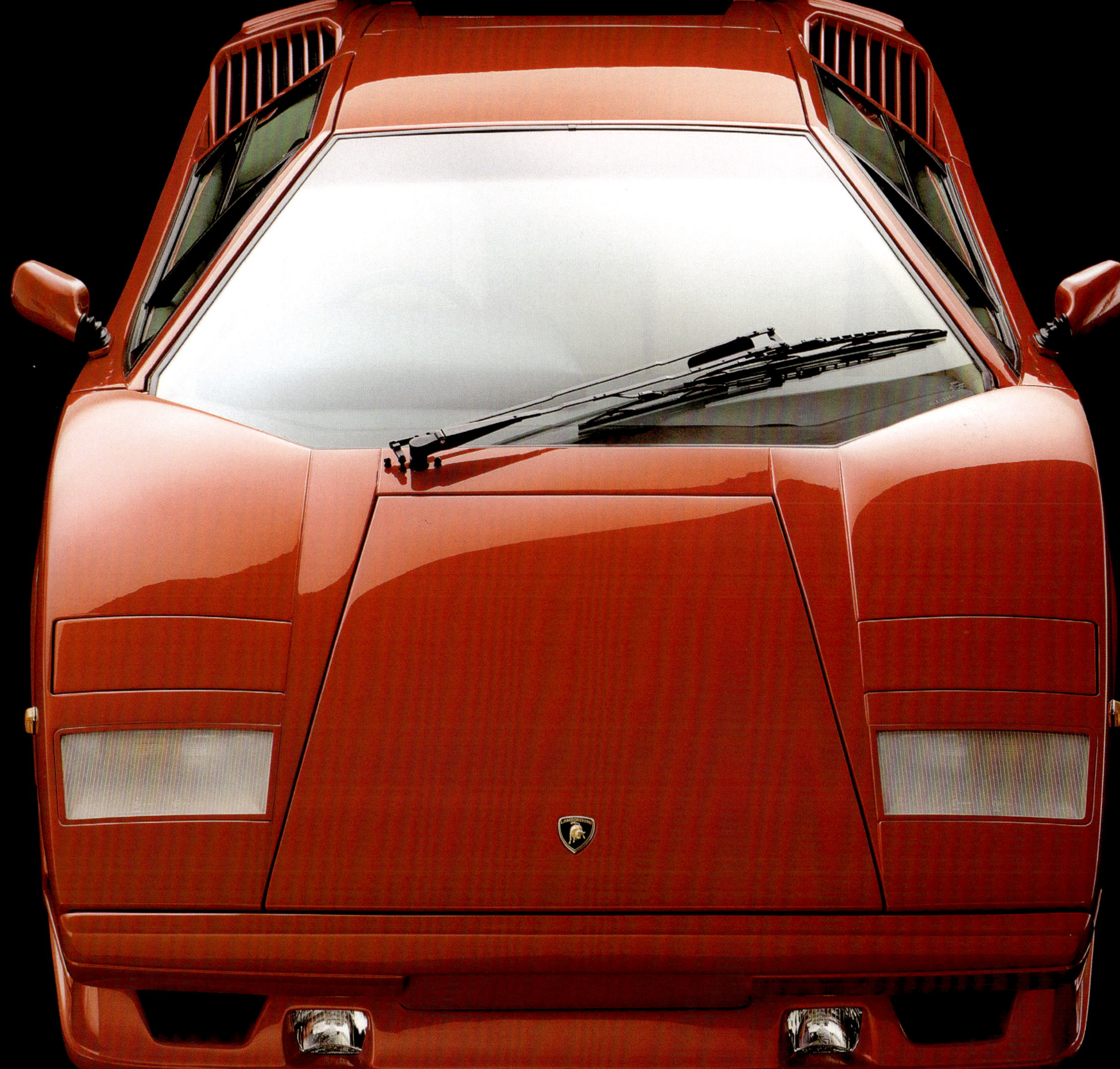

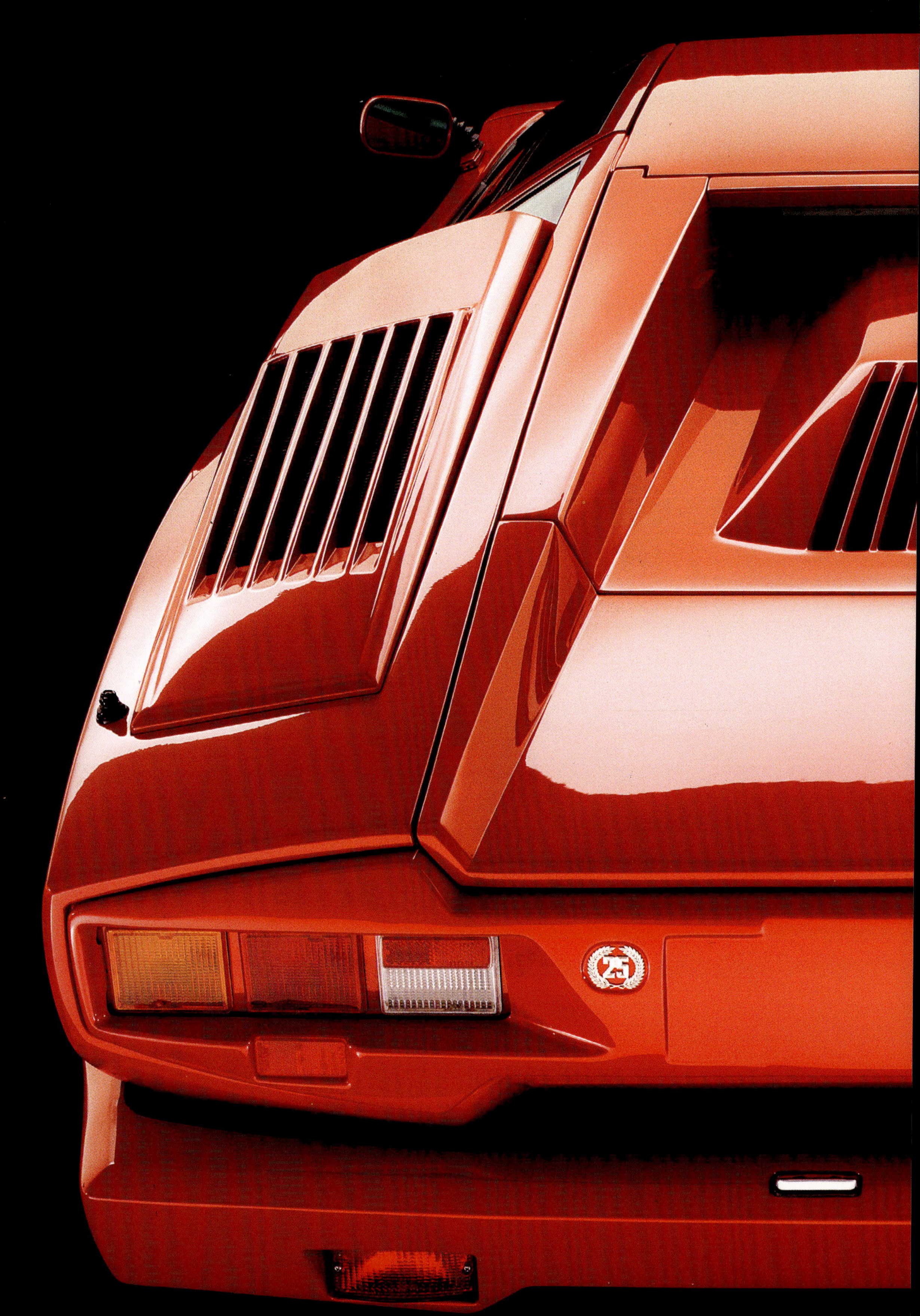

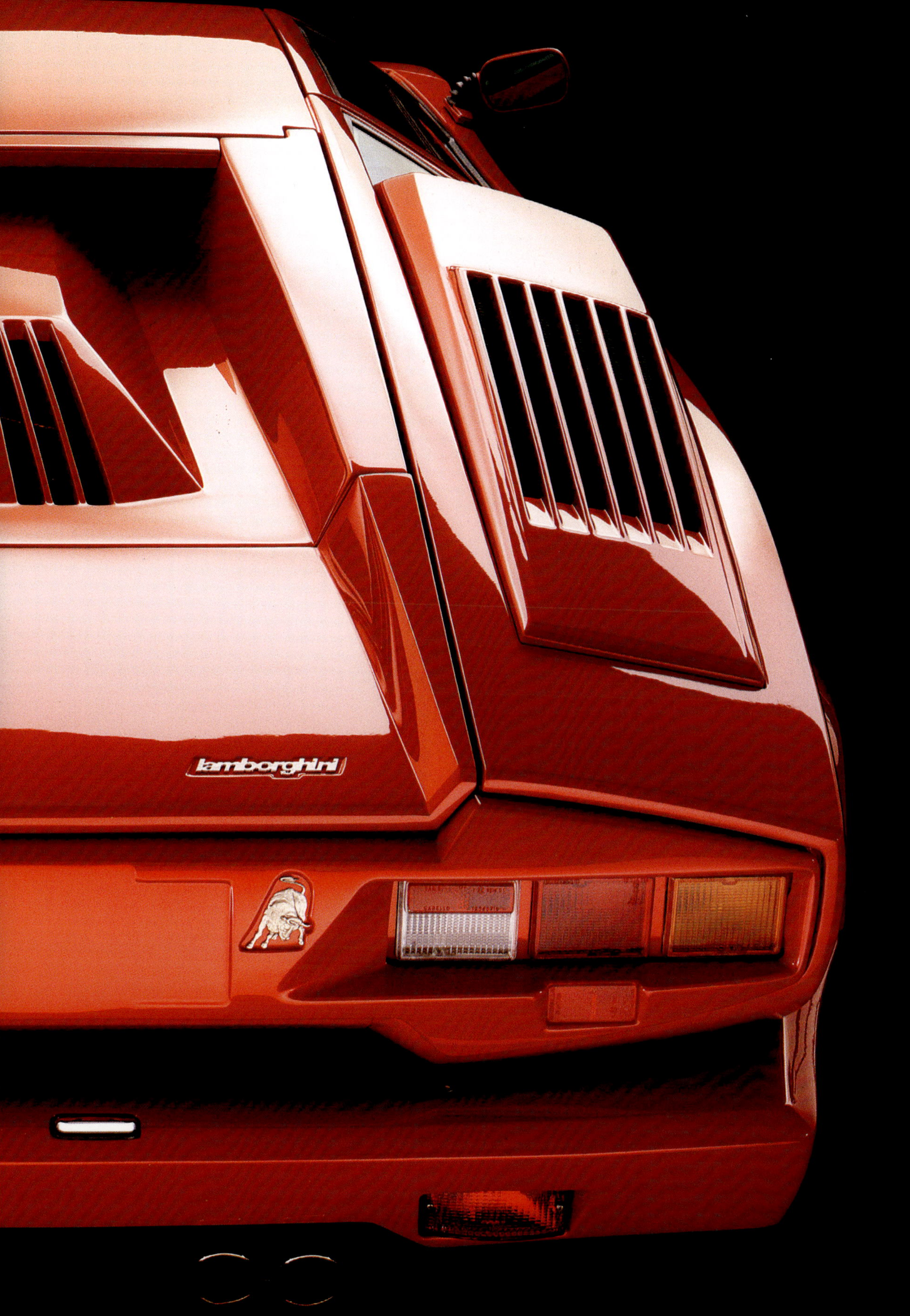
lamborghini

FERRARI 308

Cars were stars in the '70s, quite literally in the case of Magnum PI's *Ferrari*

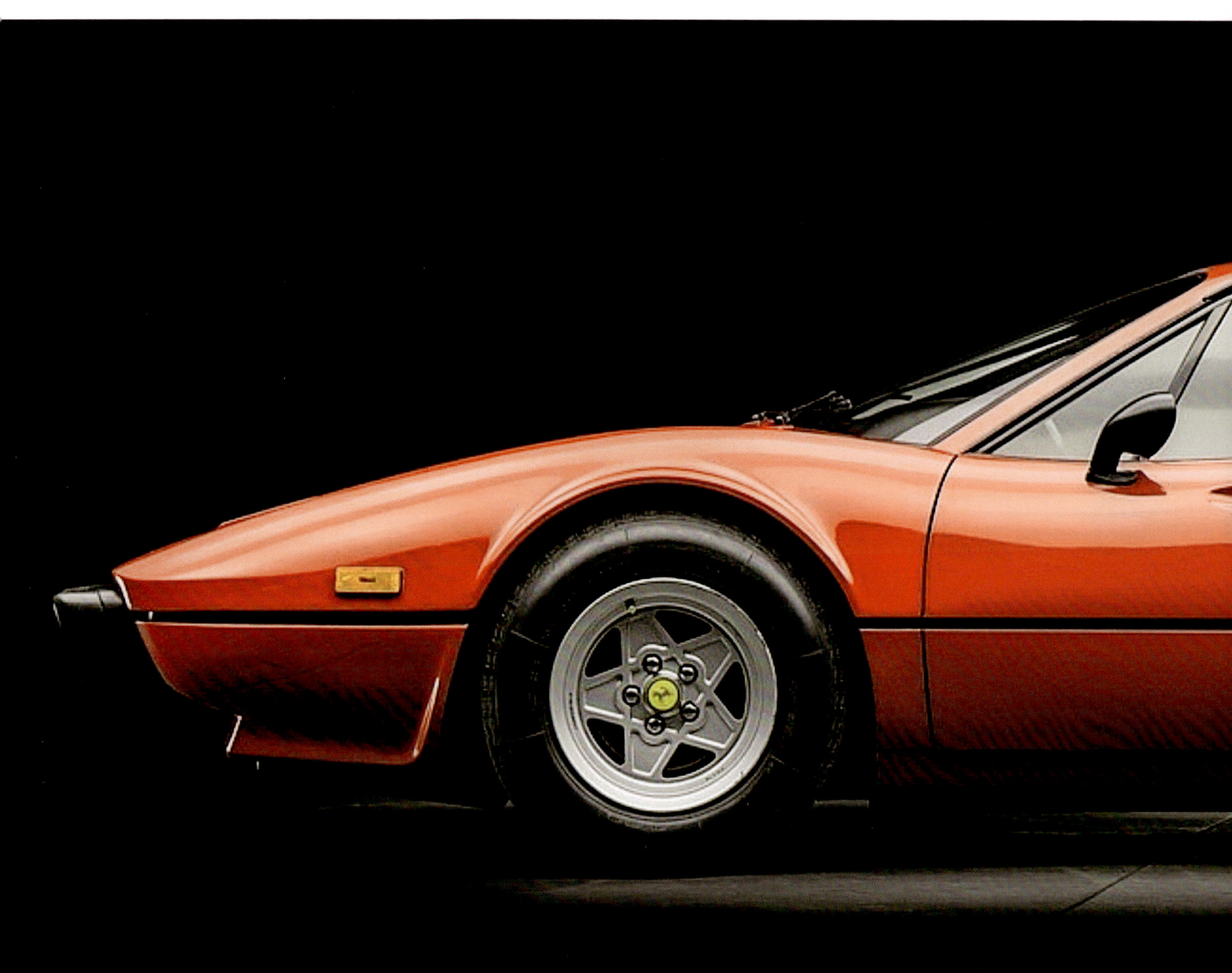

1970 ➤ 1979

It seems redundant to write "famous Ferrari" because seemingly every car to ever roll out of the workshop Enzo Ferrari created in Modena, Italy, has become famous and coveted by car collectors. Take your pick: race cars that won in Formula One and at Le Mans, road cars from the original 125 S to the 166 MM to the 500 TR, the 250 California, the Dino, the 365 Daytona, the 512 BB, the GTO, Testarossa, F40, F50, the Enzo, FXX, La Ferrari, and so many more, each of them loved by the *tifosi* of the Ferrari faithful.

But there is one Ferrari that was loved by many more, by television audiences who otherwise might not have known a Ferrari from a Ford. This car was the 308, the one driven across television screens by actor Tom Selleck, who played the title role in the *Magnum PI* series (the original series, which aired each week from 1980 to 1988 and then in syndication; it is still in syndication, even though a new *Magnum PI,* this one with a different cast [and a Ferrari 488 Spider] launched on TV screens in 2018).

While the 308 is best known as Magnum's Ferrari, it actually wasn't his car. According to the television show's script, the Ferrari was owned by Robin Masters,

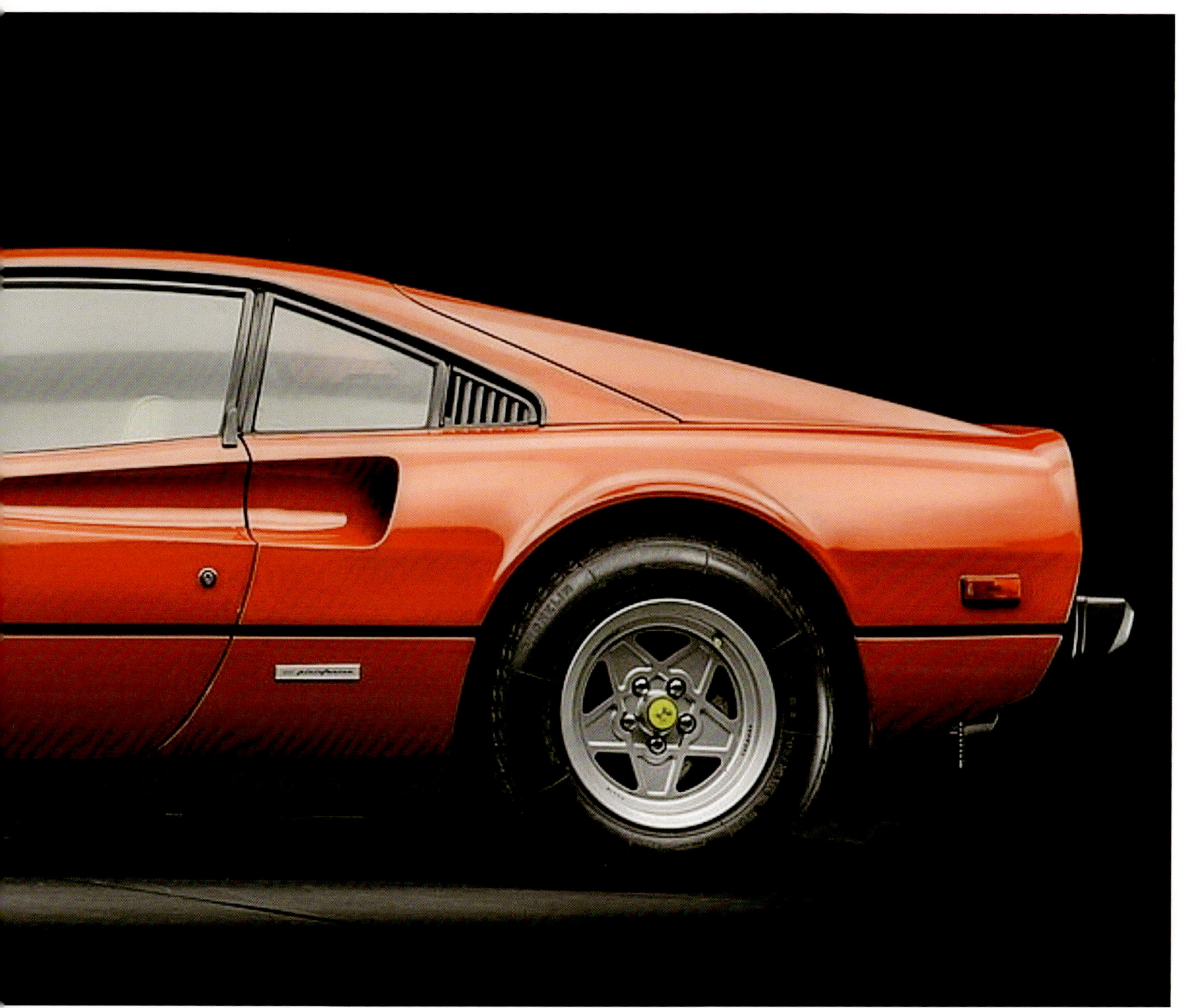

a wealthy and reclusive author, or by Magnum's employer, Higgins, who manages the "Robin's Nest" Hawaiian estate on which Higgins and Magnum reside.

In 2024, Britain's *Car* magazine's website shared a "love letter" from writer Mark Walton to Magnum's car, pointing out that what began in the first season as a carbureted 308 GTS gave way to a fuel-injected GTSi for Season 2, and then to a four-valve QV for the final two years of production:

"*Magnum PI* arrived on British TV in 1981, which makes me feel old but also nostalgic and fuzzy inside. This show had a profound effect on me, a boy who was just deciding that cars were more interesting than dinosaurs. I loved the way it 'normalized' the Ferrari 308 GTS—the way Magnum didn't actually own the car, he only borrowed it; and he used it as his daily driver, which made the Ferrari seem so much more real."

After years of dreaming, Walton finally got to drive a vintage 308 GTS. "I can't tell you the relief! I didn't want my memories ruined...and thankfully [it] didn't disappoint...It's still an amazingly engaging car, so emotional compared to today's fat by sterile supercars."

As usual, Ferrari contracted the Pininfarina design studio and Leonardo Fioravanti styled the 308, which replaced the Dino 246 in the company's sports car lineup. The GTS model came with a Targa-style removable panel (necessary for a driver such as Selleck, who stood six-foot-four and likely wouldn't fit in the hardtop GTB [Berlinetta]).

Power came from Ferrari's 2.9-liter V8, originally rated at 250 plus or minus horsepower depending on whether the customer was in Europe (252) or the United States (237).

"The 308 is a dramatic demonstration of how well Ferrari has coped with the pressing demands of emissions, safety, higher fuel prices, and lower speed limits while retaining all the prestige and fun for which this marque has become famous," *Road & Track* magazine reported in 1977.

Magnum's Ferrari remained in production until 1985, when the company introduced the 328.

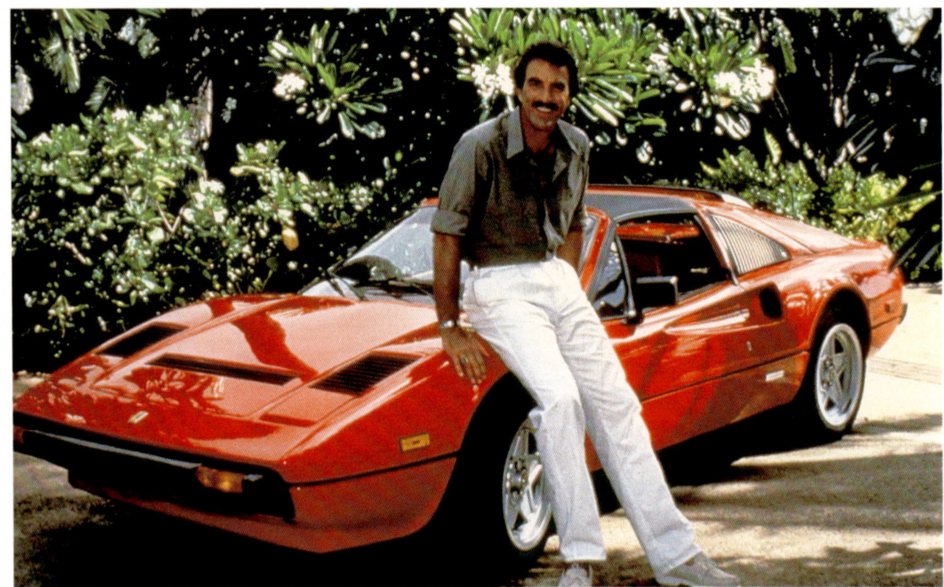

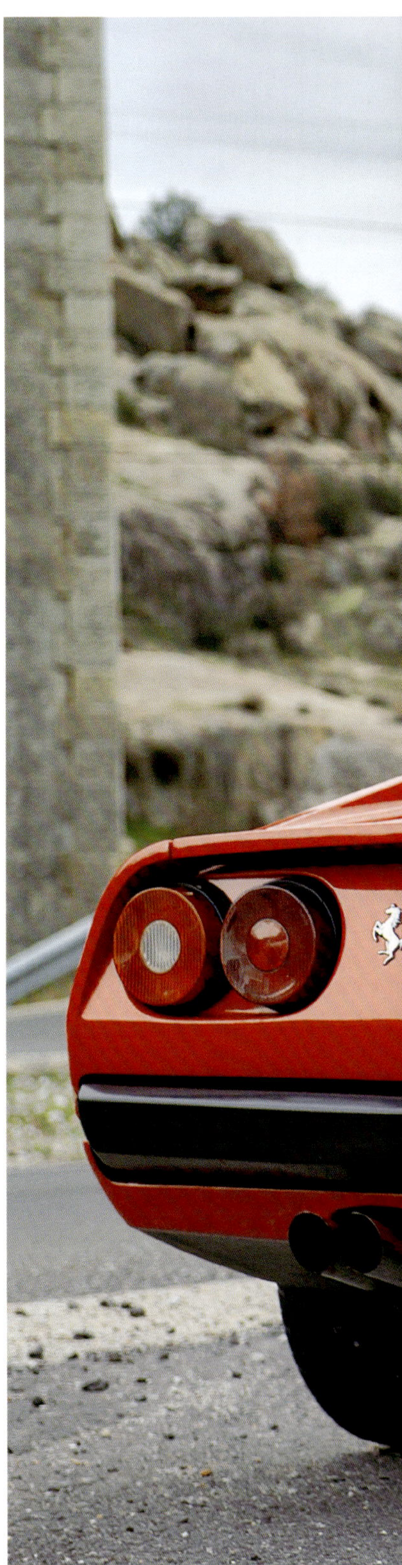

Previous and opposite pages ■ Leonardo Fioravanti of Pininfarina was responsible for the design of the Ferrari 308, which became an automotive superstar when it was selected as the ride for television private eye Thomas Magnum, as portrayed by the American actor Tom Selleck.
These pages ■ Thanks to its role in an American television series, the 308 might be the most famous of all Ferraris.

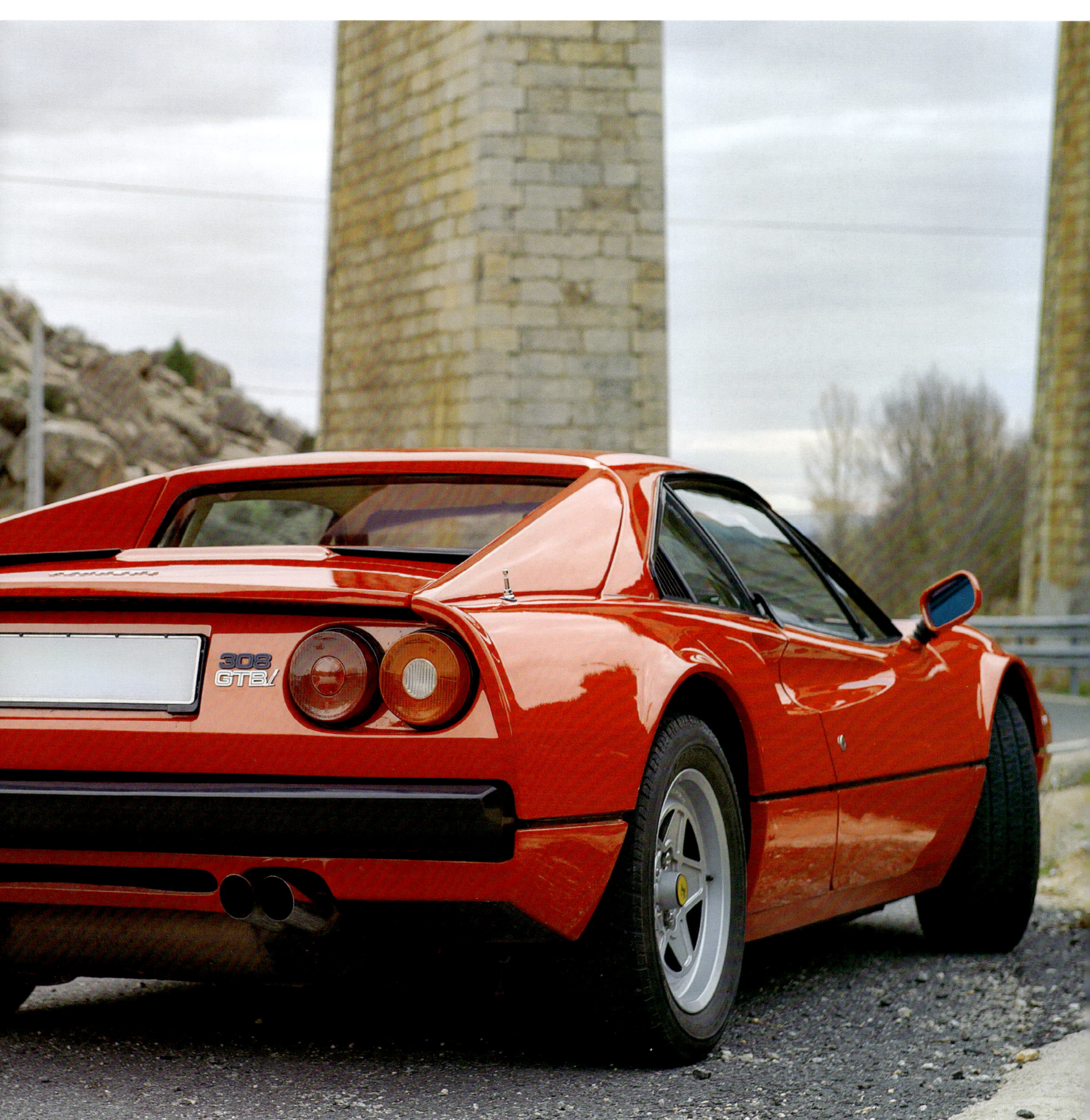

BMW
M1

Created to celebrate its hometown as host of the Olympic Games, the M1 truly was an artistic achievement

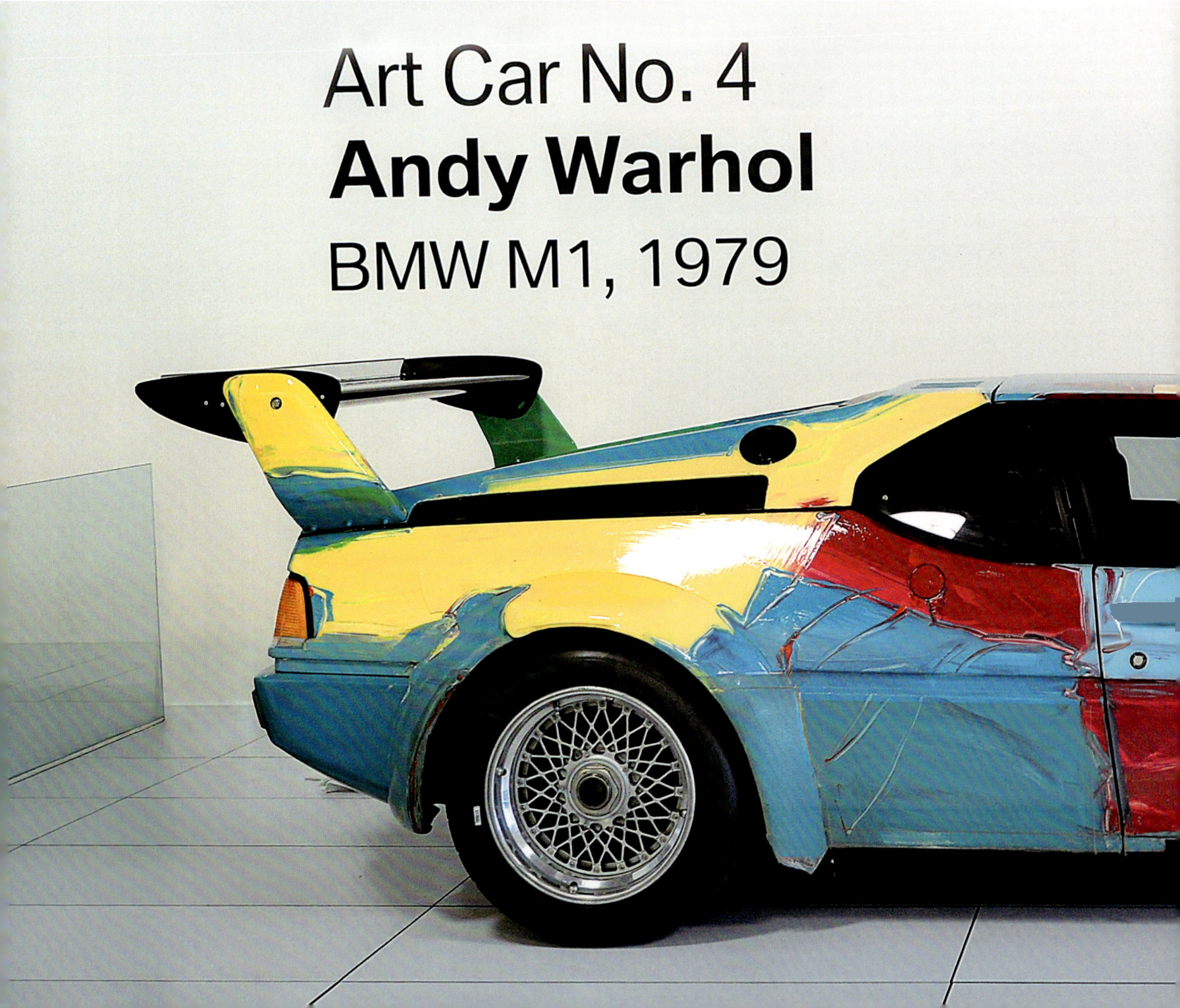

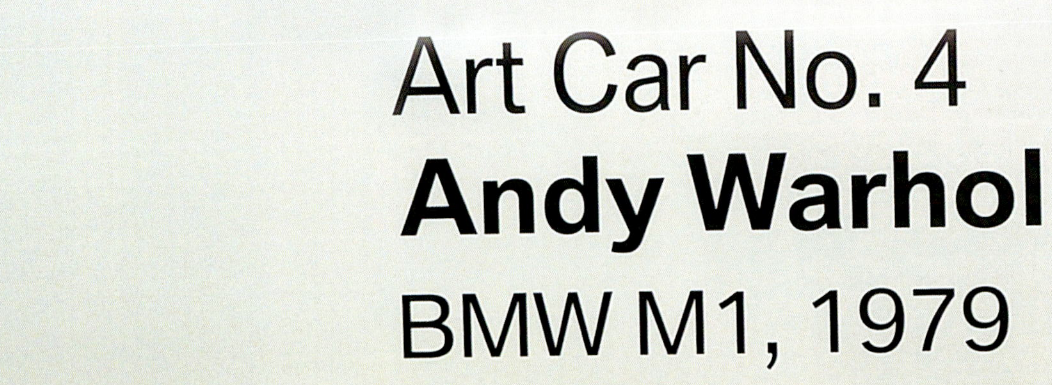

1970 ➤ 1979

Racing in horse-drawn chariots was a part of the Ancient Olympic Games held in Greece starting in 776 BC, but its modern equivalent, automobile racing, has yet to be included since the games were revived near the end of the nineteenth century. However, there is a car that has a modern Olympics connection. It is the BMW M1.

When Munich, West Germany, hosted the Olympic Games in 1972, German automaker BMW celebrated the selection of its headquarters' hometown by commissioning a special concept car. Designed by the automaker's design director Paul Bracq, the BMW Turbo was presented as an experimental safety vehicle, albeit one with a low-slung and wedge-shaped body that looked much like an exotic supercar.

Among the vehicle's notable features were BMW's first use of mid-engine architecture and a new turbocharged 4-cylinder engine that would soon go into production powering the German automaker's new 2002 sports coupe.

Move the calendar ahead a few years and BMW needed to make changes to remain competitive as new regulations were written for the World Manufacturers' Championship in endurance sports car racing. By 1975, Bracq had returned to his native France to design for Peugeot, so BMW turned to Italian design star

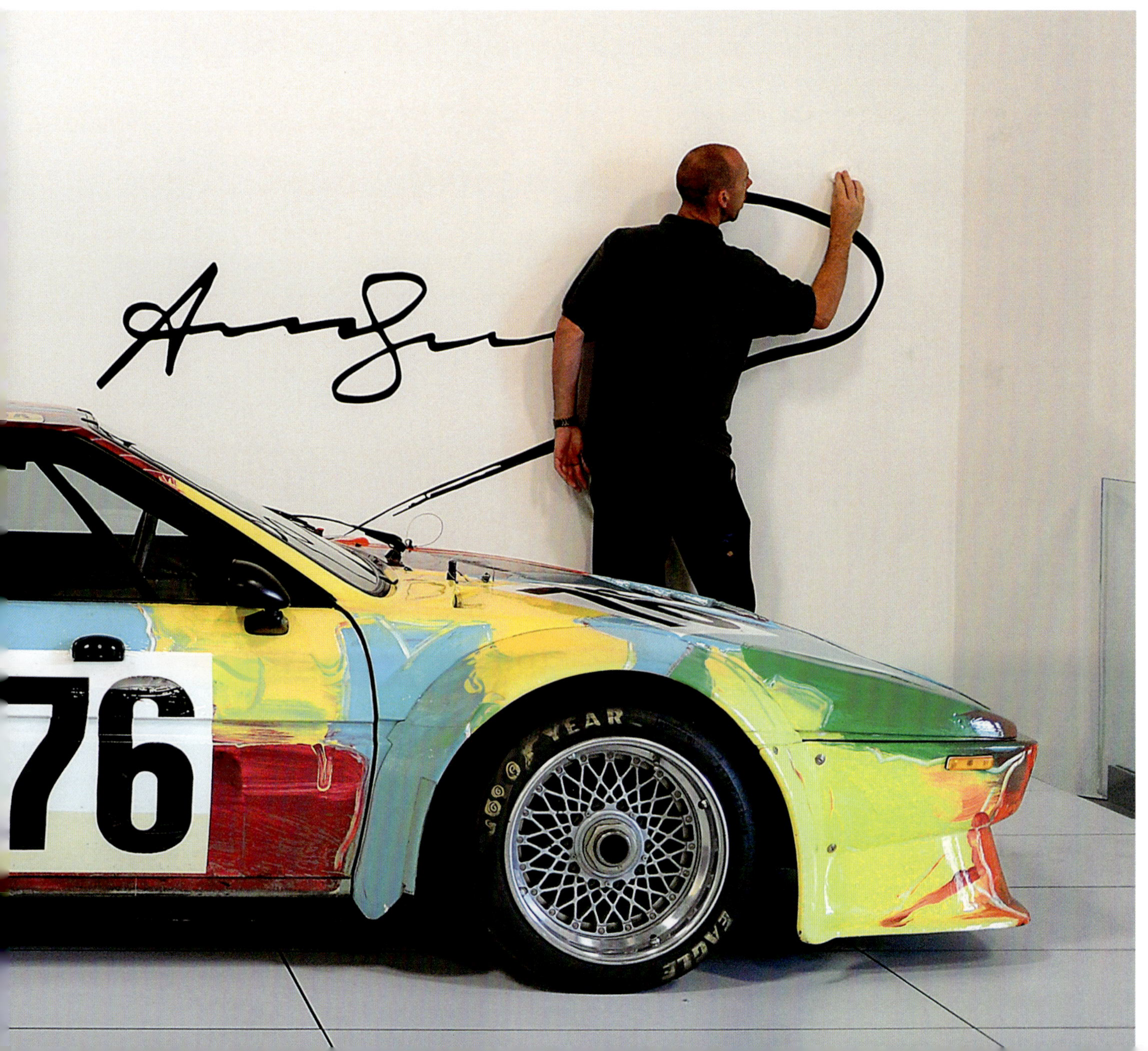

Giorgetto Giugiaro to make some track-ready revisions to Bracq's Olympic concept. BMW also contracted another Italian, Lamborghini, to engineer a tube-frame chassis and to build the 400 examples of the car to homologate it (make it eligible) for the racing series. Financial problems at Lamborghini eventually had BMW turning to Giugiaro and his Italdesign and other Italian companies to also do vehicle production, including the fiberglass coachwork, with final assembly in Germany by the coachbuilding company Baur.

While the Olympic car's turbo-4 was fine for use in the 2002 sports coupe, more power was needed for big-time auto racing, so BMW Motorsport GmbH created a 24-valve, double-overhead cam 3.5-liter inline 6-cylinder engine that provided nearly 500 horsepower on the racetrack—and 270 horsepower for the 400 road-going versions of what BMW labeled as the M1.

Previous pages ■ French racer and auctioneer Hervé Poulain came up with the idea of the "art car," the first a BMW 3.0 CSL painted by Alexander Calder. Among the fleet was a BMW M1 with an Andy Warhol paint scheme.
■ BMW design director Paul Bracq styled the M1, which BMW created to celebrate Munich hosting the 1972 Olympic Games.

Although it looked like a futuristic exotic sports car, BMW presented the M1 as a concept for an advanced safety car.

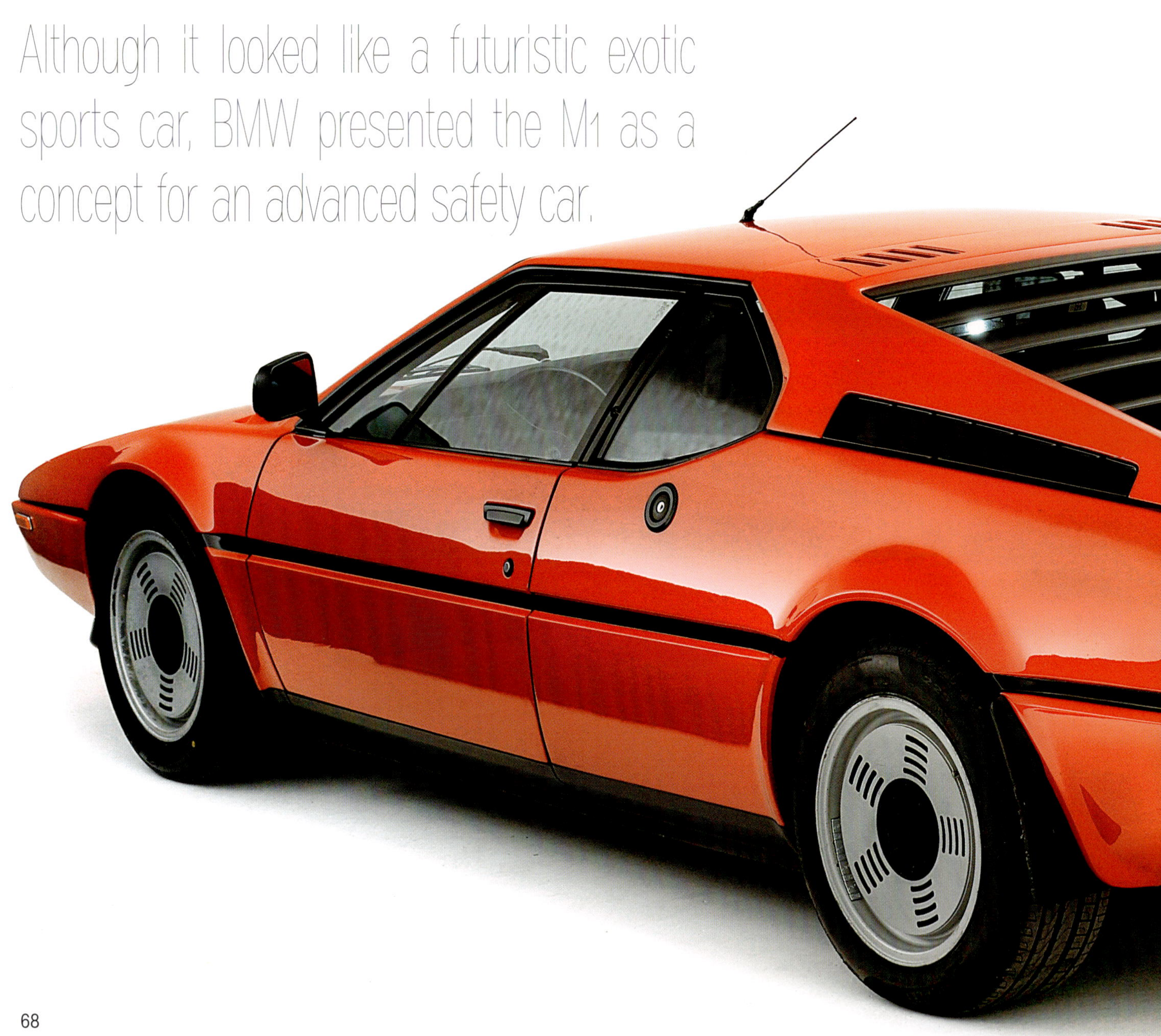

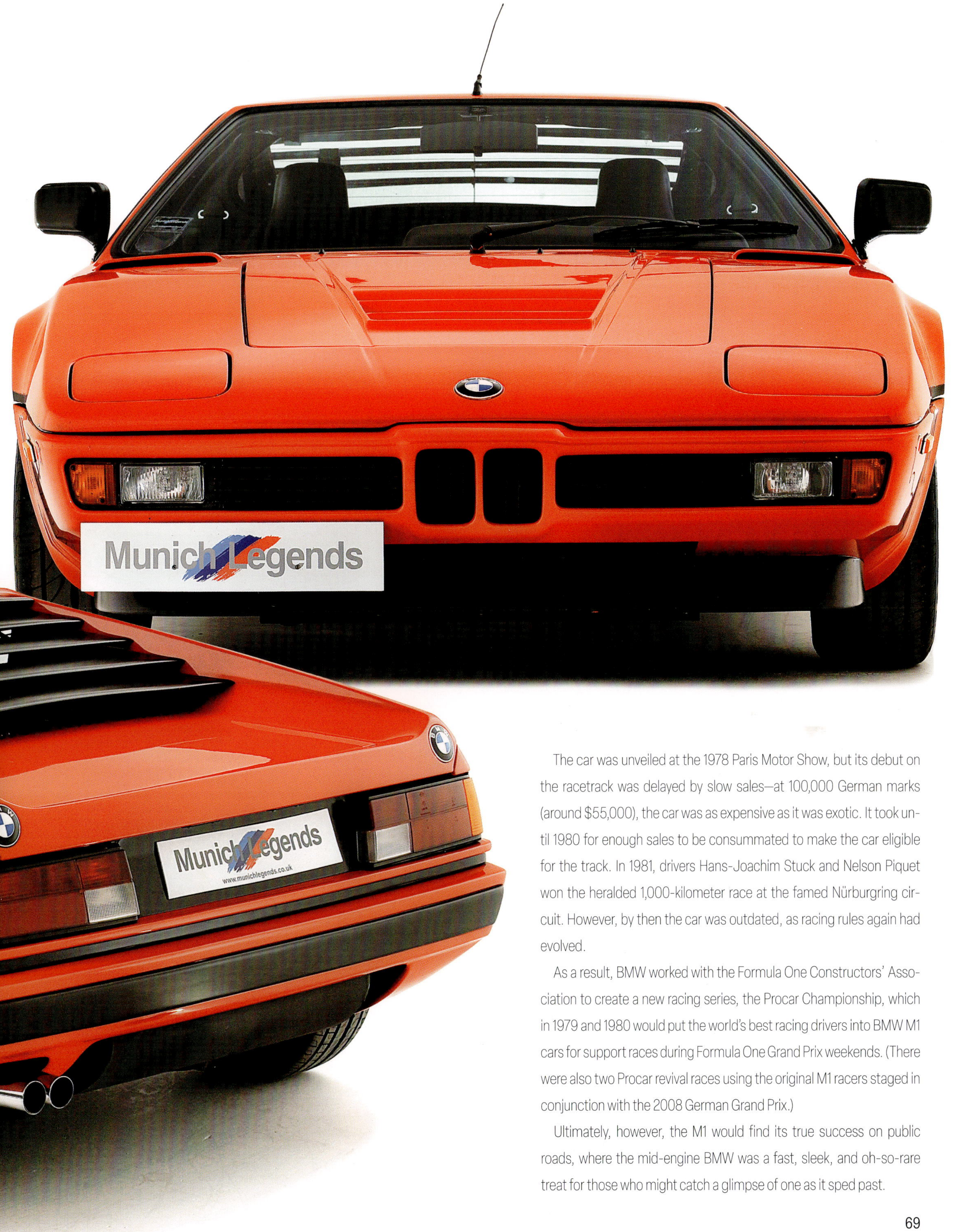

The car was unveiled at the 1978 Paris Motor Show, but its debut on the racetrack was delayed by slow sales—at 100,000 German marks (around $55,000), the car was as expensive as it was exotic. It took until 1980 for enough sales to be consummated to make the car eligible for the track. In 1981, drivers Hans-Joachim Stuck and Nelson Piquet won the heralded 1,000-kilometer race at the famed Nürburgring circuit. However, by then the car was outdated, as racing rules again had evolved.

As a result, BMW worked with the Formula One Constructors' Association to create a new racing series, the Procar Championship, which in 1979 and 1980 would put the world's best racing drivers into BMW M1 cars for support races during Formula One Grand Prix weekends. (There were also two Procar revival races using the original M1 racers staged in conjunction with the 2008 German Grand Prix.)

Ultimately, however, the M1 would find its true success on public roads, where the mid-engine BMW was a fast, sleek, and oh-so-rare treat for those who might catch a glimpse of one as it sped past.

MAZDA RX-7

This sports car proved the viability of the (quite revolutionary) rotary engine

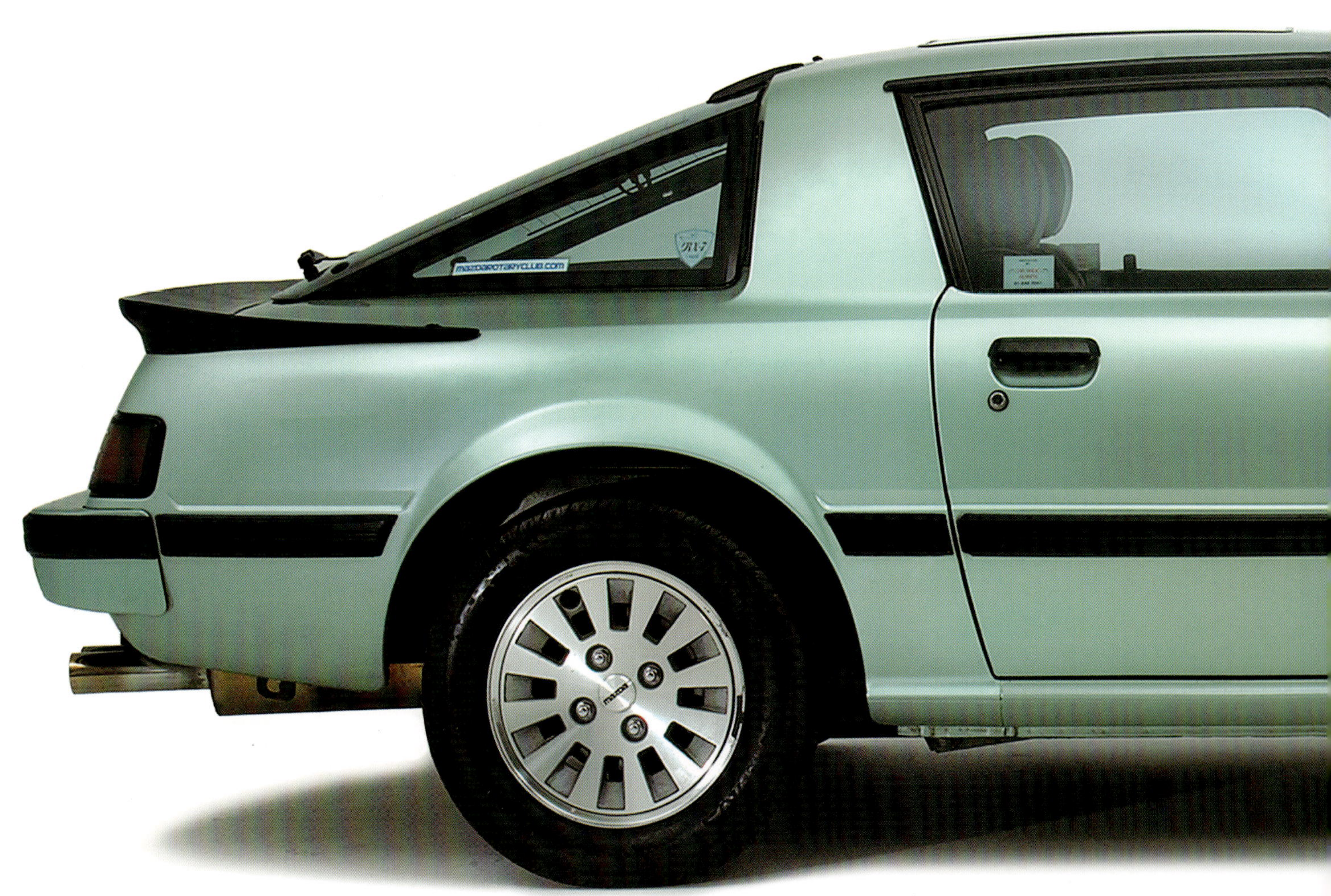

1970 ➤ 1979

In the early years of the automobile, they were propelled by a variety of powerplants. In the early 1900s, steam engines and electric batteries competed with the petroleum-fueled internal combustion engine for dominance. Even after the so-called ICE (internal combustion engine) won out (well, at least until the recent resurgence in electric motors and advancements in battery technology), there were alternatives to the traditional arrangement of pistons that would move up and down within cylinders and thus turn a crankshaft, which in turn would drive the mechanism to turn the vehicle's wheels.

In the 1920s, a German engineer named Felix Wankel created a "rotary compressor" engine. Instead of the traditional engine block with pistons in cylinders, Wankel's engine had what amounted to a block that was more of an oval shape. Within this oval, what appears to be a bulging triangle rotates around a fixed-toothed shaft, creating three zones for fuel compression, ignition, and exhaust.

The engine was lighter yet more powerful than the typical ICE powerplant, albeit one with issues to work out, such as lubrication, sealing, and fuel efficiency.

It wasn't until the mid-1950s that the Wankel rotary was used in a production automobile. Various traditional automobile manufacturers experimented with the rotary technology, but none as serious or successful as Mazda, which presented

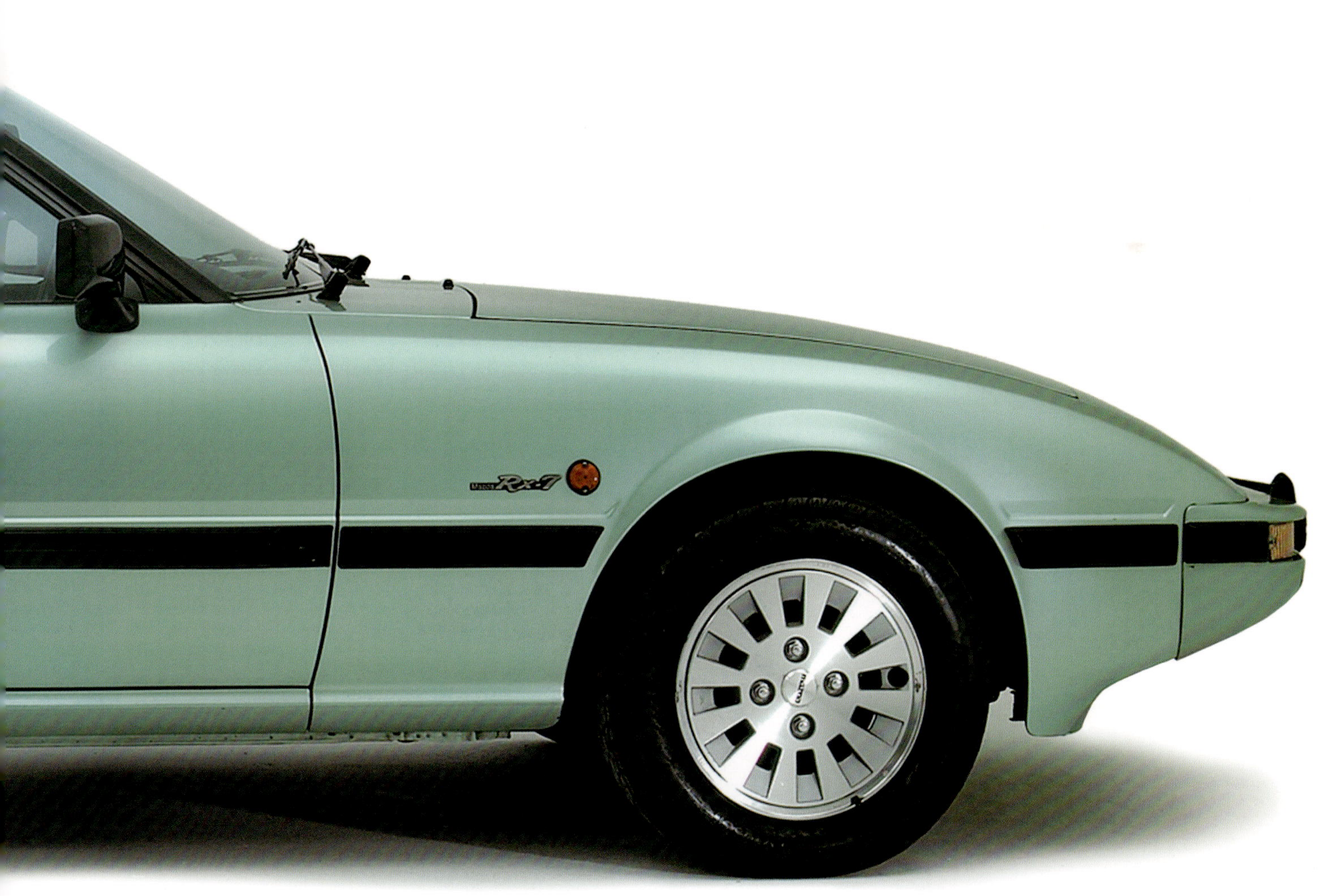

two prototypes at the Tokyo Motor Show in 1967. That same year, Mazda unveiled its Cosmo 110S, a rotary-powered sports car with a design as exotic as its engine.

Other applications followed, though none drew that much interest until the launch in 1978 of the Mazda RX-7. The RX-7 was a true sports car with design and performance that rivaled that of the Datsun 280Z or Porsche 924. Its lightweight and two-rotor powerplant produced more than 100 horsepower, and turbocharging the engine could boost output to more than 150 and top speed to nearly 150 mph (241.5 km/h).

The RX-7 proved particularly popular with sports car enthusiasts and amateur racers; around 500,000 units were purchased before the car got new coachwork for its second generation, which launched in 1985.

The second-gen version might be considered more of a grand touring than a true sports car, even offering 2+2 seating and a convertible top. Nonetheless, the car continued to do very well on the racetrack, winning the International Motor Sports Association GTU (under-2-liter class) championship eight years in succession.

Although Mazda championed the rotary engine in its RX-7, it stuck with traditional ICE for its mainstream models.

Previous and these pages ■ The Mazda RX-7 looked like the typical '70s sports car, but that was just the car's body shell and interior. Under the hood was an engine that forsook traditional pistons moving up and down in cylinders for a triangular rotor that spins among zones for fuel compression, ignition, and exhaust.

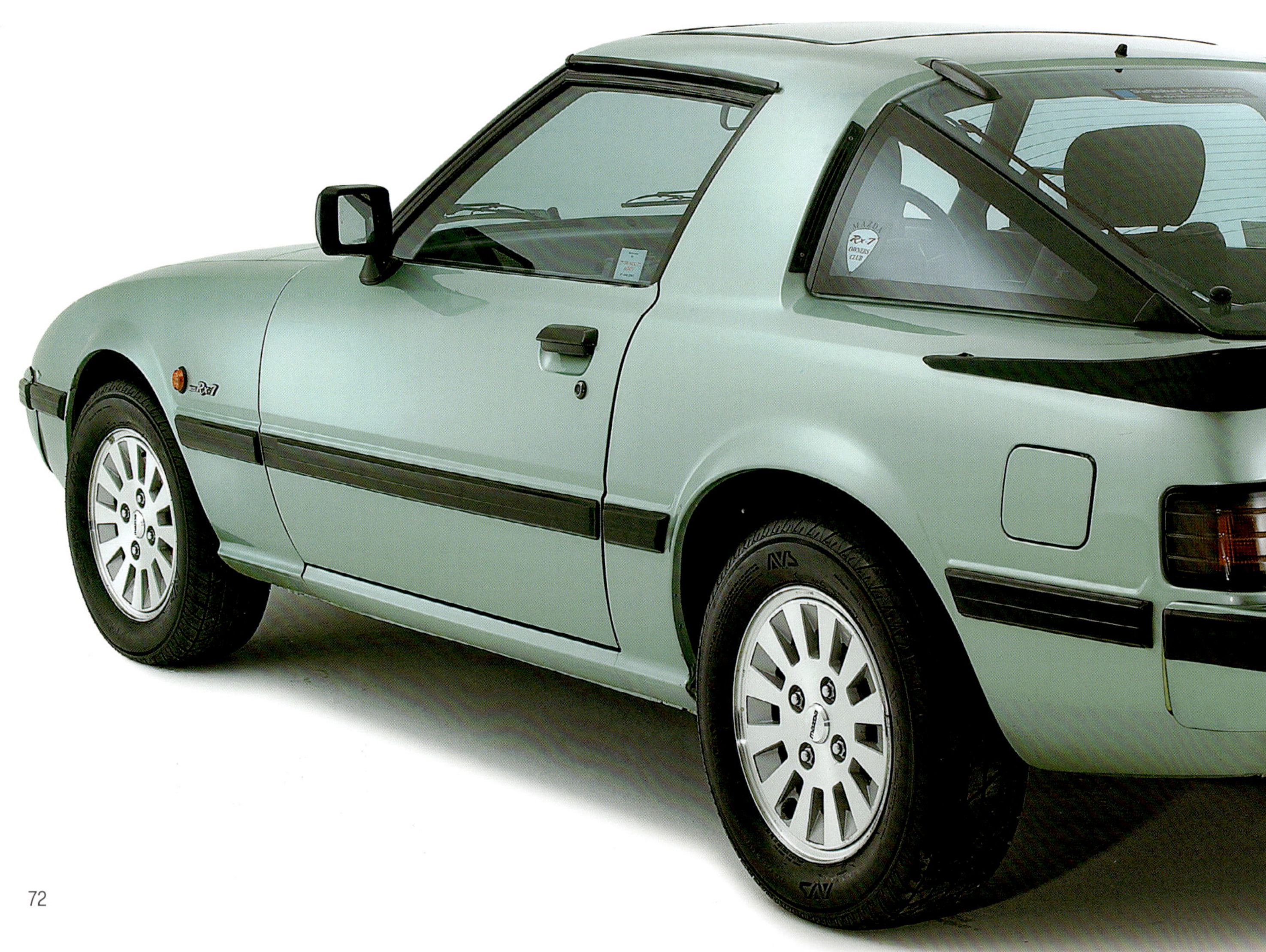

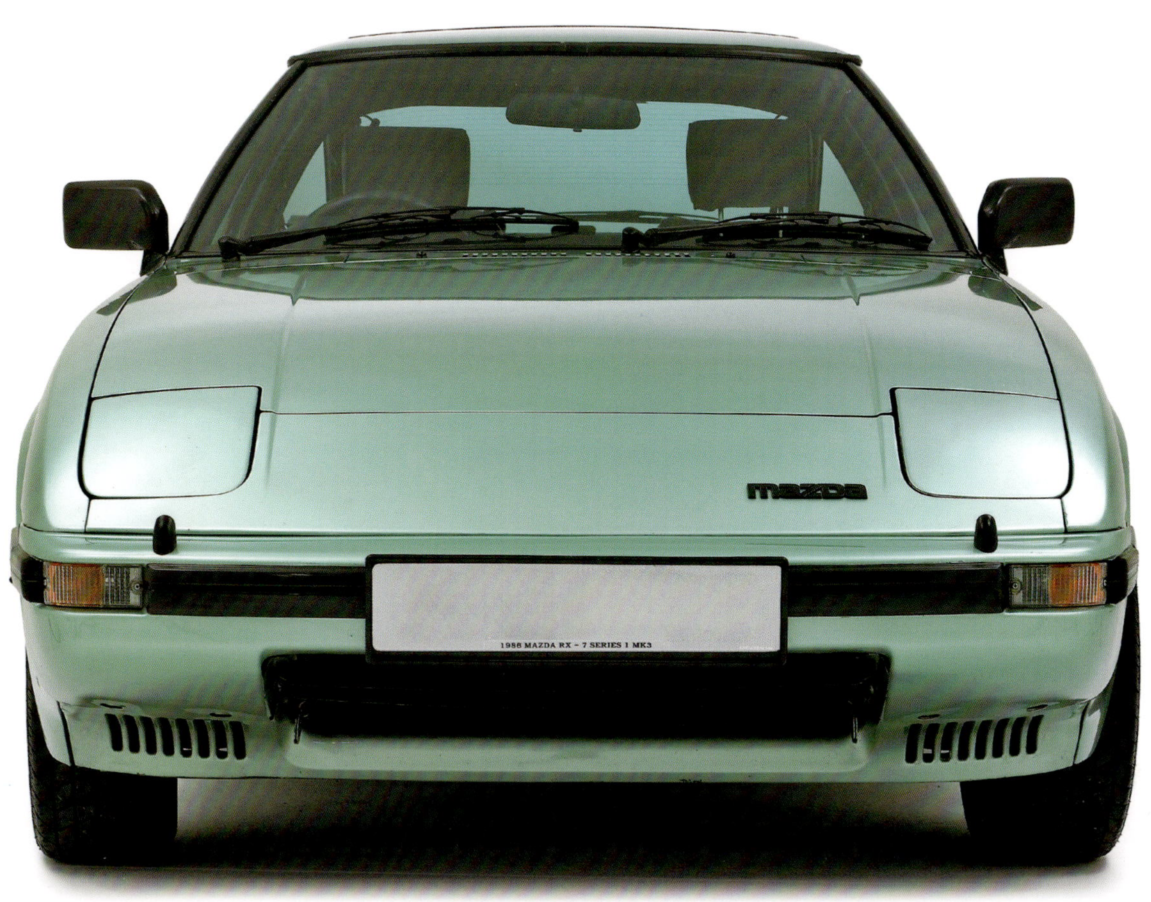

The RX-7 and its rotary engine was a forerunner for the Mazda 787B that won the 24 Hours of Le Mans in 1991.

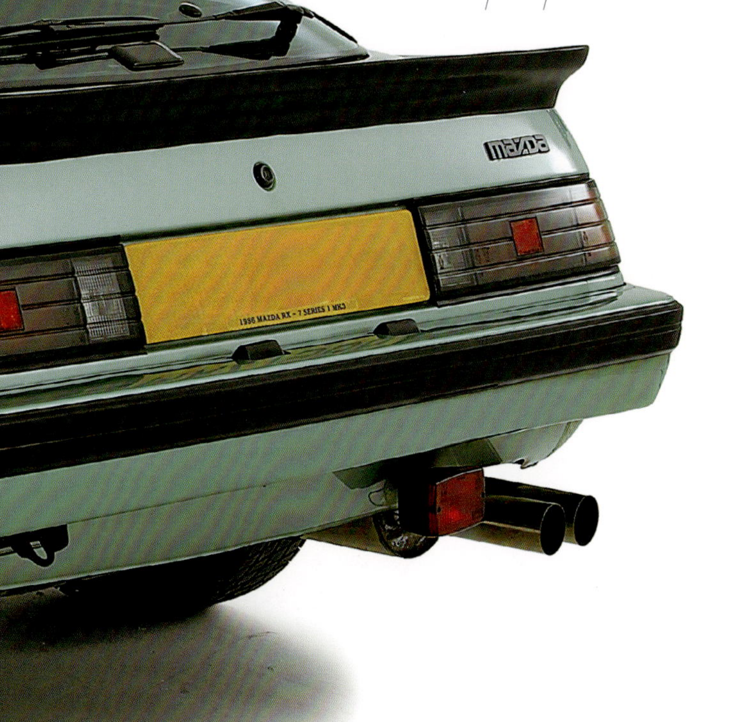

But it also proved the viability of the rotary in 1991 when it became the first Japanese automaker to win what many see as the most important auto race in the world, the 24 Hours of Le Mans. Mercedes-Benz and Jaguar were heavily favored in the race, but it was a rotory-powered Mazda 787B, wearing the bright orange and green colors of the Mazdaspeed team's racing sponsor, the Japanese store chain Renown, that was first across the finish line, and by a margin of two laps after the round-the-clock competition.

A third-generation road-going RX-7, again with new coachwork, was in production from 1991 to 2002, when it was succeeded by a new rotary-powered RX-8 model, a car notable in part for its unusual three-door architecture.

PORSCHE 928

Engine in front (and a V8 at that), trailer hitch at the rear

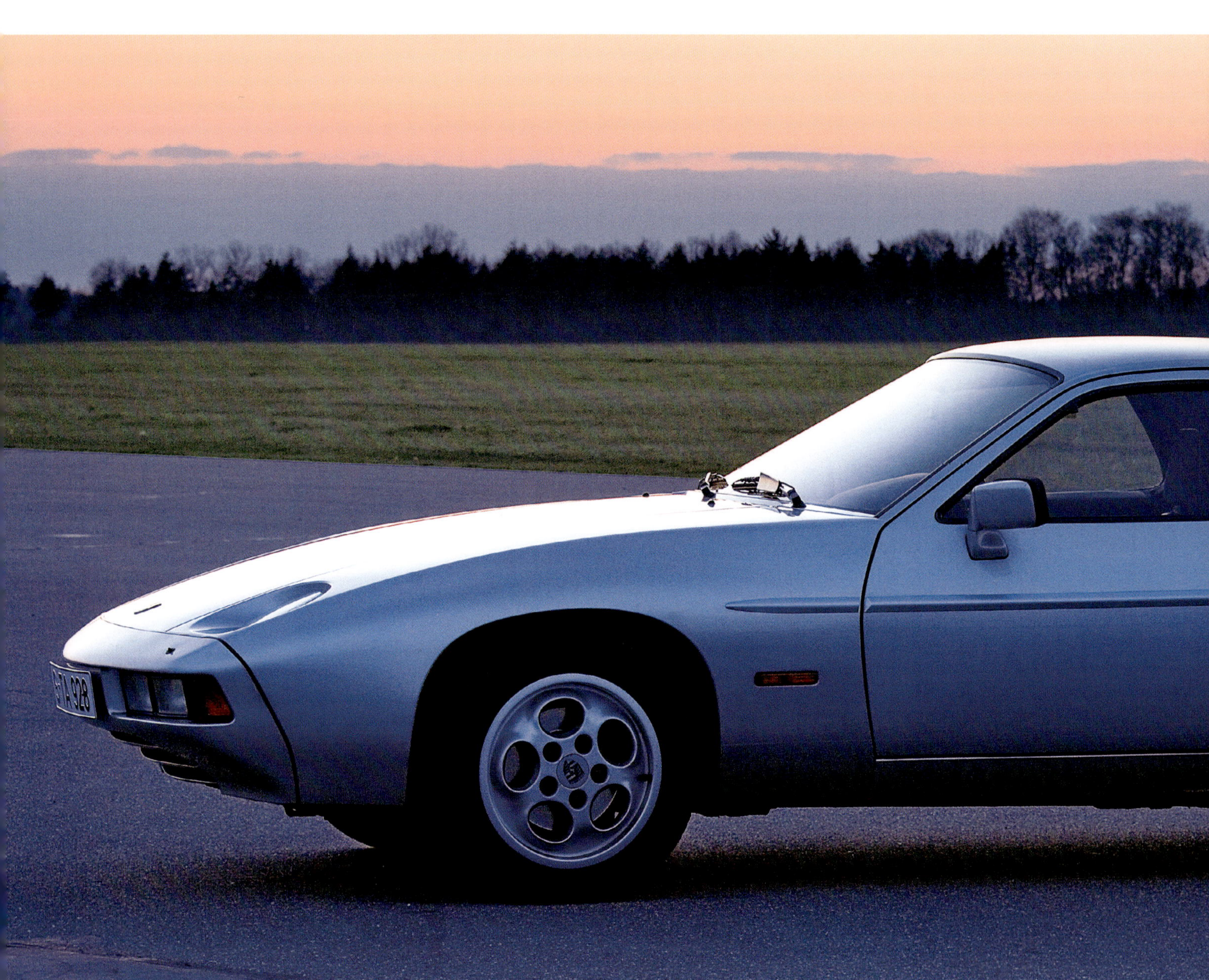

1970 ➤ 1979

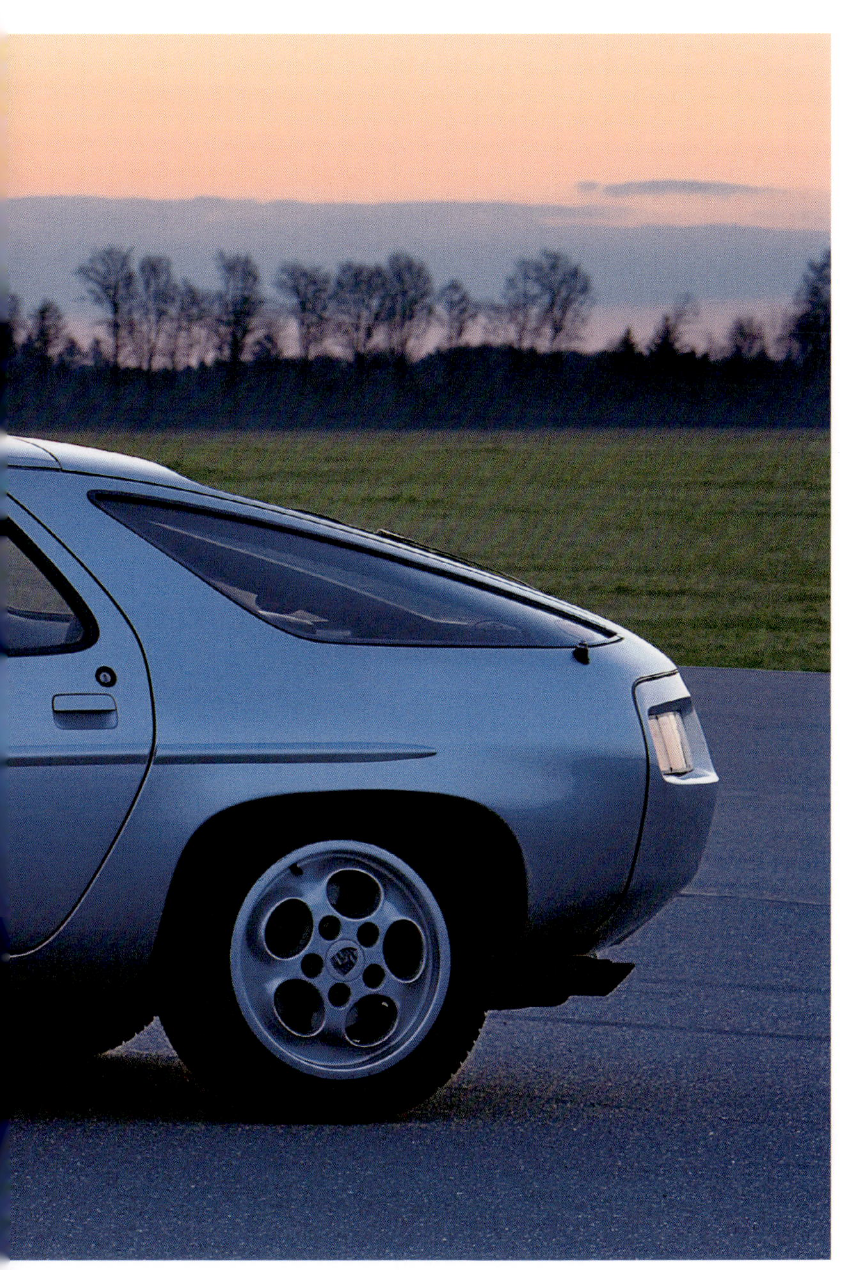

With the exception of the first Porsche automobile, built early in the twentieth century with electric motors mounted within its wheel hubs, and the Porsche farm tractors with their conventional engine in front of the steering wheel, Porsche's cars were engineered with their powerplants located behind the passenger compartment. Well, until the 928.

There were at least three things remarkable about this low-slung sports car: Its engine was in front. That engine was not an air-cooled and horizontally opposed 4- or 6-cylinder as in the 356 and 911, nor even the liquid-cooled inline 4 from the 924, but a 4.5-liter V8 rated at more than 200 horsepower even without the boost of turbocharging. The back of the car (like the Porsche farm tractor) could be equipped with a trailer hitch to pull a horse trailer or a boat, something that wouldn't be repeated by the German sports car producer until decades later when it saved its very existence by entering the sport utility vehicle (SUV) marketplace with the Cayenne.

In the mid-1970s, Porsche's iconic 911 sports car was aging. It had been evolved from the 356, which itself had been evolved from the original Volkswagen Beetle, and it appeared the rear-engine architecture and air-cooled engines may be reaching their limit. Besides, customers increasingly wanted more luxury in their vehicles' interiors while also demanding better fuel economy in the aftermath of global fuel crises.

■ The 928 looked like a 911 had been stretched from bumper to bumper.

Porsche's solution was the 928, which it created as a potential replacement for the venerable 911. This new Porsche would be more luxurious, a grand touring car with a sports car's styling (and room for a couple of children to ride along with their parents) as well as the sort of performance that a V8 engine could provide.

The 928 was unveiled at the 1977 Geneva Auto Show and became the first (and to date, the only) sports car to be awarded European Car of the Year.

Decades later, *Motor Trend* magazine called the 928 the most underrated Porsche car of all, adding that back in its time "it had seemed an impossibly fast and effortlessly competent machine, a 165-mph continent-crusher that made almost every other grand turismo on the planet seem fussy and fragile."

But, the article continued, with its engine an air-cooled V8 and mounted in front, "the 928 was heresy incarnate for the Porsche purists." (Another issue with Porsche purists: The 928 cost a third again more than the 911.) And yet *Motor Trend* noted that before long, all Porsche engines would be liquid-cooled and that

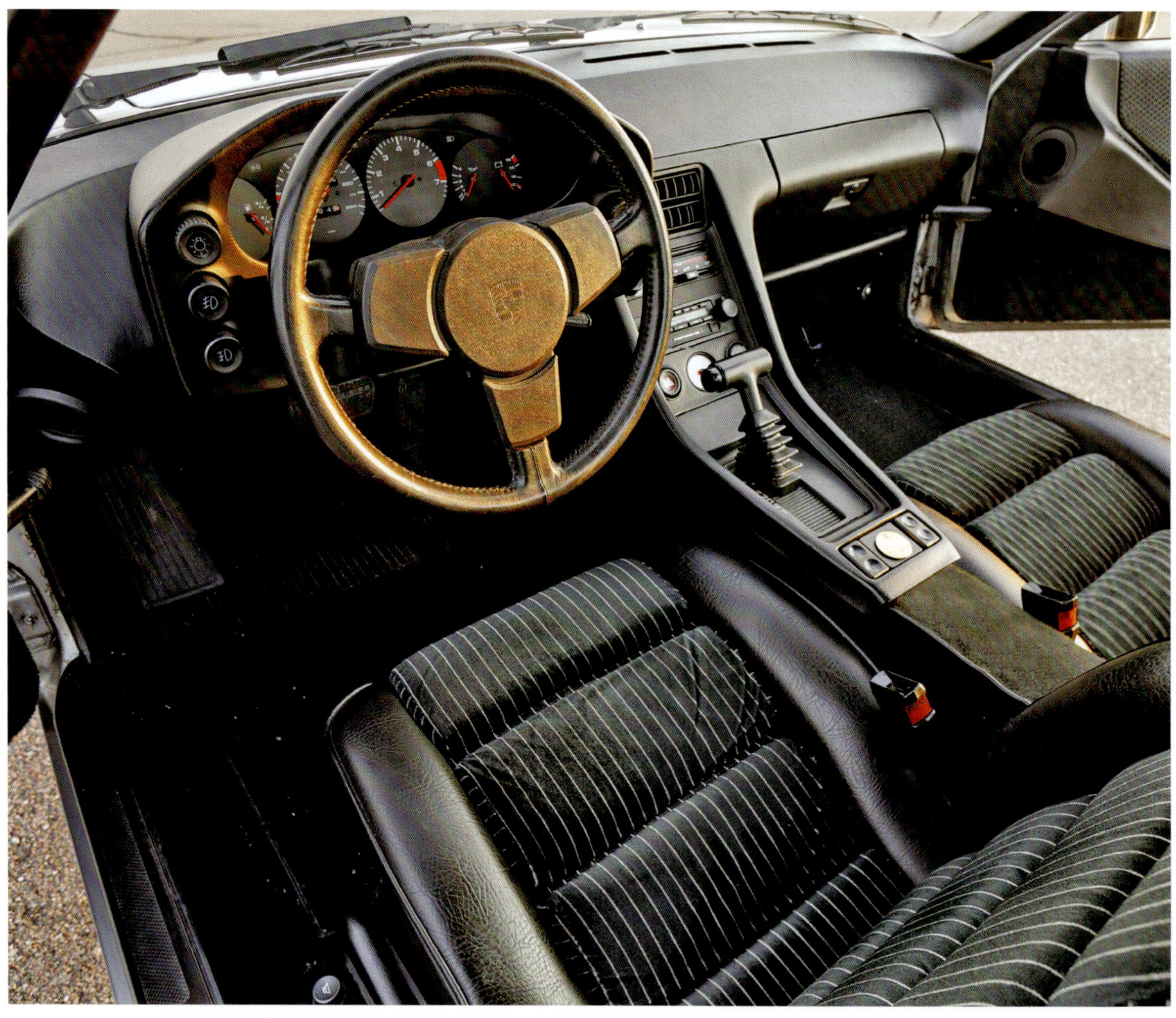

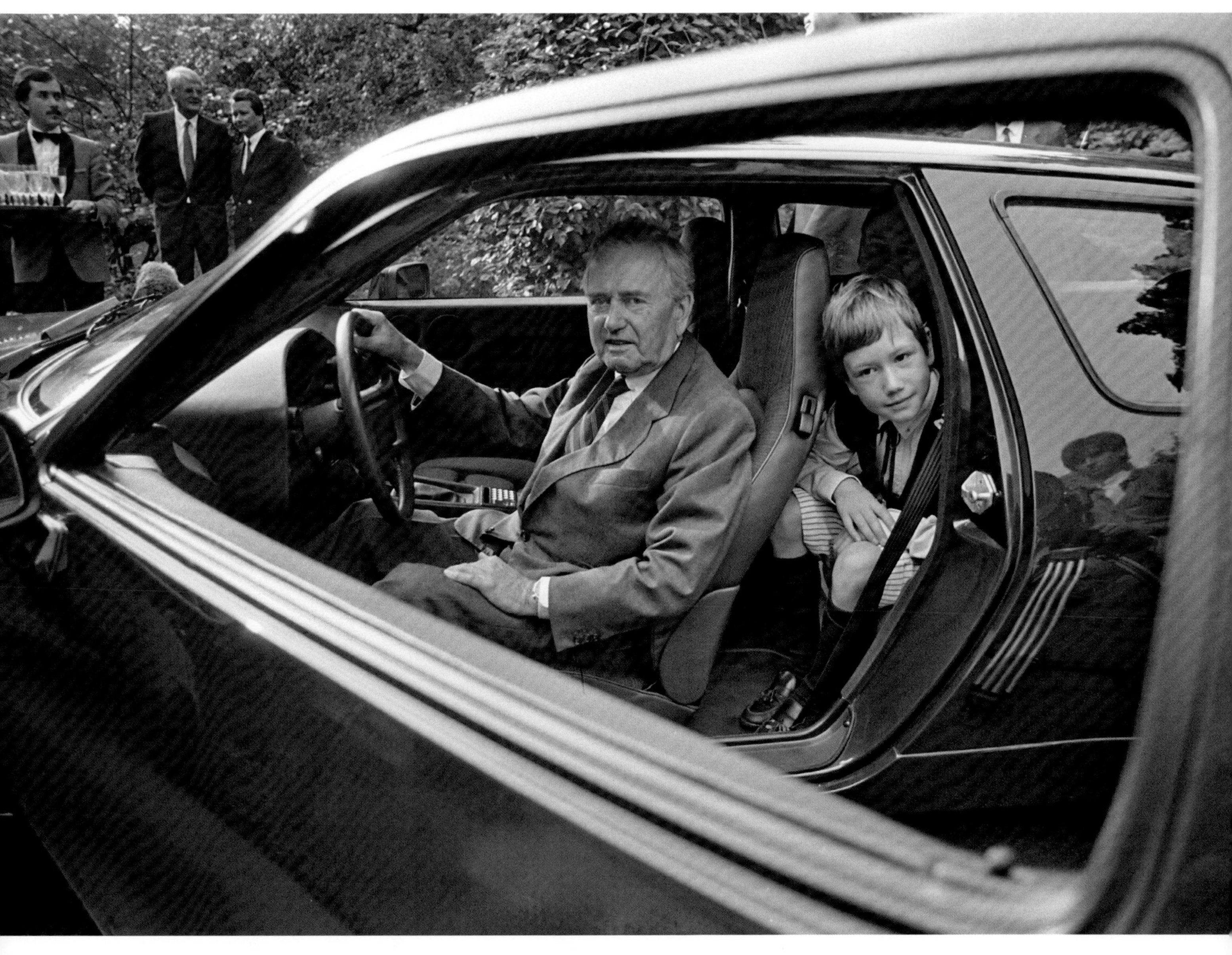

Opposite page ■ The passenger compartment of the Porsche 928 was more luxurious than in the 911.
This page ■ Ferdinand "Ferry" Porsche in the driver's seat of a 928. His grandson Daniel was in the back seat.

"front-engine V8-powered vehicles are acknowledged as having been Porsche's savior."

The headline on its review called the 928 "the most underrated" Porsche car of all.

The 928 would evolve through nearly two decades of production, with larger and more powerful V8 engines and higher-performance S, S4, and GTS variations. It soon would be joined in the Porsche stable by another front-engine sports car, albeit a water-cooled 4-cylinder that powered the 944.

And in a bit of irony, while the 928 wasn't the vehicle that saved Porsche, which underwent a resurgence (albeit temporary) under new management, it was the precursor to the V8-powered, trailer-towing SUV that did. And in the process, the 928 itself would become popular with Porsche collectors.

Top ■ Pop-up headlamps illuminated the way through the dark and gave the car a sharper profile when retracted during the daytime.
Bottom and opposite pages ■ The 928 was the first Porsche automobile with a liquid-cooled and front-mounted engine of 8 cylinders.

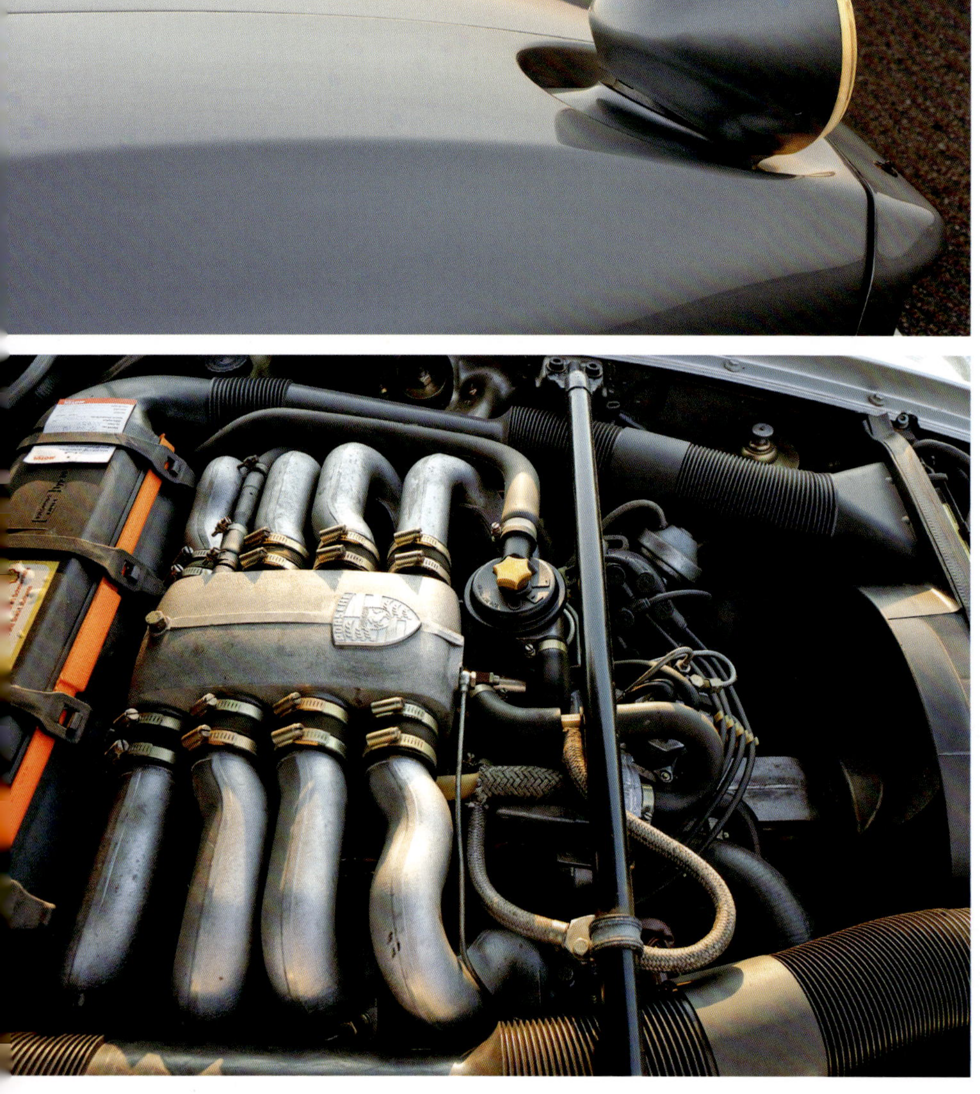

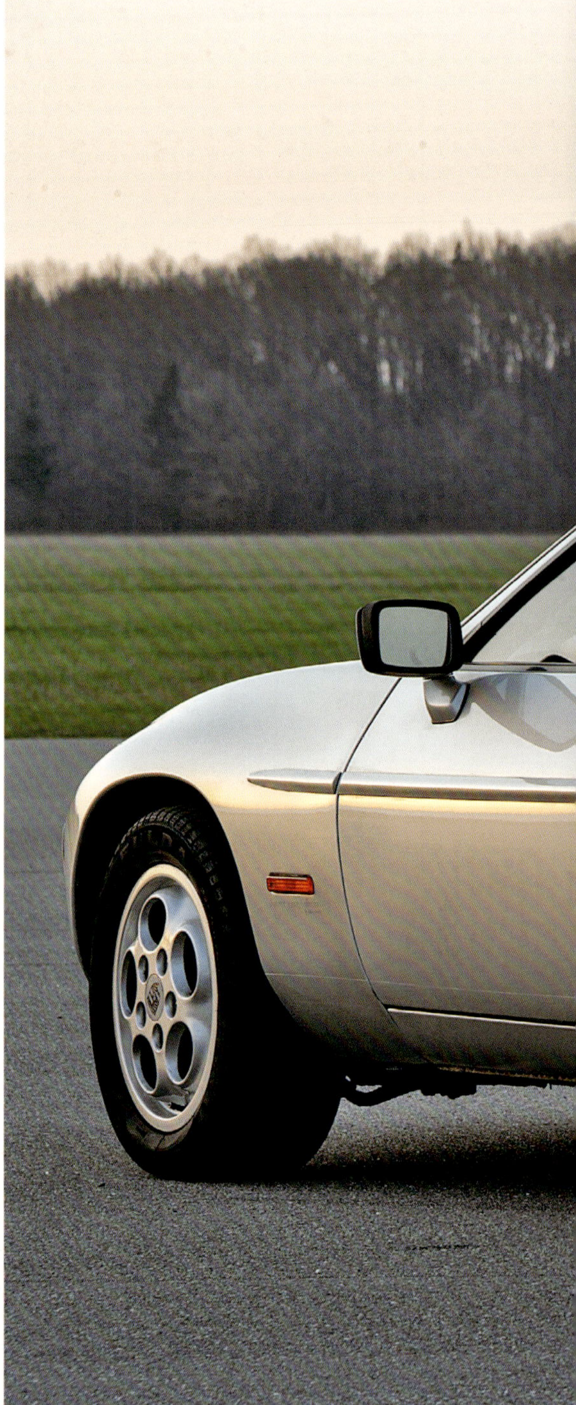

With a front-mounted V8 engine, the 928 could pull a horse, a boat trailer, or a caravan.

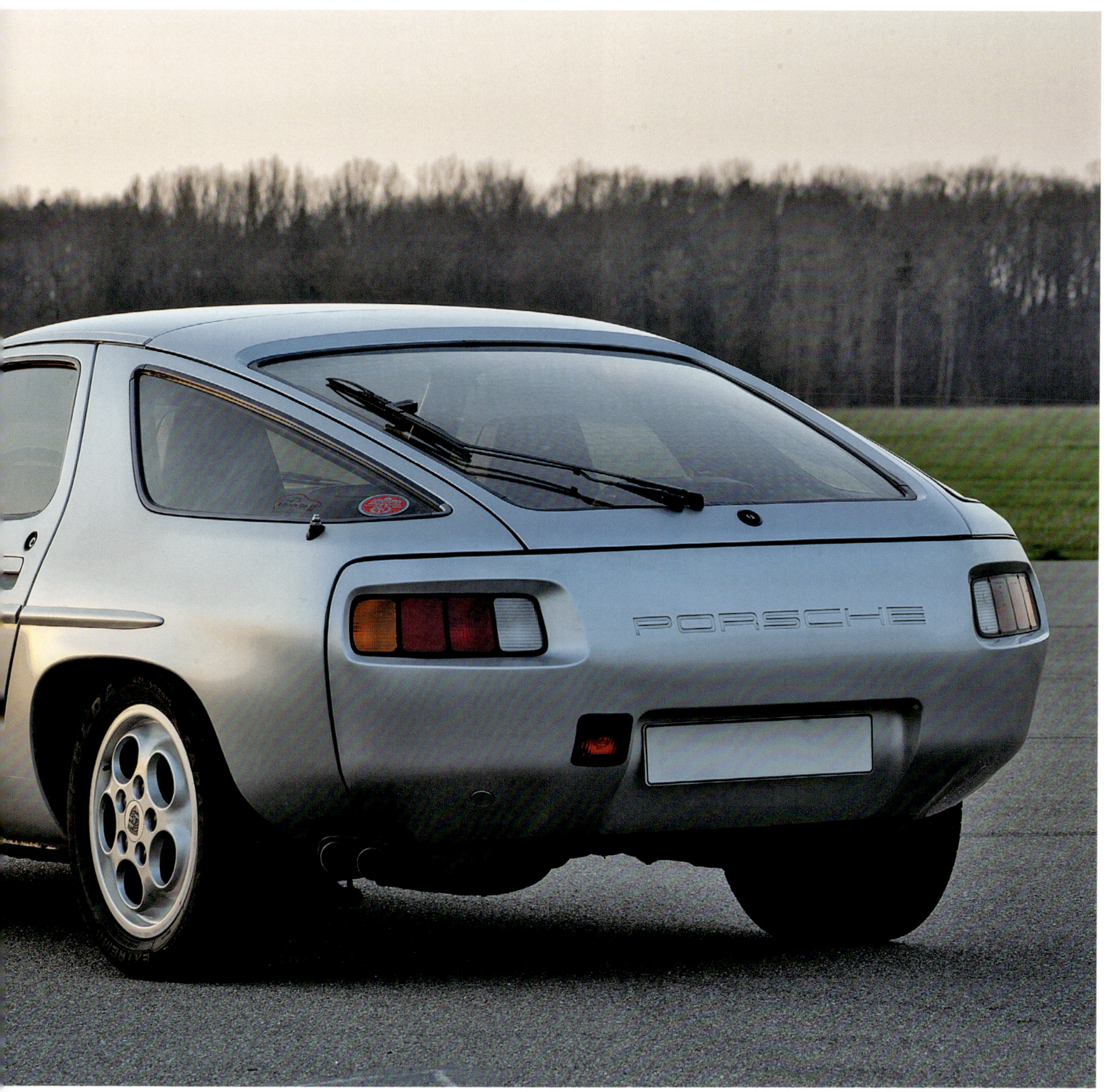

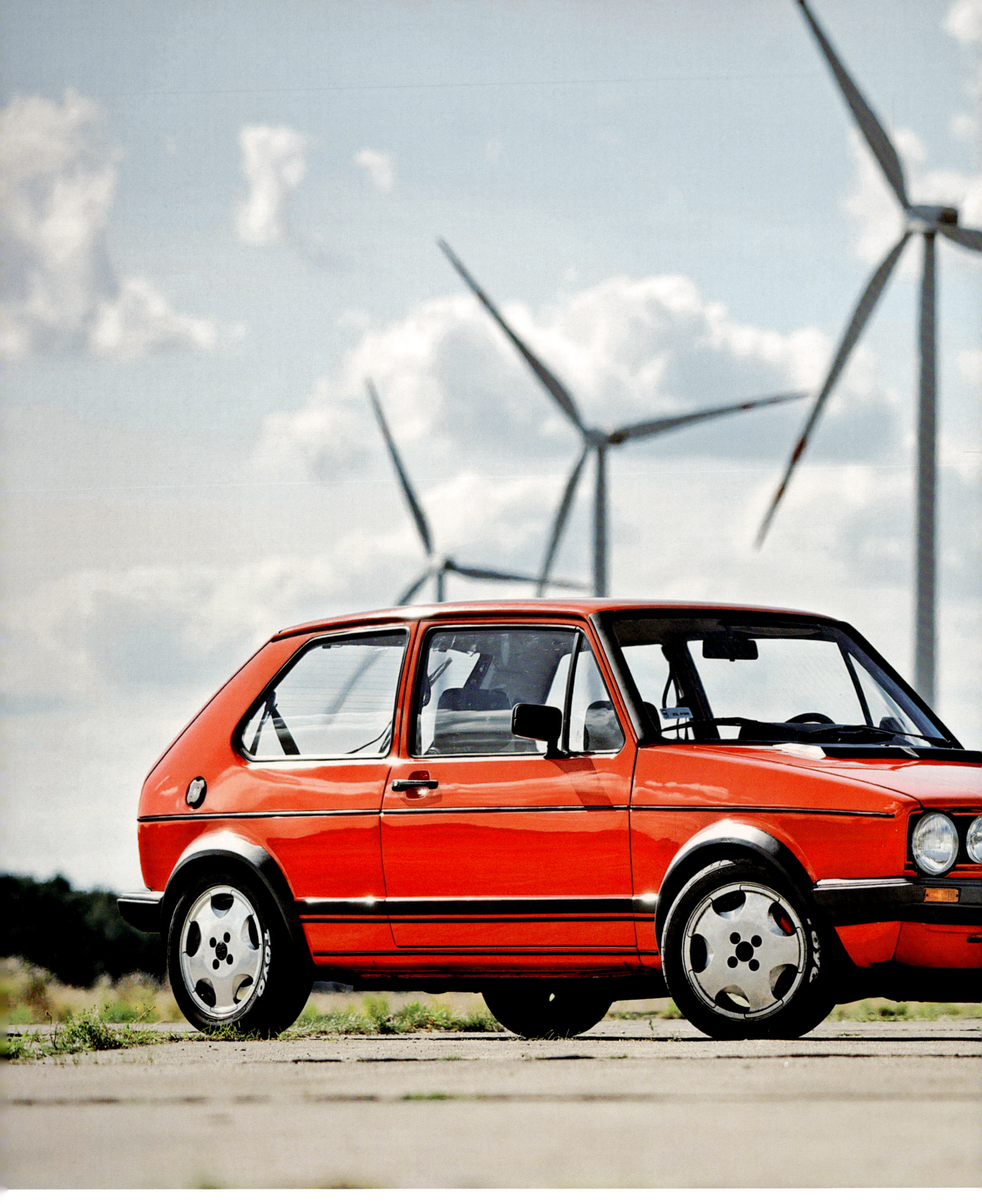

1970 ➤ 1979

VOLKSWAGEN GOLF GTI

"The quintessential hot hatchback" excites on road or track

By the mid-1970s, the Volkswagen Type 1—the people's car that had launched in 1938 and was not only the planet's all-time bestseller, but globally cherished as the beloved "Beetle"—had finally become, well, outdated. Its petite size and air-cooled and rear-mounted engine just didn't make sense in a world that needed cars to be safer and cleaner.

Volkswagen was already considering a replacement for the Beetle in the late 1950s. The new car would need an efficient water-cooled engine that would be mounted in front of the passenger compartment. A series of proposals were considered. Finally, after the 1969 Turin Auto Show in Italy, Volkswagen hired Giorgetto Giugiaro and his Italdesign studio to create a possible Beetle successor.

Where the Beetle was semicircular in its shapes, Giugiaro's proposal showed his "folded-paper" styling cues.

His hatchback design was approved, but the car needed a name. Caribe and Blizzard were suggested but lost out to Golf, which has been sourced to (pick your favorite):

- the Gulf Stream (*Golfstrom* in German),
- the name of a horse owned by Volkswagen's head of purchasing and ridden one weekend by VW's chairman,
- or the game of golf, the name inspired when a Volkswagen executive mounted a golf ball atop the shift lever during the car's development.

While the Beetle would remain in production somewhere in the world for at least two more decades, the new Golf started rolling down VW assembly lines in the late spring of 1974. (The vehicle would be alternatively known as the Rabbit in the United States and Canada and as the Caribe in Mexico.)

■ While the Beetle was a series of circles and semicircles, the Golf featured "folded-paper" styling cues.

Created as a replacement for the VW Beetle, the Golf in its GTI form provided a new level of driving dynamics.

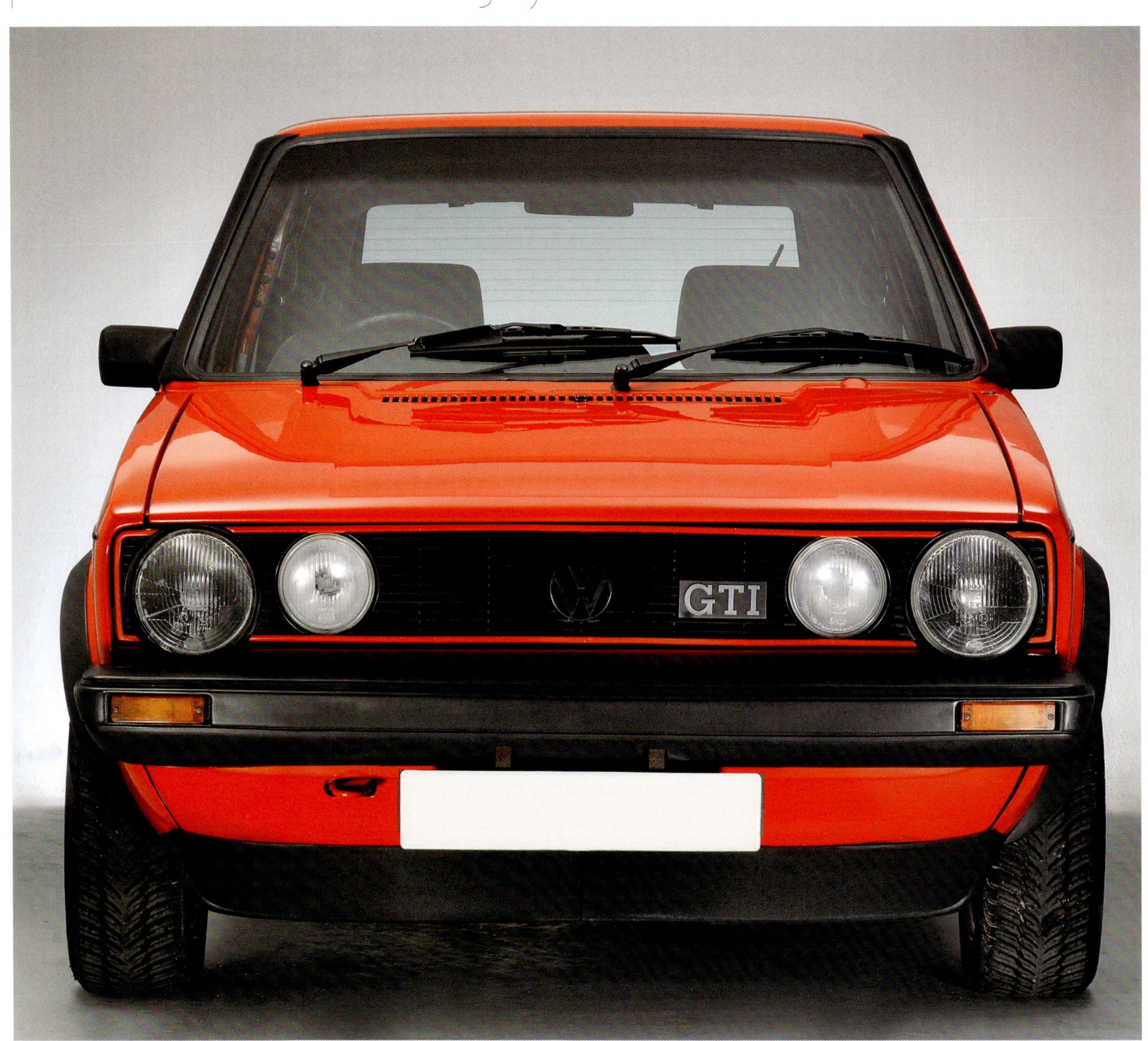

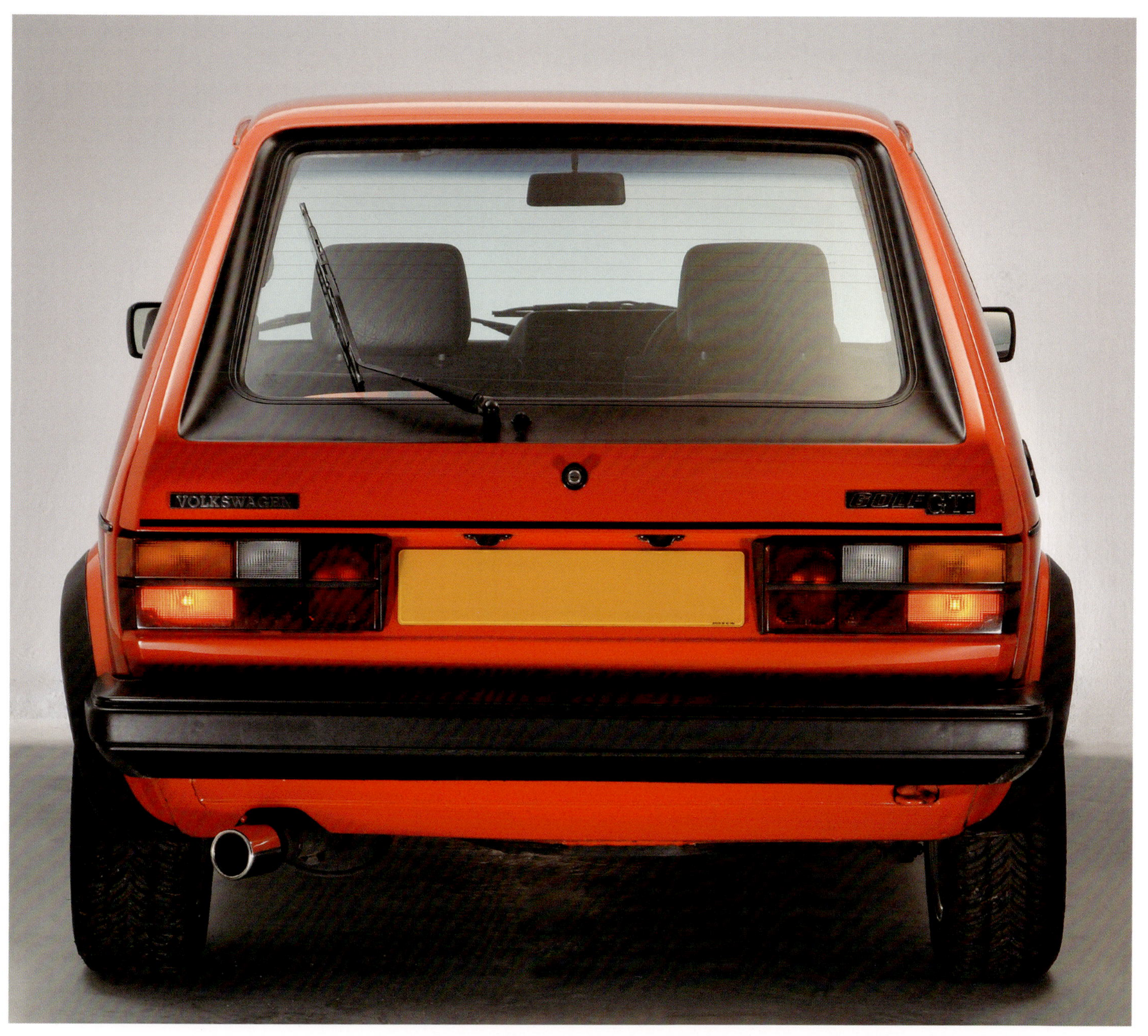

■ Volkswagen transformed its Golf with a fuel-injected engine previously used by Audi and backed up the powerplant with wider wheels, disc brakes, lowered suspension, and a 4-speed (and later a 5-speed) manual transmission.

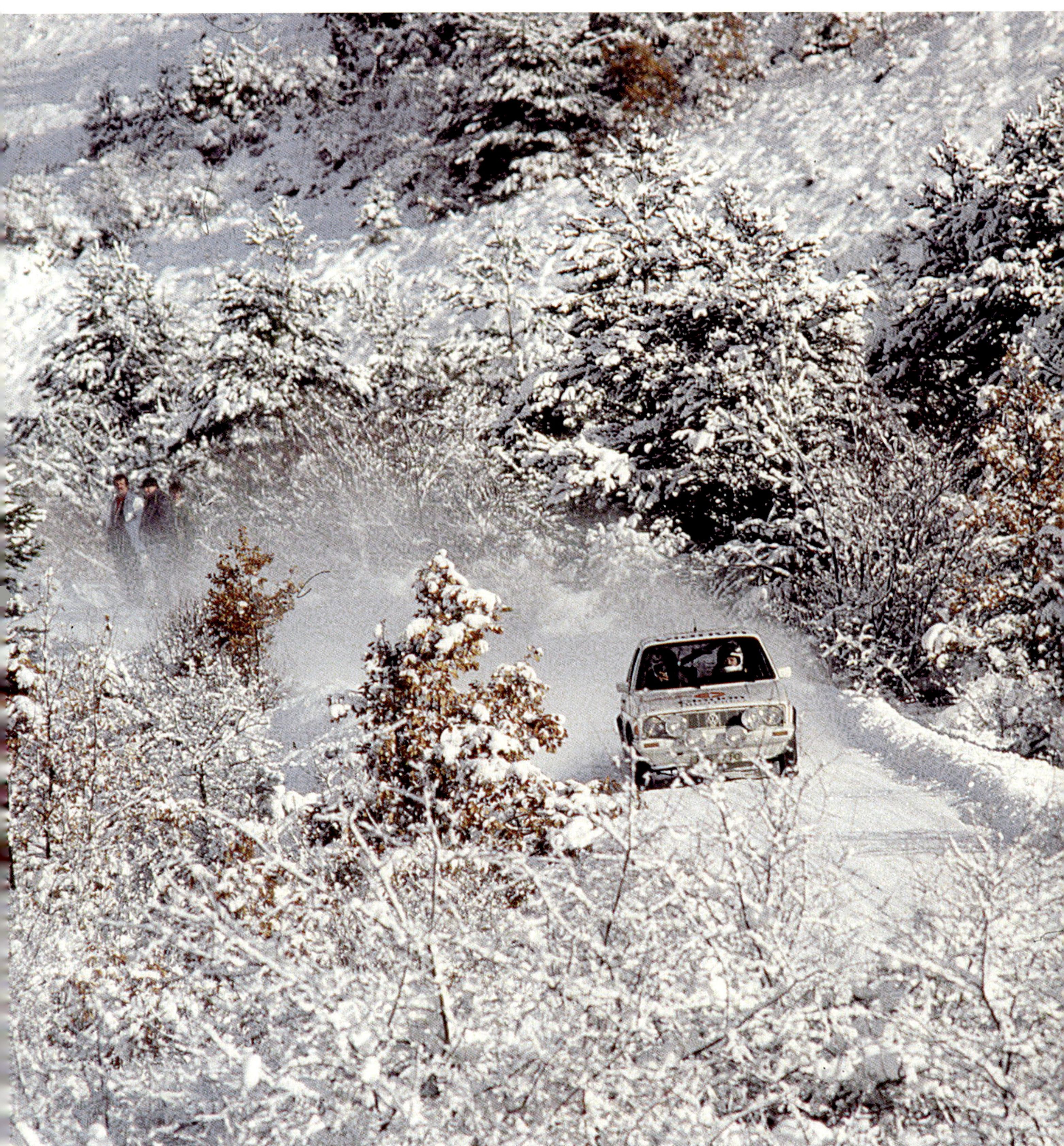

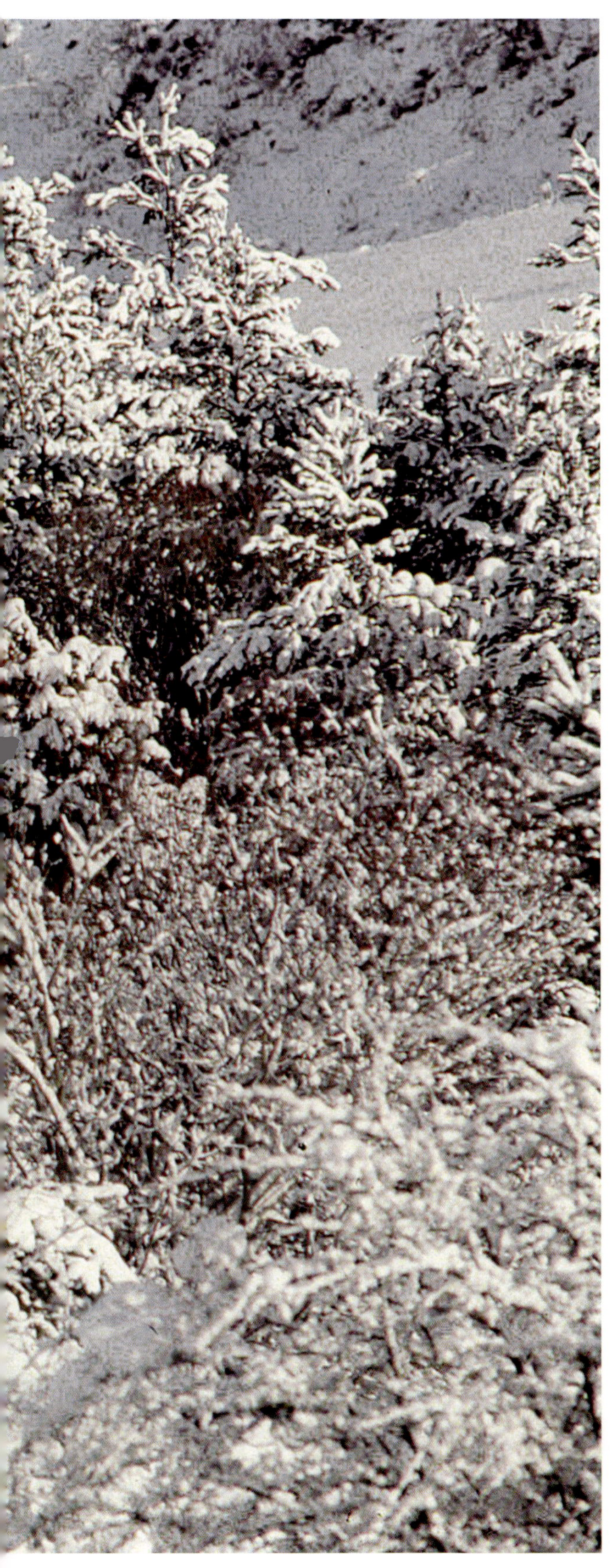

■ Volkswagen's Golf GTI provided a relatively low-cost entry into motorsports, whether on the paved racetrack or rallying along forest trails.

But even before the first one arrived at a dealership, Volkswagen employees were working, albeit in secret, on higher-performance modifications. Nearly two years later, they were ready to come out from hiding and present their work to Volkswagen management.

Project EA195 was unveiled as the Volkswagen Golf GTI in the fall of 1975 at the Frankfurt Motor Show and went on sale in the fall of 1976. The car's badge traced to the Italian *Gran Turismo Iniezione* (Grand Tourer Injection in English).

Visually, the car featured blistered wheel wells, a front spoiler, matte-black and red trim, more aggressive tires, front ventilated disc brakes, stiffened and lowered suspension, and a 1.6-liter fuel-injected 4-cylinder engine rated at nearly 110 horsepower that flowed to the front wheels through a 4-speed manual transmission (which in the summer of 1979 was replaced by a 5-speed unit).

Car and Driver magazine has called the Golf GTI "the quintessential hot hatchback."

"The Golf GTI's 1976 launch was a disruptive occurrence: VW had dumped the 110-hp 1.6-liter inline-four, previously offered at Audi, into the super-light and compact Golf. It upended hierarchies in more ways than one, as even entry-level Porsches couldn't keep up...Top speed: more than 110 mph."

Adds Hagerty, classic car insurer and value tracker, "While there certainly were fast hatches before the...debut of the GTI, it was the Golf that truly popularized the breed and spurred rival companies to create their own souped-up versions of mainstream hatches."

The GTI became a popular choice for low-cost motorsports, both on the racetrack and in rallying.

The Golf has remained in production since its debut, and the GTI has entered its eighth generation, now powered by a 241-horsepower, 2.0-liter turbocharged 4-cylinder engine.

LANCIA DELTA INTEGRALE

Compact family hatchback transforms into the rage of the rally circuit

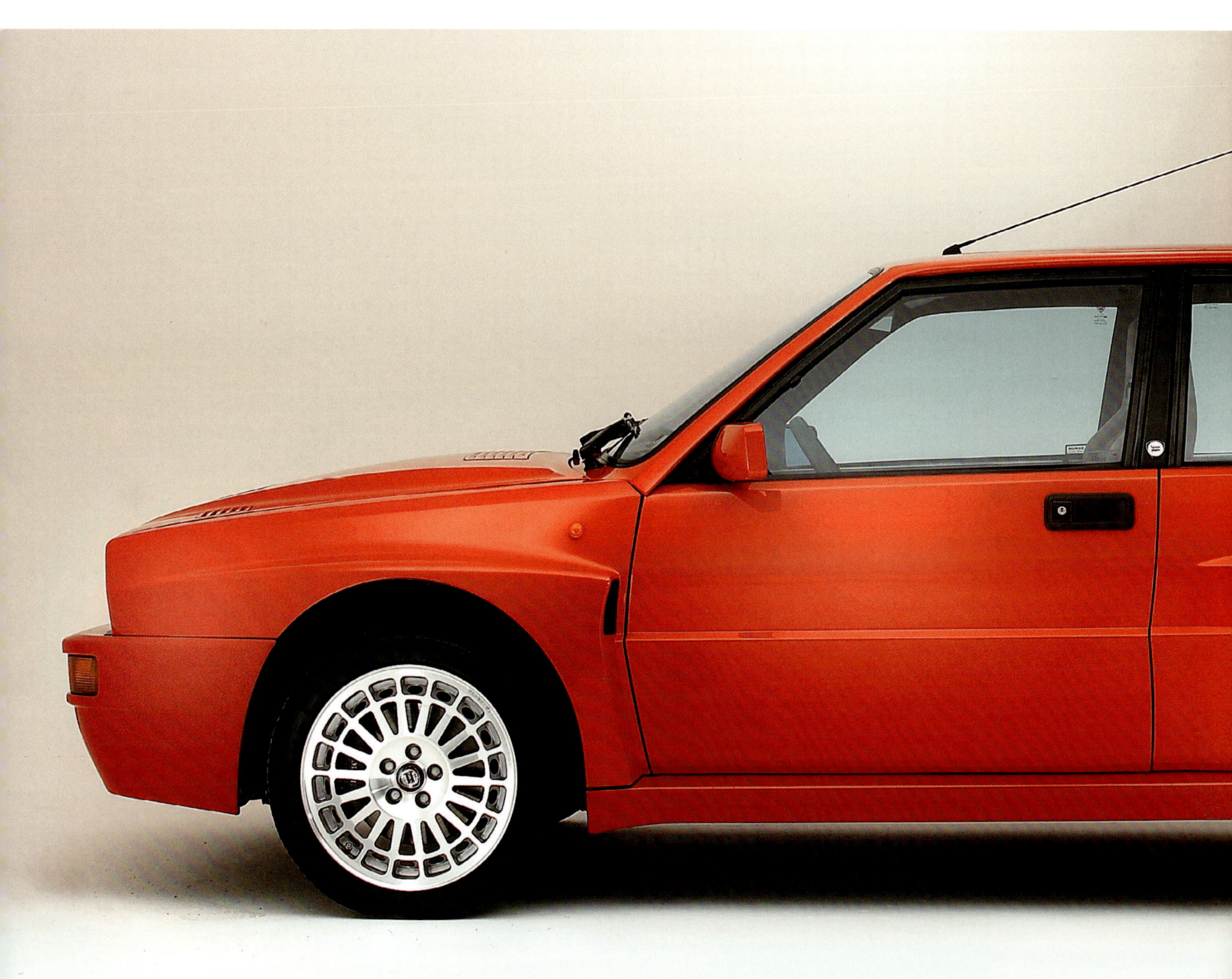

1970 ➤ 1979

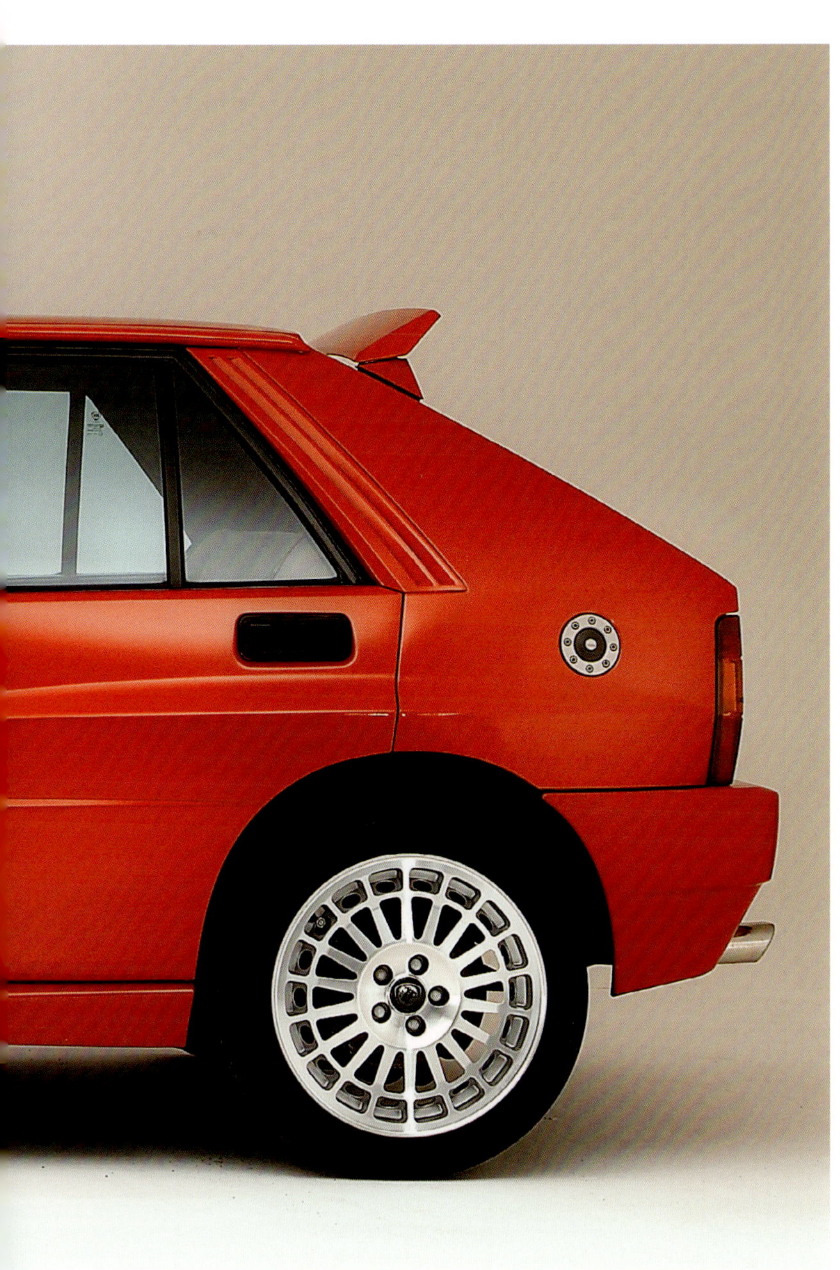

Lancia had dominated the World Rally Championship in the mid-1970s, its purpose-built Stratos racing to the title in 1974, 1975, and again in 1976, and then carrying Lancia driver Sandro Munari to the inaugural driver's championship in 1977, when the makers' title went to Lancia's parent and Italian rival, Fiat.

Lancia would take the makers' title again in 1983 with its Rally 037 model. But by then Audi with its quattro and then Peugeot with its 205 T16 had became the cars of choice.

At the 1979 Frankfurt Motor Show, Lancia unveiled its new compact family car. Designed by Giorgetto Giugiaro and his Italdesign studio, it was a front-driven hatchback badged as the Delta.

The cars used Fiat 4-cylinder engines but with power-boosting enhancements by Lancia engineers. Almost immediately it was selected as the European Car of the Year by the panel of automotive journalists representing sixteen countries.

So-called hot hatches were popular in Europe and in many cases supplemented the family-oriented version with higher-performance variations. Thus for Lancia in 1985 came the Delta S4, with 4-wheel drive and a turbocharged engine. Basically, the car was a homologation special that made it possible for Lancia to compete with the Delta S4 in the World Rally Championship's Group B category, which it did from the final race of 1986 and throughout the 1987 season.

■ Giorgetto Giugiaro created the hatchback styling that Lancia unveiled at the Frankfurt Motor Show in 1979.

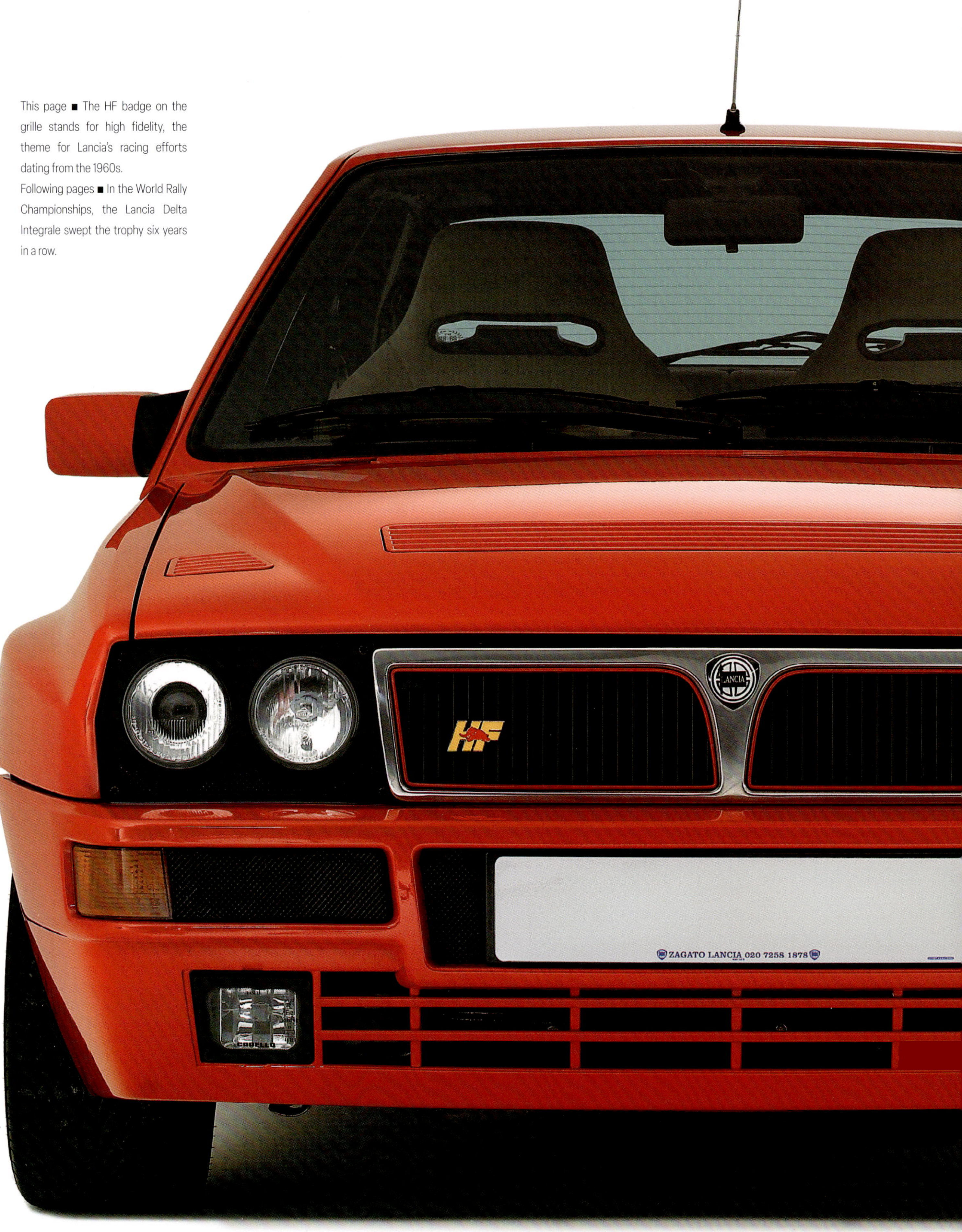

This page ■ The HF badge on the grille stands for high fidelity, the theme for Lancia's racing efforts dating from the 1960s.
Following pages ■ In the World Rally Championships, the Lancia Delta Integrale swept the trophy six years in a row.

When the rules of rallying required new hardware, Lancia was ready with its made-for-rally Delta Integrale.

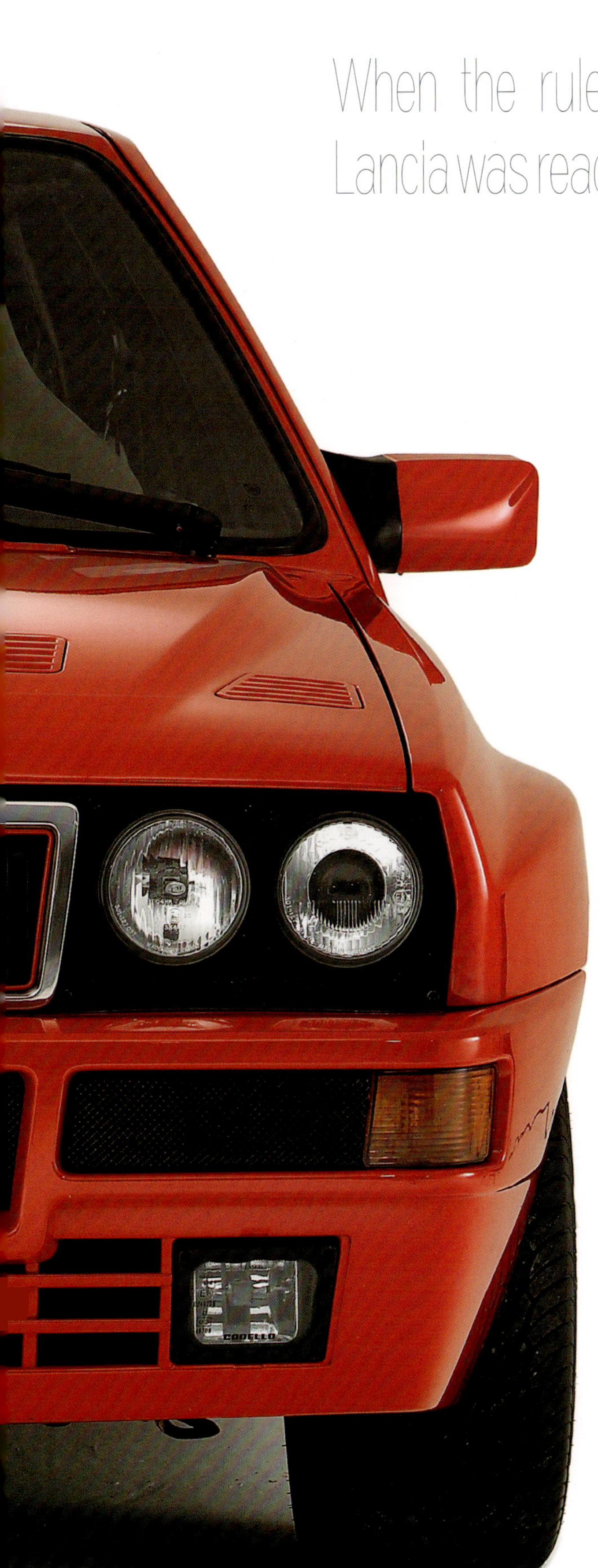

In rally trim, the S4 reportedly could sprint from a standing start to 100 km/h (62 mph) in a remarkably quick 2.3 seconds, and on a gravel road at that! But such cars—nicknamed the Killer Bees—proved too dangerous even for the world's most skilled rally drivers, and the rules were changed for 1987.

But Lancia was ready. It rolled out its new Group A entry, the made-for-rallying Delta HF Integrale (HF short for high fidelity, a badge that had been employed on sports and racing Lancias since the mid-1960s).

Lancia won the manufacturers' trophy that year and then again each year for the next five years. Lancia's Juha Kankkunen won the driving championship in 1987 and 1991, and Lancia driver Miki Biasion drove off with that trophy in 1988 and 1989.

In 2020, the website Petrolicious did a road test of a vintage Lancia Delta S4. In that report, Mario Escudero wrote, "I had always been interested in the mechanical aspects of the cars I counted as my favorites, but fine engineering coupled with elegant aesthetics is even better. I doubt anyone would disagree with a statement as simple as that, but there are some machines that don't need to exude beauty in a traditional sense to win over enthusiast hearts and minds. The Lancia Delta S4 is a prime example.

"Does it live up to that hype?" he continued, immediately answering his own question. "In short, absolutely. It forces you to pay attention in every regard. Its looks are arresting, and the seriousness conveyed by its form prepares you for a driving experience that requires your utmost focus…It is even more perfect than my years of fantasizing could have predicted."

Lancia's Delta remained in series production into the mid-1990s.

Coachbuilder Zagato was contracted by a Dutch car enthusiast and restorer to create a more streamlined two-door coupe version of the Delta Integrale. The car was known as the Lancia Hyena, and two dozen copies were produced between 1992 and 1996.

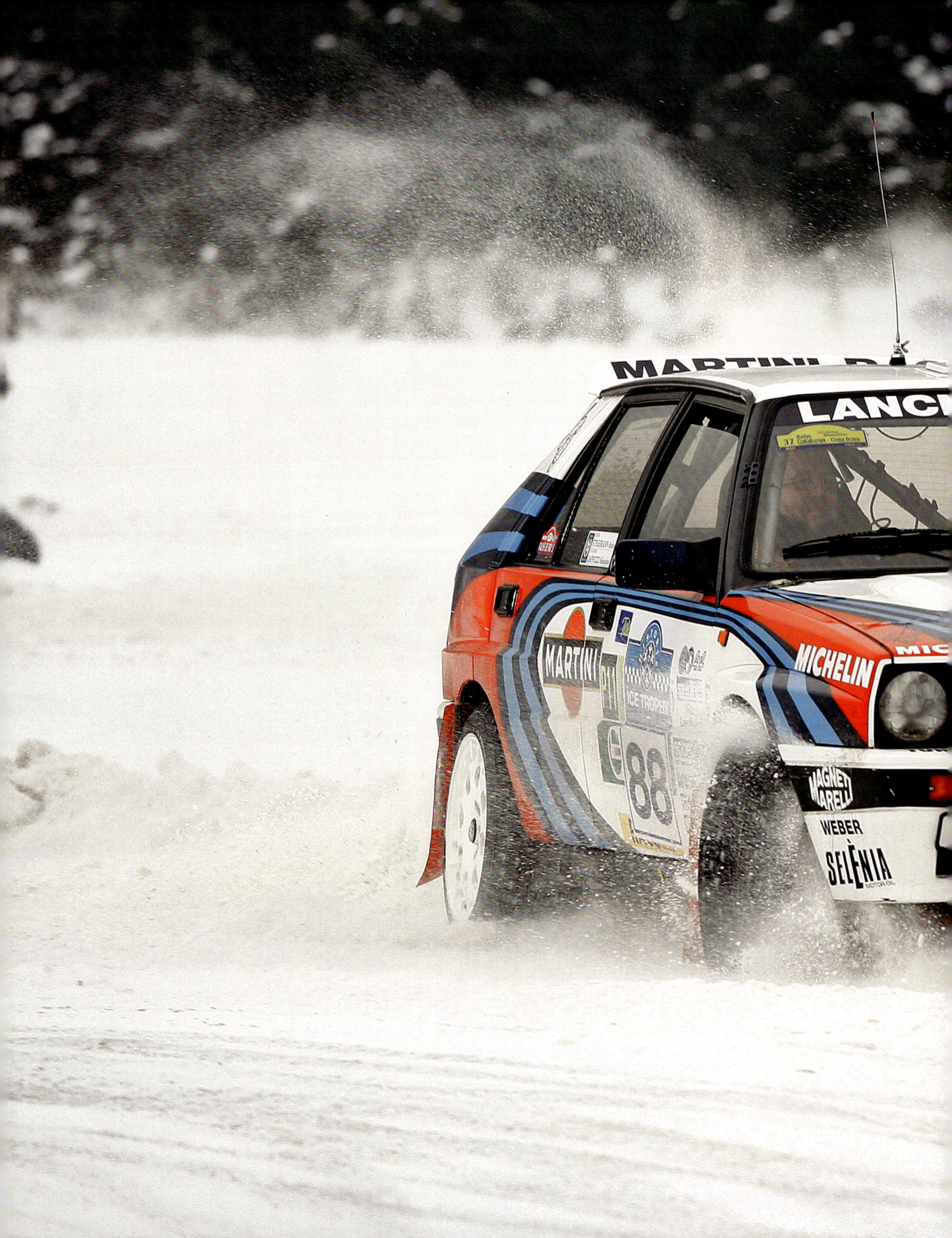
MARTINI
MICHELIN
ICE TROPHY
88
MAGNETI MARELLI
WEBER
SELENIA

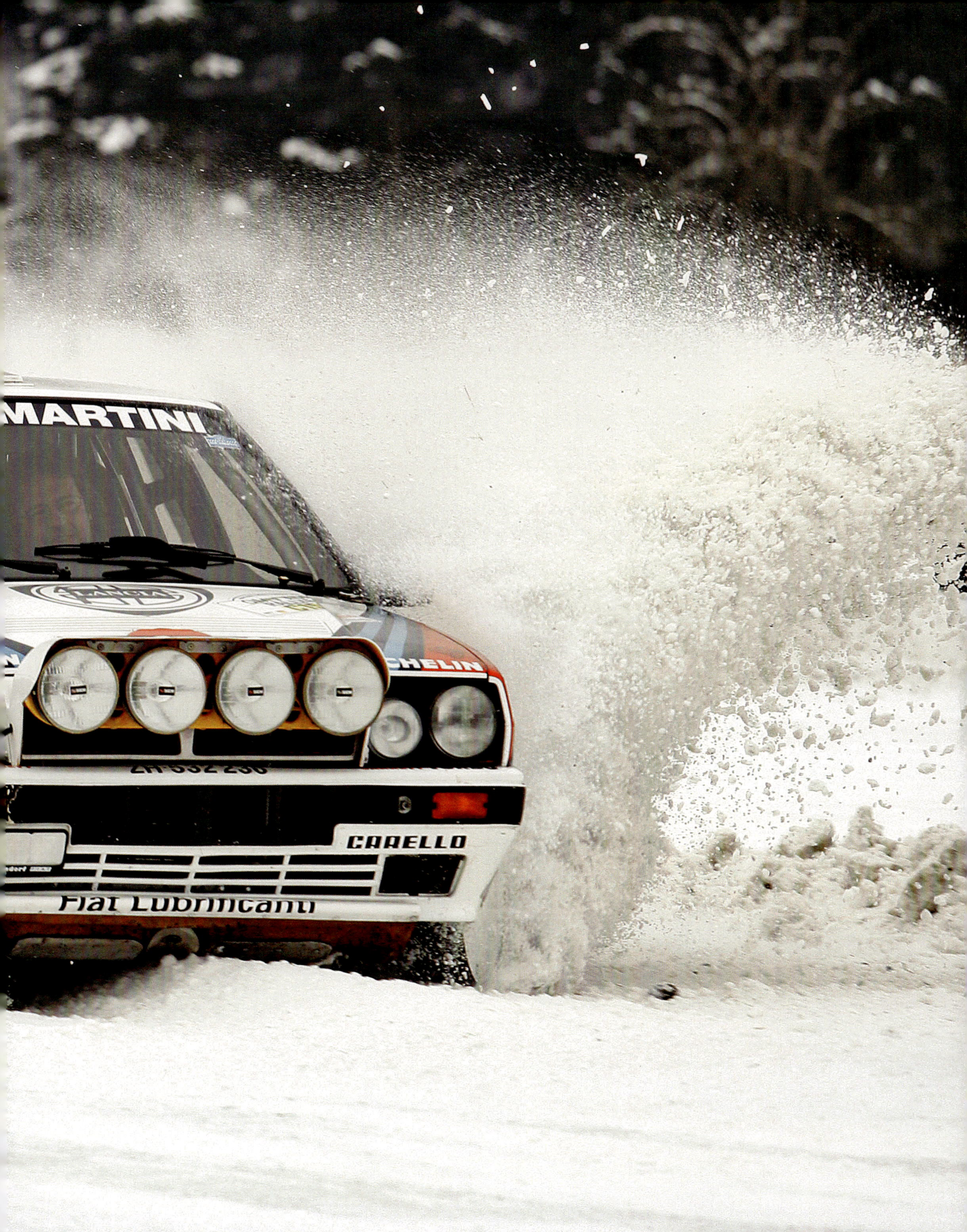
MARTINI
CARELLO
Fiat Lubrificanti

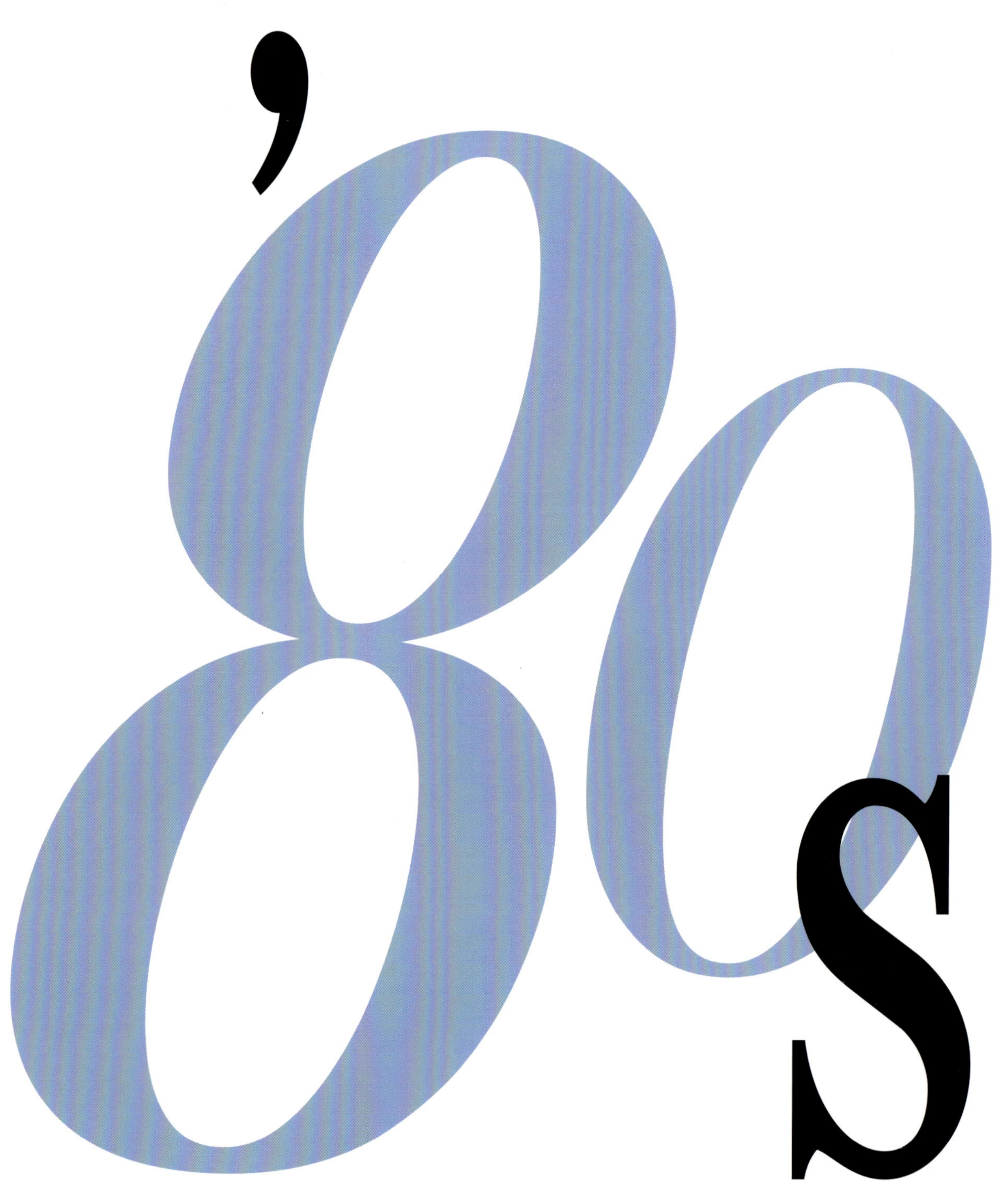

"No good cars came from the 1980s"
the headline claimed.
But we've identified quite a few.

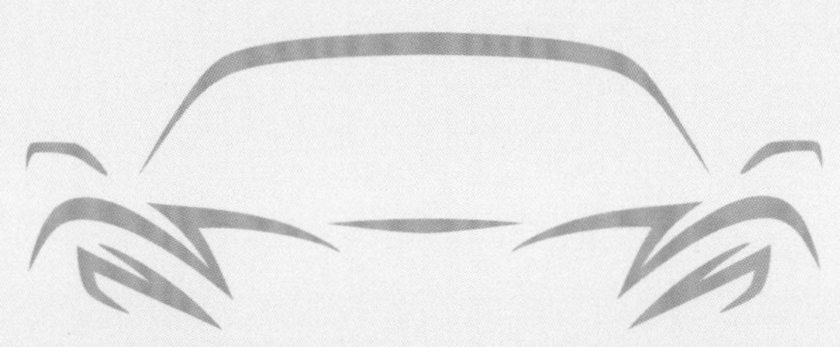

The 1980s were an odd mix. On one hand, they were the decade of decadence, with *Wall Street* movie character Gordon Gekko declaring "greed is...good." On the other hand, there was turmoil and instability around the world: war in the Middle East, war over small islands in the southern Atlantic, civil wars and famine, the AIDS epidemic, Chernobyl, the mid-air bombing of Pan Am flight 103, a protest in Tiananmen Square, the fall of the Berlin Wall.

The decade also presented us with the World Wide Web, MTV, Yuppies, and Prozac.

Early in 2025, *The New York Times* headlined an article, "The 1980s are back, and not in a good way."

From an automotive perspective, we'll mention two other recent headlines. In 2024, thedrive.com proclaimed, "1980s cars were great. Here's why" and motortrend.com offered, "Basically, no good cars came from the 1980s."

Nonetheless, there were at least two significant developments within the automobile industry in the 1980s, though each might be termed aspects of economic globalization.

In late 1979, Japanese automaker Honda opened an auto manufacturing plant in the United States. Within a few years, Nissan and Toyota followed suit. Toyota also launched a joint-manufacturing facility with General Motors, and Mitsubishi did the same thing with Chrysler. Meanwhile, automotive production was ramping up significantly in South Korea, India, and Latin America.

At the same time, there was the emergence of the so-called world car.

"National differences in automobile design reflecting unique domestic market conditions have all but disappeared, and design is now fairly well standardized worldwide," professor and cultural historian James J. Flink wrote in his book, *The Automobile Age*, in 1988. He noted that such vehicles were assembled from components sourced in a variety of countries.

Meanwhile, in her book *A Century of Car Design*, historian and professor Penny Sparke notes, "The financial difficulties of the 1980s had the effect of creating a 'designer culture' in the area of domestic goods—furniture interior items and home economics—in response to consumers' belief that they could either buy themselves out of the recession or forget about it through the creation of and absorption into their own individual 'lifestyle.'"

However, she adds, the automobiles of the 1980s were largely unaffected—at the time.

"It did not reach the motor car in that decade, however," she added. But she noted, "When it finally did, in the 1990s, the results were dramatic."

Later in this book, we'll get to the cars of the 1990s—when engineers finally figured out how to generate more power within emission regulations. Immediately following, we present cars that made their mark in the 1980s. Some were still very much products of their national culture. Some were developed with global appeal. One became known for using an assembly line that stretched across an ocean.

But they all have one thing in common: They are still cherished by car enthusiasts and collectors four decades later.

1980 ➤ 1989

AUDI QUATTRO

An all-wheel-drive solution for all-weather traction

Ancestry is a hobby that fascinates (but also frustrates) many people as they search to find their roots and trace their family trees. Car companies also have histories, and they can be just as fascinating. Take Audi, for example.

As early as 1896, German engineer August Horch went to work for Karl Benz, the man credited with the invention of the automobile. After three years managing the Mannheim factory for the automobile's founding father, Horch started his own company, A. Horch & Co., and in 1900 he began producing his own motorcars.

In 1906, one of his cars beat those that were more powerful and expensive, including those from Benz, to win the Herkomer Trial, a 500-mile test that included hill climbs and speed runs.

Soon, however, Horch had a falling out with partners who were the & Co. of his company. In the process he lost the corporate rights to his name, which derived from the German word for listen. He started a new company, Audi, the Latin word for listen.

Horch's Audi won the Alpine Trial road rally so often that it got to keep the traveling trophy.

After a decade at Audi, Horch left to join the German Ministry of Economics. In 1932 Audi was enfolded into Auto Union (and thus the four-ring emblem). It became part of the Volkswagen Group in 1972, and a year later Ferdinand Porsche's grandson Ferdinand Piëch arrived to head Audi's engineering department. He had been involved in motorsports at Porsche and wanted to get Audi involved in auto racing.

While working on a four-wheel-drive system for a future Jeep-style vehicle for Volkswagen, Piëch's team created quattro, a full-time all-wheel-drive setup that not only worked on snow-covered roads but on racetracks as well.

The innovative system was lighter than traditional four-wheel-drivetrain technology and was unveiled at the Geneva Motor Show in 1980. That fall it helped Audi win the Portuguese Rally a full half-hour ahead of the runner-up.

Soon the system went into series production underpinning the Audi quattro, a coupe powered by a turbocharged 5-cylinder engine.

■ Audi's quattro was both a vehicle model and an engineering system that benefited from the traction of all four wheels providing propulsion.

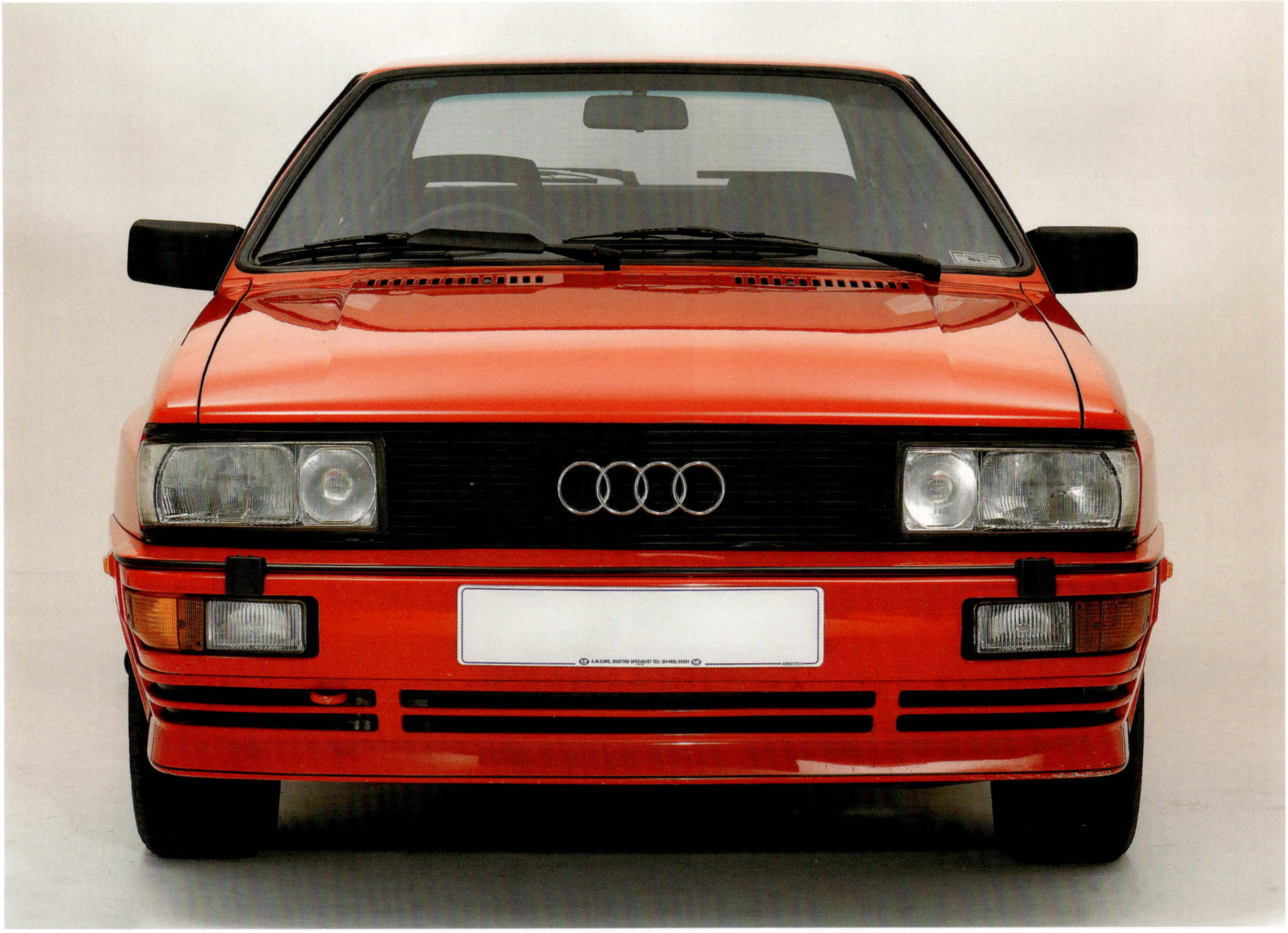

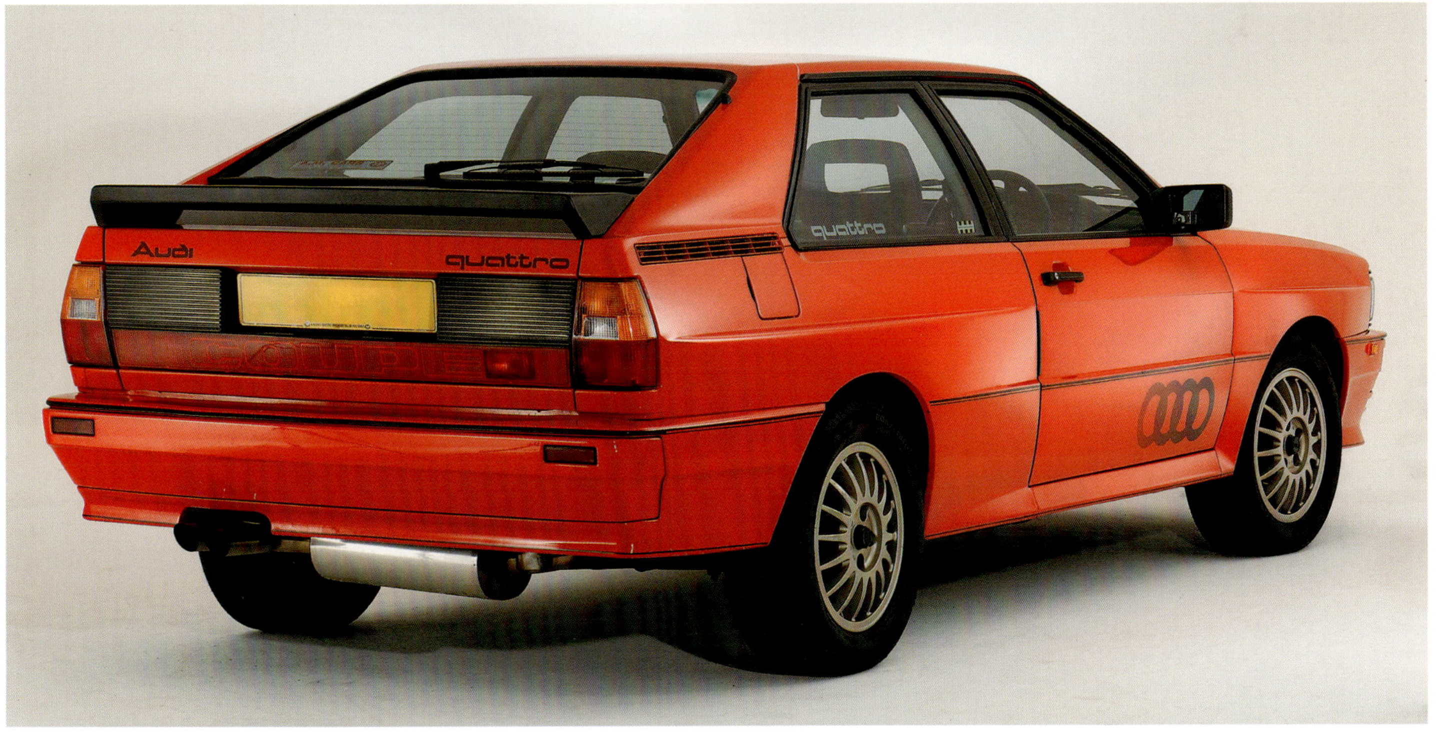
Audi
quattro
quattro

RENAULT 5 TURBO

Unheralded hatchback transformed into mid-engine motorsports monster

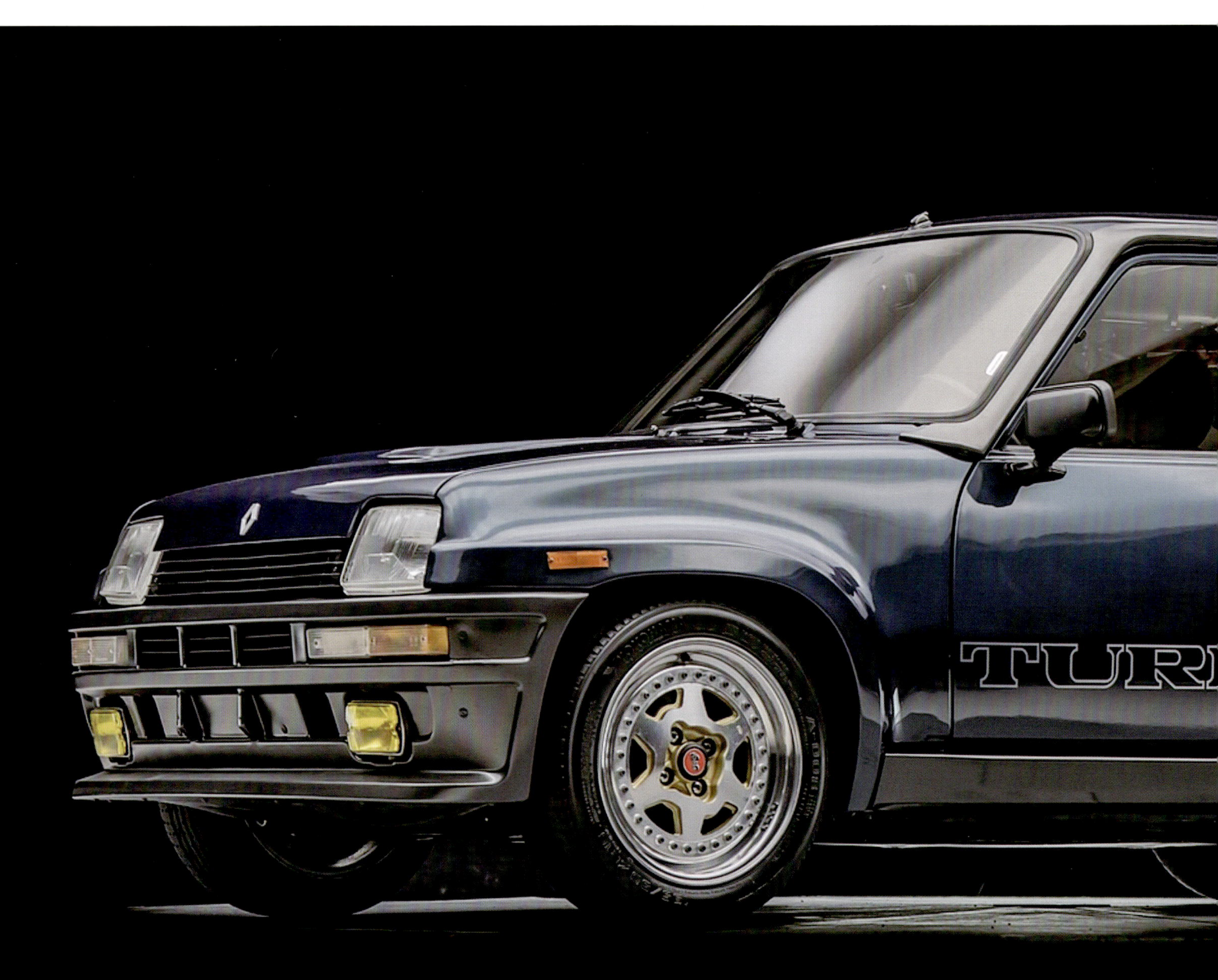

1980 ➤ 1989

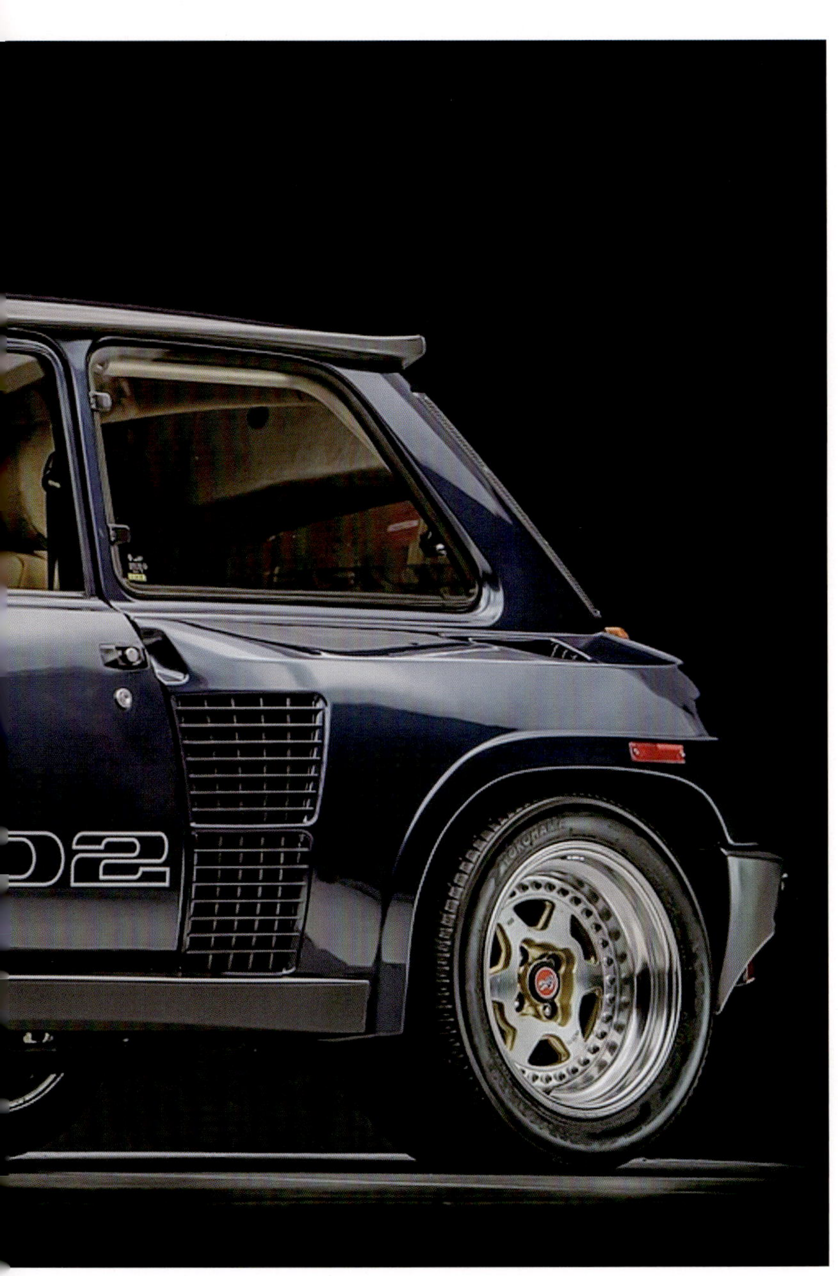

The Renault 5 dated to the early 1970s and was sold in North America from 1976 to 1983 as Le Car.

Driving.ca, a Canadian website, took a spin in a survivor from 1986 and noted that "even in French-speaking Quebec, most average folks perhaps don't have the fondest memories of Renault," even if the car "attacks a sweeping corner with terrier-like tenacity." Nonetheless, "French mechanical quirkiness... lost a bit of its charm in the face of unrelenting Japanese-made reliability."

Eager to prove its competitiveness, Renault presented the 5 Turbo prototype in Paris in 1978 and the model at the 1980 Brussels Motor Show. Known simply as the R5 Turbo, the car traced its roots loosely to that unheralded Renault 5.

The rally car, and the road-going versions needed for homologation, got new hatchback coachwork designed at Bertone by Marc Deschamps and Marcello Gandini. Not only did the studio redo the sheet metal, but it also created a distinctive interior, which, as Britain's *Evo* magazine noted, featured "a mad red and blue color scheme covering every surface, and an asymmetrical steering wheel that looks like the controller from an arcade machine."

Where the standard 5 had a lackluster 4-cylinder engine mounted at the front that pulled the car around, the R5 Turbo

■ The Renault 5 (sold as Le Car in North America) was a rather mundane hatchback that the company morphed into a mid-engine motorsports powerhouse.

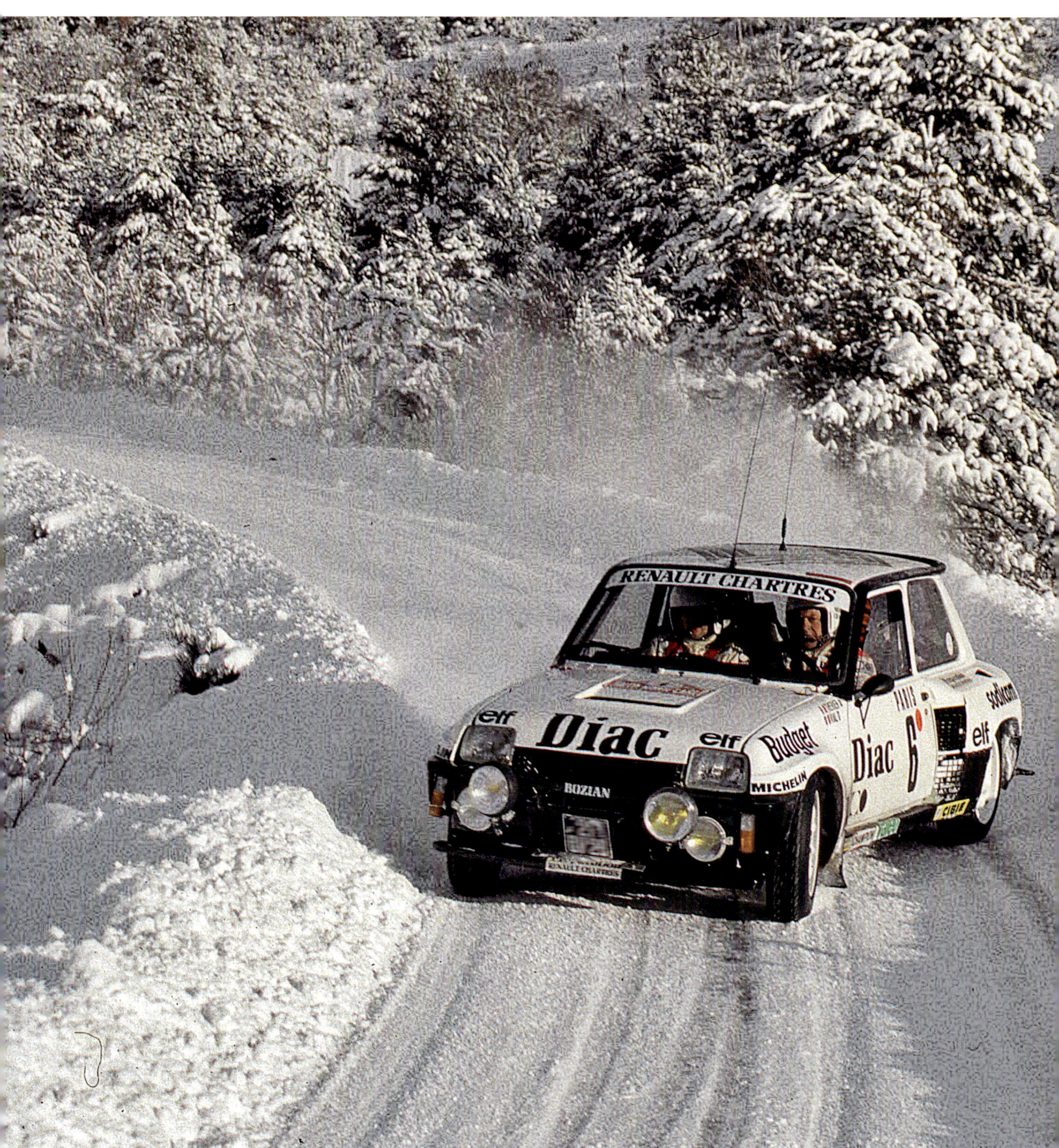
RENAULT CHARTRES
elf
Diac
elf
Budget
Diac
6
MICHELIN
BOZIAN
elf
CIBIE

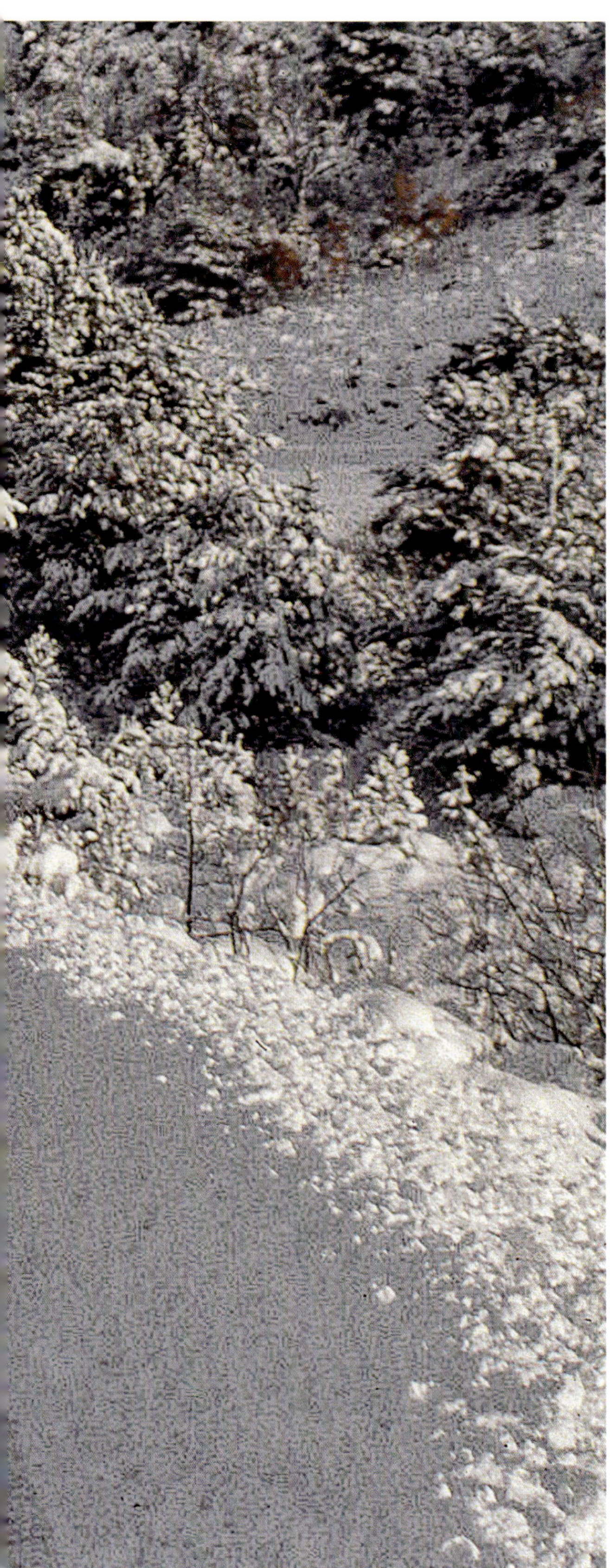

■ The Renault 5 Turbo excelled in the slick conditions of events such as the Monte Carlo Rally and also showed its capabilities on dry racetracks.

had its boosted 1.4-liter 4 mounted mid-body behind seats for the driver and a single passenger (or rally navigator), providing nearly 160 horsepower and 221 Nm of torque to the rear wheels, more power than any other French automobile in production.

The R5 Turbo made its competitive debut in the 1981 Monte Carlo Rally, where Jean Ragnotti drove it to victory. For motorsports events, power was boosted to 180 and then 207 and eventually to 385 in 1987, when the R5 Turbo won the French Supertouring Championship.

"Imagine if today's hot-hatches out-accelerated and out-handled today's mid-engine Ferrari," insurer and car evaluator Hagerty suggested in 2023. "The R5 Turbo beat up on the contemporary Ferrari 308—as well as every other supercar—by moving its turbocharged engine to the back, where rear seats used to be...What a car it was."

Or as Britain's *Evo* magazine had put it a year earlier, "Today's WRC cars are deeply impressive and the drivers as skilled as ever, but you'll search in vain for a true road-going equivalent for any of the series' top cars.

"Things were different in the early 1980s. Before Group B came Group 4, where Lancia Stratos battled Escorts, Fiat 131s, and one of the era's most distinctive cars, the Renault 5 Turbo. Rather than fight with front-wheel drive, Renault's engineers dropped their 1.4-liter turbocharged engine between the rear wheels instead and pumped up the bodywork to turn their shopping car into a stage-ready monster.

"Tarmac ace Jean Ragnotti took the competition car to three Monte Carlo Rally victories and achieved several strong results elsewhere. But while the Turbo was eventually out-competed by four-wheel-drive Group B machines, its legacy as one of the greats has endured to this day. It's clear that the model had a strong impact, too, with Renault capitalizing on the nostalgia with the revival of the 5 in all-electric forms in 2022."

DeLOREAN DMC-12

A car made famous on film from a man whose life was the stuff of a Hollywood script

A couple of decades before his name would become known around the world for a stainless steel over fiberglass-bodied sports car that carried actor Michael J. Fox *Back to the Future*, John Z. DeLorean was an American automotive engineer working at Chrysler, and then at Packard, and finally at General Motors.

DeLorean rose quickly through the ranks of executives at GM's Pontiac Division, becoming chief engineer in 1959 and general manager, and thus a General Motors vice president, in 1965; four years later he became general manager at Chevrolet, GM's largest and most important division, then to head all GM car and truck development.

As Pontiac's general manager, DeLorean helped to develop the GTO, an American sedan and convertible that became the first "muscle car," and helped create the buzz that, at Pontiac, "We Build Excitement."

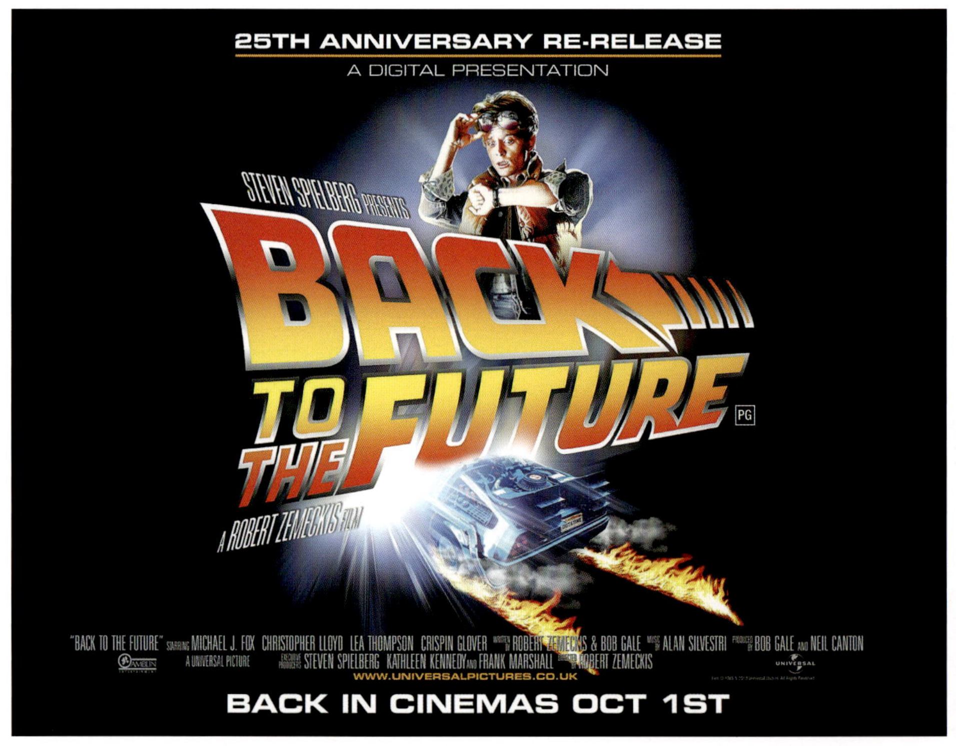

■ The DeLorean DMC-12 was featured in *Back to the Future*, but its creator, John Z. DeLorean, was the subject of at least four other Hollywood treatments: *Car Crash: The DeLorean Story* in 2004, *Driven* in 2018, *Framing John DeLorean* in 2019, and *DeLorean: Living the Dream* in 2020.

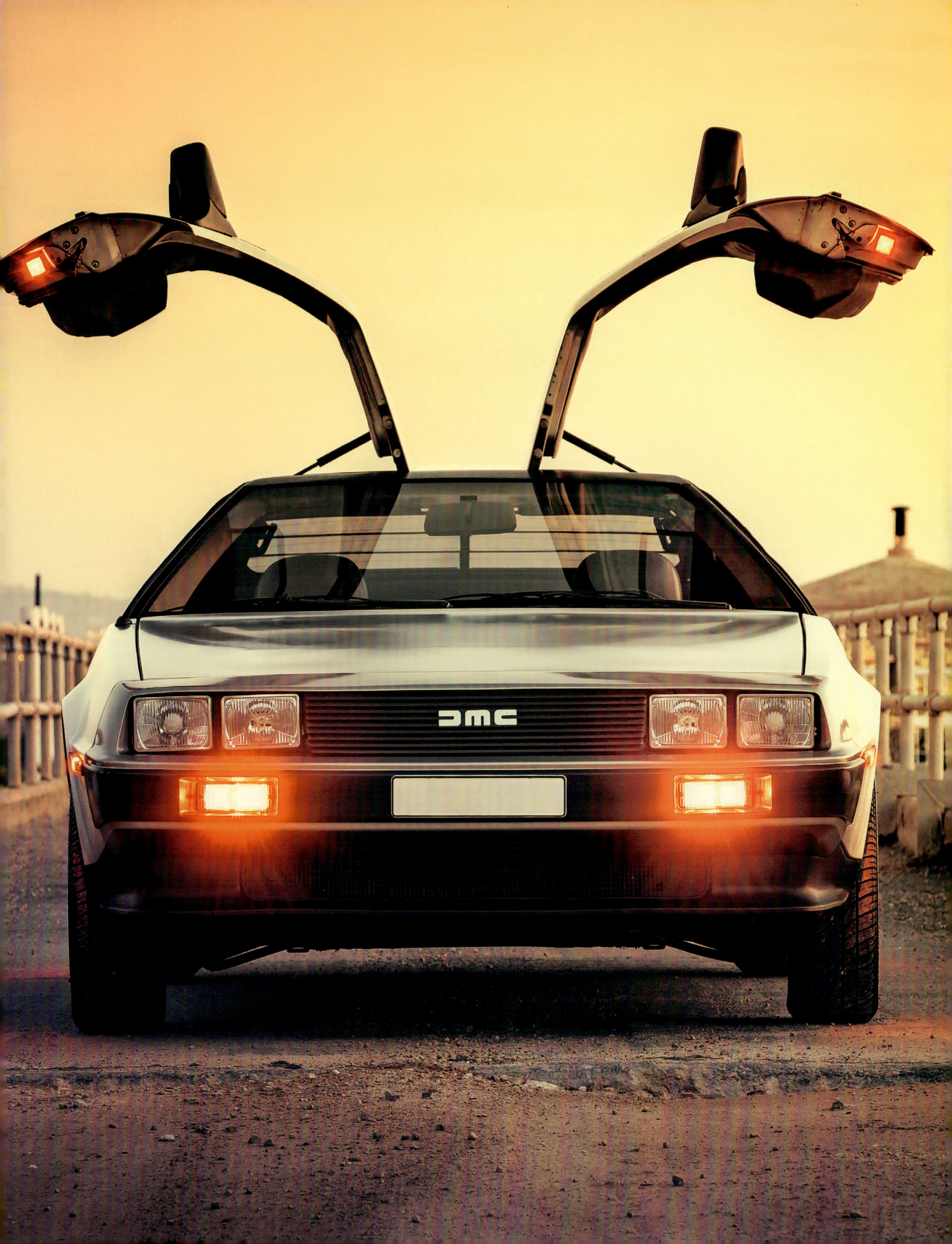
DMC

Times were also exciting for DeLorean. He changed his style (even undergoing plastic surgery), got divorced, married an actress and model, got divorced again, left GM, married again, and moved to Northern Ireland to pursue his team of building his own cars.

He recruited the world's foremost car designer, Giorgetto Giugiaro, to do the styling for his car, and perhaps the most famous of automotive engineers, Colin Chapman, to redo one of his own Lotus models to become the DeLorean DMC-12.

Giugiaro's wedge-shaped design included gullwing doors with windows that had only small areas that retracted for access to fresh air or a toll booth.

DeLorean's goal was the so-called ethical sports car with an advanced plastic chassis and powered by a mid-mounted Wankel rotary engine. Instead, it was built around a modified Lotus Esprit chassis and powered by the V6 shared by Peugeot, Renault, and Volvo, an engine that provided only 130 horsepower and less dynamic performance than expected in a sports car.

There also were build-quality issues, including leaking doors, a hard-to-repair stainless steel veneer, and all-electronic dashboard glitches.

Production finally began in 1980, sales began in 1981, and the company went into receivership and filed for bankruptcy in 1982 after DeLorean was arrested on drug-trafficking charges (from which he was acquitted). The company produced 7,500 cars but had sold fewer than half that number when it entered receivership.

Motor Trend magazine reported that "stylistically, the DeLorean was a tour-de-force, but mechanically, it fell as flat as its side profile. That 2.8-liter PRV V6 pushed out a wheezy 130 horsepower and 153 lb-ft of torque, just enough to shuffle the 2,700-pound car to 60 mph in around 9 seconds when fitted with the 5-speed manual transmission; the deed took around 11 seconds with the 3-speed automatic. DeLorean owners would have done well to leave the restaurant after all the Lamborghini Countachs had gone to avoid being caught at a light next to one. Top speed was a low-for-the-form-factor 109 mph."

Bottom ■ Unlike the time-traveling movie car with its flux capacitor, the DeLorean DMC-12 was powered by a 130-horsepower V6 also used by Peugeot, Renault, and Volvo.

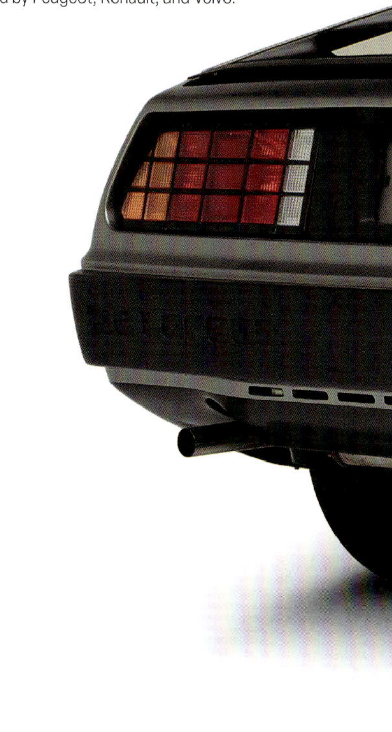

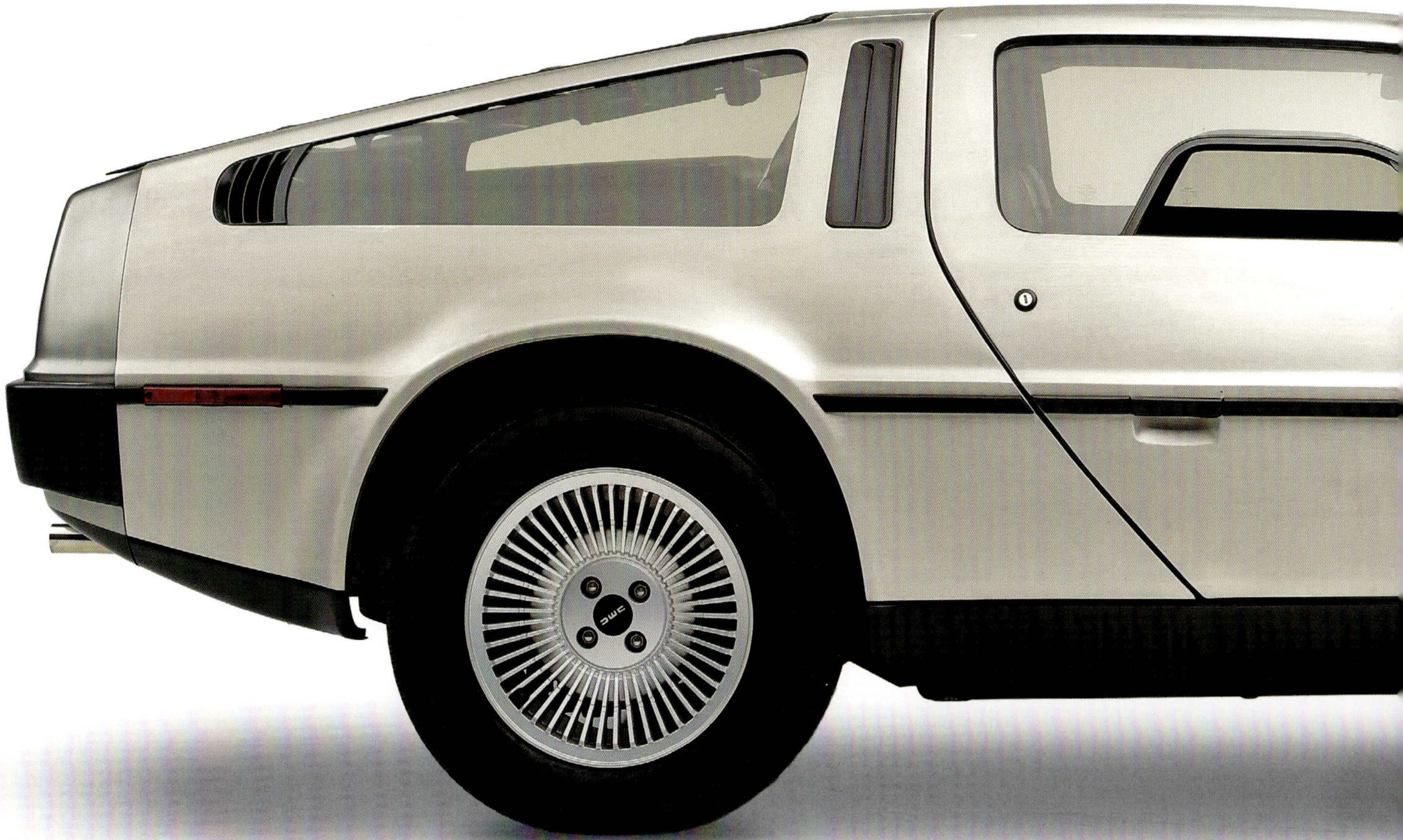

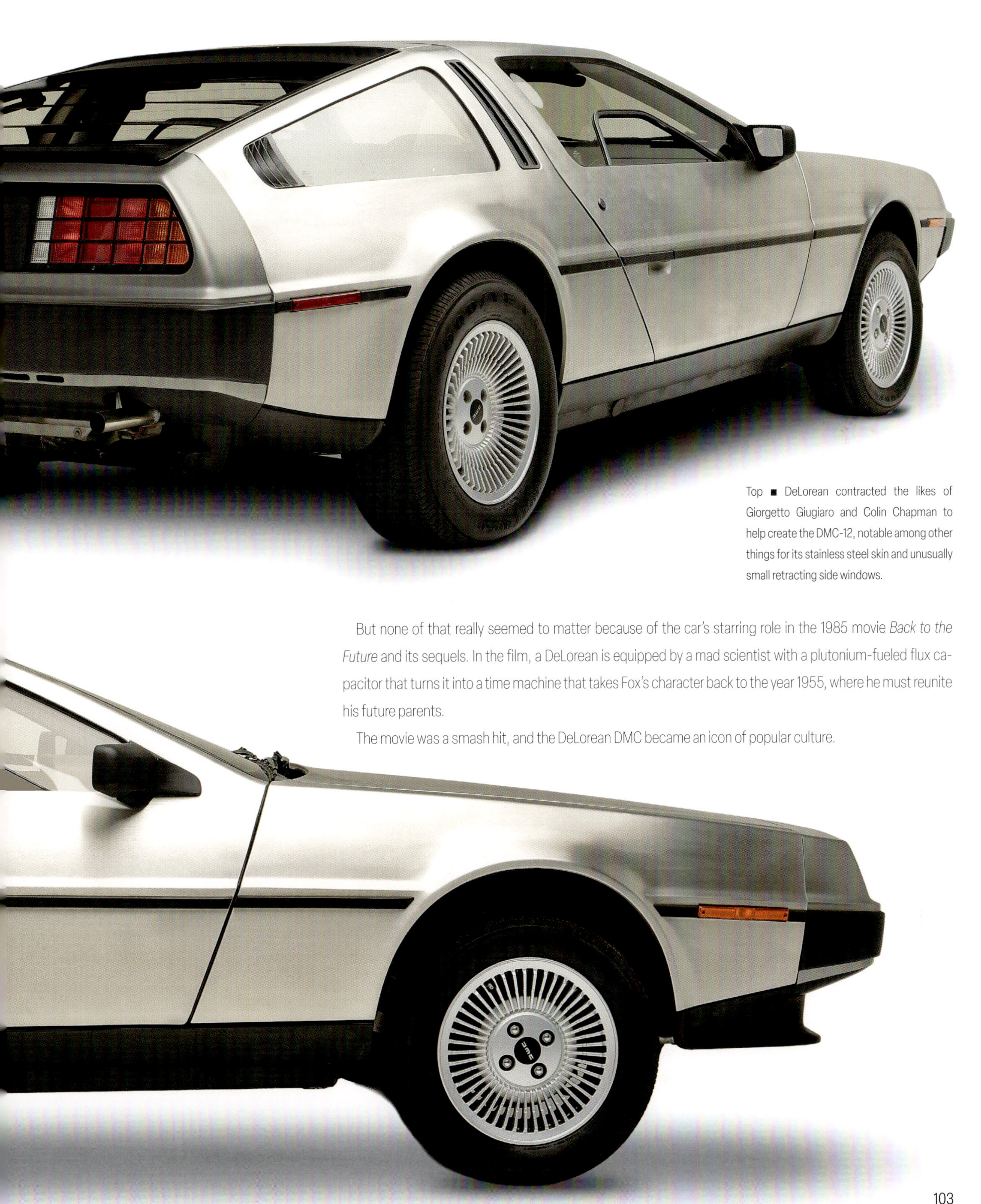

Top ■ DeLorean contracted the likes of Giorgetto Giugiaro and Colin Chapman to help create the DMC-12, notable among other things for its stainless steel skin and unusually small retracting side windows.

But none of that really seemed to matter because of the car's starring role in the 1985 movie *Back to the Future* and its sequels. In the film, a DeLorean is equipped by a mad scientist with a plutonium-fueled flux capacitor that turns it into a time machine that takes Fox's character back to the year 1955, where he must reunite his future parents.

The movie was a smash hit, and the DeLorean DMC became an icon of popular culture.

PORSCHE 944

Porsche's entry-level sports car beat rivals from Lotus and Ferrari in an import car comparison test

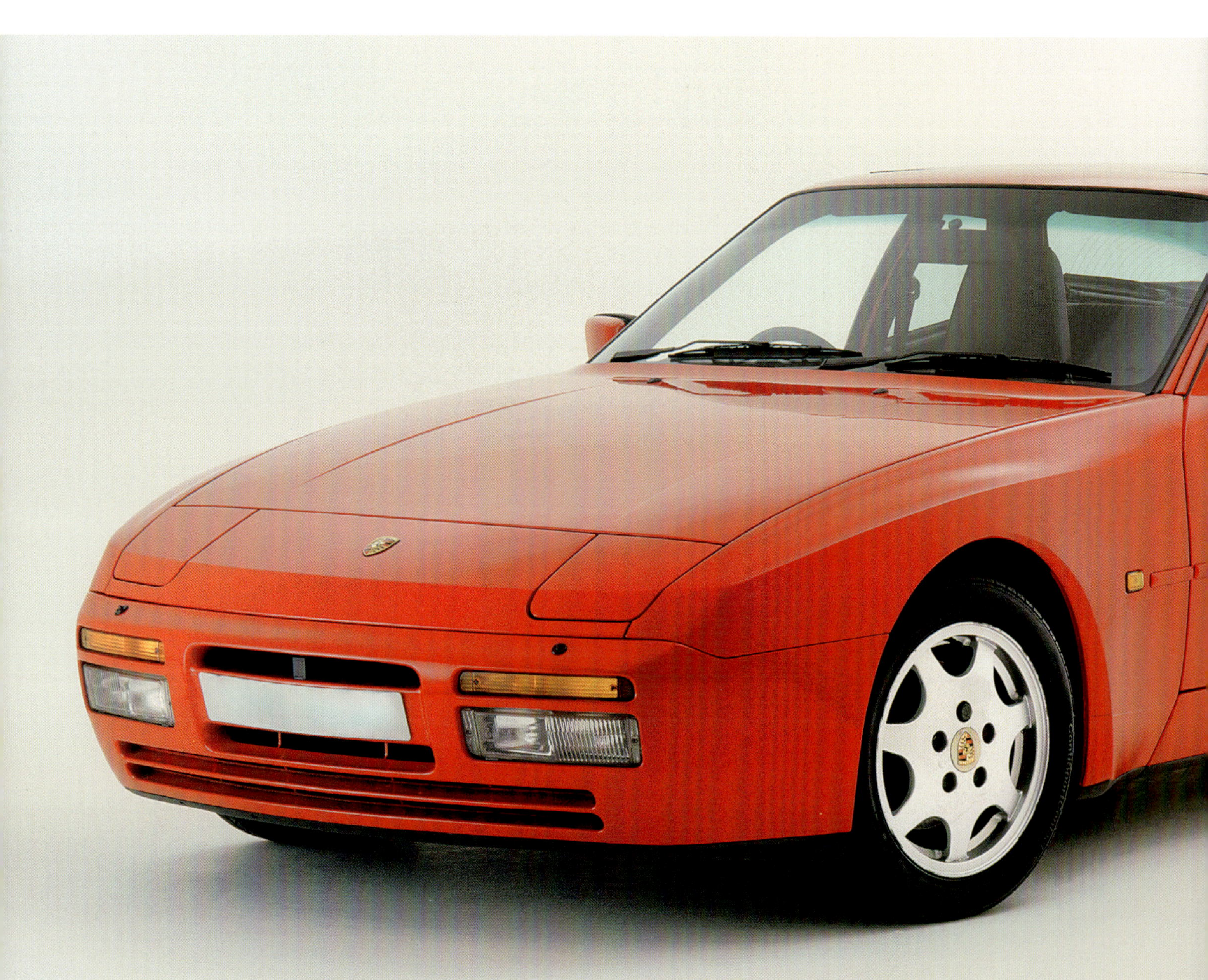

1980 ➤ 1989

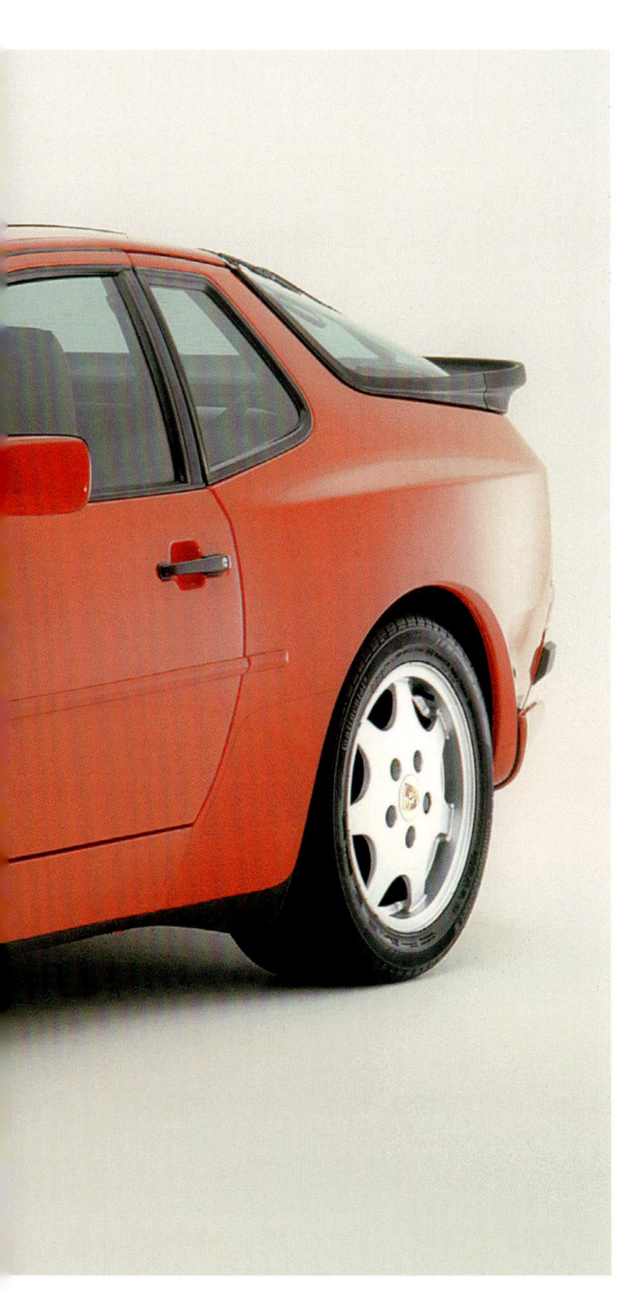

To remain viable, Porsche needed an entry-level sports car. Not everyone needed (or could afford) a 911, and the short-lived 912 (a 911 with a 4- rather than 6-cylinder engine) wasn't the answer. Next came the 914, a mid-engine two-seater with a Targa roof.

The 924 followed. Working with corporate partner Volkswagen, a sports coupe with a front-mounted and water-cooled engine was developed; originally the idea was that each of the partners would get its own version. But Volkswagen changed its mind, leaving Porsche alone with its version.

The 924 would evolve into the 944, which would evolve again and be badged as the 968. The 944/968 would emerge as Porsche's bestseller until the success in the late 1990s and early 2000s of a new mid-engine sports car, the Boxster.

Unlike the rear-engine 911, the 944 was a more conventional sports car: liquid-cooled engine in front, power transferred from there to the rear wheels. The engine was a 2.5-liter 4-cylinder, basically half of the V8 Porsche had developed for its 928. A turbocharged option would become available.

The 944 also looked more like other sports cars, its wedge shape emphasized when the pop-up headlamps were retracted and with a rear-sloping hatchback cover. A convertible version was available.

Although the car's official unveiling was at the Frankfurt Motor Show in the fall of 1981, it actually had been shown earlier that year when it raced in the guise of the 928 GTP at the 24 Hours of Le Mans, where Jürgen Barth and Walter Röhrl drove a turbocharged version to a seventh-place finish.

In 1984, American automotive magazine *Car and Driver* tested eight imported cars, including the Audi quattro, Ferrari 308, Lotus Esprit Turbo, even the Porsche 911 Carrera, and declared the Porsche 944 the best of them all.

■ To power the entry-level 944, Porsche created an engine that basically was one-half of the V8 in the Porsche 928.

BUICK GN/GNX

The racing-inspired but brief revival of the American muscle car

■ The Buick GNX was faster than a Ferrari F40 in 0-to-60 mph and quarter-mile sprints.

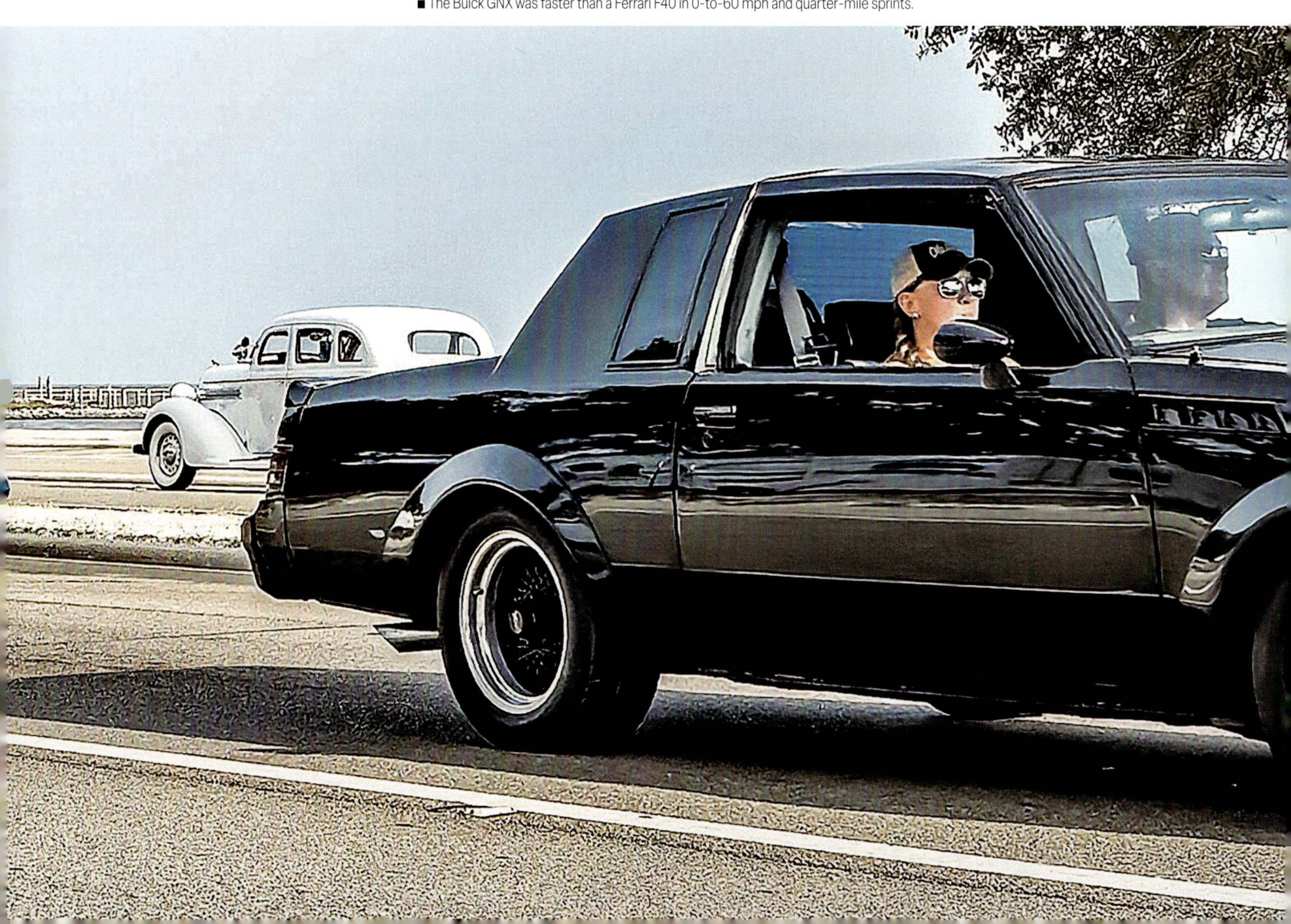

1980 ➤ 1989

In the 1960s, American automakers unleashed a succession of what became known as "muscle cars." It began at Pontiac, where engineers stuffed the largest, most powerful V8 engine under the hood of a midsize family sedan to create the Pontiac GTO—yes, the name "borrowed" from an exotic Ferrari sports car.

Others soon joined the race—and quite literally. Factory engineers and then customers raced away from stoplights to show whose car was the fastest, be it the GTO, Chevrolet Chevelle 396, Oldsmobile 442, Mercury Cyclone, Dodge Charger, or Plymouth GTX.

By the early 1970s, the muscle cars went into a forced atrophy thanks to the fuel crisis, new emission regulations, and increasing insurance fees.

General Motors' Buick Division had entered the race with its Gran Sport model, powered by V8 engines as large as 7.4 liters (455 cubic inches). It also supplied the pace car, the Regal Turbo, for the 1981 Indianapolis 500, but instead of a V8, the Regal Turbo featured a V6, turbocharged to demonstrate that a more fuel-efficient engine could still be quite powerful.

Buick went a step further, taking advantage of the rules of Indy car racing to produce a turbocharged V6 racing engine that proved fast enough to power the pole-winning (fastest qualifier) at the 1985 500 race.

In 1981 a Buick won the NASCAR (stock car) racing championship in the United States, and the automaker celebrated in 1982 with a new limited-production model, the Grand National, powered by a V6 engine. Later the V6 would be turbocharged to provide as much as 235 horsepower (and 447 Nm of torque).

Succeeding the Grand National in 1987 was the Buick GNX, the X short for experimental. It was a true if brief muscle car revival, produced with help from the American arm of McLaren. A few more than 500 were built, each painted in black and supplied with more than 300 horsepower and more than 550 Nm of torque.

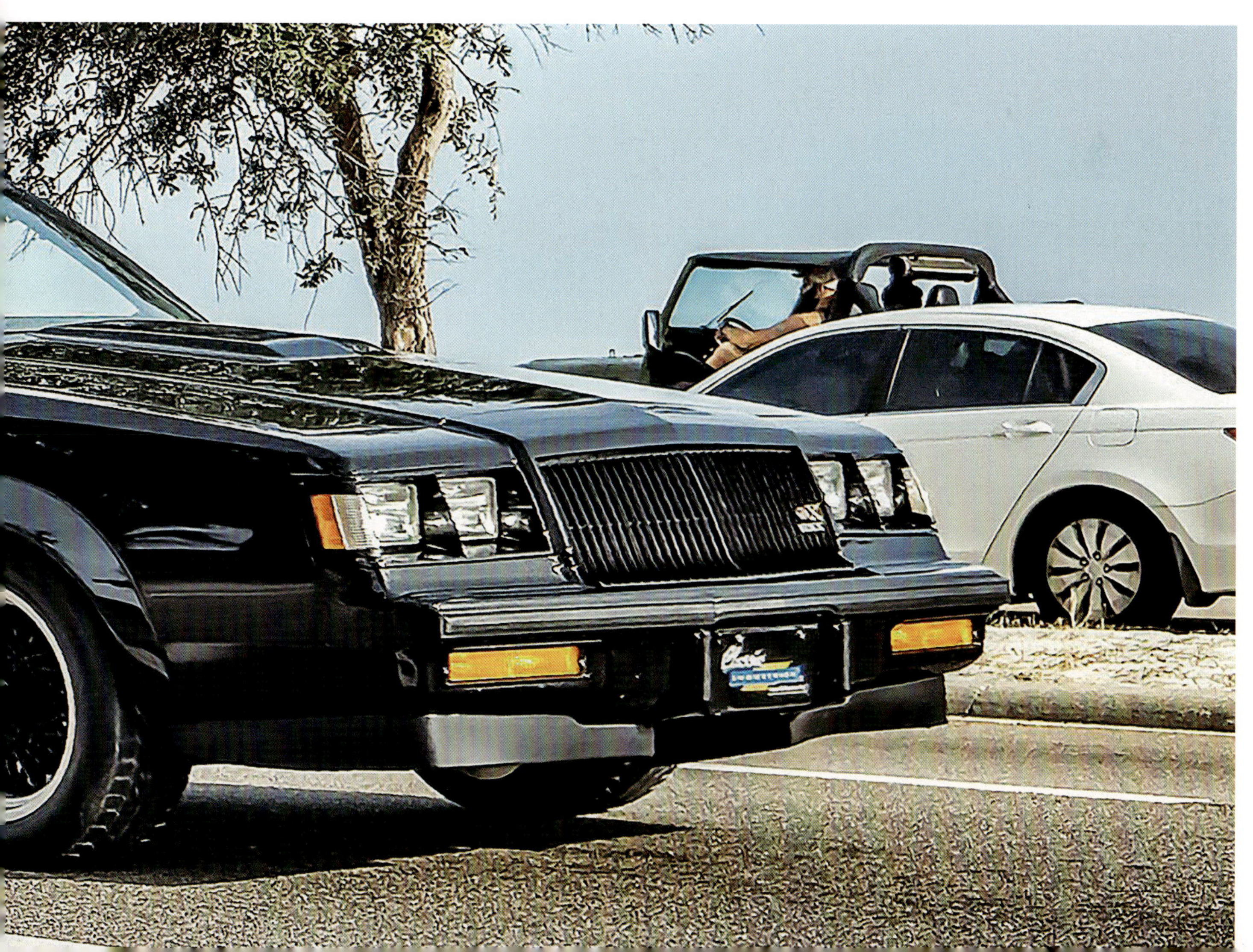

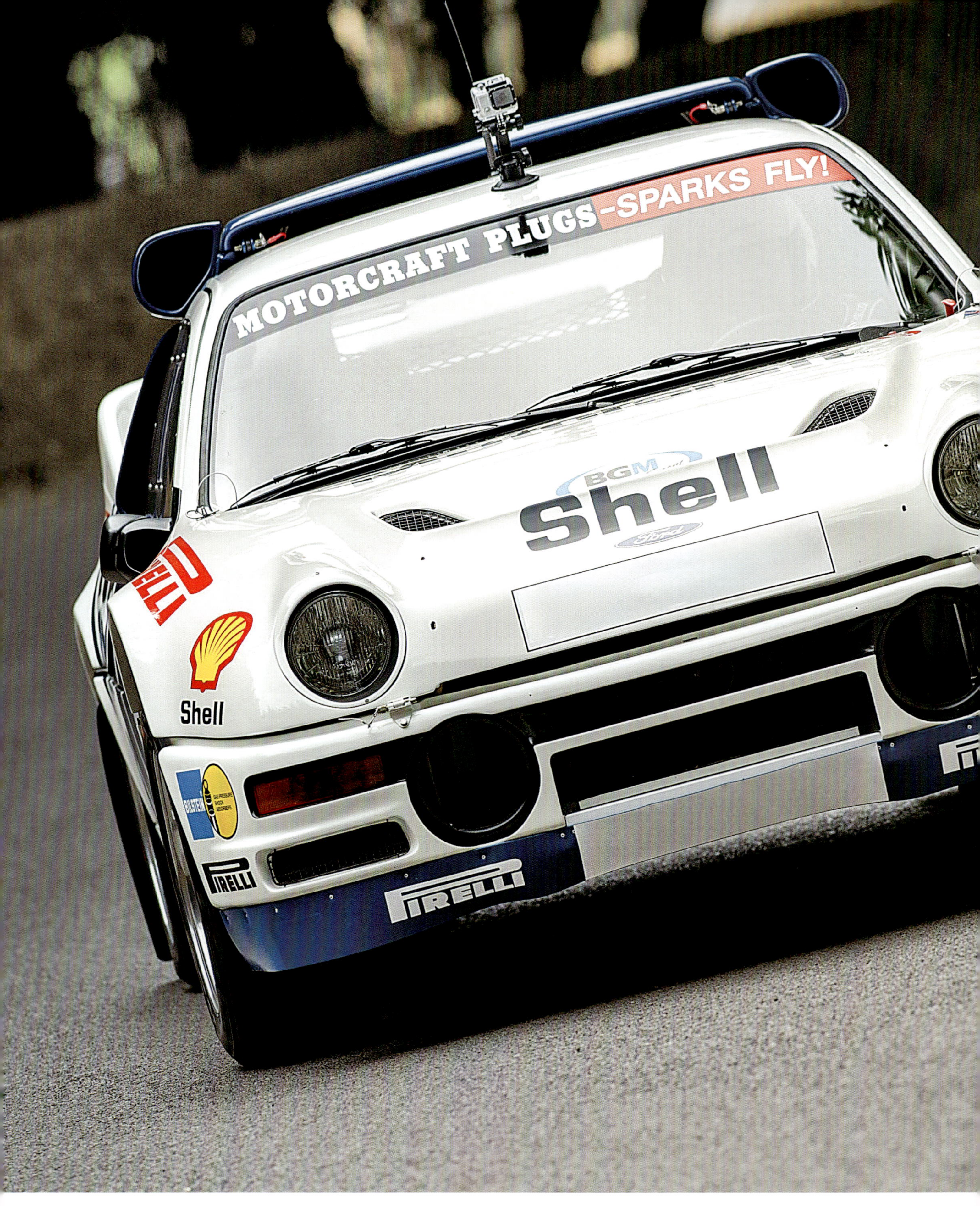
MOTORCRAFT PLUGS-SPARKS FLY!
Shell
Shell
PIRELLI
PIRELLI
BILSTEIN

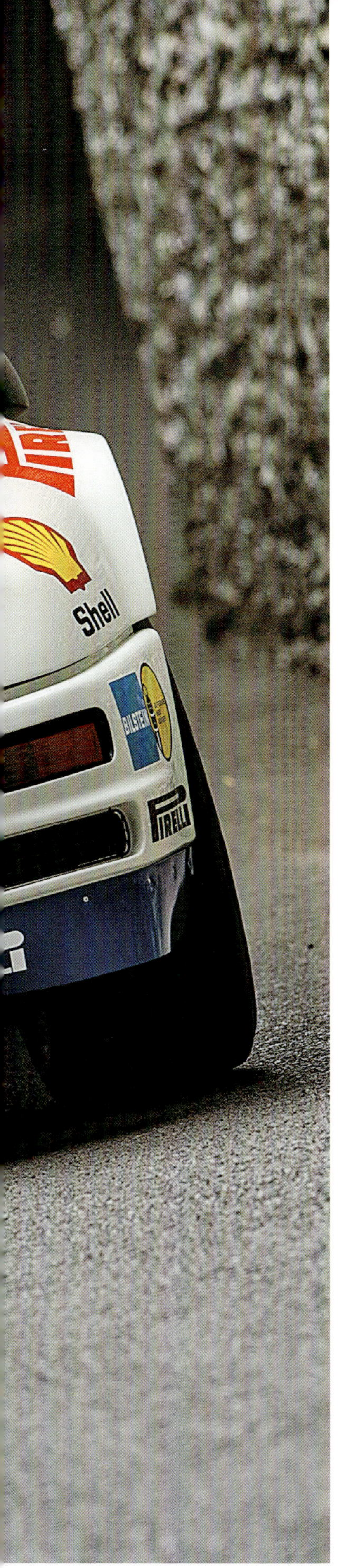

FORD RS200

The Ford that "looked—and drove—like no other Ford before or since"

"Ask any rally fan to name their favorite era and chances are that the wild Group B years will be at the top of most people's list," Britain's *Evo* magazine reported in 2019.

"It was a time of uncompromising and completely unhinged machinery," the magazine continued, "with designers and engineers really pushing the envelope when it came to interpreting the rules and endowing these four-wheel-drive turbocharged monsters with the maximum possible performance. And with the rules stipulating 200 road-going examples of the rally cars had to be produced, the Group B era spawned some stunning road cars too.

"And perhaps the wildest of them all was Ford's RS200."

The RS200, *Evo* explained, was a purpose-built model "that looked—and drove—like no other Ford before or since."

Ford had won the 1979 World Rally Championship with a version of its Escort compact sedan, a model that was being phased out of production. To be competitive under the Group B rules taking effect for 1982, Ford needed something special, so it pretty much started from scratch and created the RS200.

This new Ford featured an aluminum chassis (by former Lotus F1 designer Tony Southgate), a mid-mounted turbocharged 4-cylinder engine (rated at nearly 250 horsepower in street examples and nearly 450 in full rally guise), and new suspension hardware, all of it wrapped by an exotic body (in Kevlar for rally versions and fiberglass for street machines) designed in Italy at the Ghia studio by Filippo Sapino (with help from Ian Callum).

The rally team's cars were late arriving, and there was little success beyond a third-place finish at the Swedish Rally. Years later, however, former rally champion Stig Blomqvist drove an RS200, albeit one with more than 900 horsepower available, to victory in the 2004 Pikes Peak International Hill Climb.

■ A bespoke creation for rallying, the RS200 used only a windshield and tail lamps from Ford's parts bin.

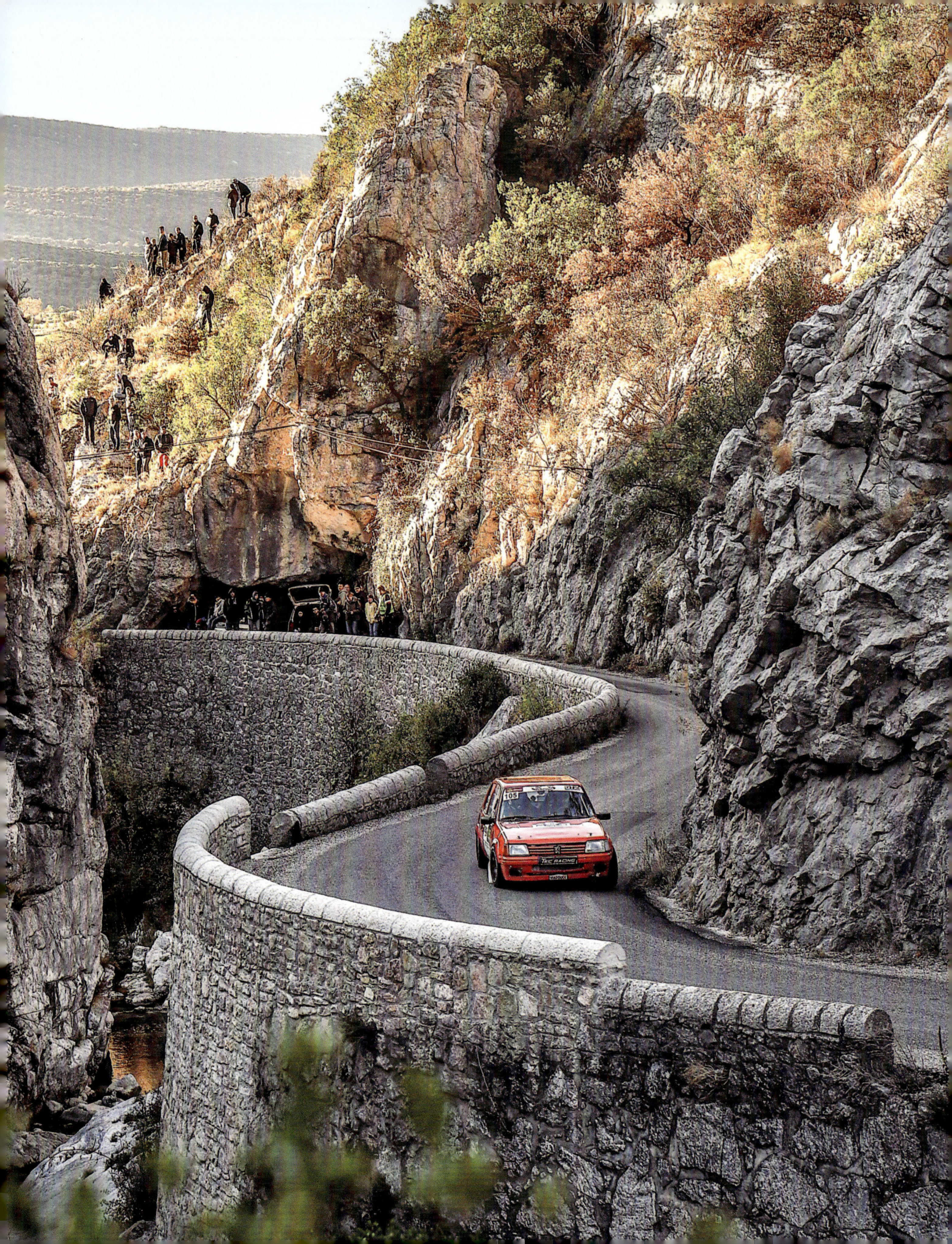

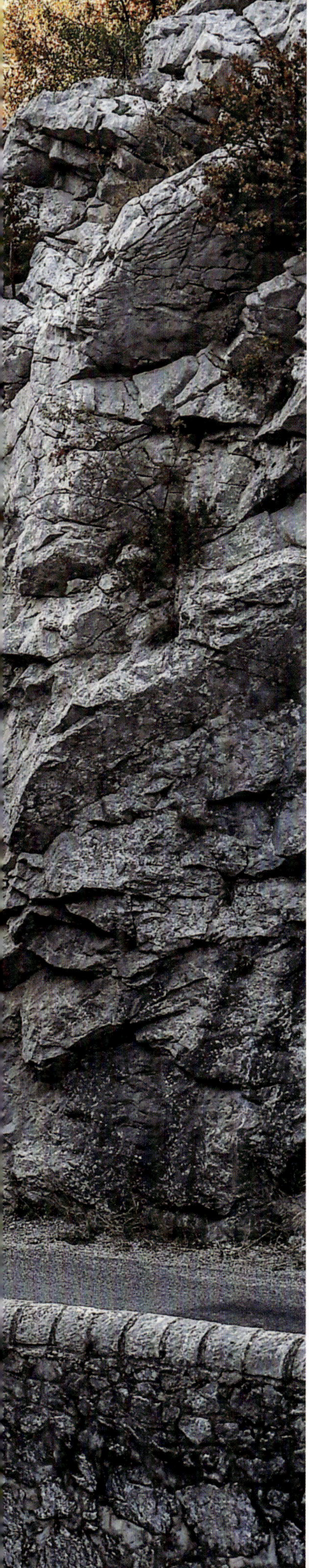

1980 ➤ 1989

PEUGEOT 205 GTI

A truly hot hatchback from France's most conservative automaker

The automobile may have been created in Germany, but the automobile industry started in France, where Panhard & Levassor and Peugeot each were involved in vehicle production as early as 1890.

Armand Peugeot's family had been involved in manufacturing since 1810, first in steel production and later in making saw blades, hand tools, coffee grinders, and bicycles.

Early on, Peugeot demonstrated the viability of its motorized vehicles by racing them. The first auto race, 126 kilometers from Paris to Rouen in 1894, was won by a Peugeot, and all five Peugeots entered in the race finished the full distance.

Though considered the most conservative of France's Big 3 automakers, in 1983 Peugeot rolled out a rather stunning successor to its model 104. This new and slightly larger 205 was designed in-house and was termed "a visual masterpiece—pert, curvaceous, and delicately proportioned," by Britain's *CAR* magazine, which later would acclaim the 205 as the Car of the Decade for the 1980s.

The 205 was available as a 3- or 5-door hatchback and with a variety of powertrain and trim versions. Among them were the GT, the Turbo 16 4x4 for use in rally sports, and for 1984 the 205 GTI, a 3-door model with a manual transmission and either a 1.6- or 1.9-liter 4-cylinder engine.

Peugeot 205 Turbo 16s carried Timo Salonen and Juha Kankkunen to the World Rally Championships in 1984 and 1985, respectively.

Auto insurer and valuation tracker Hagerty suggested the "feisty and fabulous" 205 GTI as the hot hatchback of the 1980s even in the presence of the Volkswagen Golf GTI and the Renault 5 GT Turbo. Why the Peugeot? "Nothing else gets that magic mix of driver interaction, good looks, mechanical toughness, and sheer fizz quite as perfectly right."

■ In its Turbo 16 guise, the 205 took Timo Salonen and Juha Kankkunen to back-to-back World Rally Championships.

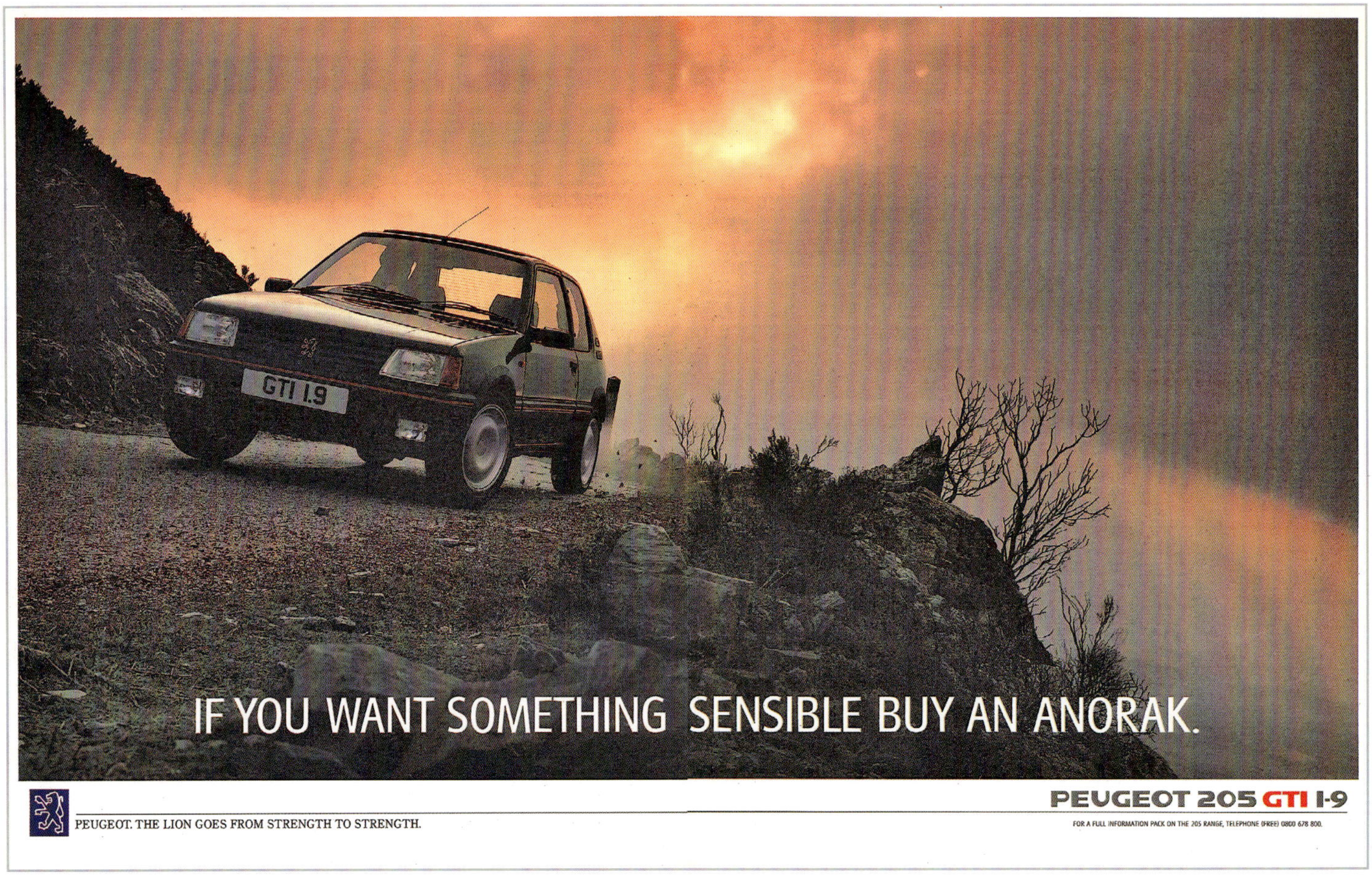

IF YOU WANT SOMETHING SENSIBLE BUY AN ANORAK.

PEUGEOT 205 GTI 1·9

PEUGEOT. THE LION GOES FROM STRENGTH TO STRENGTH.

FOR A FULL INFORMATION PACK ON THE 205 RANGE, TELEPHONE (FREE) 0800 678 800.

Typical European hatchbacks were as practical as a hooded waterproof rain jacket, but Peugeot's was "feisty and fabulous."

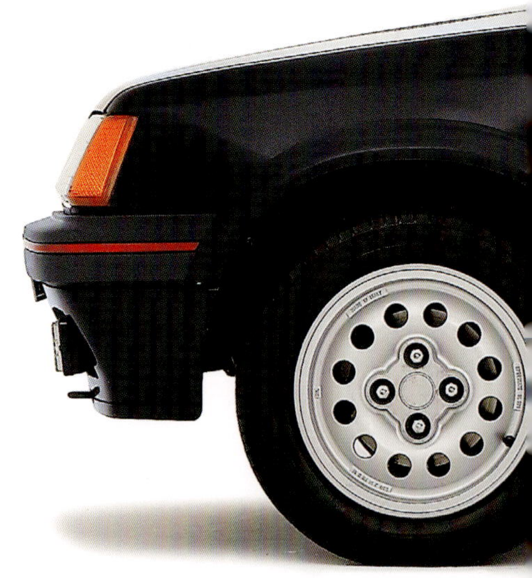

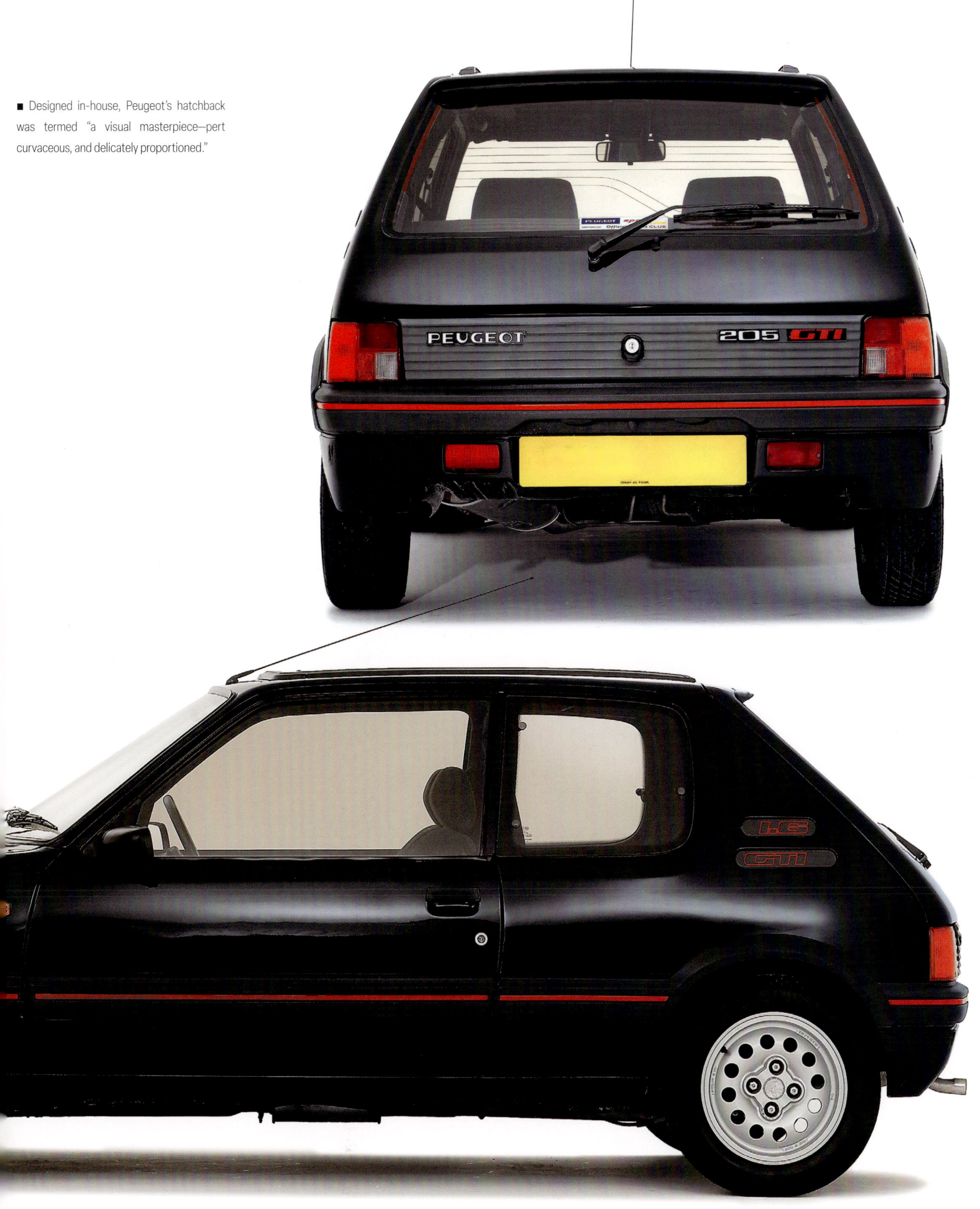

■ Designed in-house, Peugeot's hatchback was termed "a visual masterpiece—pert curvaceous, and delicately proportioned."

FERRARI TESTAROSSA

There was nothing at all subtle about this head-turning redhead

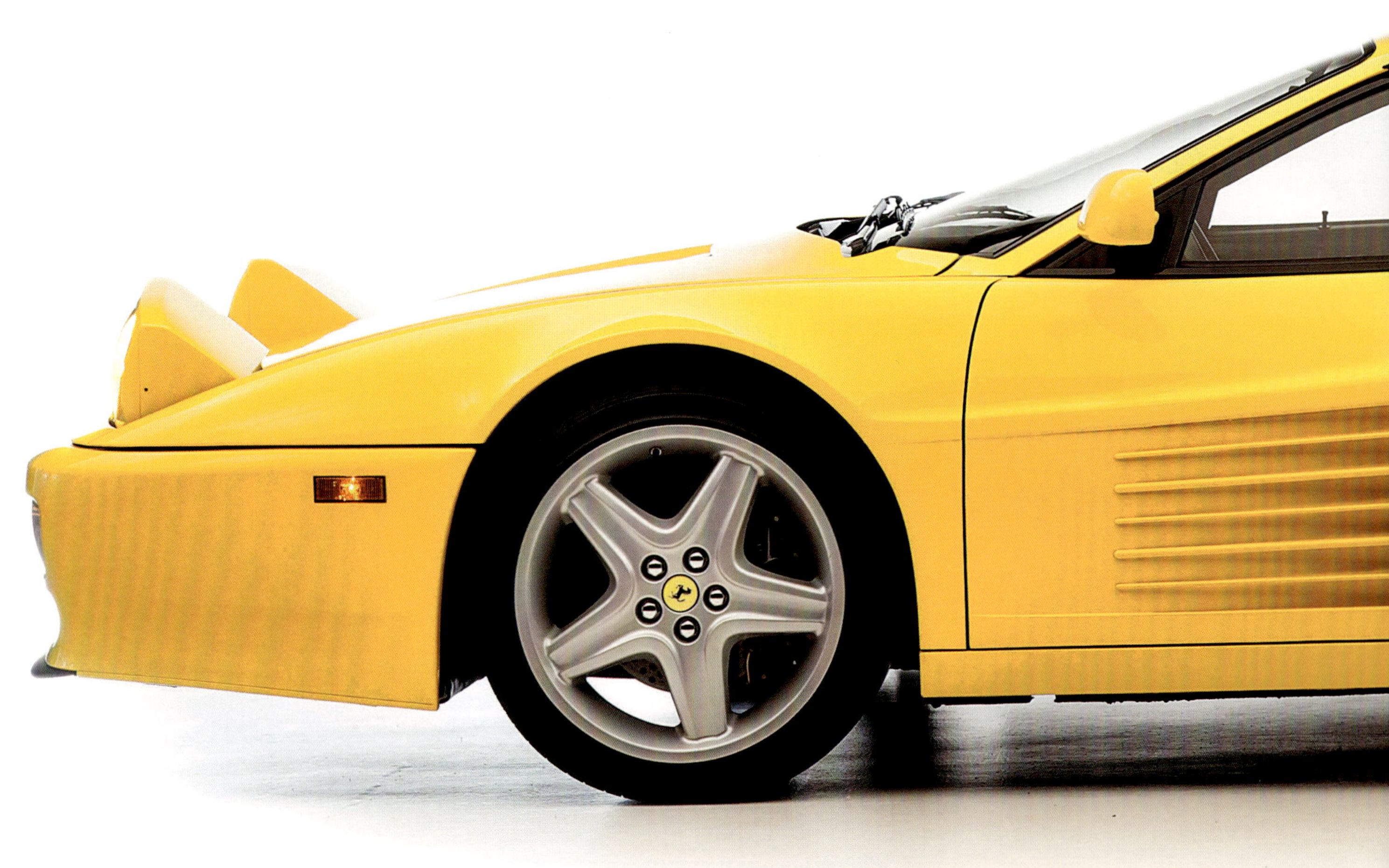

1980 ➤ 1989

Testarossa is the Italian word for redhead. Enzo Ferrari's sports car company first applied it in 1956 to the 500 TR, the TR short for Testa Rossa, so named for the red color painted on the 4-cylinder engine's cam cover.

Revised racing rules would require a new Ferrari after the 1957 season. That car would be the Ferrari 250 Testa Rossa, also known as the 250 TR, still with red cam cover but now there were two of them, one for each bank of the V12 powerplant. The 250 TR was entered in the World Sports Car Championship racing series starting in 1958. It won ten races, including the 24 Hours of Le Mans three times, and three season championships.

The nameplate would be back on a Ferrari sports car in the 1980s, but this time as a single word.

As Ferrari expressed on its website, "With its low nose, flamboyant body-side 'strakes,' and wide hips, Ferrari's design partner Pininfarina wasn't just embracing the zeitgeist, it was accelerating it. The new car—with a contracted version of a famous old name—received its world debut at the Lido cabaret club on the Champs-Élysées ahead of the 1984 Paris Motor Show. This is a car that was total showbiz."

Indeed. There was nothing subtle about this Testarossa, which was designed to turn heads as it was driven down the roadway.

Introduced in 1984 and going into production into 1996, the styling led by Leonardo Fioravanti for Pininfarina featured dramatic strakes that ran across the body sides. Basically vents to direct cooling air to the radiators for the rear-mounted 12-cylinder engine, some may have likened the strakes to cheese graters or egg slicers; regardless, they could not go unnoticed.

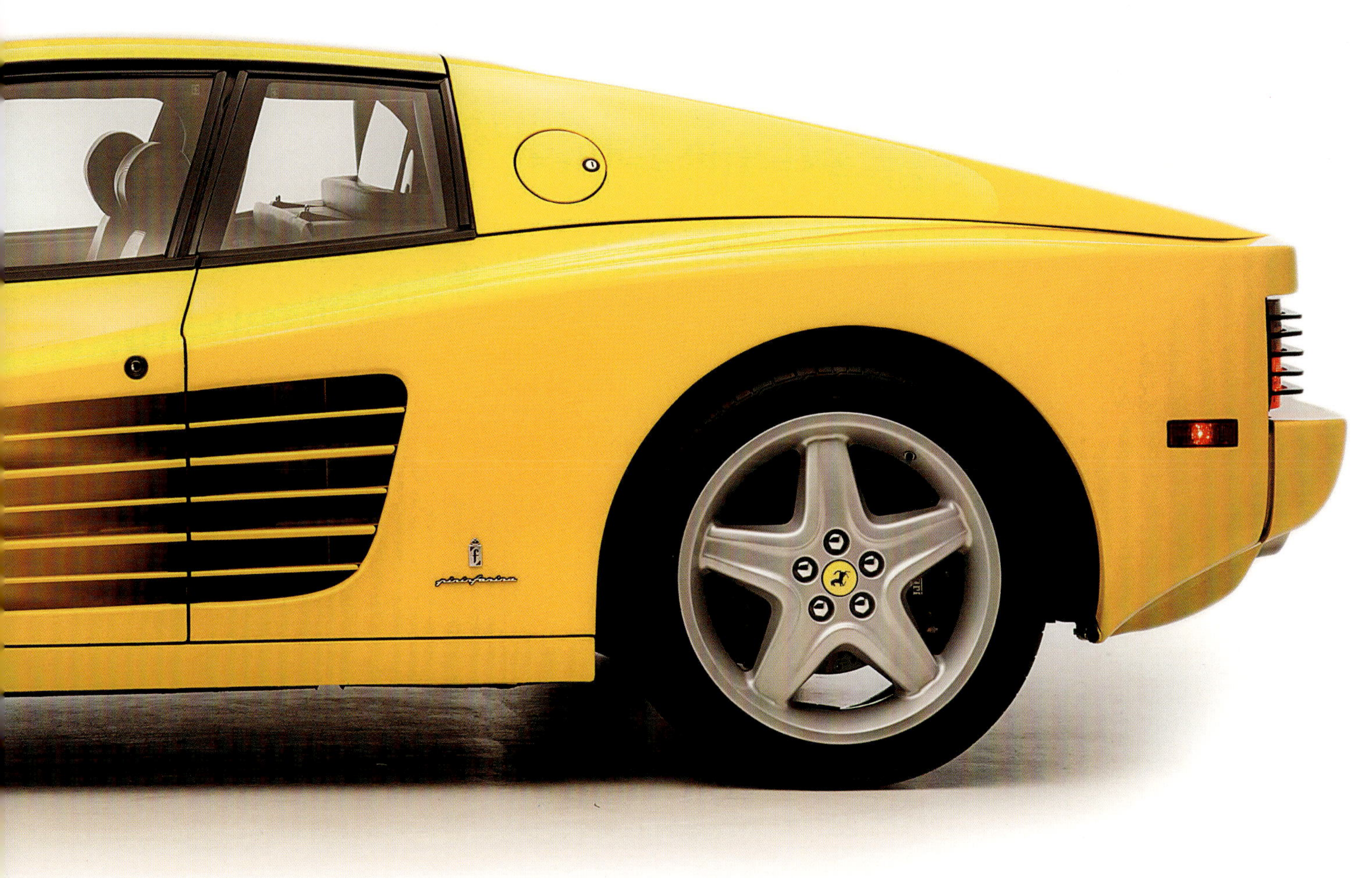

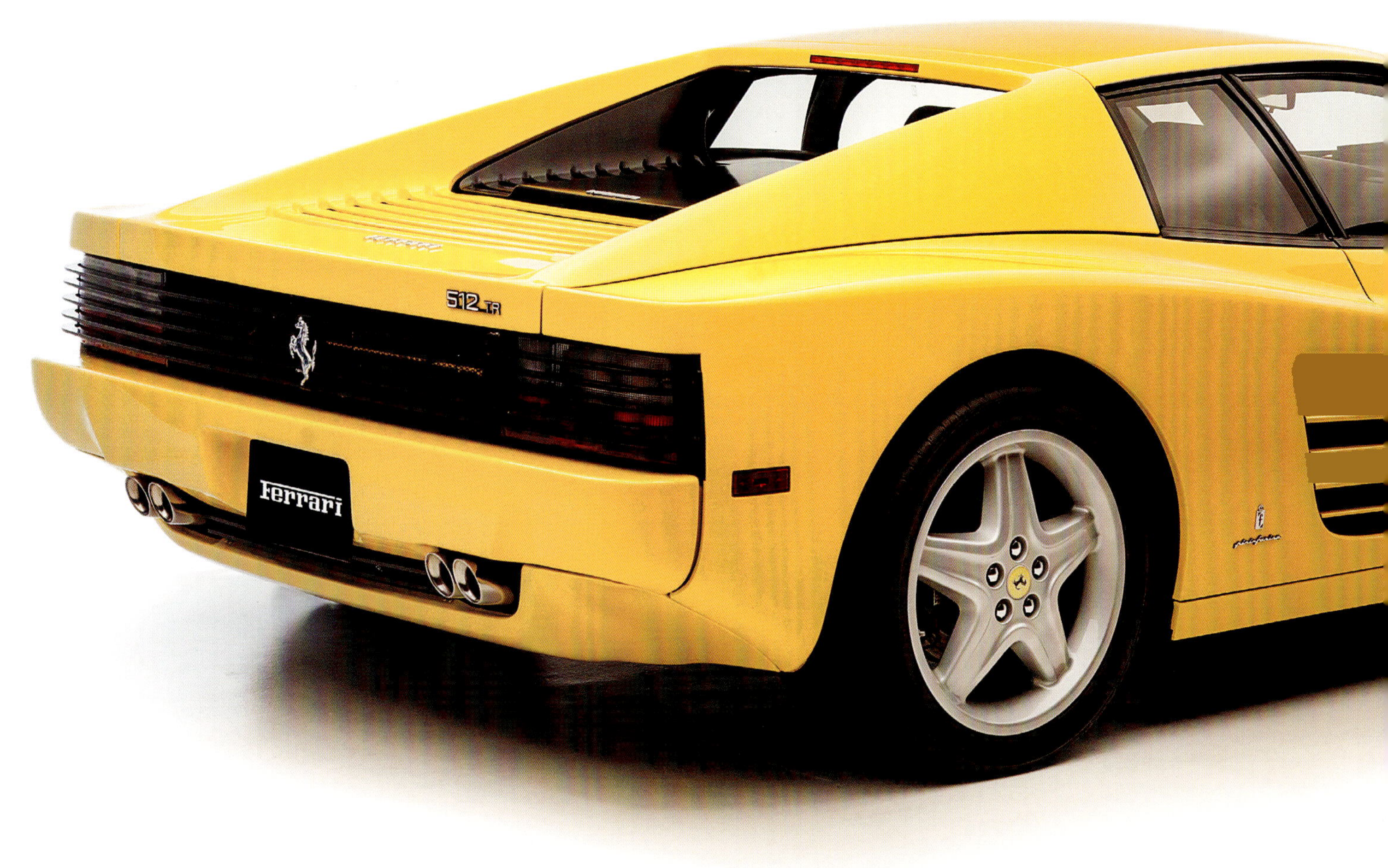

This fabulous Ferrari took its name from the red-colored cylinder heads on its 390-horsepower 12-cylinder engine.

Nor could the Testarossa with its low nose, its wide rear, and the sound of its 4.9-liter flat-12—or if you prefer, 180-degree V—engine that pumped out 390 horsepower, propelling the car to speeds of up to 180 mph (290 km/h).

In 2017, *Road & Track* magazine asked, "We all know the Ferrari Testarossa is gorgeous, but what's it like to drive?" adding that there must be a reason the car appears on millions of bedroom wall posters.

To answer, the magazine drove a 1991 example and reported, "Hop into a well-kept Testarossa...and all will be well in your world. The 12-cylinder engine likes to sing; the Italian leather is perfect. And Pininfarina's classic styling makes sure you rule the scenery, no matter where you drive. This comically wide Ferrari is a true icon for all the right reasons."

The author got to drive an example at about the time that the 1991 model was

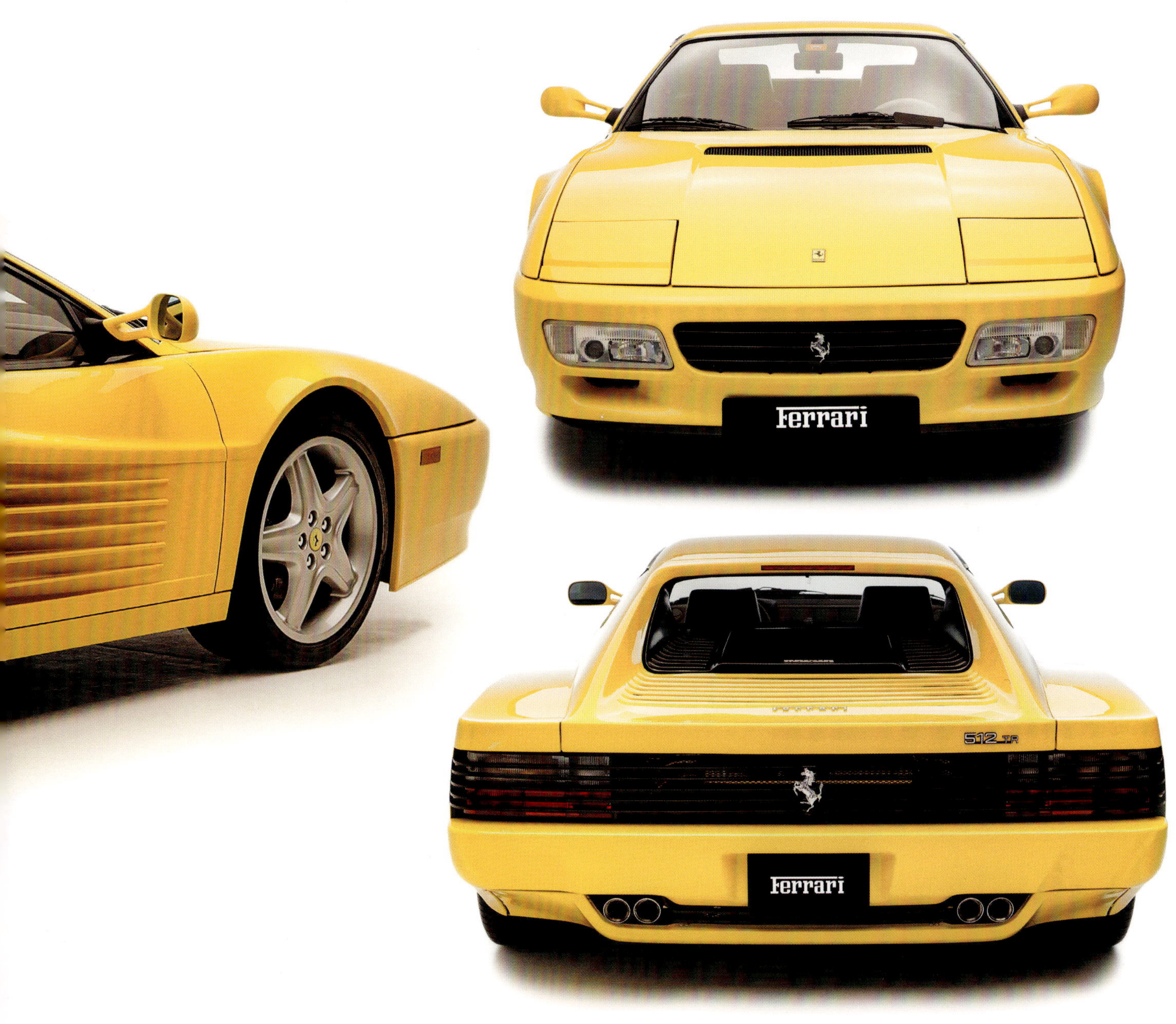

Previous, these, and following pages ■ Stunning body-side strakes were more than a dramatic part of the design—they directed cooling air to the wide, 4.9-liter engine cradled between wide rear tires.

brand-new. I wrote that it made the driver begin to understand how an Olympic-class sprinter might feel, especially one running the curve of the 200-meter race, or perhaps the way a top American football halfback feels powering his way around those who would try to stop him short of the goal line.

Though instead of having to run past or around, you sat there, in air-conditioned comfort on a leather-covered seat, gripping the steering wheel and grinning from ear to ear. The car didn't have a radio, but it didn't matter; the wonderful exhaust tones from the 12-cylinder engine provided the soundtrack.

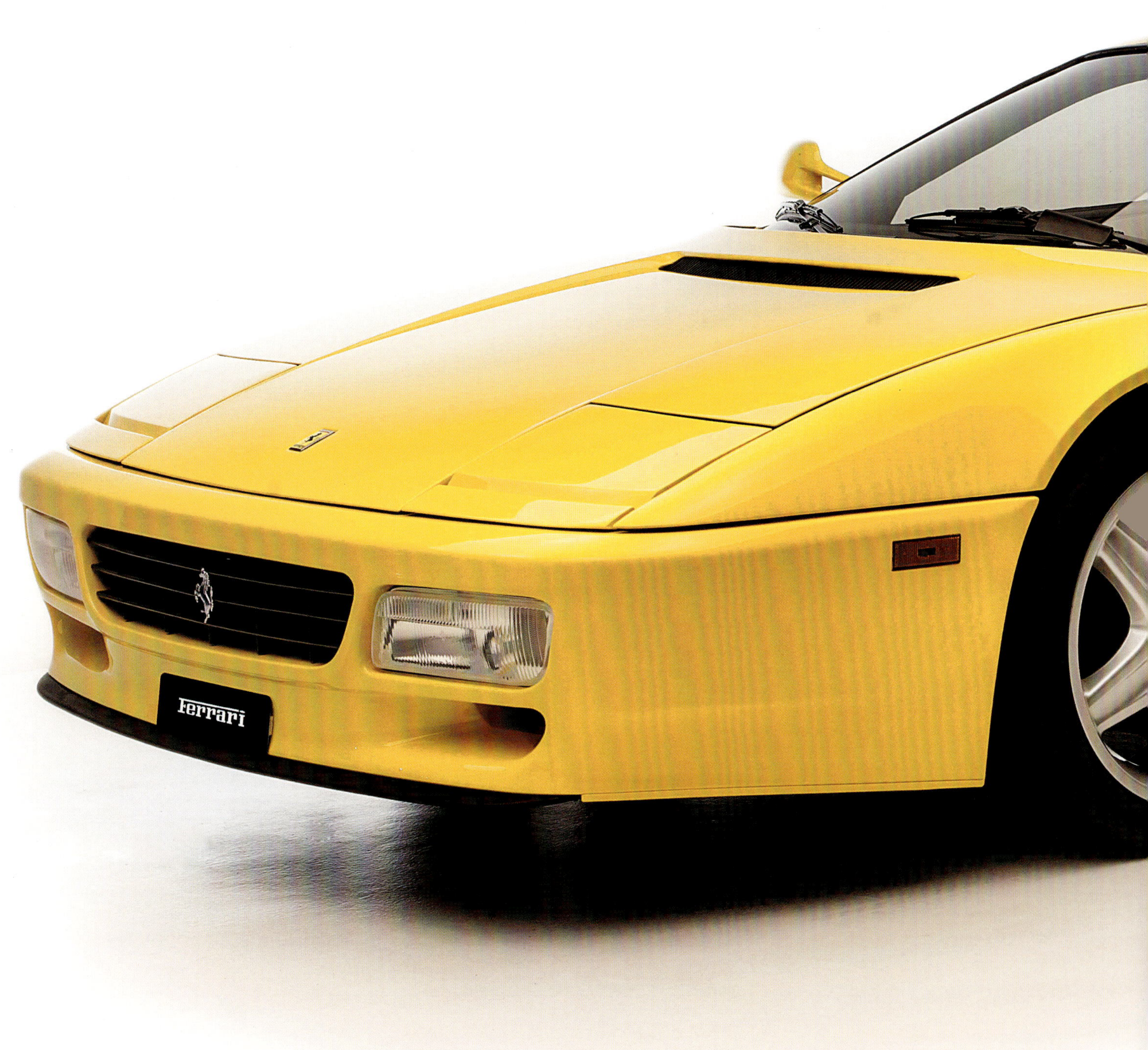
Ferrari

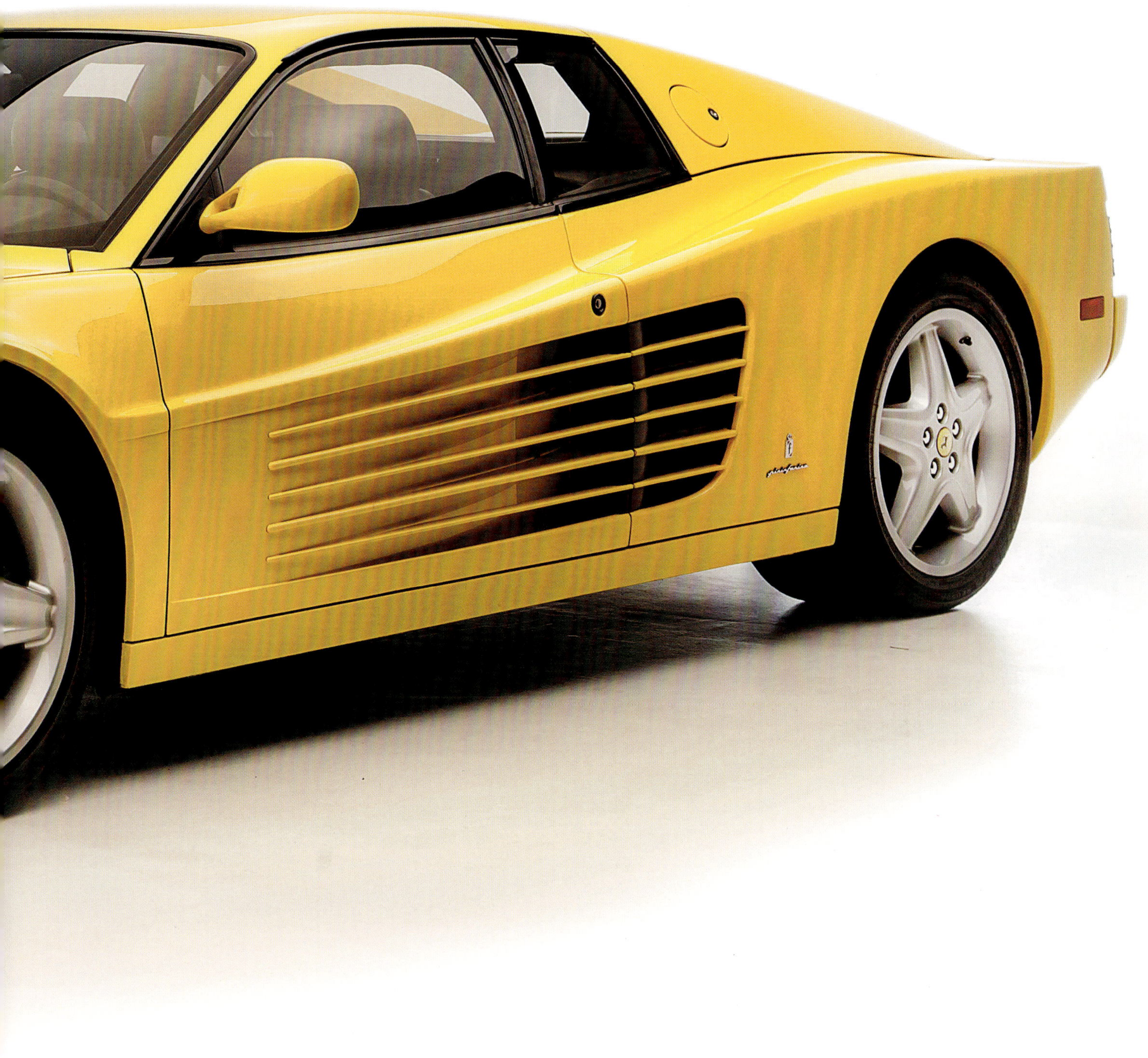

CHEVROLET CORVETTE C4

The C4 marked the fourth generation of America's sports car and brought it into the modern era

Late in 1951, General Motors design head Harley Earl assigned a team in his studio to create a proposal for the American version of the two-seat European sports car, but with a proviso. Should the proposal be approved for production, he specified not a metal body but one made of the same composite fiberglass-reinforced plastic already in use for aircraft and boat skins.

The result—the Chevrolet Corvette—was displayed at General Motors' annual Motorama showcase in January 1953 at the Waldorf Astoria hotel in New York City, where it proved to be so popular (and without the wait for pressing steel body panels) that it went into production just a few months later.

A decade later, the car entered its second generation in the guise of what would become an iconic split-window fastback coupe. Five years later, the third generation launched, its design inspired by the dramatic Mako Shark concept car.

As the mid-1980s approached, the Corvette was due for a complete makeover. At the same time, production of the sports car was moving to a new assembly plant in Bowling Green, Kentucky. There were delays that meant there would not be a 1983 model, but the 1984 car, the so-called C4, certainly proved to be worth the wait.

The Autopian website called the C4 "a seminal moment in Corvette history," adding, "The C4 Corvette isn't just another eighties techno-wedge. It set the template for the following three decades, defining what the Corvette could, and should, be.

"The C4 is a groundbreaking design," the article continued, lamenting "the Corvette had gone soft, going from lean rock and roll star to overweight lounge singer."

The transformation included a more modern body design so sleek (the windshield was raked at a 64-degree angle) that it reduced drag by an amazing 25

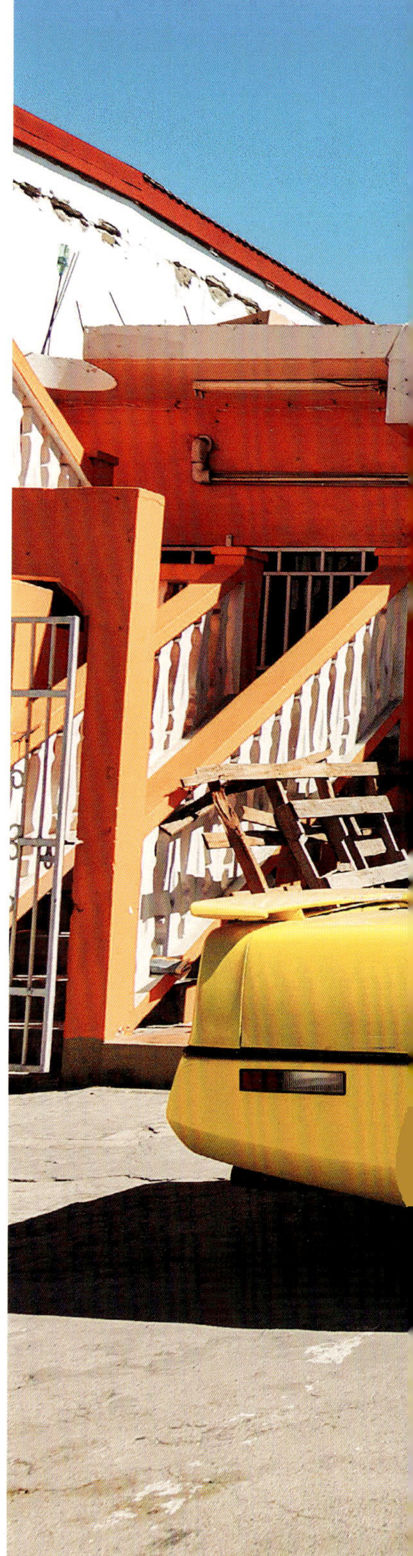

■ For its fourth generation, the Chevrolet Corvette got a more aerodynamic shape, new technology, and even a new assembly plant.

1980 ➤ 1989

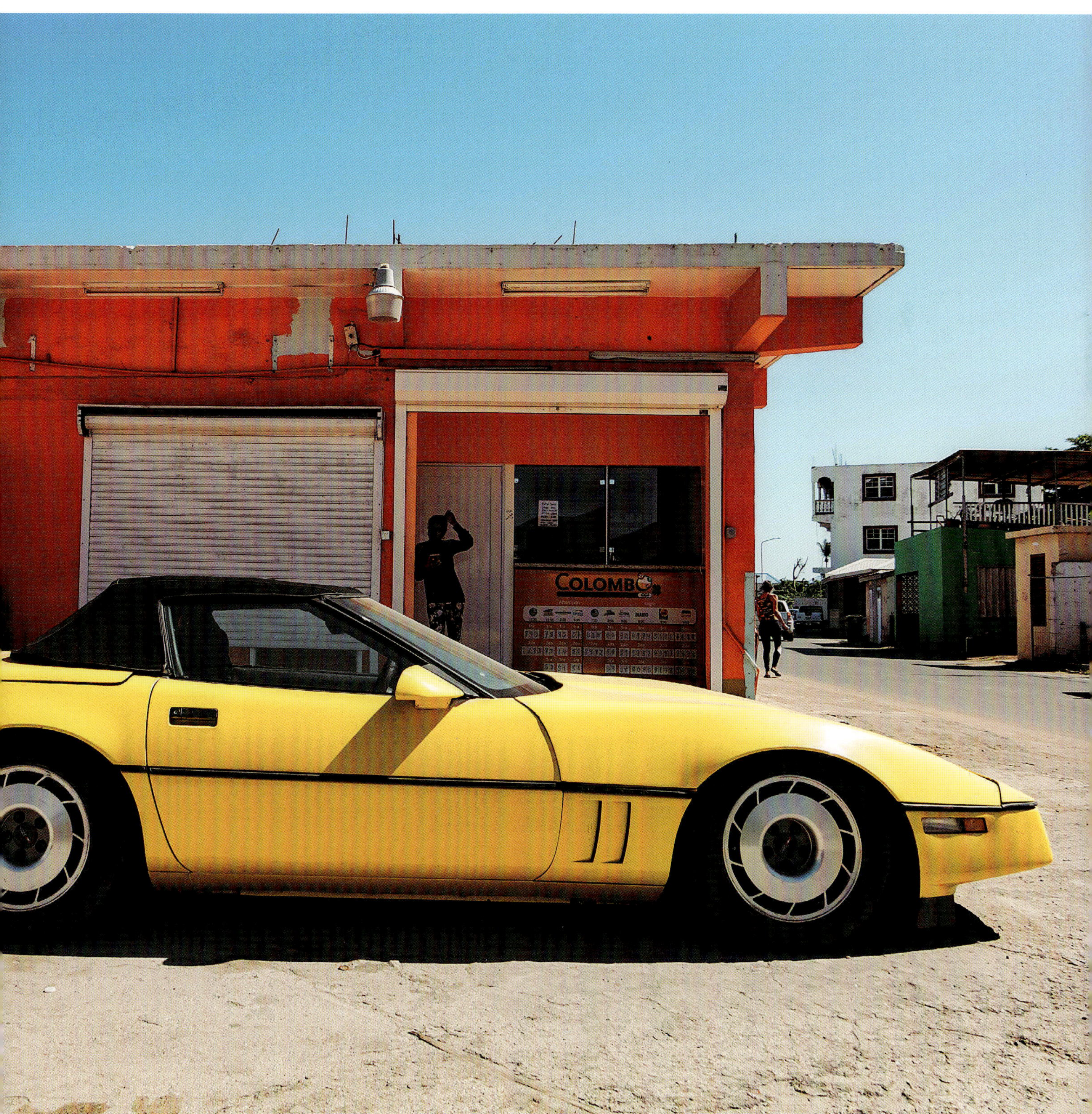

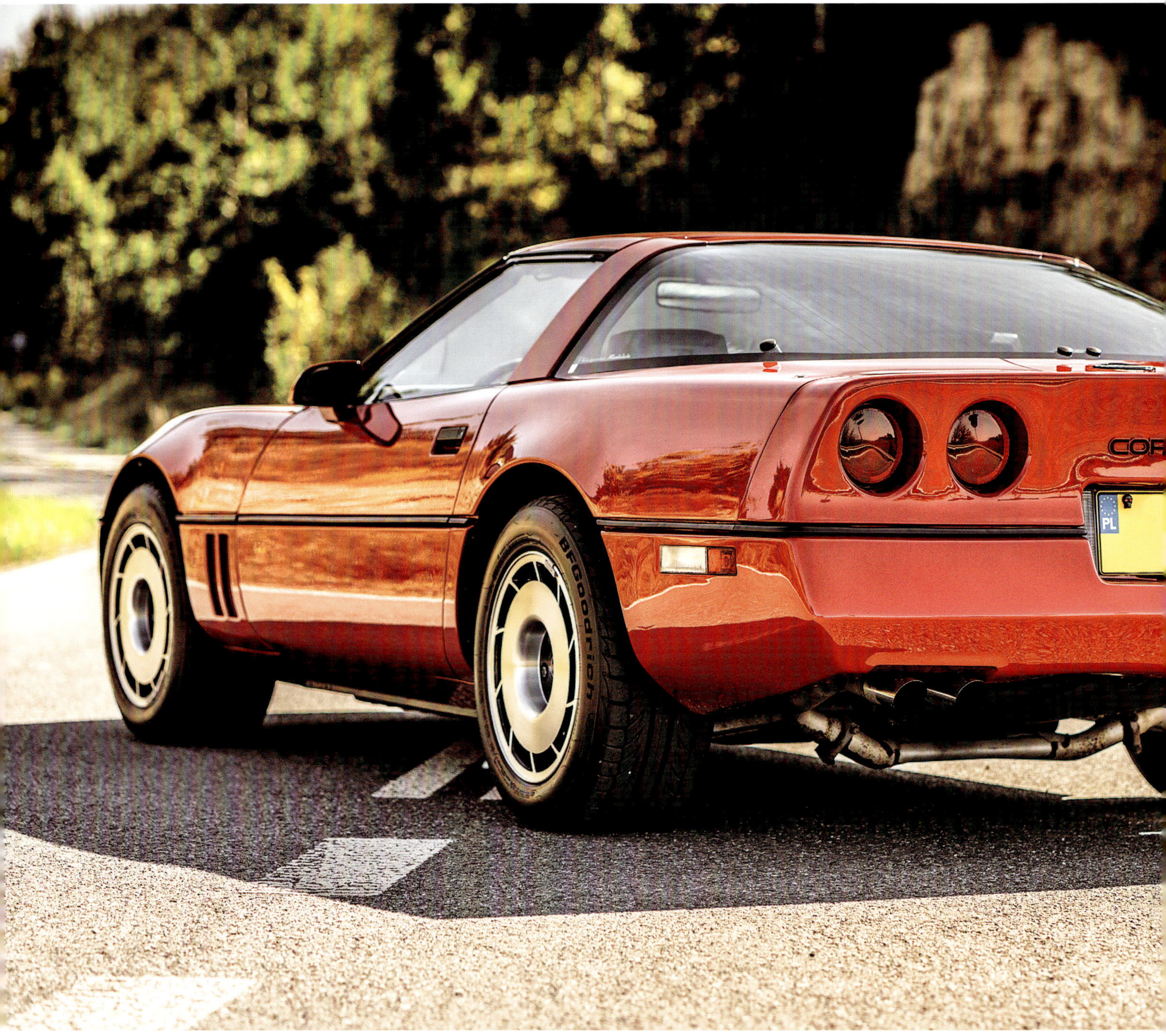

The C4 Corvette could carry you at 140 mph for less than half the price of the least-expensive Ferrari.

percent. The body included a lift-away Targa-style top, and a full convertible model would be available for the 1986 model year.

The chassis was improved; the interior was new and updated. The car was nearly 9 inches shorter but 2 inches wider and more than 200 pounds lighter (thanks in part to aluminum suspension components) than the C3 version. While the engine remained the 5.7-liter V8, it was now tuned to provide 205 horsepower and 393 Nm of torque, and a 4-speed manual transmission was also offered for the first time in several years.

Sports car enthusiasts responded, buying more than 50,000 of the cars during the 1984 model year.

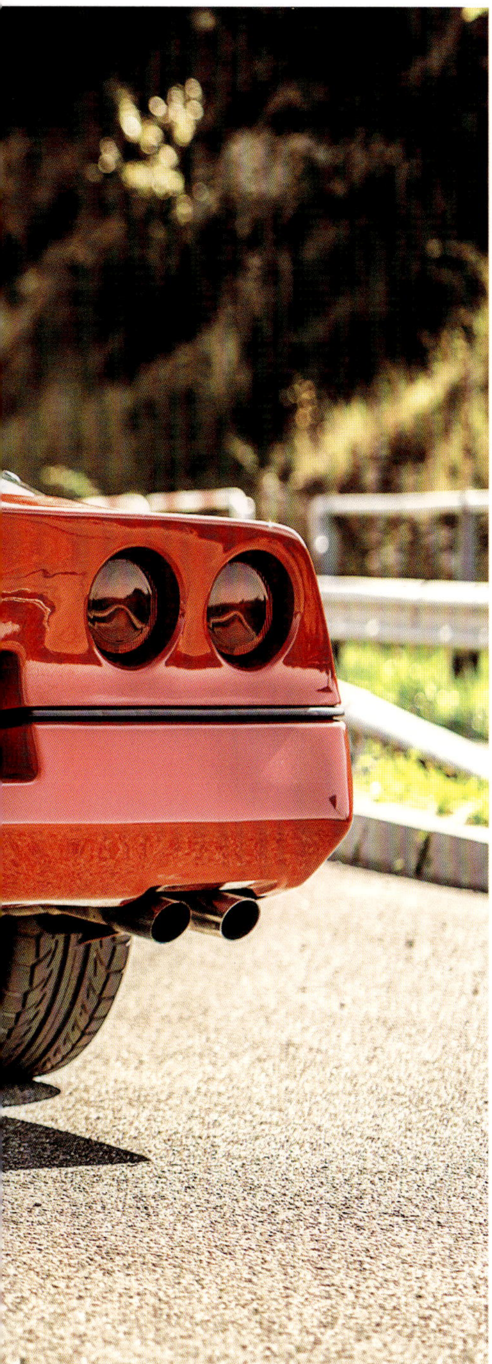

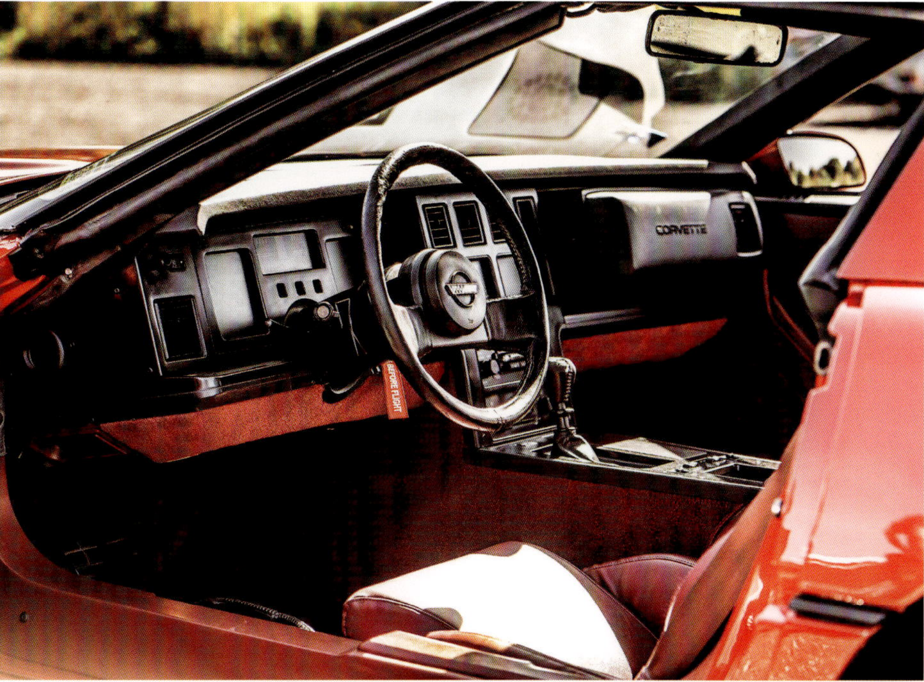

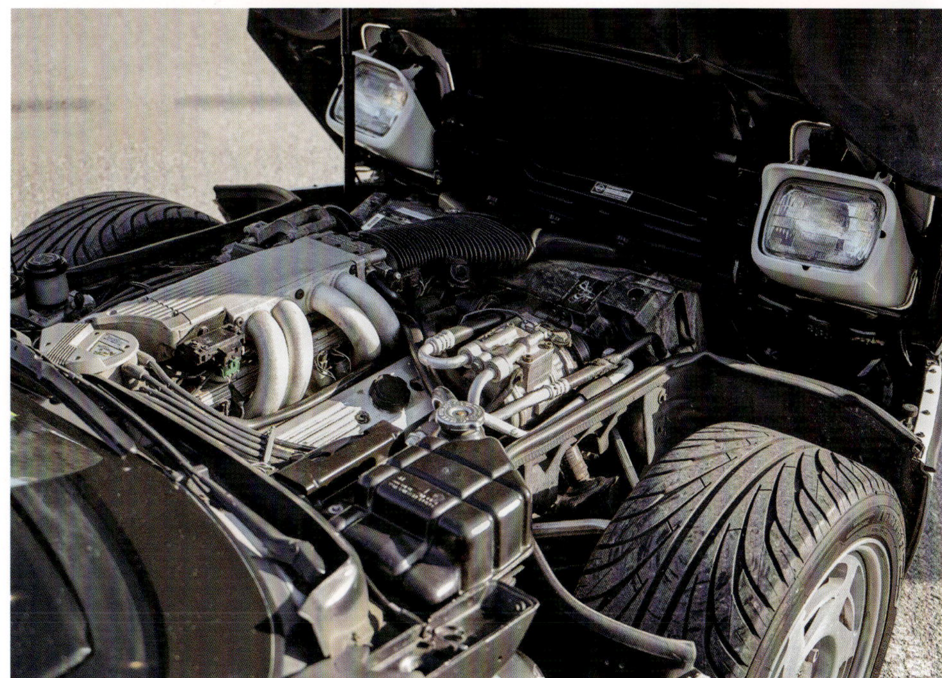

These pages ■ The C4 was two inches wider than before but also more than 200 pounds lighter.

Top ■ The car featured a new interior with more use of electronic displays.

Bottom ■ Unlike many of Europe's fastest sports cars, the Corvette had its engine at the front.

Car and Driver magazine proclaimed, "America takes on all comers" and called the C4 "a true-born, world-class sports car loaded with technical sophistication." Capable of speeds up to 140 mph (225 km/h), it said the new Corvette was one of the "half-dozen fastest production automobiles in the entire world!"

As impressive as that 1984 version was, *Motor Trend* magazine noted in a retrospective that "the thirteen-year trajectory of the platform is really a continuum of steady improvement...and important changes came fast and furious during C4's tenure," listing such innovations as a 6-speed manual transmission, the launch of the high-performance ZR1 model in 1990 and new 300-horsepower small-block V8 for 1992, and that engine's output reaching 340 horsepower for 1996, which would be the final year of production for the fourth-generation of America's sports car.

TOYOTA MR2

From Japan, an affordable mid-engine sports car

Have you ever pondered the ideal place to put the engine in an automobile? Sure, most cars have the engine in front, people in the middle, and a cargo area in the back. But putting the engine in the back certainly worked for Volkswagen and Porsche. And then there are those cars constructed with the engine in the middle, tucked tightly behind the passenger compartment, albeit likely leaving room for seating for only a driver and a single occupant.

Positioning the weight of the engine, the transmission, and even the occupants between the front and rear axles provides balance front-to-rear and side-to-side, thus allowing steering, suspension, and braking capabilities to be optimized. Such placement also can enhance aerodynamics by not requiring a tall hood around the typical front-placed engine.

Exotic (and expensive) sports cars often have mid-engine architecture, but from time to time automakers

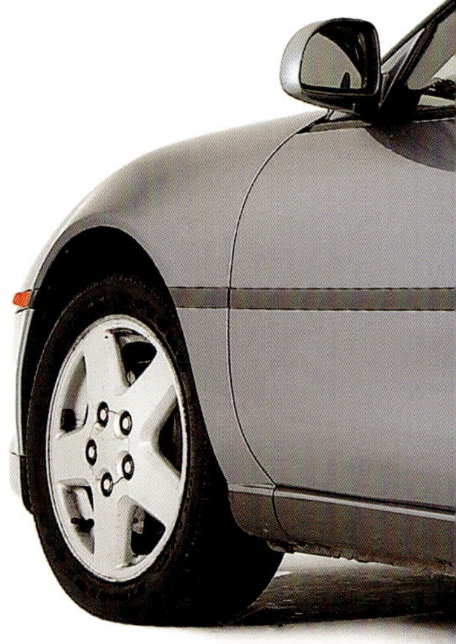

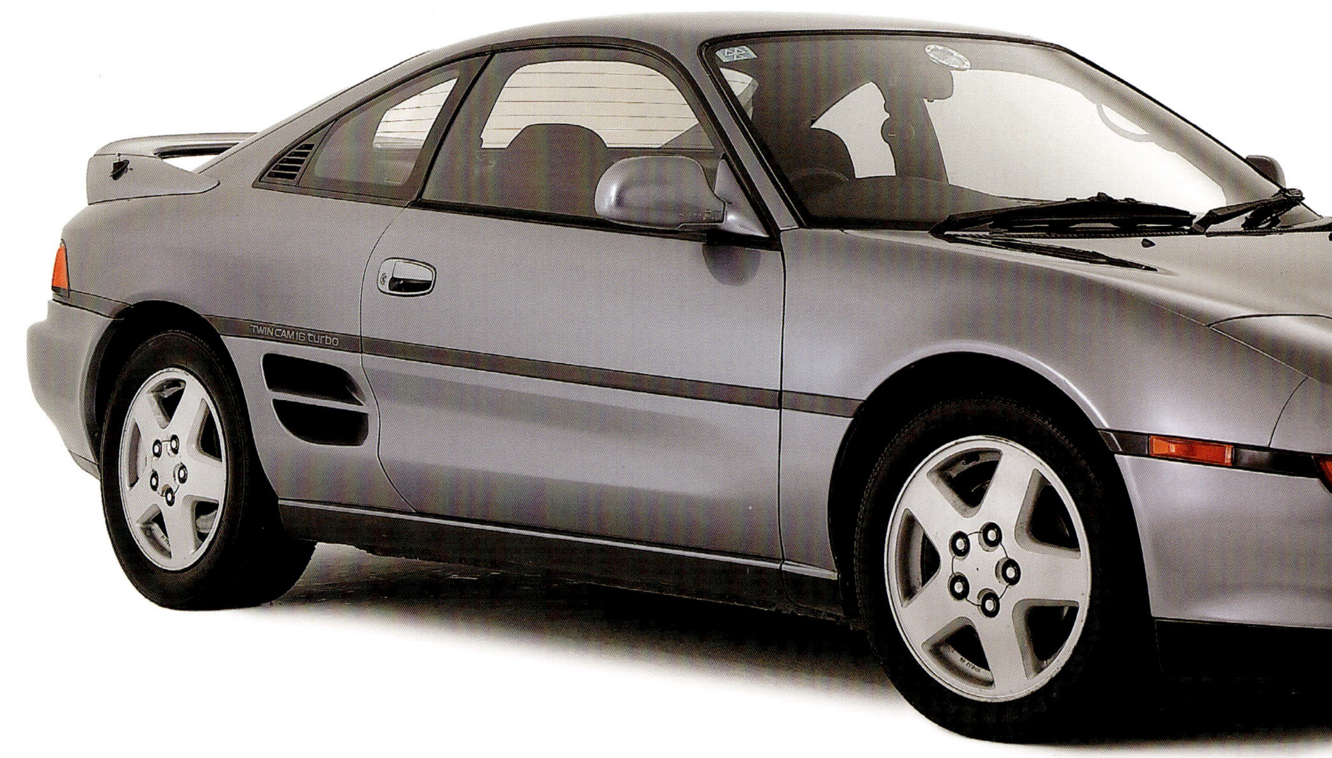

■ Toyota set out to produce a car with good fuel economy that might be fun to drive, but the result proved to be a true sports car.

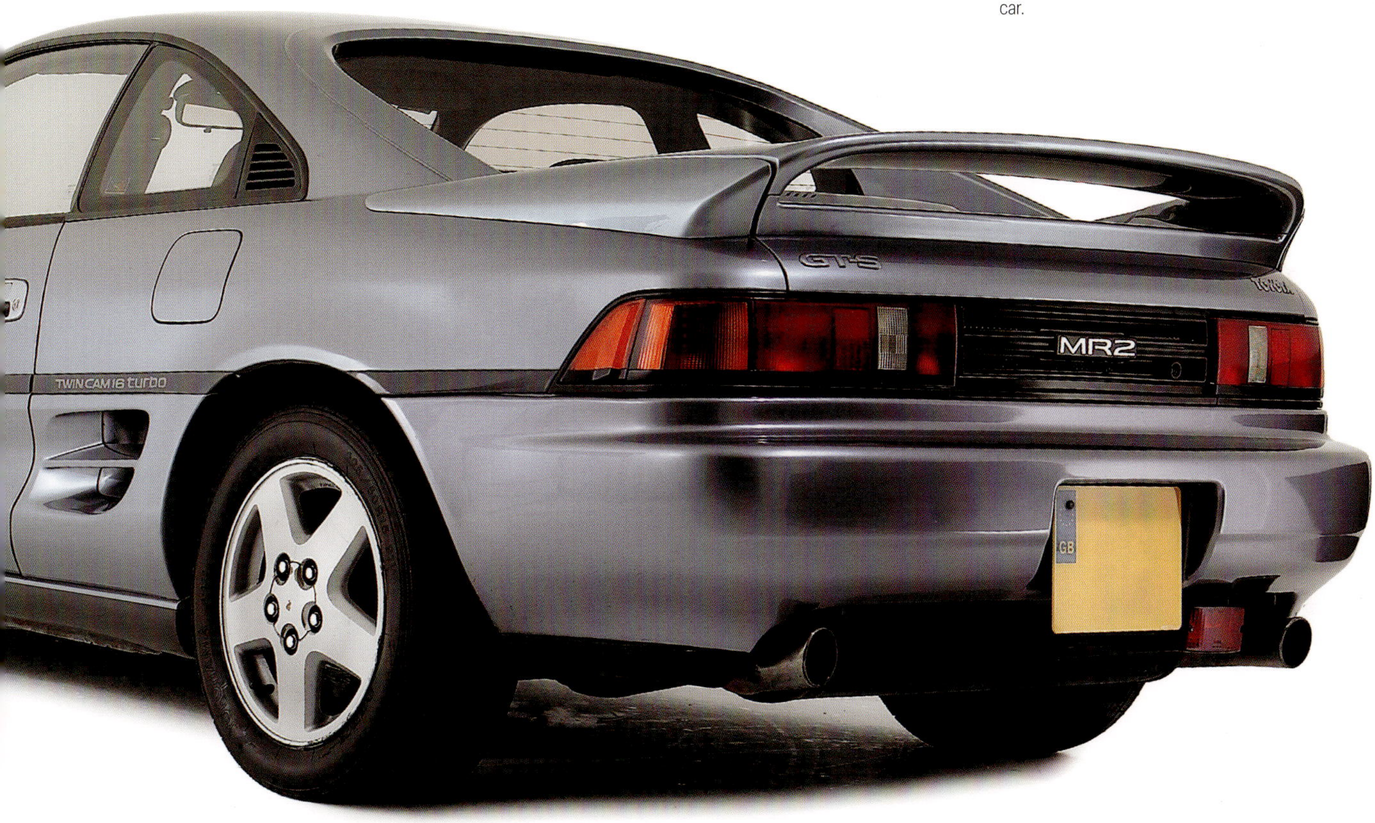

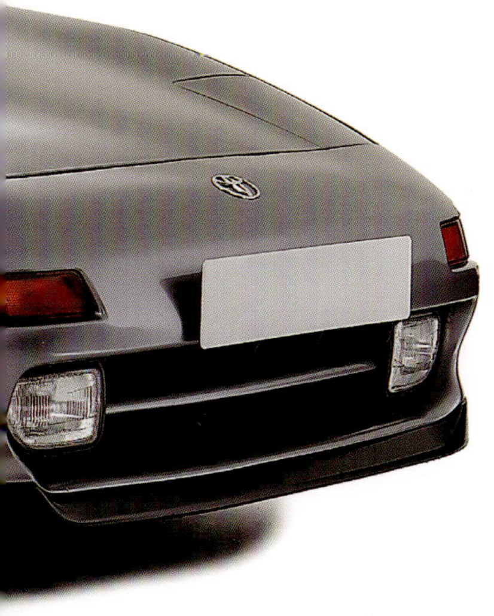

take the effort to apply this style to more affordable offerings. Take, for example, the 1970s and '80s when Fiat offered the X1/9, Porsche the 914, Pontiac the Fiero, and Lancia the Scorpion.

In 1983, Toyota displayed at the Tokyo Auto Show a mid-engine concept car, the SV-3. A year later, that concept moved into production as the Toyota MR2, the name likely traced to Midship Runabout (with) 2 seats, though in English-speaking countries it typically was called the "Mister 2."

The original goal was to build a car that was affordable, offered good fuel economy, and was fun to drive, though not necessarily a real sports car, which the MR2 turned out to be, thanks in part to the use of a 1.6-liter twin-cam 4-cylinder engine, 5-speed manual transmission, and disc brakes at all four corners.

Car and Driver magazine immediately included it in its annual list of the ten best cars. *Motor Trend* magazine said the MR2 "was essentially a budget exotic car." *Automobile* magazine matched it against a Ferrari 308 in a comparison test.

BMW M3

Bavarian automaker adds performance and an M badge to its compact car

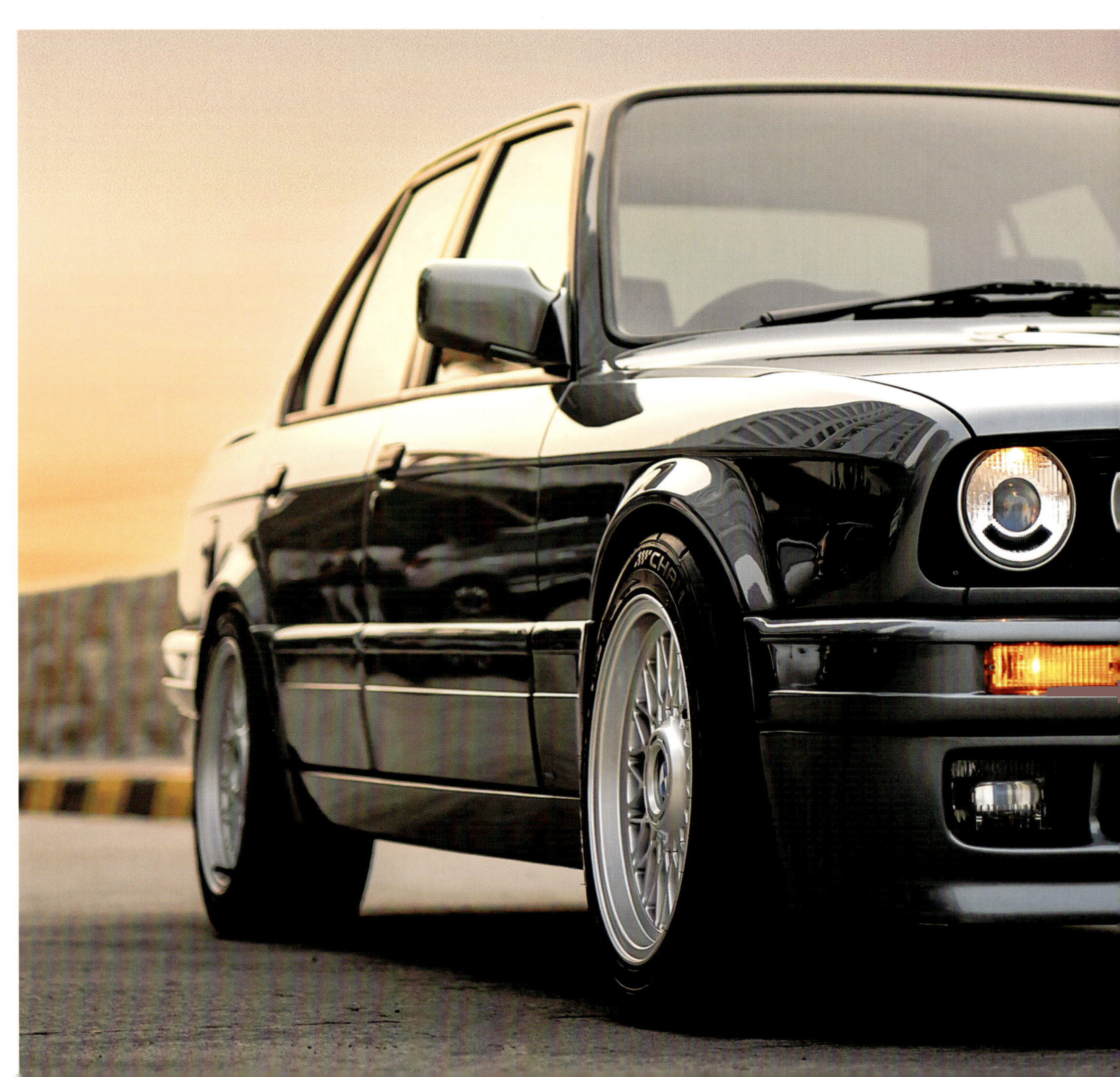

1980 ➤ 1989

In the spring of 1972, German automaker BMW launched BMW Motorsport. Eight employees were assigned to the company's auto racing effort, starting with the entry of a 3.0 CSL coupe in the German and European touring car series.

Success in auto racing bred interest in high-performance models among the company's customers, so at the 1978 Paris Motor Show, BMW unveiled its first M-badged offering, the M1, a mid-engine sports car designed for racing. A year later the M badge was back, and this time on the M535i, a high-performance version of BMW's 5 Series sedan.

The most popular of the M cars would launch in 1986. It was the M3, which was based on the E30 second generation of BMW's 3 Series compact coupe and convertible.

While the standard 325 was equipped with straight-6 engines rated at 170 horsepower, the M3 got high-revving 2.3-liter inline 4s that offered 195 horsepower in 1986 and '87, 220 horsepower in 1988, and 238 horsepower in 1989 and '90. The M versions also were equipped with enhanced transmissions, suspension, and braking systems.

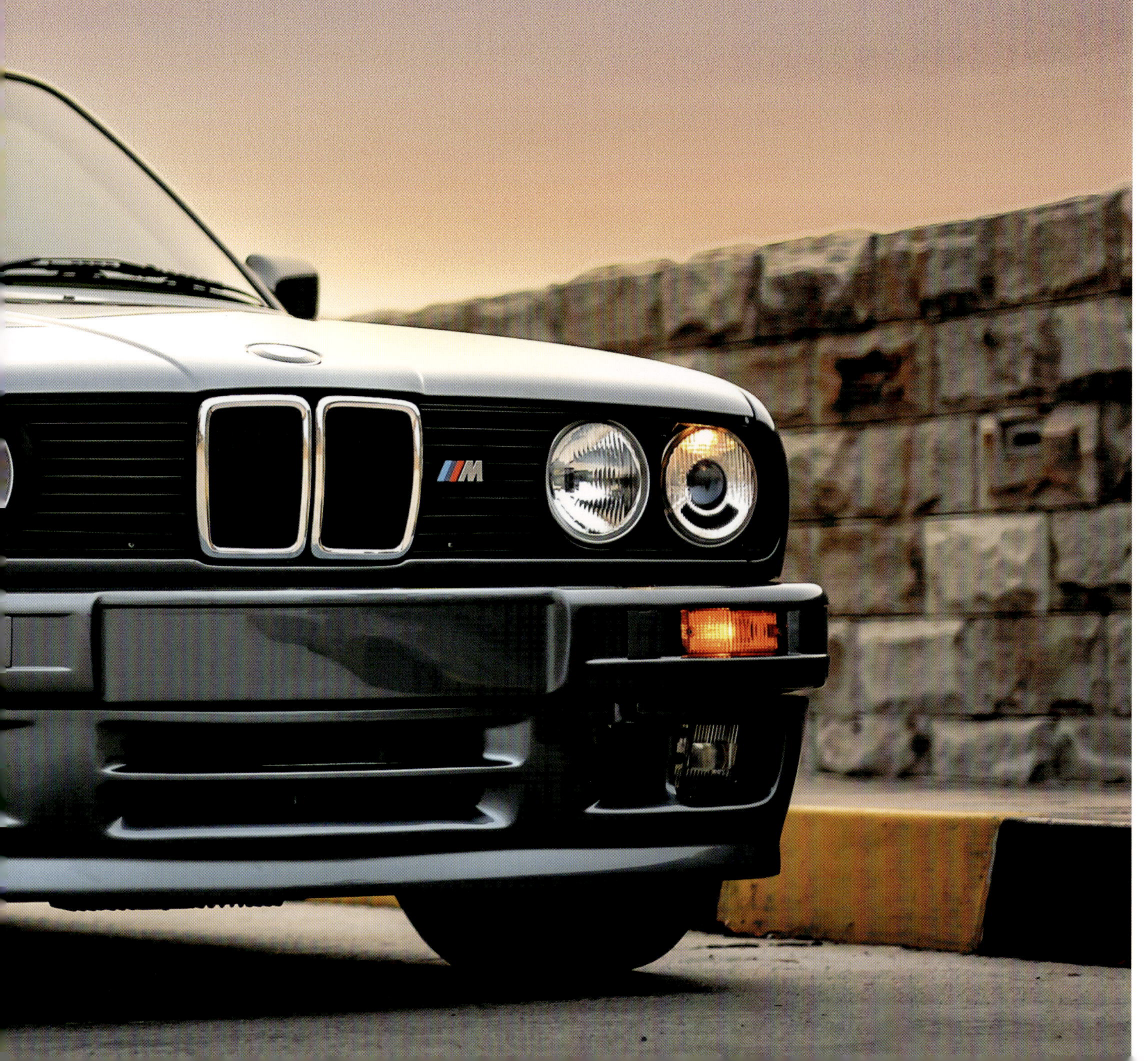

In 1987, *Car and Driver* magazine did a road test of the 1988 M3: "The Bavarian Motor Works is back on track with a fleet of drivers' cars, and the M3 is potent proof of its new direction. The M3 is the most recent of the broad-shouldered BMW Motorsport models to reach our shores. For those not yet fluent in M-speak, the M-machines are limited edition, high-performance versions of the 3-, 5-, and 6-series sedans. For several years the M-cars were a treat reserved for European buyers, but since early this year they have been trickling into the hands of hungry American enthusiasts."

The magazine thanked the homologation rules for Group A racing for making such a car available, adding, "The M3's racing heritage is immediately apparent in its steroid-injected bodywork. With its aggressive assortment of air dams, body flares, and spoilers, the M3 will quicken the pulse of any boy (or girl) racer lucky enough to catch a glimpse of one...

"The sub-skin makeover is equally impressive... Formula 1 fans will think they've died and gone to Monaco the first time they lift the M3's hood. Inside sits a naturally aspirated, 2.3-liter version of BMW's

■ The original M3 engine had only 4 cylinders, not the standard 6, but it produced more horsepower, and the car also had other performance enhancements to deal with that power.

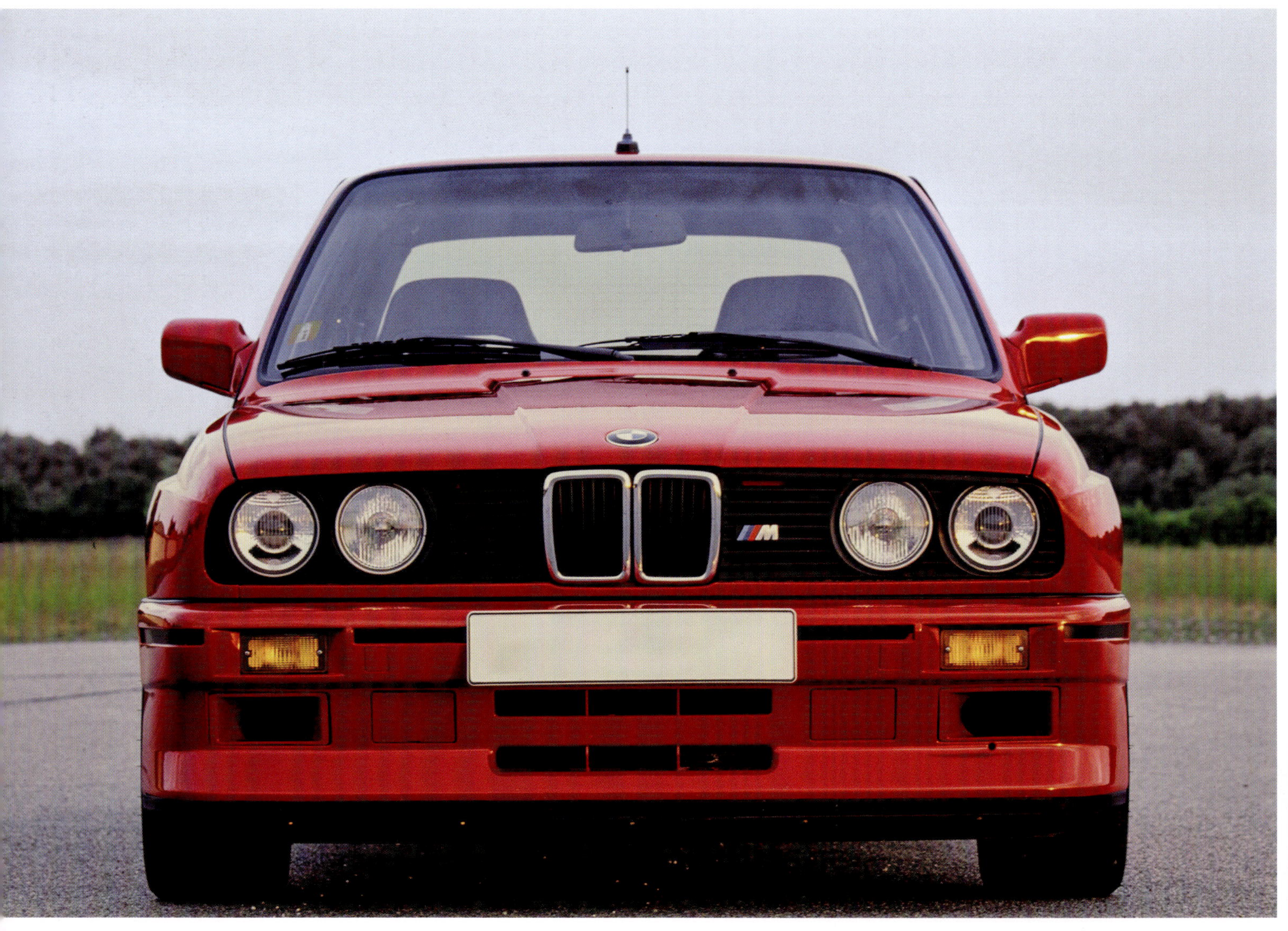

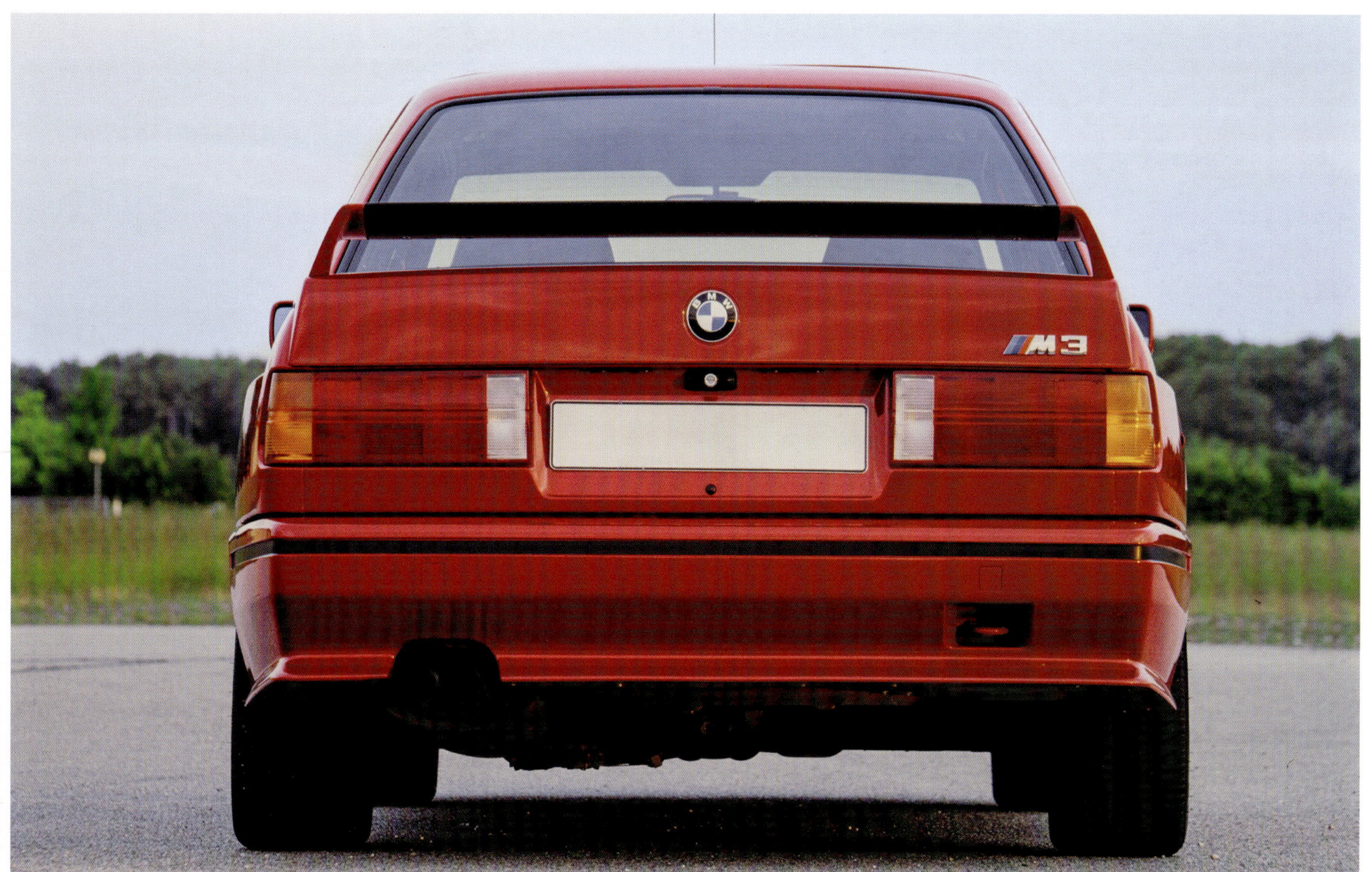

Driving enthusiasts were 'smitten,' and still are as original M3s are highly collectible.

brutal turbocharged 4-cylinder Grand Prix engine...What looks impressive on paper feels equally stirring on the road... enough punch to blow off the Mercedes-Benz 190E 2.3-16 and stay neck and neck with the Porsche 944S... All in all, we're smitten."

So was collector car insurer and value tracker Hagerty: "Modern classic cars don't come much more sought after and revered than the original BMW M3."

In the early 1990s, the E36 replaced the E30, and along came the M versions, now including a four-door sedan as well as the M3 coupe, convertible, and sedan. Each was powered by inline 6s with 282 horsepower and 320 Nm of torque, and the fun has since continued through the 3 Series generational advancements.

The availability of such performance in the sedan architecture also helped boost sales. The E30 M version sold nearly 18,000 copies while the E36 model hit more than 71,000 in sales, although more than half of those were still the coupe version.

PORSCHE 959

"To call it perfect is the mildest of overstatements"

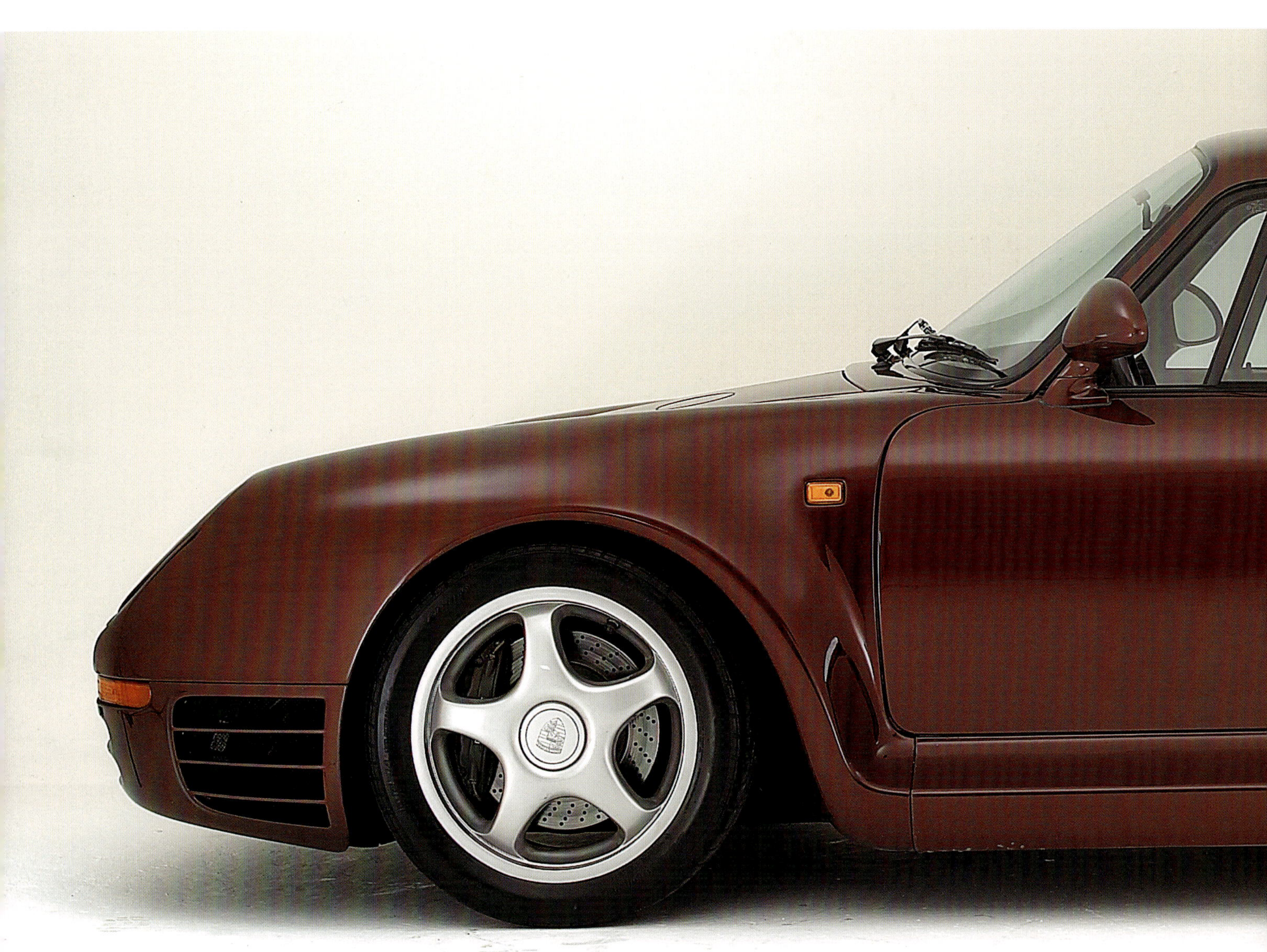

1980 ➤ 1989

By the 1980s, Porsche's 911 was an aging yet still viable sports car, and the company was looking ahead to what might be next. At the same time, it was considering an entry into Group B motorsports,using the rally events as a place to test a new all-wheel-drive system that could automatically adjust the torque distribution among the four wheels.

The result was the 959, which was based on the 911 but with the twin-turbocharged engine from the 956 and 962 race cars, a height-adjustment suspension system, a new aerodynamic body made of aluminum and Kevlar, and a chassis floor of Nomex instead of steel.

Three prototypes (without the twin-turbo engines) were entered in the 1984 Paris-Dakar Rally across parts of Europe and Africa; one of them won, another was sixth, and the third was twenty-fifth. The following year (with the more powerful engine), one of the Porsches won the Rallye des Pharaons, and in 1986 a trio placed first, second, and sixth again in the Paris-Dakar. That same year, Porsche entered a 959-based 961 in the 24 Hours of Le Mans; it finished seventh overall and first in class (trailing only Porsche's all-out sports prototype racers).

Next to come was Group B rallying, only to have that category canceled. However, all was not lost for the Porsche project. For one thing, the all-wheel-drive system proved its capability to deal with high-powered turbocharged engines and was used on all future 911 Turbo models. For another, the 959 was produced not only in a Sport version for racing but in a Komfort model for public roads and with more creature-comfort features than would be desirable on the racetrack.

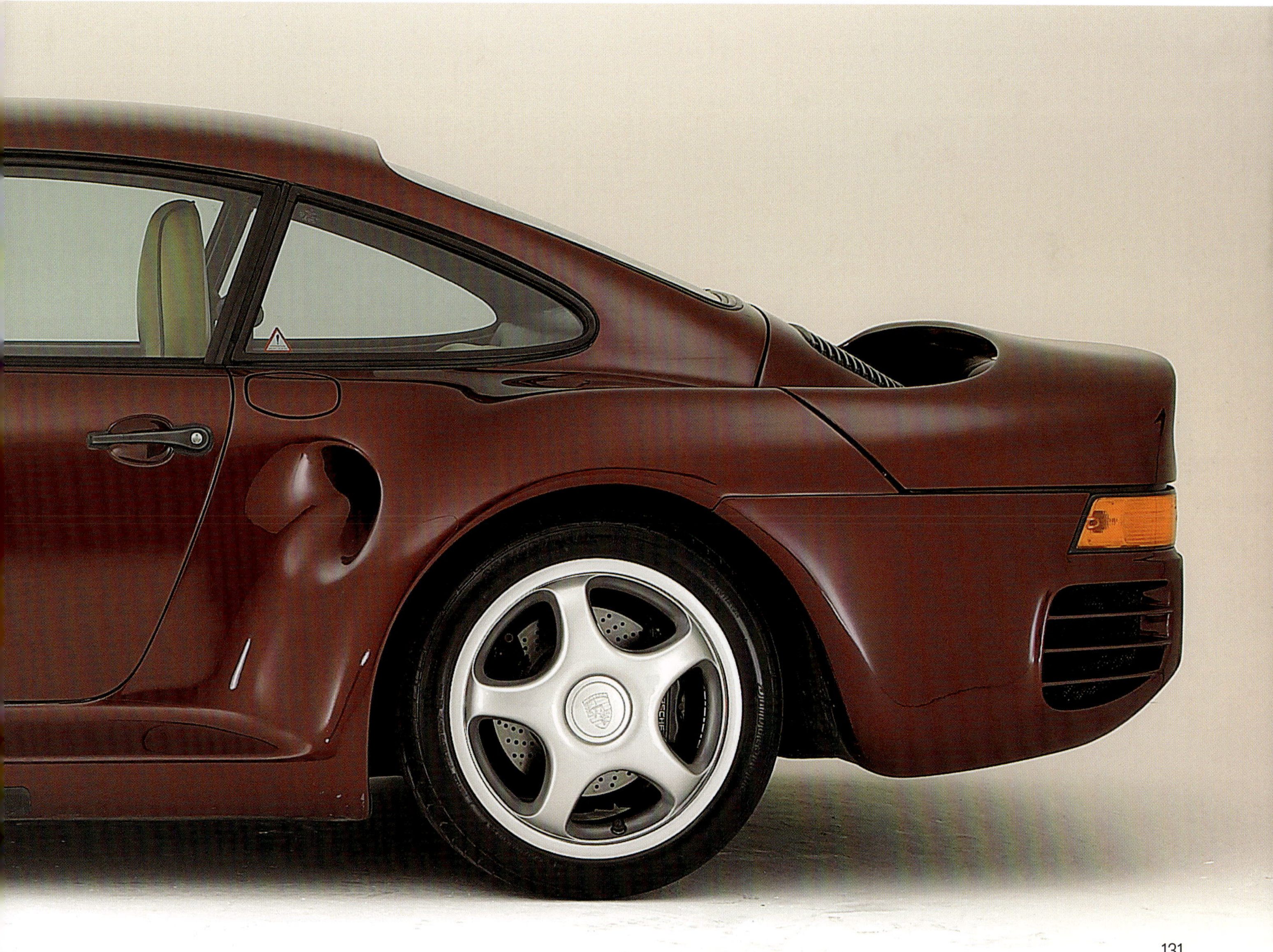

Porsche noted that when presented at the 1985 Frankfurt Auto Show, the 959 "was the most expensive, most technologically advanced, and fastest series production car in the world."

With its twin-turbo engine rated at 450 horsepower and 500 Nm of torque (and 680 horsepower for the race-track), the car was capable of speeds up to 196.9 mph (317 km/h).

In 1987, *Car and Driver* magazine tested the 959. "We hesitate to call any car perfect. The absence of flaws in any product of human endeavor is extraordinarily rare," it reported. "But we have just returned from West Germany, where we finally got a chance to drive a Porsche 959 on the street, and the word 'perfect' is difficult to avoid.

"What single word more accurately describes a car that combines race-car performance with luxury-sedan comfort, that is equally adept at commuting through rush-hour traffic, profiling in jet-set locales, negotiating

■ While based on the 911, the 959 offered all-wheel drive, a lighter and more aerodynamic body, and a twin-turbocharged engine rated at 450 horsepower.

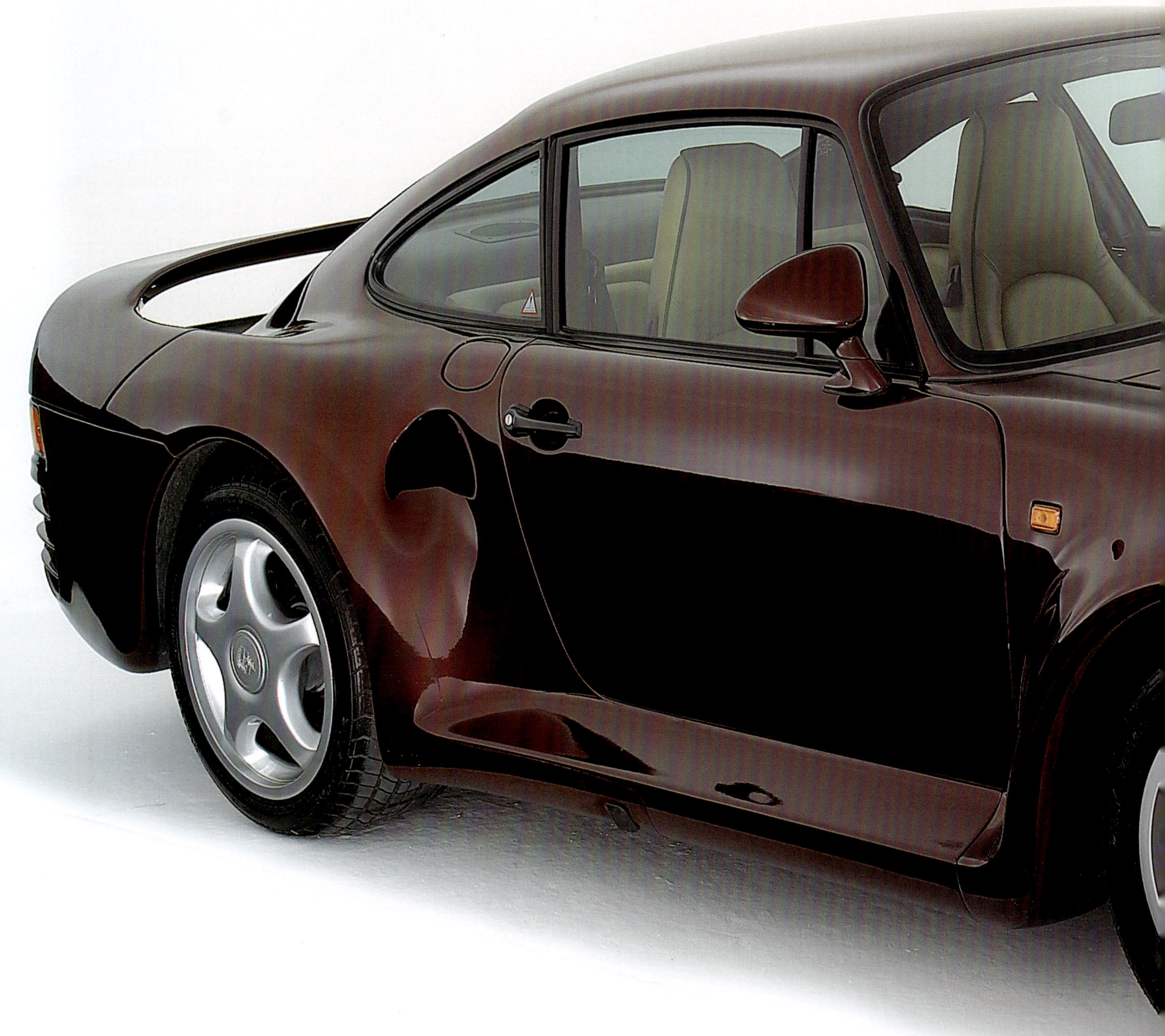

blizzard-swept mountain passes, and outrunning light airplanes?

"The Porsche 959 can accomplish almost any automotive mission so well that to call it perfect is the mildest of overstatements.

"Power and speed are the core of the 959's excellence. With rocket-sled acceleration and the highest top end we've ever measured, the 959 stands alone at the pinnacle of production-car performance."

However, it added, "Unlike most ultra-performance cars, the 959 is astonishingly easy to drive." It quoted the 959 project director as saying speed without security and stability is senseless, and added that runs at 190 mph on the autobahn were "completely comfortable in the 959."

And in conclusion, the magazine found that to compare the 959 to a typical car is like comparing "the F-15 (military fighter jet) to a hang glider."

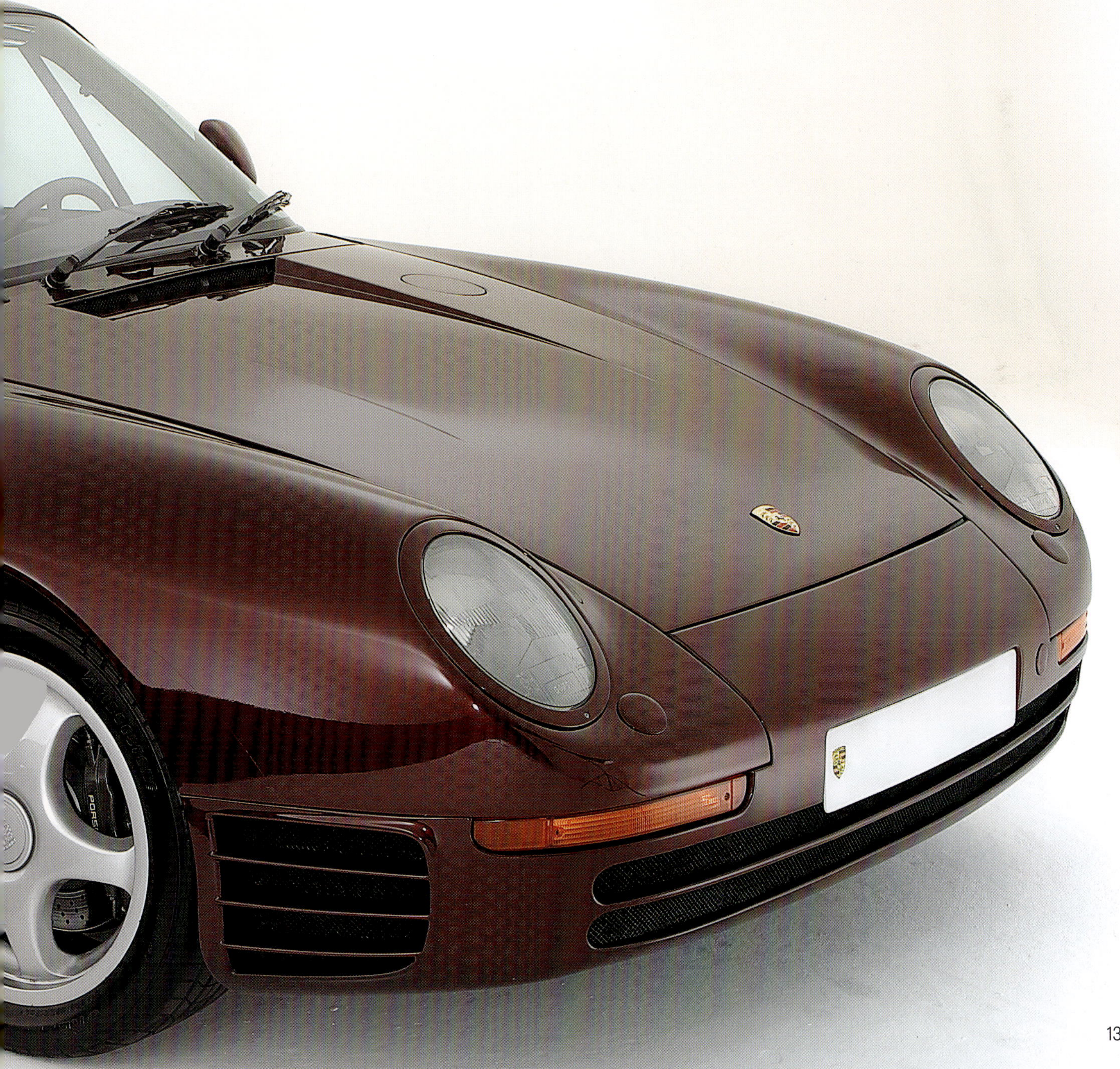

FERRARI F40

The car that represents the culmination of Il Commendatore's career

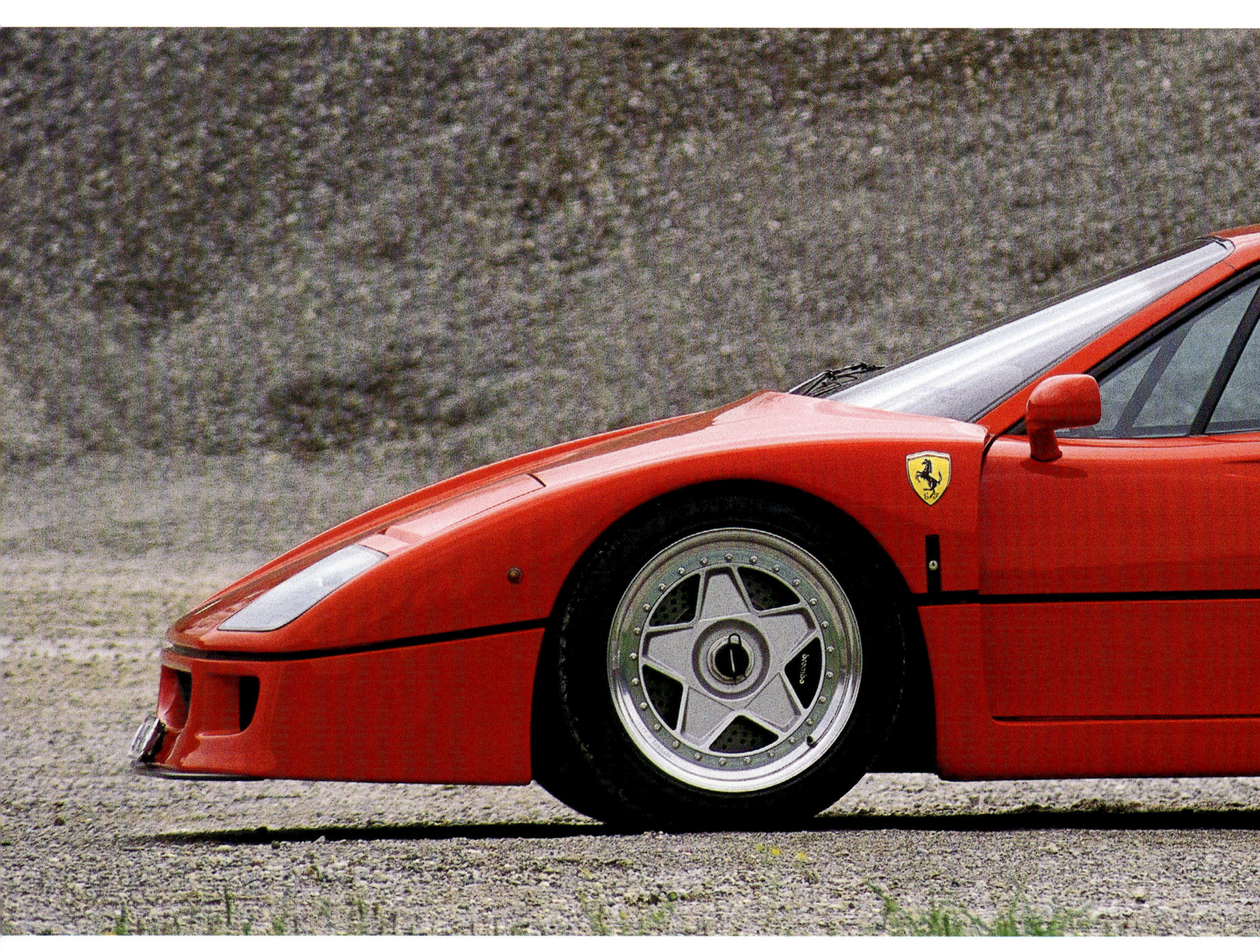

Enzo Ferrari—or Il Commendatore, the nickname traced to his British rivals on the road and the track—died in August 1988 at the age of ninety. The last car in which he was directly involved was presented the previous year. It was named the Ferrari F40 in celebration of Ferrari's fortieth anniversary as an automaker.

And while so many of that company's products were exotic and perhaps even bold, the F40 was audacious, all the way from its high rear wing to being not only the fastest Ferrari, indeed the fastest of all street-legal production cars, but also the most expensive.

At the F40's unveiling, Il Commendatore said he had expressed his desire for his last car to leave a legacy, "a wish that we produce a car which would remind us of Le Mans and the GTO."

Leonardo Fioravanti, who at that time was in charge of design at Pininfarina, told England's *Classic & Sports Car* magazine, "In the 1960s, it was possible for the private driver to buy a car that was very similar to the racing cars. What we have done with the F40 is build a machine which pays little respect to the limitations of modern times..."

The F40 was, in part, Ferrari's alternative to the technologically advanced Porsche 959. "Certainly the Italian car's whole ethos couldn't have been further

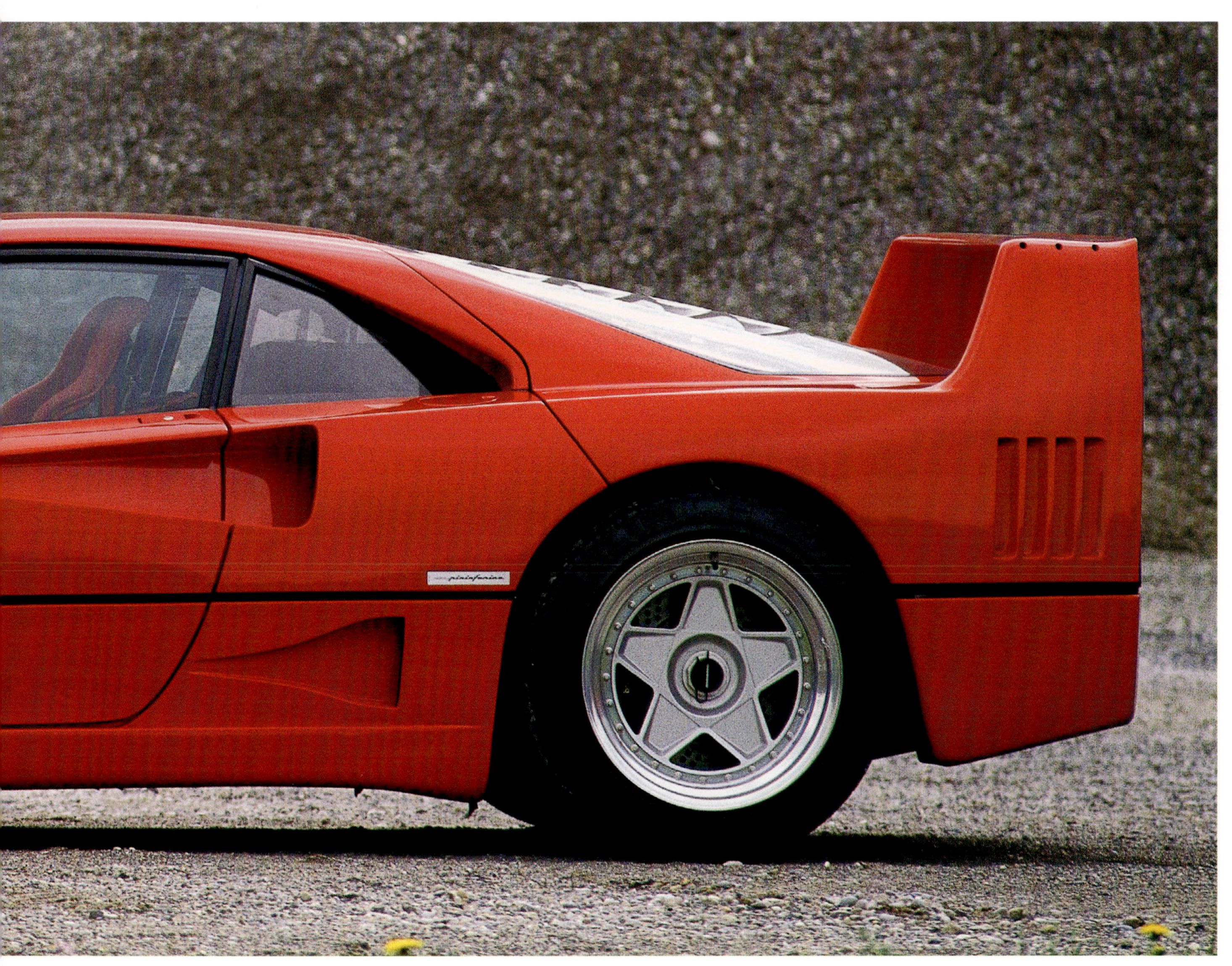

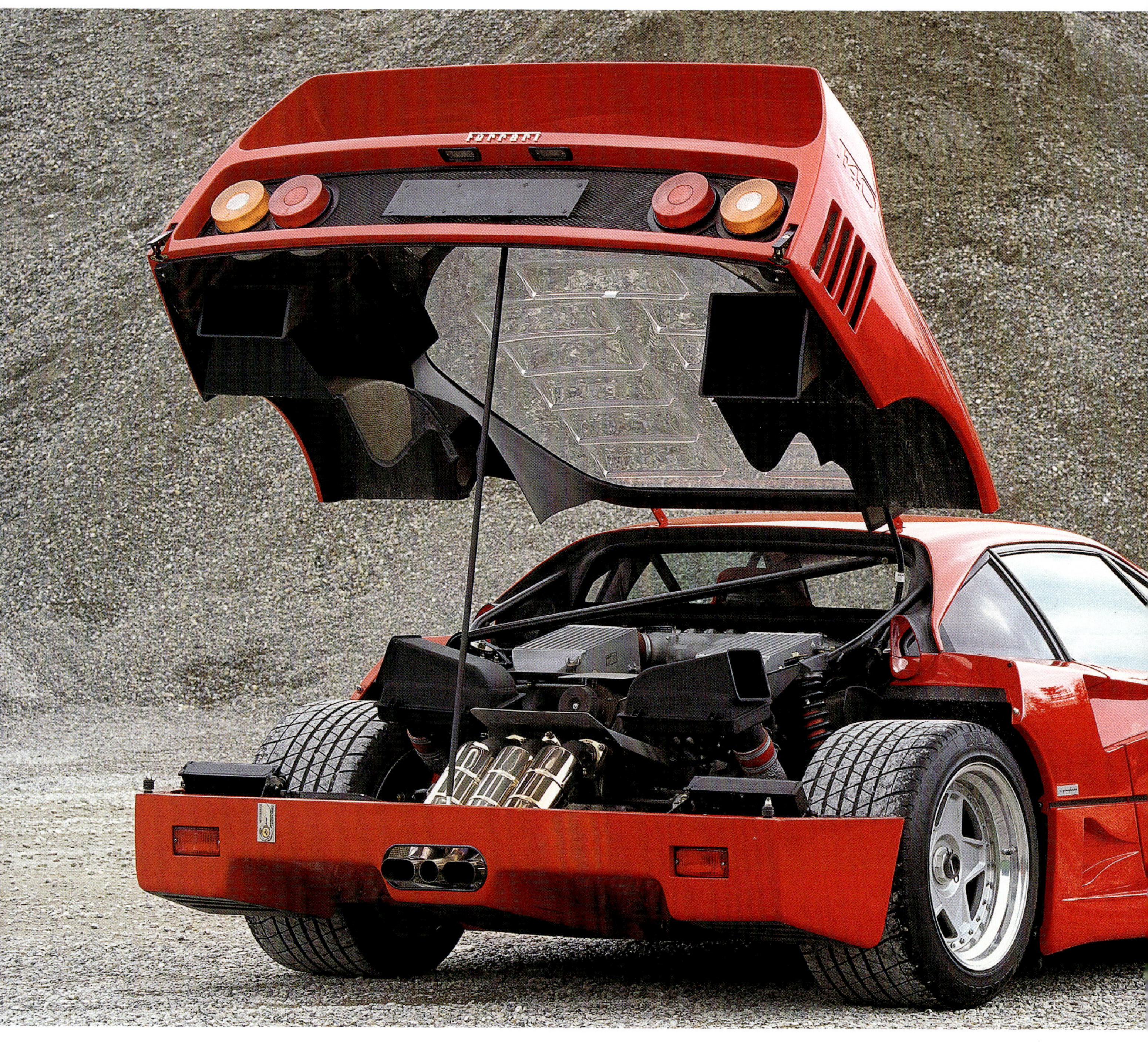

removed from that of its Weissach rival," *Classic & Sports Car* magazine suggested.

"This car, for us, has a special meaning," Fioravanti continued. "This world has too many computers, too much technology, and here we have recovered the design of a car as an emotion, just as in the old days. It is not nostalgia, but we prove that even today it is possible to make a car with a human approach."

The F40 was the spiritual successor to the Ferrari 288 GTO, itself an homage to the original Gran Turismo Omologato, the Ferrari 250 GTO.

The F40 was built on a racing-style tubeframe chassis and carried a mid-mounted 3.0-liter V8, twin-turbocharged engine to provide 471 horsepower and 577 Nm of torque beneath its coachwork of carbon fiber and Kevlar, with the engine visible beneath its clear plastic cover. The car could sprint from a standing start to 60 mph (96 km/h) in 3.9 seconds and could reach 124 mph (200 km/h) in just 12 seconds on its way to a top speed of 201 mph (323 km/h), the suspension lowering automatically for aerodynamic efficiency.

True to its racing heritage, the interior was Spartan, with minimal air conditioning, no radio, no glove box, no carpets, and no interior door panels.

American magazine *Car and Driver* finally got its hands on an F40 in the early 1990s, reporting, "After two days on the road and an afternoon at the test track,

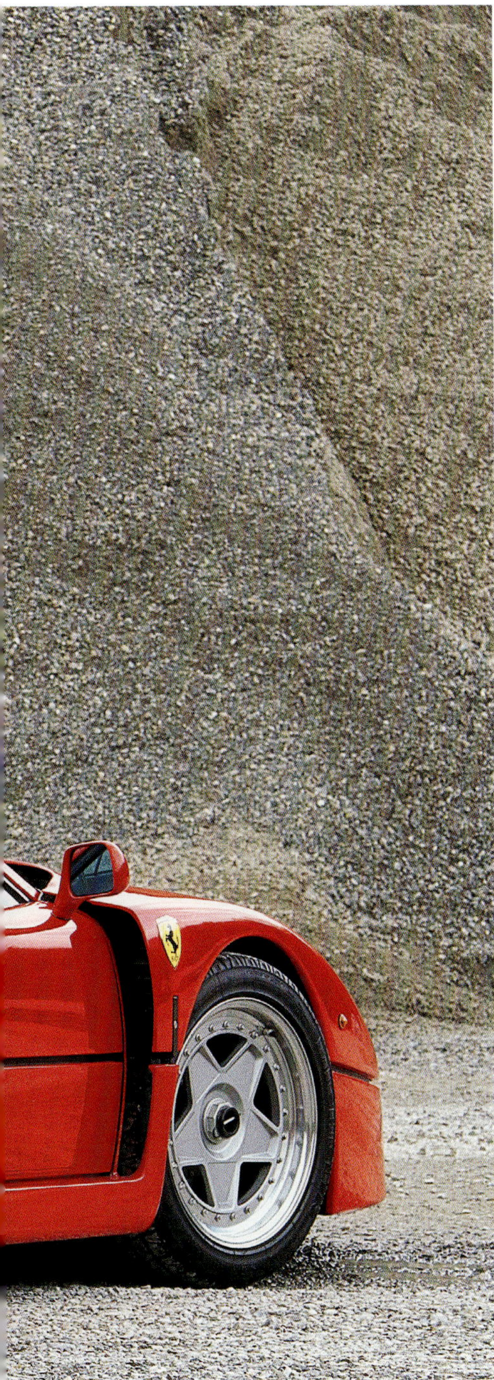

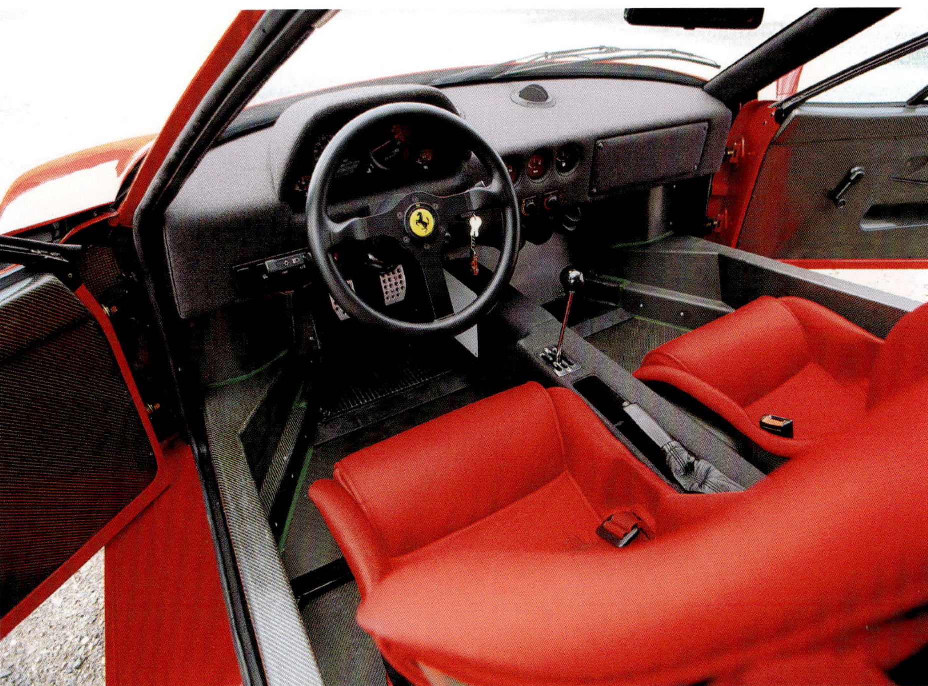

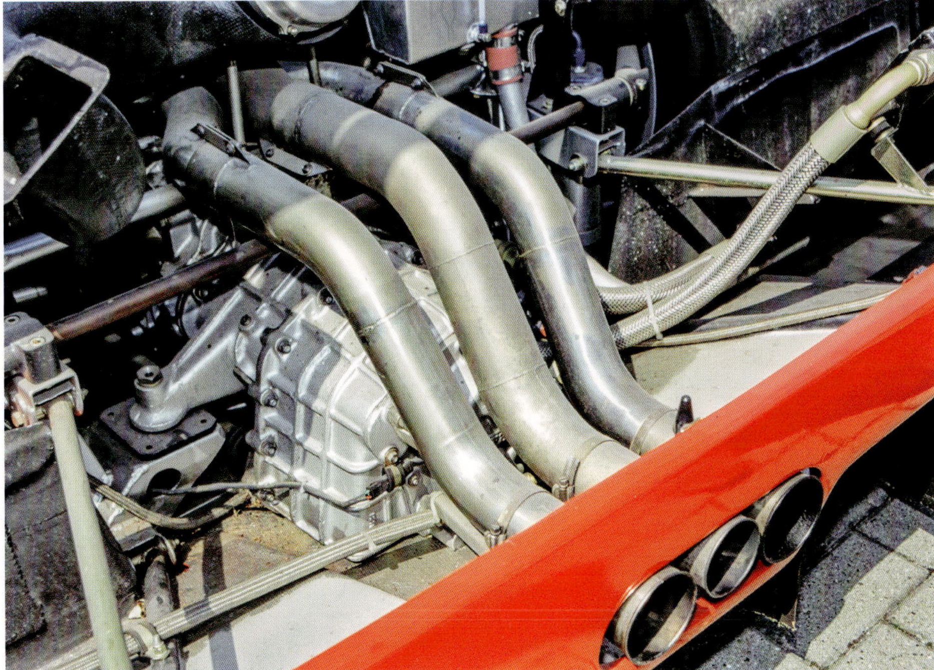

These pages and bottom ■ The F40's V8 engine displaced only 3.0 liters but was twin-turbocharged to pump out 471 horsepower and was visible through a window or by elevating the entire rear section of the car.

Top ■ The interior reflected racing cars—no radio, no carpet, and no door panels, though with some degree of air conditioning.

we can report that nothing we've ever driven can match the mix of sheer terror and raw excitement...

"You see, a Ferrari F40 isn't like other current exotic cars. In the last twenty years, the cars with the mile-high price tags and headache-inducing acceleration have gone through a remarkable metamorphosis: They've become thoroughly domesticated.

"Not so for the F40. It harks back to a time—the late 1950s and before—when makes like Ferrari, Maserati, Jaguar, and Porsche built sport and GT cars for the road that could be raced with a minimum of modifications. Some started life as high-strung racers and were barely tamed for the street...None of them were comfortable, tractable, or reliable. What they offered was unvarnished excitement—the raw, elemental race-car experience for the street. The F40 is like that."

Enzo Ferrari called the F40 his legacy, rooted in the GTO and racing at Le Mans.

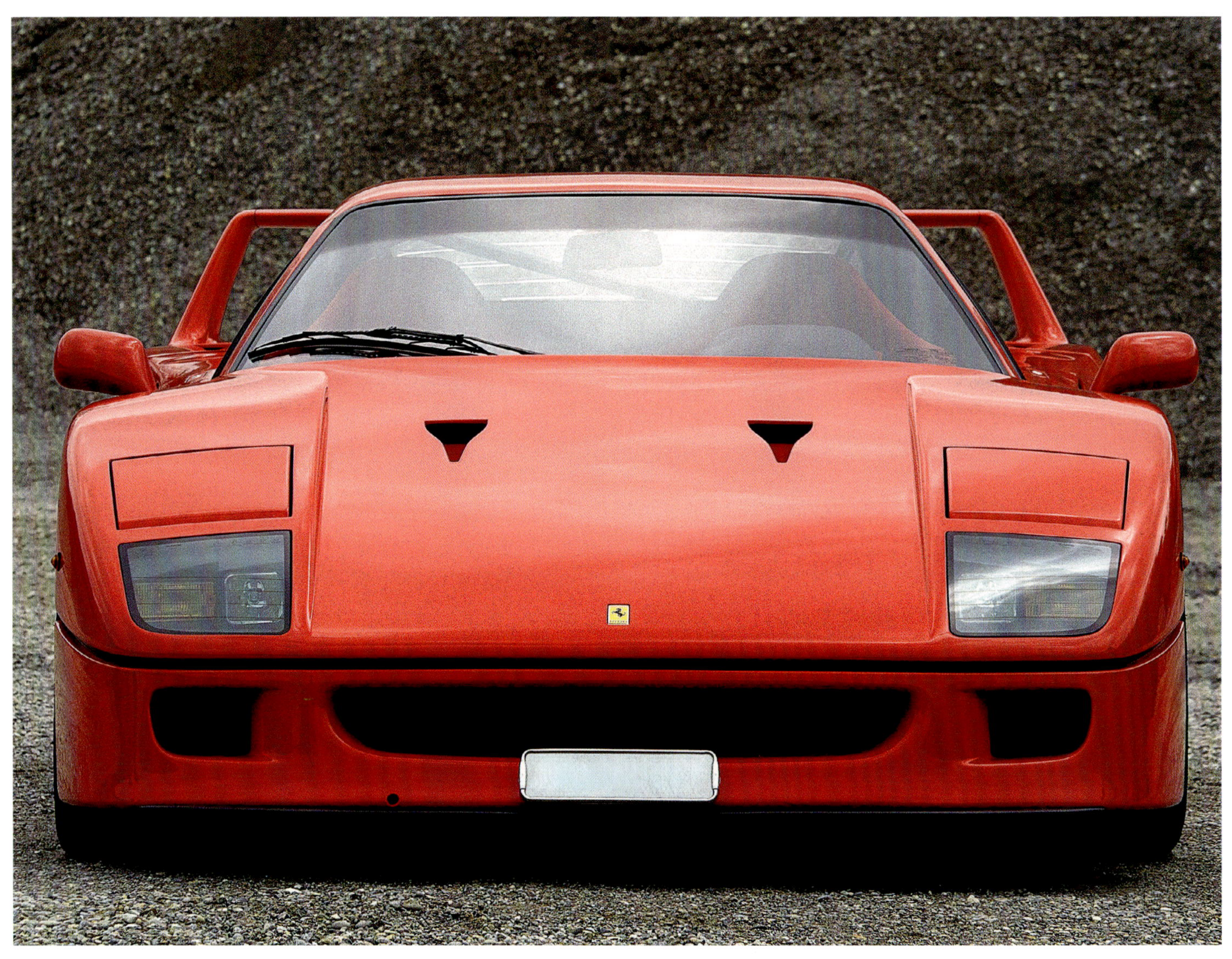

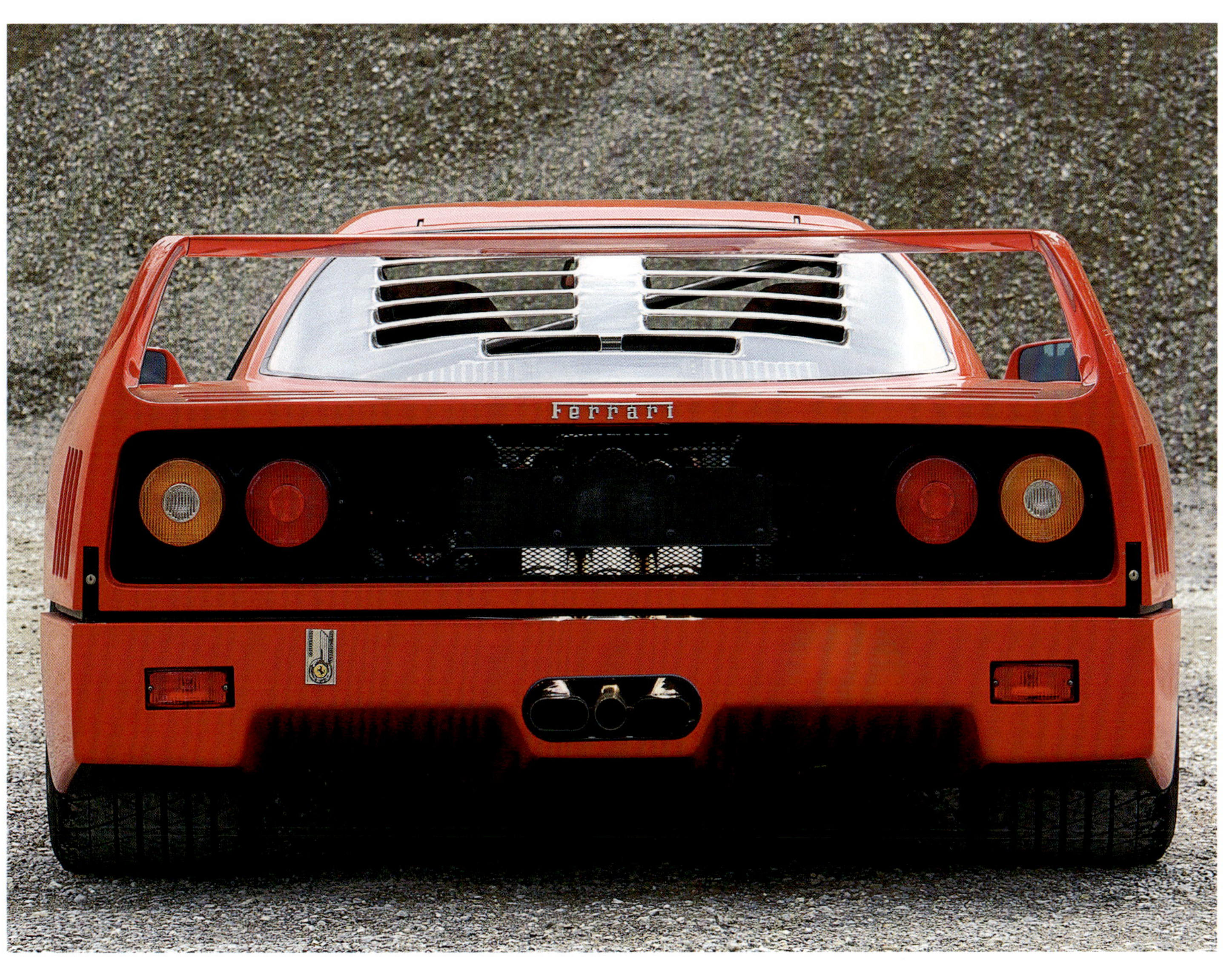

■ The F40 was a modern interpretation of the classic Ferrari, favoring analog and the emotion of human control over computerization.

CADILLAC ALLANTÉ

A car that quite literally created an air bridge between Italy and the United States

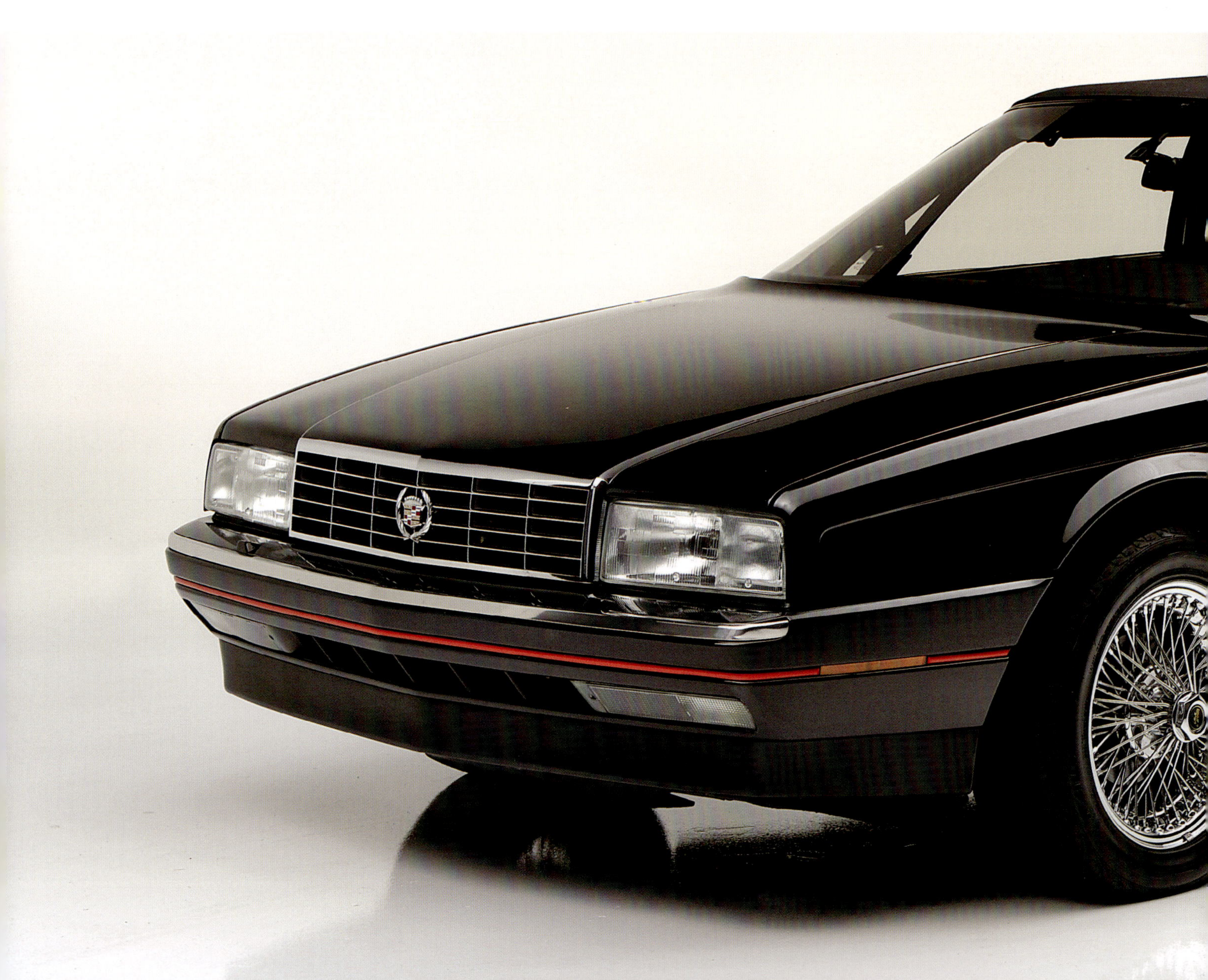

1980 ➤ 1989

Between downsizing for better fuel economy and increased competition in the luxury segment from import brands, Cadillac desperately needed a new star car. To get one, it set up perhaps the most unusual (and expensive) assembly process in automotive history.

Cadillac management came up with the idea of combining American engineering with European design and contracted Pininfarina of Italy as a partner in the project to create a new halo car, a luxurious two-seat roadster.

Under the agreement, the car was designed and bodies were built and painted by Pininfarina in Italy. Then they were loaded into specially outfitted 747 aircraft and flown to Michigan, where the chassis, engines, and interiors were installed. On the return flights to Italy, the aircraft carried the more than seventy-five Cadillac-supplied components needed for car body assembly.

Aircraft traveled on this nearly 7,000-mile "Air Bridge" three times a week, and for five years the car's chief engineer flew back and forth monthly between the US and Italy. The Allanté went on sale in the spring of 1987. It was priced at $54,700, nearly $20,000 more than Cadillac's top-of-the-line Fleetwood sedan.

Cadillac produced the Allanté into 1993, putting nearly 21,500 of them on the road. The original engine, which drove the front wheels, was a 4.1-liter V8 rated at 170 horsepower. In 1989 that engine was replaced with a larger V8 rated at 200 horsepower, and just a year before production ended, the car got Cadillac's new Northstar V8 with 290 horsepower.

Car and Driver magazine reported that the new engine "makes the Allanté finally worth taking seriously" just months before GM decided to end this trans-Atlantic experiment and the car's production.

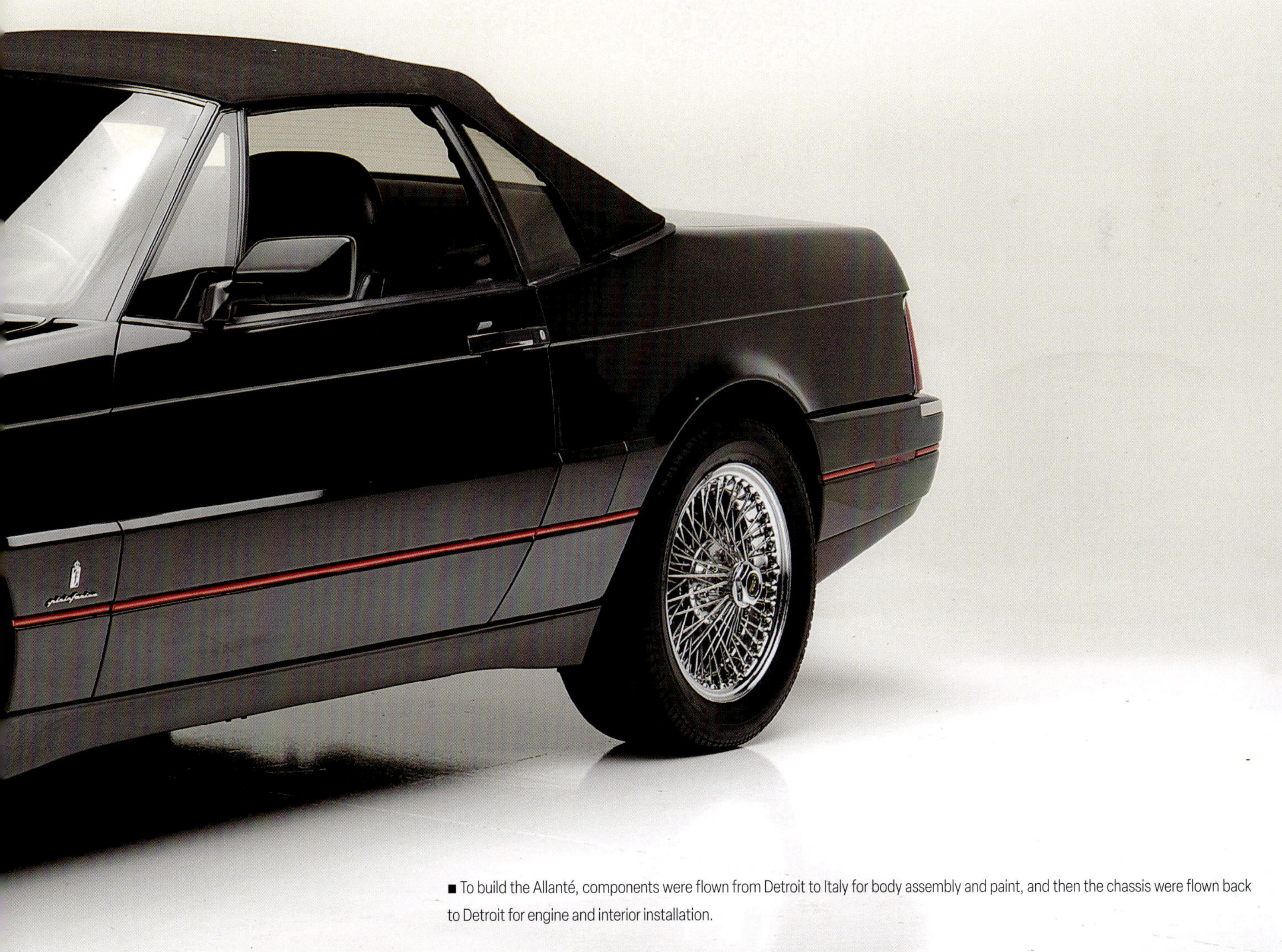

■ To build the Allanté, components were flown from Detroit to Italy for body assembly and paint, and then the chassis were flown back to Detroit for engine and interior installation.

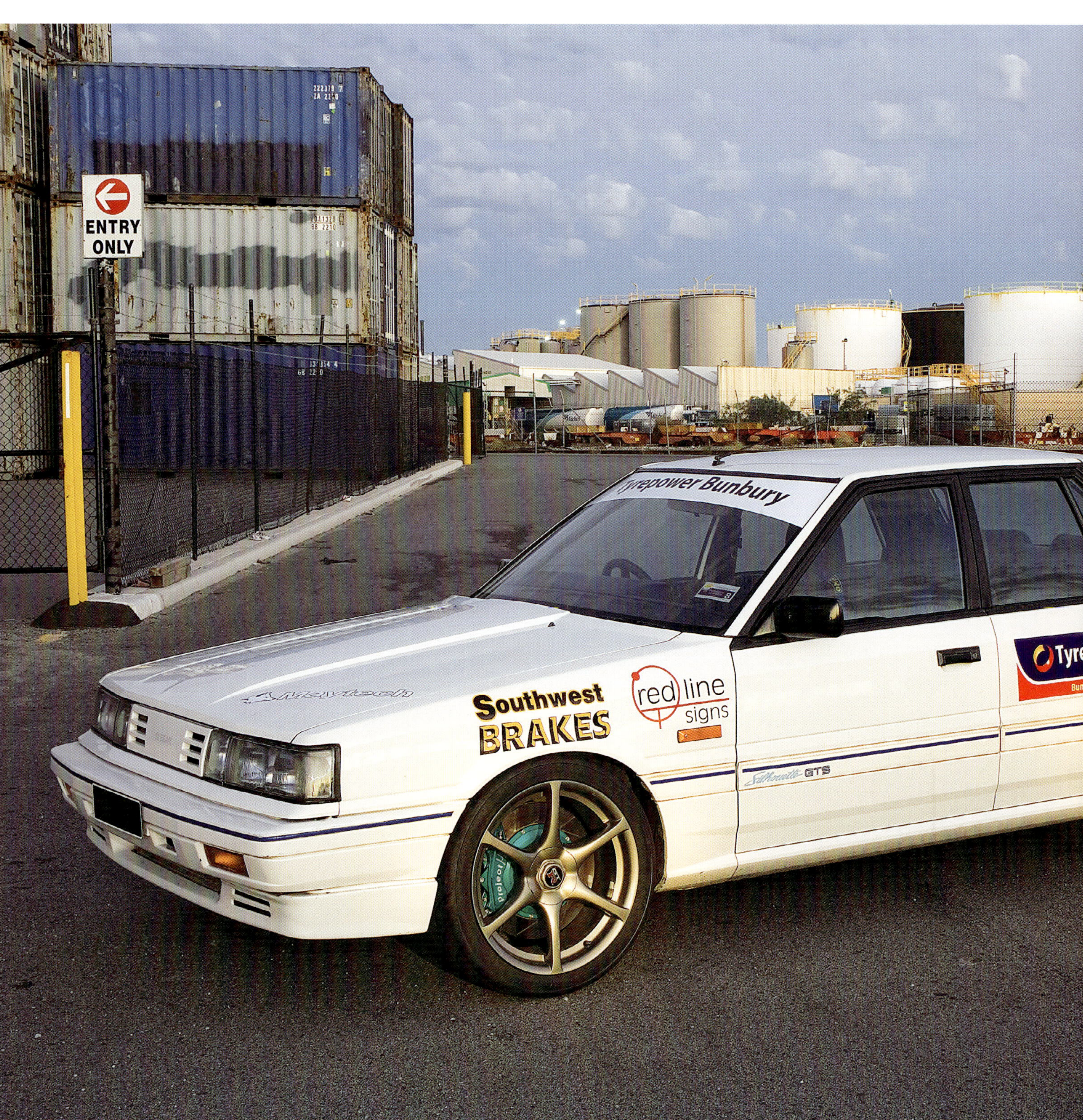
ENTRY
ONLY
Tyrepower Bunbury
Southwest
BRAKES
red line
signs
Silhouette GTS
Tyre

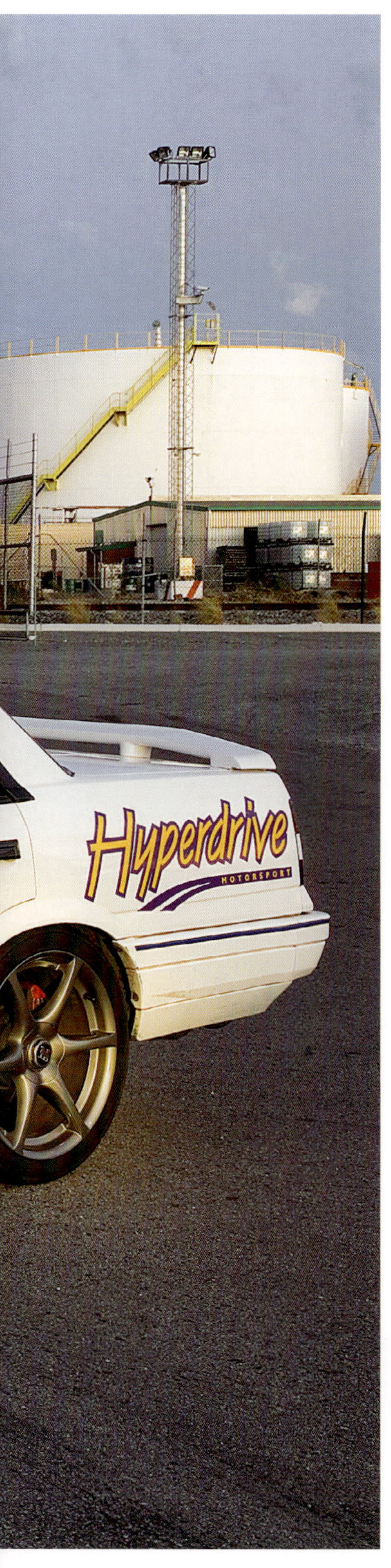

NISSAN SKYLINE GT-R

The muscle car for the millennial generation

Japan's Prince Motors introduced its Skyline model in 1956. Although a rather mundane sedan, the Skyline was the first Japanese car promoted in Europe, shown at the 1957 Paris Salon. When Prince became part of Nissan in 1967, the new owners kept the Skyline in production.

For three years beginning in 1969, Nissan offered a high-performance version called the Skyline GT-R (GT for Gran Turismo and R for Racing).

The nameplate then went on hiatus for sixteen years, until 1989 when a new Skyline GT-R launched. This version truly lived up to its initials. It immediately won the Japanese Touring Car Championship trophy four years in a row—never losing a race in the process—and added two titles in the Australian Touring Car Series for good measure.

Australia's *Wheels* automotive magazine nicknamed the GT-R "Godzilla" and praised it as "the best handling car we have ever driven."

Though not sold in the United States or Europe, the GT-R became extremely popular through its appearance in *Gran Turismo* and other video games and in *The Fast and the Furious* movie series. Its fame also spread along with drifting, a motorsports competition that showcases car control at speed while racing side by side around the track; the sport started in Japan but has since become popular with the millennial generation in other countries.

In 2016, Nissan celebrated the newest GT-R and the model's legacy by displaying an array of vintage GT-R versions at the New York Auto Show. *Car and Driver* magazine said the day "upstaged many of the new-car debuts of other manufacturers" showcasing their new vehicles at the event.

■ With initial sales restricted to its Japanese homeland, video games and movie roles spread word of the Godzilla car around the world.

MAZDA MX-5

Created in America and built in Japan, the rebirth and modernization of the British roadster

■ Mazda's Miata was so popular that automakers around the world responded with their own two-seat roadsters.

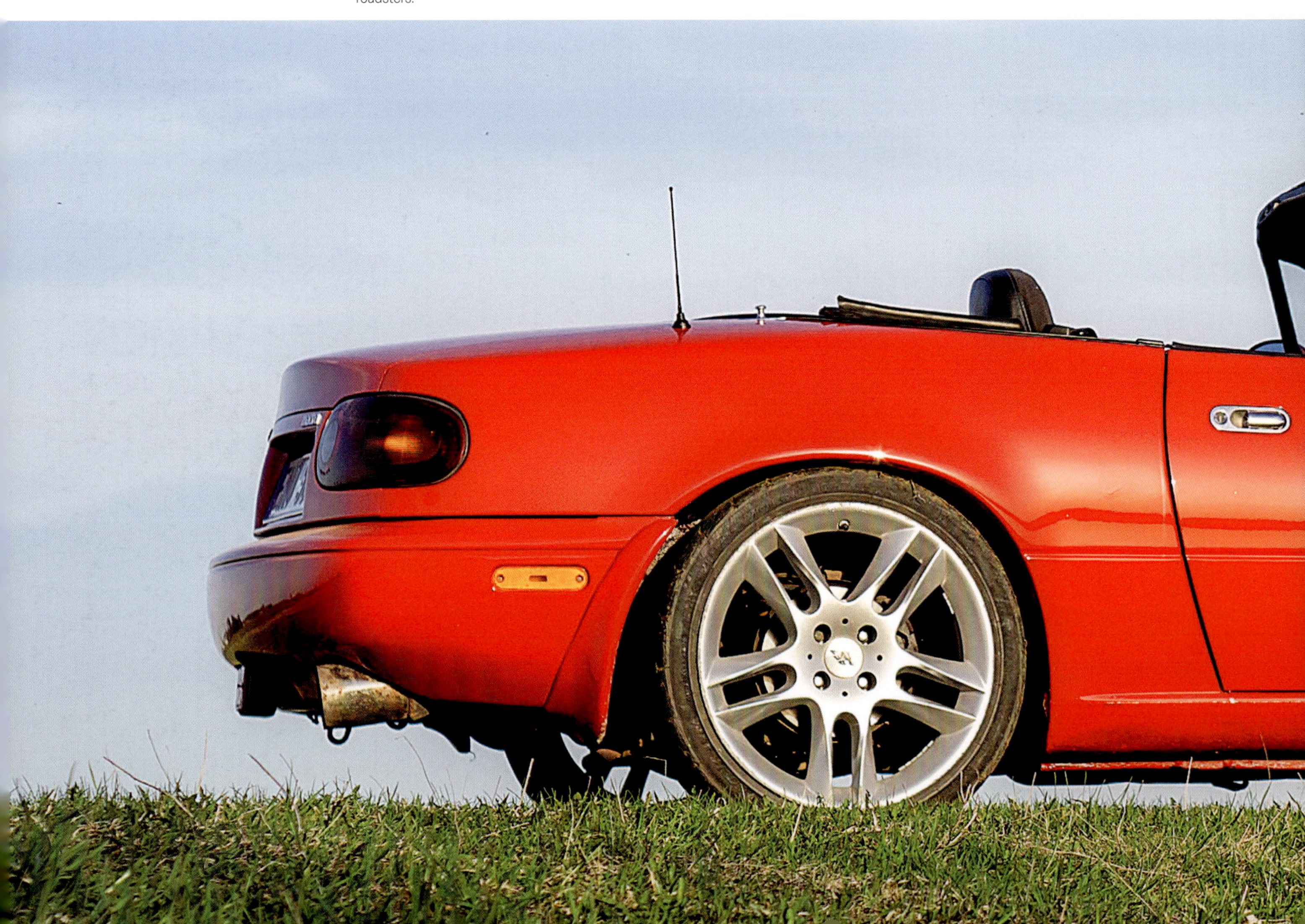

1980 ➤ 1989

American GIs brought many things back from their time in Europe during and immediately after World War II. Among those things were small, nimble, two-seat sports cars with canvas convertible tops. The most popular of them had been manufactured in England.

Fast forward to 1989 and the rebirth of the British roadster, except this one wasn't from England. It was from Japan, where it was known as the Eunos Roadster but had debuted at the 1989 Chicago Auto Show as the Mazda MX-5 and with a badge that proclaimed it the Miata, the Old High German word that translated to "reward."

Indeed, the MX-5 would prove to be a reward for those who owned one, not only for those who had suffered the leaks and other foibles of those earlier British roadsters and now had the updated version with contemporary technology and build quality, as well as for a new generation of drivers who were experiencing the joy of a top-down sports car for the first time.

That experience proved so popular that other automakers eagerly joined the party, including Porsche (Boxster), BMW (Z3), Honda (S2000), Mercedes-Benz (SLK), Saturn (Sky), Pontiac (Solstice), and Audi (TT).

Though a Japanese car, the Miata's roots were in the United States. In the early 1980s, Miata launched the LWS (Lightweight Sports Cars) study and assigned two teams in Japan and one at its US office in California. But the actual idea hadn't come from within Mazda but instead from American automotive journalist Bob Hall, who had been a foreign exchange student in Japan and had enjoyed riding in his father's British sports cars as a youngster. He suggested to Mazda that it was time for someone to resurrect the genre.

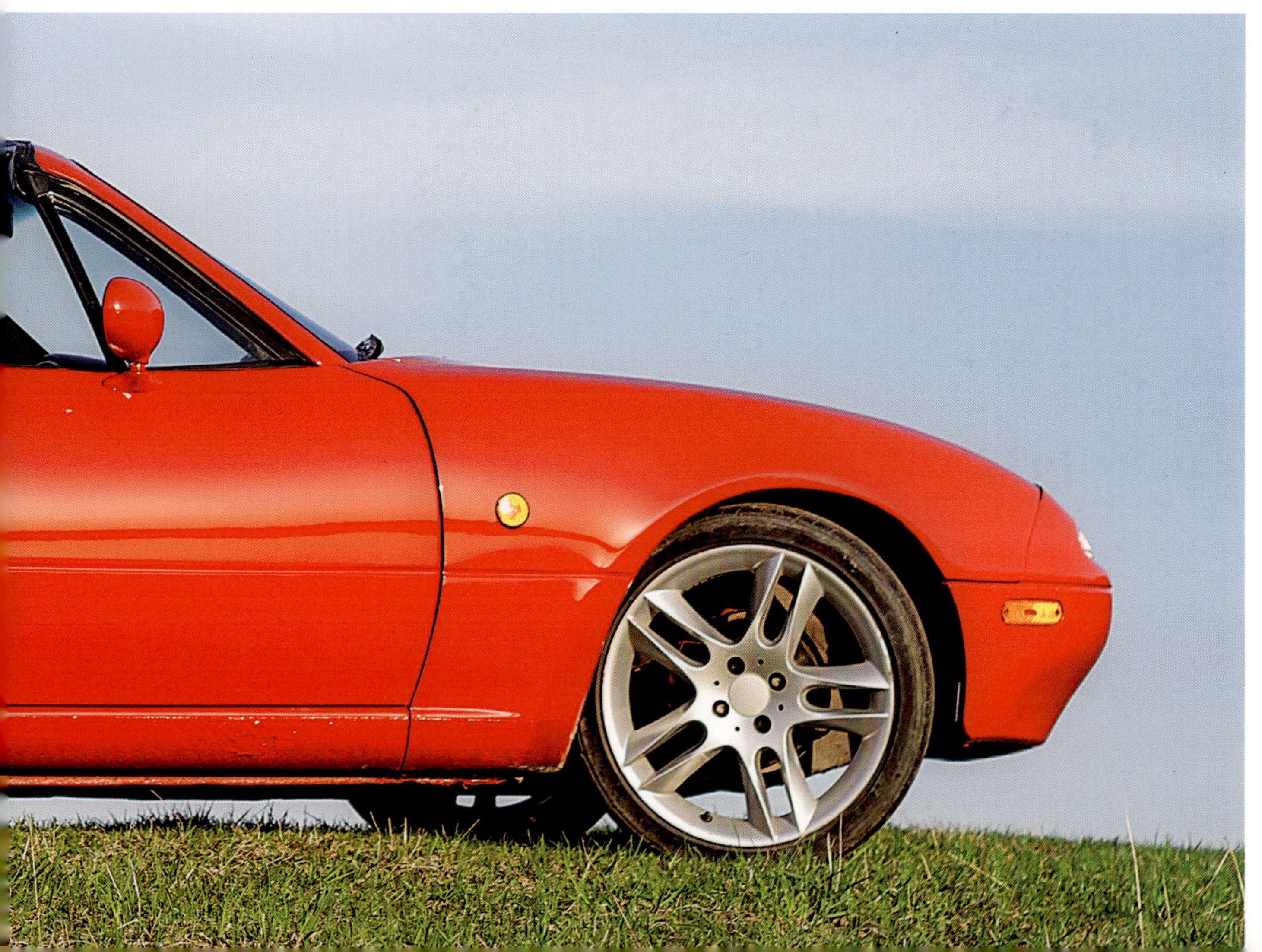

1980 ➤ 1989

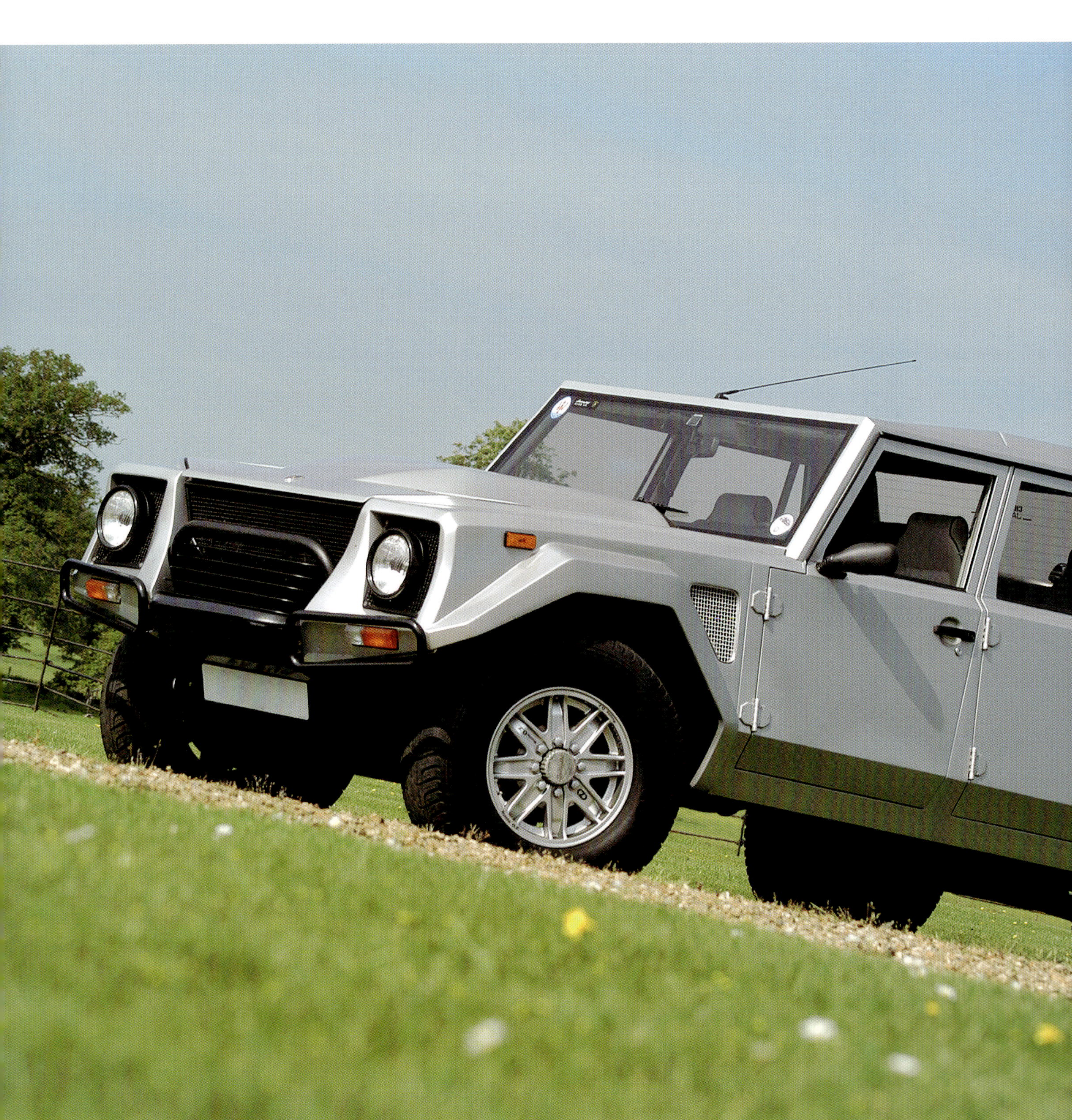

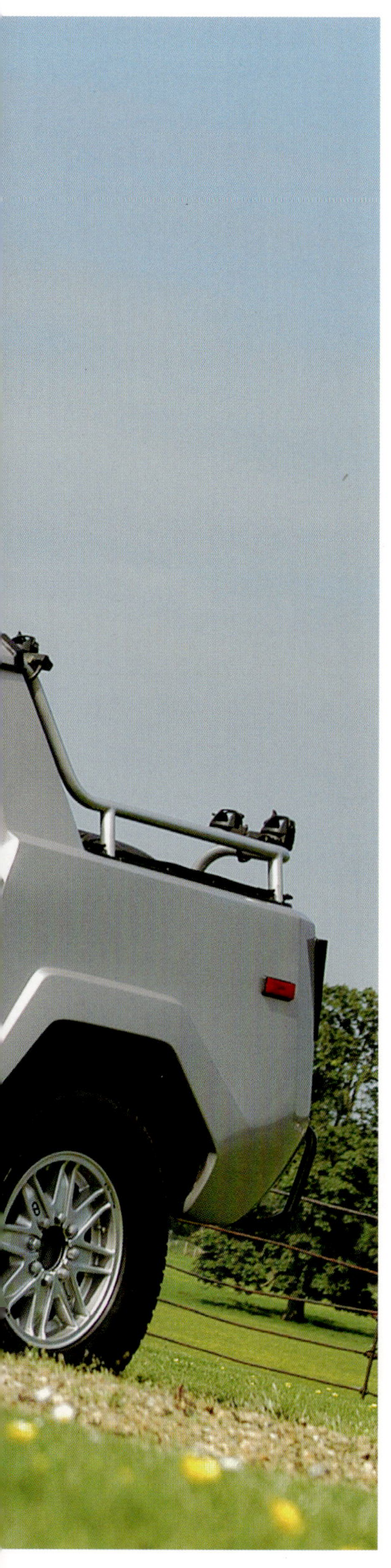

LAMBORGHINI LM002

"Heart of a Countach, capability of a Humvee, more exotic than either"

What, you may wonder, is a sport utility vehicle doing punctuating this book filled with exotic sports cars and high-performance sedans? Yes, we know that SUVs and their "crossover" cousins are everywhere on the roads and trails these days, but can any of them really be considered a new classic?

Well, if any of them might, it is the Lamborghini LM002, a vehicle perhaps better known as the "Rambo Lambo," a nickname inspired by the *Rambo* movie series that starred actor Sylvester Stallone as a misunderstood American special forces veteran of the Vietnam War battling corruption and cartels.

By the way, Stallone bought an LM002 (some referred to the exotic SUV as the La Moo Too), as did the likes of Tina Turner, Malcolm Forbes, Keke Rosberg, and even Muammar Gaddafi, among other celebrities. Former American football star turned television host Michael Strahan has owned three of the exotic Lamborghini SUVs, one of which was displayed at the 2024 New York Auto Show.

Like Rambo the movie character, the LM002 also had military history. Back in 1977, the US Army was looking for a contemporary replacement for its venerable World War II–era "jeep," that word short of what was a general purpose all-terrain troop transporter.

US-based Mobile Technology International was among those responding, turning to Lamborghini, the Italian sports car maker (but with a history of producing farm tractors) for the assembly of what was called the Cheetah, an off-roader powered by a mid-mounted Chrysler V8 engine.

The Army's contract eventually went to AM General and its Humvee. Lamborghini kept at it, doing another prototype, the LM001, now with a rear-mounted AMC V8. Neither mid- nor rear-engine placement work well in off-pavement environments, so at the

■ The "Rambo Lambo" began as a proposal for a replacement for the venerable military Jeep.

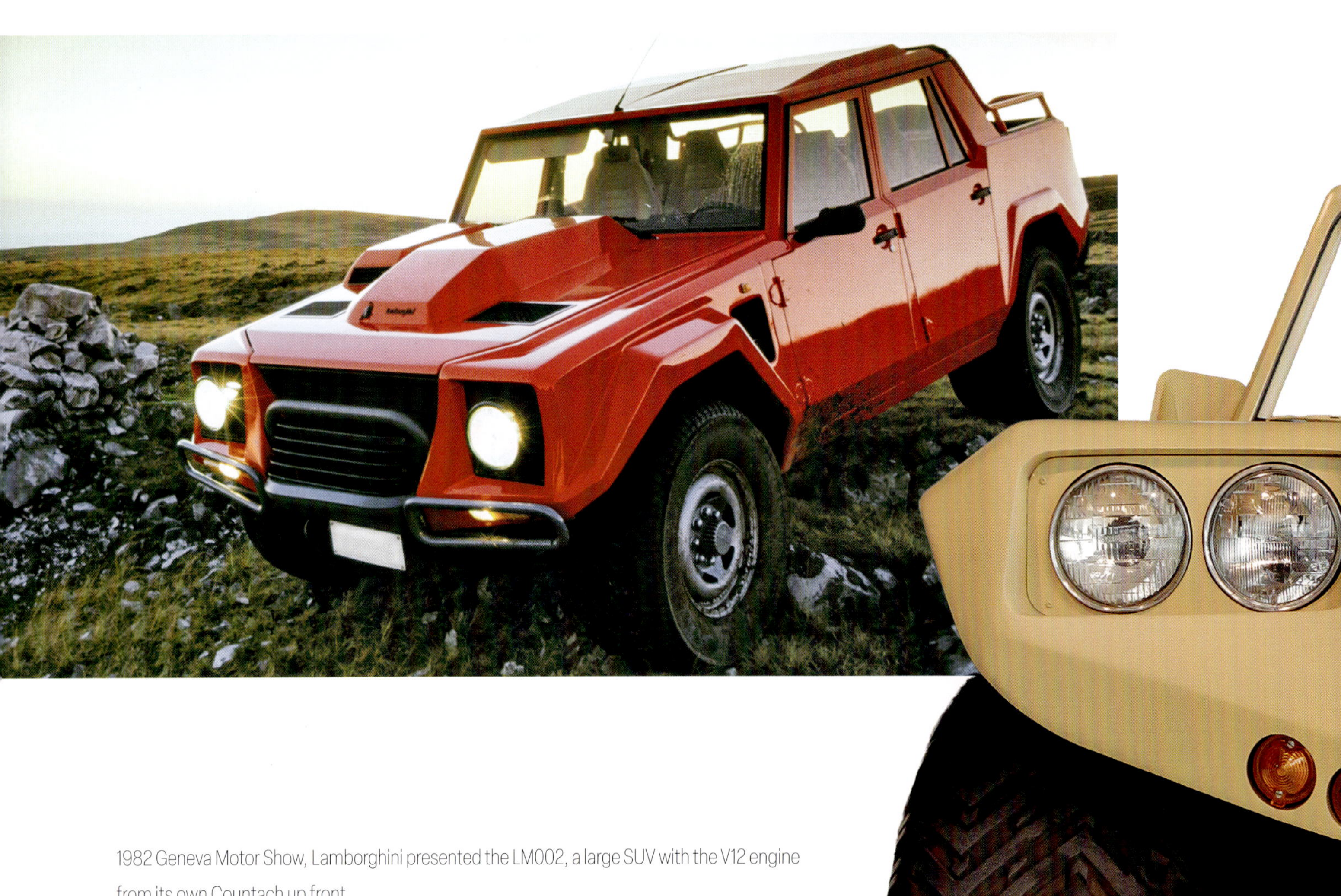

1982 Geneva Motor Show, Lamborghini presented the LM002, a large SUV with the V12 engine from its own Countach up front.

While no military orders followed, Lamborghini went back to work, redoing the LM002 as a civilian machine shown at the Brussels Auto Show in 1986. Only 301 were produced over the course of seven years, but wow, did they have an impact.

As forbes.com reported, "In the LM002 the company had created a wild PR machine. It had the heart of a Countach, the capability of a Humvee, and was arguably more exotic than either."

The Countach engine could supply as much as 700 horsepower and special Pirelli Scorpion tires could be inflated or deflated onboard—and reportedly could survive running over concrete Jersey barriers at 60 mph (96 km/h). All the while, you and your passengers were enjoying the air conditioning and encased in a luxurious leather-lined compartment.

In 1987, *Car and Driver* magazine proclaimed, "Let us introduce you to a vehicle that is to chi-chi off-road boutique items what the LA Raiders (a professional American football team known for the outrageousness of its fans) are to the Joffrey Ballet. Meet the *Mad Max* machine. Meet the closest thing to a street-legal Tiger tank known to man. Meet the Lamborghini LM002.

"Never before in recent memory have we driven a vehicle that has turned as many heads, blown as many minds, freaked as many citizens, or been as much insane, outrageous fun as the Rambo Lambo."

■ Rare (only 301 produced) and aggressive on the outside but luxurious inside, the LM002 appealed to Hollywood entertainers, sports stars, and even a dictator or two.

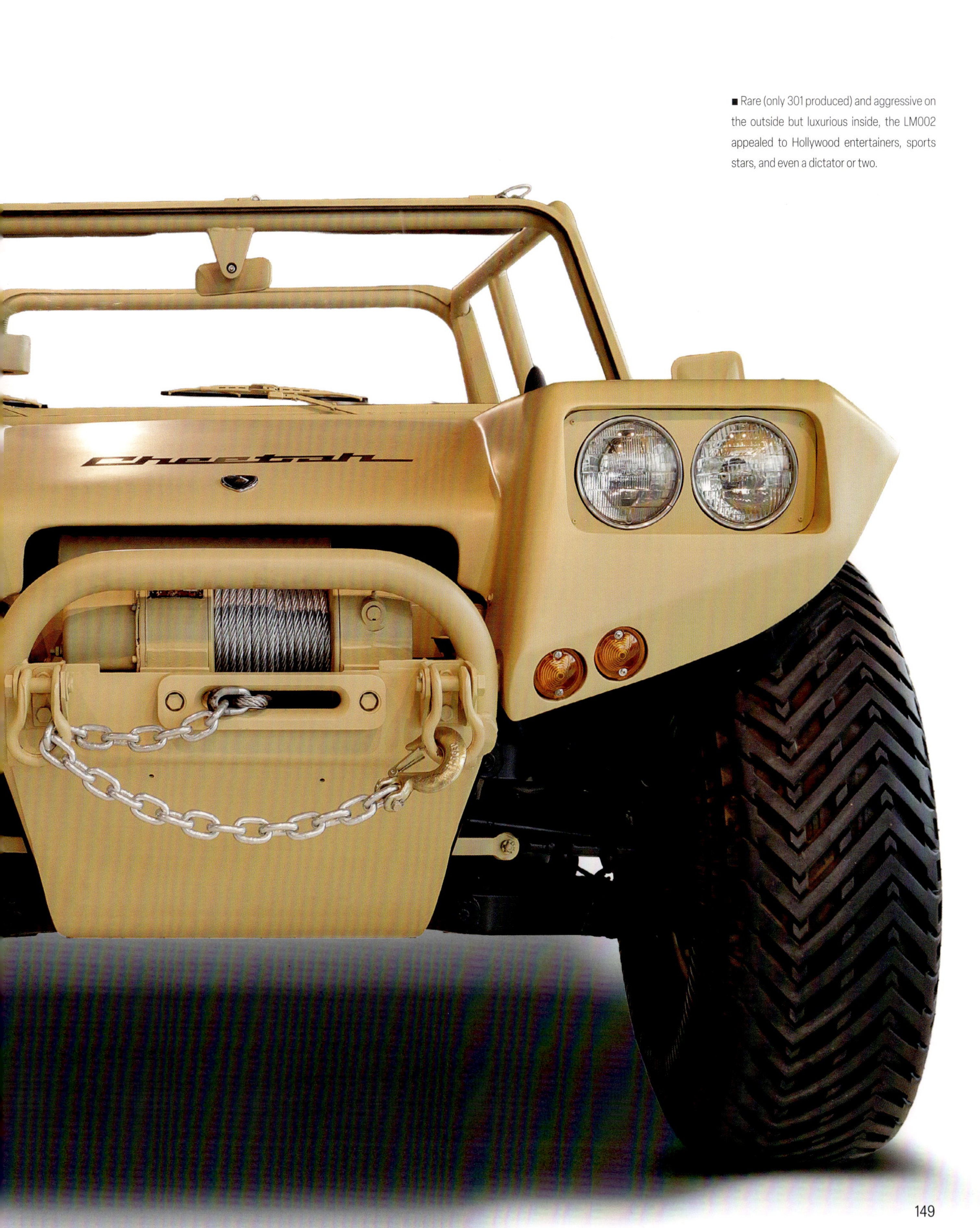

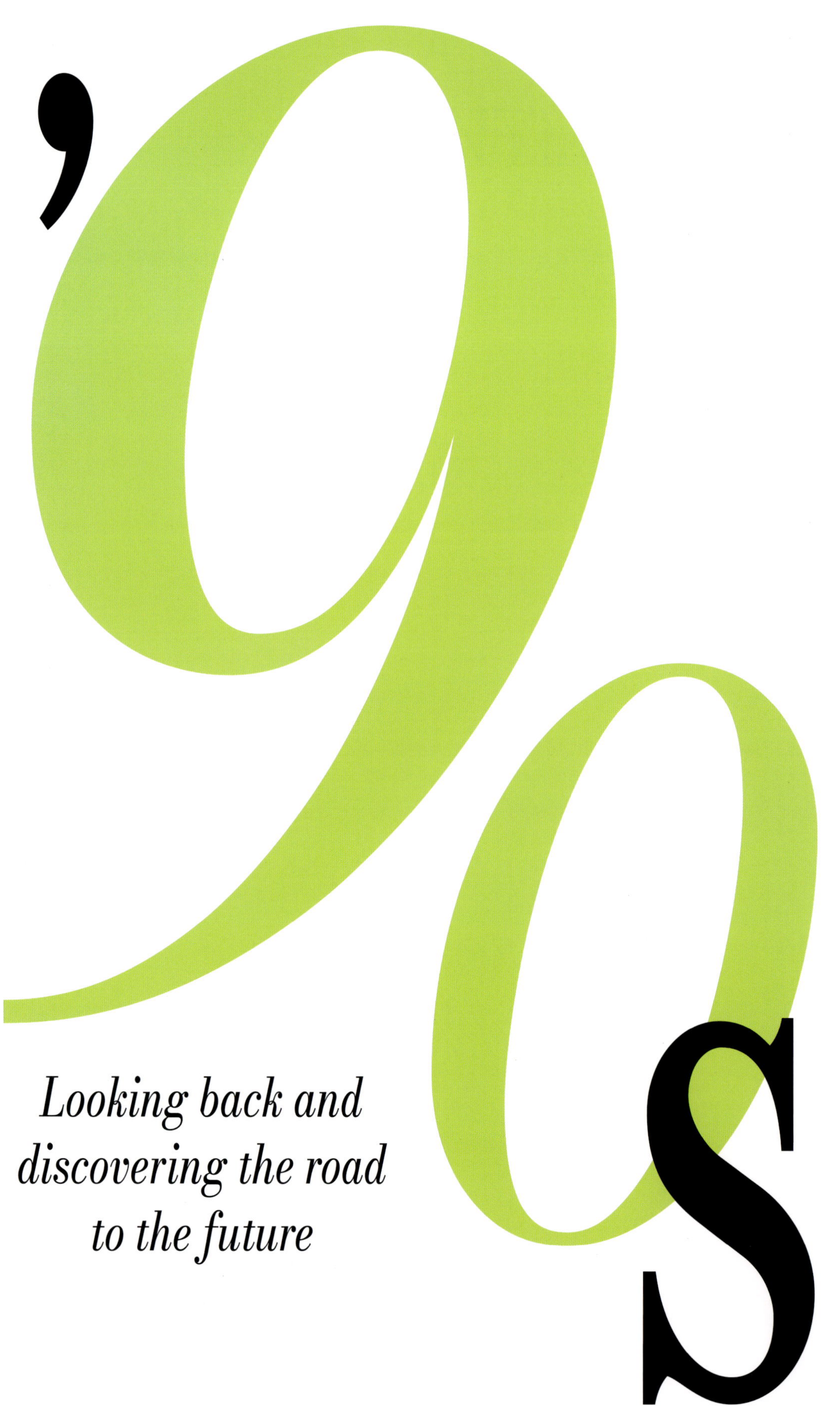

Looking back and discovering the road to the future

The 1990s was a decade of tumult and technology. It began with the Gulf War as Iraq invaded Kuwait and ended with the uncertainty and turmoil of Y2K.

In between, Germany reunified, the Soviet Union dissolved, ethnic hatred rekindled in Yugoslavia, Rwanda, and elsewhere, and yet anti-apartheid activist Nelson Mandela was released from a South African prison and was elected the country's president.

The Human Genome Project launched. Dolly the sheep was cloned. The Chunnel, an undersea railroad link, opened between France and England. Globalization became a theme for corporations, which also created information technology departments and became concerned about their carbon footprints.

We got cable television, the internet, the World Wide Web (and so many websites), and personal computers. We watched a movie about the *Titanic* and an animated film about toys. Our musical tastes diversified as we listened to everything from grunge to gangsta rap, from electronic dance music to county and western, and even to The Wiggles.

Wikipedia devoted an entire section of its review of the decade to automobiles, noting loss of market share at General Motors, financial troubles at Chrysler, cars in general tending to be increasingly similar in design, the popularity of the sport utility vehicle, and that "Japanese cars continued to be highly successful during the decade," including new luxury brands such as Lexus and Infiniti.

As noted in the introduction to our previous chapter, historian and professor Penny Sparke reported in her book *A Century of Car Design* that '80s financial issues "did not reach the motor car in that decade; however, when it did, in the 1990s, the results were dramatic."

She continued, "Japan was responsible for reenergizing the arena of car design in the 1990s. Its manufacturers and designers achieved this in two ways: first by introducing the idea of the 'retro' car, which, by looking back at the heroic period of the automobile, succeeded in reviving its contemporary culture; and secondly, by realizing that the market for cars was fragmented—as was the lifestyle to which they had to conform—and that the days of undifferentiated cars were over."

She pointed out that the Japanese automakers created new typologies, producing cars that would have enhanced appeal to women and younger customers, and that automakers in the United States and Europe followed suit.

"The recognition that the car was no longer an icon of modernity but rather a lifestyle accessory gave designers a new sense of freedom, and they were swift to rise to the challenge."

At the same time, engineers were figuring out that the electronic software needed to meet government requirements to reduce emissions and improve fuel economy could also be used in these more efficient engines to generate even more power without increasing the toll on the environment.

In the ensuing chapter, you'll find cars ranging from sporty two-seaters to comfortable four-door sedans to exotic supercars that do not look like identical jelly beans but were capable of providing driving thrills with minimal emissions and enhanced safety features. They indeed were among the New Classics.

1990 ➤ 1999

HONDA/ACURA NSX

An exotic yet practical (and affordable) sports car from Japan

Soichiro Honda was a teenager working in a Japanese automotive repair garage when his boss suggested that Honda build a race car, which he did—quite successfully until the mid-1930s, when he was involved in an on-track mishap that seriously damaged his left eye.

A year later Honda started manufacturing piston rings for cars and aircraft. His factory was destroyed during World War II, but he acquired 500 small military-surplus generator engines that he used to motorize bicycles. That led to the production of complete motorcycles.

To promote his products and motivate his employees, Honda entered his machines in important racing events, taking the title in the prestigious Isle of Man TT in 1959 and wining the 125cc and 250cc World Championships in 1961.

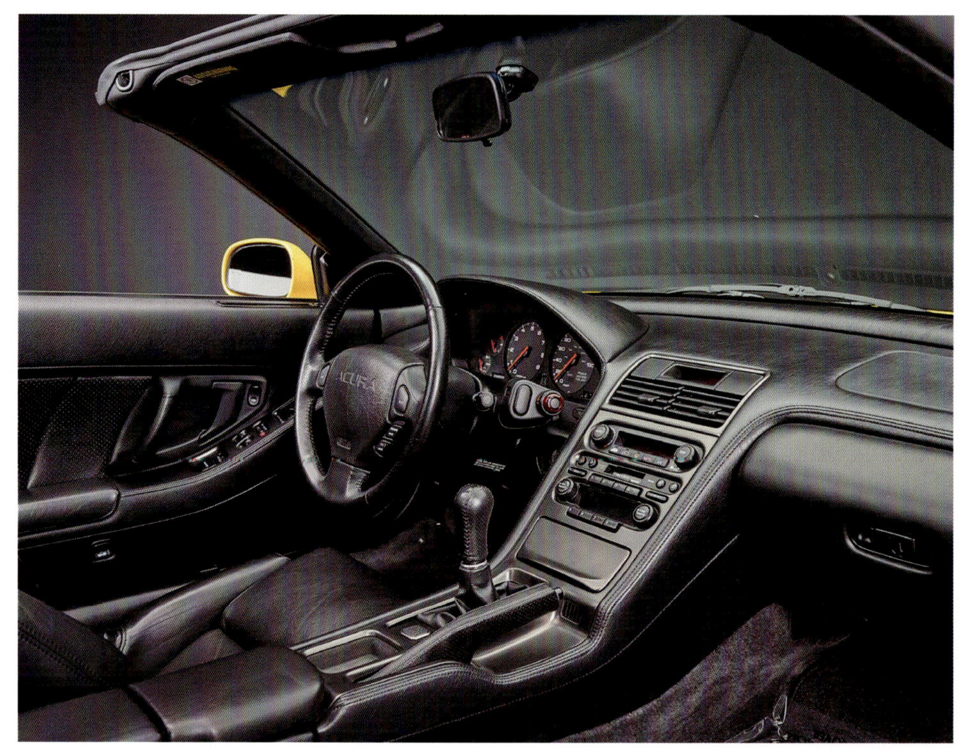

■ Automotive magazine road testers praised the NSX not only for its dynamic performance but for its everyday practicality: a comfortable interior and the rationality of its V6 engine.

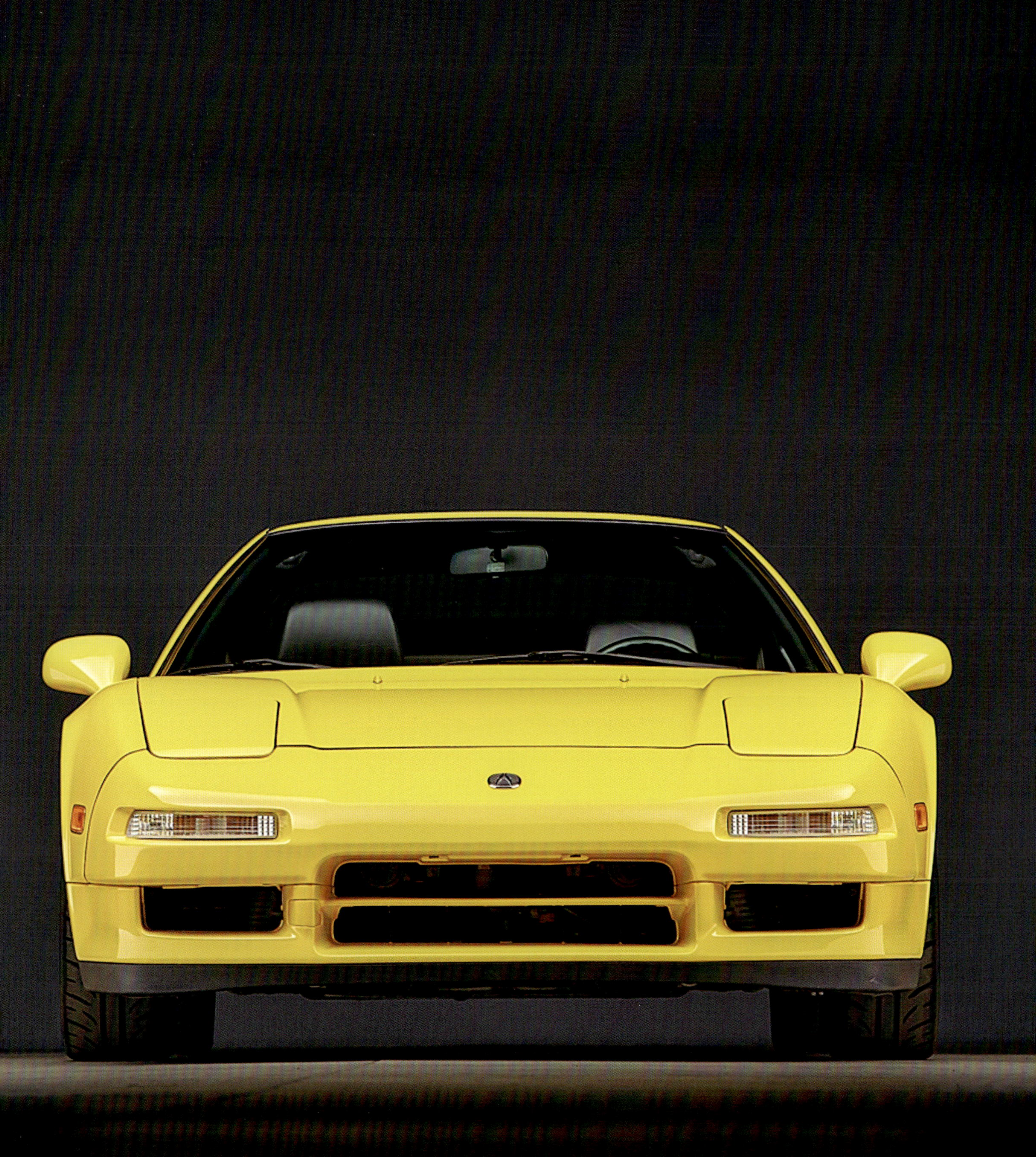

By 1962 Honda was the world's largest motorcycle manufacturer and started producing automobiles.

It entered Formula One auto racing in 1964 and achieved its first victory the following year, its RA272 racer winning in Mexico. It withdrew after the 1968 season but returned in 1983 as an engine supplier powering Nelson Piquet, Ayrton Senna, and Alain Prost to a sweep of the drivers' championships from 1987 to 1991.

To compete with the likes of Ferrari not only on the track but on the road, Honda teamed up with Italian design house Pininfarina to present at the Turin Auto Show the HP-X (Honda Pininfarina eXperimental), a wedge-shaped, mid-engine sports car concept powered by a 2.0-liter Honda V6 engine.

After an in-house redesign, insertion of a 3.0-liter Honda V6, and development input from Formula One racing champion Senna, the HP-X would evolve into the NSX (New Sportscar eXperimental), which was unveiled at the Chicago Auto Show in 1989 and launched into the automotive marketplace in 1990, selling in some markets with a Honda badge and in others by Honda's luxury division, Acura.

"We *C/D* testers are unanimous," *Car and Driver* magazine proclaimed in its 1994 review. "The NSX is our top choice for pure driving pleasure. Yet despite our enjoyment of its moves and our admiration for the all-aluminum construction that puts it on the good side of the F=ma equation, the NSX remains widely misunderstood, neither coveted nor respected in fair proportion to the joy it delivers."

Why not? Because other exotic sports cars post higher numbers on the test track but, the magazine continued, "track numbers say nothing about usable performance. Exotics are notoriously tricky to drive, and street-usable

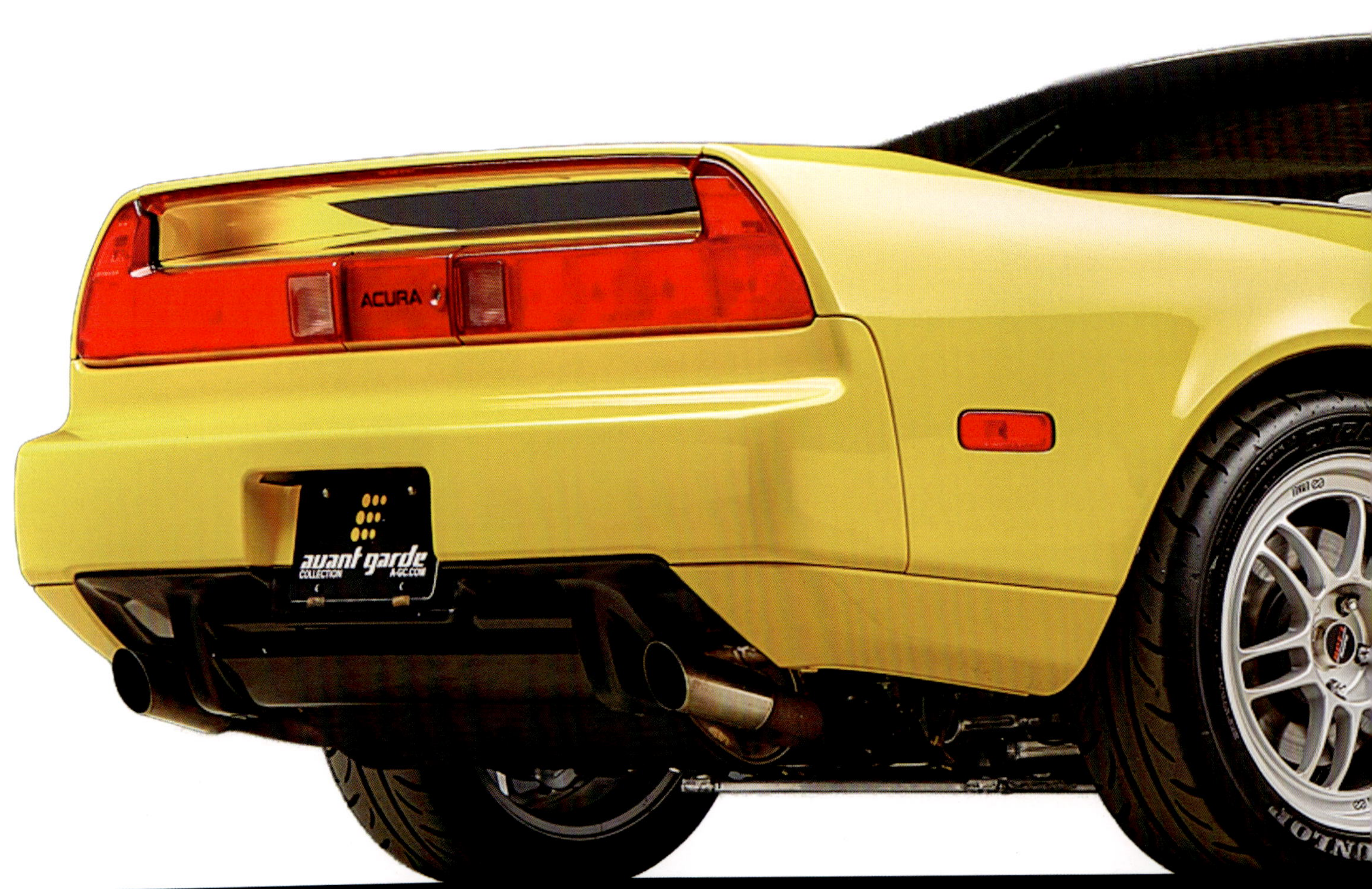

■ The final design was done in-house at Honda but was inspired by an earlier concept "show" car by Pininfarina.

performance is typically well below the track numbers. Except for the NSX. This machine is so honest and predictable in its responses that most of its track performance is also use-ful performance. Out in the world, the NSX's no-sweat capabilities top the charts.

"Imagine a mid-engined sportster with every ergonomic detail as correct as in an Accord (Honda's standard family sedan). It's simply never been done before. The NSX starts from that level. Then it excels."

The magazine then referred to the NSX as the F-16 (military jet fighter) for the road rather than for the sky and added, "The NSX is the most precise and attuned mid-engined machine we've ever driven."

The original NSX was in production into 2005. Two years later Honda announced plans for the ASCC (Advanced Sports Car Concept) with a V10 engine, but changed its mind, and at the 2012 North American International Auto Show in Detroit unveiled a new NSX concept, this one to be a gas/electric hybrid and built at Honda's assembly plant in Ohio, USA.

Formula 1 racing champion Ayrton Senna did much of the test driving during the NSX development process.

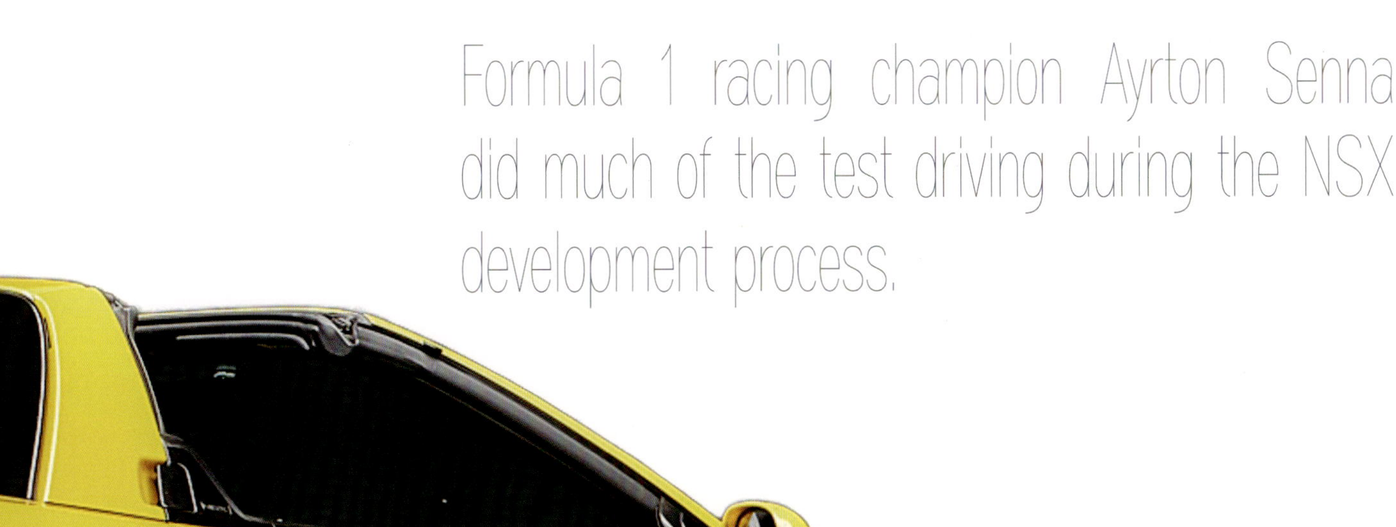

1990 ➤ 1999

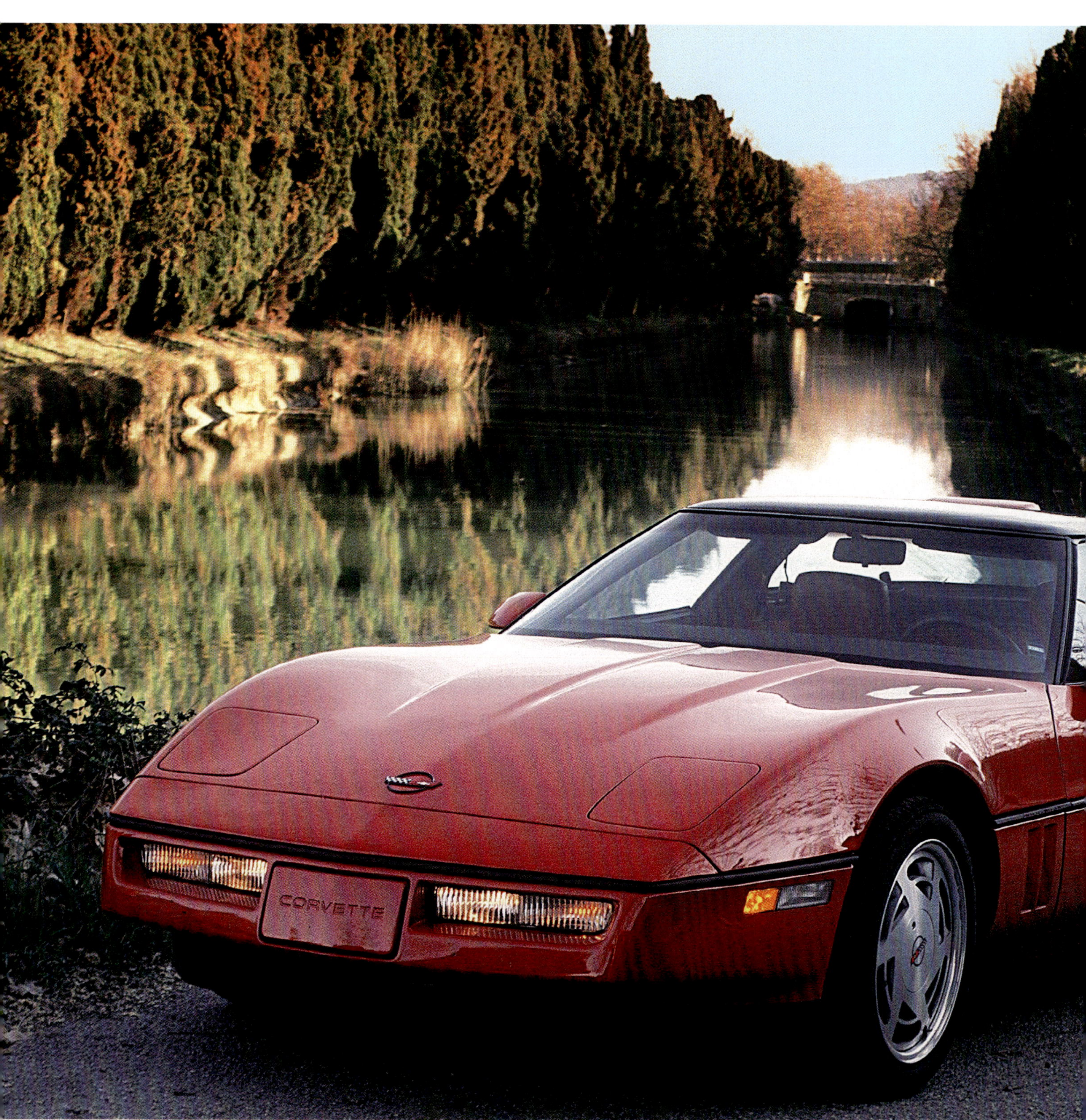

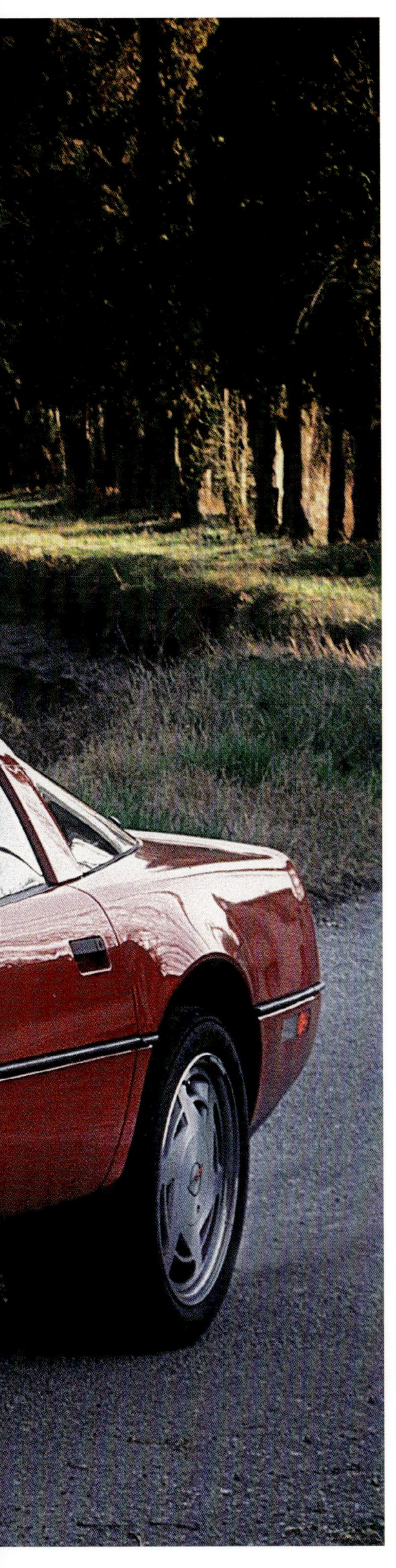

CHEVROLET CORVETTE ZR1

With outrageous horsepower and torque, this one claimed the title of King of the Hill

"The ZR1 makes the statement that we can do things today that no one even dreamed could be done ten or twenty years ago," Dave McLellan, chief engineer for the Chevrolet Corvette, told *Car and Driver* magazine in the summer of 1989. "We've achieved a spectacular level of performance and are still able to meet or exceed all government standards for fuel economy, safety, noise, emissions, and so on."

Starting in the late 1960s, concern over automotive emissions, fuel economy, and safety (or lack thereof) had led national governments to set new parameters, within which the products of auto producing companies had to operate, and require onboard computer controls to verify whether the various mandates were being met.

It took some time, but engineers eventually found ways to make cars more efficient and use software to enhance performance while still operating well within the emission and fuel economy restrictions.

One case in point was the introduction for the 1990 model year of the Chevrolet Corvette ZR1, the so-called King of the Hill.

As *Car and Driver* explained, "The new ZR1 can provide the best driver in the world with all the slam-bam power that he could ask for, yet its personality and demeanor are such that drivers who are less than world-class—a group that, by our observation, includes a great many owners of high-performance cars—are remarkably well protected from themselves."

To showcase its engineering capabilities, General Motors set out to produce what would be the world's fastest production car, the new King of the Hill. It had launched the fourth-generation of its Corvette sports car in 1983, and three years later

■ The ZR1 was more than just another version of the C4 Corvette—it was a true transformation.

it had acquired British automotive specialist Lotus. The 5.7-liter V8 in the standard C4 Corvette was rated at 245 horsepower, but the trans-Atlantic effort, which included powerboat engine producer Mercury Marine, created the LT5, a 5.7-liter V8 that pumped out 370 horsepower and more than 500 Nm of torque.

The ZR1 underwent several modifications from the standard C4 to control such power, including adjustable suspension and wider tires. Chevrolet put the ZR1 through a series of speed tests that resulted in a variety of FIA-certified records, including a 24-hour run covering 4,221 miles at an average of more than 175 mph (283 km/h).

For the 1993 model year, the LT5 was updated to 405 horsepower and 522 Nm.

As reported by American automotive magazine *Motor Trend*, "General Motors bet big on electronics

■ With help from Lotus and Mercury Marine, Chevrolet engineers found ways to generate horsepower efficiently and cleanly.

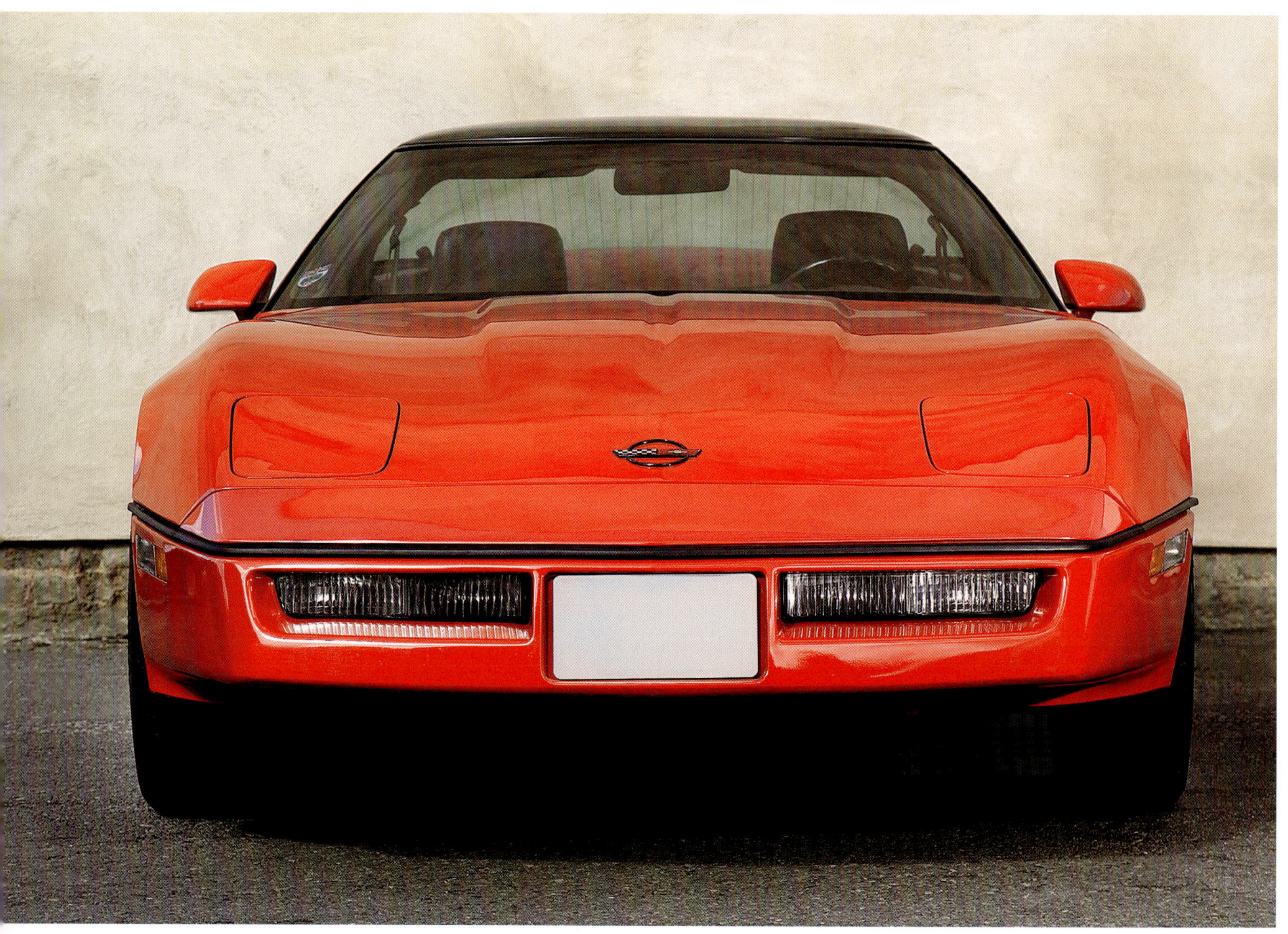

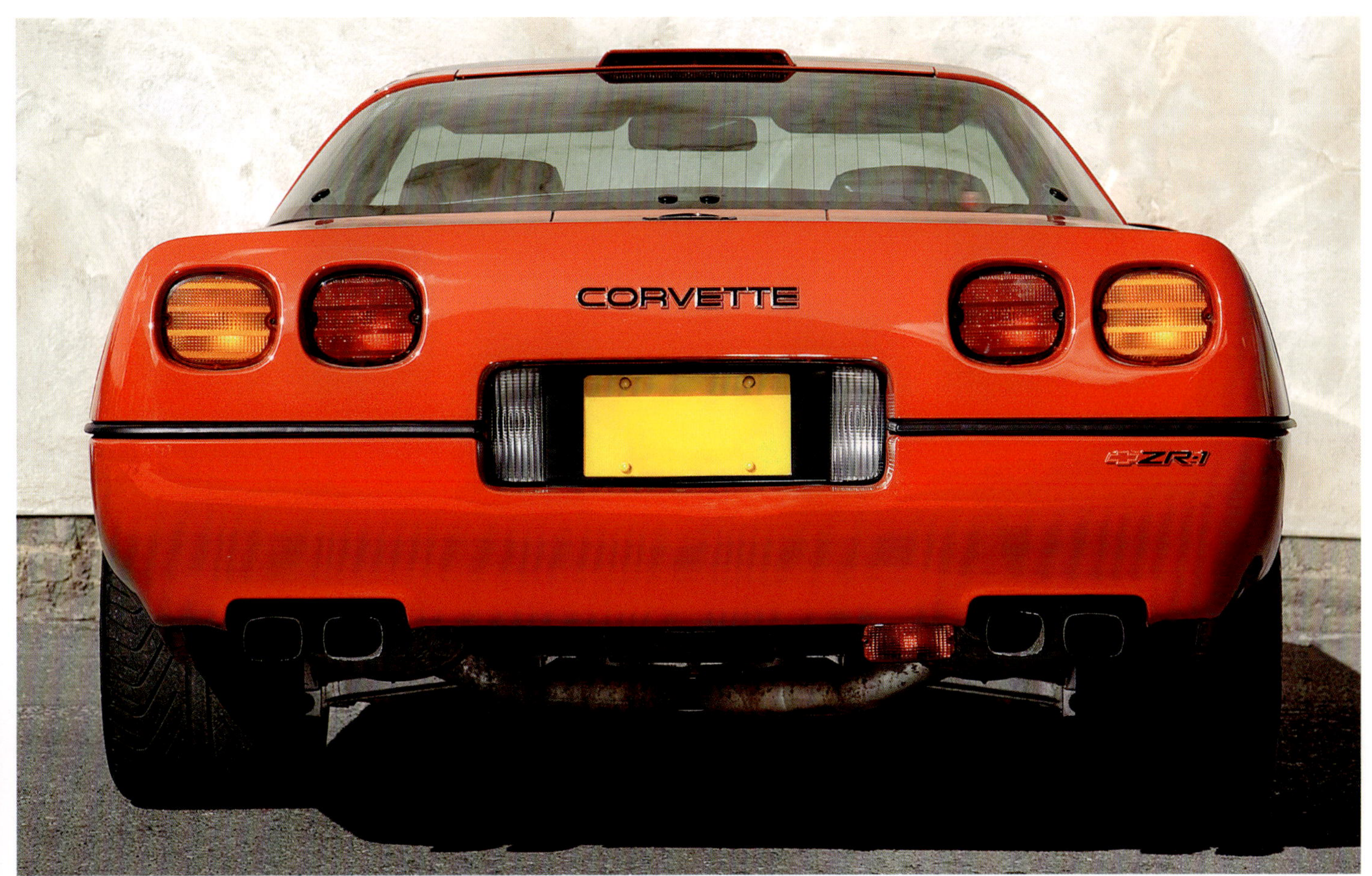

The ZR1 transformed America's sports car into a world-beating triumph of engineering for the first time.

and advanced technology in the 1980s as it looked to put the energy crisis, performance-choking emissions regulations, and Japanese brands in its rearview mirror."

"Chevrolet Corvette engineers received an assignment as ambitious as it was simple: Build the world's best-performing production car. They delivered the 1990 Chevrolet Corvette ZR1, a monstrously powerful and furiously quick car that kept pace with exotic supercars costing tens of thousands of dollars more...The ZR1 transformed America's sports car into a world-beating triumph of engineering for the first time."

Even Britain's *Top Gear* recalled the time "when the C4 ZR1 had a V8 that was arguably better than a Ferrari V12."

ZR1 (or ZR-1 depending on which generation) has been signified the highest performance of what is known as "America's sports car." The first ZR1 was an engine package on the C3 Corvette in the early 1970s. The most recent is the ZR1 version of the C8 and mid-engined 2025 Corvette.

MERCEDES-BENZ 500E

The badge said Mercedes, but the driving dynamics were delivered by Porsche

The author's recollection is that in the fall of 1990, Mercedes-Benz's annual technology showcase for visiting automotive journalists included a side trip to a round of the DTM, the German Touring Car championships, so *Autoweek* magazine assigned its motorsports editor (the author) to the trip.

One afternoon during the multi-day event, we were presented with the array of cars Mercedes would introduce during the following year, and I was pulled aside by the company's public relations specialist for the United States. He told me that he had made arrangements for me to drive the sedan positioned at the far end of the line and on the next-to-last rotation.

He instructed that there would be a place on the route where a flagman would signal to exit the autobahn and return to the parking area. He said to ignore the flagman and to keep going, but to try to return the vehicle as the last driving rotation was ending.

I'll never forget the look on that flagman's face when I blew past him at probably 130 mph (209 km/h).

Oh, there was one other thing he told me, well, actually what he couldn't tell me: He couldn't tell me anything about this sedan, at least not yet, but that my experience with it would be important for our magazine's car-enthusiast subscribers.

As it turned out, the car was the prototype for the 1991 Mercedes-Benz 500E, the ultra-performance version of its executive-class W124 sedan and a joint venture with German sports car specialist Porsche. (The car would be badged E500 from 1993 to 1995.)

This being a prototype of the future production car, it was equipped with a manual rather than automatic transmission, as well as a suspension system that lowered the car the faster it was traveling. And with

■ Mercedes engineers were busy developing the next S Class sedans, so Porsche was recruited to create a highest-performance version of the E Class.

1990 ➤ 1999

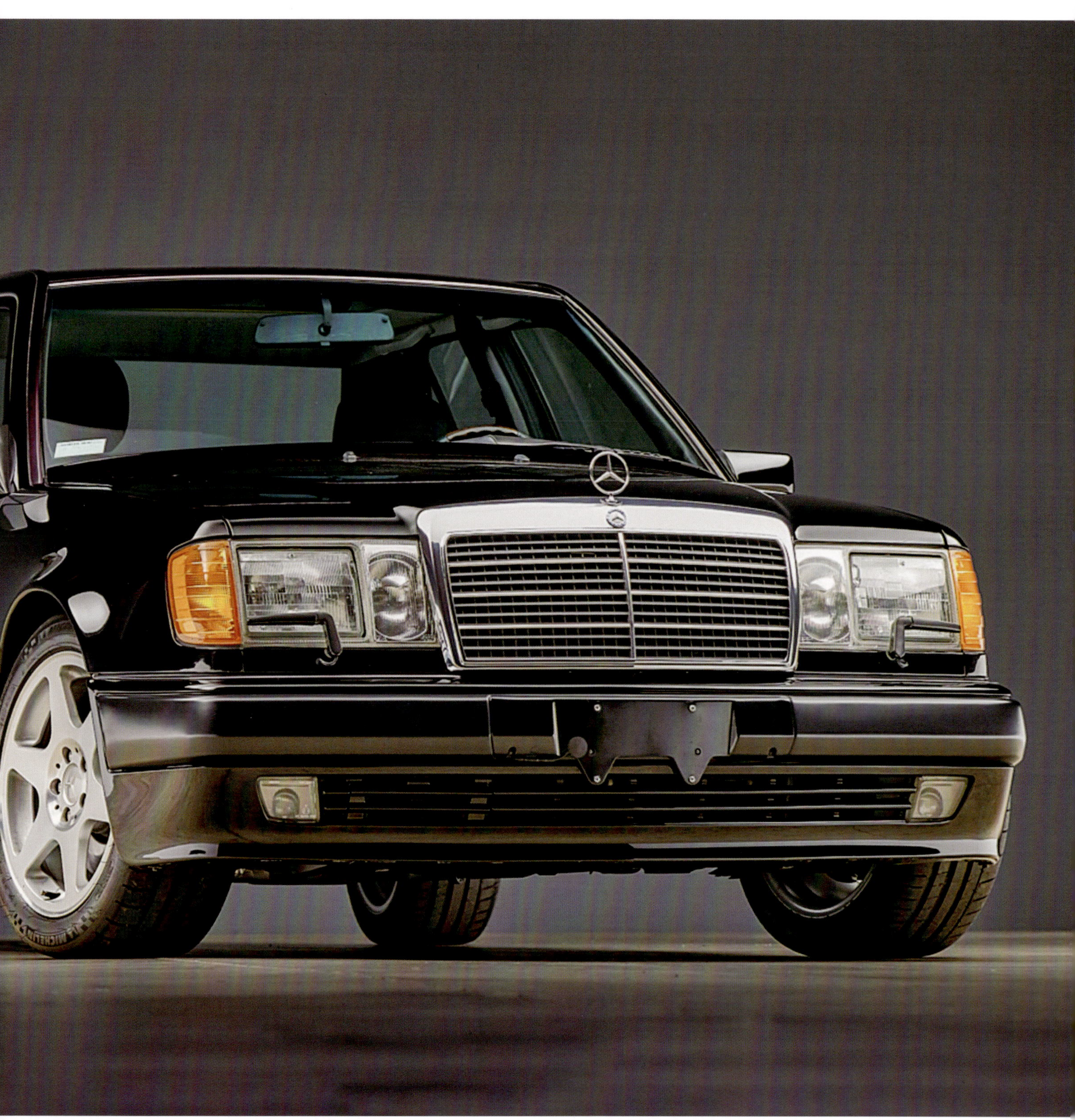

a 5.0-liter V8 engine pumping out more than 300 horsepower and nearly 500 Nm of torque, this sedan could travel in excess of 150 mph (250 km/h).

Not only did Porsche engineer the 500E, in many ways re-engineering the W124 E Class sedan to accommodate a larger engine and rear axle, wider wheels, larger brakes, etc., but it also built them on one of its own assembly lines.

So while at first glance the 500E looked like a regular Mercedes E-Class sedan, it performed like a Porsche sports car.

As one of our veteran car-testing editors put it in our official test drive article, "The 500E is anything but a tail-out, slash-and-burn boy racer. It is smoothness, stability, and flexibility defined. You probably will not look fast driving it...[But] it is fast, also easy and secure...The 500E is one of a kind. If not the best car in the world, it may be the best compromise of utility, comfort, safety, and thrilling performance."

Car and Driver praised how the 500E "devours twisty roads like a car half its size." And while "it's as composed and refined as any other Benz...it's damned good at going slow...The 500E...reveals its supercar status when you ask it to flex its muscles."

More than a quarter of a century later, Mercedes-Benz describes the 500E as "one of the most highly sought-after young classic cars."

For its part, Porsche's website recalls that the 500E combined "the comfort of a touring saloon with the performance of a sports car."

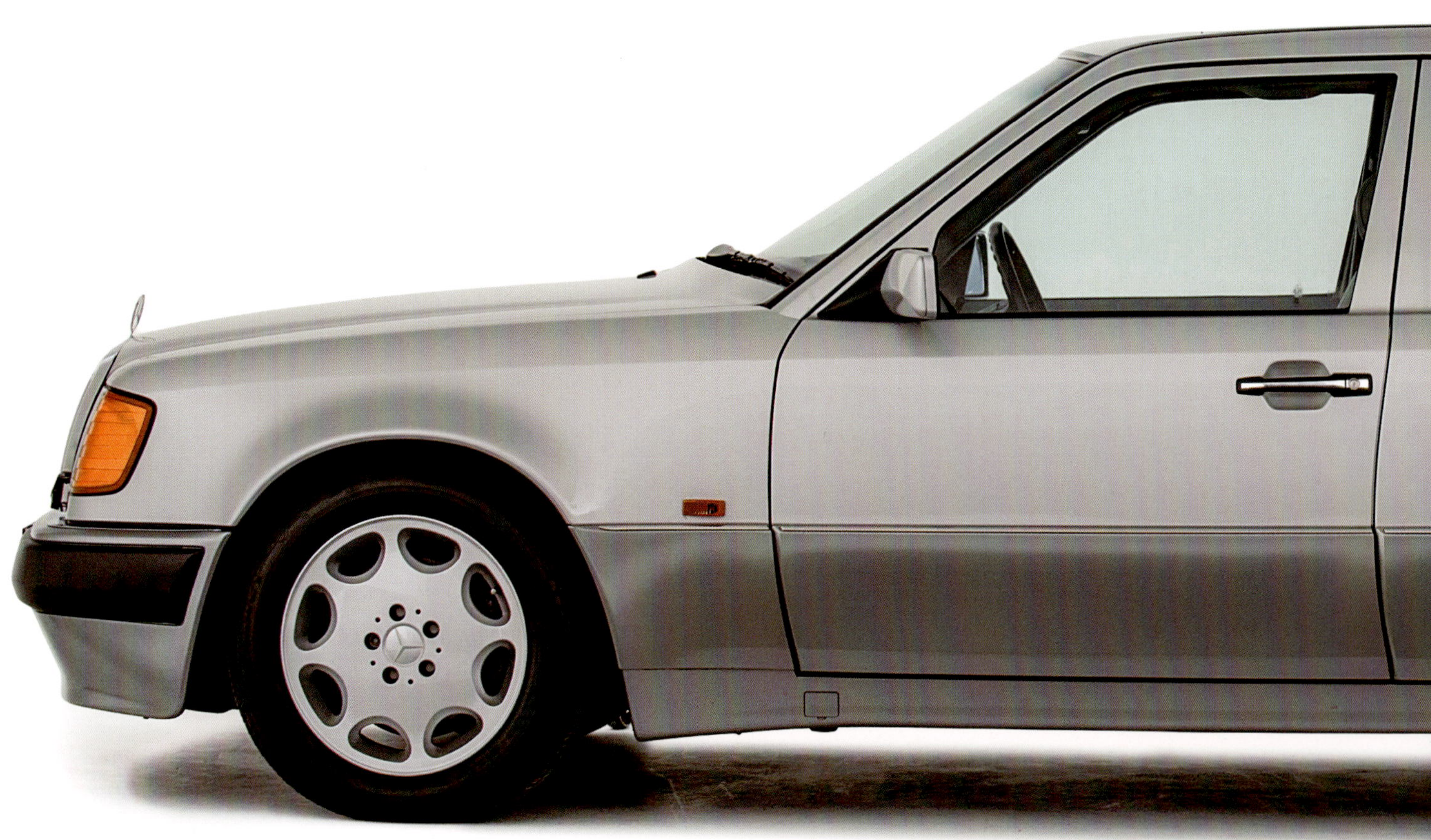

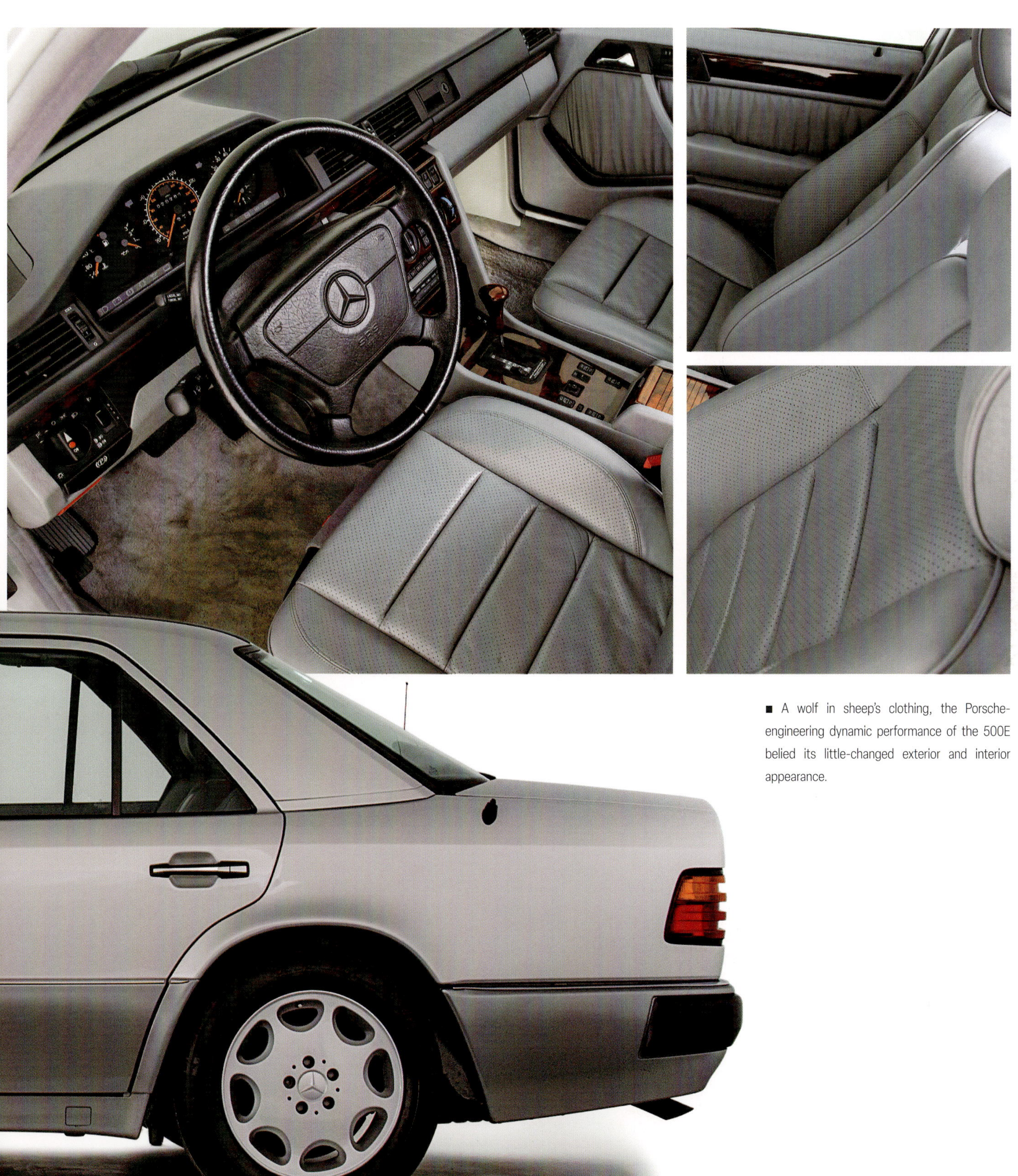

■ A wolf in sheep's clothing, the Porsche-engineering dynamic performance of the 500E belied its little-changed exterior and interior appearance.

LAMBORGHINI DIABLO

All-wheel drive helps keep this raging bull under control

In 2023, classic car insurer and value tracker Hagerty commissioned for its website a series of articles to celebrate the sixtieth anniversary of Italian sports car maker Lamborghini. The series was titled "Lamborghini Legends," and one of its headlines flatly declared "The Diablo 6.0 VT is the best Lamborghini ever built."

Introduced in 1990, the Diablo (the name is Spanish for "devil," which in keeping with Lamborghini tradition was the name of a famous Spanish fighting bull) was developed as the replacement for Lamborghini's Countach, and thus also a successor to the Miura, the original "supercar."

Like the Miura and Countach, the Diablo was designed, at least initially, by Italian styling superstar Marcello Gandini, who was just twenty-five years old when he penned the Miura for Ferruccio Lamborghini.

Lamborghini's car company would go through a series of owners in the 1970s and '80s. When the Diablo was commissioned, the Italian maker of exotic vehicles was owned by a pair of wealthy Swiss brothers, but by 1987 it had become part of the Chrysler Corporation (which in turn sold the Italian automaker in 1994; eventually, Lamborghini would find itself enfolded into the Volkswagen Group).

Upon taking control at Lamborghini, Chrysler had the design of the Diablo redone in-house under design director Tom Gale (with Luc Donckerwolke, working out of a Chrysler-managed studio located at Lamborghini, doing the 6.0 VT as well as the Murcielago that replaced the Diablo).

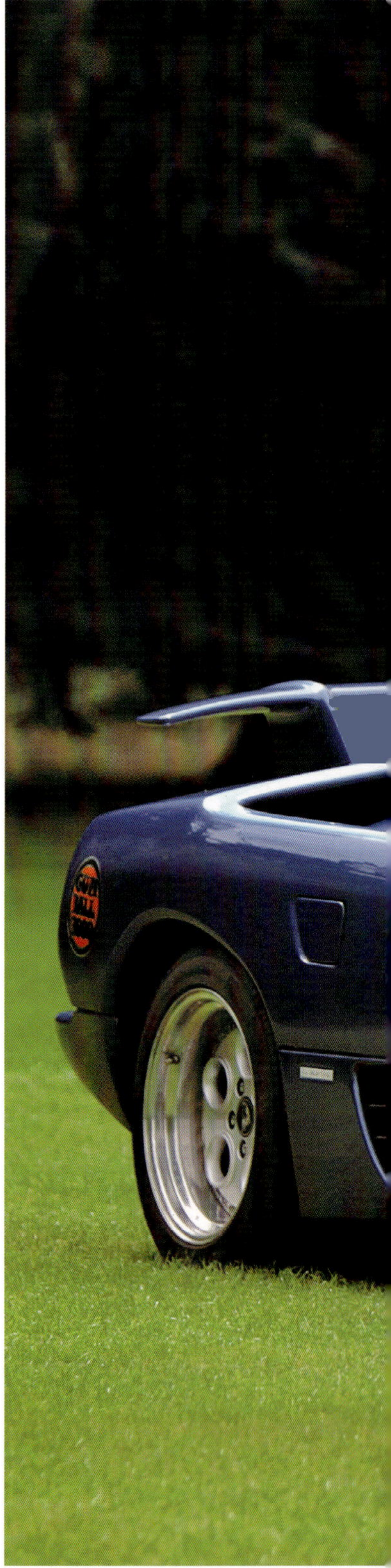

■ Special hinges allowed the Diablo's doors to open like butterfly wings.

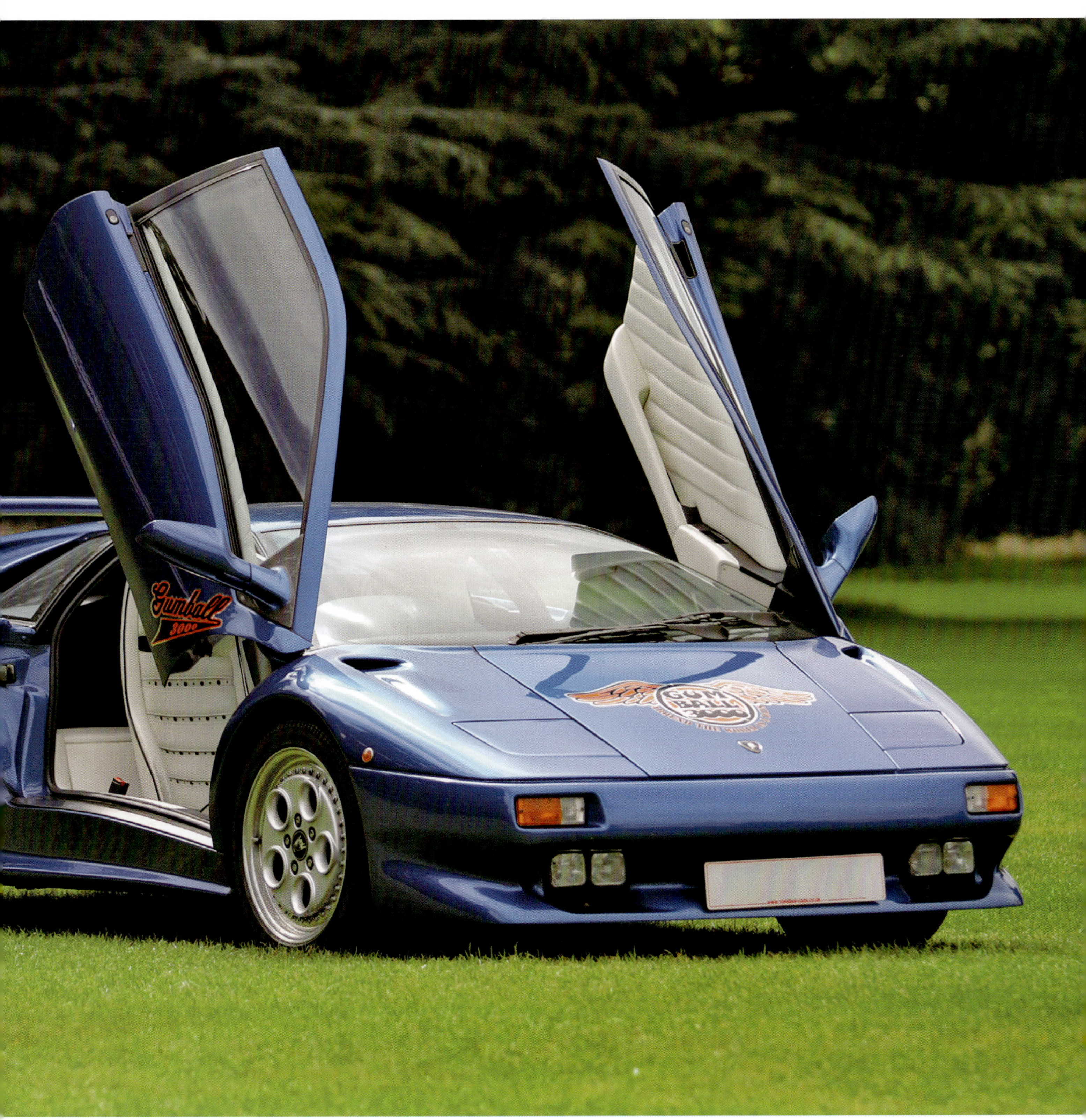
Gumball 3000

Lamborghini created the first supercar, the Miura, which was succeeded by the Countach and then the Diablo, which brought the concept into the modern era of automotive technology.

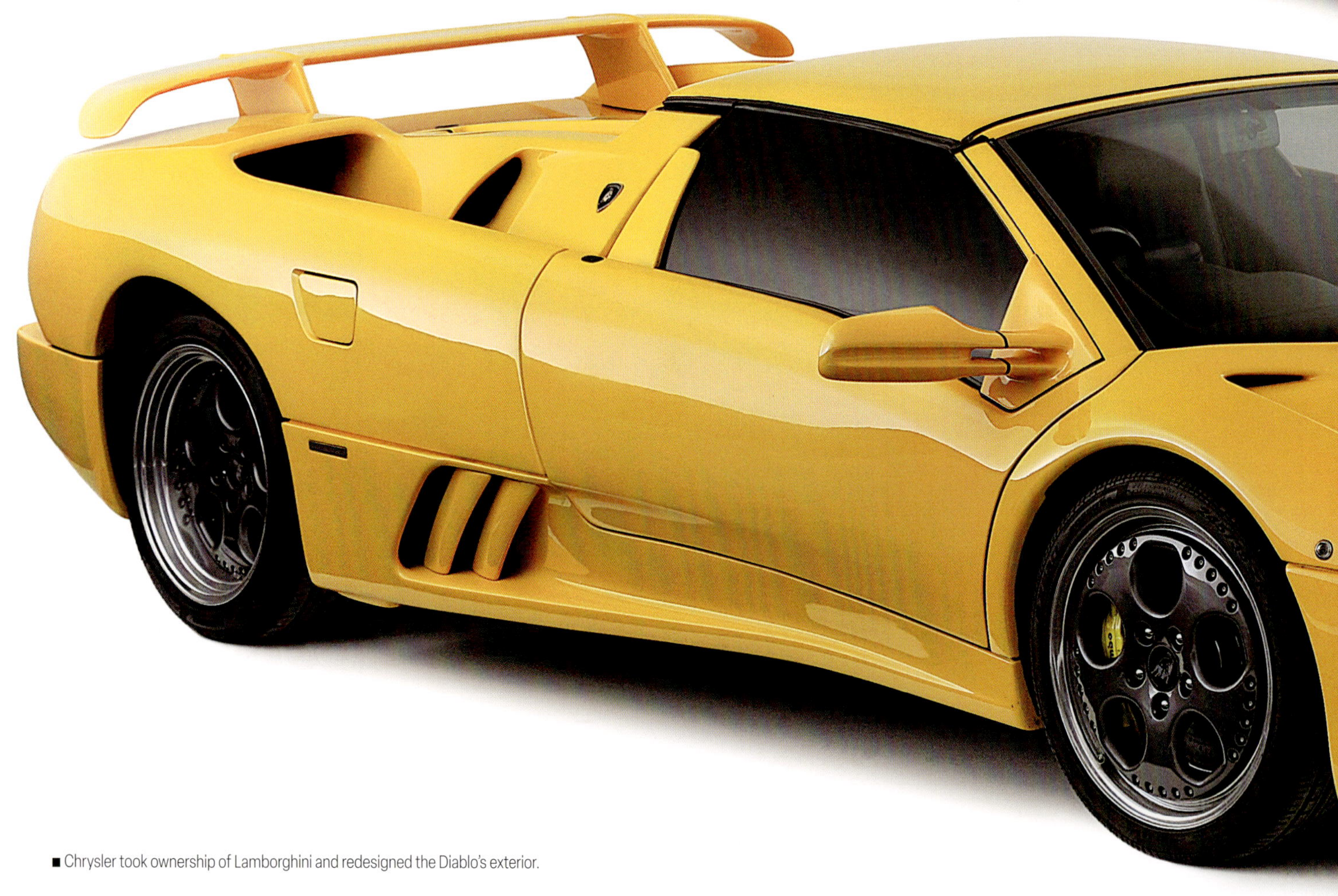

■ Chrysler took ownership of Lamborghini and redesigned the Diablo's exterior.

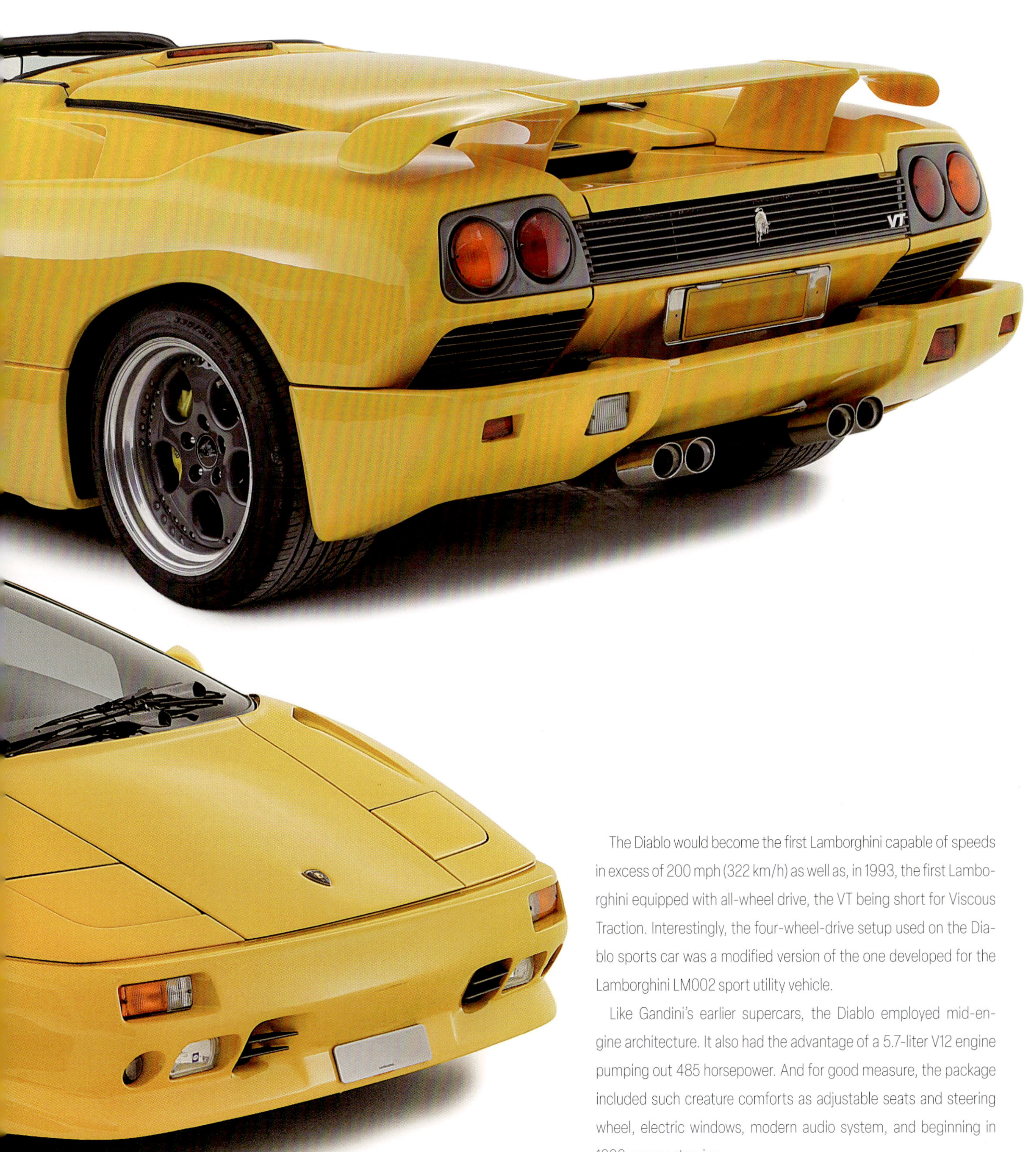

The Diablo would become the first Lamborghini capable of speeds in excess of 200 mph (322 km/h) as well as, in 1993, the first Lamborghini equipped with all-wheel drive, the VT being short for Viscous Traction. Interestingly, the four-wheel-drive setup used on the Diablo sports car was a modified version of the one developed for the Lamborghini LM002 sport utility vehicle.

Like Gandini's earlier supercars, the Diablo employed mid-engine architecture. It also had the advantage of a 5.7-liter V12 engine pumping out 485 horsepower. And for good measure, the package included such creature comforts as adjustable seats and steering wheel, electric windows, modern audio system, and beginning in 1993, power steering.

Lamborghini showed a convertible version of the Diablo at the 1992 Geneva Motor Show. The concept car included the scissor-style door hinges even though the car lacked a permanent metal roof.

A German specialist company was licensed to do convertible conversions for customers until 1995, when Lamborghini introduced its own open-to-the-sky Diablo VT roadster.

In 1998, under Volkswagen ownership and management by VW's Audi division, the Diablo VT 6.0 launched. The car got a design update, and the engine was enlarged to 6.0 liters that provided 549 horsepower.

As the Hagerty website noted, "When it launched in 1990, the Diablo was almost as hardcore as the Countach it replaced. There was no power steering, for example, and the 5.7-liter V12 drove the rear wheels without any driver aids. However, by the end of its run, with Audi now at the helm of Lamborghini, the Diablo had metamorphosed into a civilized, yet no-less-staggering supercar."

Car and Driver magazine agreed in its period road test, terming the 1994 Diablo VT "a more civilized bull" and noting the "adoption of all-wheel drive gives it the traction to match its raging V-12."

A devilish delight: Diablo is the Spanish word for devil.

Bottom ■ Not only did all-wheel drive help manage vehicle dynamics, but the Diablo interior offered a surprising degree of creature comforts.
Opposite page ■ With V12 power, the Diablo was the first Lamborghini sports car that could exceed 200 mph (322 km/h).

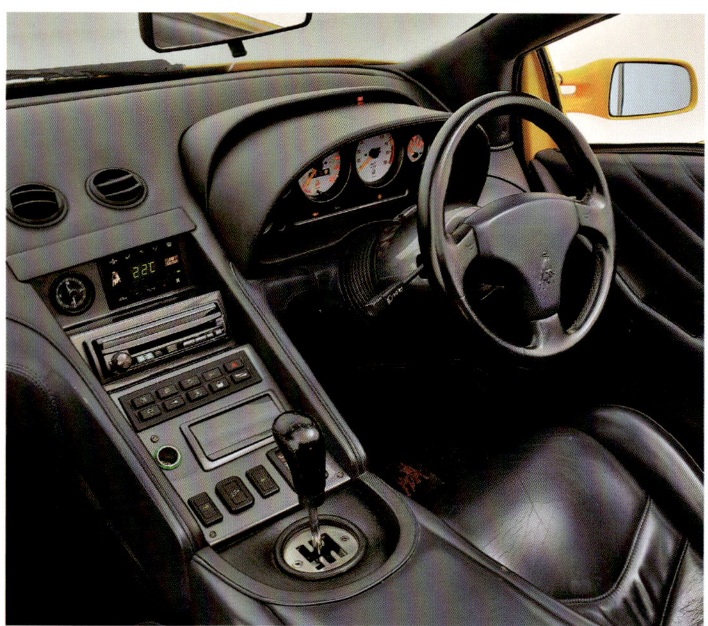

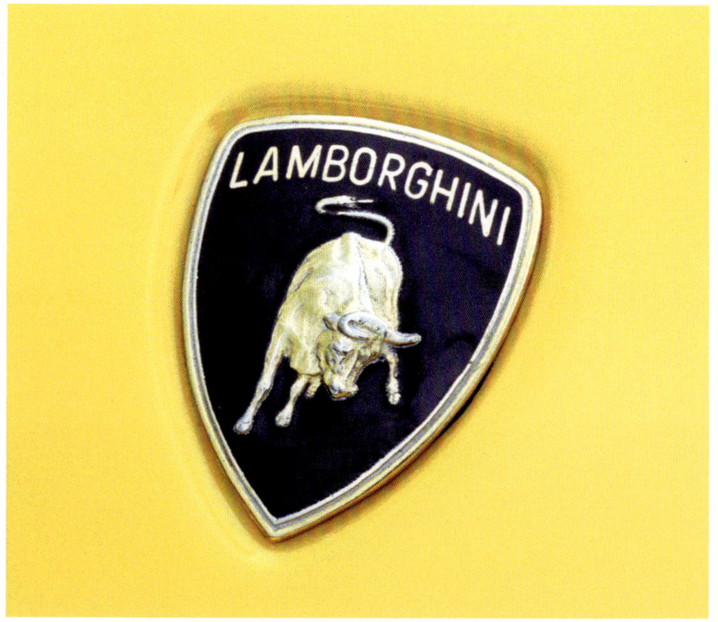

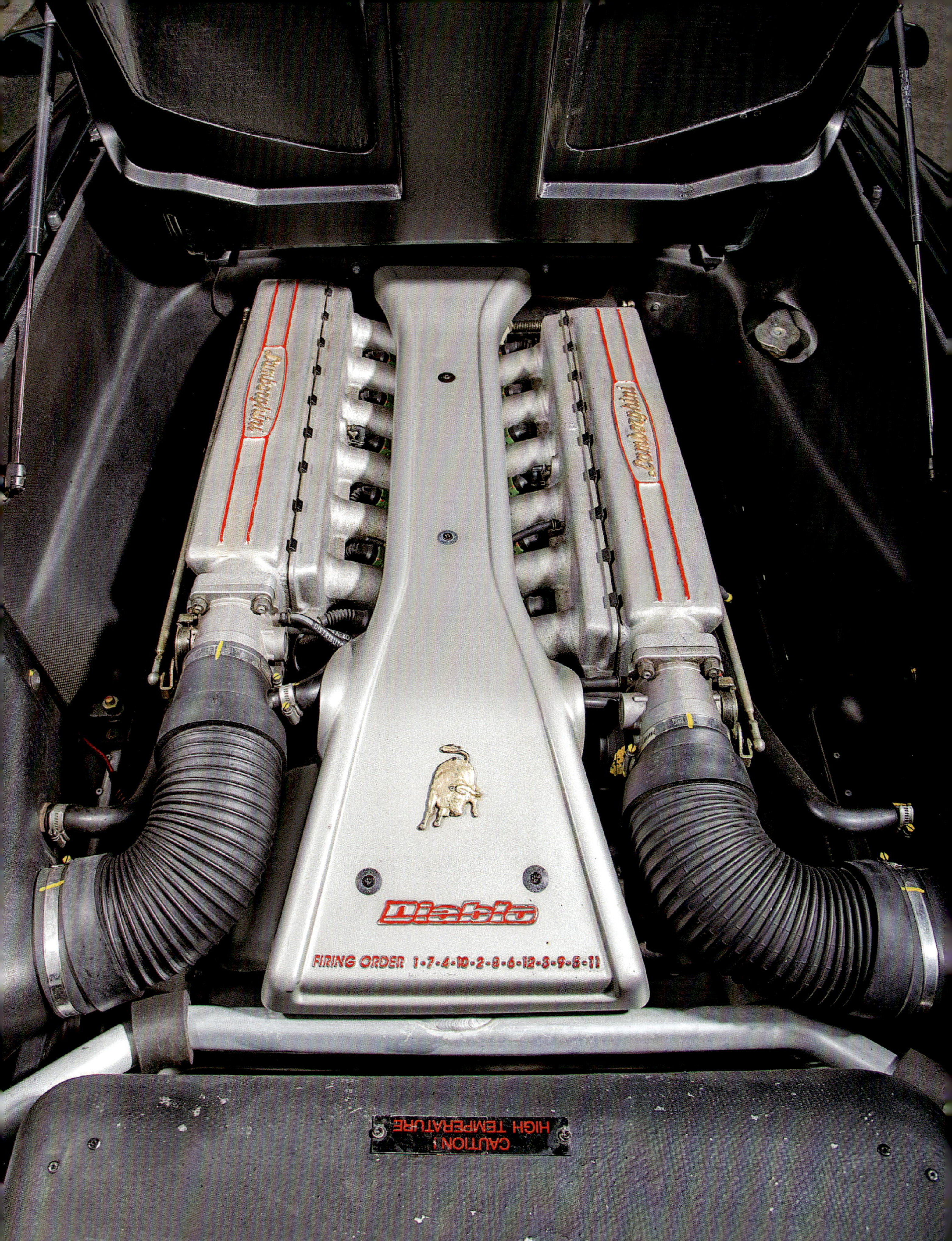
Lamborghini
Lamborghini
Diablo
FIRING ORDER 1-7-4-10-2-8-6-12-3-9-5-11
CAUTION !
HIGH TEMPERATURE

DODGE VIPER RT/10

The outrageous result of undertaking to build a contemporary Shelby Cobra

Were there a dictionary that included photographs of cars to illustrate words, the Dodge Viper would be a good choice to show alongside the word *audacious*, which typical dictionaries define with words and phrases such as "rude boldness," "shameless," "foolishly adventurous," "risk-taking," and even "impudent."

The open roadster coachwork with side-mounted exhaust pipes looked like something from Pixar's *Cars* animated movie, although it would be nearly a decade before we'd meet the likes of Lightning McQueen and company.

Even more outrageous was this car's engine, basically a Chrysler V10 truck engine reworked by Lamborghini, the Italian exotic sports car maker that had become part of the Detroit automaker's portfolio.

The Viper's creation traces to a conversation early in 1988 between Carroll Shelby, Le Mans–winning

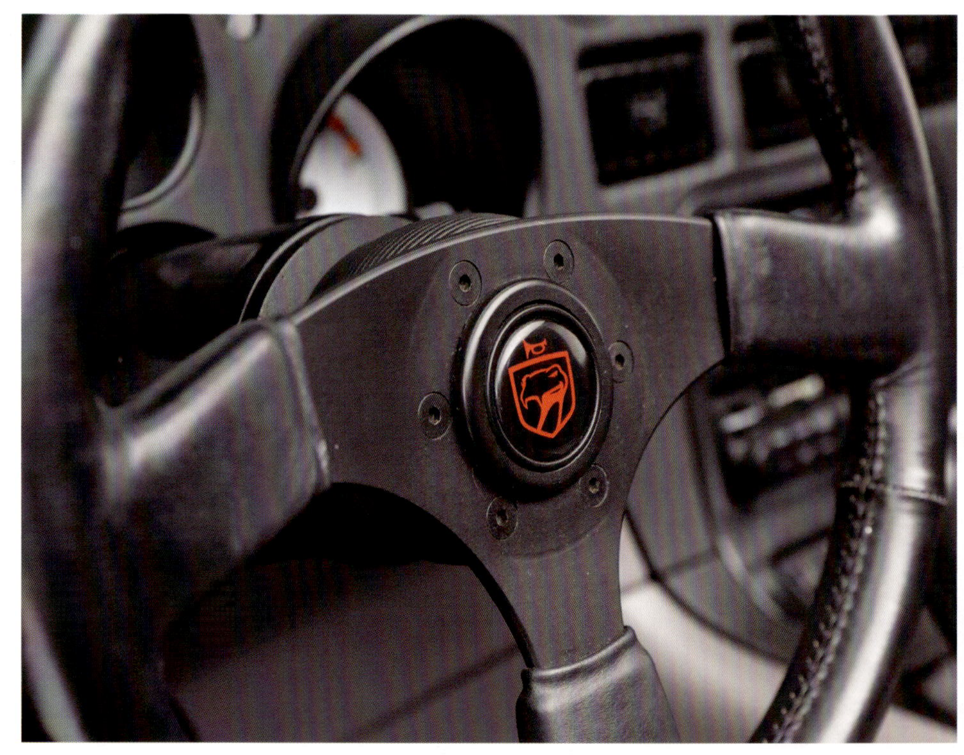

This page ■ Shelby did his Cobra and decades later helped Chrysler create its Viper.
Opposite page ■ Originally only offered as a roadster, the GTS coupe version was added in 1996, in part for motorsports competition.

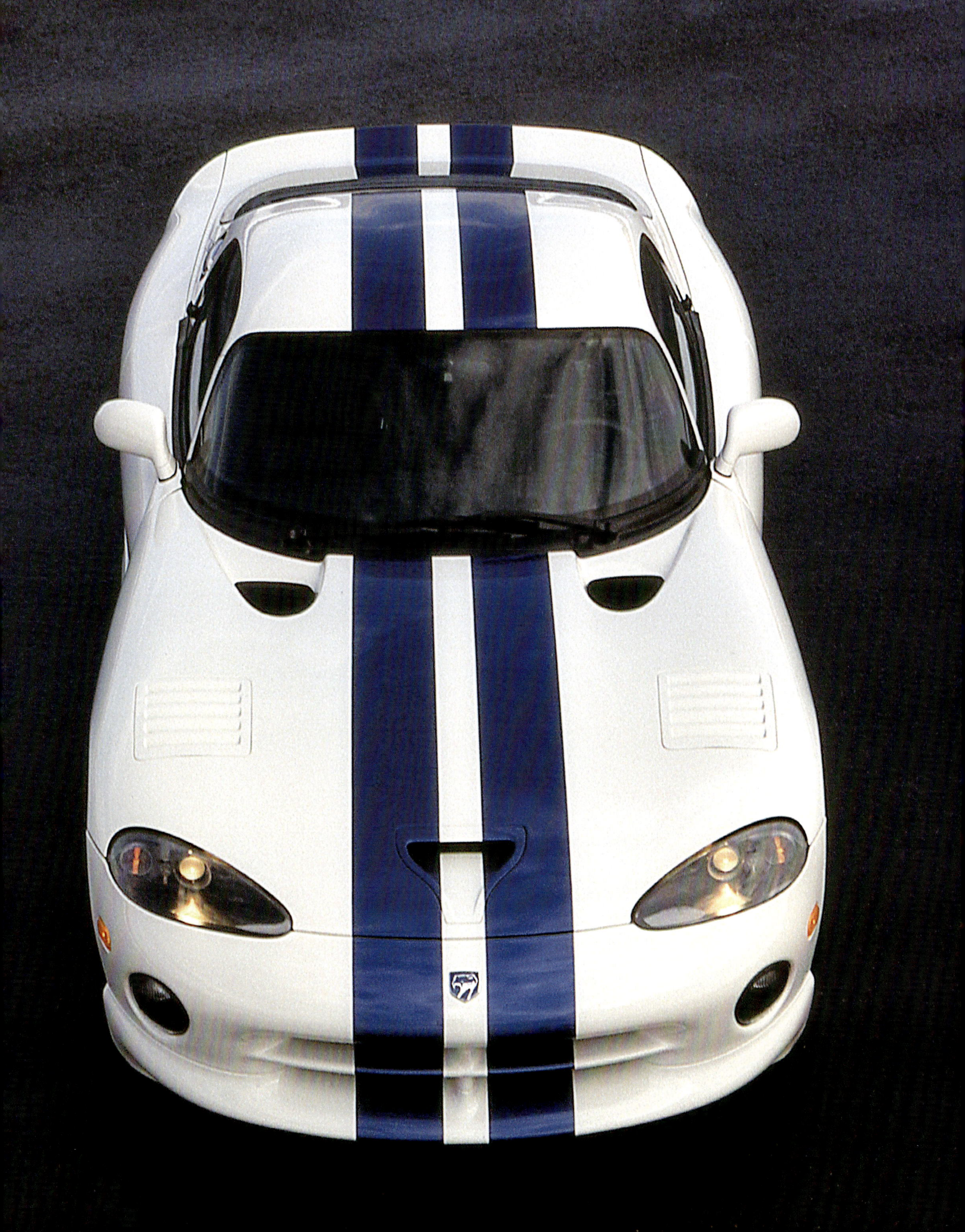

driver and creator of the Cobra sports car who'd had a falling out with his friends at Ford, and Bob Lutz, former US Marine Corps fighter pilot and BMW and Ford executive who'd recently become the president of Chrysler Corporation.

During the course of their conversation, the topic of a new and contemporary Cobra-style sports car came up, and that such a car should favor good ol' American wind-in-your-face fun and fury hardware instead of software-enabled computerized wizardry.

Lutz invited Chrysler engineering chief François Castaing into the conversation. Castaing had a history that included Formula One and Le Mans racing, and his team was working on a new 10-cylinder heavy-duty truck engine.

Meanwhile, Chrysler design director Tom Gale and his team were sketching a new and more aggressive face for Chrysler's Dodge division. That face, with its crosshair grille, was unveiled in January 1989 on a bulging, bright-red sports car, the Dodge Viper VM-01, albeit supposedly only a concept vehicle unlikely to ever go into production.

But three years later at the Detroit show, Chrysler displayed the production-ready Viper RT/10, which a few months later served as the pace car for the seventy-fifth anniversary of the Indianapolis 500, and with sixty-eight-year-old Shelby himself as its driver even though he was just a few months post-surgery for a heart transplant!

The heart of the Viper was its 8.0-liter V10, pumping out 400 horsepower and 450 pound-feet (610 Nm) of torque. A 6-speed manual transmission relayed that power to huge, 13-inch-wide rear tires.

The Viper had a steel backbone chassis and a fiber-reinforced composite body. There were no side windows or exterior door handles; you reached inside to unlatch the doors. There were no side windows, but side curtains just as on the earliest of sports cars. A sheet of canvas could be stretched above the two seats in case of rain. The GTS, an enclosed coupe version of the Viper, became available in 1996.

So what was it like to drive this retro roadster? In 1992 *Car and Driver* magazine reported, "With the wind ripping new configurations in your eyebrows and the engine in full honk, you're not going to give one whit about absent windows or door handles. Because this Viper is one of the most exciting rides since Ben-Hur discovered the chariot.

"That's the whole point of the Viper," it added. "It's intended to go fast, stop hard, hang on to corners, and give everyone in sight—driver, passenger, and bystanders—a thrill that will make their day."

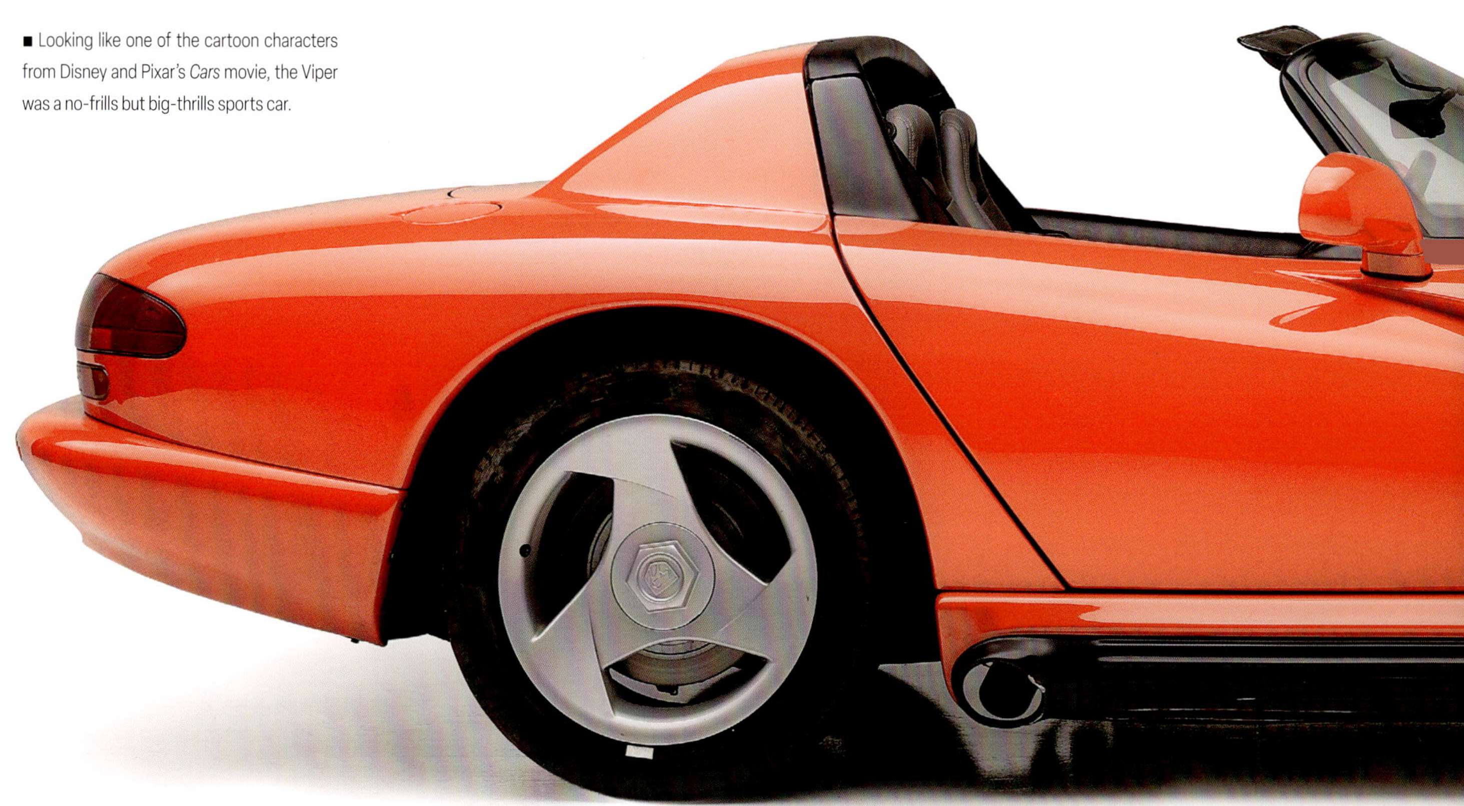

■ Looking like one of the cartoon characters from Disney and Pixar's *Cars* movie, the Viper was a no-frills but big-thrills sports car.

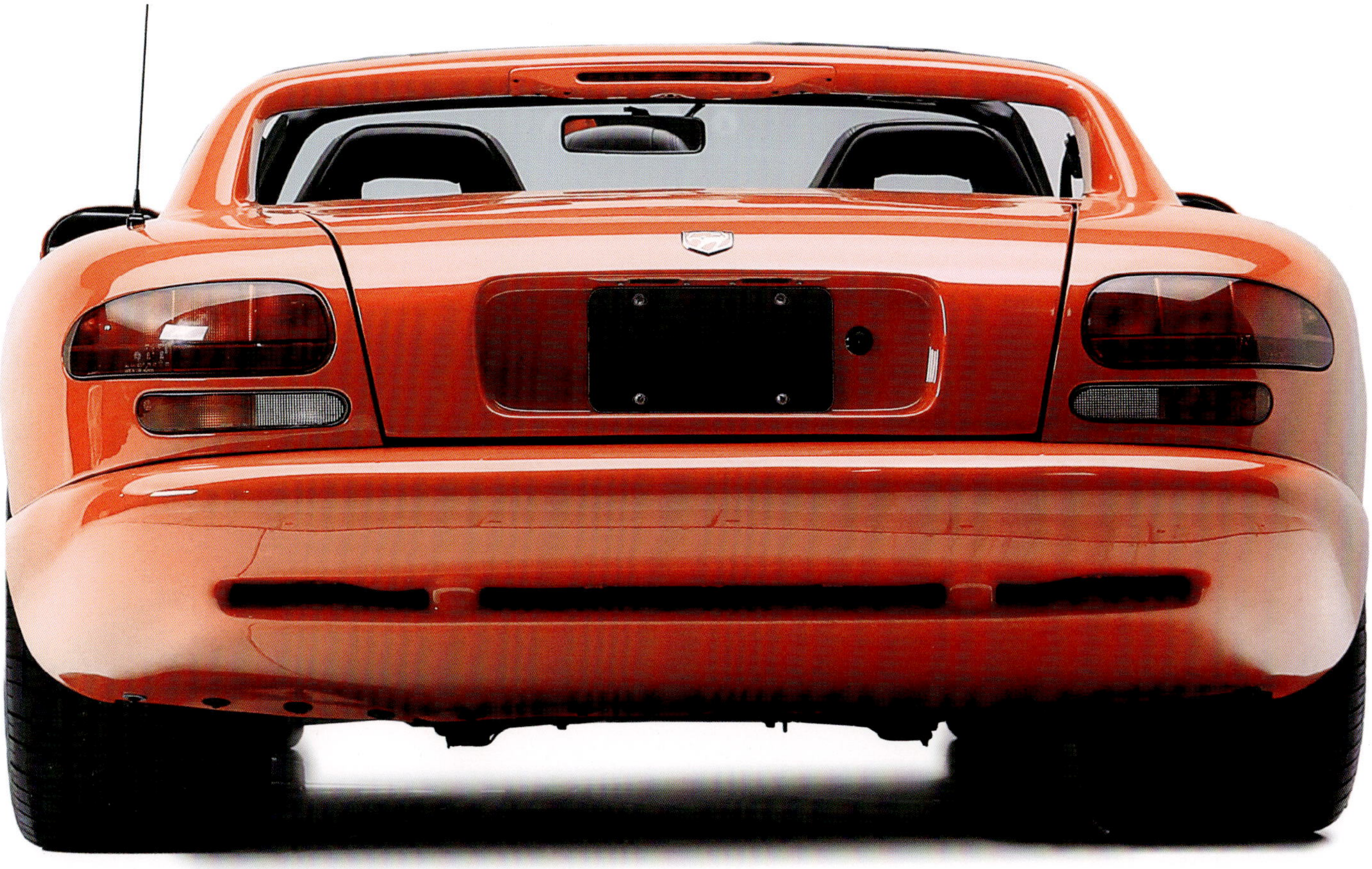

One road tester reported the Viper to be "one of the most exciting rides since Ben-Hur discovered the chariot."

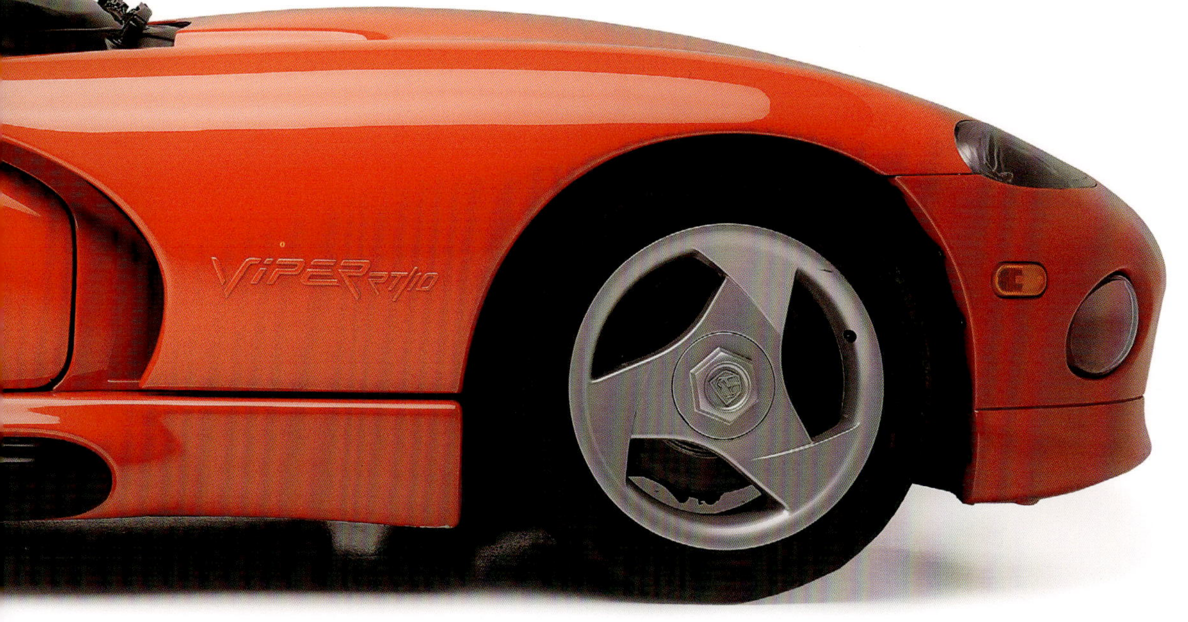

BUGATTI EB110

Historic auto company is reborn in the form of a modern supercar

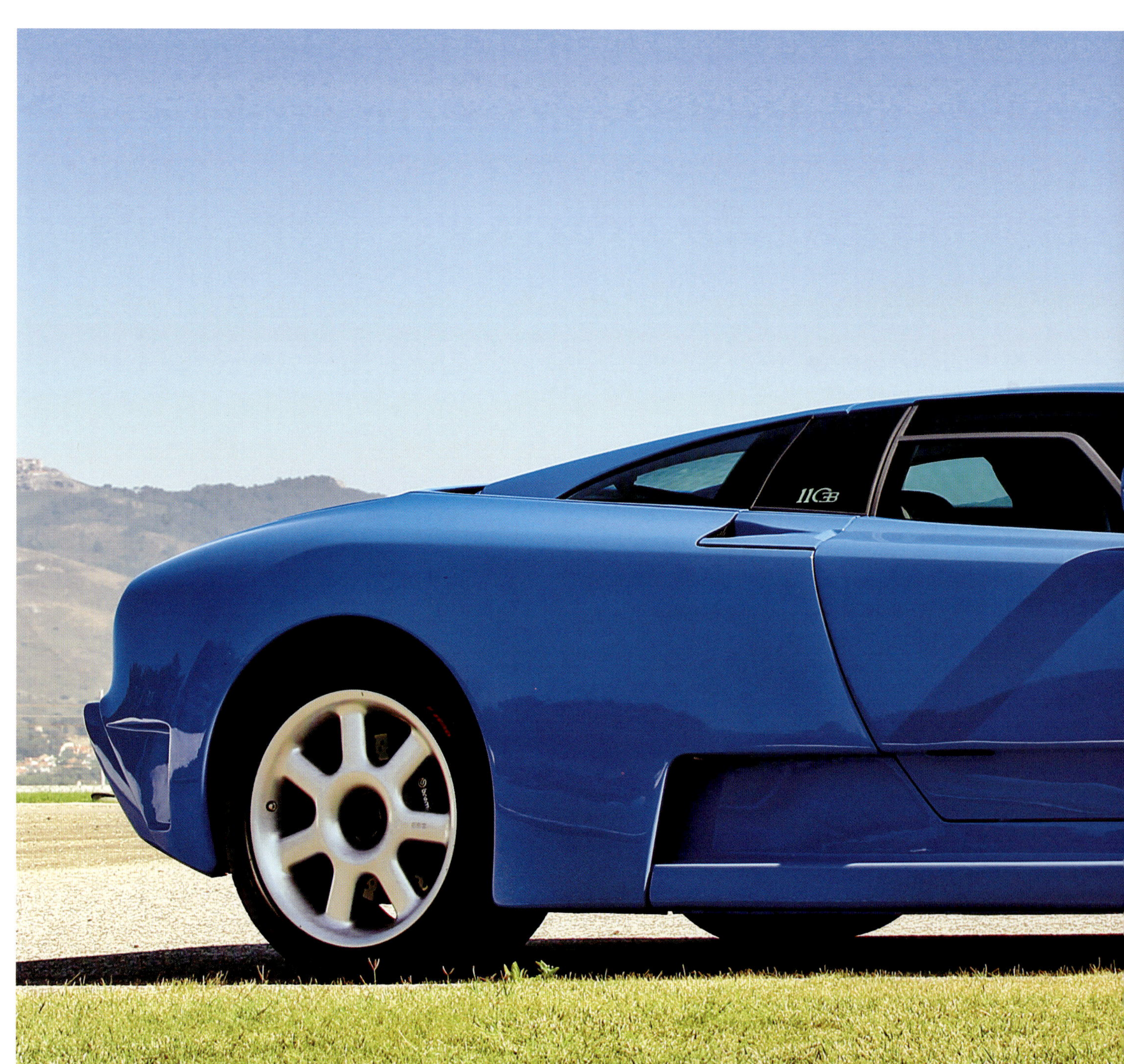

1990 ➤ 1999

"No make of car has earned such a charismatic reputation on such a small output (about 7,800) as Bugatti" is how the four-volume, 2,192-page *Beaulieu Encyclopedia of the Automobile* opens its presentation on the automobile company founded in the south of France in 1909 by Ettore Bugatti.

Bugatti was born into an artistic family in northern Italy in 1881. His grandfather was an architect. His father, Carlo, was a famous designer and builder of furniture, musical instruments, and jewelry. Ettore's brother, Rembrandt, was an acclaimed sculptor, best known for his animal figures.

But Ettore's passion was automobiles. He built his first motorcar when he was a teenager, and he worked for several German automakers before setting up his own workshop in Molsheim, a historic city on the French-German border, in his late twenties. Bugatti built cars that would reach new levels in speed and luxury. His race cars posted victories in more than 2,000 events, and his road cars were elegant and expensive and were owned by royals and movie stars.

His son, Jean, joined him at the automobile company and created several gorgeous machines but died in a crash while testing a car in 1939.

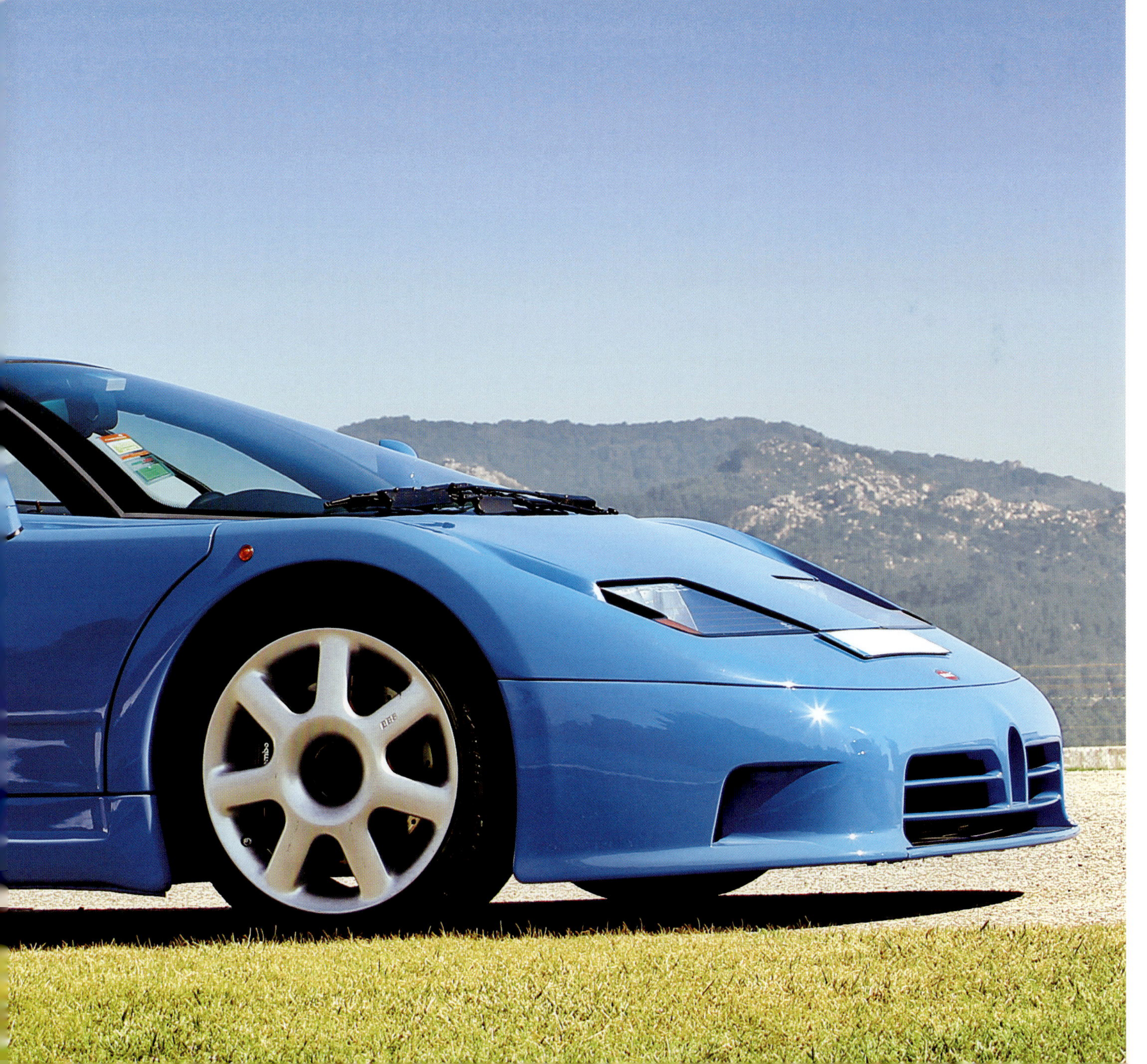

Ettore died in 1947. Another son, Roland, kept things going. Two new cars were displayed at the Paris Salon in 1951, but the company was shuttered in 1956.

There were several efforts for a Bugatti revival. Finally, rights to the name were purchased in 1987 by Romano Artioli, Italy's largest Ferrari dealer and importer of Japanese cars. He built a new Bugatti factory near Modena, Italy, and hired famed engineer Paolo Stanzani and designer Marcello Gandini to create a modern Bugatti. During development, the project was code-named FL12, short for Ferruccio Lamborghini 12-cylinder, but would be unveiled as the Bugatti EB110, the name including Bugatti's initials and the car's unveiling in Paris to celebrate the 110th anniversary of his birth.

The EB110 was a modern supercar. It was built from carbon fiber with a steel roof and aluminum body panels, scissors-hinged doors, and a modern interpretation of Bugatti's historic trademare, its horseshoe-shaped grille.

The car was underpinned by four-wheel drive technology, a system capable of controlling the power output of its quad-turbocharged 3.5-liter V12 engine rated at 550 horsepower or 611 in the Super Sport model. Either way, the EB110 was the fastest production car in the world, reaching 221 mph (356 km/h).

According to a 2010 report in *Motor Trend*, "In the early '90s...the 110 was King of the Hill. With a 3.5-liter, 553-horse V-12, a 0–60 mph time of 3.4 seconds and a 213-mph top speed, it outpaced the

Previous and these pages ■ With its 12-cylinder engine pumping out 550 horsepower, the EB110 was the fastest production car in the world, reaching 221 mph (356 km/h).

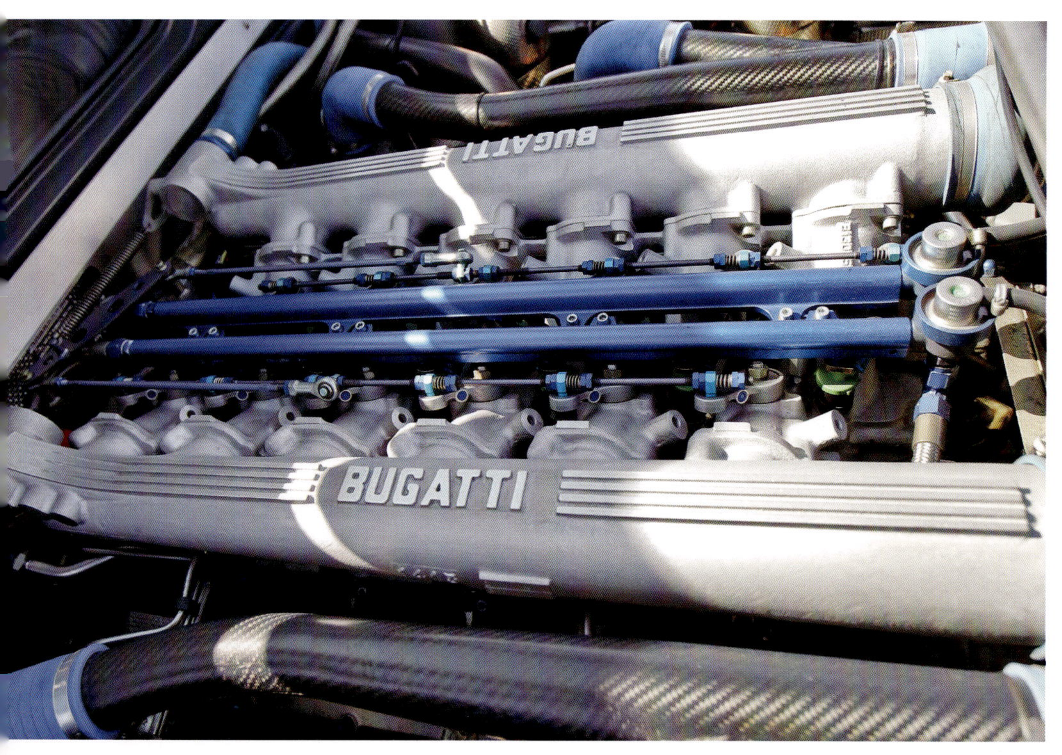

Ferrari F40, and it's still faster than many of the newer machines you'll find occupying internet ultimate-supercar fantasy lists...Launched in 1991, it was the first production car with a carbon-fiber monocoque (just nipping the McLaren F1), the first with quad turbos, and featured full-time four-wheel drive."

Bugatti would produce nearly 130 examples of the EB110 by the time production (and the company's funding) ended in 1995. Before the end of the decade, the rights to Bugatti would be purchased by the Volkswagen Group, which in 2005 would unveil a new (and even faster) Bugatti, the Veyron EB 16.4.

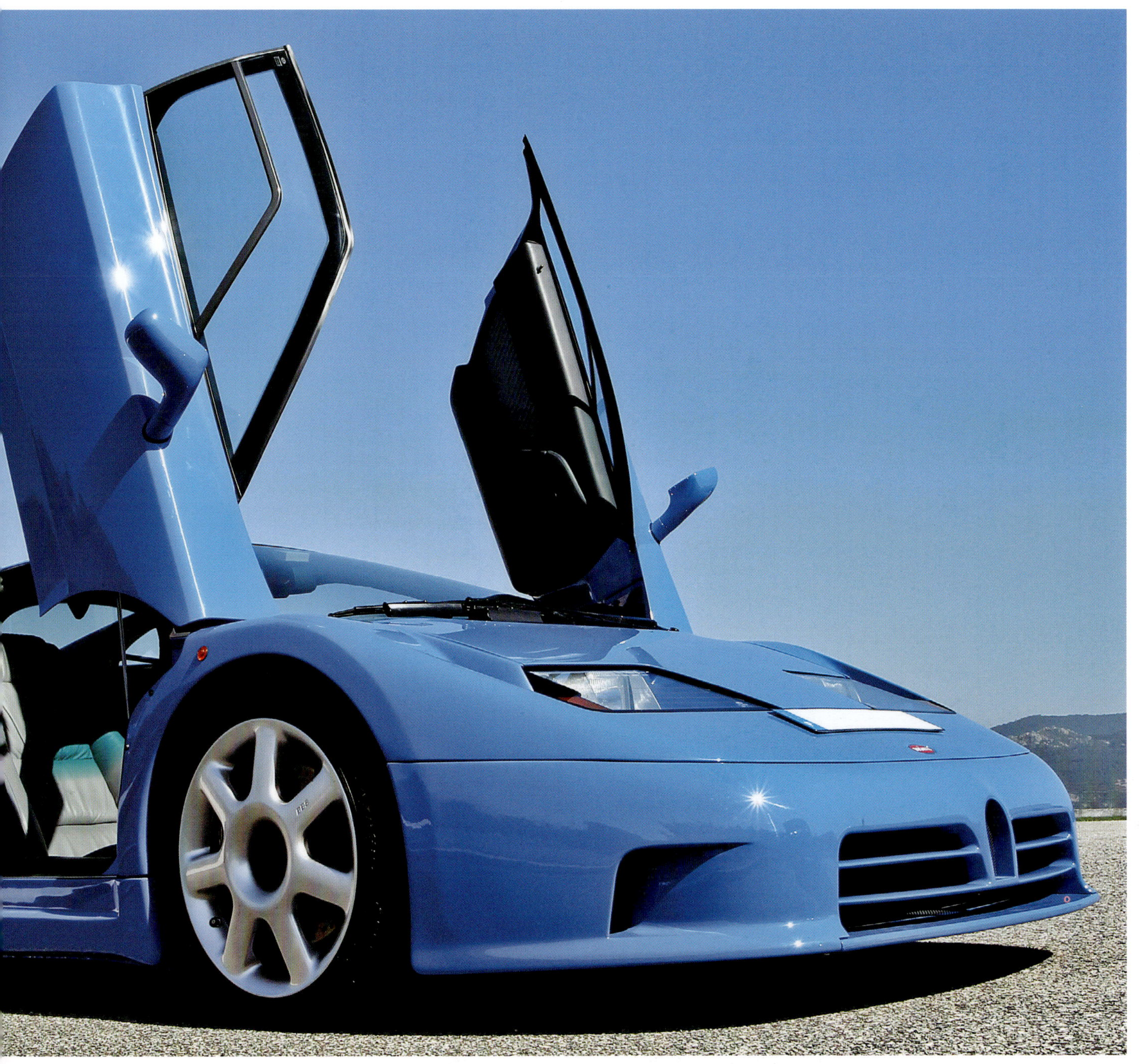

JAGUAR XJ220

A supercar that nearly lived up to the numbers in its name

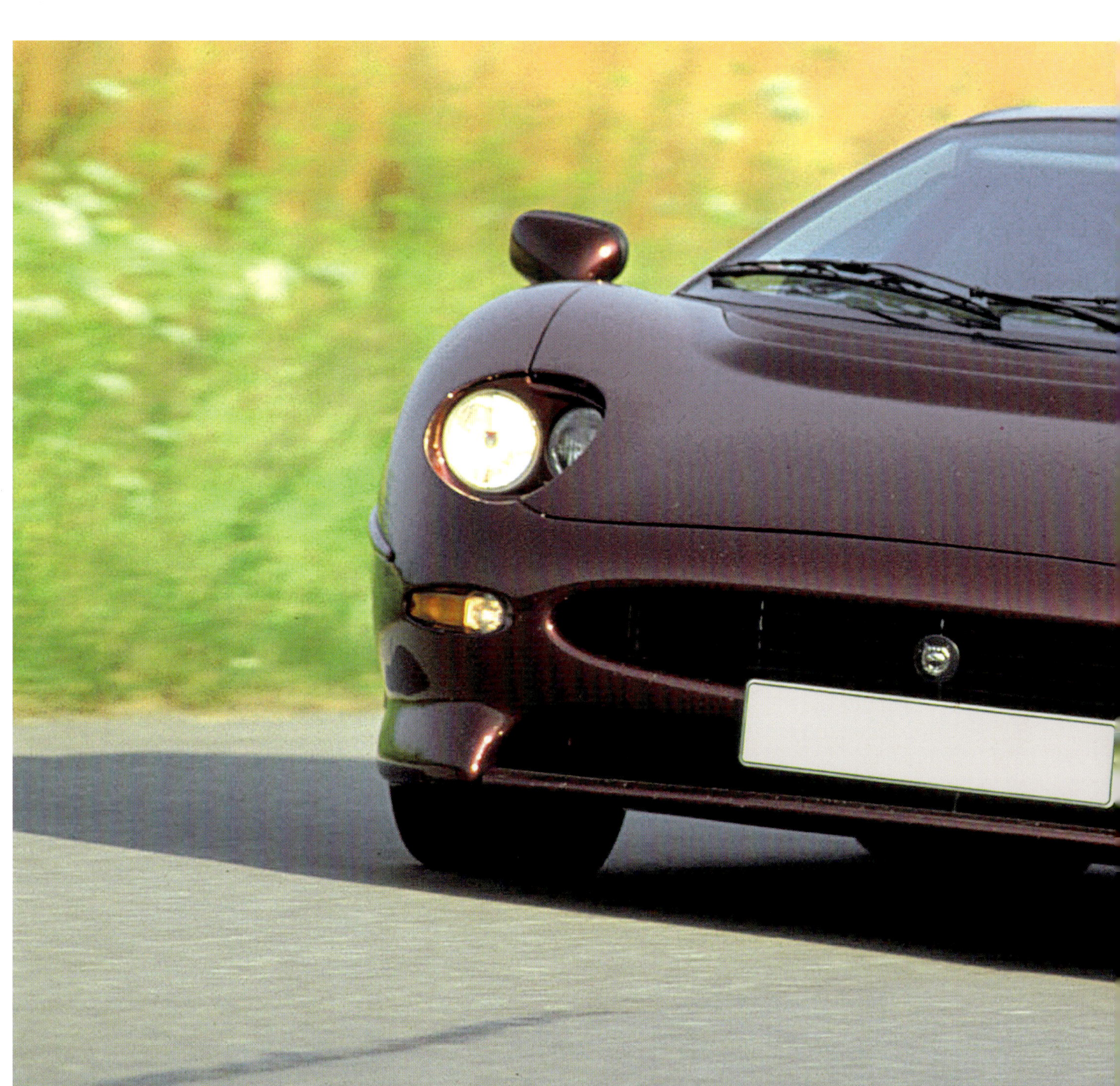

1990 ➤ 1999

Back in 1946, composer Irving Berlin penned a line that went "anything you can do, I can do better" for the Broadway musical *Annie Get Your Gun*. That lyric would become something of a theme for exotic sports car manufacturers in the early 1990s.

As Britain's *Top Gear* reported in 2012, "Conceived by an informal group called 'The Saturday Club,' Jaguar's chief engineer Jim Randle wanted to make a Jaguar that could beat the supercars of the time, the Ferrari F40 and Porsche 959."

Randle reportedly began work on what would become the XJ200 supercar during his Christmas holiday in 1987 when he constructed a 1:4 scale model from cardboard. He showed the model around when he returned to work after the holiday, and The Saturday Club was organized to push forward on the project during off hours.

The club's work resulted in a mid-engine, all-wheel-drive concept car named the XJ220 in homage to the famed and historic mid-1950s Jaguar XK120, which was so-named because of its 120-mph top speed (Randle and The Saturday Club expected their contemporary supercar to be capable of speeds up to 220 mph).

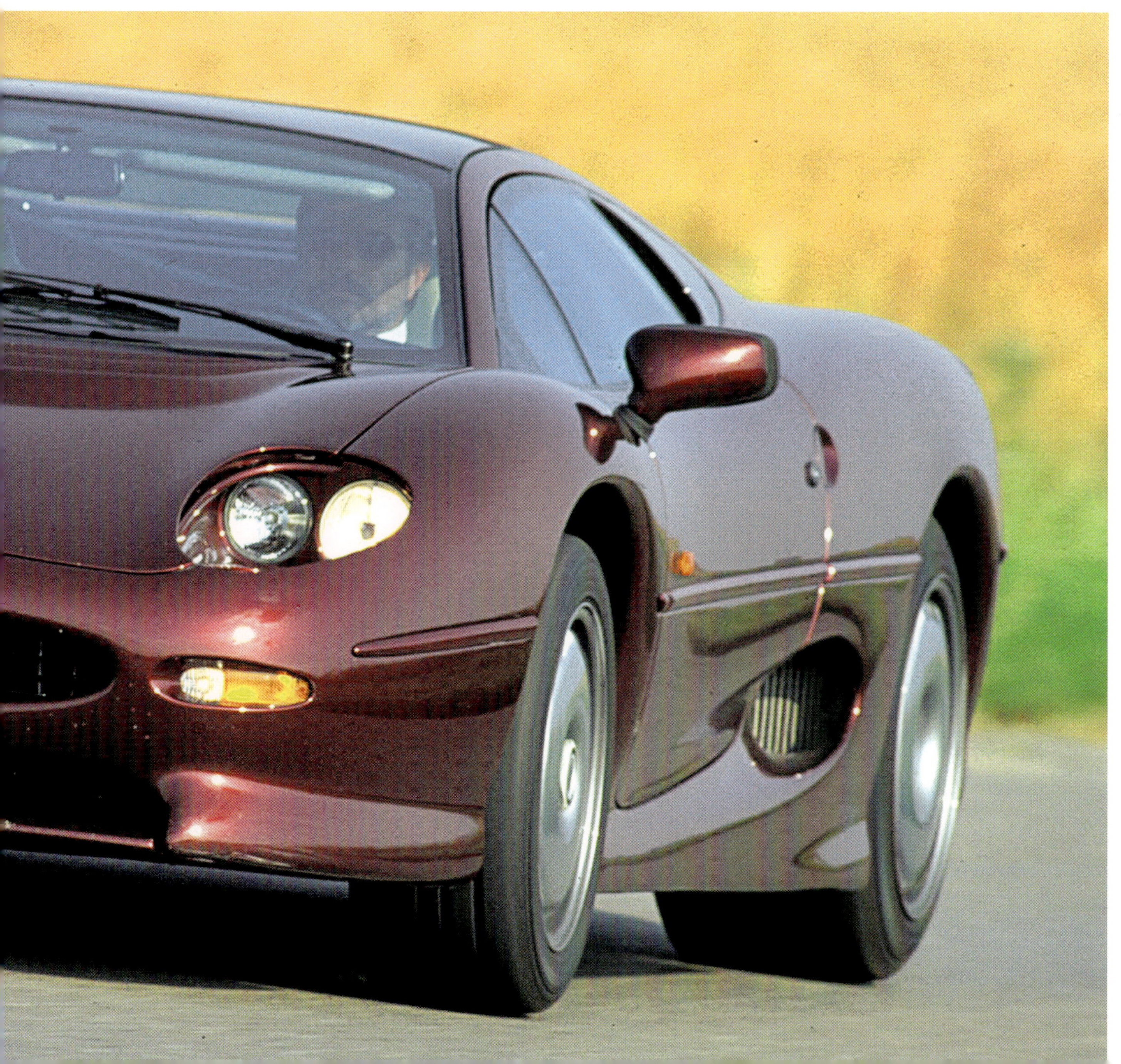

With coachwork styled by the Jaguar design department, a V12 engine prepared by Jaguar specialist Tom Walkinshaw Racing, and with four-wheel-drive help from specialist FF Developments, the concept was displayed at the British Motor Show in Birmingham in the fall of 1988.

The car went into production in 1992, with 282 produced over a two-year period. By the start of production, the XJ220 had shrunk in both overall size and weight and was equipped not with a V12 but with a twin-turbocharged V6, nonetheless rated at more than 540 horsepower, enough to propel the car from a standing start to 60 mph (96 km/h) in just 3.5 seconds, setting a lap record at the famed Nürburgring circuit in Germany and reaching a production-car speed record of 212.3 mph (341.7 km/h) on a test track in Texas.

All that was particularly impressive for what was still a rather large vehicle, "the world's widest production car," Britain's *CAR* magazine reminded. "It's also roomy [inside]...There's decent legroom and plenty of shoulder room.

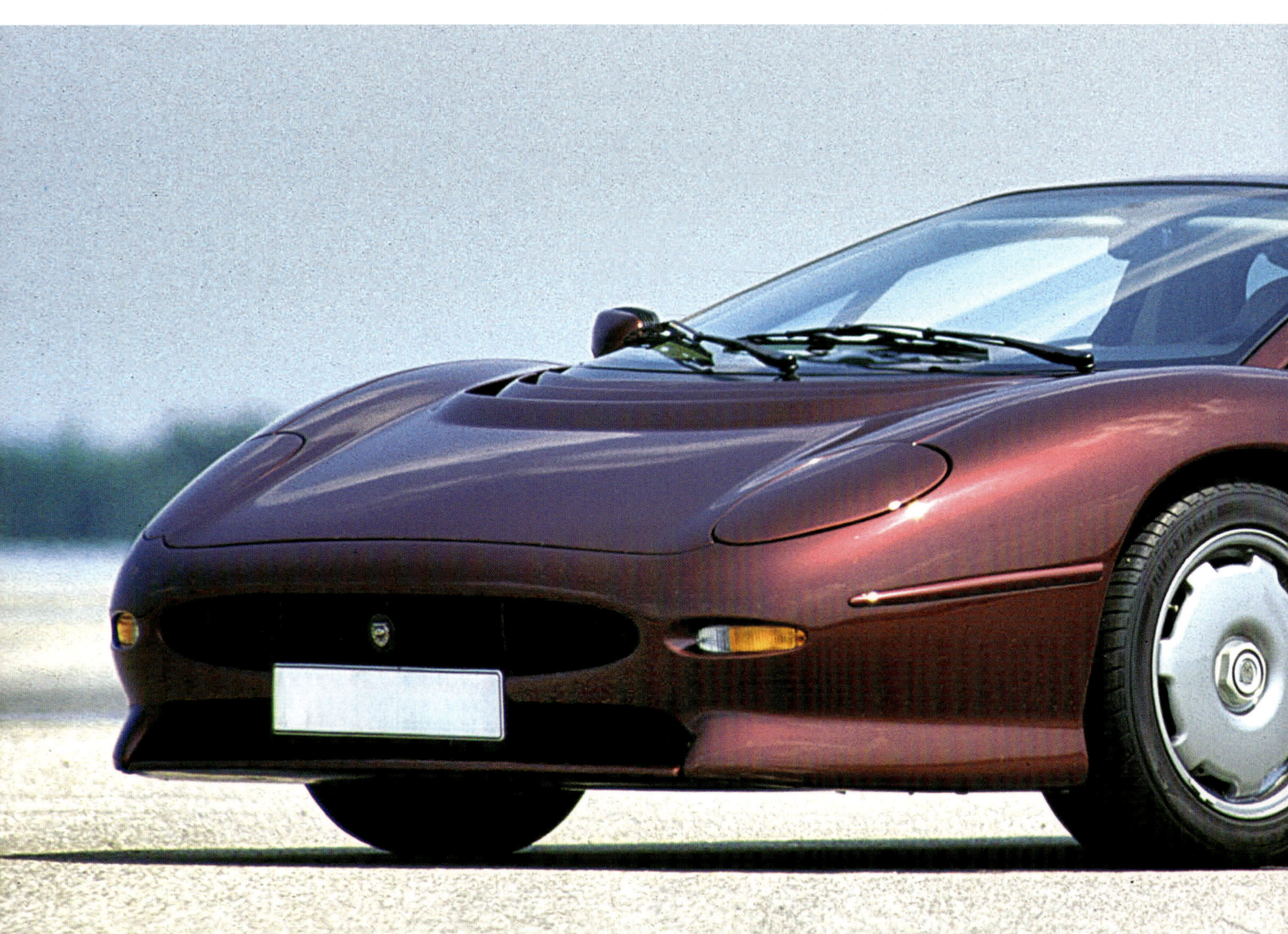

"Here is a 200-mph monster that could fusslessly transport you and a friend to the south of France."

However, *CAR* continued, "Like all the best performance cars, this one shrinks as the speed builds. You always know, deep down, that you're wearing a set of XXL clothes. Yet when going fast, the XJ200 feels small...This is an easier car to punt hard on long runs than any seriously fast supercar rival."

While fast, it turns out, the XJ220 also was luxurious, with a leather interior and air conditioning. But it was also very expensive, to the point that a dozen of the cars that went unsold were offered to a made-for-television auto racing series called the *Fast Masters*. The concept was to put famous race car drivers aged fifty and older into identical cars and set them loose on the track.

Ah, the best laid plans, as they say. The series devolved into a high-speed demolition derby, with former Indianapolis 500 winner Bobby Unser emerging as champion.

In a 2021 retrospective, Britain's much-respected *Goodwood Road & Racing* summarized Jaguar's XJ220 as "the most unloved supercar."

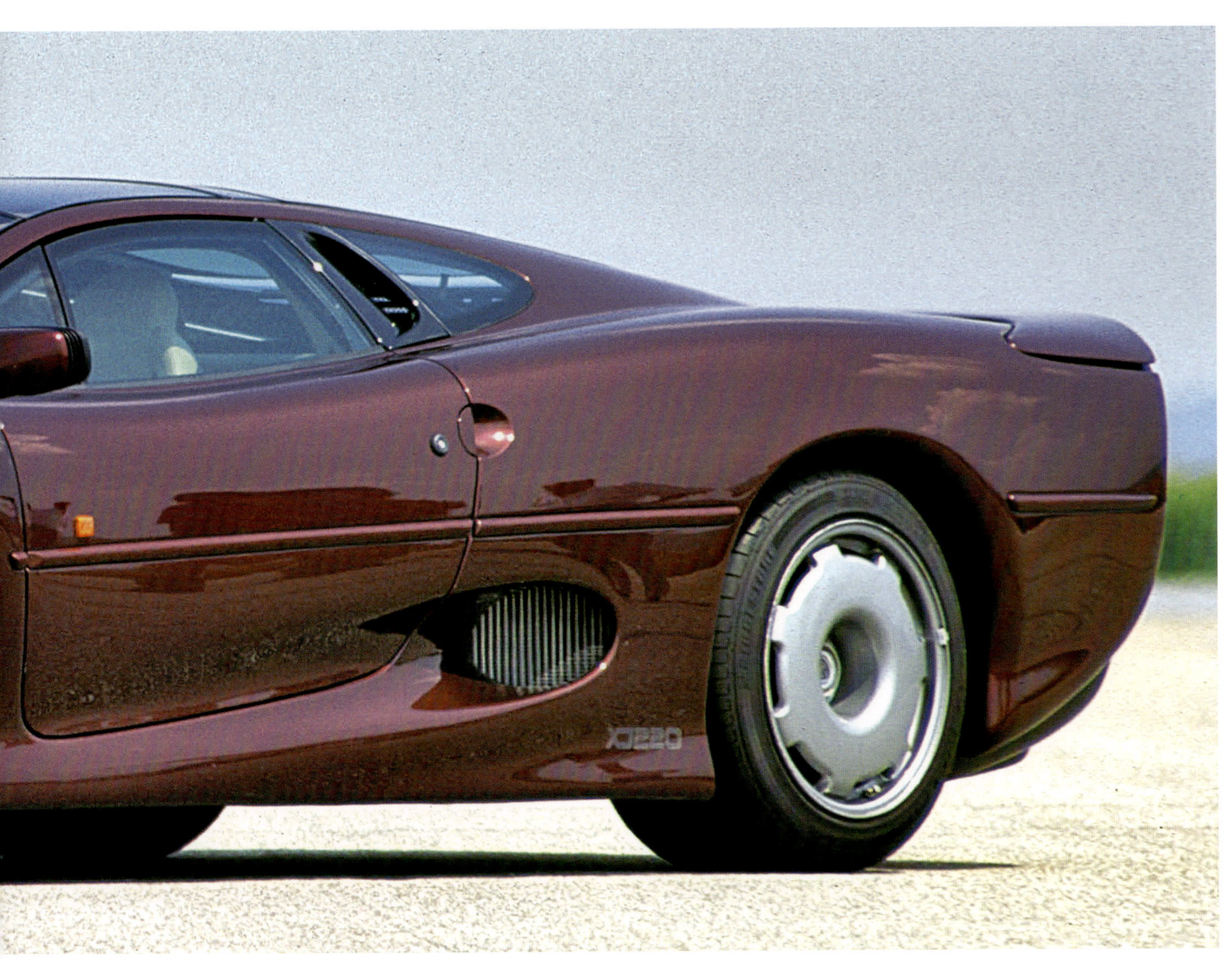

Previous and these pages ■ In the 1950s, Jaguar badged one of its sports cars as the XK120 because it could be driven at 120 mph (193 km/h). Decades later, the company's supercar was called the XJ220 because its targeted top speed was 220 mph (354 km/h).

TOYOTA SUPRA

Ferrari F40 looks (and very good dynamic performance) for one-seventh of the price

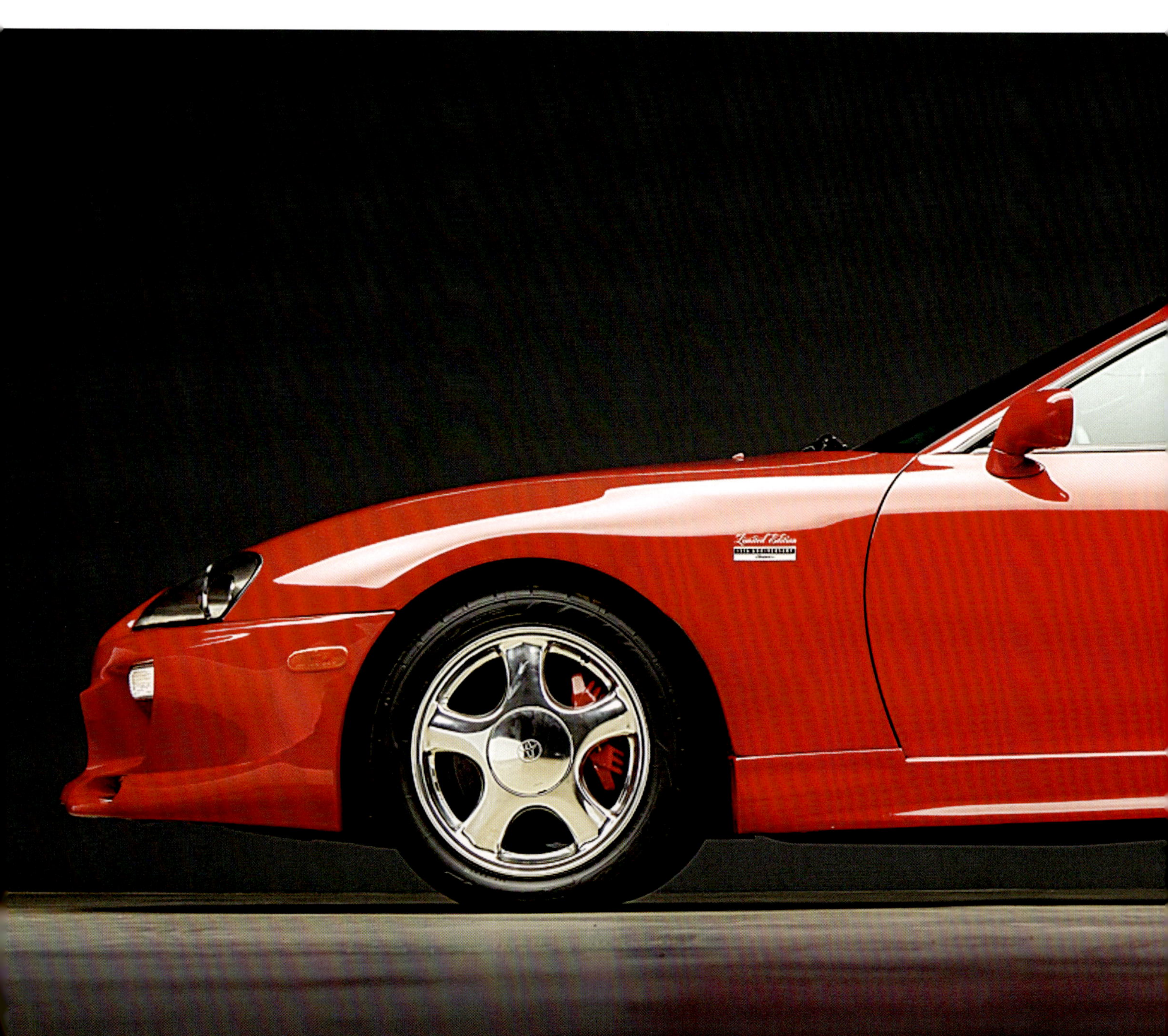

1990 ➤ 1999

In the 1920s, Japanese inventor Sakichi Toyoda created a series of powered looms that revolutionized the textile industry. In 1936, his son, Kiichiro Toyoda, constructed a car, and what would become known as the Toyota Motor Corporation was founded.

(While the family name was Toyoda, a word which in Japanese means "fertile rice paddies," the corporation's name became Toyota, reportedly because that word could be written in *katakana* letters with what was considered to be a "lucky" number of brush strokes and at the same time also was easier for native Japanese speakers to pronounce.)

Automotive production did, indeed, prove lucky for Toyota, which in the twenty-first century would become the world's most prolific automobile producer.

In the aftermath of World War II, Toyota returned to passenger car production, and by the late 1950s was exporting vehicles. For the most part, they were mundane sedans. However, in 1967 Toyota worked with Yamaha to create a spectacular sports car, the Toyota 2000GT. Toyota created the stunning fastback design, and Yamaha developed the straight-6 engine.

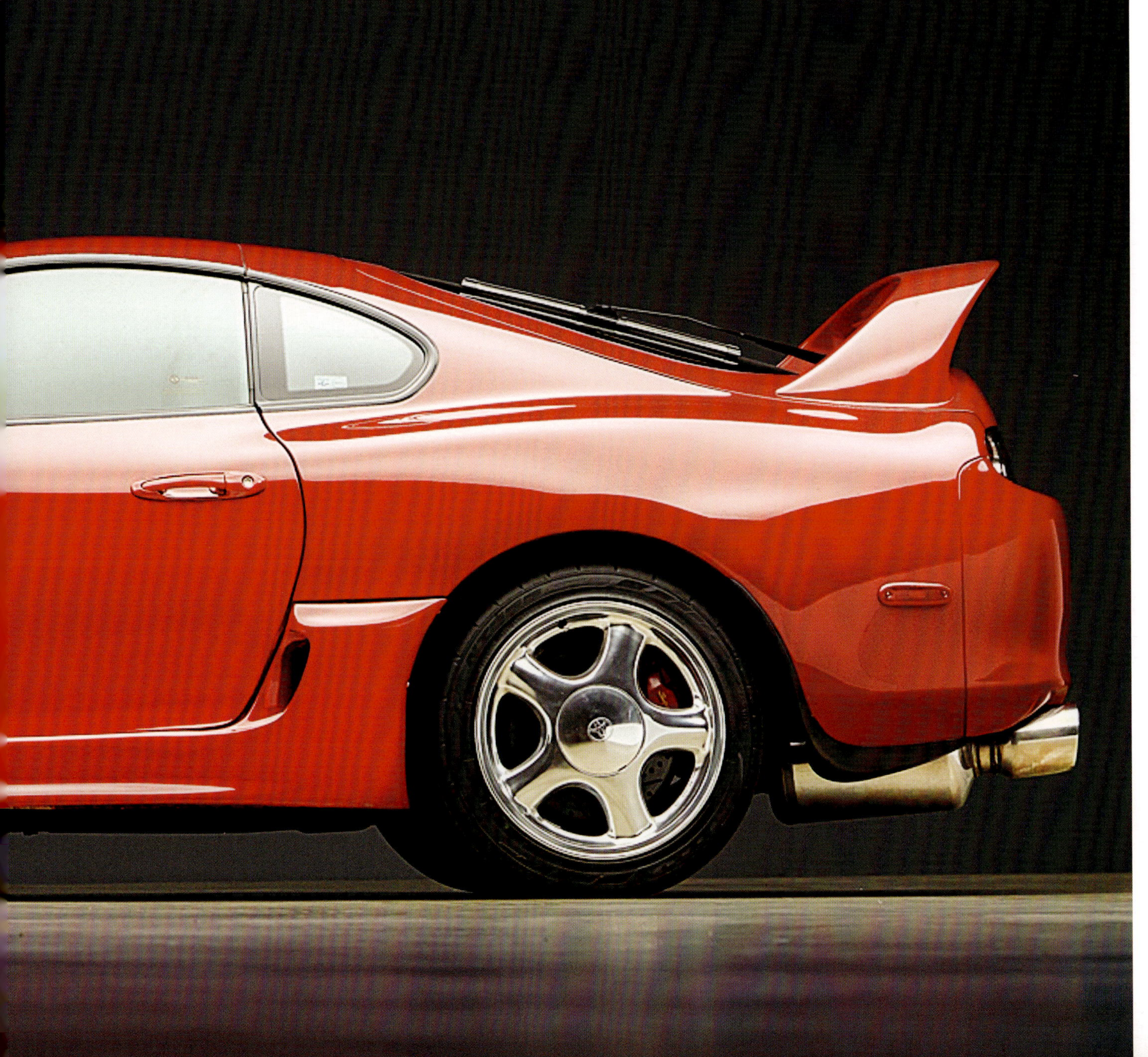

Road & Track magazine called the stunning limited-production vehicle "one of the most exciting and enjoyable cars we've driven" and said it compared favorably with the heralded Porsche 911.

In the early 1970s, Toyota developed a two-door sports coupe, the Celica, which was designed to compete with vehicles such as Ford's Mustang in the United States and its Capri in Europe.

By 1978, and in part to meet American dealers' request for a car that could compete with the Datsun 280Z, Toyota developed a higher-performance version of the Celica. This new version was badged as the Supra (the name derived from the Latin term for "surpass" or "go beyond").

While Celicas were propelled by 4-cylinder engines, the Supra got an inline-6 rated at 200 horse-

Previous and these pages ■ Turbocharging boosted the output of the Supra's 6-cylinder engine, making the sports coupe faster than many more expensive purpose-built sports cars.

The F40-like rear wing wasn't out of place on a sports coupe with surprisingly impressive capabilities.

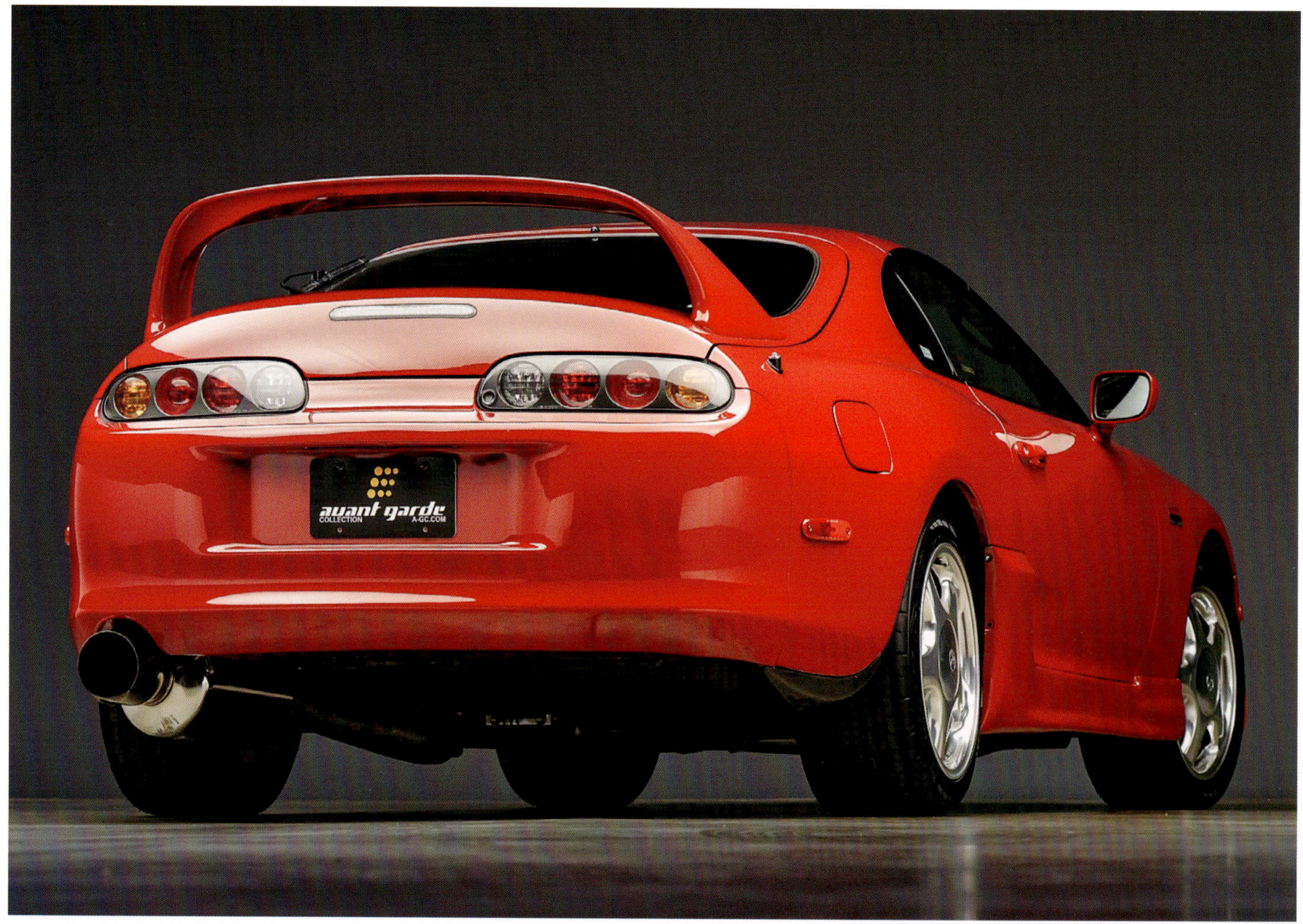

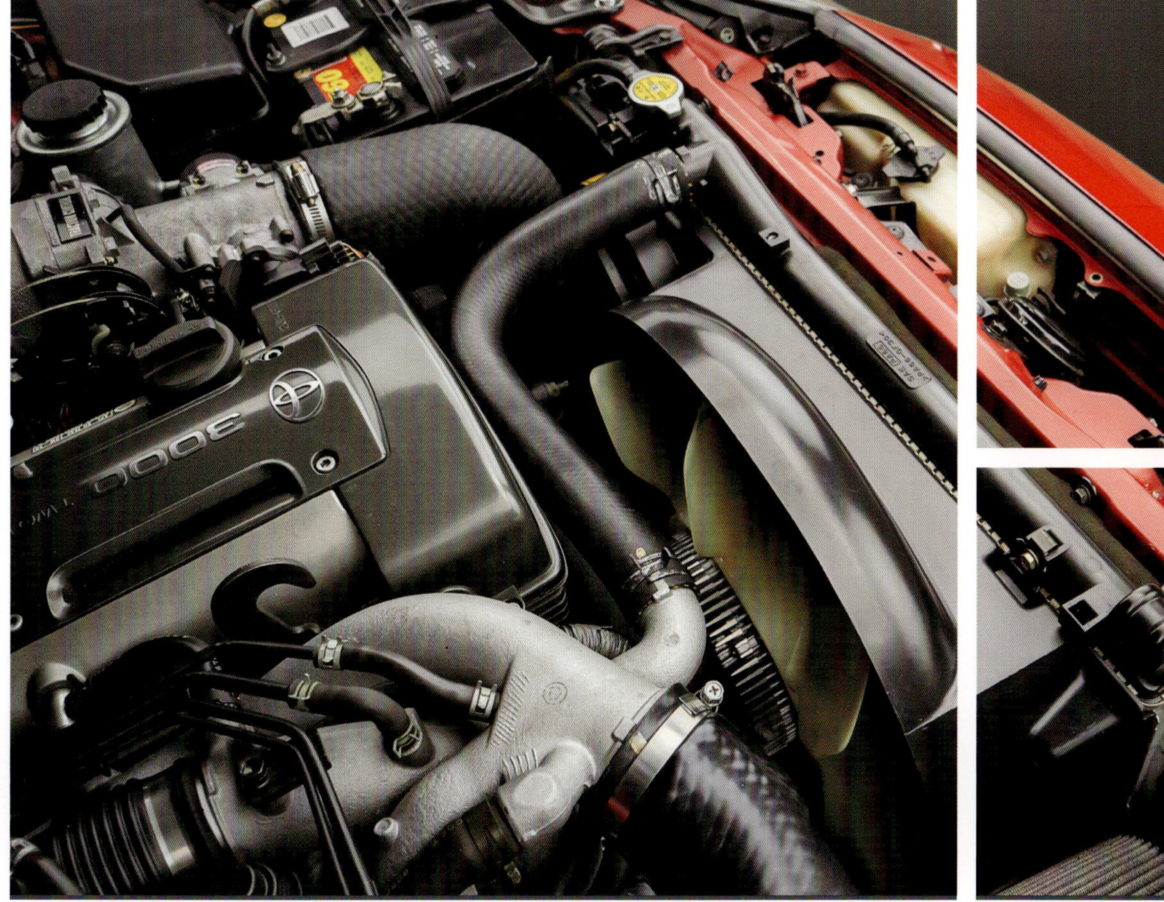

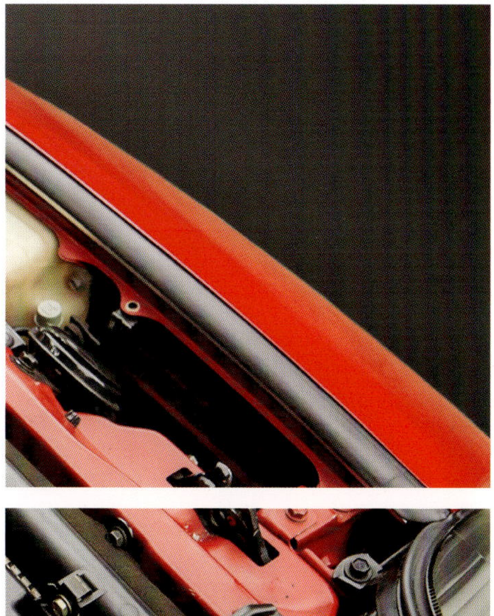

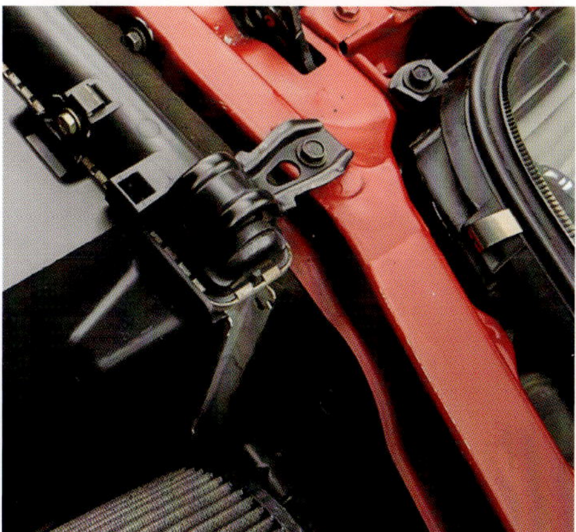

power and rode on a longer wheelbase so the engine fit beneath the lengthened hood.

By the Supra's third generation (1986–1993), horsepower was boosted to 230 by a pair of turbochargers. In 1993, the fourth generation launched, this one more closely related to the Lexus SC model from Toyota's luxury division.

Car and Driver magazine said it saw styling similarities between the 1993 Supra and not the Lexus but the Ferrari F40. It noted, however, that the 1993 Supra shared its 3.0-liter inline 6-cylinder engine with its Lexus cousin, and that the engine was good for 230 horsepower in standard guise or for 320—and a walloping 315 pound-feet (433 Nm) of torque—when equipped with a pair of turbochargers.

Thus equipped, the magazine reported, the sports coupe could propel itself to 60 mph (96 km/h) in a tick more than 4.6 seconds, which it noted was quicker than an Acura NSX, Porsche 928 GT, Mazda RX-7, or your basic Chevrolet Corvette. And it could post such a sprint for a price ($42,000) far below that of the look-alike F40.

Motor Trend magazine also appreciated the Supra's speed but added this: "Like the Supra Turbo's acceleration, its handling and braking prowess are close to the best we've ever seen, regardless of cost...A Supra with this magnitude of road rocket performance could be history in the making."

And it was, at least through the end of production of that fourth-generation version. Toyota then put the Supra badge on hiatus until it launched a fifth-generation version in 2019.

MCLAREN F1

Decades later and "still the definition of the perfect supercar"

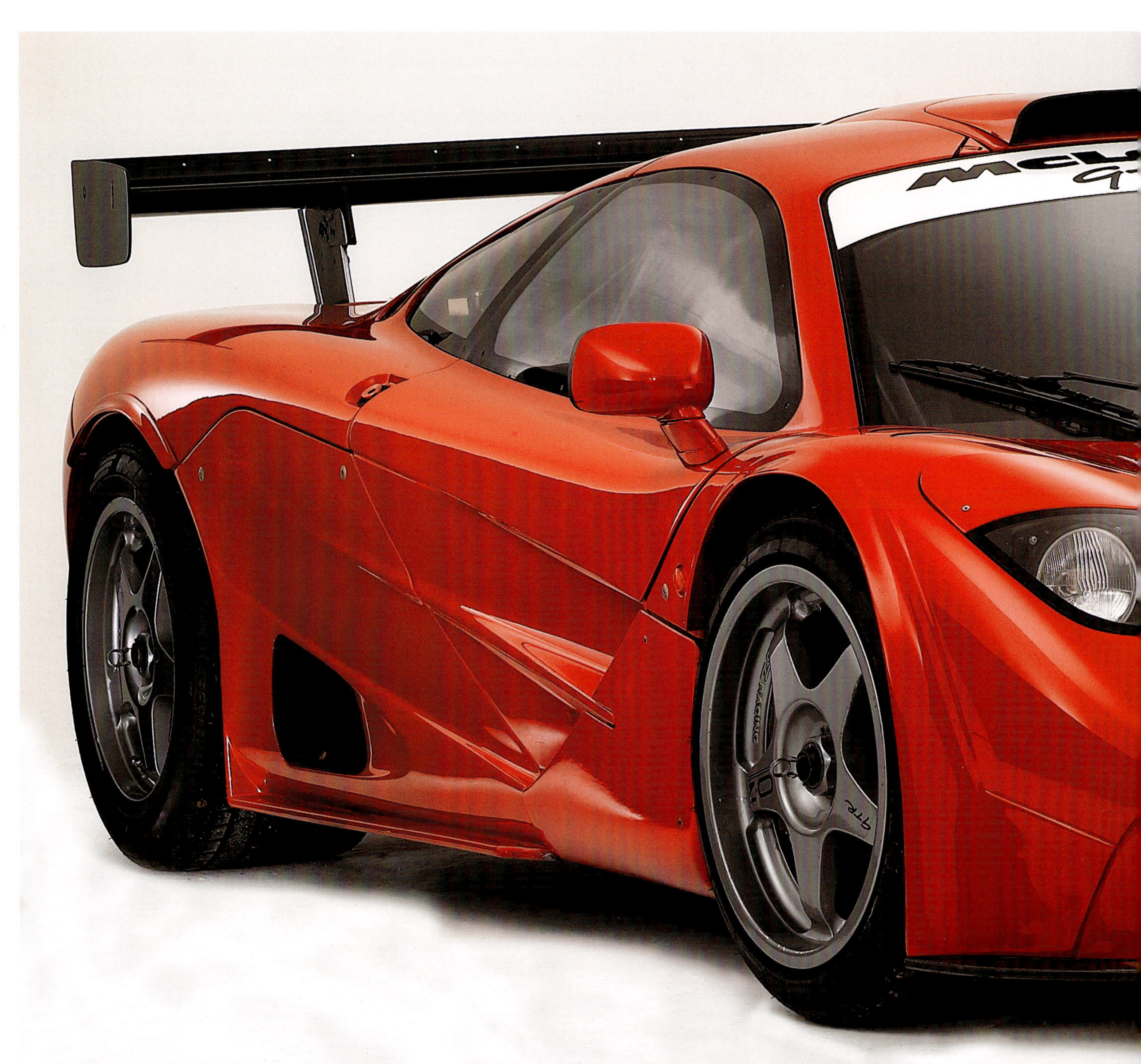

"McLaren F1 humbles all other supercars," *Car and Driver* magazine praised in its period road test.

After its turn in one of the supercars, Britain's *CAR* expounded: "The 627-horsepower F1, which humbles all previous slingshot exotics, is just what design director Gordon Murray pledged it would be: the ultimate motoring experience, the closest sensation to a street-legal grand prix car. Forget Porsche's 959, Ferrari's F40, Jaguar's XJ220, Bugatti's EB110. They're overweight, underpowered pussycats compared with McLaren's BMW-powered blockbuster. The F1...trounces them emphatically."

In 2020, decades after the McLaren F1 production had ended, *Road & Track* declared, "The McLaren F1 is still the definition of the perfect supercar."

At on the thirtieth anniversary of the car's unveiling, *Evo* proclaimed, "All these years on, the world has yet to welcome a better packaged, better finished, or more habitable supercar. Or one that's as potent, light, and tactile."

Bruce McLaren moved from New Zealand to England in 1958 to pursue his career in motorsports. A decade later, he and teammate Denis Hulme dominated the Can-Am Challenge Cup series.

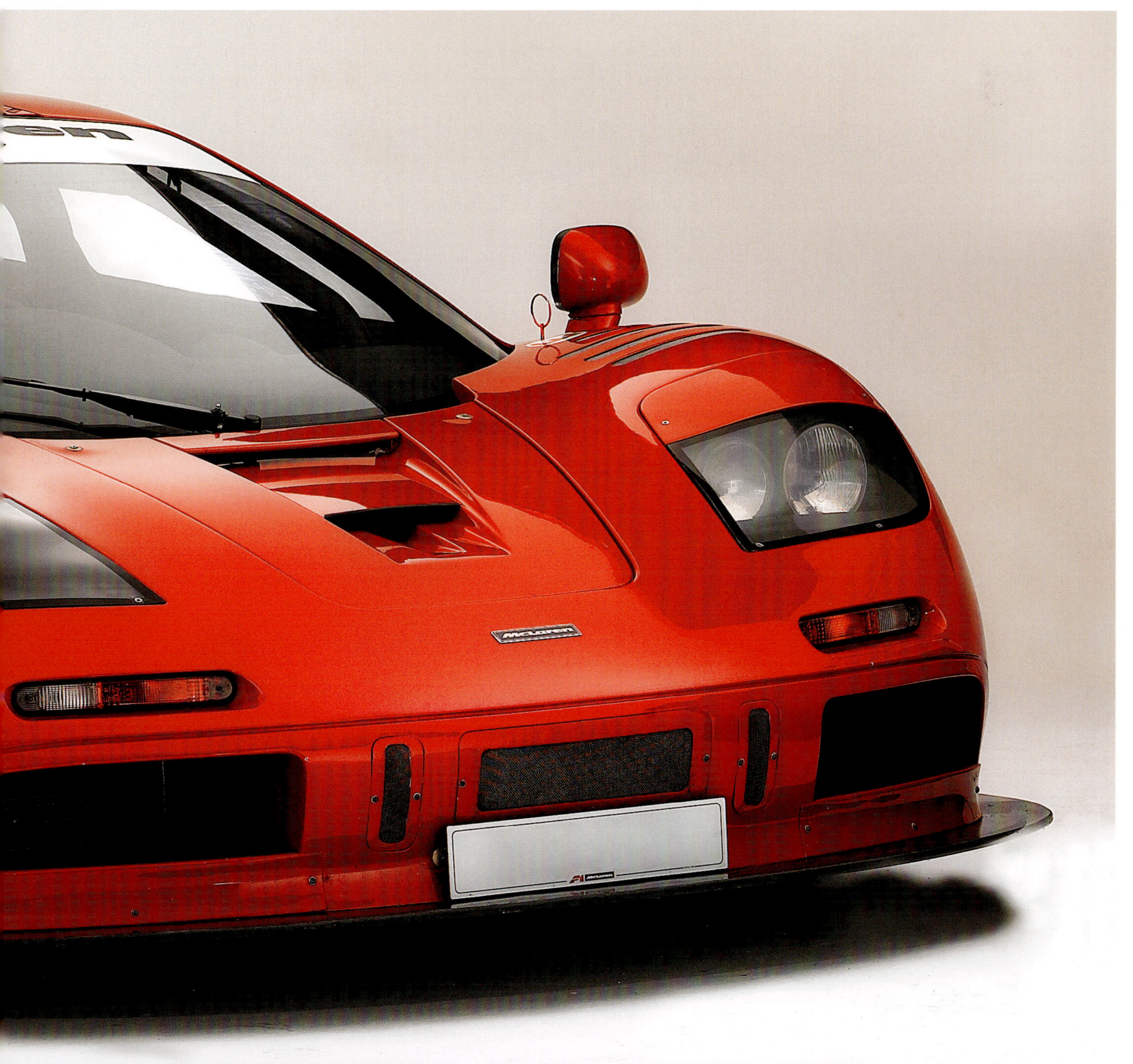

McLaren also built and drove at Indianapolis and in Formula One. McLaren died in a crash while testing a race car in 1970, but McLaren Racing went on to win the F1 championship seven times in eight seasons from 1984 to 1991.

At that point, team leadership felt ready to produce the ultimate road car and handed the assignment to its racing car designer/engineer Gordon Murray.

Murray left his native South Africa for England in hopes of working for Lotus. Instead, he designed guided missiles before landing on with the Brabham racing team, where one of his innovative designs was so successful it was banned by a rules change. From Brabham, Murray moved to McLaren.

To be faithful to the spirit of F1 racing, Murray built the McLaren F1 road car around the driver, who sat in the middle of the cockpit with passenger seats on either side and slightly behind so as not to interfere with the driver's peripheral vision.

Just behind the cockpit, which featured air conditioning, power windows, an audio system, Connolly leather, and custom luggage fit into panels just ahead of the rear wheels, was the engine. It was a 6.1-liter V12 from BMW that was naturally aspirated, producing its power (650 Nm of torque) without turbo or supercharging. To help control such power, Murray used a technology from his outlawed Brabham F1 car—a pair of small fans literally sucked the McLaren to the roadway. To enhance braking, an airfoil brake emerged from the car's tail.

The McLaren F1 was unveiled at the Monaco Grand Prix in 1992. The following year, the prototype reached 231 mph (372 km/h) in testing at the circular track in Nardo, Italy. In 1998, racer Andy Wallace achieved a record-setting two-way average of 240.14 mph at the Volkswagen test track in Germany.

McLaren produced a reported 106 examples of its marvellous F1 supercar between 1992 and 1998.

For the bottom line, we return to *Car and Driver* magazine's report from 1994: "Forget the Jaguar XJ220, Bugatti EB110, Ferrari F40—until now cars deserving to be called rapid. The McLaren blitzes them all. We're talking about a road car that surpasses the performance of most of the racers that will line up for this year's 24 Hours of Le Mans race."

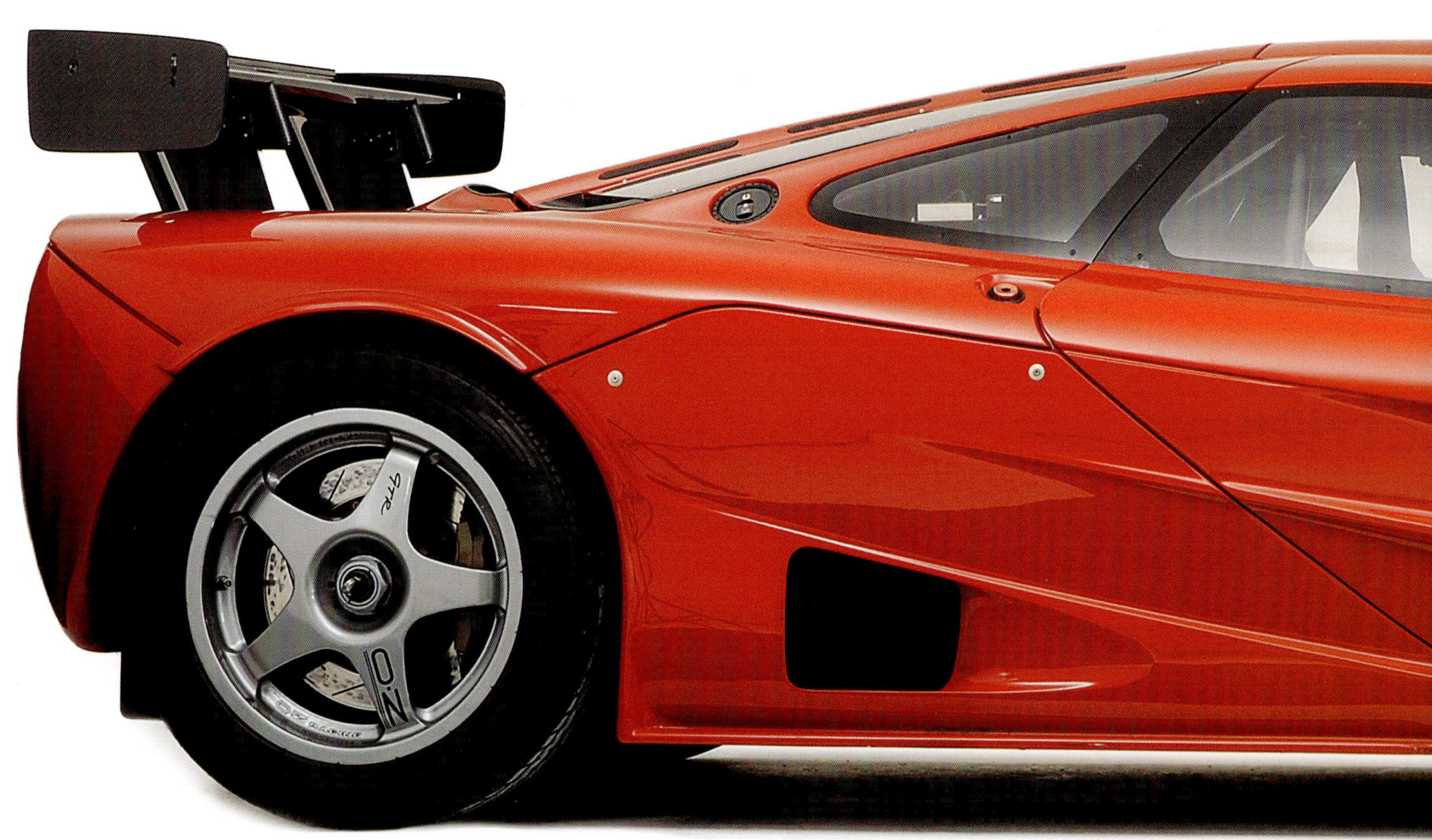

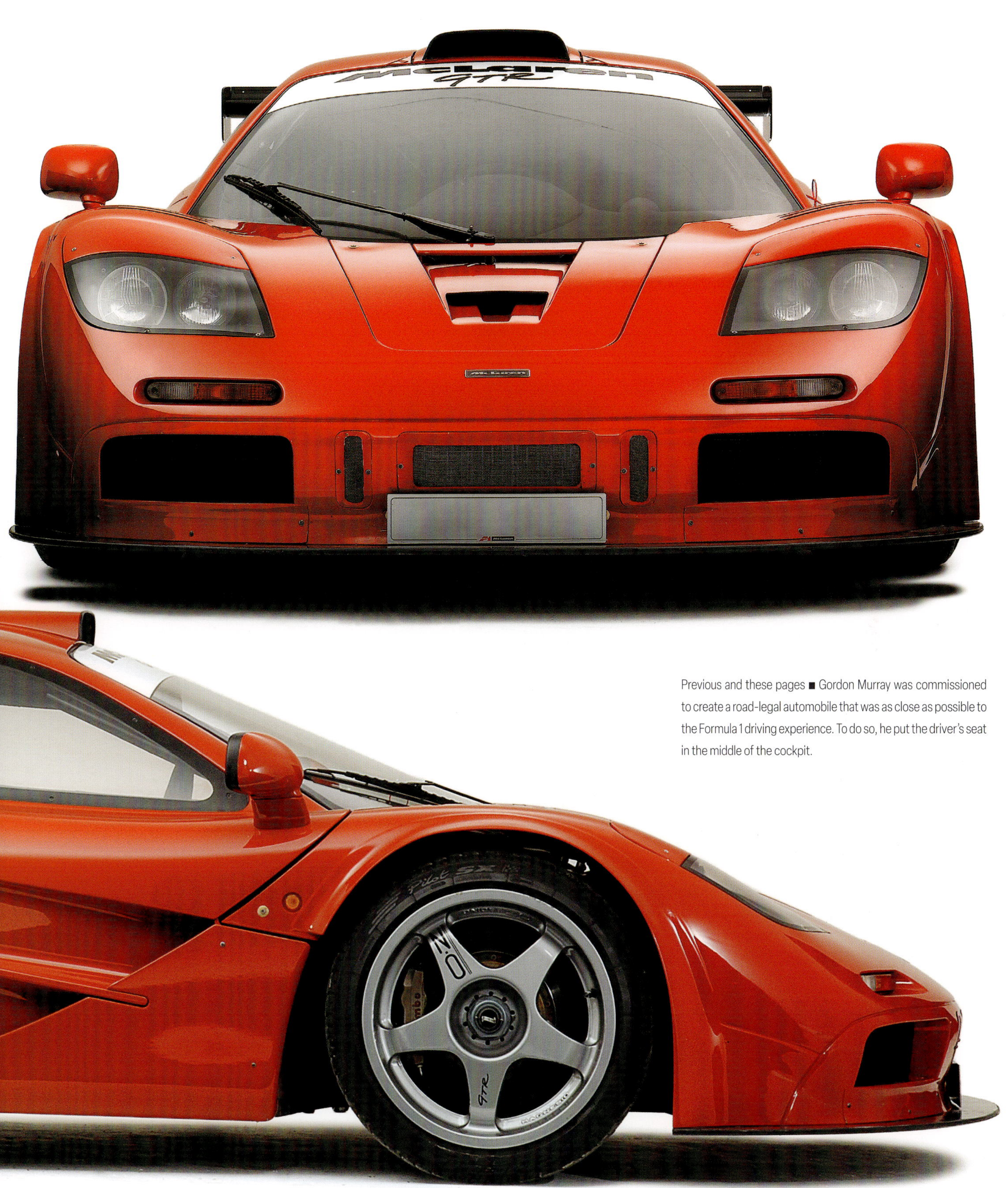

Previous and these pages ■ Gordon Murray was commissioned to create a road-legal automobile that was as close as possible to the Formula 1 driving experience. To do so, he put the driver's seat in the middle of the cockpit.

The McLaren F1 was bred in racing but featured air conditioning, power windows, Connolly leather, and other luxury comforts for its occupants.

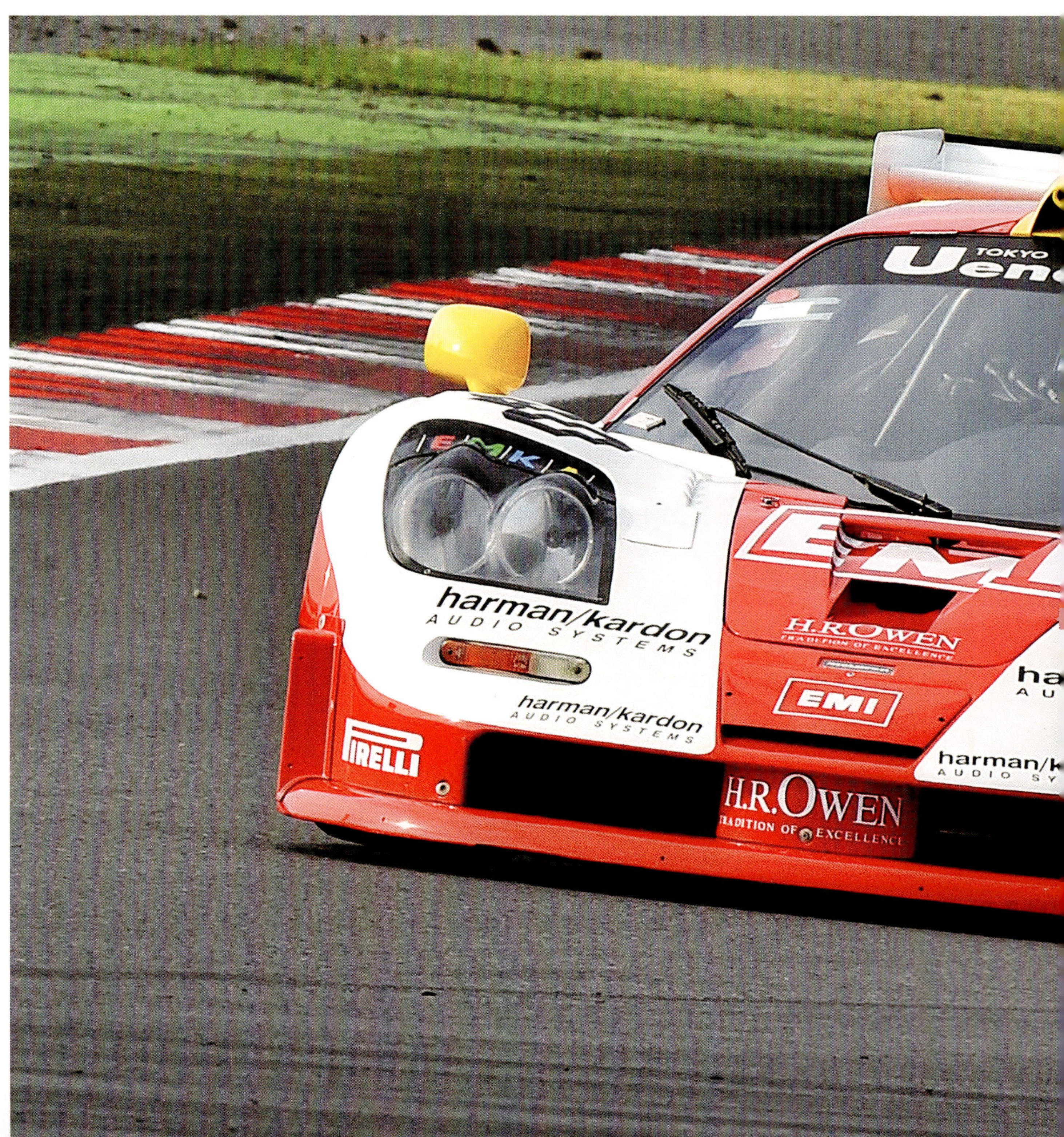

■ The McLaren F1 GTR was the version of the supercar specially prepared for motorsports competition. In 1995 one such car won the 24 Hours of Le Mans race.

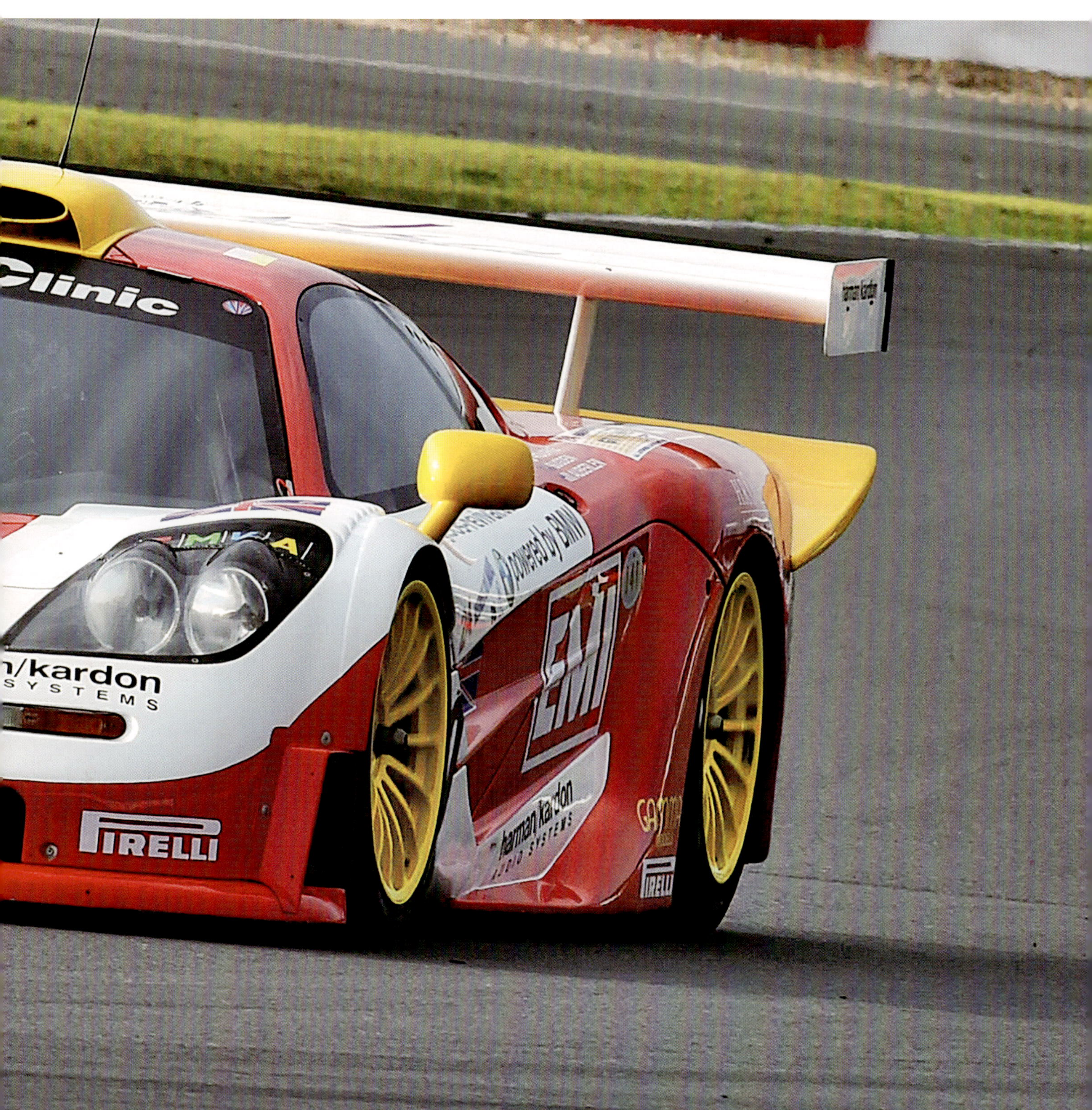

PORSCHE 911 (993)

The end of an era: the last Porsche with an air-cooled engine

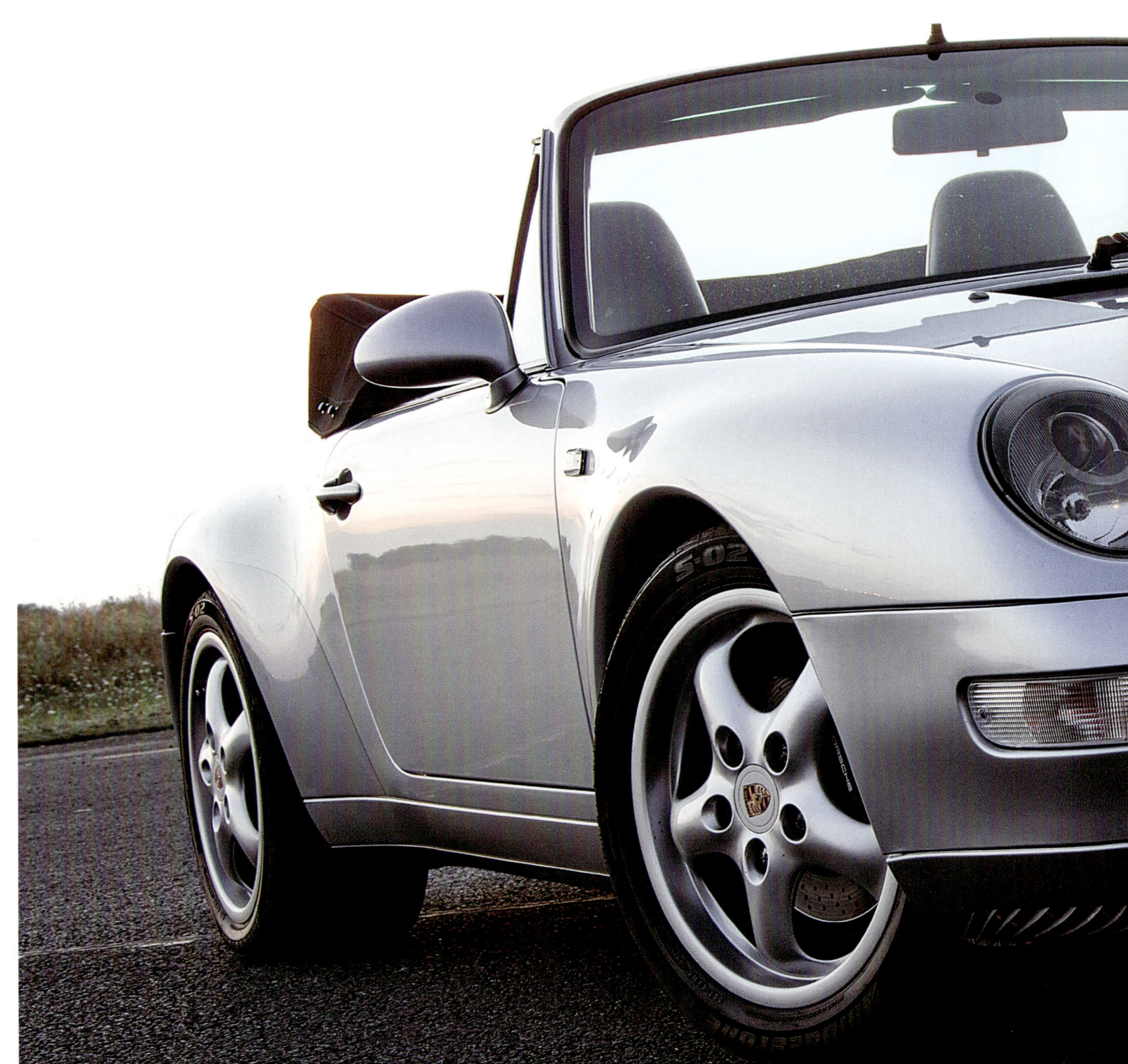

1990 ➤ 1999

Ferdinand Porsche created some of the world's fastest racing cars and was the chief engineer for the Volkswagen Type 1, the car that became beloved around the world as the "Beetle."

His son, Ferry Porsche, used the Type 1 as the basis for a sporty offspring, the Porsche 356. Ferdinand's nephew and Ferry's cousin, F.A. "Butzi" Porsche, studied design rather than engineering.

When in the mid-1960s it came time for the 356 to be succeeded by a new Porsche sports car, Butzi designed the 911, which in addition to a more streamlined body featured a horizontally opposed 6-cylinder "boxer" engine rather than the previous 4-cylinder, as well as a 5-speed transmission, enhanced suspension, and steering and four-wheel disc brakes.

Porsche had a modern sports car, albeit one with its engine still at the rear of the car and cooled by air rather than liquid.

Since then, the 911 has been in continuous production, maintaining its basic profile throughout while being updated mechanically and in features to improve its occupants' experiences.

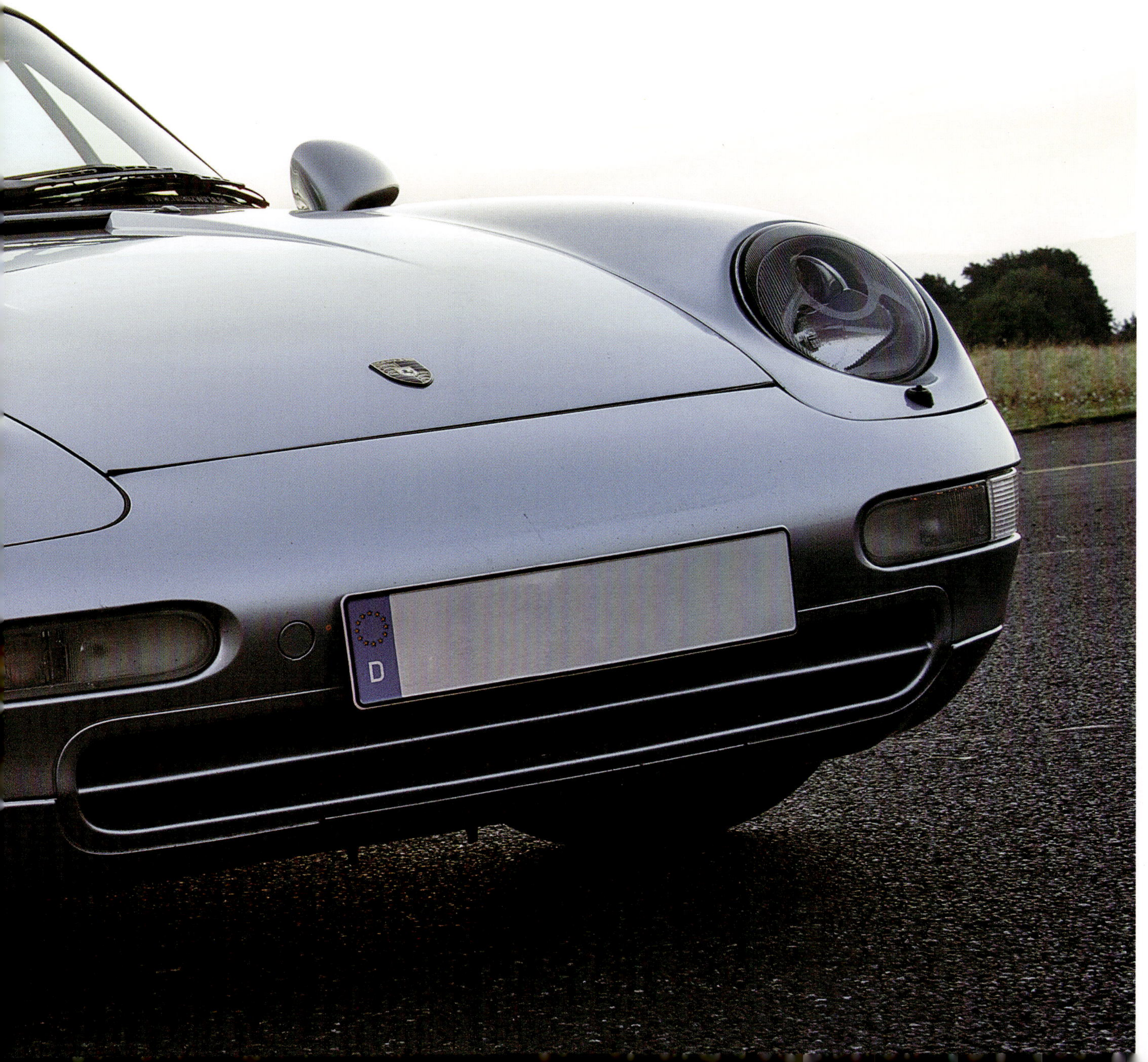

Porsche realized the importance of the 993 to its customers and thus delayed the launch of its successor.

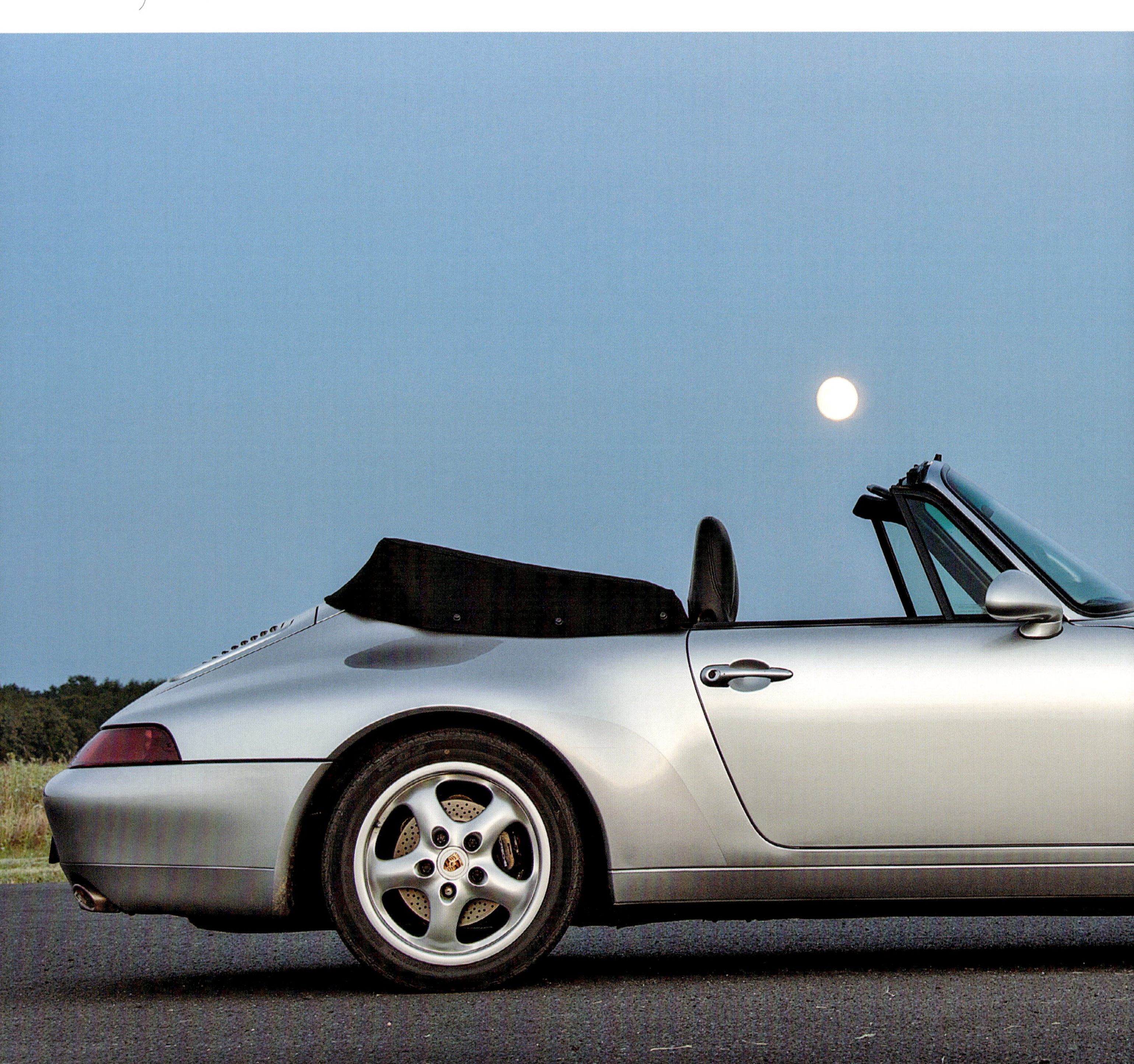

Previous and these pages ■ The "pinnacle of the breed" of air-cooled Porsches, the 993 became cherished by collectors.

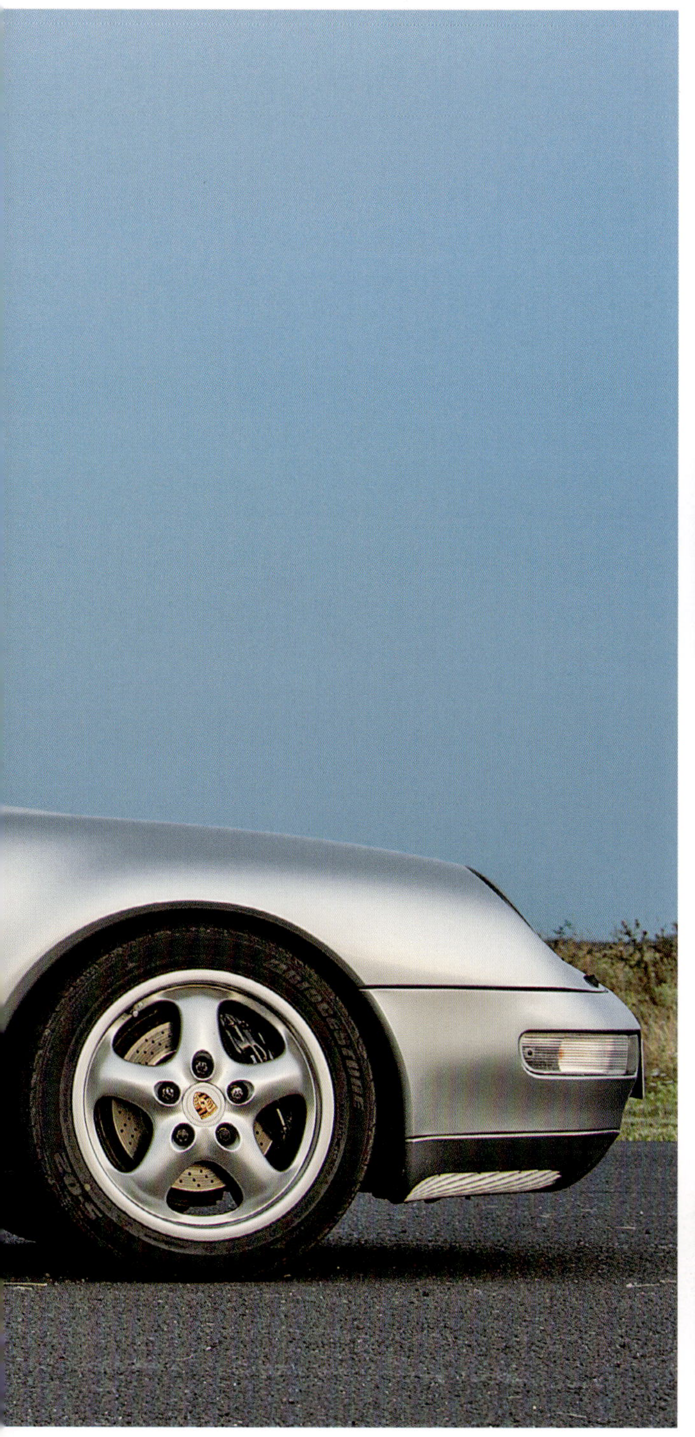

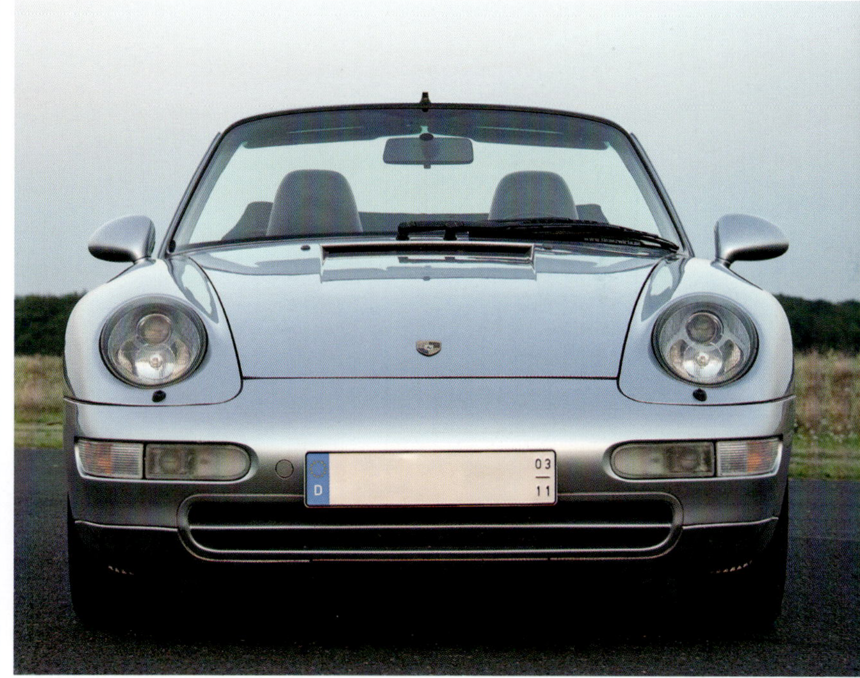

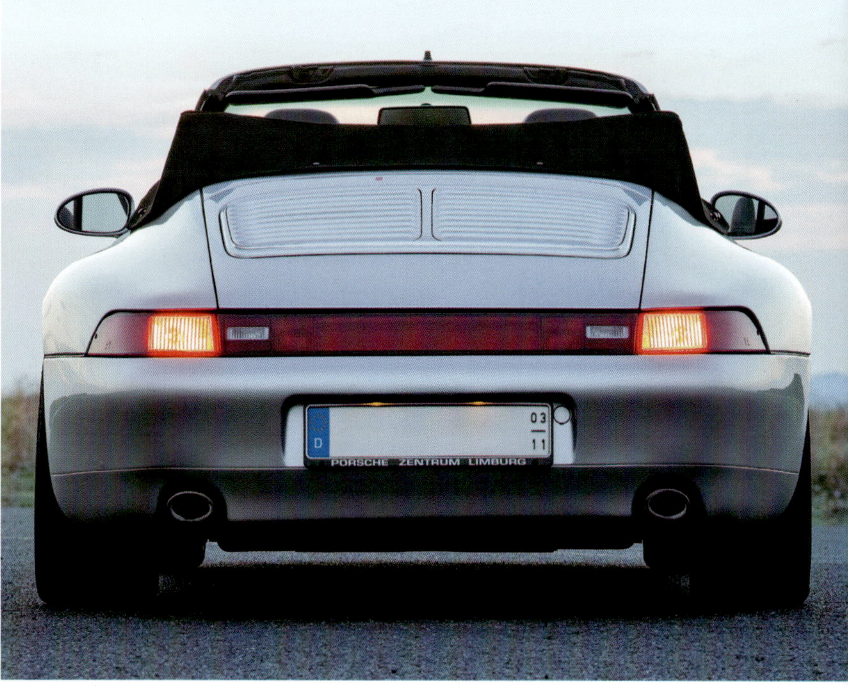

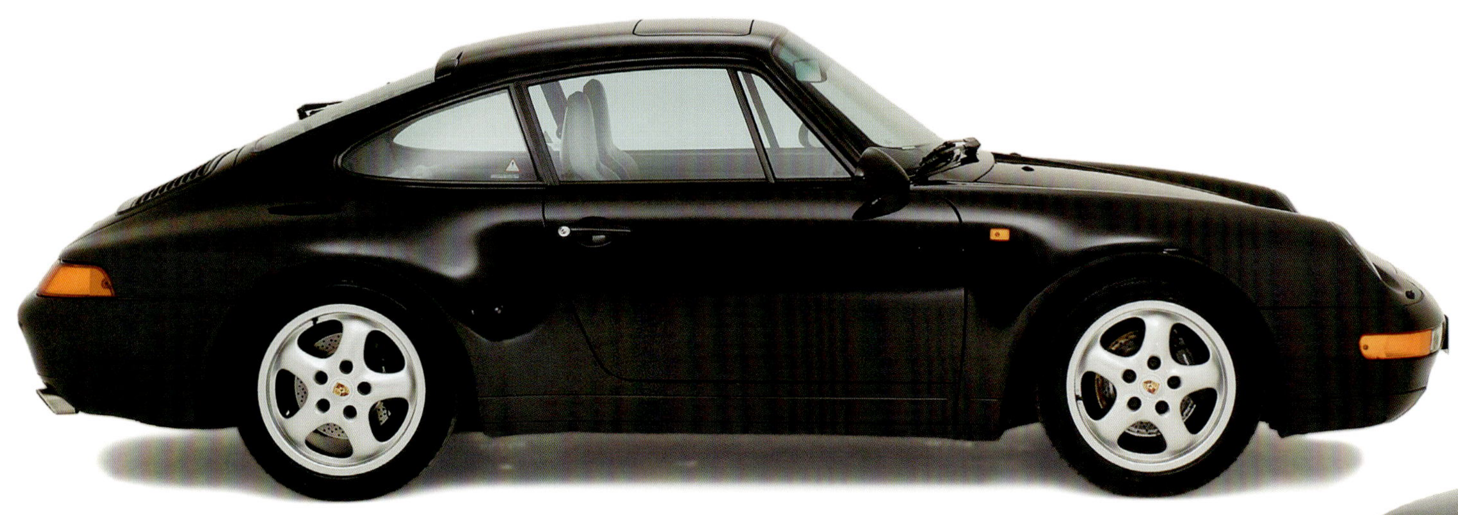

Porsche had taken air-cooled engine technology as far as it could, so the next 911—the 996—would incorporate liquid cooling.

As a senior engineer for a rival company expressed it, while others invested in making their cars look different from generation to generation, Porsche retained the car's iconic styling and focused on the details, on enhancements to design and component technology that propelled its 911 closer and closer to automotive perfection.

The fourth generation of the 911's attention-to-detail evolution was the 993. At first, its 3.0-liter engine provided 272 horsepower. Before long that figure would increases to 300, or to 408 in the form of the turbocharged 3.6-liter unit in the 911 Turbo.

But even Porsche could extract only so much from an air-cooled engine, even with turbocharging and even while taking advantage of the engine's smaller size and weight. But in the face of new fuel-economy and emission regulations and the need for even more power to operate onboard electronics, air-conditioning equipment, and such, even Porsche realized it was time to make a change.

Thus the 993 version of the 911 was in production only from 1994 to 1998. It was then replaced by the 996 edition, which would have its 6-cylinder engine water cooled.

The 993 would be the last of the air-cooled Porsches, and with its brief production run would emerge as something of an instant classic and a car cherished by collectors.

Even Porsche was aware that it had produced something special, and it delayed the launch of the 996 so it could take full advantage of the appeal of the 993 and the subsequent versions—convertible, four-wheel-drive, and Turbo—that would arrive to round out the lineup.

Classic car insurer and value tracker Hagerty looked back at the 993 in 2024.

"As the final air-cooled 911, it's seen as the pinnacle of the breed by many, especially as it was the model charged with keeping Porsche's flagship relevant against ever more sophisticated and capable opposition from the likes of the Ferrari F355 and Honda NSX," it suggested.

"The 993 never slipped in value in the same way its successor, the water-cooled 996, did, and that means surviving 993s tend to have been better cared for. As a result, it's been a solid classic Porsche choice almost since the day the last version of the 993 went off sale in 1998."

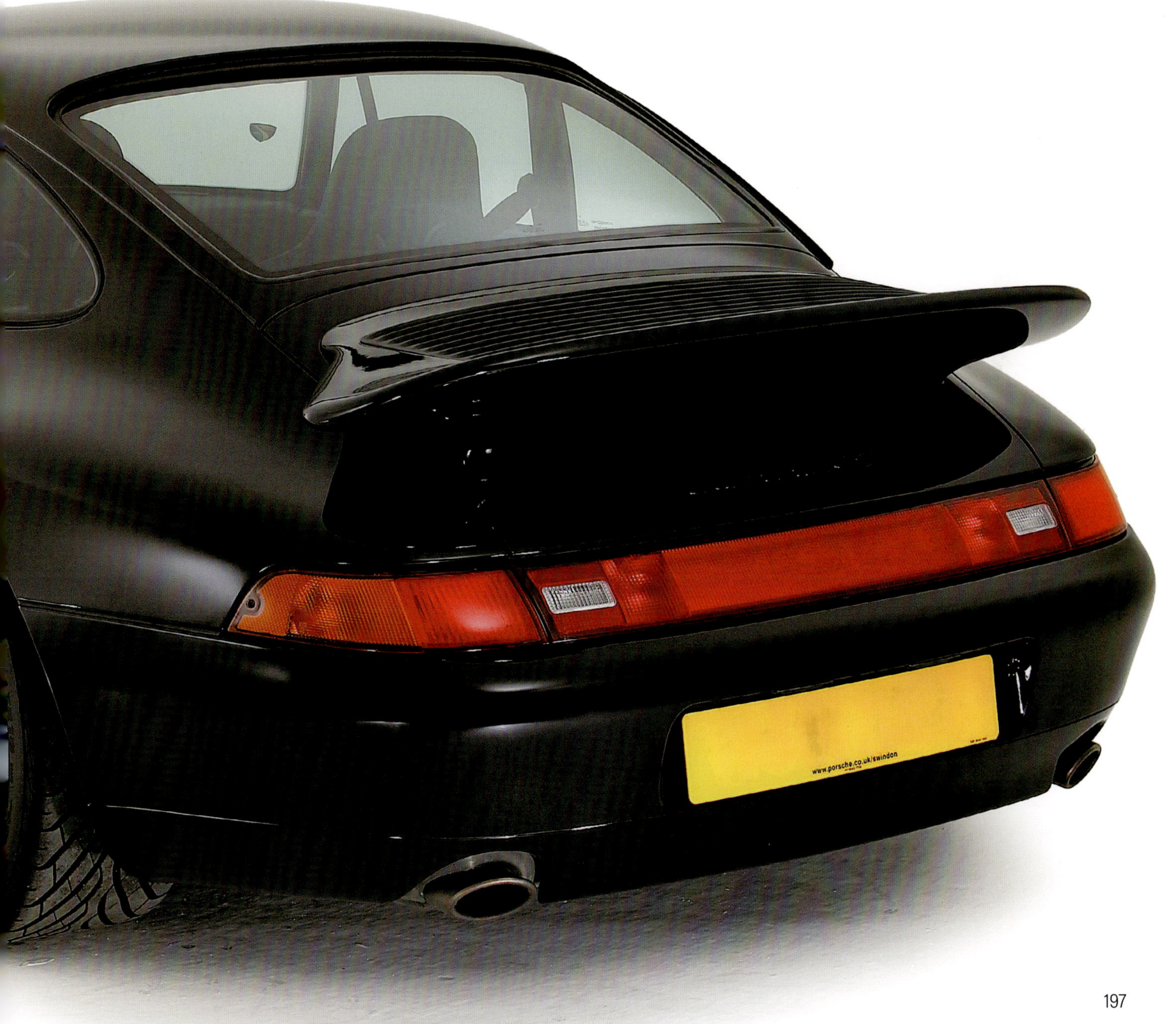

■ The "whale tail" spoiler on the engine cover signified the Turbo version of the car, with performance boosted to more than 400 horsepower.

1990 ➤ 1999

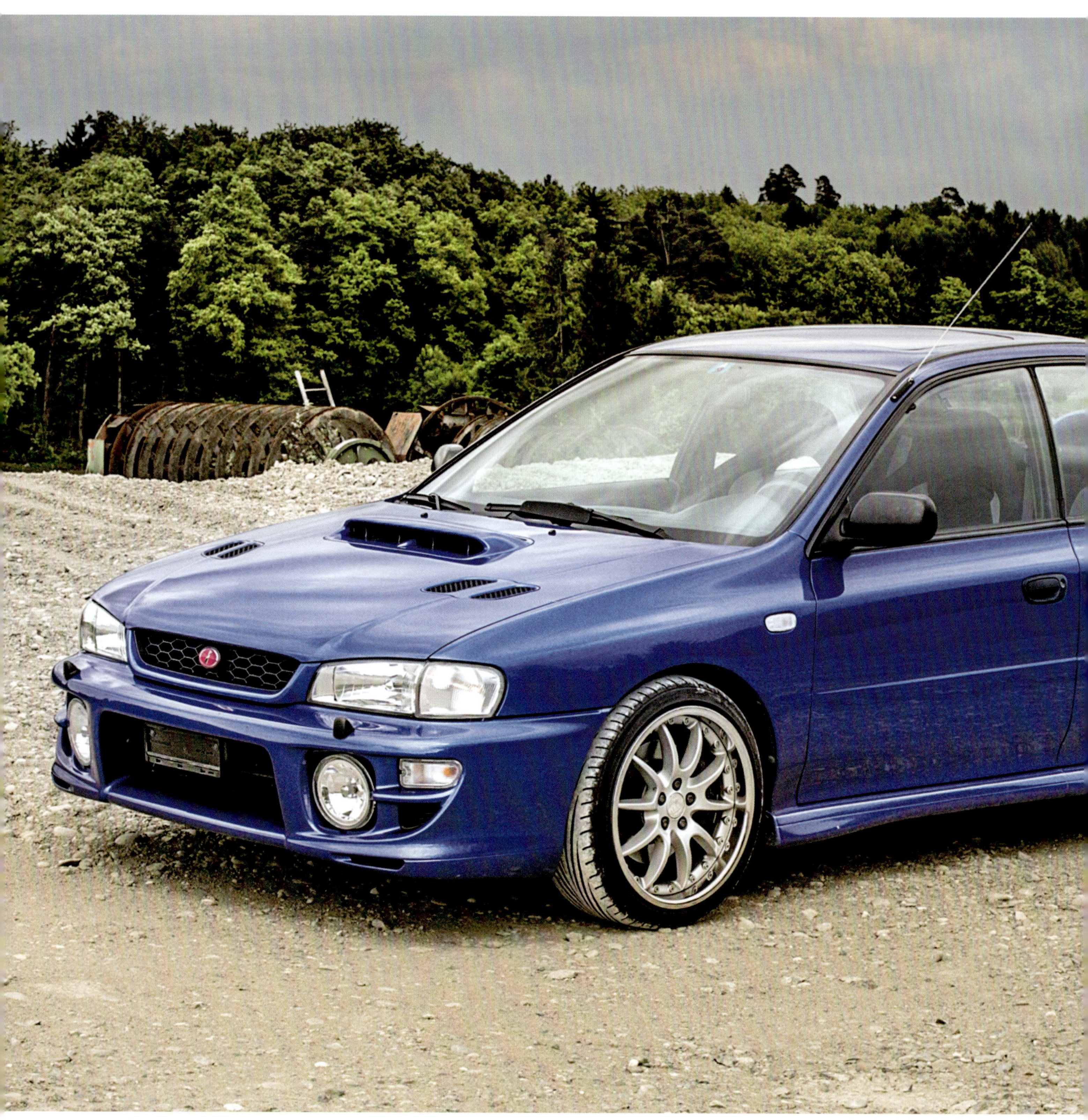

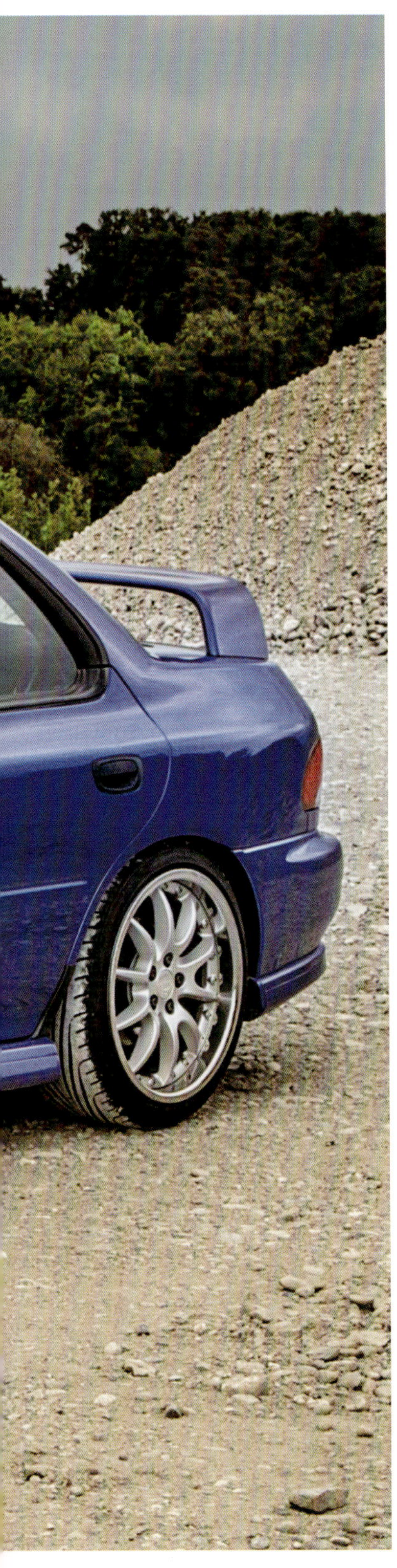

SUBARU IMPREZA WRX STI

The quite impressive transformation of compact sedan into motorsports champion

What the Detroit muscle cars of the 1960s were to the baby boomer generation, Japanese vehicles such as the Nissan Skyline GT-R and Subaru Impreza WRX STI were to the millennial generation.

Perhaps not as powerful or as fast as the earlier American machines, the later Japanese cars were nimble and quick and exciting, and in the case of the Subaru's Impreza WRX STI, that excitement extended beyond the pavement.

Like the Lancia Stratos and Delta Integrale and Ford RS200 of previous decades, the Subaru Impreza WRX STI was a street-legal rally car. The initials that followed the Impreza model name stood for World Rally eXperimental and Subaru Tecnica International.

After World War II, Japanese companies with experience in manufacturing aircraft, engines, and even motor scooters joined to create Fuji Heavy Industries. In the late 1950s they produced their first automobiles under the Subaru brand, which would become known for its 4-cylinder "boxer" style engines (small in size at 2.0 liters but pumping out nearly 250 horsepower) and sure-footed symmetrical (and permanent) four-wheel drive system.

Subaru had entered its cars in rally events as early as 1970, but it wasn't until the 1990s—when it linked with the Prodrive team from England and a major sponsor—that it would secure the first of a series of major-event victories.

Subaru carried Colin McRae to the World Rally Championship drivers' title in 1995 and that same year began a string of WRC manufacturers' titles that ran through the 1997 season.

Australia's *Which Car?* magazine touted the Impreza WRX STI of the late 1990s as "The ultimate STI—a performance watermark so high that modern Subarus are still yet to surpass it."

■ Cosmetic changes designed for rally competition gave the car a special presence on the street.

FERRARI F50

Ferrari couldn't wait to celebrate its fiftieth anniversary

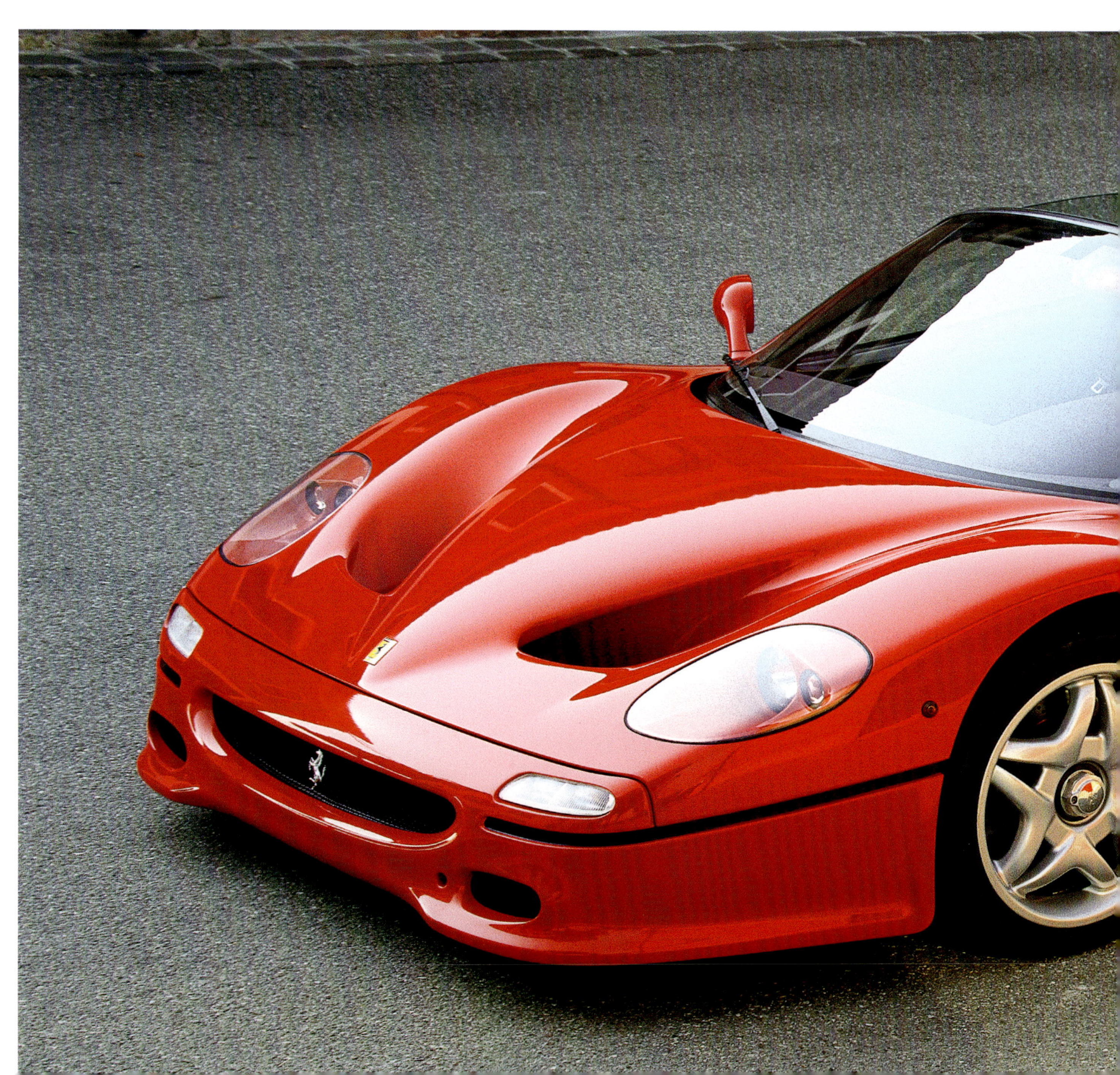

1990 ➤ 1999

In the previous chapter on the New Classic Cars from the 1980s, we met the Ferrari F40, the last car with which Enzo Ferrari was directly involved and presented in 1988 in celebration of the company's fortieth anniversary.

Enzo Ferrari died months after the F40 launch. It would seem then that the subsequent Ferrari F50 would be a celebration of the company's fiftieth anniversary, which it was, except that it went into production in 1995 after its debut that spring at the Geneva Motor Show. So perhaps we should consider it an early anniversary present.

In fact, the F50 was a Ferrari Formula One race car that could be driven legally on public roads, not just on racetracks. No, it didn't look like an F1 racer. Its wheels were not uncovered; instead they were enclosed along with other components within coachwork designed at Pininfarina.

Again in contrast with the Ferrari's Grand Prix racing magazine, it didn't have a single-seater cockpit but an enclosed occupant compartment with room for a driver and a passenger.

But it did have a V12 engine based on the one in the Ferrari F1 racer, and that

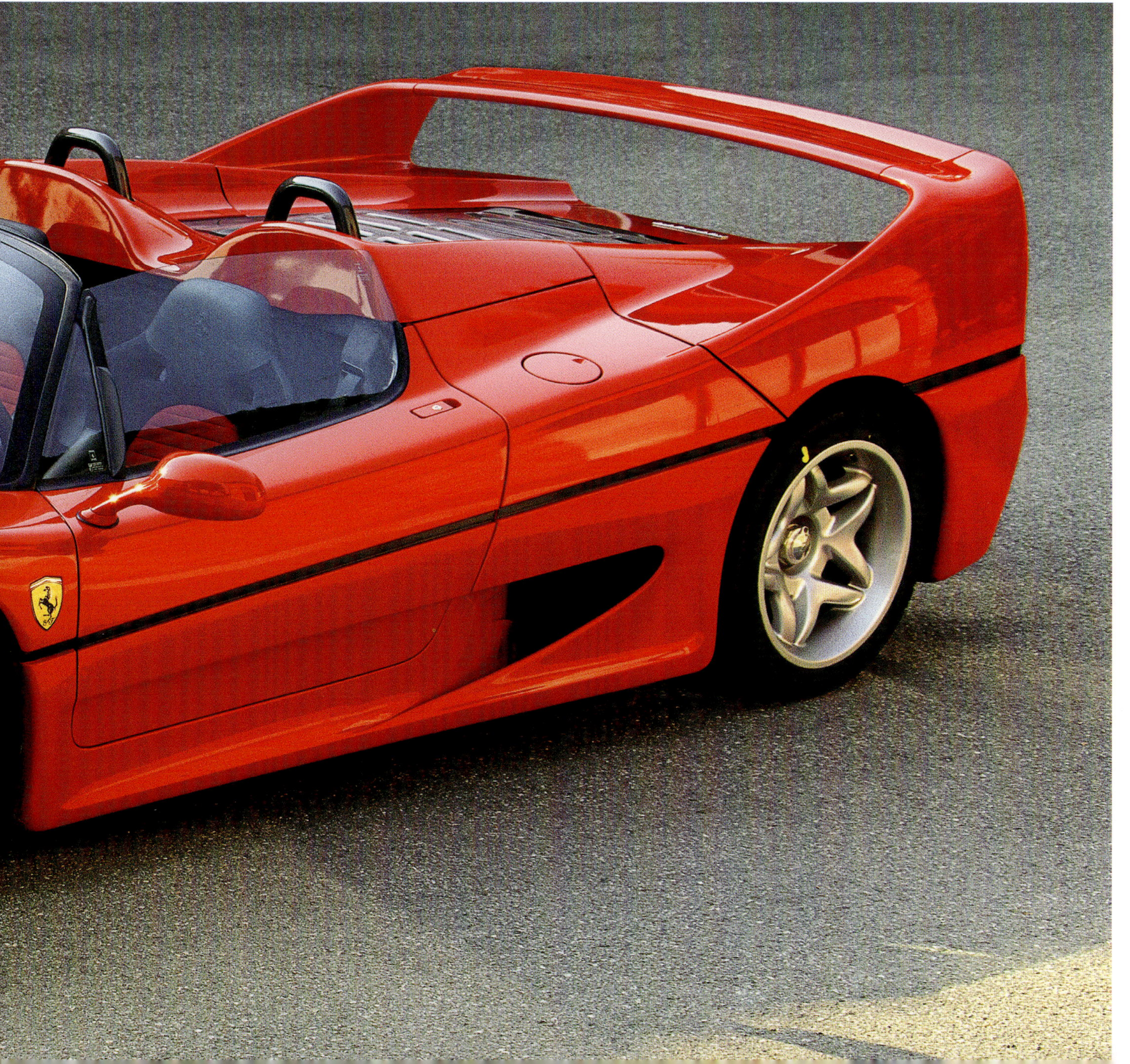

engine was mounted behind the cockpit and could propel the F50 to speeds in excess of 200 mph (322 km/h). And while F1 regulations limited the engine's displacement to 3.5 liters, for the F50 the engine would be enlarged to 4.7 liters, providing 520 horsepower, albeit nearly 300 less than what was available to Gerhard Berger and Jean Alesi in the Ferrari 651 F1 racers.

The F50 also was comprised primarily of carbon fiber, employed F1-style suspension, underbody panels, fuel cell-style gas tank, and had a huge rear wing to provide road-gripping downforce. It also had a removable roof panel so its occupants could enjoy an open-cockpit experience.

At its launch, Ferrari's new president, Luca di Montezemolo, noted that all the years of Ferrari racing experience had gone into the F50's development, and this likely would be the last time his or any company could truly base a road car on its F1 racer because of increasingly stringent emission regulations.

Ferrari also announced that the F50 would be a limited-production car, limited to 349 examples, the last produced in 1997. Why 349? Because Ferrari's research indicated that there might be only 350 buyers around the world for such a car. And because Ferraris should always be hard to obtain, the decision was made to build one car fewer than the market might demand.

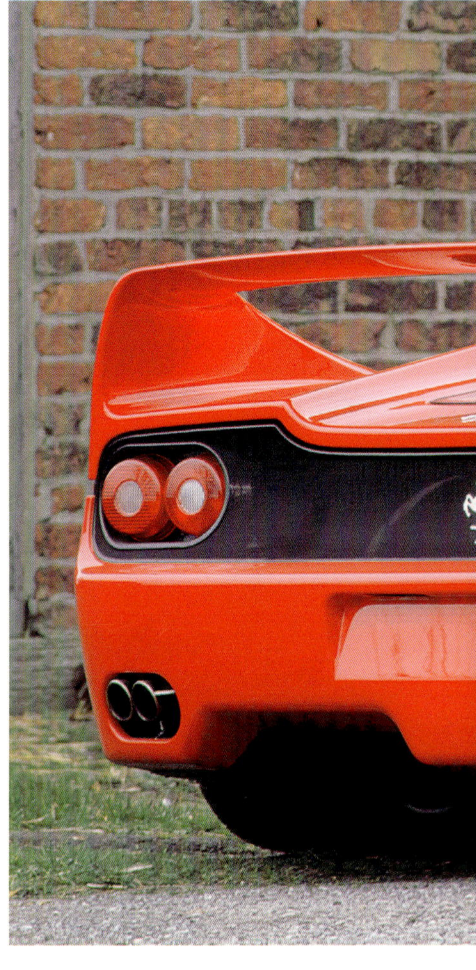

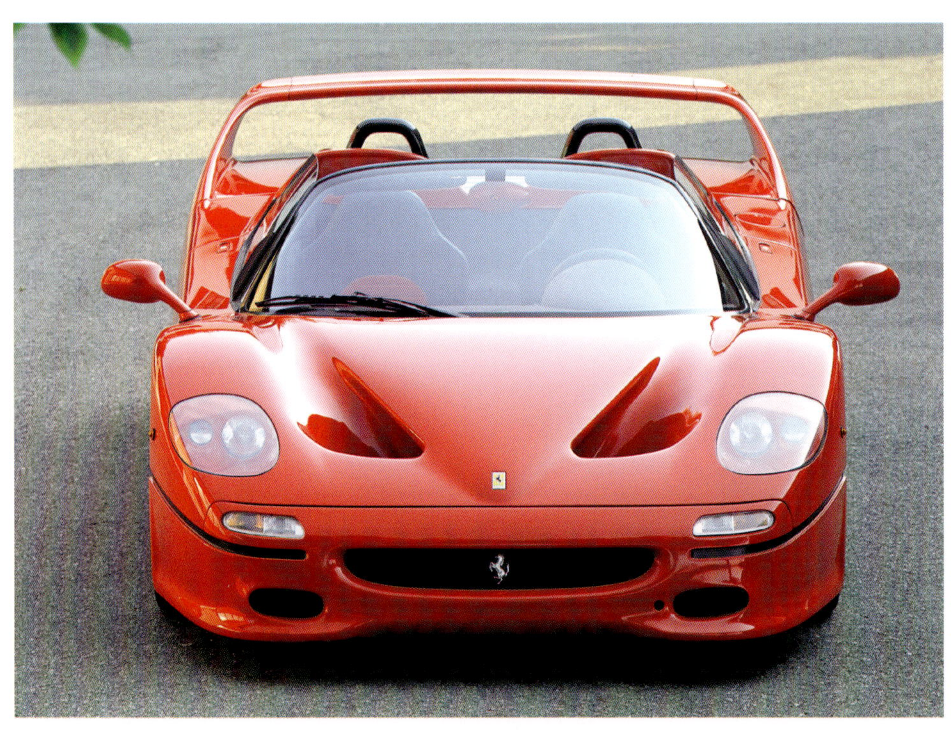

Previous and these pages ■ The F50 followed in the tire tracks laid down the previous decade by the F40 and brought along nearly a decade of technological evolution.

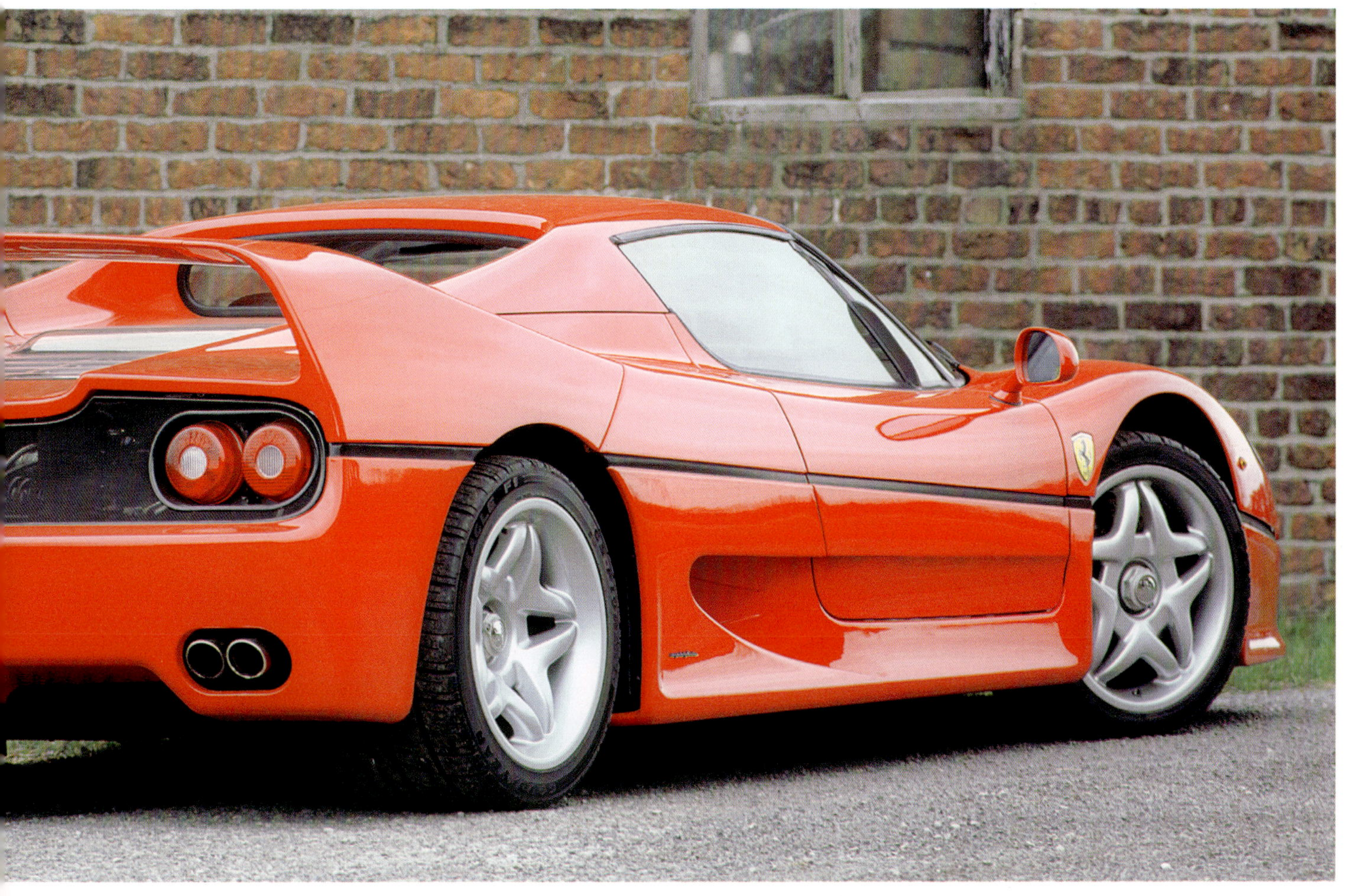

Unlike Ferrari's F1 race car, the F50 had side-by-side seats, meaning a passenger could share the thrill ride.

"Packed full of Formula 1 tech, the F50 was a gloriously balanced supercar, and with a never-to-be-repeated combination of an F1-derived V12 and a gated manual gearbox, it was one of the greatest ever analogue supercars," praised Britain's *Evo* magazine.

In 1997, *Car and Driver* magazine took an F50 around Ferrari's own test track.

"Amid the wails, howls, and whoops from the engine and gearbox—yes, and a few from the driver—it comes as a surprise to find Ferrari's 513-hp F50 a benign and even friendly car," it reported. "And it's clear after two laps around Ferrari's Fiorano test track that there's enough of a racing flavor in the roadgoing Grand Prix car to make the driver feel like a hero."

Ferrari's new president said regulations likely meant the F50 would be the last example of a street-legal grand prix racer.

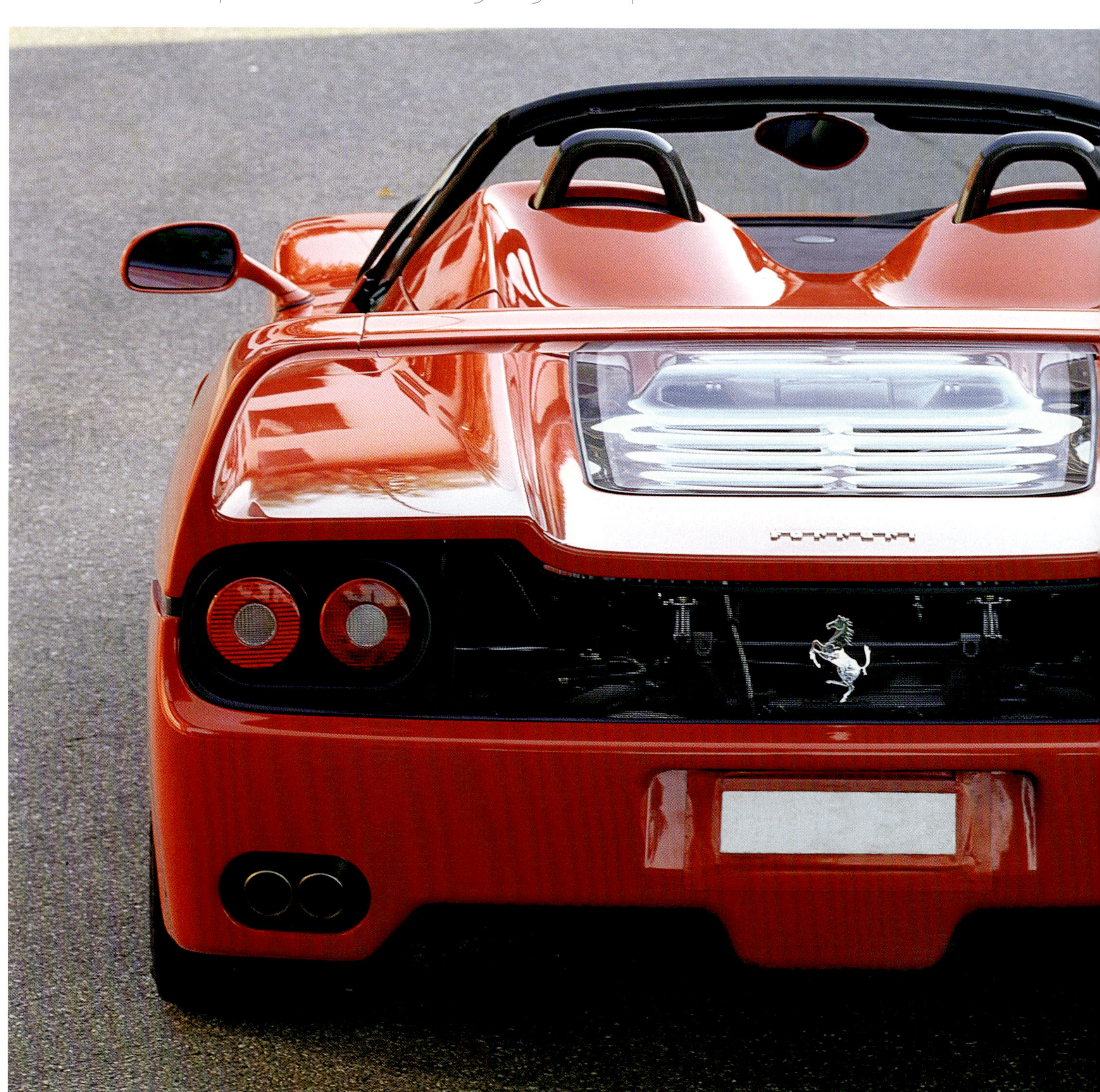

■ Beneath sleek coachwork by Pininfarnia, Ferrari installed road-legal versions of the hardware from its Formula 1 racing cars.

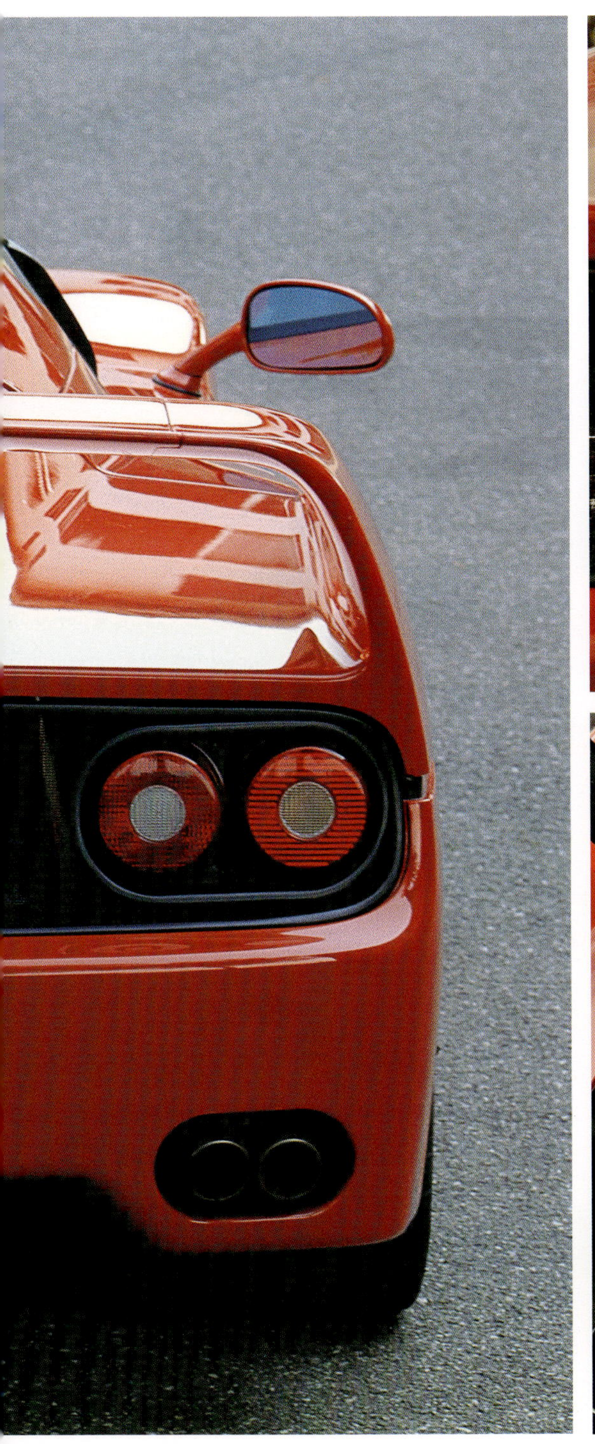

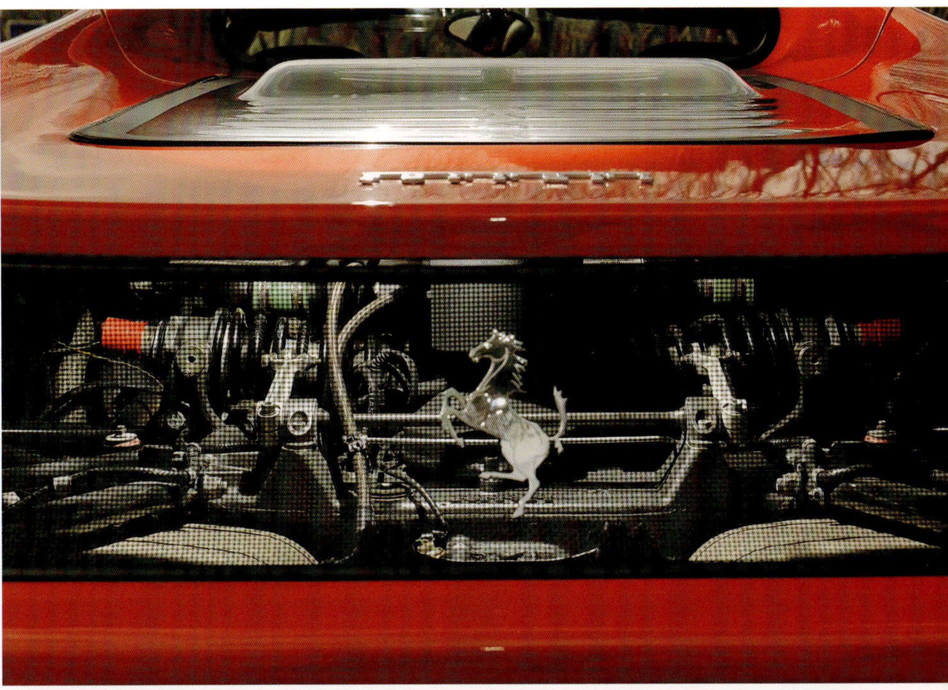

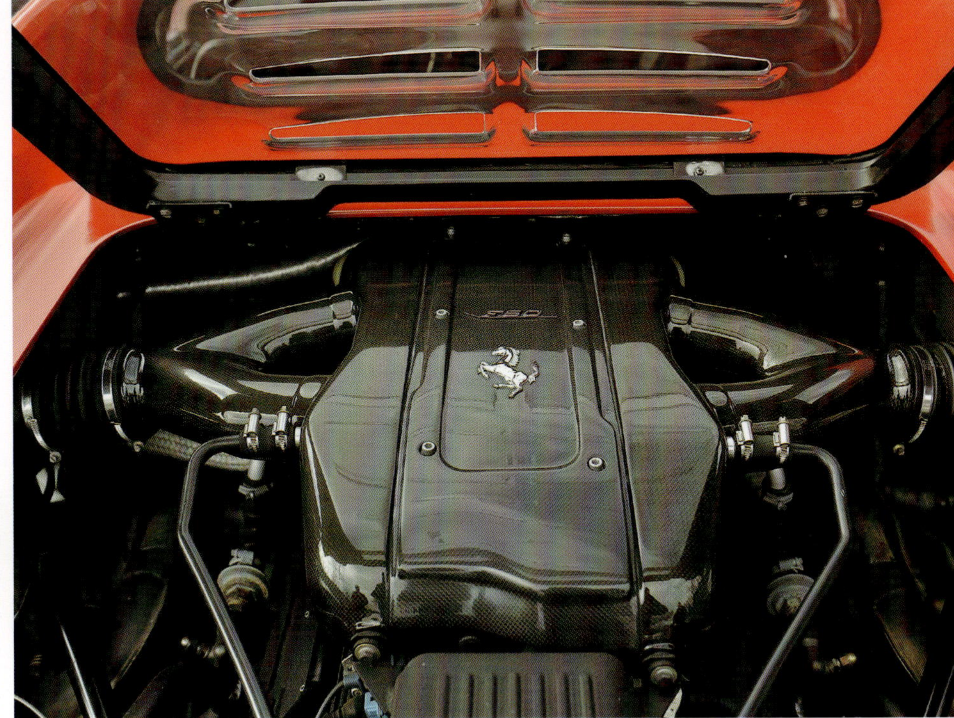

BMW
Z3

Globalization: a British-style roadster from a German automaker but built in the United States

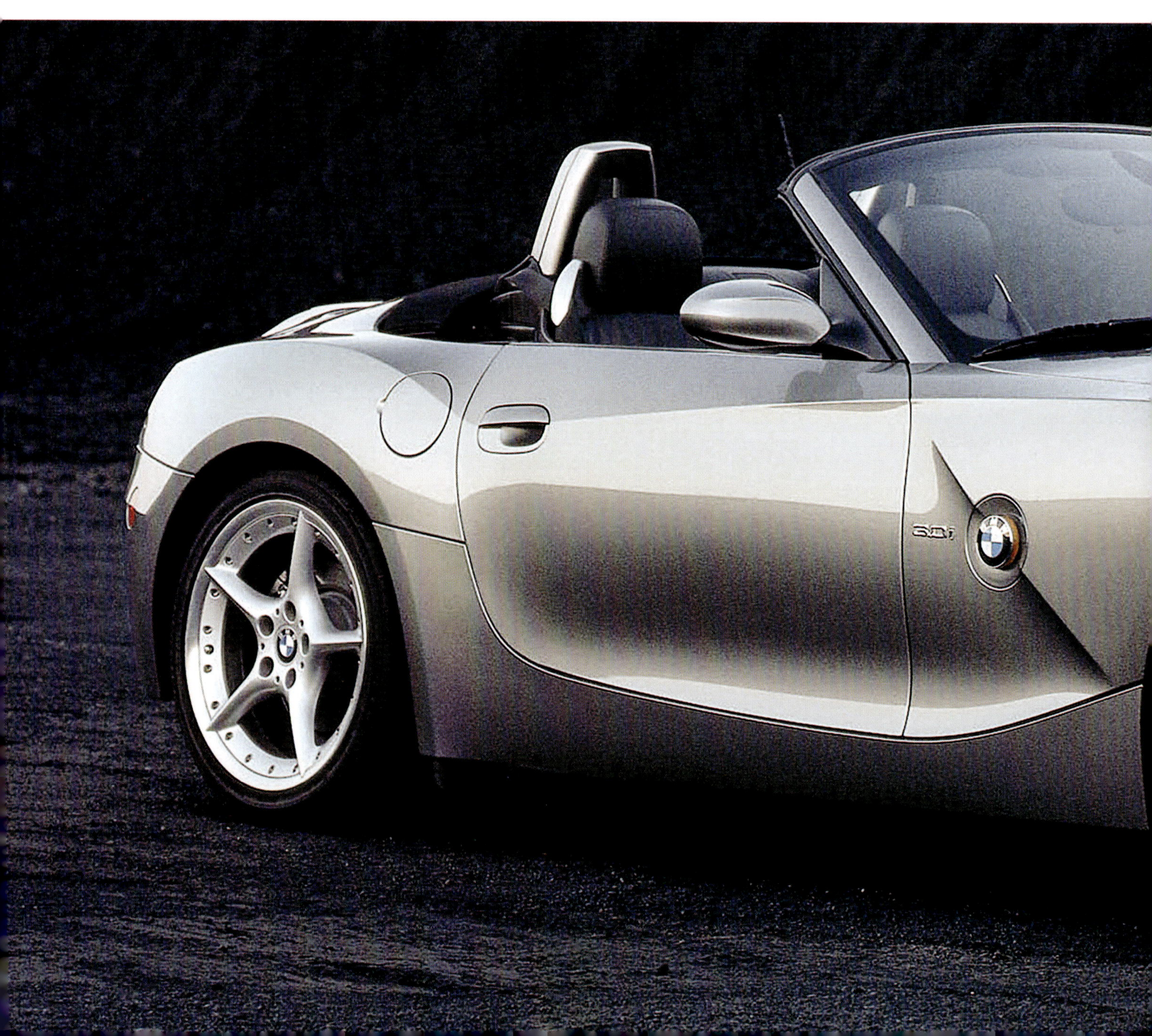

Mazda's reinvention of the classic British roadster triggered a party that seemingly all automakers were eager to join. BMW's entry was the Z3, which got a rather spectacular introduction with a role in the 1995 James Bond movie *Golden-Eye*, and not only in the film itself but also in two brief appearances in the movie's pre-release trailer.

BMW actually got something of a head start on the roadster revival. In 1987 it unveiled the Z1, a two-seat open-top concept that went into low-volume production and was offered for sale only in Europe. The most striking part of the car was doors on either side of its plastic composite body. The doors were electrically operated, and not only were their windows power operated but the entire door retracted into the lower body sill panel on its side of the car.

The Z3 had its official debut at the 1996 North American International Auto Show in Detroit. It was based on mechanicals from BMW's 3 Series and was propelled by a 1.9-liter 4-cylinder engine rated at 138 horsepower.

One benefit, *Car and Driver* magazine explained, was that the Z3 could be sold for less than $30,000. "The company intends this new Z3 Roadster to be a BMW

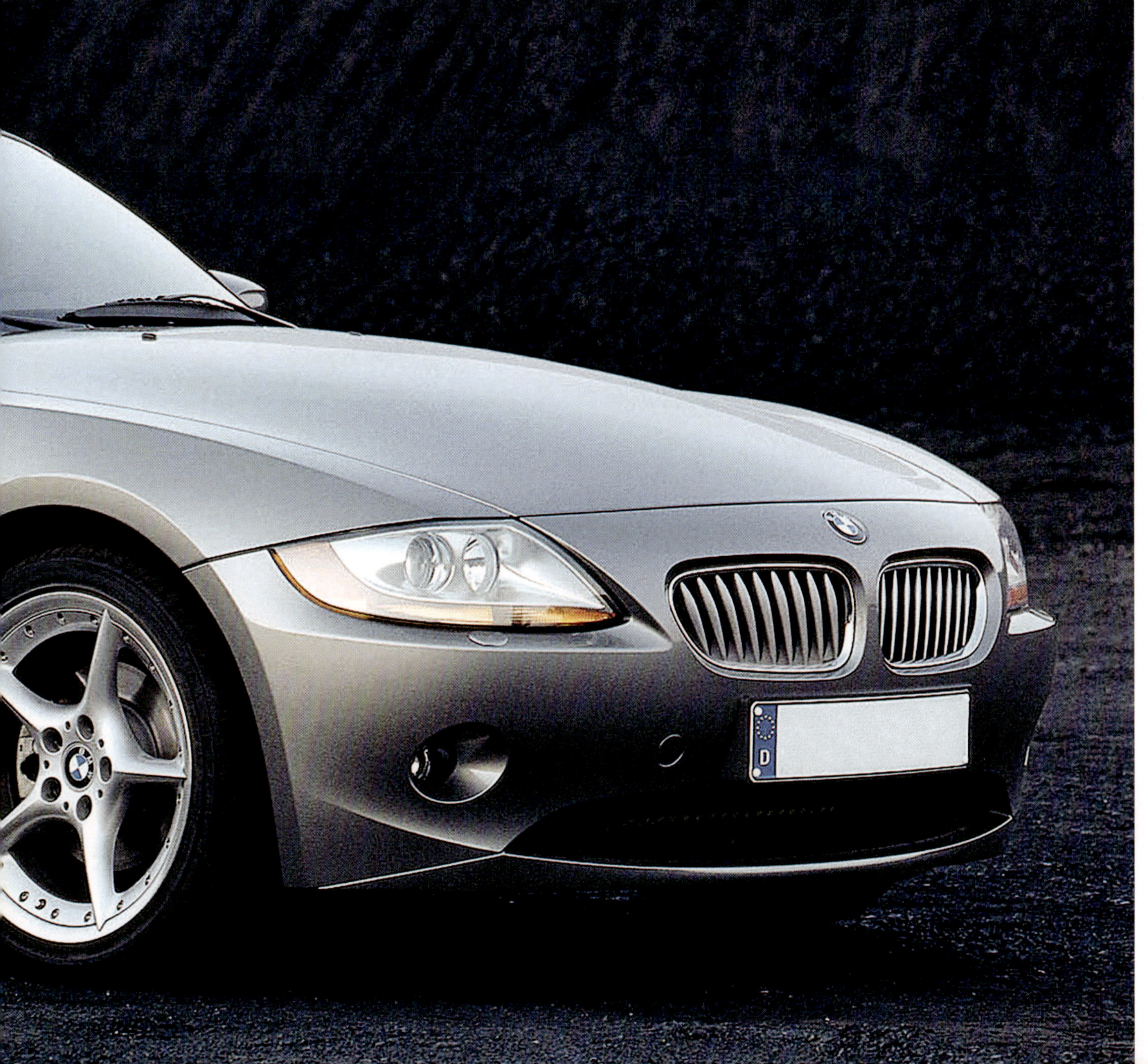

for the many rather than a BMW for the few," the magazine suggested.

Also helping to keep the price in reach of the many was a surprise worthy of a Bond movie script. BMW announced that the Z3 would be the first BMW-badged car not built in Germany but in a new manufacturing facility in South Carolina, USA, from where it would be exported to 100 markets around the globe.

Nonetheless, customers and critics sought more power. BMW responded by offering an optional 190-horsepower, 2.8-liter straight 6. Early in 1998 it also added a hatchback-style Z3 coupe to the model mix and high-performance M versions from its motorsports group. The Z3 M arrived in Europe with 316 horsepower (240 in US spec).

Supposedly just to see if the engine fit, the M team found it could wedge BMW's 5.4-liter V12 beneath one Z3 roadster's hood. The engine provided 322 horsepower but also added excessive weight to the front of the car. The car reportedly reached 163 mph (263 km/h) in testing.

Meanwhile, the standard Z3 M was promoted as "adrenaline for two."

The M Coupe and M Roadster were featured on *Car and Driver* magazine's 1999 "10 Best" list, where they joined BMW's 3 and 5 Series sedans.

"The addition of a steel roof may do nothing for the Z3's lines, but it does provide a huge improvement in stiffness," the magazine said of the M Coupe. "As a result, the car feels rock solid, and the driver, seated low in the tiny cabin, feels like an integral component.

"This oneness between driver and machine combines with the lively steering, precise shifter, and 240-hp M engine to produce an uncanny harmony between the driver's desires and the car's instant reflexes. After a half hour behind the wheel of an M coupe, our doubts about the exterior styling were forgotten.

"For those willing to trade some stiffness for daylight, the M roadster provides most of the coupe's benefits. Either way, to drive these cars is to love them."

Previous and these pages ■ The Z3 made its debut not at an auto show but in the James Bond movie *GoldenEye*.

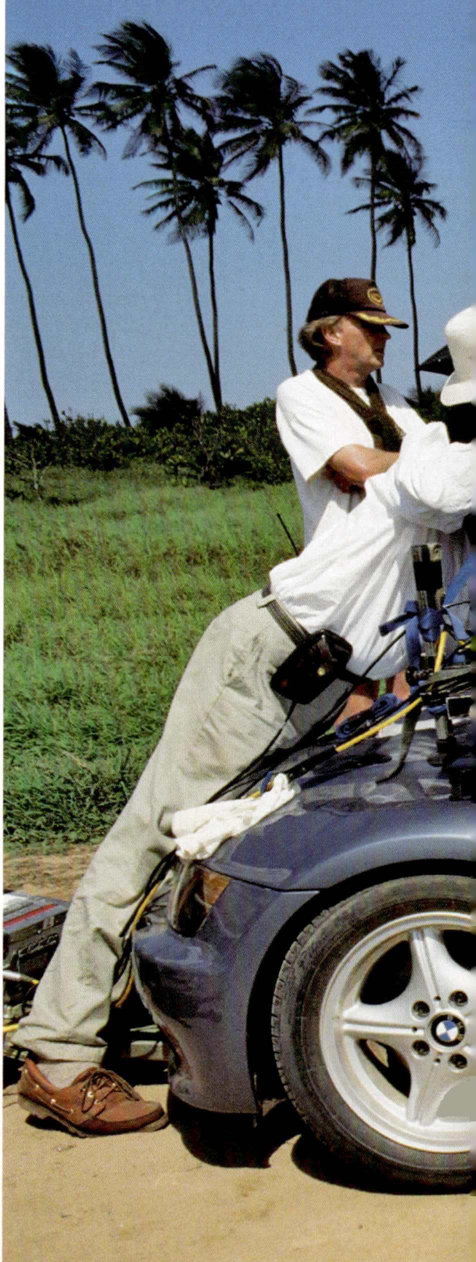

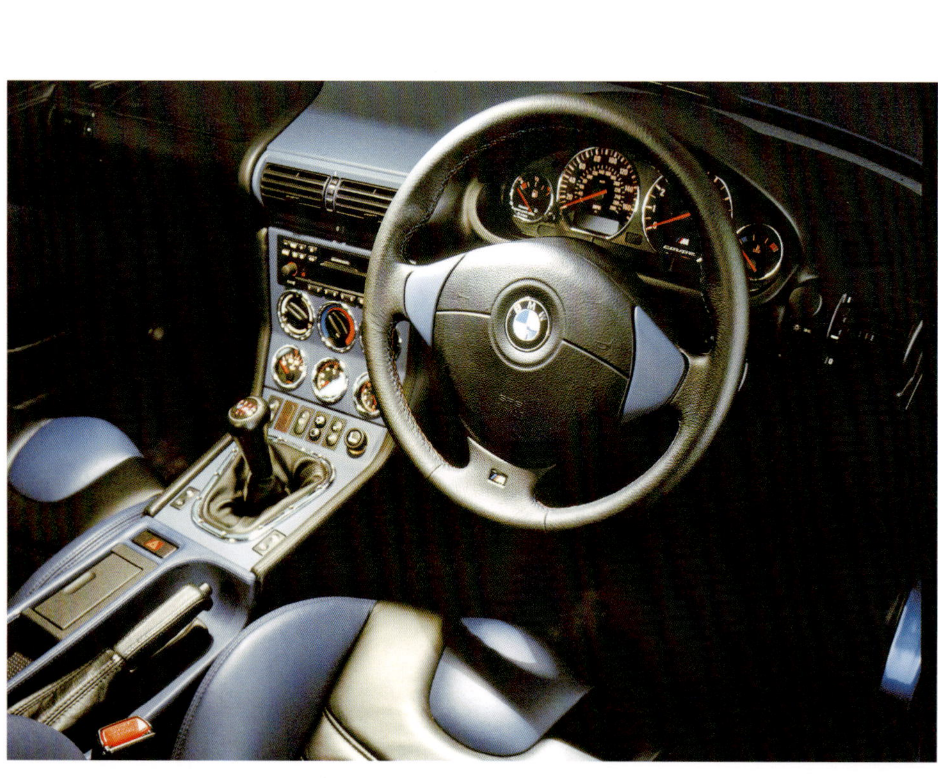

Unlike the expensive Aston Martin, with the Z3, many more would-be 007s could afford to drive their fantasies.

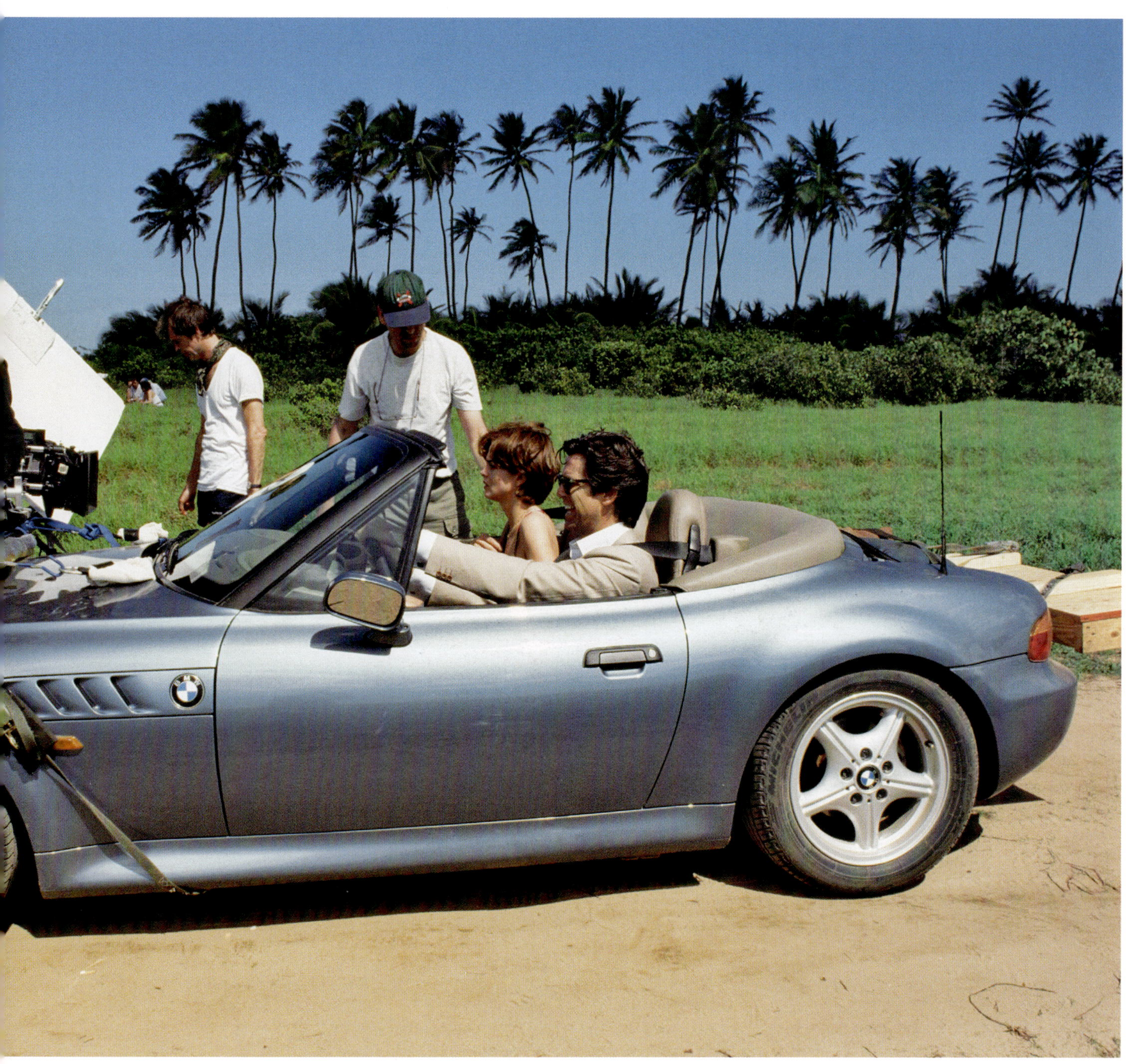

1990 ➤ 1999

"The early 1990s was a time of global recession," German automaker Porsche recalls on its corporate website. "Porsche, with its high production costs and particular susceptibility to the ups and downs of the failing US economy, had more to fear than most."

That was especially true as the 928 and 968 were nearing the end of their lives, and even the venerable 911 was undergoing a significant redesign.

There were expectations that Porsche's press conference at the 1993 North American International Auto Show in Detroit would focus on finances. But then Porsche took the cover of a concept car that breathed new life into the brand.

The concept, and the production model that followed three years later, was the Boxster, its name a blend between its "boxer" style horizontally opposed 6-cylinder engine and the original Porsche Speedster of the mid-1950s.

With its engine placed immediately behind a seat for the driver and single passenger, the Boxster also had roots in the mid-engine 914 of the early 1970s.

"Here," recalled designer Harm Lagaay, "was a car which nobody had expected."

And according to Hagerty, auto insurer and value tracker, here also was "the concept that saved the brand...The Boxster concept signaled something even more critical than a

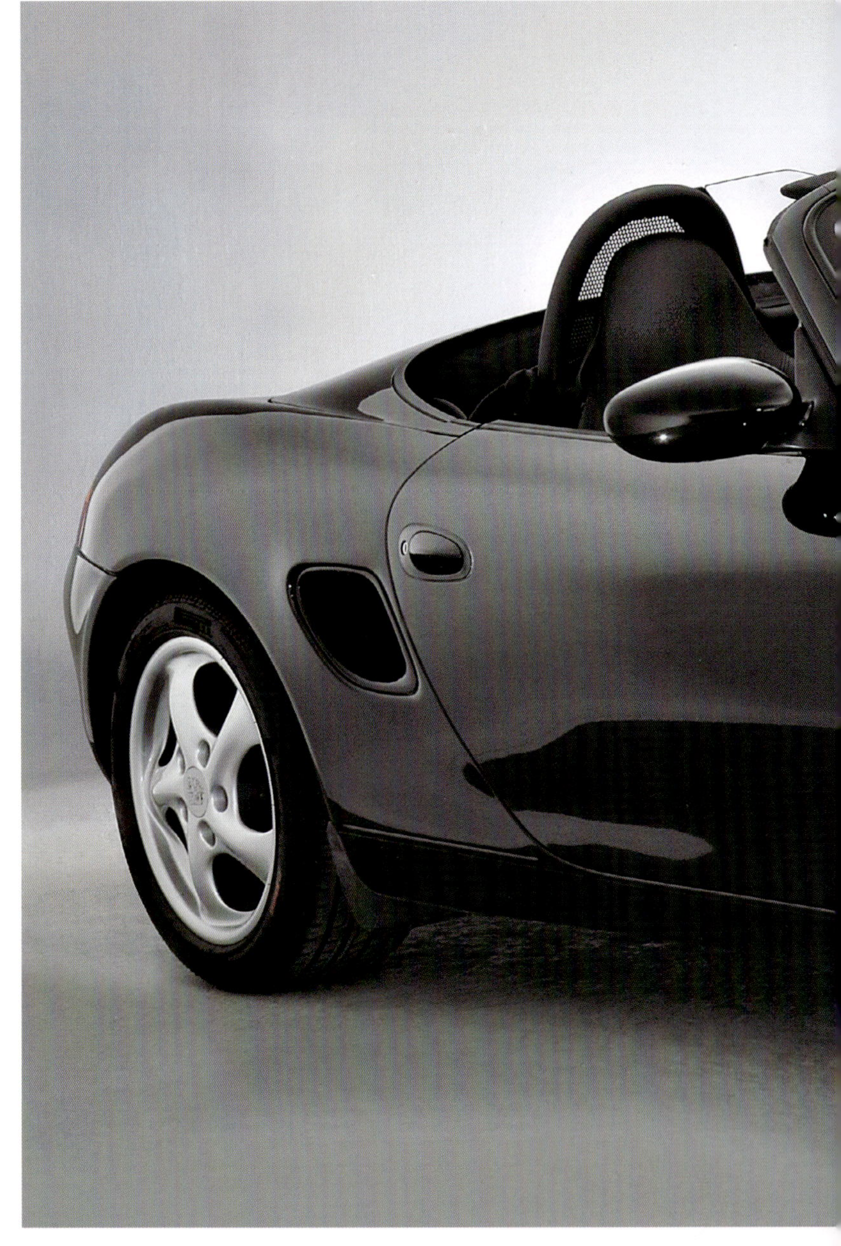

■ The Boxster brought back memories of the Porsche Speedster of the 1950s.

PORSCHE BOXSTER

Was Porsche about to fail? Not with this unexpected delight

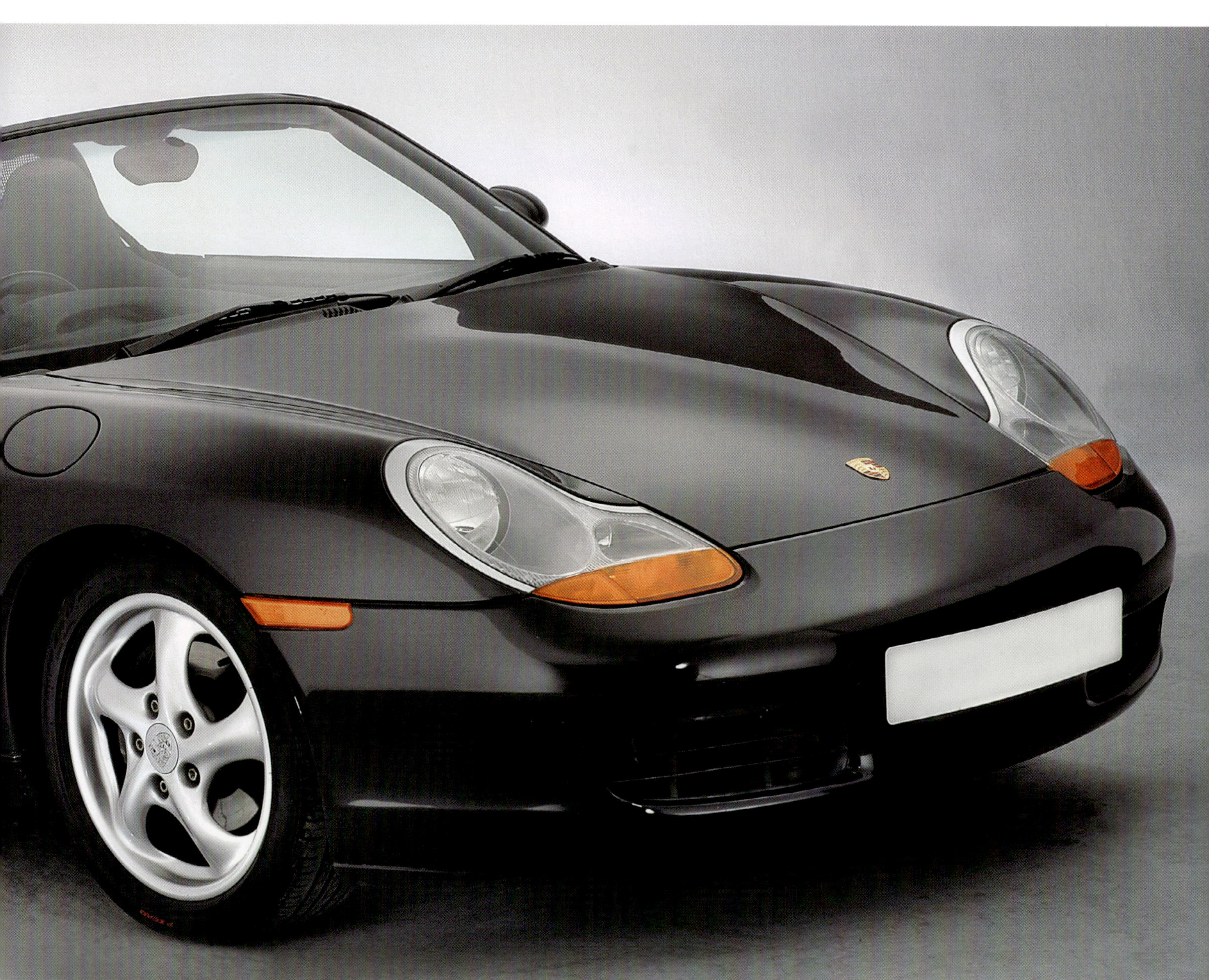

new design direction. This was about survival. The Boxster offered the promise of a new, more affordable Porsche sports car at a time when the company's future was a question mark.

"In the late 1980s, Porsche was in trouble. Sinking, in fact. The marque's affair with front-engine cars—the 928 grand tourer and 924/944/968 four-cylinder models—was coming to a necessary end. Negative economic trends, an unfavorable exchange rate, lower-priced competition, and Porsche's own production inefficiencies had put the carmaker in a difficult spot. Selling out to another brand seemed possible."

Customers would have to wait some three years before the concept went into production and was made available at Porsche dealerships. It was offered at first with a 2.5-liter flat-6 engine rated at 201 horsepower. Before long, that engine was upgraded to a 2.7-liter version with 217 horsepower, and a Boxster S model joined the lineup, this one with a 3.2-liter 6 rated at 250 horsepower.

These and following pages ■ An intriguing feature of the Boxster concept displayed at the Detroit show was zippers in the outboard surface of the shoulder area of each seat. Inside each zippered pocket was a special windbreaker jacket.

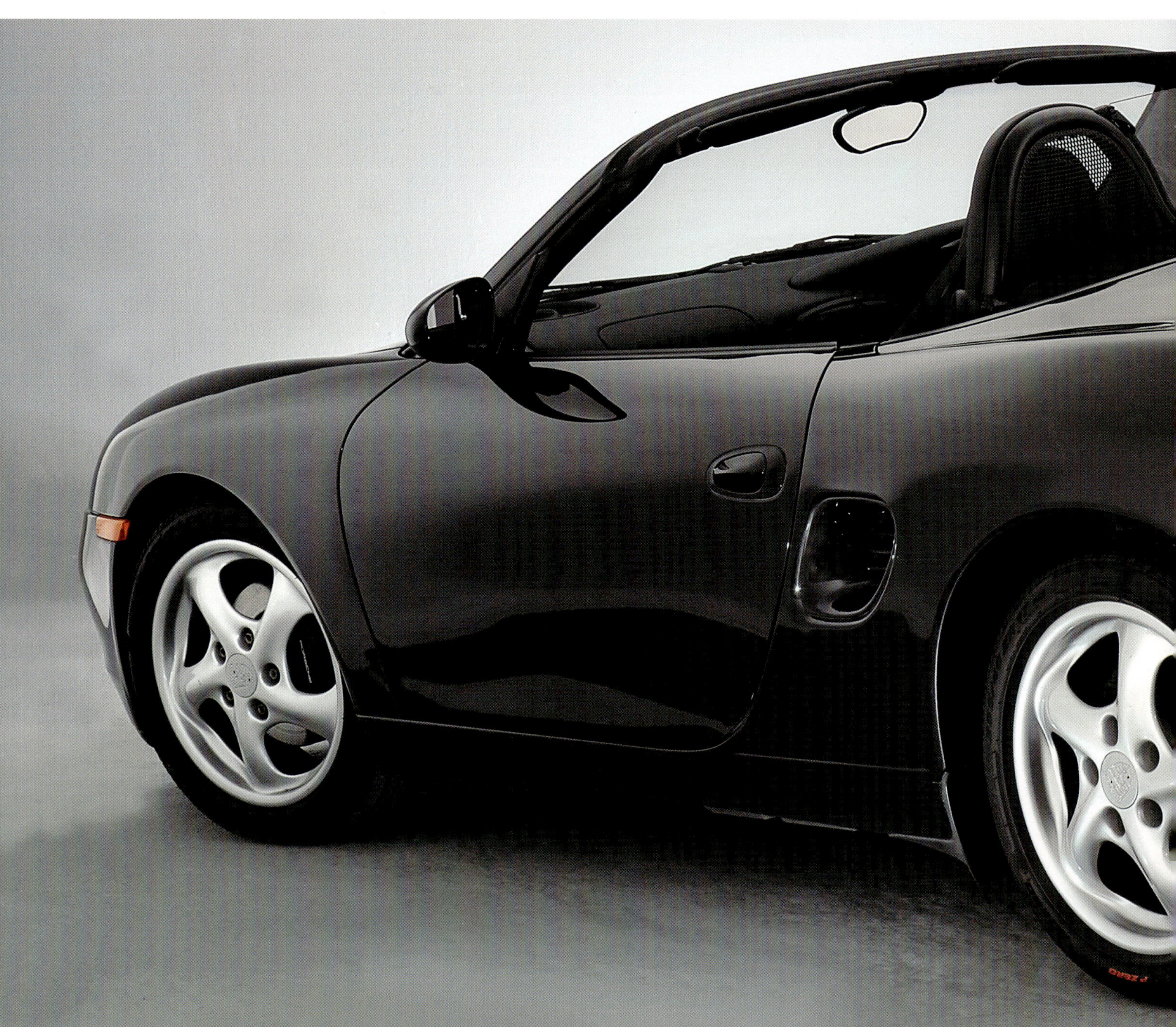

Motor Trend magazine praised the car as an entry-level model that "delivers a full dose of the Porsche experience. It"s all Porsche, all the time." It praised the design as dimply, "yet rewardingly elegant...and these aesthetics translate into function, as well... The Boxster's eager-revving 2.5-liter sets a new performance bogey for the current wave of entry-level German roadsters...On the road, the drivetrain, suspension, brakes, and rack-and-pinion steering work in concert like a well-rehearsed philharmonic. Each element fuses with the next to create a rewarding, communicative link between driver and car."

It also noted how the electric-powered soft top opened or closed quickly and that the Boxster offered cargo storage both under its front hood and in a compartment behind the mid-mounted engine. (The author once drove a Boxster to visit his mother in Florida and had room on the way home for his luggage as well as twelve full grocery bags of fresh-picked grapefruit from her trees).

In 2005 Porsche would offer the Cayman, a full-enclosed coupe version of the Boxster roadster.

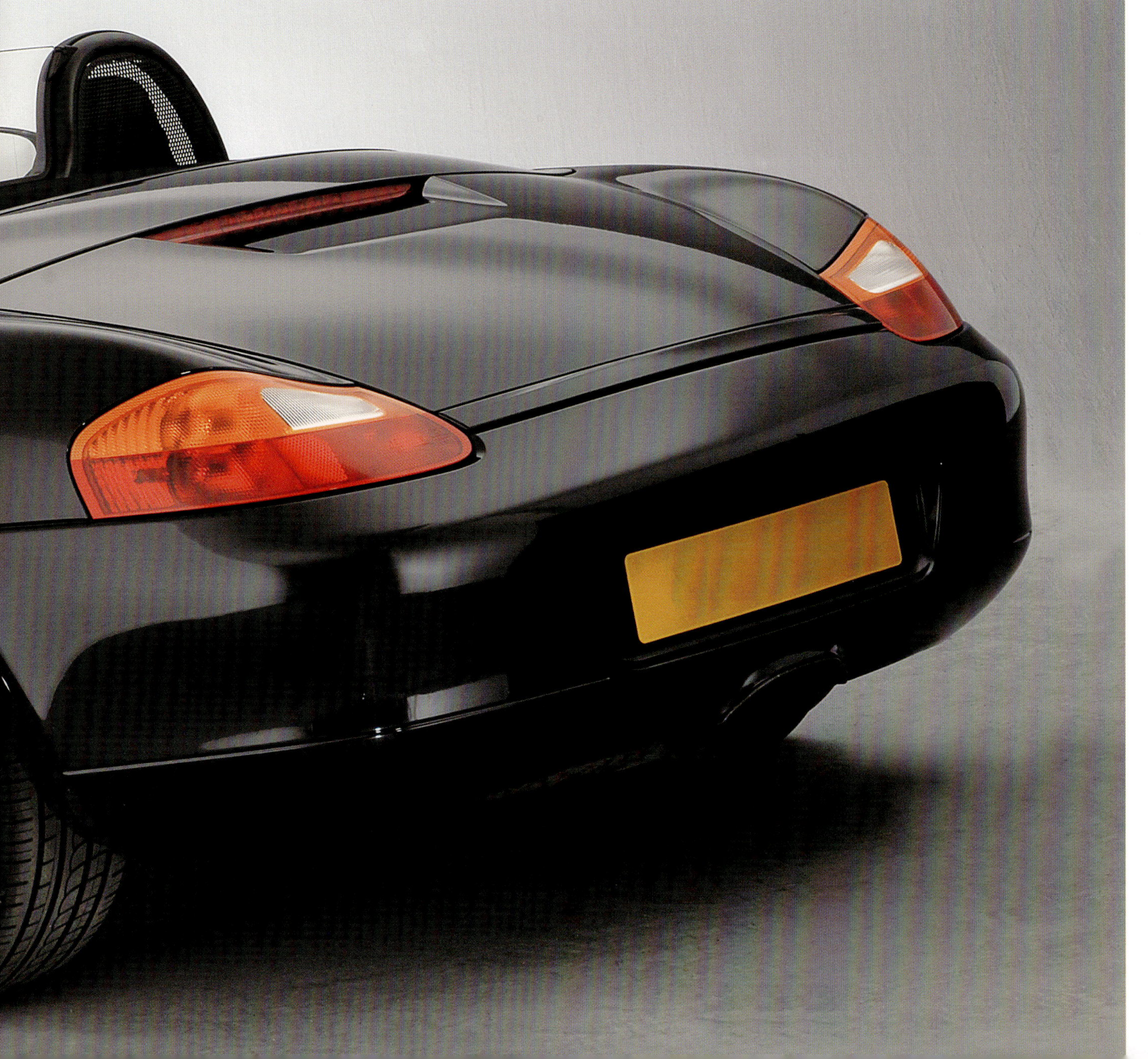

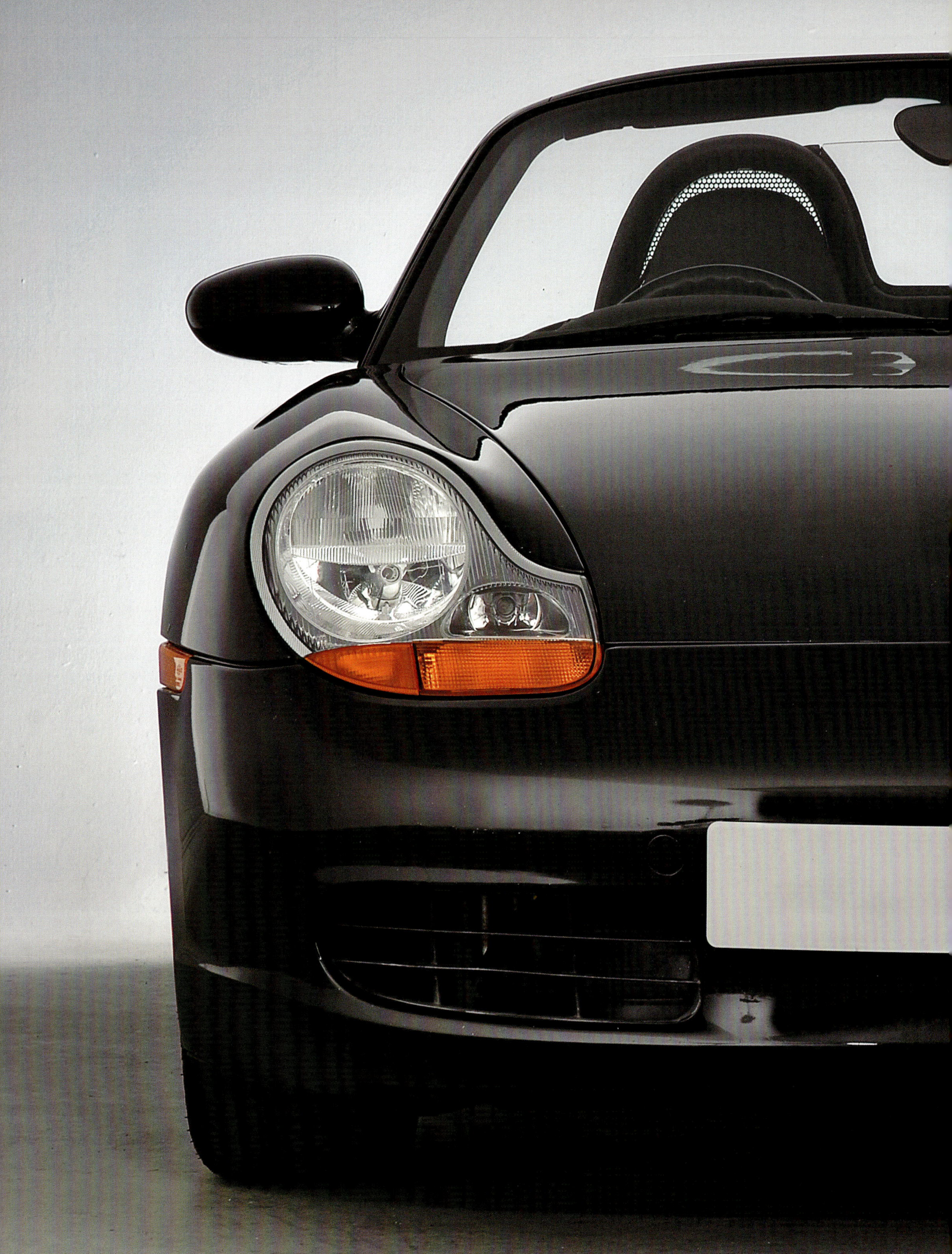

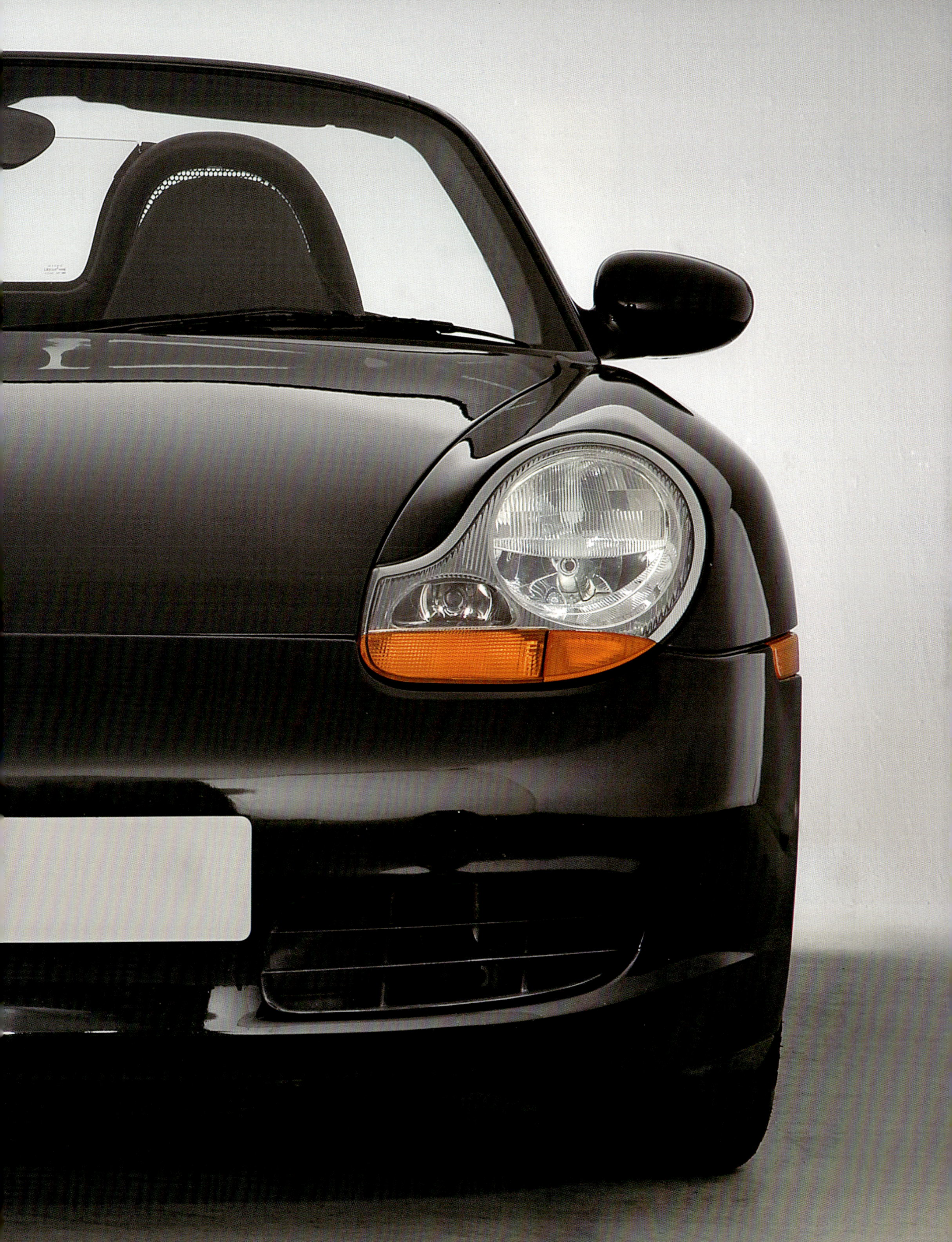

1990 ➤ 1999

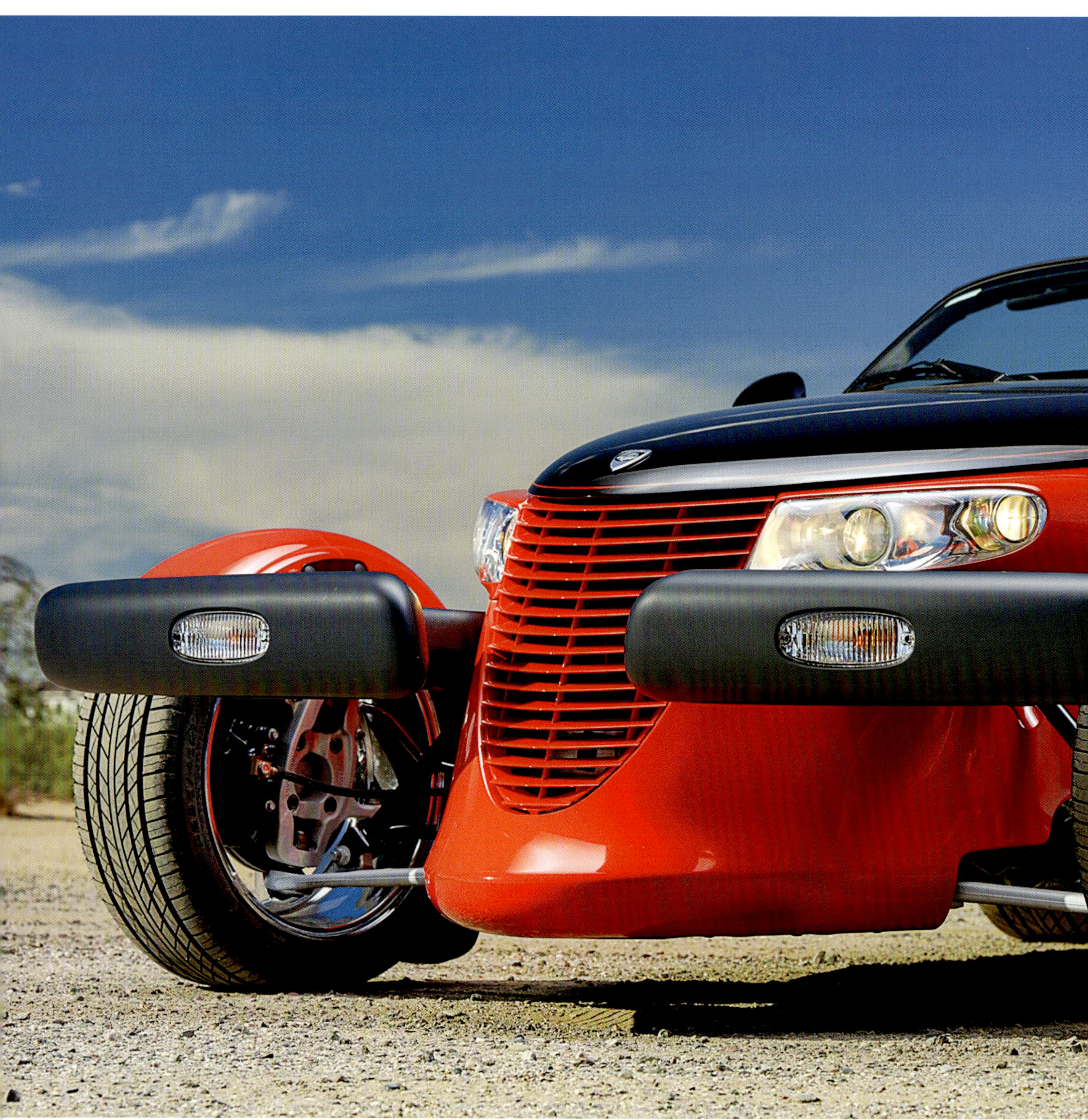

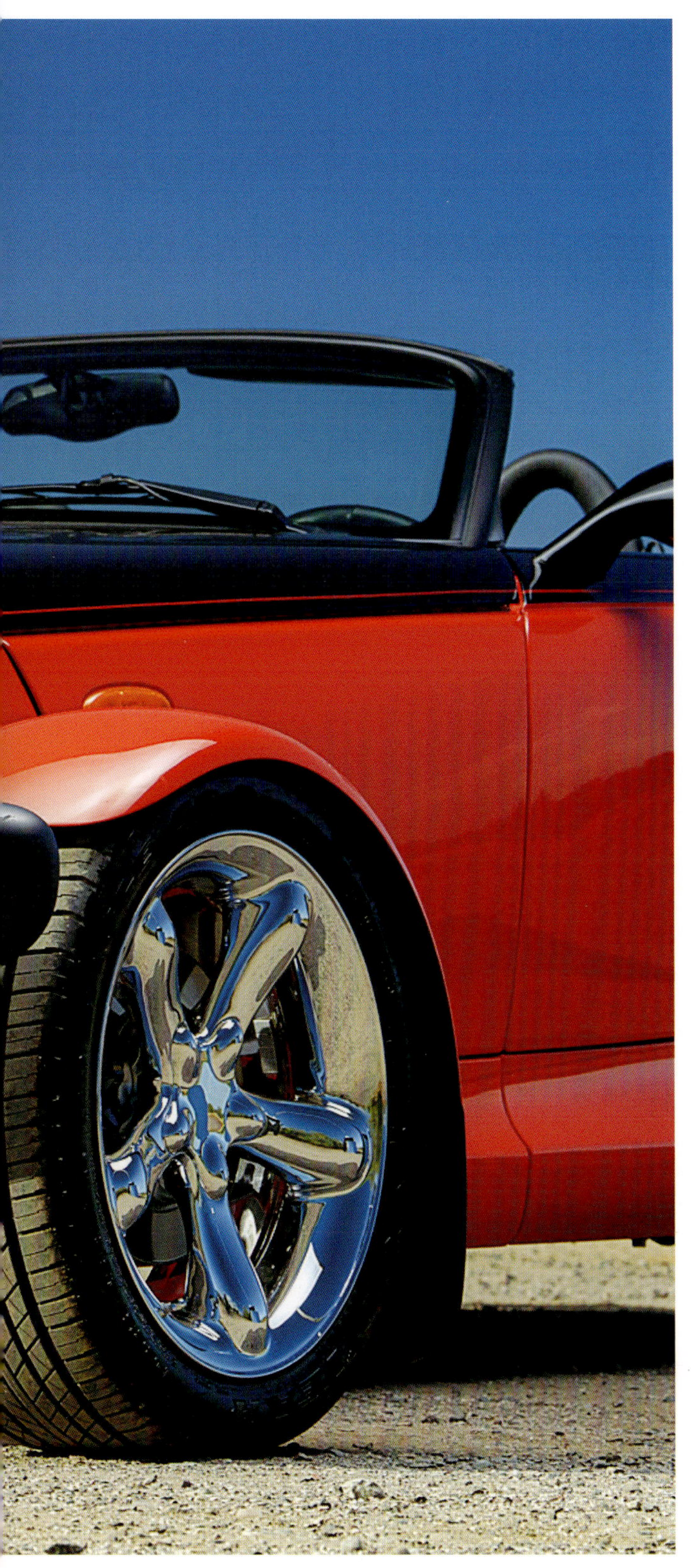

PLYMOUTH PROWLER

Could factory assembly match the magic of the hot-rodder's garage?

Back to the Future was the title of a blockbuster 1985 movie that starred a futuristic car as a time machine. But "back to the future" also became something of a theme for car designers.

Consider the rebirth of the British sports car in the form of Mazda's Miata. The New Beetle from Volkswagen. The Fiat Cinquecento was updated and reintroduced as the Fiat 500.

What Ford called "Retrofuturism," and which emerged in the form of new production cars with nostalgic designs—the Thunderbird, Mustang, and Ford GT—and concepts such as the Forty-Nine. General Motors presented the Buick Blackhawk concept and Chevrolet SSR pickup truck.

The Bugatti Atlantic inspired the Chrysler Atlantic, the Shelby Cobra was reborn as the Dodge Viper, the vintage sedan delivery vehicle begot the Chrysler PT Cruiser, and the classic American postwar hot rod took the form of the Plymouth Prowler.

The Prowler was unveiled as a concept car at the Detroit Auto Show in 1993 and immediately received the "Most Fun" award from *AutoWeek* magazine.

The design of the Prowler was led by Chrysler's studio chief Tom Gale, who

■ With motorcycle-style front wheels, the Plymouth Prowler's design tried to capture the spirit of the homebuilt hot rod.

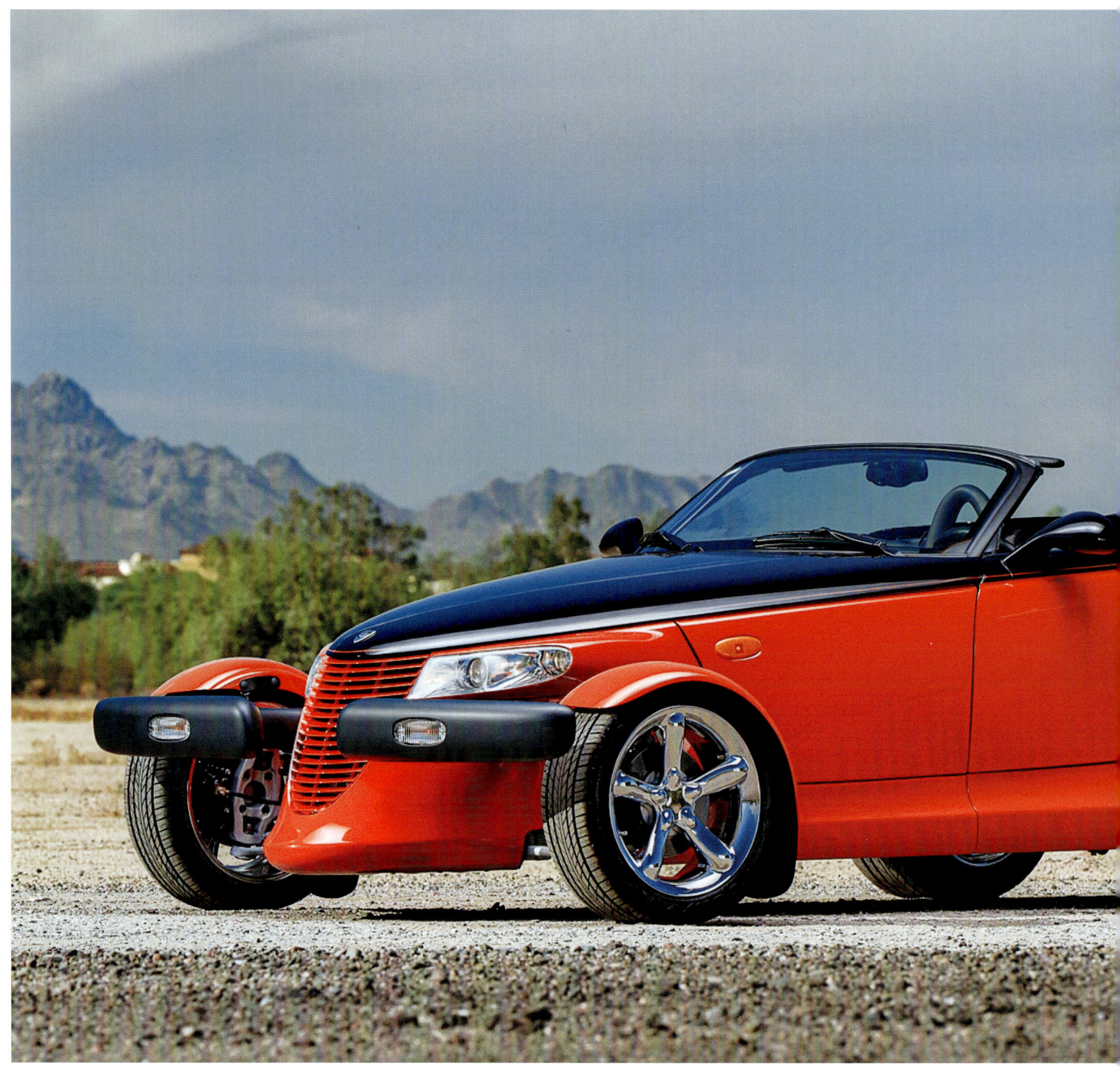

recalled the days in his garage when he built a classic American hot rod based on a 1932 Ford.

The idea behind the Prowler was two-fold: First, to re-create Chrysler's Plymouth brand to appeal to a younger audience, and second, to re-create the classic American hot rod, except you didn't have to build it yourself and it came with a factory warranty.

But while the Prowler may have looked spectacular, its dynamic performance was found lacking. While hot-rodders built their creations around the original Ford V8 or the later Chevrolet "small-block" V8 or perhaps even a Chrysler "Hemi" V8—and maybe even supercharged versions of those engines—the Prowler was equipped with the 3.5-liter V6 otherwise used in Chrysler's family sedans, and instead of a manual transmission, the Prowler came with a 4-speed automatic.

The engine in the Prowler concept was tuned to provide 240 horsepower, but when the car went into production for 1997, the V6 produced only 214 horsepower (though it was replaced in 1999 by one with 253 horsepower).

Motor Trend magazine noted that the car lacking in power and in sound: "The metallic rap of eight cylinders filling two [exhaust] pipes with syncopated

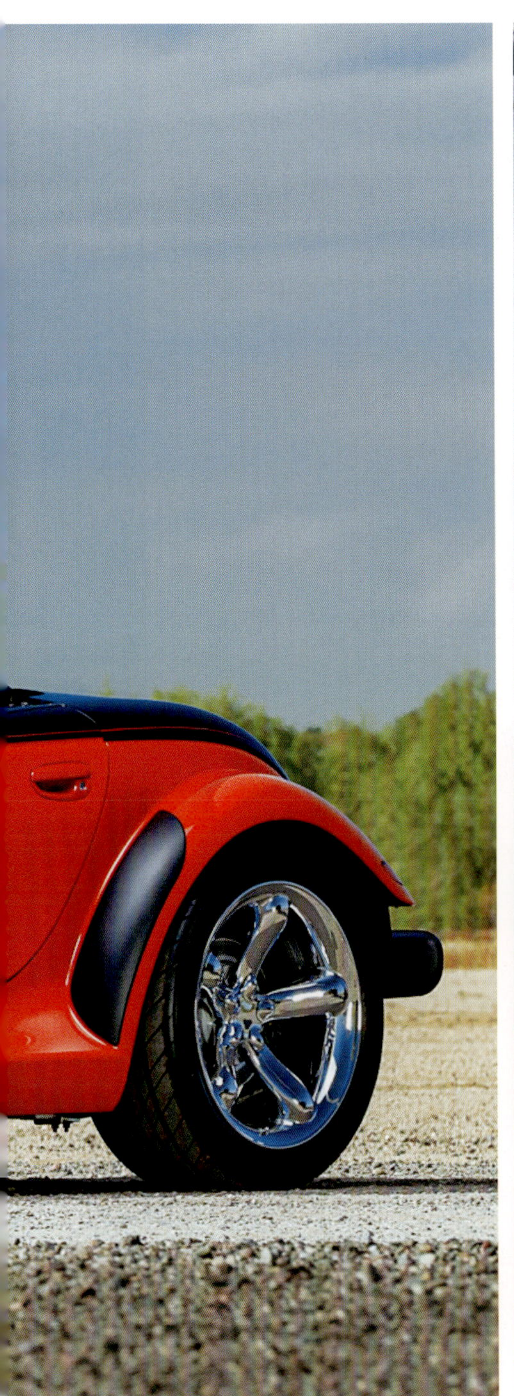

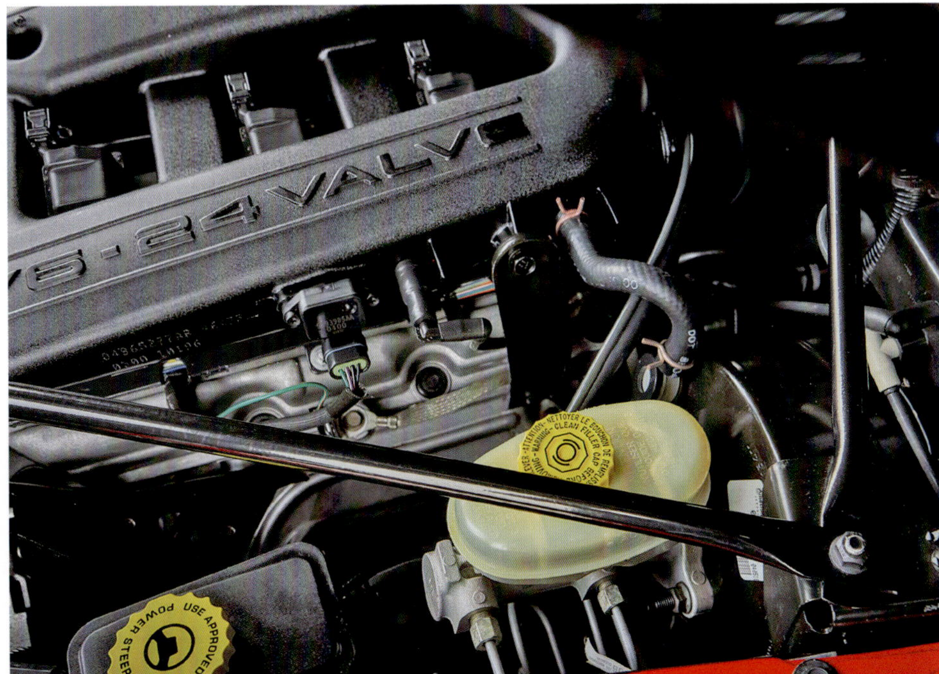

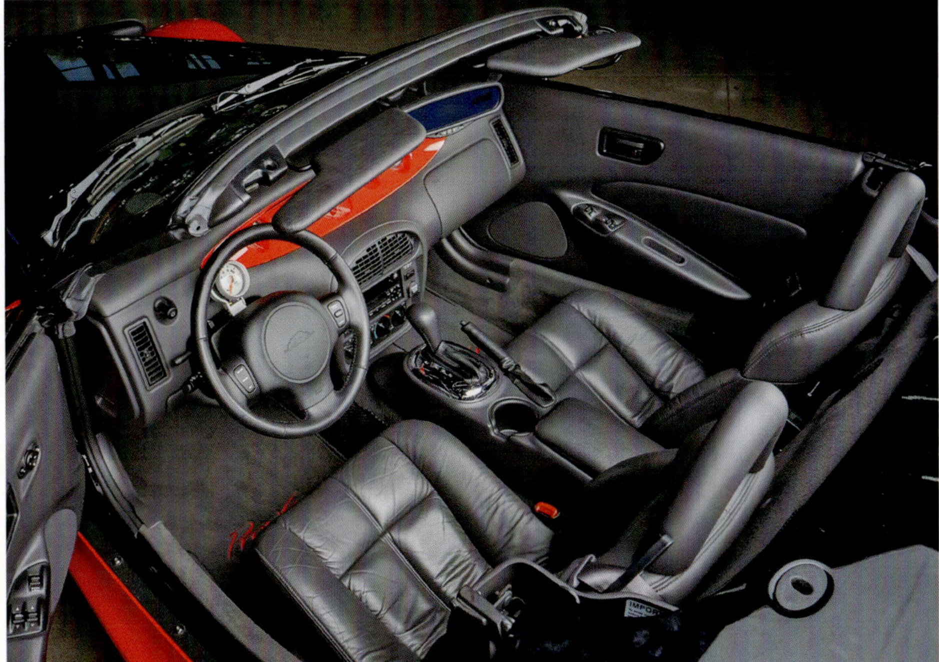

■ While it resembled the hot-rodder's home build, the Plymouth Prowler offered only a V6 engine, not Chrysler's popular Hemi or other V8, nor was a manual transmission offered.

rhythm is baked so deeply into America's hot-rod soul that some enthusiasts will shun Chrysler's cool cat simply because it lacks the right rumble."

That report was a retrospective and also pointed out that anyone hoping for a more powerful V6 or even a V8 from factory were out of luck, "as by the end of the 2000 model year, the Plymouth brand was no more."

The Prowler did last until 2002 but was badged as a Chrysler. Ironically, in 1999 at the SEMA show, an auto show of automotive aftermarket parts of manufacturer concepts, Chrysler displayed what it called the Plymouth Howler, which was based on the Prowler but with a small pickup truck–style bed at the back, a 4.7-liter V8 engine at the front, and a 5-speed manual shifter in between.

The Plymouth Prowler looked like a real hot rod but lacked the power and the sound of a V8 engine.

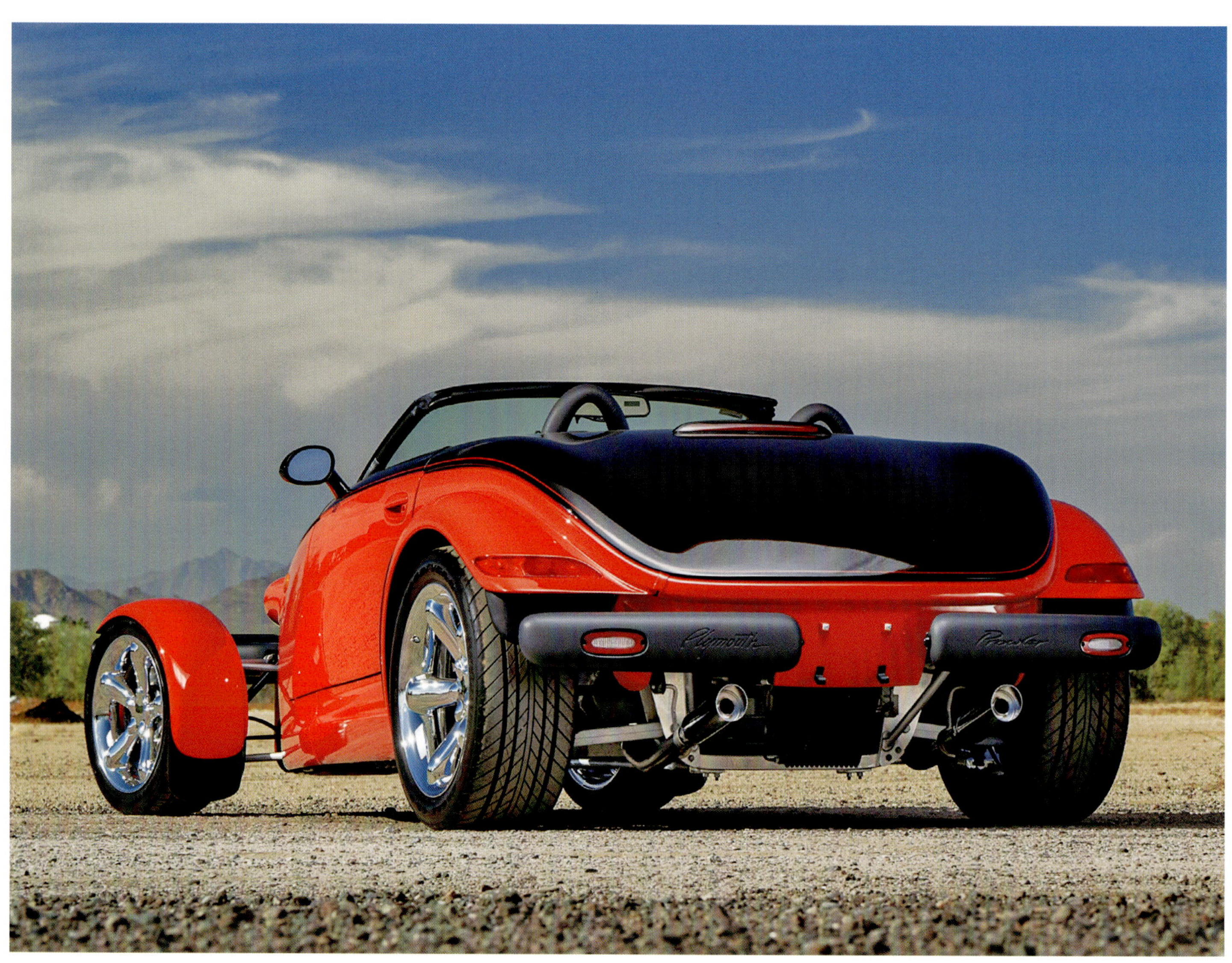

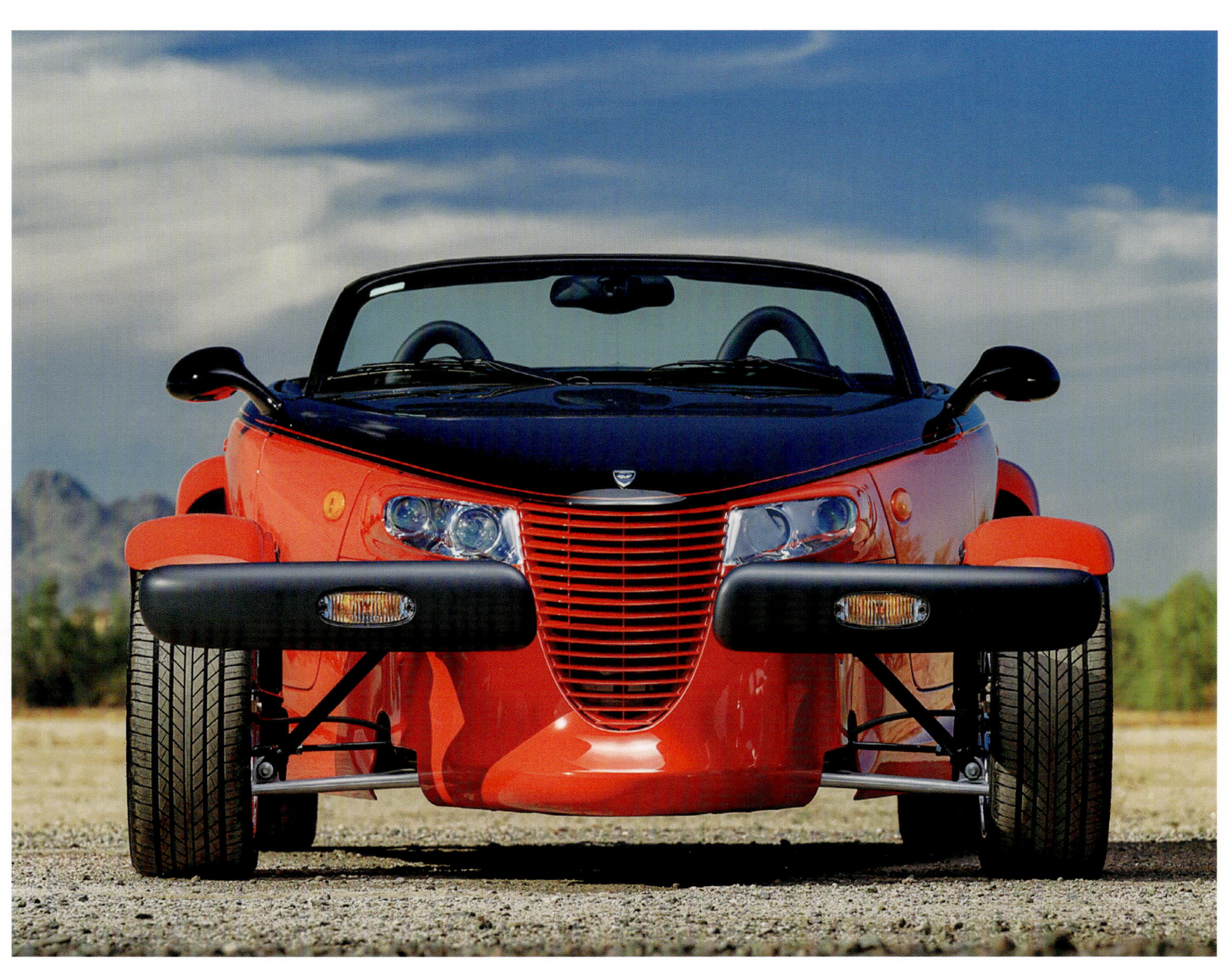

■ The Plymouth Prowler was a case of style over substance, the right look but not the performance to match.

1990 ➤ 1999

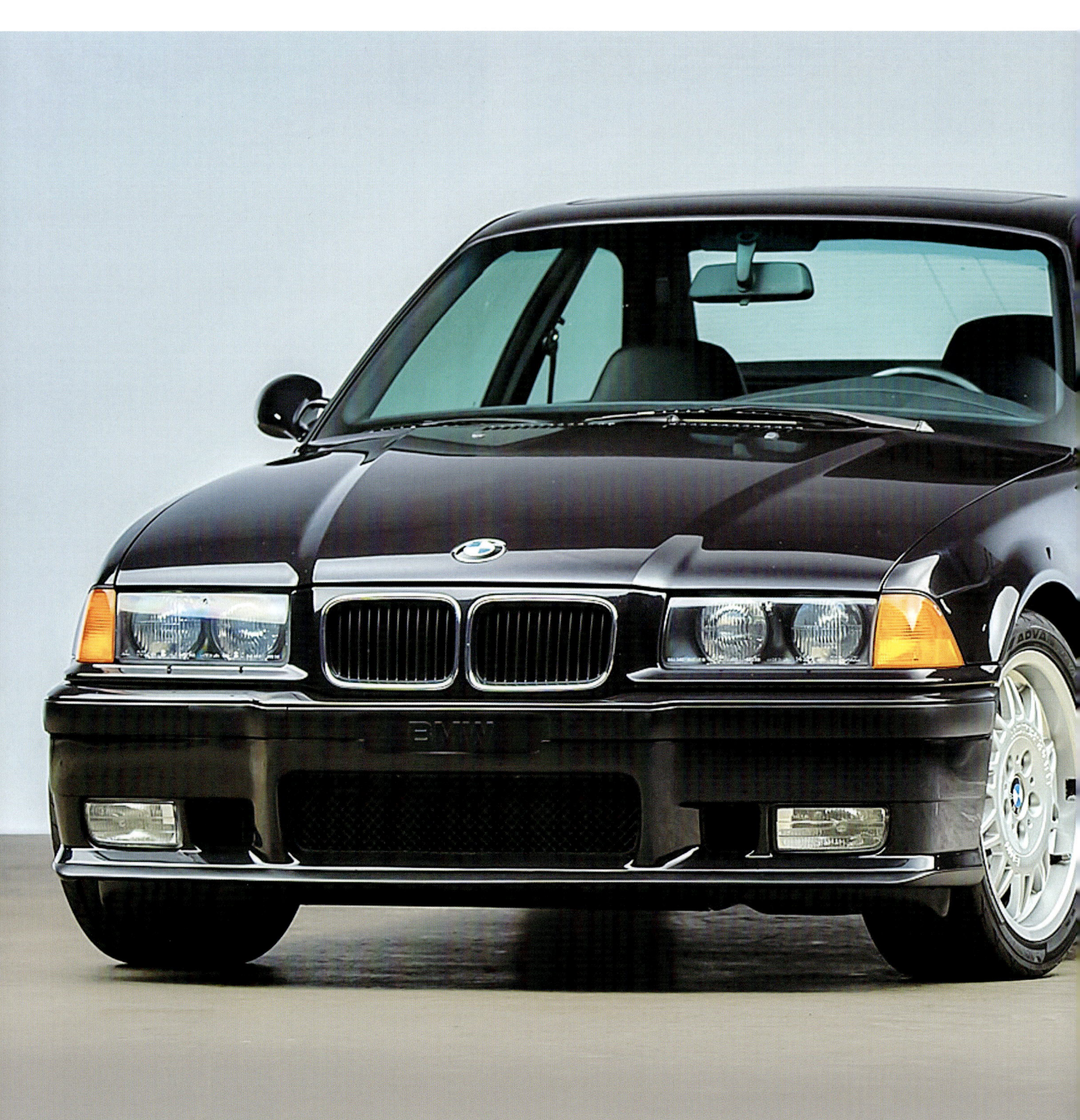

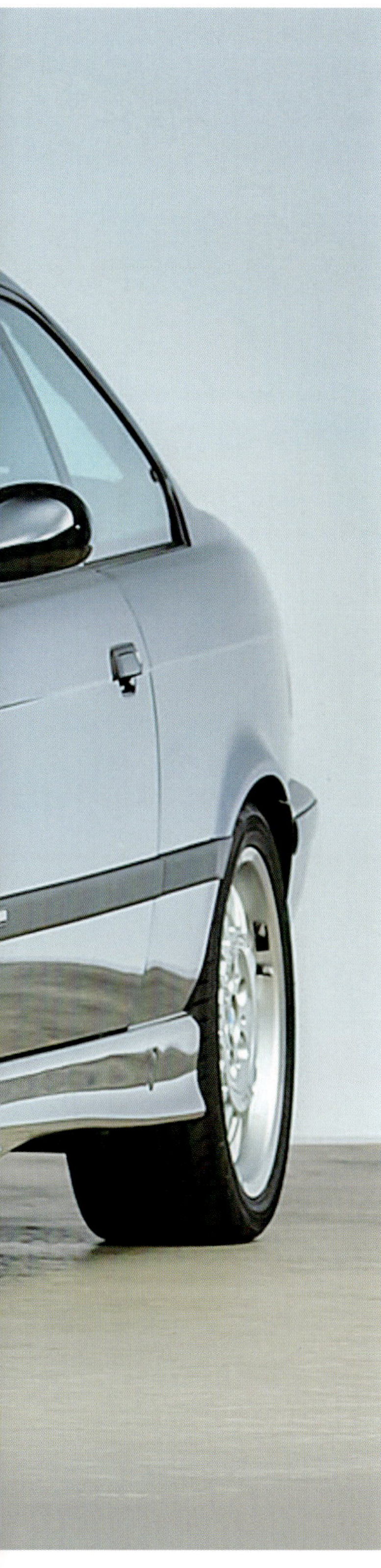

BMW M3

Two more doors, two more cylinders, and more interior space enhance the appeal of BMW's sporty compact

Early on, BMW's M3 had been available only as a coupe or convertible, but with the introduction of the E36 generation of the German automaker's compact car in 1992, it wasn't long before the M3 lineup expanded to include a 4-door sedan. While the coupe remained the most popular with buyers, sales of the M3 sedan exceeded those of the convertible version.

The arrival of the E36 platform meant that the M3 would be equipped for the first time with an inline 6-cylinder engine, BMW's venerable 3.0-liter unit rated at 282 horsepower.

Not long before the M3 sedan arrived, the bodywork for the M3 coupe and convertible was updated. That change also brought another change in powertrains, 3.2-liter inline 6-cylinder engines good for 316 horsepower, and 6-speed rather than 5-speed manual transmissions. For those who preferred not to have to bother with a clutch pedal, there was the option of BMW's new Shifttronic gearbox, a 6-speed SMG (sequential manual transmission) technology designed to provide shifts quicker than those achieved with a standard 6-speed/3-pedal setup.

The E36 generation of BMW's 3 Series was in production from 1992 to 1999. Two decades later, Britain's *CAR* magazine did a retrospective on the M3. Lamenting that unlike the previous E30 M3, the E36 version's roots were not in auto racing, and thus the car was bigger, heavier, and more luxurious.

"But hold on a second," the magazine continued. "While it's true that the E36 is bigger...and doesn't have the pure motorsport pedigree, it counters with a simply stunning 6-cylinder engine, a broader operating range, and because over 70,000 were produced, you can still buy one for sensible money. They even made a saloon version if you want to buy a really sensible car."

■ With the launch of the E36 version of its 3 Series model, BMW could offer an inline 6-cylinder engine and other enhancements for its M3.

1990 ➤ 1999

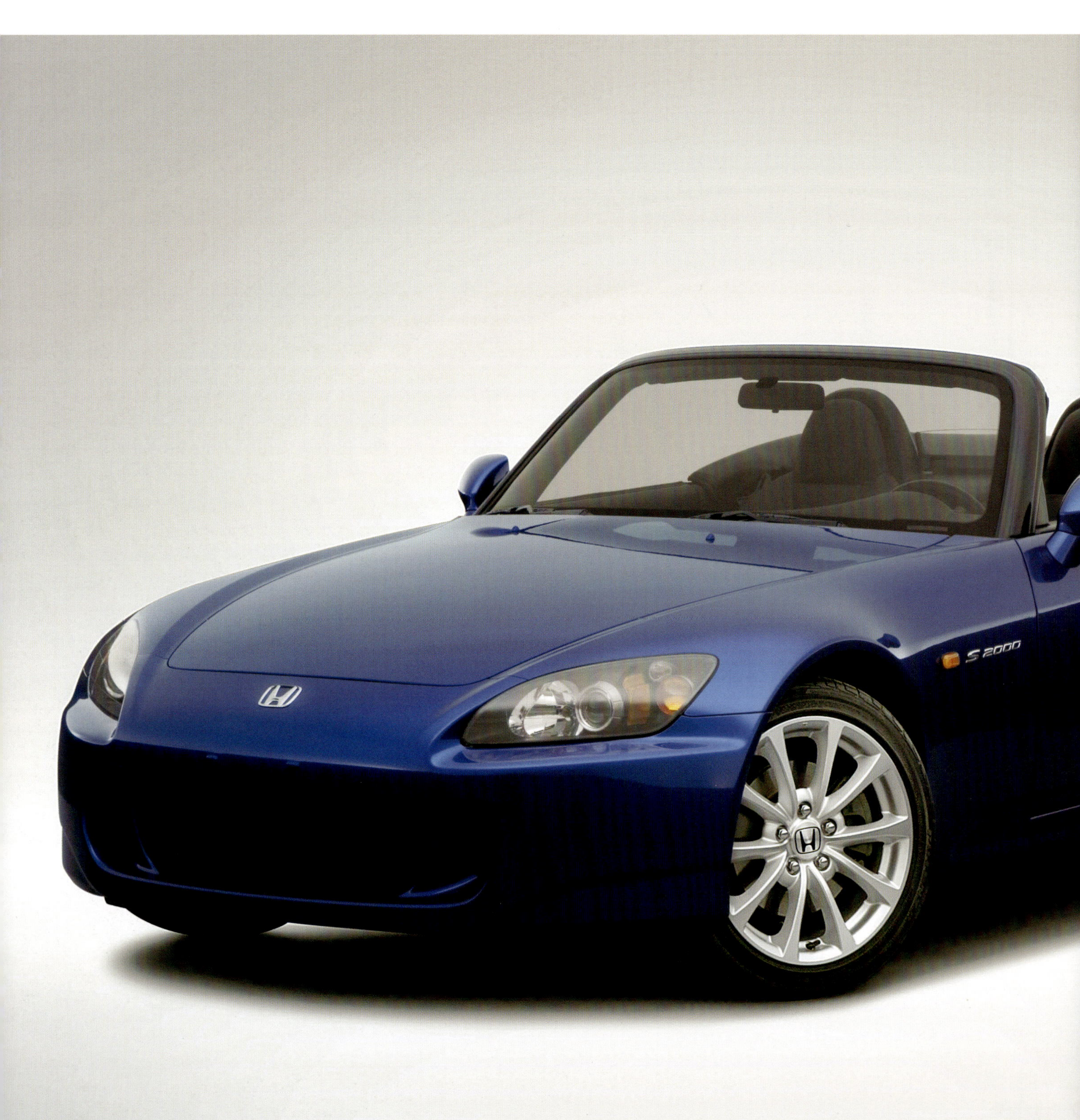

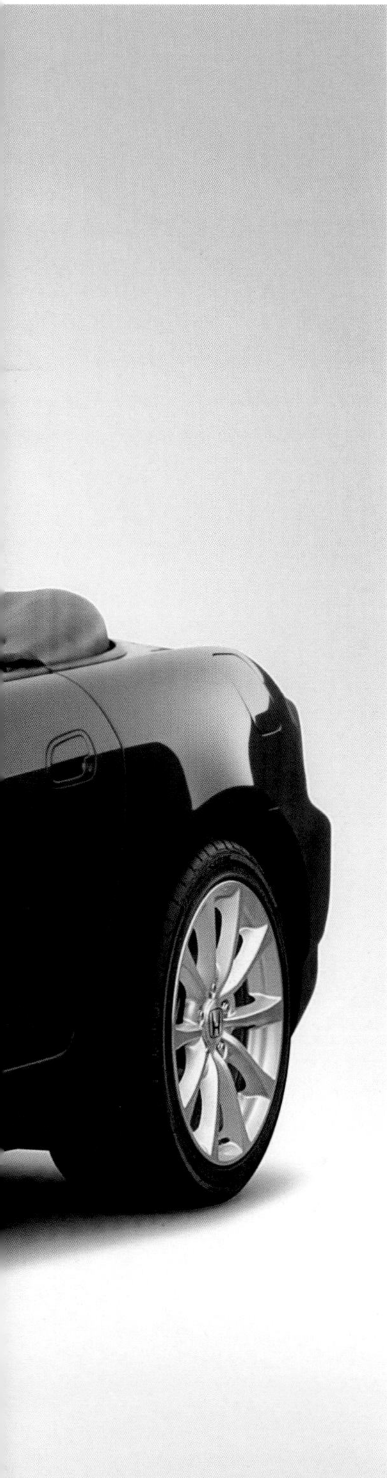

HONDA S2000

Honda may have been a little late to the roadster revival, but perfection takes time

In 1998, Honda Motor Company celebrated its fiftieth anniversary with a pageant, a parade, and a party at the Twin Ring Motegi racetrack sixty-five miles north of Tokyo. The 50,000 people invited to attend the event saw famous Honda racing motorcycles and automobiles in motion around the track, some of them driven in tire-smoking donuts to delight the crowd.

Honda also used the occasion to give a group of American automotive journalists a quick sneak peek at the S2000 roadster, which was scheduled to have its official unveiling in the spring of 1999 at the New York Auto Show and then go on sale later that year.

Honda might have been a little late in rolling out its version of the reborn British roadster, but as Soichiro Honda had said decades earlier of his first automobile, the S500 roadster, "I didn't want to build a car like everyone else's."

Actually, Honda had displayed a concept car, the SSM (Sport Study Model) at the Tokyo show back in 1995. Since then, Honda engineers had taken control, creating the sort of car they would want to drive, especially on mountain roads with the occasional lap around a race track.

To enhance balance, the 4-cylinder engine, a brand-new 2.0-liter unit rated at more than 237 horsepower, was set mid-front, aft of the front wheels, and was mated to a 6-speed manual transmission (no automatic gearbox was available) and limited-slip differential. The chassis featured racing-style double-wishbone suspension.

The cockpit had two seats and a dashboard inspired by the one in the McLaren-Honda Formula 1 racing car; there was a key to turn on the electrical system and a red button to actually start the engine, which had a 9,000 rpm redline.

■ The S2000 did set itself apart in design and in what was offered within the roadster's package.

The Honda S2000 remained in production into 2009. Throughout its production, it was powered by engines that provided about 2 horsepower per cubic inch of displacement, the highest figure among all mass-production automobiles with normally aspirated engines.

"Sports car fans, the car of your dreams will finally arrive," *Car and Driver* proclaimed after its first test drive. "Honda's S2000 comes to market with one goal: driving fun.

"It has the stuff sports-car fantasies are made of: a front-engine, rear-drive layout; a 6-speed, close-ratio manual transmission; an unequal-length control-arm suspension all around; disc brakes; and supportive, firm bucket seats—in a package that weighs less than 2,800 pounds. The S2000's crown jewel, however, is a 2.0-liter naturally aspirated 4-cylinder engine pumping out an incredible 240 horsepower at 8,300 rpm and revving to an 8,900 rpm redline."

"The chassis tuning is nearly perfect," the praise continued, "and the weight distribution rounds to an ideal 50/50. The tires always feel precisely planted. The car communicates a clear picture of what's happening at the contact patch."

But wait, there's more: While a compact roadster, "as icing on the cake, Honda eliminated some traditional sports-car vices. There's plenty of legroom, even for six-footers."

Classic car insurer and value tracker Hagerty did a retrospective in 2023, listing the various roadsters produced after the Mazda MX-5, and noted, "Leave it to Honda, however, to take the Miata's formula of sports car purity and add a dozen of high-revving thrills...Twenty years on, Honda's S2000 leads the pack."

"It has the stuff sports-car fantasies are made of," one magazine's road test proclaimed. "Honda's S2000 leads the pack."

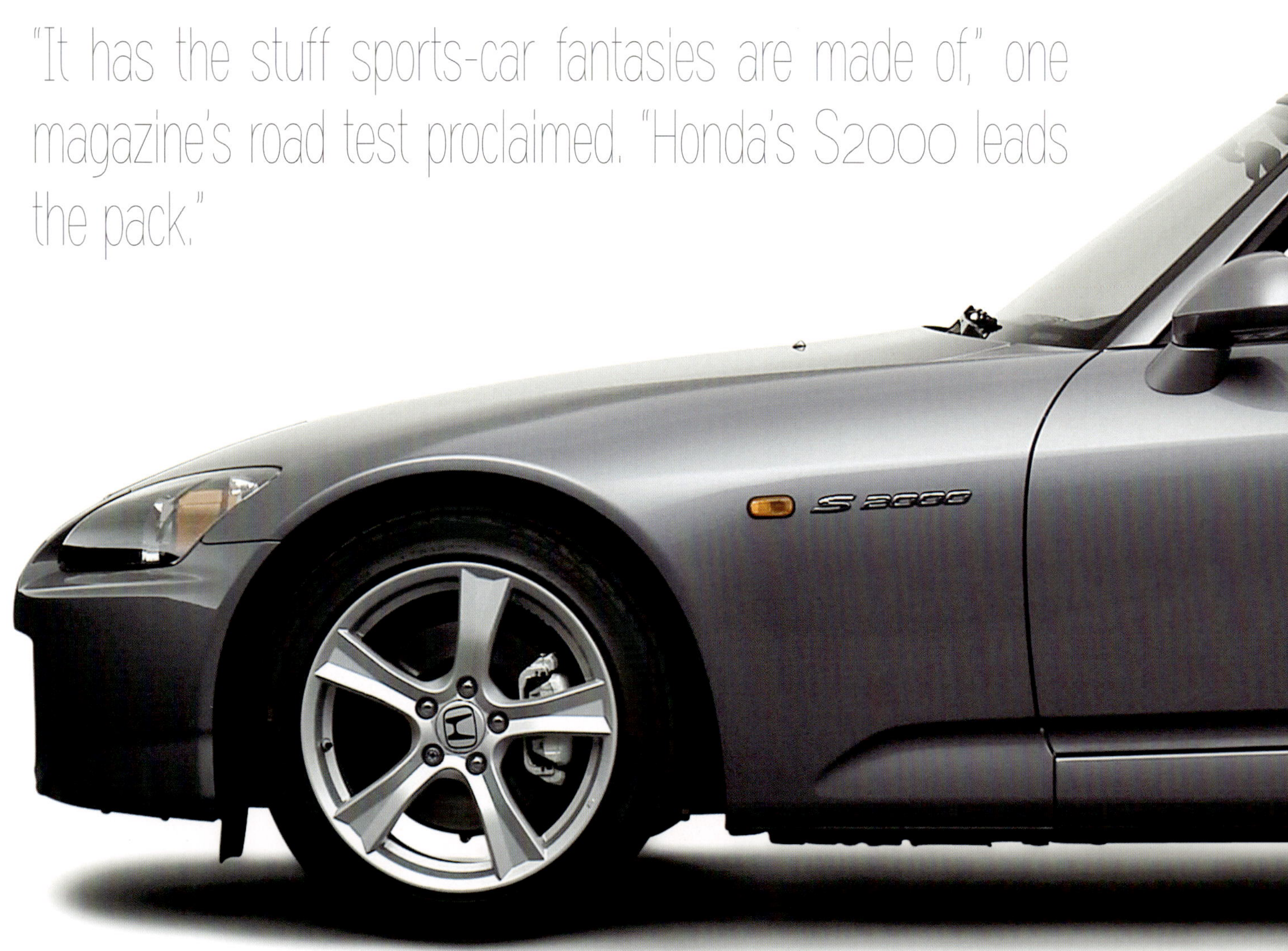

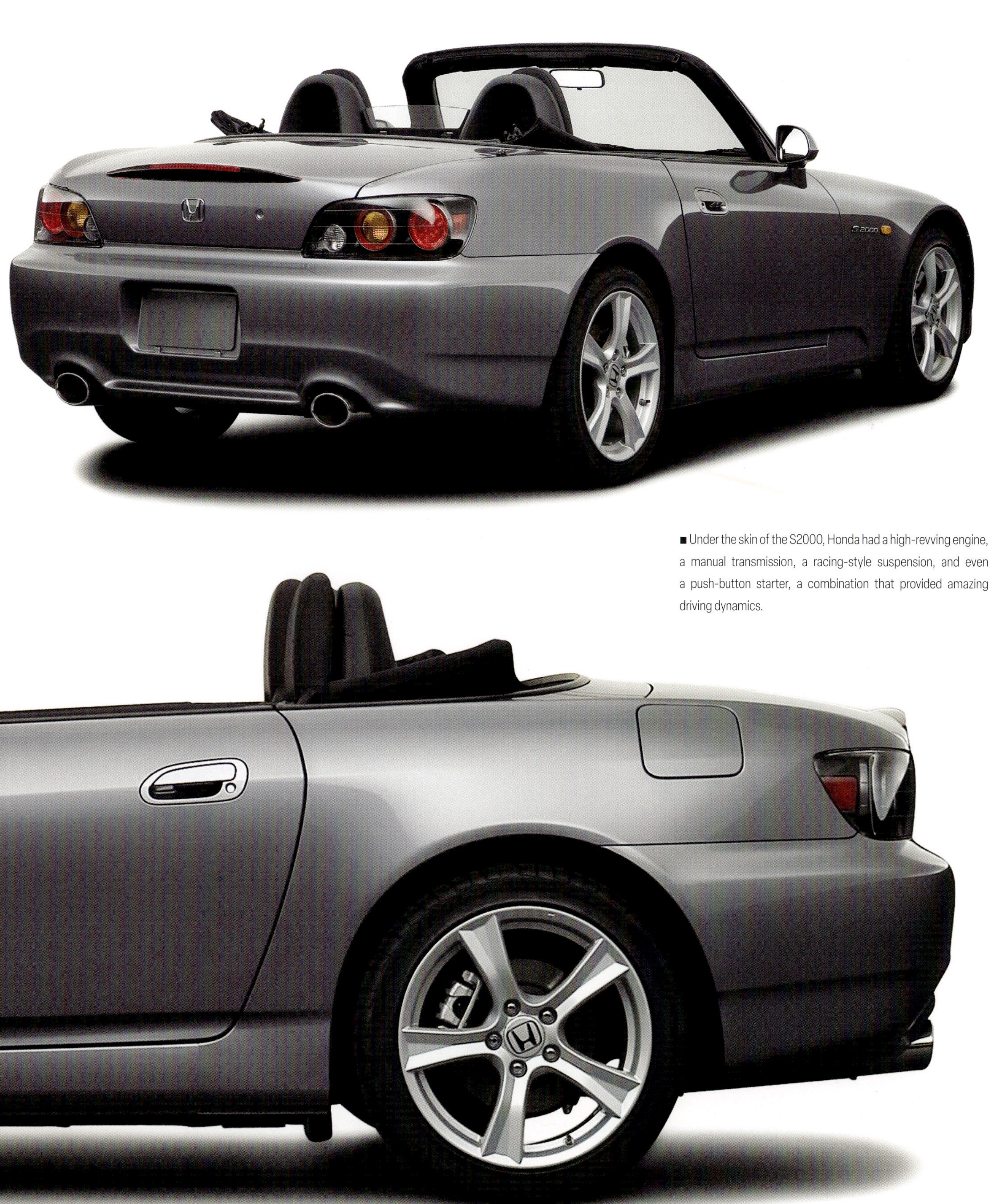

■ Under the skin of the S2000, Honda had a high-revving engine, a manual transmission, a racing-style suspension, and even a push-button starter, a combination that provided amazing driving dynamics.

LOTUS ELISE

Lotus finds its soul, and other automakers find a platform for their own vehicles

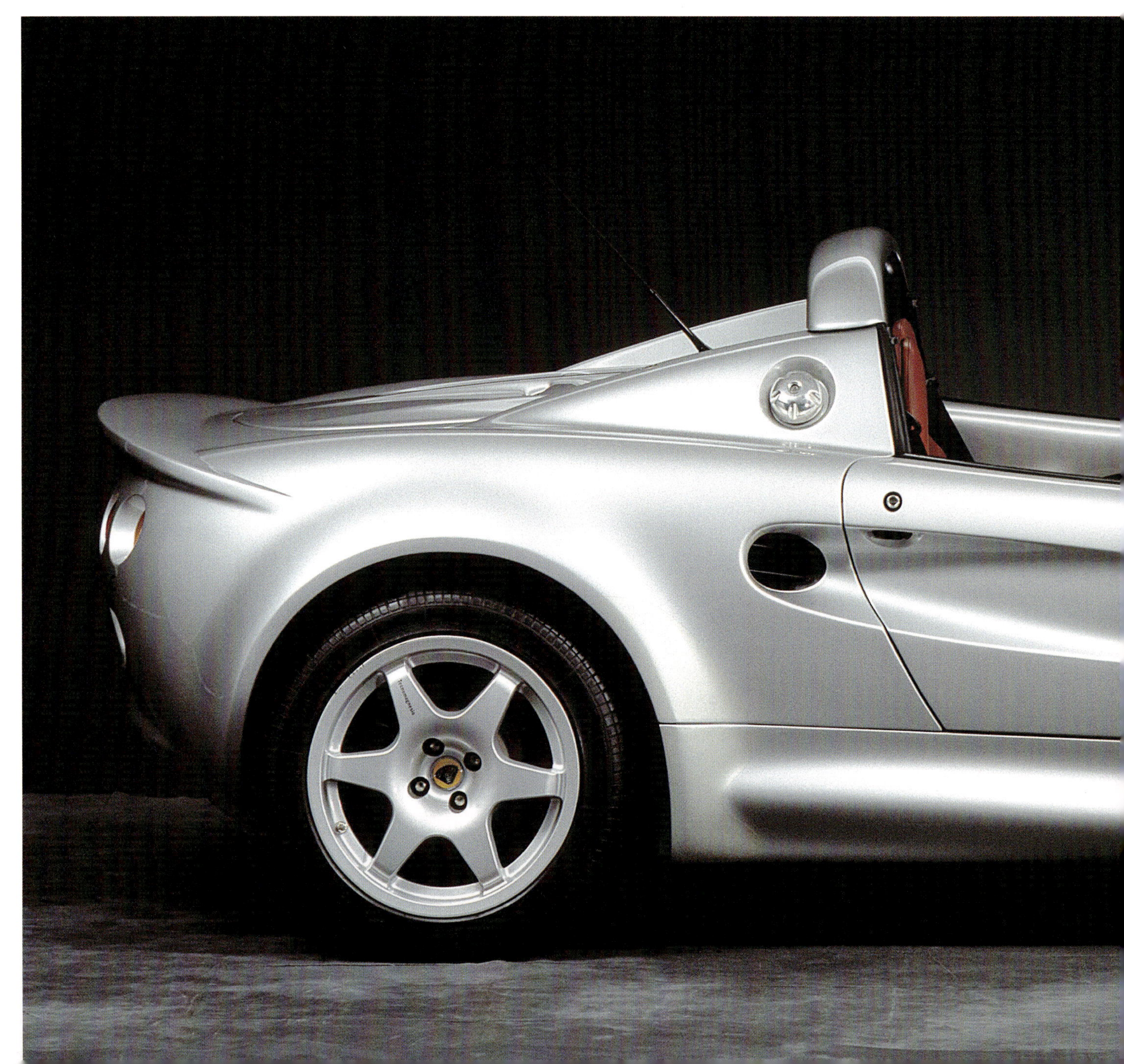

1990 ➤ 1999

Austrian businessman Emil Jellinek bought a motorcar from Daimler-Motoren-Gesellschaft in 1896 and then ordered several more, which he sold to his wealthy neighbors in Nice on the French Riviera. As his sales total grew, so did his influence, to the point that he was able not just to have a new vehicle named in honor of his eleven-year-old daughter, Mercedes, but the entire pioneering German automobile manufacturing company changed its name to the now familiar Mercedes-Benz.

But young Miss Jellinek wasn't the only daddy's daughter to receive such an honor. Well, technically Elisa Artioli was the granddaughter of Romano Artioli, who purchased the rights to the Bugatti automotive brand in 1987 and to Lotus in 1993.

In 1996 Lotus Cars launched a new sports car, the Lotus Elise, named after Artioli's granddaughter, Elisa, who was two years old when her automotive namesake was unveiled.

Built atop a rigid and bonded extruded aluminum chassis that weighed only 70 pounds (31.7 kilograms), even complete with coachwork, engine, two seats,

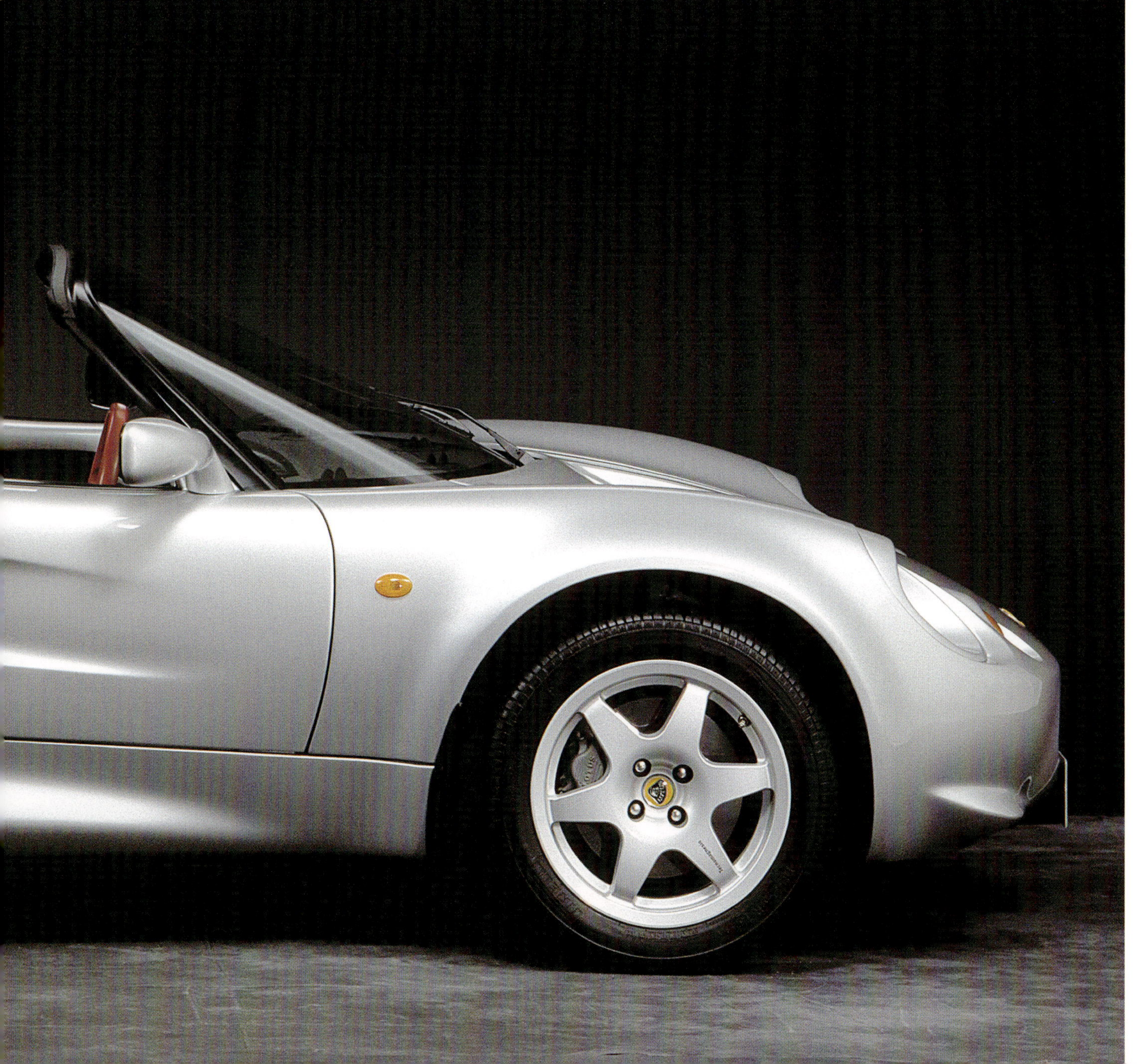

Previous and these pages ■ Elise's rigid but lightweight chassis was true to Colin Chapman's original cars and provided a basis for other vehicles from Lotus as well as from Opel, Hennessey, and Tesla.

tires, etc., the Lotus Elise still weighed in at less than 1,600 pounds (725 kilograms). That was light enough that the mid-mounted 1.8-liter 4-cylinder engine rated at a mere 118 horsepower could propel the car from a standing start to 60 mph (96 km/h) in less than six seconds.

"The Elise found a ready audience, and it was widely felt that Lotus had found its soul once more," *The Beaulieu Encyclopedia of the Automobile* reported in a reference to the belief of Lotus's founder, the late Colin Chapman, and his philosophy of "Simplify, then add lightness," which he followed in producing cars for the racetrack and the roadway.

The Elise's roadster coachwork was designed by Julian Thompson, and its interior featured a driver's seat set slightly ahead of the passenger's seat to help enhance the car's dynamic balance. New European crash-test standards led to a redesign for 2001. The redesigned version not only was used by Lotus, but would be the basis for the Opel Speedster, Hennessey Venom GT, and Tesla Roadster as well as for the Lotus Exige, 2-Eleven, and Europa S.

At first, the Elise's 4-cylinder engine had come from British automaker Rover, but Lotus later sourced 4-cylinder engines from Toyota. The result was a bump in horsepower, to as much as 217, with a 0-to-60 sprint in less than five seconds, and in top speed to 145 mph (233 km/h).

"Flung at the world at the 1995 Frankfurt Motor Show, the Elise was something of a return to the purity of Lotus's roots," America's *Road & Track* magazine reported.

"The tiny car was based around a new bonded extruded aluminum chassis, with fiberglass body panels, new lightweight brakes, and a new lightweight motor. It showed that you didn't need huge brawn and high price tags to turn heads. And though both the concept Audi TT and Ferrari F50 were at the same show taking a large chunk of the limelight, the Elise grabbed headlines all over the planet.

"As a package, it was pretty alluring, a simple handling-biased low-power sports car for the modern."

The magazine said the Elise wasn't fast but was very, very quick, and with steering "outside of a race car, you won't find anything quite as pure."

"The thing was very obviously designed to be driven hard as often as takes your fancy."

The lightweight and versatile Elise would remain in production until 2021, when it was succeeded by the Lotus Emira.

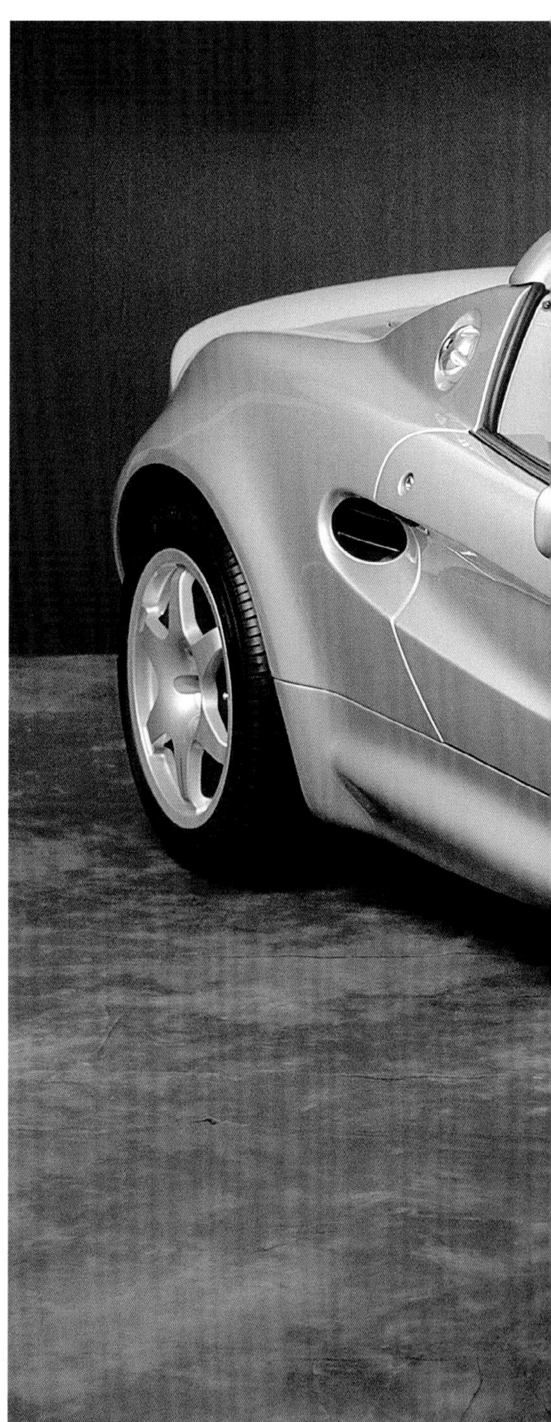

The Elise was so light and nimble that 118 horsepower was enough to provide an exciting thrill ride.

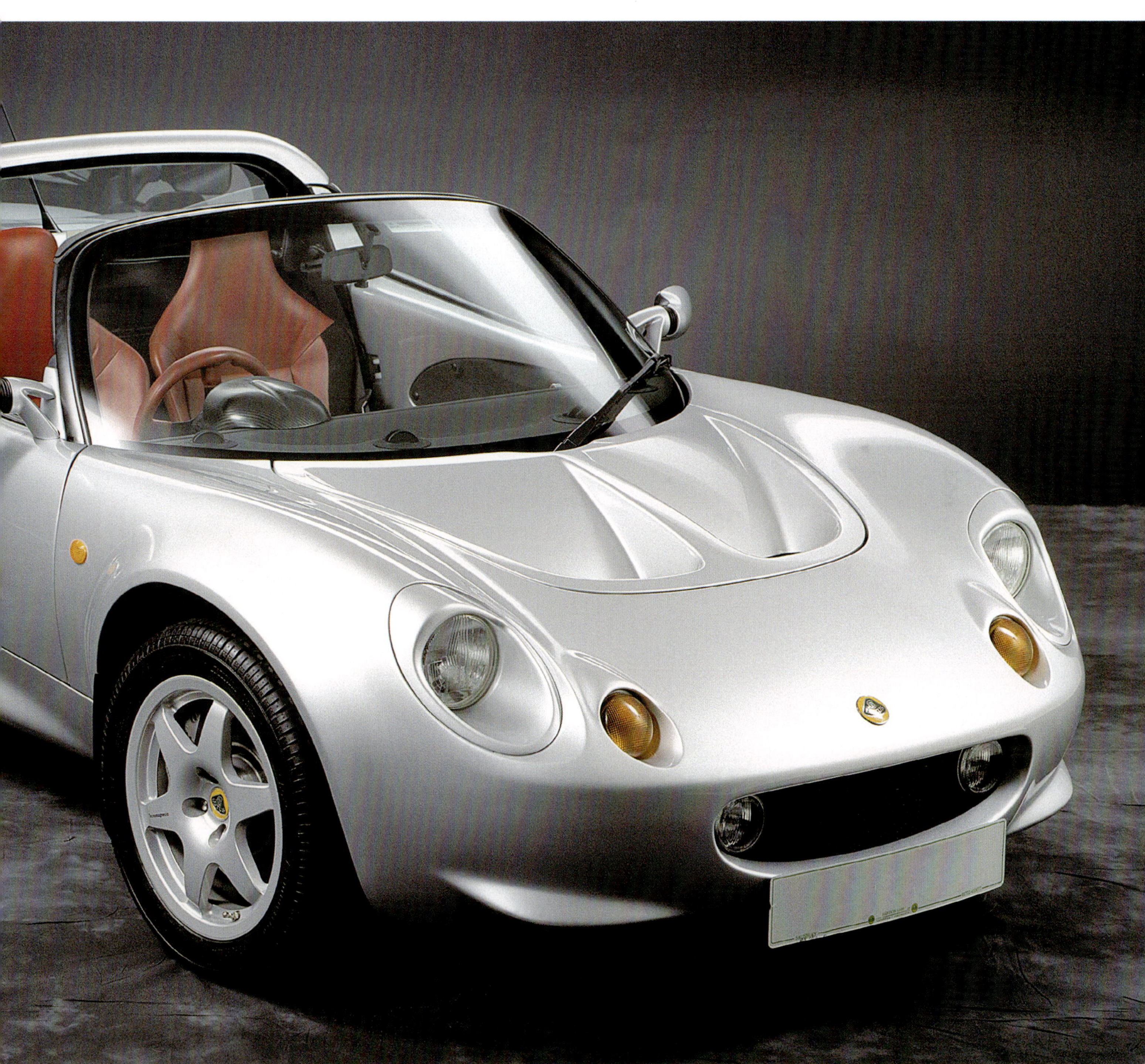

PAGANI ZONDA C12

Blending art and science to make a modern supercar

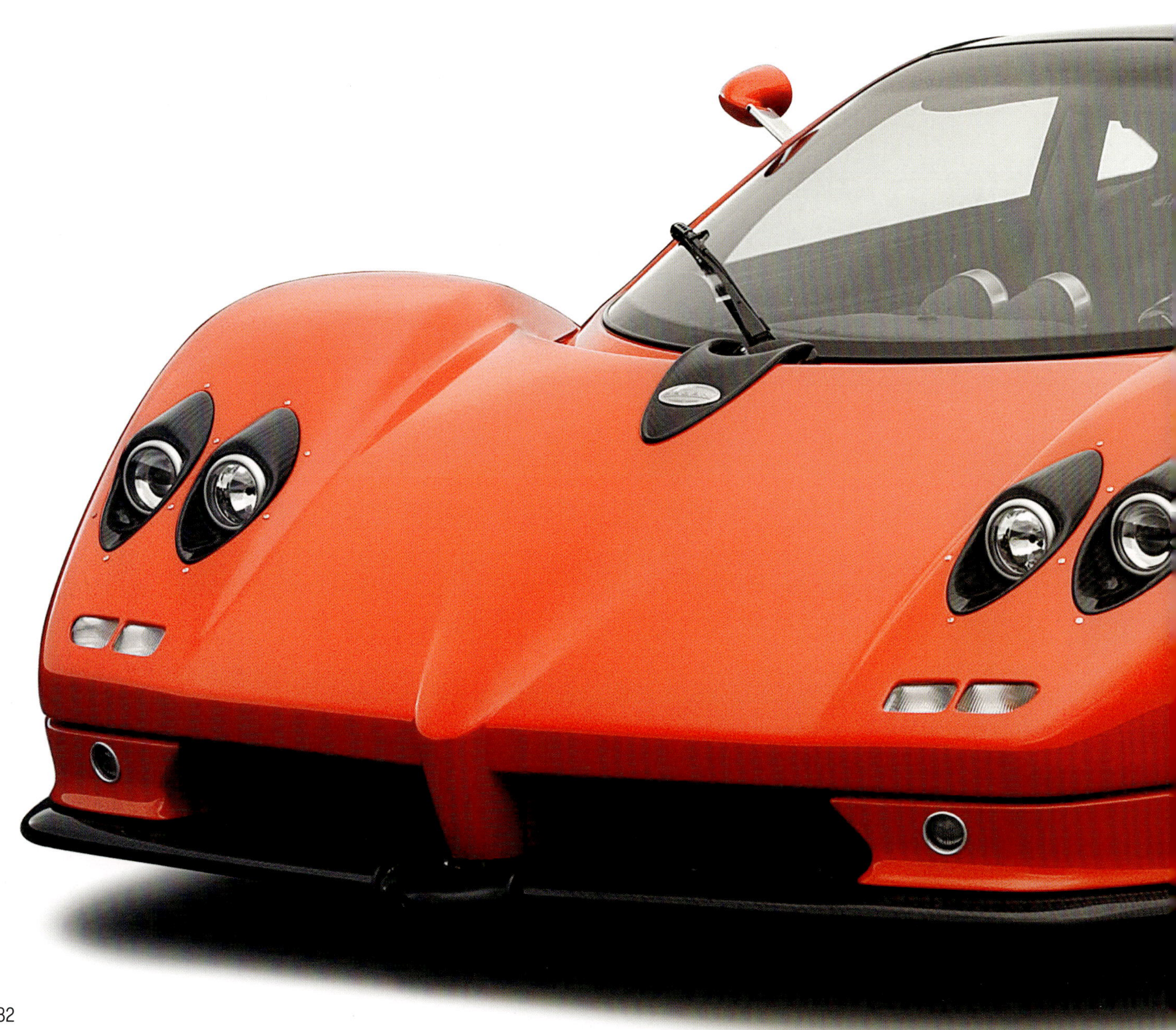

1990 ➤ 1999

Horacio Pagani was born in Argentina to Italian parents; his father was a baker, his mother an artist. As a child, Horacio crafted model cars from wood and read as much as he could about exotic European cars.

One day, while reading an article in *Reader's Digest*, he was inspired by a quote from Leonardo da Vinci, who said, "Art and science are two disciplines that must walk together hand in hand." By the age of twenty, Pagani had combined art and science, building his own small formula racing car, and he soon was befriended by the great Argentine racing champion Juan Manuel Fangio.

In 1982, at the age of twenty-seven and armed with a letter of introduction from Fangio, Pagani moved to Europe, where he was hired at first as a mechanic and then promoted to a position as an automotive design engineer by Lamborghini. In 1985 he became the head of the company's new composite material department and helped create the lightweight carbon fiber coachwork for the Lamborghini Countach Evoluzione.

Pagani suggested that Lamborghini buy its own autoclave to produce carbon fiber components. When the company balked at that idea, Pagani went to a bank

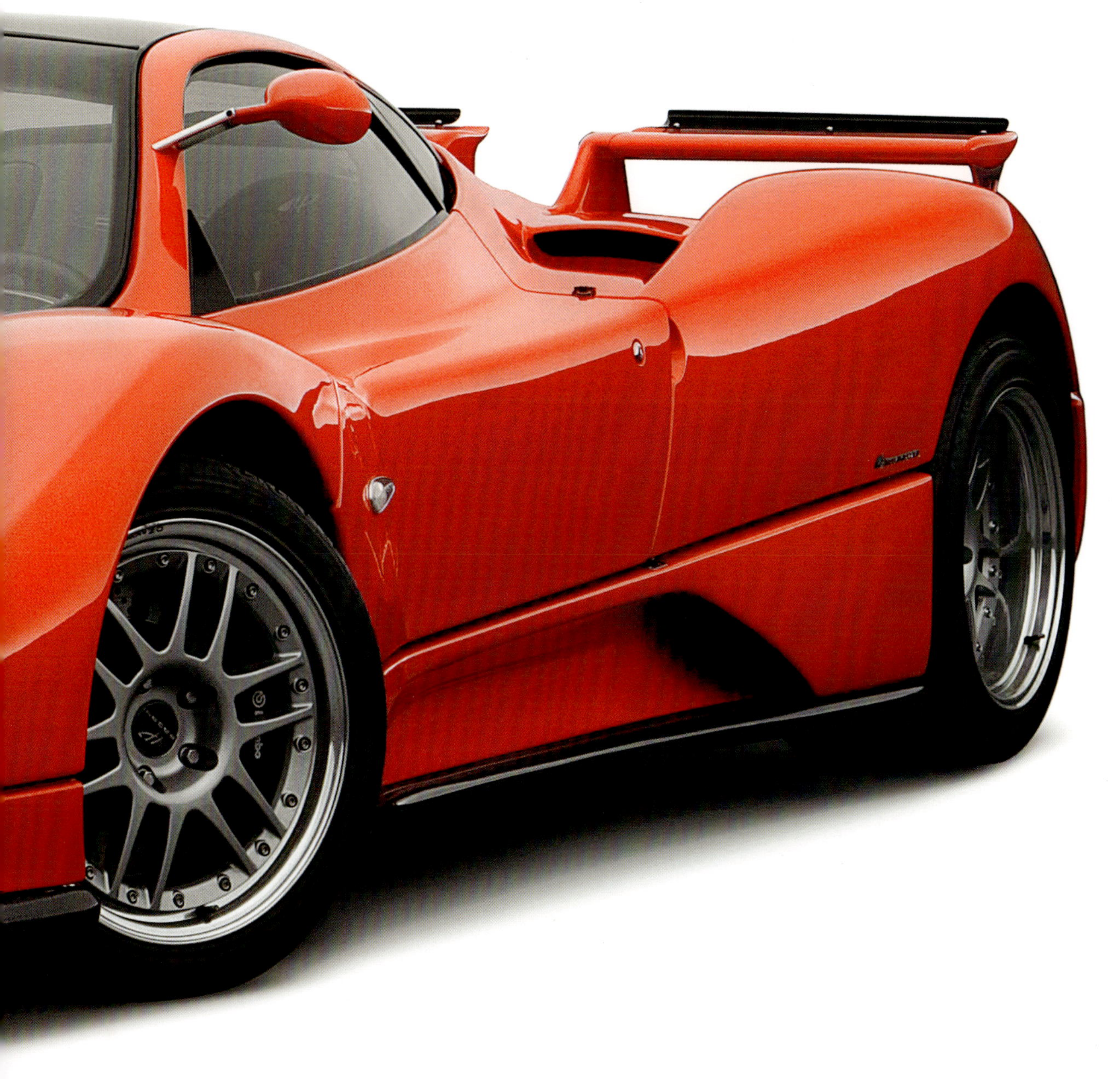

and obtained a loan to establish Modena Design, where he produced composites for companies including Renault, Daihatsu, Dallara, Aprilia, and even Ferrari's Formula 1 racing team.

At the same time, he was working on his own supercar, which he planned to name in honor of Fangio. But after Fangio's death, Pagani unveiled the car as the Zonda, the Spanish name for the strong, fast wind that blows on the eastern slopes of Argentina's Andes Mountains.

Because of his own success while racing for Mercedes-Benz in the 1950s, Fangio had encouraged Pagani to secure engines for his budding supercar project from the German company. Pagani had a meeting with Mercedes' chief engineer in 1993 and showed him his prototype.

"It looks like a timeless car!" he was told.

"Thank God!" Pagani responded. "Because I don't have any money, and I'll need a lot of time to make it."

Several months later, Mercedes agreed to let its 450-horsepower V12 engine propel Pagani's Zonda C12 (C for Pagani's wife, Cristina, 12 for the engine's cylinder), which was unveiled at the Geneva Motor Show in 1999.

Britain's *Evo* magazine reported that compared to the McLaren F1 or Lamborghini's Diablo, "the Zonda felt like a supersized Lotus Elise. Supple and beautifully poised, with pinpoint steering and immense performance, it gave the lie to supercar lore that demanded exotica should be belligerent and/or intimidating to drive."

Upon the twentieth anniversary of the Zonda, Petrolicious praised, "To many... the Zonda seems like it was unveiled yesterday. It holds its own among the latest ranks of exotic autos with three times the horsepower of respectable sports cars, and yet it is now *two decades* old. To give the car some context, auto mags at the beginning of the twenty-first century featured cars like the Ferrari 360 Modena. Line that up side by side with a Zonda to see just how radical the first Pagani was and still is."

The Zonda would evolve through its two decades in production and would be joined in the Pagani stable by the Huayra and Utopia.

Left and opposite page ■ Horacio Pagani had plans for his supercar, but they couldn't come to fruition unless he found an engine. He did, a V12 from Mercedes-Benz, which was fitting since the car's shape was inspired by the Silver Arrows of Group C auto racing.

Right ■ While the C12 may be considered small in size, its interior was designed for occupant comfort.

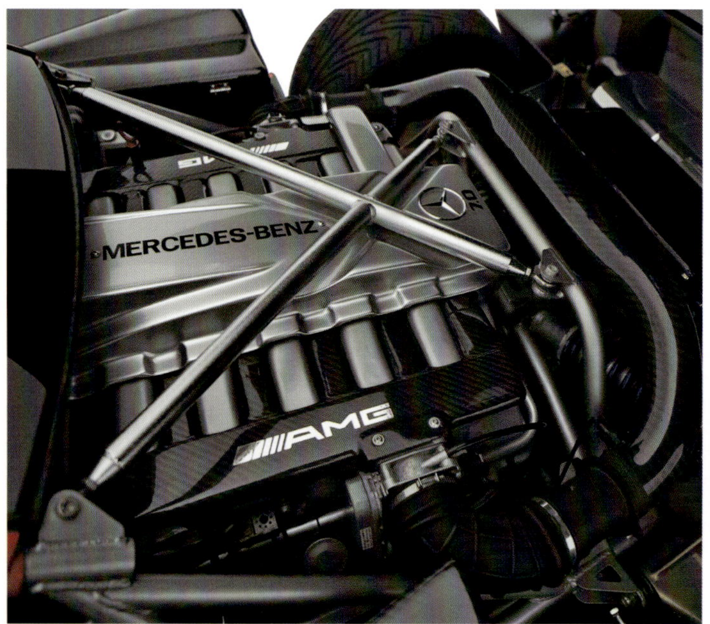

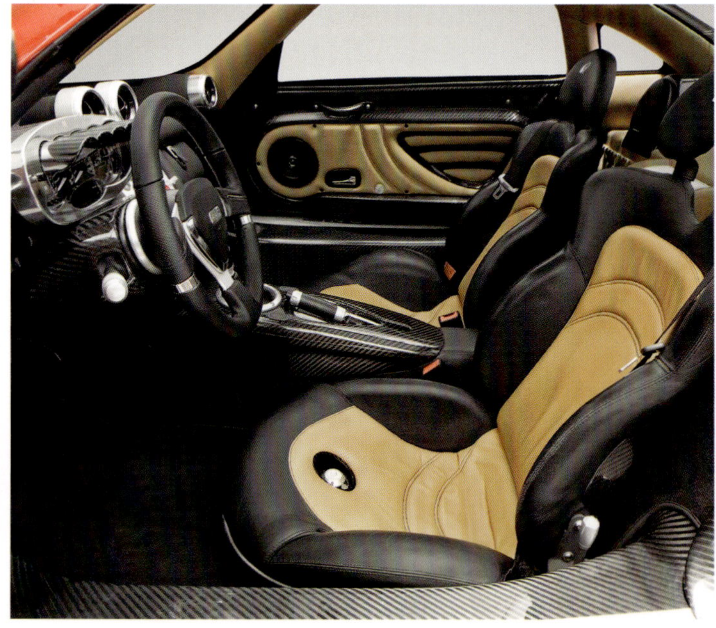

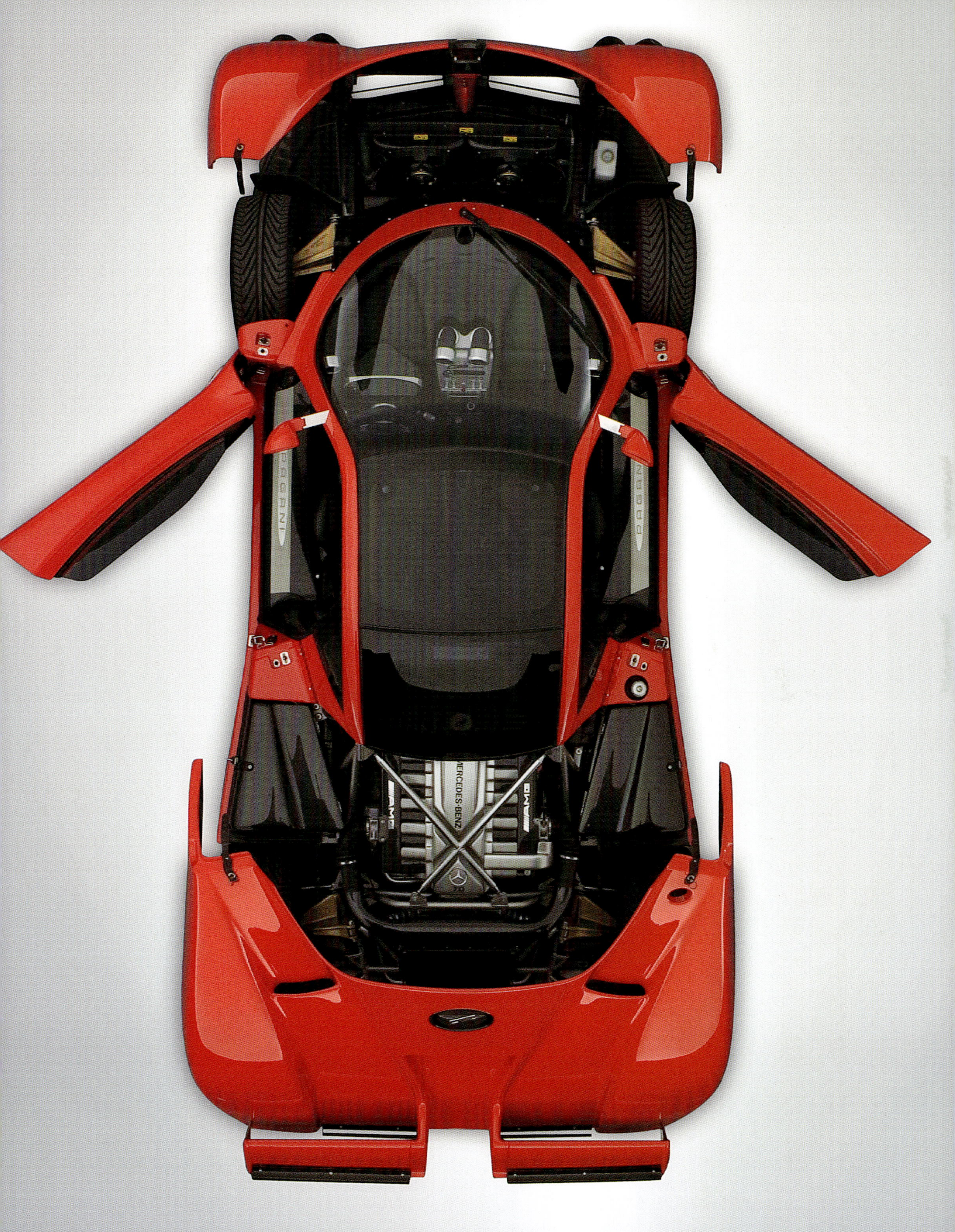
PAGANI
PAGANI
MERCEDES-BENZ
AMG
AMG

Even two decades after the car's introduction, "it holds its own among the latest ranks of exotic autos."

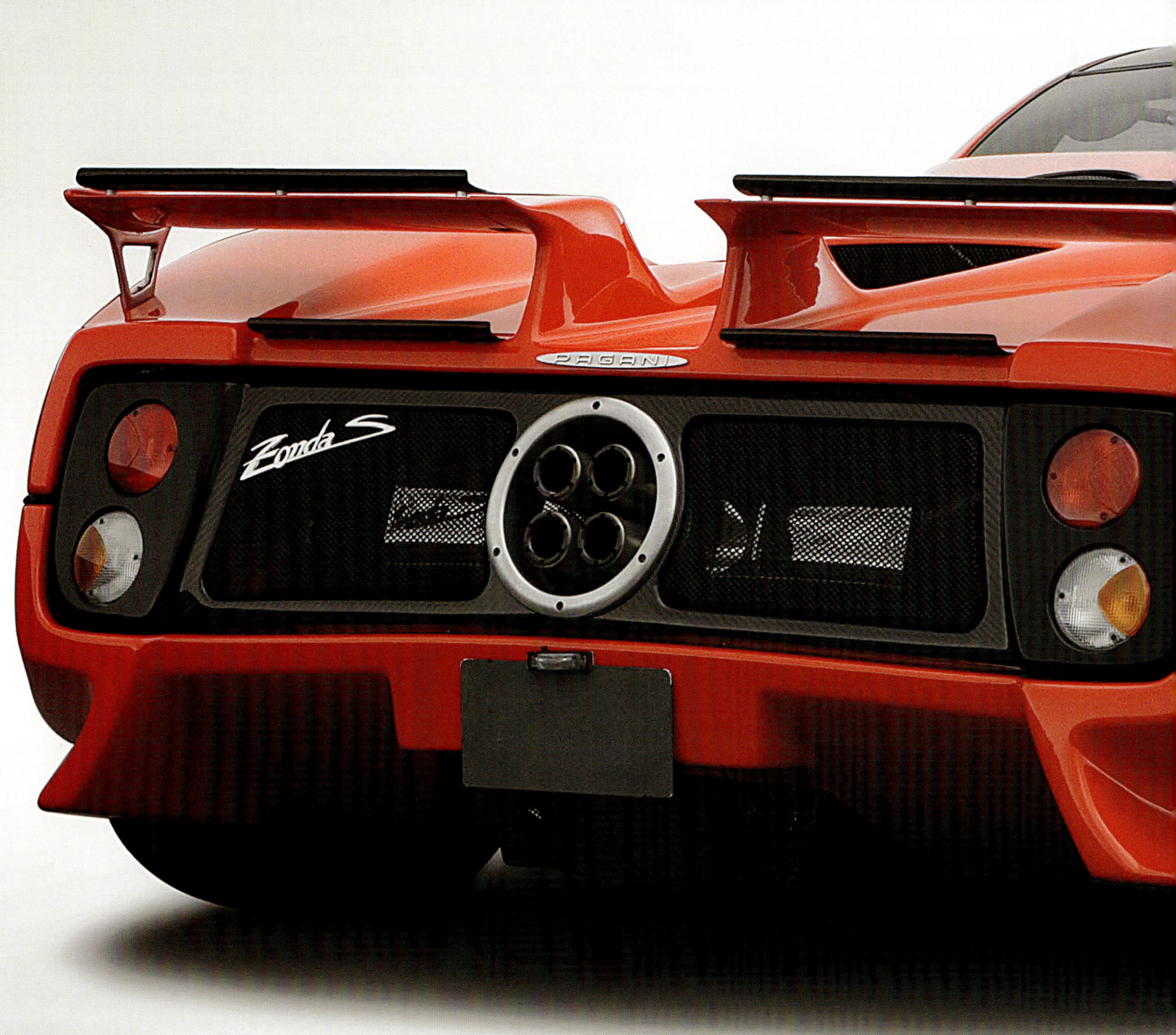

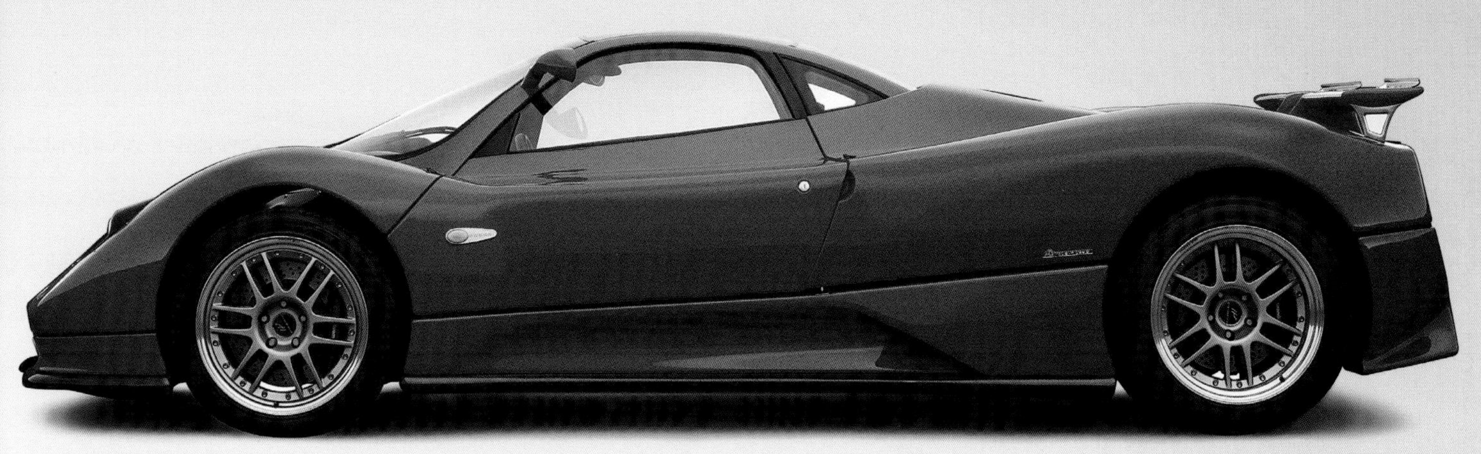

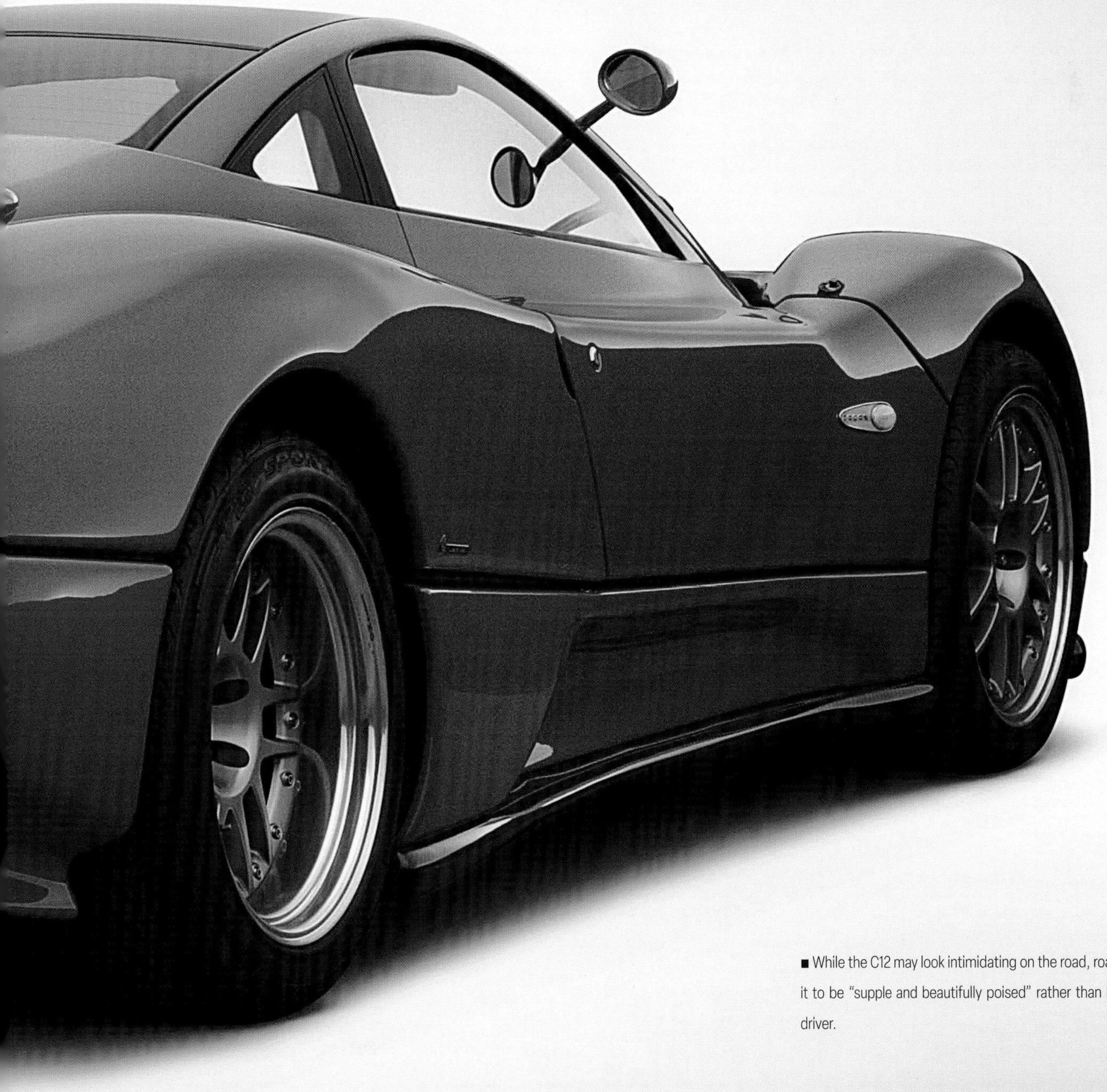

■ While the C12 may look intimidating on the road, road testers report it to be "supple and beautifully poised" rather than belligerent to its driver.

AUTHOR

LARRY EDSALL is a journalist who specialized for five decades in covering the automotive industry. He was the managing editor at *AutoWeek* magazine, wrote about automotive subjects for *The New York Times* and *Detroit News*, and was the chief editor of the iZoom.com and ClassicCars.com websites.

PHOTO CREDITS

Pages 10-11: National Motor Museum/Heritage Images/Getty Images
Pages 14-15: Pierre Jean Durieu/Shutterstock.com
Pages 16-17, 17, 18-19, 20-21,22-23,23: Tom Wood/Alamy Photo Stock
Pages 24-25: JoshBryan/Shutterstock.com
Pages 26-27, 28: Tom Wood/Alamy Photo Stock
Page 29: JoshBryan/Shutterstock.com
Pages 30-31: Rainer Schlegelmilch/Getty Images
Pages 32-33: DPPI Media/Alamy Photo Stock
Pages 34-35: JoshBryan/Shutterstock.com
Pages 36-37: Grzegorz Czapski/Alamy Photo Stock
Page 37: National Motor Museum/Heritage Images/Getty Images
Pages 38-39: imageBROKER.com/Alamy Photo Stock
Pages 40-41: Rod Kirkpatrick/Alamy Photo Stock
Page 42: mauritius images GmbH/Alamy Photo Stock
Page 43: Girardo Archive/Alamy Photo Stock
Pages 44-45: National Motor Museum/Heritage Images/Getty Images
Page 46: Screen Archives/Getty Images
Page 47: National Motor Museum/Heritage Images/Getty Images
Pages 48-49: Gestalt Imagery/Shutterstock.com
Pages 50-51: arda savasciogullari/Shutterstock.com
Page 51: Fin Costello/Redferns/Getty Images
Pages 52-53, 54-55, 55: National Motor Museum/Heritage Images/Getty Images
Pages 54-55: National Motor Museum/Heritage Images/Getty Images
Pages 56-57: Kim Sayer/Alamy Photo Stock
Page 58: Scott Sim/Alamy Photo Stock
Pages 59, 60-61: Kim Sayer/Alamy Photo Stock
Pages 62-63: JoshBryan/Shutterstock.com
Page 64: Photo 12/Alamy Photo Stock
Pags 64-65: FernandoV/Shutterstock.com
Pages 66-67: Frederic J. Brown/Afp/Getty Images
Pages 68-69: National Motor Museum/Heritage Images/Getty Images
Page 69: Heritage Image Partnership Ltd/Alamy Photo Stock
Pages 70-71, 72-73,73: National Motor Museum/Heritage Images/Getty Images
Pages 74-75, 76: Rainer Schlegelmilch/Getty Images
Page 77: Roland Holschneider/picture alliance/Getty Images
Pages 78, 78-79: Rainer Schlegelmilch/Getty Images
Pages 80-81: Tom Wrzesień/Alamy Photo Stock
Pages 82, 83: National Motor Museum/Heritage Images/Getty Images
Pages 84-85: Girardo Archive/Alamy Photo Stock
Pages 86-87, 88-89: National Motor Museum/Heritage Images/Getty Images
Pages 90-91: imageBROKER.com/Alamy Photo Stock
Page 95: Motoring Picture Library/Alamy Photo Stock
Pages 96-97: JoshBryan/Shutterstock.com
Pages 98-99: Girardo Archive/Alamy Photo Stock
Page 100: FlixPix/Alamy Photo Stock
Page 101: myphotobank.com.au/Shutterstock.com
Pages 102-103: Barrett-Jackson/Getty Images
Pages 104-105: National Motor Museum/Heritage Images/Getty Images
Pages 106-107: Brian Welker/Alamy Photo Stock
Pages 108-109: Scott Dennis/Alamy Photo Stock
Pages 110-111: DPPI Media/Alamy Photo Stock
Page 112: Retro AdArchives / Alamy Photo Stock
Pages 112-113, 113: National Motor Museum/Heritage Images/Getty Images
Pages 114-115, 116-117, 117, 118-119: Faisal Khatib/Alamy Photo Stock
Pages 120-121: Hugh Mitton/Alamy Photo Stock
Pages 122-123: Jacek Piotrowski/Shutterstock.com
Page 123 top: Jacek Piotrowski/Shutterstock.com
Page 123 bottom: Wirestock, Inc./Alamy Photo Stock
Pages 124-125: National Motor Museum/Heritage Images/Getty Images
Pages 126-127: Je_Cekrek/Shutterstock.com
Page 128, 129: Rainer Schlegelmilch/Getty Images
Pages 130-131, 132-133: National Motor Museum/Heritage Images/Getty Images
Pages 134-135, 136-137, 137 top, 138, 139: Rainer Schlegelmilch/Getty Images
Page 137 bottom: Maggi & Maggi/Getty Images
Pages 140-141: Barrett-Jackson/Getty Images
Pages 142-143: Richard McDowell/Alamy Photo Stock
Pages 144-145: Jurgis Mankauskas/Alamy Photo Stock
Pages 146-147: Alvey & Towers Picture Library/Alamy Photo Stock
Page 148: LAT Images/Getty Images
Pages 148-149: Joshua Claro/Alamy Photo Stock
Pages 152, 153, 154-155: JoshBryan/Shutterstock.com
Pages 156-157, 158, 159: Goddard Archive/Alamy Photo Stock
Pages 160-161: JoshBryan/Shutterstock.com
Pages 162-163: National Motor Museum/Heritage Images/Getty Images
Page 163: Motoring Picture Library/Alamy Photo Stock
Pages 164-165: Jonathan Tennant/Alamy Photo Stock
Pages 166-167: National Motor Museum/Heritage Images/Getty Images
Page 168 left: National Motor Museum/Heritage Images/Getty Images
Page 168 right: Phil Talbot/Alamy Photo Stock
Page 169: Matthew Richardson/Alamy Photo Stock
Page 170: Barrett-Jackson/Getty Images
Page 171: Goddard Archive 2/Alamy Photo Stock
Pages 172-173, 173: Barrett-Jackson/Getty Images
Pages 174-175, 176, 176-177: Jos Bispo/500px/Getty Images
Pages 178-179,180-181: culture-images GmbH/Alamy Photo Stock

Pages 182-183, 184, 185: JoshBryan/Shutterstock.com
Pages 186-187, 188-189, 189: National Motor Museum/Heritage Images/Getty Images
Pages 190-191: CJM Photography/Alamy Photo Stock
Pages 192-193, 194-195, 195: Rainer Schlegelmilch/Getty Images
Pages 196, 196-197: Heritage Image Partnership Ltd/Alamy Photo Stock
Pages 198-199: areyouben/Shutterstock.com
Pages 200-201, 202: Rainer Schlegelmilch/Getty Images
Pages 202-203: National Motor Museum/Heritage Images/Getty Images
Pages 204-205: Rainer Schlegelmilch/Getty Images
Page 205: FernandoV/Shutterstock.com
Pages 206-207: BMW AG/Getty Images
Page 208: National Motor Museum/Heritage Images/Getty Images
Pages 208-209: Keith Hamshere/Getty Images
Pages 210-211, 212-213, 214-215: National Motor Museum/Heritage Images/Getty Images
Pages 216-217, 218-219, 219, 220-221, 222-223: JoshBryan/Shutterstock.com
Pages 224-225, 226-227, 227: Drive Images/Alamy Photo Stock
Pages 228-229, 230-231: National Motor Museum/Heritage Images/Getty Images
Pages 232-233, 234, 235, 236-237, 237: Drive Images/Alamy Photo Stock

Cover: Simon Newbury/Alamy Photo Stock

BIBLIOGRAPHY

BOOKS

A Century of Car Design, Penny Sparke, Barron's Educational Services, Hauppauge, New York, USA, 2002

24 Heures du Mans: 1923–1992, Christian Moity / Jean-Marc Teissedre / Alain Bienvenu, Editions D'Art J.P. Barthelemy, Automobile Club de L'Ouest, Besancon Le Mans, France, 1992

Camaro 2016: Chevrolet's Modern Performance Car, Larry Edsall, Quarto Publishing Group, Minneapolis, Minnesota, 2016

Corvette Stingray: The Seventh Generation of America's Sports Car, Larry Edsall, MBI Publishing Company, Minneapolis, Minnesota, USA, 2013

Ferrari, Larry Edsall / Dennis Adler, MBI Publishing Company, Minneapolis, Minnesota, USA, 2011

Legendary Cars: Cars That Made History from the Early Days to the 21st Century, Larry Edsall, White Star, Vercelli, Italy, 2005

Masters of Car Design, Larry Edsall, White Star, Vercelli, Italy, 2008

Miata 20 Years, Larry Edsall, MBI Publishing Company, Minneapolis, Minnesota, USA, 2008

Never Stop Driving: A Better Life Behind the Wheel, Larry Webster / Zach Bowman / Jack Baruth / Brett Berk, Hagerty Media Properties, Traverse City, Michigan, USA, 2019

Standard Catalog of Imported Cars: 1946–2002, updated by Mike Covello, Krause Publications, Iola, Wisconsin, USA, 2002

Standard Catalog of American Cars, 1946–1975, edited by Ron Kowalke, Krause Publications, Iola, Wisconsin, USA, 1997

Standard Catalog of American Cars, 1976–1999, James M. Flammang / Ron Kowalke, Krause Publications, Iola, Wisconsin, USA, 1999

The Automobile Age, James J. Flink, The MIT Press, Boston, Massachusetts, USA, 1993

The Beaulieu Encyclopedia of the Automobile, edited by Nick Georgano, Fitzroy-Dearborn Publishers, Chicago, Illinois, 2000

PERIODICALS

AutoWeek magazine, Crain Communications, Detroit, Michigan

WEBSITES

autoweek.com
britannica.com
caranddriver.com
carmagazine.co
classicandsportscar.com
driving.ca
dupontregistry.com
evo.co
forbes.com
goodroad.com
hagerty.com
imdb.com
journal.classiccars.com
mercedes-benz.com
motortrend.com
nytimes.com
octane-magazine.com
pagani.com
petrolicious.com
porsche.com
roadandtrack.com
theautopian.com
thedrive.com
topgear.com
volkswagen-newswroom.com
wikipedia.org

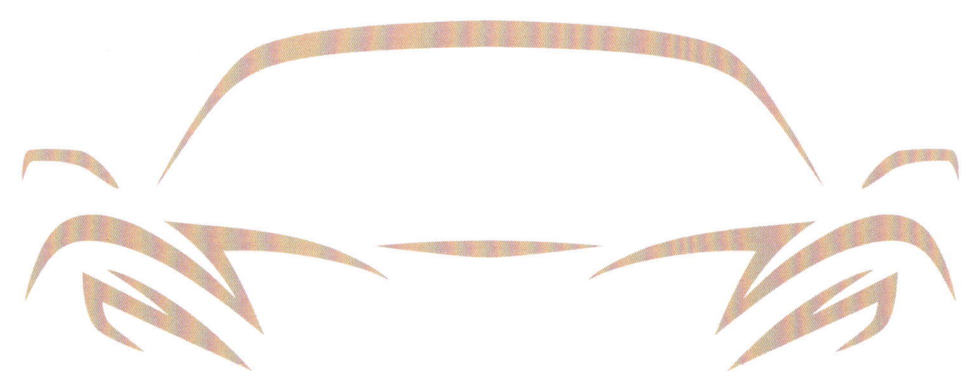

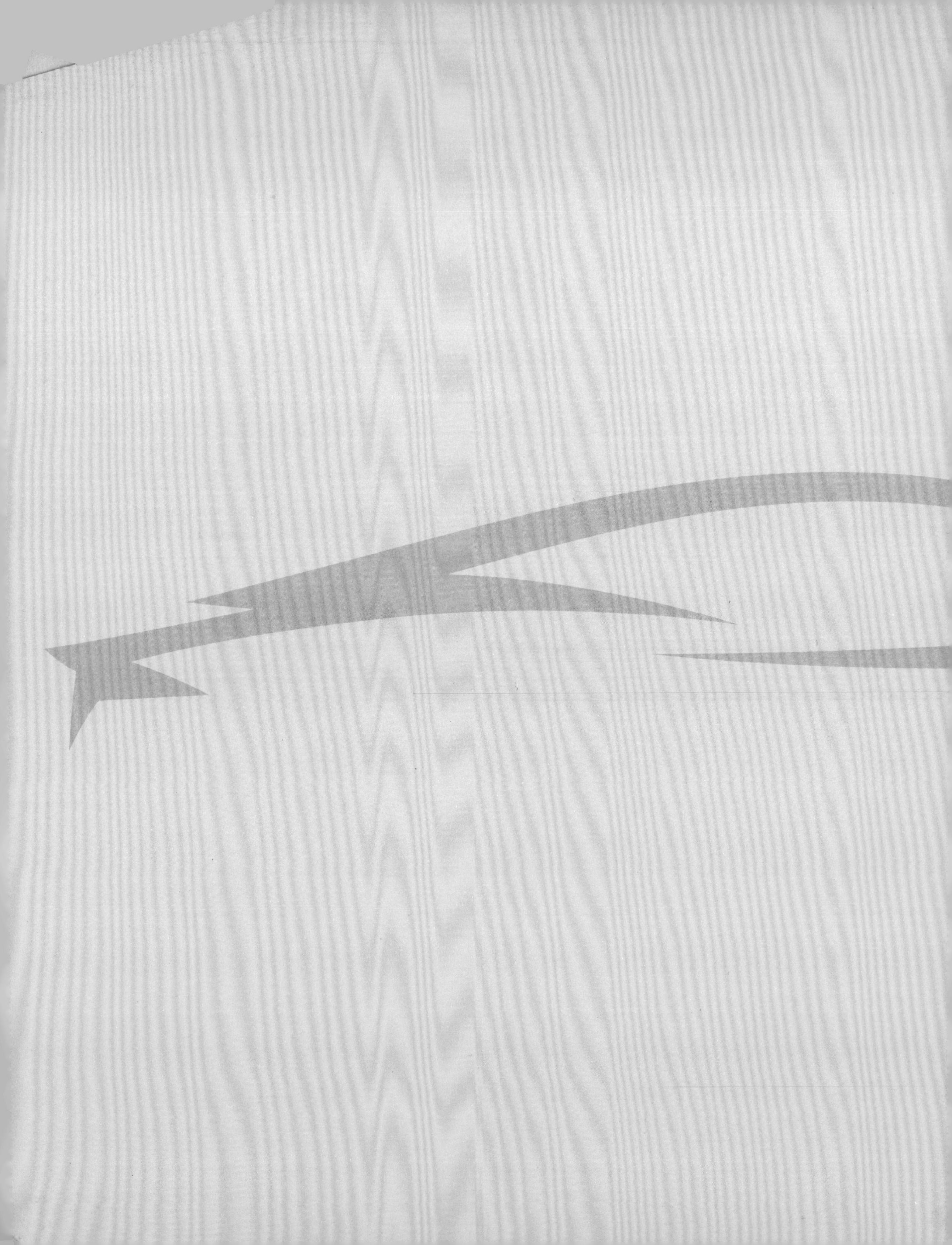